Man's inhumanity to man

By

William K. Mackie

ISBN: 979-8-52945-836-5

Introduction

The murder of George Floyd on 25th. May 2020 turned the World on its head. Black Lives Matter, which had been on the go for eight years prior to Floyd's murder, jumped on this situation of once again African Americans are being killed or persecuted by white cops. The BLM have unfortunately started to destroy property, they started burning cars, and tearing down statues, then the Reverend Al Sharpton and the Reverend Jessie Jackson joined in the conversation. Unfortunately, because of the hatred and lack of trust of white folks stirred up by Black Lives Matter, even these two fine upstanding Men of God, started spouting out statements that only served to fuel the fire of hatred. They both claim to be continuing the work of the late Dr Martin Luther King Jr., but if you take the time to listen to what they say, then you realise that what they are saying today, has no comparison to what Dr King advocated. Dr King was an advocate of Peaceful, Non-Violent Protesting. Jessie Jackson should know this better than most, he was on the balcony of the Lorraine Motel in Memphis, Tennessee, when Dr King was assassinated on 4th. April 1968. Andrew Young was there also, but I have yet to hear Andrew Young spout any of the rubbish that comes from Sharpton or Jackson.

In the United States of America, it was not ONLY Black people who were enslaved, it was not only Black people who suffered from Racial Inequality. The Native Americans were hounded by the White Americans until their right to live peacefully and retain their own culture, and even down to where they could live, was all decided by White Americans for the sole Benefit of White Americans. But as you read through this book, you will discover that Native Americans were being massacred long before Christopher Columbus arrived. They were being massacred by fellow Native Americans.

Long before the American War of Independence (April 19, 1775 – September 3, 1783), slaves were being sent to the "New World" by the English Government, White Slaves, both from Ireland and Scotland. They were sent out to America because they dared to challenge the outlandish laws of the English King and Government. Emancipation of the slaves didn't cause the American Civil War, emancipation of slaves, started in England in 1772, when a runaway slave asked for protection from his Master. Slavery was abolished in 1807, when the English Parliament voted to end the slave trade. Sadly, it took 30 years to eradicate it completely.

In the struggle between the English Government and the Irish, the struggle was mainly because the Island of Ireland was predominantly Roman Catholic, and the

Protestant Kings of England, sent protestants from England to take over the ownership of much of the lands in Ireland. As you can imagine this did little to please the farmers or the farm workers.

It is my aim by means of this book, to help the reader fully understand the struggle of the Black American following the emancipation of slaves, is not a modern concept. Globally man has been inhumane towards other human beings almost since time began. Man has been brutal towards other members of the human race, irrespective of their Colour, Creed or Social status.

Man's inhumanity towards other men, was a greed for more, be that more Power, more Lands, more Possessions or just a simple case of I can so I will. In other words, bully boy tactics.

I need to take you back to the time of the white slaves, many people in the U. S. A. today, do not realise that the first slaves in many parts of what is now the United States of America, were Irish slaves, there were also Scottish slaves. I also want to take reader back in time to remember that long before the New World was discovered that, the Native Americans were being massacred in their own land, and they were being massacred by other Native Americans.

Outside of the New World, the Jews were being hounded and downtrodden, and this started long before Hitler came to power.

Even now Jews are not safe anywhere in the world. They could be attacked anywhere. Back in 1976/77, I had a part-time job every Saturday I was employed as a Security Officer, by a Synagogue that met inside a Jewish School in Mill Hill East, in London. Now when I started, I was told by the Cantor, basically if they don't look Jewish, they don't get in. Those adult males that came in had made to measure silk suits, and drove Mercedes or BMWs, so when this rust bucket of an old Ford drove into the car park, and this tall guy in a Gestapo styled full length leather coat carrying a Carpet bag, got out of the car, and tried to gain access I said no. He insisted that I let him in, but he didn't look anything like the rest of the men who were already inside. I locked him out of the building, and I went to get the Cantor. The Cantor came to the front door with me, and as he approached the front door, he started laughing and said, "Yes, you'll do, can you do this job regularly?" He unlocked the door, and apologised to the Rabbi, and then locked the door again.

Not just the Jews have been subject to Racial inequality. In the United States in 1882 they banned Chinese from coming to America.

Japanese Prisoners of War during WWII were treated worse than dogs, both men and women, but soldiers who became prisoners because they were ordered to surrender, were the lowest of the low, in the eyes of their Japanese captors.

In China today, Muslims are being rounded up, pretty much in the same way as the Nazis did to the Jews.

In the Arabian states, they are buying and selling slaves in large scale Sex Trafficking. Even in Eastern Europe, Sec Trafficking has become big business.

In recent years in England, gangs of Eastern Europeans and Pakistanis have been convicted of grooming under aged girls, passing them around their friends like pieces of meat in a butcher's shop.

Racial Inequality is NOT something that happens exclusively in the United States of America, nor as this introduction and the rest of this book, I hope will show, but Racial Inequality is NOT exclusively something that happens to African Americans.

In truth, knowing where to start this book, and then knowing what to give as a title for this book, was a long hard thought-out process. It has also been hard to decide what facts and events to add and which to leave out. If I were to list every human conflict and every act of inhumanity to his fellow man, then this book would no doubt been a work covering several volumes, but I decided not to go that far. I decided that as I have always in the past looked out for the underdog as best as I could, I felt that now that I am part of the Special Monitoring Mission of the International Human Rights Commission, I just felt that I had to speak out about racial inequalities (not just black versus white) and set the record straight as best as I could, that man has been treating his fellow man with jealousy, mistrust, greed and loathing since it was first written in the Bible.

It is also still going on today where supposed Civilised Societies are treating their citizens as being lower than dogs. Slavery still exists, human trafficking is on the rise, not just women, but men and even children are being pimped off so that some War Lord or dictator can hide behind his armed guards and make a fortune out of the misery of others. Human trafficking is rampant in many nations, China, Russia, America, Britain, and in many E. U. Countries.

Most of what is contained in this book can be found online, but when people decide to rise up against authority, or turn on the hate machine and point it at certain Faiths or colours or communities, they don't want to check out what history says, because they may just find out that the cause they claim to be fighting for, either isn't a new cause, or that there may be a more peaceful way to make the changes that they desire. Destroying history will not make an issue go away, it just means that in the future history will reflect the upon how you as the protagonist, have gone down in history as a thug, a bully oh yes and as a racist. Don't think that if you have darker skin than the next guy, that you aren't a Racist. Racism doesn't depend on the colour of your skin; it depends on the purity of your heart.

The author is now a member of the Special Monitoring Mission
of the International Human Rights Commission
as part of the Danish International Team

"The only thing necessary for the triumph of evil, is for good men to do nothing."
Edmund Burke.

"The greatest deception that men suffer, is from their own opinions."
Leonardo da Vinci.

A wise man was once asked,

"Tell me sir, in which field could I make a great career?"

The man replied with a smile,

*"Be a good human being. There is a lot of opportunity, in this area.
And very little competition*

**Man's inhumanity to his fellow man is mentioned in the Bible
Genesis, Chapter 4. King James Version**

And Adam knew Eve his wife; and she conceived, and bare Cain, and said, I have gotten a man from the Lord.

2 And she again bare his brother Abel. And Abel was a keeper of sheep, but Cain was a tiller of the ground.

3 And in process of time it came to pass, that Cain brought of the fruit of the ground an offering unto the Lord.

4 And Abel, he also brought of the firstlings of his flock and of the fat thereof. And the Lord had respect unto Abel and to his offering:

5 But unto Cain and to his offering he had not respect. And Cain was very wroth, and his countenance fell.

6 And the Lord said unto Cain, Why art thou wroth? and why is thy countenance fallen?

7 If thou doest well, shalt thou not be accepted? and if thou doest not well, sin lieth at the door. And unto thee shall be his desire, and thou shalt rule over him.

8 And Cain talked with Abel his brother: and it came to pass, when they were in the field, that Cain rose up against Abel his brother, and slew him.

9 And the Lord said unto Cain, Where is Abel thy brother? And he said, I know not: Am I my brother's keeper?

Contents

Chapter one

England

The Act of Settlement 1701

I am starting with this chapter about the English Government, because the English, their greed, and their superiority complex, saw them treat almost every other nation, Race or Creed, with contempt.

This Act of Parliament demonstrates how the Roman Catholics were to be treated by the fact that from the passing of this Act ONLY Protestants could become Monarchs in England, and after 1707, that English throne, became a British throne.

The Act of Settlement is an Act of the Parliament of England that was passed in 1701[1] to settle the succession to the English and Irish crowns on Protestants only. This had the effect of deposing the descendants of Charles I (other than his Protestant granddaughter Princess (later Queen Anne) as the next Protestant in line to the throne was the Electress Sophia of Hanover, a granddaughter of James VI and I. After her, the crowns would descend only to her non-Catholic heirs.

The Act of Supremacy 1558 had confirmed the Church of England's independence from Roman Catholicism under the English monarch. In the political crises known as the Glorious Revolution of 1688 one issue was perceived assaults on the Church of England by King James II, a Roman Catholic. James was deposed in favour of his daughter Mary II and her husband William III. The need for the Act of Settlement was prompted by the failure of William and Mary, as well as of Mary's sister – the future Queen Anne – to produce any surviving children, and the Roman Catholic religion of other members of the House of Stuart. The line of Sophia of Hanover was the most junior among the Stuarts but consisted of convinced Protestants willing to uphold the Church of England. Sophia died on 8 June 1714, before the death of

---

[1] The act received Royal Assent in 1701. However, it is formally dated as 1700 in official use, such as the listing for the act in the *Chronological Table of the Statutes*, because acts passed before the Acts of Parliament (Commencement) Act 1793 came into force are dated by the year in which the relevant parliamentary session began, which, in this case, was 1700 (OS).

Queen Anne on 1 August 1714. On Queen Anne's death, Sophia's son duly became King George I and started the Hanoverian dynasty in Britain.

The act played a key role in the formation of the Kingdom of Great Britain. England and Scotland had shared a monarch since 1603 but had remained separately governed countries. The Scottish parliament was more reluctant than the English to abandon the House of Stuart, members of which had been Scottish monarchs long before they became English ones. English pressure on Scotland to accept the Act of Settlement was one factor leading to the parliamentary union of the two countries in 1707.

Under the Act of Settlement anyone who became a Roman Catholic, or who married one, became disqualified to inherit the throne. The act also placed limits on both the role of foreigners in the British government and the power of the monarch with respect to the Parliament of England. Some of those provisions have been altered by subsequent legislation.

Along with the Bill of Rights 1689, the Act of Settlement remains today one of the main constitutional laws governing the succession not only to the throne of the United Kingdom, but to those of the other Commonwealth realms, whether by assumption or by patriation.[2] The Act of Settlement cannot be altered in any realm except by that realm's own parliament and, by convention, only with the consent of all the other realms, as it touches on the succession to the shared crown.[3]

Following the Perth Agreement in 2011, legislation amending the act came into effect across the Commonwealth realms on 26 March 2015, and removed the disqualification arising from marriage to a Roman Catholic. Other provisions of the amended act remain in effect.

The Act also laid down the conditions under which the Crown could be held. No Roman Catholic, nor anyone married to a Roman Catholic, could hold the Crown. The Sovereign now had to swear to maintain the Church of England (and after 1707, the Church of Scotland).

The Act of Settlement not only addressed the dynastic and religious aspects of succession, it also further restricted the powers and prerogatives of the Crown.

---

[2] Toporoski, Richard (1998). "The Invisible Crown". *Monarchy Canada*. Toronto: Monarchist League of Canada (Summer 1998). Archived from the original on 9 February 2008. Retrieved 16 May 2009.
[3] The Statute of Westminster 1931", *legislation.gov.uk*, The National Archives, 1931 c. 4

Under the Act, parliamentary consent had to be given for the Sovereign to engage in war or leave the country, and judges were to hold office on good conduct and not at Royal pleasure – thus establishing judicial independence.

The Succession to the Crown Act (2013) amended the provisions of the Bill of Rights and the Act of Settlement to end the system of male primogeniture, under which a younger son can displace an elder daughter in the line of succession. The Act applies to those born after 28 October 2011. The Act also ended the provisions by which those who marry Roman Catholics are disqualified from the line of succession. The changes came into force in all sixteen Realms in March 2015).

Now we can start to look at the Segregation and Racial inequalities that were meted out to the Catholic Irish, as well as the Catholic Scottish.

If you have seen the movie "Braveheart" you will know that there was animosity between the English and the Scots. But "Braveheart" whilst it did much in Scotland to fuel the debate about Scottish Independence, it was not historically accurate.

Chapter two

Ireland

The Irish Rebellion of 1641

If you were to ask anyone other than an Irishman, about the Irish Rebellion, they will tell you about the Easter Uprising of 1916. But there were in fact several uprisings before that.

The Irish Rebellion of 1641 was an uprising by Irish Catholics in the kingdom of Ireland, who wanted an end to anti-Catholic discrimination, greater Irish self-governance, and to partially or fully reverse the plantations of Ireland. They also wanted to prevent a possible invasion or takeover by anti-Catholic English Parliamentarians and Scottish Covenanters, who were defying the king, Charles I. It began as an attempted *coup d'état* by Catholic gentry and military officers, who tried to seize control of the English administration in Ireland. However, it developed into a widespread rebellion and ethnic conflict with English and Scottish Protestant settlers, leading to Scottish military intervention. The rebels eventually founded the Irish Catholic Confederacy.

The rebellion began on 23 October. The plan to seize Dublin Castle was foiled, but the rebels swiftly captured numerous towns, forts and fortified houses in the northern province of Ulster. Within days they held most of the province. Rebel leader Felim O'Neill issued a forged proclamation claiming he had the king's blessing to secure Ireland against the king's opponents. The uprising spread southward and soon most of Ireland was in rebellion. In November, rebels besieged Drogheda and defeated an English relief force at Julian town. The following month, many Anglo-Irish Catholic lords joined the rebellion. In these first months especially in Ulster some Catholic rebels drove out or killed thousands of Protestant settlers (most notably the Portadown massacre), and settlers responded in kind. Reports of rebel massacres outraged Protestants in Britain and left a lasting impact on the Ulster Protestant community.

King Charles and the English parliament both sought to quell the rebellion, but parliament did not trust the king with command of any army raised to do so. This was one of the issues that led to the English Civil War. Charles ordered forces to be raised in Ireland, and the English parliament drafted a bill to give *itself* the power to raise armed forces. Eventually in April 1642, following negotiations between the English and Scottish parliaments, the Scots sent a Covenanter army to Ireland. It swiftly captured most of eastern Ulster, while a Protestant settler army held north-western Ulster.

Government forces meanwhile recaptured much of the Pale, and held the region around Cork. Most of the rest of Ireland was under rebel control.

In May 1642, Ireland's Catholic bishops met at Kilkenny, declared the rebellion to be a just war and took steps to control it. With representatives of the Catholic nobility in attendance, they agreed to set up an alternative government known as the Irish Catholic Confederacy and drew up the Confederate Oath of Association. The rebels, now known as Confederates, held most of Ireland against the Protestant Royalists, Scottish Covenanters and English Parliamentarians. The rebellion was thus the first stage of the Irish Confederate Wars and part of the wider Wars of the Three Kingdoms, which would last for the next ten years.

The roots of the 1641 rebellion lay partly in the Elizabethan conquest and colonisation of Ireland, and partly in the alienation of Anglo-Irish Catholics from the newly-Protestant English state in the decades following that conquest. Historian Aidan Clarke writes, "the religious factor was merely one aspect of a larger problem posed by the Gaelic Irish, and its importance was easily obscured; but religious difference was central to the relationship between the government and the colonists".[4]

The pre-Elizabethan Irish population is usually divided into the Gaelic Irish, and the Anglo-Irish or 'Old English', descendants of medieval English and Anglo-Norman settlers. These groups were historically antagonistic, with English settled areas such as the Pale around Dublin, south Wexford, and other walled towns being fortified against the rural Gaelic clans.[5] By the 17th century, the cultural divide between these groups, especially at elite social levels, was narrowing. An account in 1614, wrote, "the Old English race as well in the Pale as in other parts of the Kingdom, despised there mere Irish, accounting them to be a barbarous people, void of civility and religion and the other of them held the other as a hereditary enemy" but cited intermarriage "in former ages rarely seen", education of the Gaelic Irish and "the late plantation of New English and Scottish all part of the Kingdom whom the natives repute a common enemy; but this last is the principal cause of their union".[6] Many Old English lords not only spoke the Irish language, but extensively

---

[4] Aidan Clarke, "Plantation and the Catholic Question 1603–1623", in TW Moody, FX Martin FJ Byrne (editors), *A New History of Ireland: Early Modern Ireland 1534–1691*, p. 188
[5] Colm Lennon, *Sixteenth Century Ireland, The Incomplete Conquest* pp 67–68

patronised Irish poetry and music, and have been described as *Hiberniores Hibernis ipsis* ("More Irish than the Irish themselves"). Intermarriage was also common. Moreover, in the wake of the Elizabethan conquest, the native population became defined by their shared religion, Roman Catholicism, as opposed to the Protestantism of the new settlers (Church of England, Church of Scotland and Church of Ireland).[7]

During the decades between the end of the Elizabethan wars of re-conquest in 1603 and the outbreak of rebellion in 1641, the political position of the wealthier landed Irish Catholics was increasingly threatened by the English government of Ireland.[8]

The Tudor conquest of Ireland during the late 16th and early 17th century saw the Plantations of Ireland: where Irish-owned land was confiscated and colonised with settlers from Britain. The Ulster was the biggest, and saw the confiscating of vast amounts of forfeited land from the Irish lords who fled in the Flight of the Earls in 1607. Of this territory 20% was granted to "deserving" native Irish lords and clans.[9] The new settlers were required to be English-speaking and Protestant. By the time of the 1641 rebellion, native Irish society was not benefiting from the plantation, and this was exacerbated by the fact many grantees had to sell their estates due to poor management and the debts they incurred.[10] This erosion of their status and influence saw them prepared to join a rebellion even if they had more to lose.[11]

Many of the exiles (notably Eoghan Ruadh Ó Néill) found service as mercenaries in the Catholic armies of Spain and France. They formed a small émigré Irish community, militantly hostile to the English-run Protestant state in Ireland but restrained by the generally good relations England had with Spain and France after 1604. In Ireland itself the resentment caused by the plantations was one of the main causes for the outbreak and spread of the rebellion. Moreover, the Irish Parliament's legislation had to be approved by the English privy council, under a 15th-century Act of the Irish Parliament, known as Poynings' Law. The Protestant settler-

---

[6] A Discourse on the Present State of Ireland, Cited in Nicholas Canny, Making Ireland British, Oxford, 2003, pp.411–412
[7] Darcy, Eamonn. *The Irish Rebellion of 1641 and the Wars of the Three Kingdoms*. Boydell & Brewer, 2015. p.6
[8] The Gaelic Irish and Old English were increasingly seen by outsiders and increasingly defined themselves, as undifferentiated Irish." Padraig Lenihan, *Confederate Catholics at War*, pp 4–6.

[9] Robinson, Philip (2000); *The Plantation of Ulster*, page 86. Ulster Historical Foundation. ISBN 978-1-903688-00-7.
[10] Robinson, Philip (2000); *The Plantation of Ulster*, p. 190. Ulster Historical Foundation. ISBN 978-1-903688-00-7.
[11] Robinson, Philip (2000); *The Plantation of Ulster*, p. 190. Ulster Historical Foundation. ISBN 978-1-903688-00-7.

dominated administration took opportunities to confiscate more land from longstanding Catholic landowners.[12] In the late 1630s Thomas Wentworth, the Lord Deputy of Ireland, proposed a new round of plantations,[13] though these had not been implemented by 1641. In 1641, 60% of land still belonged to Catholics.[14]

Religious discrimination:

Most of the Irish Catholic upper classes were not opposed to the sovereignty of Charles I over Ireland but wanted to be full subjects and maintain their pre-eminent position in Irish society. This was prevented by their religion and by the threat of losing their land in the Plantations. The failed Gunpowder Plot of 1605 had led to further discrimination against, and mistrust of, Catholics.

Anglicanism, a branch of Protestantism, was the only approved form of worship. Practicing Catholicism in public could lead to arrest, and non-attendance at Protestant church services was punishable by recusant fines. Catholics could not hold senior offices of state or serve above a certain rank in the army. The Irish privy council was dominated by English Protestants. The constituencies of the Commons gave Protestants a majority.[15]

In response, the Irish Catholic upper classes sought 'The Graces', and appealed directly to the King, first James I and then Charles I, for full rights as subjects and toleration of their religion. On several occasions, the kings seemed to have reached an agreement with them, granting their demands in return for raising taxes. Irish Catholics were disappointed when, on paying the increased taxes after 1630, Charles postponed implementing their last two demands until he and the Privy Council of England instructed the Irish Lords Justices on 3 May 1641 to publish the required Bills.

The advancement of the Graces was particularly frustrated during the time that Wentworth was Lord Deputy. On the pretext of checking of land titles to raise revenue, Wentworth confiscated and was going to plant lands in counties Roscommon and Sligo and was planning further plantations in counties Galway and Kilkenny directed mainly at the Anglo-Irish Catholic families.[16] In the judgement of historian Pádraig Lenihan, "It is likely that he [Wentworth] would have eventually encountered armed resistance from Catholic landowners" if he had pursued these policies further.[17] However, the actual rebellion followed the

---

[12] Padraig Lenihan, Consolidating Conquest, pp. 56–57
[13] Padraig Lenihan, Confederate Catholics at War, p. 10, 'Wentworth saw plantation as the major instrument of cultural and religious change'
[14] Lenihan, Consolidating Conquest, p. 58
[15] TW Moody, FX Martin, FJ Byrne (editors). *A New History of Ireland: Volume III.* p.xlv
[16] Confederate Catholics at War p. 11
[17] Confederate Catholics at War, p. 12

destabilisation of English and Scottish politics and the weakened position of the king in 1640. Wentworth was executed in London in May 1641.

Conspiracy:

From 1638 to 1640 Scotland rose in a revolt known as the Bishops' Wars against Charles I's attempt to impose Church of England practices there, believing them to be too close to Catholicism. The King's attempts to put down the rebellion failed when the English Long Parliament, which had similar religious concerns to the Scots, refused to vote for new taxes to pay for raising an army. Charles therefore started negotiations with Irish Catholic gentry to recruit an Irish army to put down the rebellion in Scotland, in return for granting Irish Catholics their longstanding requests for religious toleration and land security. This army, made up mostly of Irish Catholics from Ulster, was slowly mobilised at Carrickfergus opposite the Scottish coast, but then began to be disbanded in mid-1641. To the Scots and the English parliament, this seemed to confirm that Charles was a tyrant, who wanted to impose his religious views on his kingdoms, and to govern again without his parliaments as he had done in 1628–1640. In early 1641, some Scots and English Parliamentarians even proposed invading Ireland and subduing Catholics there, to ensure that no royalist Irish Catholic army would land in England or Scotland.[18]

Frightened by this, and wanting to seize the opportunity, a small group of Irish Catholic landed gentry (some of whom were Members of Parliament) plotted to take Dublin Castle and other important towns and forts around the country in a quick *coup* in the name of the King, both to forestall a possible invasion and to force him to concede the Catholics' demands. At least three Irish colonels were also involved in the plot, and the plotters hoped to use soldiers from the disbanding Irish army.[19]

Unfavourable economic conditions also contributed to the outbreak of the rebellion. This decline may have been a consequence of the Little Ice Age event of the mid 17th Century. The Irish economy had hit a recession and the harvest of 1641 was poor. Interest rates in the 1630s had been as high as 30% per annum. The leaders of the rebellion like Phelim O'Neill and Rory O'Moore were heavily in debt and risked losing their lands to creditor'. What was more,'the Irish peasantry were hard hit by the bad harvest and were faced with rising rents. This aggravated their desire to remove the settlers and contributed to the widespread attacks on them at the start of the rebellion.

---

[18] Lenihan, Confederate Catholics at War, pp.22–23
[19] Perceval-Maxwell, Michael. *The Outbreak of the Irish Rebellion of 1641*. McGill-Queen's Press, 1994. pp.208–209

TheXXXrocers of the reb'llion were a sma'l group of Catholic landed gentry and military officers, mainly Gaelic Irish and from the heavily planted province of Ulster. The rising was to take place on Saturday 23 October 1641. Armed men led by Connor Maguire and Rory O' Moore were to seize Dublin Castle and its arsenal and hold it until help came from insurgents in neighbouring County Wicklow. Meanwhile, Felim O'Neil and his allies were to take several forts in Ulster.[20] Their plan was to use surprise rather than force to take their objectives without bloodshed, and then issue their demands, in expectation of support from the rest of the country.[21] The English garrison of Ireland was only about 2,000 strong and scattered around the country.[22] The plan to seize Dublin Castle was foiled after one of the plotters, Hugh Og MacMahon, mistakenly revealed details of the plot to his foster-brother, a Protestant convert named Owen O'Connolly. O' Connolly informed one of the Lord Justices, and MacMahon and Maguire were arrested.[23] The remaining rebels slipped out of Dublin.[24] (After the Restoration, the Parliament of Ireland made 23 October an annual day of Thanksgiving.[25])

Meanwhile, Felim O'Neill and his allies captured several forts and small towns in Ulster. Within two days, the rebels had captured most of counties Armagh, Tyrone, Fermanagh, and Monaghan. O'Neill and his men took Dungannon and Charlemont, the McCartans and Magennises took Newry, the O'Hanlons took Tandragee, the McCanns took Portadown, the O'Quinns took Mountjoy Castle.

The McMahons took Castleblaney and Carrickmacross,[26] and rebels led by Rory Maguire captured most of Fermanagh.[27] Any forts that did not surrender were

---

[20] John Kenyon, Jane Ohlmeyer, eds. *The Civil Wars, A Military History of England, Scotland and Ireland, 1638–1660*, pp. 29–30. One of his [Phelim O'Neill's] creditors, Mr Fullerton of Loughal ... was one of the first to be murdered in the rebellion".

[21] "But when they engaged in their insurrection on 22 October 1641, unquestionably they weren't intending on the destruction of the entire Plantation that had been brought into place. We don't know precisely what they intended: they presumably intended to seize the positions of strength, the military fortification of the province; having done that to, from this position of strength, to engage in some negotiation with the Crown with a view to bettering their condition in some way. But they, I think it is correct to say, that they weren't intent on destroying the Plantation." (Nicholas Canny, "The Plantation of Ireland: 1641 rebellion" Archived 22 February 2012 at the Wayback Machine BBC lecture. Accessed 12 February 2008.)

[22] Dorney, John. "Today in Irish History – First Day of the 1641 Rebellion, October 23". *The Irish Story*.

[23] Perceval-Maxwell, Michael. *The Outbreak of the Irish Rebellion of 1641*. McGill-Queen's Press, 1994. p.210

[24] Dorney, John. "Today in Irish History – First Day of the 1641 Rebellion, October 23". *The Irish Story*.

[25] 1662 (14 & 15 Chas. 2 sess. 4) c. 23". *Statutes Passed in the Parliaments Held in Ireland: 1310–1662*. George Grierson, printer to the King's Most Excellent Majesty. 1794. pp. 610–2.

[26] Liam Kennedy & Philip Ollerenshaw. *Ulster Since 1600: Politics, Economy, and Society*. Oxford University Press, 2013. p.29

[27] Perceval-Maxwell, Michael. *The Outbreak of the Irish Rebellion of 1641*. McGill-Queen's Press, 1994. pp.214–219

besieged. On 24 October, O'Neill issued the Proclamation of Dungannon, saying they were not in arms against the king, but only in defence of their freedoms, and that they meant no harm to the king's subjects.[28] Within a week, most of County Cavan had also been captured by rebels l'd by Philip O'Reilly (it's Member of Parliament) and Mulmore O' Reilly (its High Sheriff).[29] An army of at least 8,000 rebels advanced into eastern Ulster and besieged Lisnagarvey, but failed to take it.[30] At Newry on 4 November, Felim O'Neill and Rory Maguire issued a declaration, claiming the rebels were doing the king's bidding. It claimed King Charles had commissioned O'Neill to lead Irish Catholics to secure Ireland against the king's Protestant Parliamentarian opponents.[31] Though a forgery, the declaration persuaded many Catholic gentry in the rest of Ireland to support him.[32]

By early November, organized rebellion had begun outside Ulster: in County Louth, where Dundalk was captured and the Anglo-Irish Catholic gentry joined the rebellion,[33] as well as counties Leitrim and Longford.[34] Rebel forces from Ulster began advancing south towards Dublin. On 21 November, rebels under Brian McMahon began to besiege the important town of Drogheda from the north. Another rebel force under the O'Reilleys advanced through County Meath, capturing towns, before blockading Drogheda from the south. On 29 November, they defeated an English relief force sent from Dublin in the battle of Julianstown, killing 600 English soldiers.[35] By this time, rebellion had spread further south to counties Kildare,[36] Wicklow, Wexford and Tipperary.[37] In early December, the Anglo-Irish Catholic lords of the Pale joined the rebellion.[38]

The English authorities in Dublin over-reacted to the rebellion, calling it "a most disloyal and detestable conspiracy" by "some evil affected Irish Papists", which was aimed at "a general massacre of all English and Protestant inhabitants".[39] In December, the English authorities in Dublin sent troops under commanders Charles

---

[28] Corish, Patrick. "The Rising of 1641 and the Confederacy", in *A New History of Ireland: Volume III*, Oxford University Press, 1991. pp.289–296

[29] Perceval-Maxwell, p.220

[30] Perceval-Maxwell, Michael. *The Outbreak of the Irish Rebellion of 1641*. McGill-Queen's Press, 1994. pp.214–219

[31] Perceval-Maxwell, p.218

[32] *http://www.kco.ie Kco Ltd. -. "1641 Depositions". 1641.tcd.ie. Archived from the original on 31 December 2011.*

[33] Perceval-Maxwell, p.222

[34] Perceval-Maxwell, p.225

[35] Perceval-Maxwell, pp.222–223

[36] Perceval-Maxwell, p.256

[37] Perceval-Maxwell, p.245

[38] Perceval-Maxwell, p.245

[39] Richard Bellings, *History of the Confederation and War in Ireland* (c. 1670), in Gilbert, J. T., *History of the Affairs of Ireland*, Irish Archaeological and Celtic Society, Dublin, 1879. pp. 9, 18

Coote and William St Leger (both Protestants) to rebel-held areas in counties Wicklow and Tipperary respectively. Their expeditions were characterised by what modern historian Padraig Lenihan has called, "excessive and indiscriminate brutality" against the general Catholic population there[40] and helped to provoke the general Catholic population into joining the rebellion. The rebellion in Munster, the last region to witness such disturbances, was driven by the severe martial law William St Leger imposed there.[41]

Meanwhile, the breakdown of state authority prompted widespread attacks by the native Irish on the English Protestant settlers, especially in Ulster.[42] Initially, Scottish settlers were not attacked but as the rebellion went on, they too became targets.[43] O'Neill and the other rebel leaders tried to stop the attacks on settlers but were unable to control the peasantry. A contemporary (though hostile) Catholic source tells us that O'Neill "strove to contain the rascal multitude from those frequent savage actions of stripping and killing" but that "the floodgate of rapine, once being laid open, the meaner sort of people was not to be contained".[44] Many Catholic lords who had lost lands or feared dispossession joined the rebellion and participated in attacks on settlers. Such attacks usually involved the beating and robbing rather than the killing of Protestants. Historian Nicholas Canny writes, "most insurgents seemed anxious for a resolution of their immediate economic difficulties by seizing the property of any of the settlers. These popular attacks did not usually result in loss of life, nor was it the purpose of the insurgents to kill their victims. They nevertheless were gruesome affairs because they involved face to face confrontations between people who had long known each other. A typical attack involved a group of Irish descending upon a Protestant family and demanding, at knifepoint, that they surrender their moveable goods. Killings usually only occurred where Protestants resisted".[45]

---

[40] Lenihan, *Confederate Catholics at War*, p. 23

[41] Corish, Patrick. "The Rising of 1641 and the Confederacy", in *A New History of Ireland: Volume III*, Oxford University Press, 1991. pp.289–296

[42] But on the 23rd and the 24th and 25th of October 1641, the popular attacks which are relatively spontaneous, are clearly focused upon the tenants who had moved in and become beneficiaries of the Plantation; and that these actions, as well as the words which are articulated in justifying those actions – targeted attacks upon those who had moved in and benefited from the Plantation – these indicate that there was a popular sentiment of dispossession which was articulated in action as well as in words when the opportunity provided itself, when the political order was challenged by the actions which Phelim O'Neill and his associates engaged upon." (Nicholas Canny "The Plantation of Ireland: 1641 rebellion" Archived 22 February 2012 at the Way back Machine BBC lecture. Accessed 12 February 2008.

[43] Canny, *Making Ireland British*, p. 486

[44] Richard Bellings, "History of the Confederation and War in Ireland" (c. 1670), in Gilbert, J. T., *History of the Affairs of Ireland*, Irish Archaeological and Celtic Society, Dublin, 1879. pp. 14–15

[45] Nicholas Canny, *Making Ireland British*, p. 476

The motivations for the popular rebellion were complex. Among them was a desire to reverse the plantations; rebels in Ulster were reported as saying, "the land was theirs and lost by their fathers".[46] Another motivating factor was antagonism towards the English language and culture which had been imposed on the country. For example, rebels in County Cavan forbade the use of the English language and decreed that the original Irish language place names should replace English ones.[47] A third factor was religious antagonism. The rebels consciously identified themselves as Catholics and justified the rising as a defensive measure against the Protestant threat to "extirpate the Catholic religion". Rebels in Cavan stated "we rise for our religion. They hang our priests in England".[48] Historian Brian MacCuarta writes, "Longstanding animosities against the Protestant clergy were based on the imposition of the state church since its inception thirty years previously. Ulster Irish ferocity against everything Protestant were fuelled by the wealth of the church in Ulster, exceptional in contemporary Ireland".[49] There were also cases of purely religious violence, where native Irish Protestants were attacked, and Catholic settlers joined the rebellion.[50]

The number of Protestant settlers killed in the early months of the uprising is debated.[51] Early English Parliamentarian pamphlets claimed that over 200,000 Protestants had lost their lives.[52] Recent research suggests the number is much lower, in the region of 4,000 or so killed, though thousands more were expelled from their homes.[53] It is estimated that up to 12,000 Protestants may have lost their lives in total, most dying of cold or disease after being expelled from their homes in the depths of winter.[54] [55] If the upper estimate of 12,000 deaths is accurate, this would represent less than 10% of the British settler population in Ireland, though in Ulster the ratio of deaths to the settler population would have been somewhat higher, namely around 30%.[56]

---

[46] *Age of Atrocity*, p.154
[47] *Age of Atrocity*, p.154
[48] *Age of Atrocity*, p. 153
[49] *Age of Atrocity*, p. 155
[50] Canny, *Making Ireland British*, p. 177; *Age of Atrocity*, p. 154
[51] Staff Massacres and myths Archived 21 February 2008 at the Wayback Machine, University of Cambridge, Information provided by news.online@admin.cam.ac.uk, 21 October 2007
[52] *Royle, Trevor (2004), Civil War: The Wars of the Three Kingdoms 1638–1660, London: Abacus, ISBN 0-349-11564-8* p.139
[53] "William Petty's figure of 37,000 Protestants massacred... is far too high, perhaps by a factor of ten, certainly more recent research suggests that a much more realistic figure is roughly 4,000 deaths." Ohlmeyer, Jane; Kenyon, John. *The Civil Wars*, p. 278.
[54]"Modern historians estimate the number massacred in Ireland in 1641 at between 2,000 and 12,000." Marshal, John (2006). *John Locke, Toleration and Early Enlightenment Culture* Cambridge University Press, ISBN 0-521-65114-X, Page 58, footnote 10.
[55] "The Plantation of Ulster: 1641 rebellion Archived 26 October 2017 at the Way back Machine, BBC Paragraph 3. Accessed 17 February 2008.
[56] Mary O' Dowd. 1641 rebellion Archived 26 October 2017at the Way back Machine. Accessed 8 March 2008

The general pattern was that the attacks intensified the longer the rebellion went on. At first, there were beatings and robbing of settlers, then house burnings and expulsions, and finally killings, most of them concentrated in Ulster. Historian Nicholas Canny suggests that attacks on settlers escalated after a failed rebel assault on Lisnagarvey in November 1641, after which the settlers killed several hundred captured rebels. Canny writes, "the bloody-mindedness of the settlers in taking revenge when they gained the upper hand in battle seems to have made such a deep impression on the insurgents that, as one deponent put it, 'the slaughter of the English' could be dated from this encounter".[57] That month, rebels killed about 100 captive settlers at Portadown by forcing them off the bridge into the River Bann, and shooting those who tried to swim to safety. Known as the Portadown massacre, it was one of the bloodiest massacres in Ireland during the conflicts of the 1640s.[58] In nearby Kilmore parish, English and Scottish men, women, and children were burned to death in the cottage in which they were imprisoned.[59] In County Armagh, recent research has shown that about 1,250 Protestants were killed in the early months of the rebellion, or about a quarter of the settler population there.[60] In County Tyrone, modern research has identified three blackspots for the killing of settlers, with the worst being near Kinard, "where most of the British families planted... were ultimately murdered".[61] There were also massacres of settlers outside Ulster, such as the Shrule massacre in County Mayo, where dozens of Protestant prisoners were killed by their Catholic escorts.

The massacres were used to support the view that the rebellion was a Catholic conspiracy to wipe out all Protestants in Ireland.[62] This narrative was constructed in the Depositions, a collection of accounts by victims gathered between 1642 and 1655 and now housed in Trinity College Dublin.[63] [64] The accounts were outlined in a book published by John Temple in 1646, entitled *The Irish Rebellion*.[65] Temple used the massacres of Protestants to lobby for the military re-conquest of Ireland and the segregation of Irish Catholics from British Protestants.[66]

Some settlers also massacred Catholics, particularly in 1642–43 when a Scottish Covenanter army landed in Ulster. William Lecky, the 19th-century historian of the rebellion, concluded that "it is far from clear on which side the balance of cruelty rests".[67] O

---

[57] Canny, *Making Ireland British*, p. 485.
[58] Darcy, Eamon. *The Irish Rebellion of 1641 and the Wars of the Three Kingdoms*. Boydell & Brewer, 2015. pp.68–69
[59] A deposition made by one William Clarke to the effect that "about 100 Protestants (including women and children) from the nearby parish of Loughal, who were already prisoners" were killed at the bridge in Portadown in November 1641. Nicholas Canny, *Making Ireland British*, p. 485.
[60] Ohlmeyer and Kenyon, *The Civil Wars*, p. 74
[61] Lenihan, *Confederate Catholics at War*, p. 31
[62] Mac Cuarta, Brian. *Ulster 1641: Aspects of the Rising*. Institute of Irish Studies, Queen's University of Belfast, 1993. p.126
[63] "How lies about Irish 'barbarism' in 1641 paved way for Cromwell's atrocities". The Guardian. 18 February 2011.
[64] "1641 Depositions". Trinity College Dublin. Retrieved 5 March 2021.
[65] Noonan, Kathleen M. "Martyrs in Flames": Sir John Temple and the conception of the Irish in English martyrologies*. Albion, June 2004. On the website of Questia Online Library
[66] Darcy, pp.99–100

n its march through County Down, the Covenanter army killed Irish prisoners at Kilwarlin woods near Dromore and then massacred Catholic prisoners and civilians in Newry.[68] [69] James Turner records that Catholic soldiers and local merchants were lined up on the banks of the Newry River and "butchered to death without any legal process".[70] On Rathlin Island, Scottish Covenanter soldiers of Clan Campbell were encouraged by their commanding officer Campbell to kill the local Catholic MacDonnells, who were related to the Campbells' enemies in Scotland, Clan MacDonald. They threw scores of MacDonnell women over cliffs to their deaths.[71] The number of victims of this massacre has been put as low as 100 and as high as 3,000.

The widespread killing of civilians was brought under control to some degree in 1642, when Owen Roe O'Neill arrived in Ulster to command the Irish Catholic forces and hanged several rebels for attacks on civilians. Thereafter, the war, though still brutal, was fought in line with the code of conduct that both O'Neill and the Scottish commander Robert Monro had learned as professional soldiers in mainland Europe.[72]

In the long term, the killings by both sides in 1641 intensified the sectarian animosity that originated in the plantations. Modern historians argue that the killings had a powerful psychological impact on the Protestant settlers especially.[73] [74] Dr Mary O' Dowd wrote that they "were very traumatic for the Protestant settler community in Ulster, and they left long-term scars within that community".[75] Contemporary Protestant accounts depict the rebellion

---

[67] Patrick J. Corish, A New History of Ireland, Volume 3: Early Modern Ireland 1534–1691 By T. W. Moody, F. X. Martin, F. J. Byrne in, p292

[68] *Royle, Trevor (2004), Civil War: The Wars of the Three Kingdoms 1638–1660, London: Abacus, ISBN 0-349-11564-8* p. 142

[69] Ulster Archaeological Society, (1860). *Ulster Journal of Archaeology* Volume 8, London: Russell J Smith, Ireland: Hodges & Smith. p. 78–80

[70] *Royle, Trevor (2004), Civil War: The Wars of the Three Kingdoms 1638–1660, London: Abacus, ISBN 0-349-11564-8* p. 142

[71] *Royle, Trevor (2004), Civil War: The Wars of the Three Kingdoms 1638–1660, London: Abacus, ISBN 0-349-11564-8* p. 143

[72] Pádraig Lenihan, (2001) *Confederate Catholics at War, 1641–49*, Cork University Press, ISBN 1-85918-244-5. p. 211, 212

[73] Massacres and myths Archived 21 February 2008 at the Wayback Machine, University of Cambridge, Information provided by news.online@admin.cam.ac.uk, 21 October 2007. John Morrill wrote: "The 1641 massacres have played a key role in creating and sustaining a collective Protestant and British identity in Ulster."

[74] Dr Raymond Gillespie of the National University of Ireland, Maynooth, "I think in some ways it's what happens after the Plantation which is much more important for the enduring legacy. It's the fears of the Irish which are created in 1641, the fear of massacre, the fear of attack, that somehow or other accommodations which had been made before were no longer possible after that because the Irish were quite simply, as John Temple put it in his history of the rebellion 'untrustworthy'. And that book was repeatedly reprinted – I think the last time it was reprinted was 1912, so that this message (the message not of the Plantation but the message of the rebellion) is the one that persists and the one which is used continuously right through the 19th century – that the Catholics are untrustworthy; that we can't do business with them; we shouldn't be involved with them; they are part of a large conspiracy to do us down" (Raymond Gillespie Plantation of Ulster: Long term consequences Archived 24 September 2009 at the Way back Machine, BBC. Accessed 13 February 2008).

as a complete surprise; one stated that it was "conceived among us and yet we never felt it kick in the womb, nor struggle in the birth".[76] Many of them took the view that Catholics could no longer be trusted. Ulster Pro"estants commemorated the anniversary of the rebellion every 23 October for over two hundred years. According to Pádraig Lenihan, "This anniversary helped affirm communal solidarity and emphasise the need for unrelenting vigilance; [they perceived that] the masses of Irish Catholics surrounding them were and always would be, unregenerate and cruel enemies".[77] Images of rebel massacres are still shown on the banners of the Orange Order.

English and Scottish intervention:

King Charles, the English Parliament and the Scottish Parliament all agreed that the rebellion should be crushed. However, British intervention was stalled by the ongoing tension between the king and the parliaments. Charles received news of the rebellion while in Scotland on 28 October. He urged the Scottish Parliament to be ready to send troops to Ulster as soon as the English Parliament agreed to Scottish intervention. In the meantime, he bought weapons and gunpowder and had them sent to Ireland at his own expense and arranged for a small number of Scottish volunteers to be sent to Ulster. Charles "had no money to finance an expedition on his own, and had he tried to raise funds by non-parliamentary means, the Commons would have protested".[78] The king and Lords Justices in Dublin appointed James Butler, 1st Duke of Ormond, to command the King's forces in Ireland. He recruited three infantry regiments from among the refugees flooding into Dublin.[79] The King and the Lords Justices commissioned many of the leading Ulster Scots settlers to raise regiments, such as Robert and William Stewart, who formed the Laggan Army.[80]

On 4 November, the English parliament voted to send weapons and gunpowder to the English government in Ireland, and for an army of 8,000 to be raised to crush the rebellion.[81] By law, the army would be under the king's overall command. However, neither the English nor Scottish parliaments wanted the king to have command of such an army, as they feared he would then use it against them.[82] Some of them suspected that Charles was involved in the rebellion. The rebels claimed to be doing the king's bidding, and there was suspicion he would use the rebellion to gain an army for himself.[83] During the first few months, the

---

[75] Mary O' Dowd. The Plantation of Ulster: Long term consequences Archived 22 February 2012 at the Way back Machine BBC. Accessed 12 February 2008
[76] Ohlmeyer, Kenyon, *The Civil Wars*, p. 29
[77] Pádraig Lenihan, 1690, *Battle of the Boyne*. Tempus (2003) ISBN 0-7524-2597-8 pp. 257–258
[78] Perceval-Maxwell, p.262
[79] Wheeler, James. *The Irish and British Wars, 1637–1654: Triumph, Tragedy, and Failure*. Routledge, 2003. p.46
[80] Stevenson, David. *Scottish Covenanters and Irish Confederates*. Ulster Historical Foundation, 2005. p.52
[81] "House of Lords Journal Volume 4: 4 November 1641 – British History Online". *www.british-history.ac.uk*.
[82] Wheeler, James. *The Irish and British Wars, 1637–1654: Triumph, Tragedy, and Failure*. Routledge, 2003. p.46

English parliament instead ordered separate regiments to be recruited and shipped to Ireland to join the forces already there.[84] In early 1642, parliament passed the Militia Ordinance, which meant that *parliament* (rather than the king) would have command of military forces.[85] In March 1642, the English parliament passed the Adventurers' Act, which received royal assent. Under this act, wealthy Englishmen could fund the army to crush the rebellion and be repaid with land confiscated from the rebels.[86]

At the outbreak of the rebellion, the Scottish Covenanters requested funds from the English parliament for sending an army to Ulster. An army could be sent from Scotland more quickly and cheaply, and a Scottish army would not be commanded by the king nor the English parliament.[87] Some in the English parliament had misgivings about letting a large Scottish army land in Ulster, but on 21 December the House of Lords eventually agreed on sending 10,000 Scots. The Scots then insisted they should control the three biggest ports in Ulster (Carrickfergus, Coleraine and Derry), and be given Irish land for their services. This led to further delay, as there was opposition in the English parliament. Meanwhile, the rebellion in Ireland continued to spread. Eventually, in February 1642, the English and Scottish parliaments put aside their differences and agreed on sending 2,500 Scots to Ulster.[88] The army, led by Robert Monro, landed at Carrickfergus on 15 April 1642. It advanced through County Down and captured Newry on 1 May.[89]

Meanwhile, the royal army led by Ormond regained much of the Pale from the rebels in early 1642. In March his forces ended the rebel siege of Drogheda and re-took Dundalk, and in April defeated a rebel force at the Battle of Kilrush.[90]

In mid-1642, British forces totalled: 40,000-foot and 3600 horses with 300 manning the artillery. Included in this total are 10,000-foot raised by the Scottish parliament and sent to Ulster to defend their compatriots there.[91]

A quick defeat of the rebels in Ireland was prevented by the outbreak of the English Civil War in August 1642. Some English troops were withdrawn from Ireland in late 1642 and a military stalemate ensued.[92]

By early 1642, there were four main concentrations of rebel forces; in Ulster under Felim O'Neill, in the Pale around Dublin led by Viscount Gormanston, in the south-east, led by the Butler family in particular Lord Mountgarret, and in the south-west, led by Donagh

83 Perceval-Maxwell, p.264
84 Wheeler, p.49
85 Carpenter, Stanley. *Military Leadership in the British Civil Wars*. Routledge, 2004. p.36
86 Ohlmeyer, Jane. *Ireland from Independence to Occupation, 1641–1660*. Cambridge University Press, 2002. p.192
87 Stevenson, David. *Scottish Covenanters and Irish Confederates*. pp.45, 48
88 Perceval-Maxwell, pp.267–268
89 Corish, Patrick. "The Rising of 1641 and the Confederacy", in *A New History of Ireland: Volume III*, Oxford University Press, 1991. pp.289–296
90 Corish, Patrick. "The Rising of 1641 and the Confederacy", in *A New History of Ireland: Volume III*, Oxford University Press, 1991. pp.289–296
91 Ryder, *An English Army for Ireland*, p.14
92 Kenyon, Ohlmeyer, p.77

MacCarthy, Viscount Muskerry. In areas where British settlers were concentrated, around Cork, Dublin, Carrickfergus and Derry, they raised their own militia in self-defence and managed to hold off the rebel forces.[84]

Within a few months of the rebellion's outbreak, almost all the Catholic gentry had joined it, including the Anglo-Irish Catholics. There are three main reasons for this. First, local lords and landowners raised armed units of their dependents to control the violence that was engulfing the country, fearing that after the settlers were gone, the Irish peasantry would turn on them as well. Secondly, the Long Parliament and the Irish administration, and King Charles, made it clear that Irish Catholics who did not demonstrate their loyalty would be held responsible for the rebellion and killings of settlers, and would confiscate their lands under the Adventurers Act, agreed on 19 March 1642. The old policy of issuing pardons to stop conflicts was ended, and the rebel leaders were outlawed on 1 January 1642. Thirdly, it looked initially as if the rebels would be successful after they defeated a government force at Julianstown in November 1641. This perception was soon shattered when the rebels failed to take nearby Drogheda, but by then most of the Catholic gentry had already committed themselves to rebellion.[93] The Catholic gentry around Dublin, known as the "Lords of the Pale", issued their Remonstrance to the king on 17 March 1642 at Trim, County Meath.

Hugh O'Reilly (Archbishop of Armagh) held a synod of Irish bishops at Kells, County Meath in March 1642, where a majority declared that the ongoing conflict was a "holy and just war".[94]

On 10 May 1642, Archbishop O'Reilly convened another synod at Kilkenny. Present were 3 archbishops, 11 bishops or their representatives, and other dignitaries.[95] They drafted the Confederate Oath of Association and called on all Catholics in Ireland to take it. Those who took the oath swore allegiance to Charles I and vowed to obey all orders and decrees made by the "Supreme Council of the Confederate Catholics". The rebels henceforth became known as Confederates. The synod re-affirmed that the rebellion was a "just war".[96] It called for the creation of a council (made up of clergy and nobility) for each province, which would be overseen by a national council for the whole island. It vowed to punish misdeeds by Confederate soldiers and to excommunicate any Catholic who fought against the Confederation. The synod sent agents to France, Spain, and Italy to gain support, gather funds and weapons, and recruit Irishmen serving in foreign armies.[97] Lord Mountgarret was appointed president of the Confederate Council, and a General Assembly was fixed for October that year.[98]

The Confederate general Assembly was held in Kilkenny on 24 october 1642, where It set up a provisional government.[99] Present were 14 Lords Temporal and 11 Lords

---

93 Lenihan, Confederate Catholics at War, pp. 24–26
94 "Hugh O'Reilly". *www.catholicity.com*. Archived from the original on 2 April 2017.
95 Meehan, Charles Patrick. *The Confederation of Kilkenny*. 1846. p. 27
96 Meehan, p. 29
97 Meehan, p. 30
98 Meehan, p. 31
99 Meehan, p. 43

Spiritual (Bishops) from the Parliament of Ireland, along with 226 commoners.[100] The Assembly elected a Supreme Council of 24.[101] The Supreme Council would have power over all military generals, military officers and civil magistrates.[102] Its first act was to name the generals who were to command Confederate forces: Owen Roe O'Neill was to command the Ulster forces, Thomas Preston the Leinster forces, Garret Barry the Munster forces and John Burke the Connaught forces.[103] A National Treasury, a mint for making coins, and a press for printing proclamations were set up in Kilkenny.[104]

The Confederation eventually sided with the Royalists in return for the promise of self-government and full rights for Catholics after the war. They were finally defeated by the English Parliament's New Model Army from 1649 through to 1653 and land ownership in Ireland passed largely to Protestant settlers. [105]

Any sign of insurrection after this, and the perpetrators could find themselves being shipped off to the "New World" as slaves.

---

[100] Meehan, p. 41
[101] Meehan, p. 43
[102] Meehan, p. 44
[103] Meehan, p. 44
[104] Meehan, p. 45
[105] Canny pp. 562–566

Chapter three

Battle of the Boyne

The Battle of the Boyne was actually fought on July 1st. 1690 but changes made because of the Gregorian Calendar, which meant after the battle, the date was changed to 12th. July. The battle was a time in British history, a major conflict fought along the Boyne River in Ireland between King William III (William of Orange) and the exiled king James II. Having been deposed and exiled after William's landing at Brixham and subsequent English desertions, James II sought to retake his throne through an alliance with Ireland and France. A string of Irish Jacobite victories in the northern country were followed by a swift but indecisive loss on the Boyne River. Although James's escape dragged the First Jacobite Rising into 1691, the Battle of the Boyne reassured William's allies of his commitment to defeating all French-aligned forces.

The Battle of the Boyne, Ireland, between Kings James II and William III, 12 July 1690

The last half of the 17th century was a turbulent time for England. Following the English Civil War's bloody end, the country was ruled by the Puritan Oliver Cromwell and, after his death, his son Richard. The English Protectorate only ended after Richard's resignation, after which Parliament alone ruled until the house of

Stuart's restoration in 1660. Under King Charles II, the crown began to align itself with France, then an ambitious continental power and the strongest of the Catholic kingdoms. Charles was a shrewd politician, and some years before his death in 1685, he signed the Treaty of Dover. In exchange for financial assistance from France, Charles would privately convert to Catholicism and devote a number of English warships to King Louis XIV's war effort against the Protestant Dutch Republic.

Despite Charles's foreign political savvy, his domestic policy of religious tolerance did not sit well with many Irish Catholics, who had supported the exiled Stuarts at great personal risk. Under Cromwell's rule, much of their property had been stripped from them. English Protestants were also incentivized to settle in Ireland, further reducing the power of Irish Catholics. Having suffered so heavily for the Stuarts, Charles's Catholic subjects hoped for more explicitly beneficial treatment. Charles's support of his fellow believers was tacit, in contrast to that of his openly Catholic brother, James. When James II acceded to the throne in 1685, he enacted several military reforms in Ireland aimed at eliminating local Protestant influence. The Earl of Tyrconnell was tasked with disarming Protestant militias and levying an Irish army loyal not to Anglican-controlled Parliament but only to the crown.

On the other side of the North Sea, tensions escalated between France and the Dutch Republic. William III of Orange, an elected stadtholder (chief magistrate) of five major Dutch provinces, had successfully defended the Netherlands against a French invasion from 1672 to 1678. A second invasion in 1680 cemented William's opposition to an expansionist France. Setting aside religious differences, he joined the League of Augsburg alongside several Catholic powers aimed at putting a decisive end to French land grabs.

Shortly before the end of the first French invasion, William had wed his cousin Mary, who was also King Charles II's niece. In the absence of any eligible male heirs, Mary was second to an aging James in the line of succession, meaning that upon James's death, she and William could turn English firepower on France. William understood the importance of the Royal Navy in any military designs against France, and such designs would end in disaster if Charles remained a French ally with Catholic sympathies. Unfortunately for William, the line of succession changed in June 1688, when King James II's wife bore a son.

Amid doubts regarding the child's legitimacy, William rallied thousands of Dutchmen to his banner and prepared to cross the North Sea. With favourable weather conditions that stayed the English fleet, he landed that November at Brixham, located in Devonshire on Tor Bay. James's government and military splintered as men flocked to William's standard. William entered London in mid-December. By Christmas Eve, James had quietly quit his country for France, effectively ceding the throne to William.

In April 1689, Parliament crowned William and Mary joint sovereigns of Britain. Between William III's landing and coronation, however, Ireland had grown dangerously recalcitrant. Tyrconnell was able to muster his formidable army of Irish Catholics, known as Jacobites for their loyalty to the exiled James II. Tyrconnell consolidated Jacobite dominance in Ireland over a matter of months, with only a few pockets of Protestant resistance. Just weeks before William's coronation, James received enough French support to set in motion his plan to retake the throne. On March 12 he landed in the southern Irish town of Kinsale with nearly all the northern country under his control. Two major Protestant strongholds, Derry (now Londonderry) and Enniskillen, became the sites of major conflict over the next few months.

James lay siege to Derry on April 18. The city held out for three months until a Williamite relief force arrived, and by the end of July the Jacobites had retreated. Also in July, Protestants rebuffed a Jacobite army at Enniskillen and forced them to withdraw. Following Enniskillen, William dispatched a landing force of some 20,000 men from England under the duke of Schomberg, a seasoned military commander from the Holy Roman Empire. Schomberg's army was primarily Dutch, with some fresh English recruits and a few thousand Danes. At the head of this army, Schomberg landed in Northern Ireland at Bangor on August 13. He seized the town of Carrickfergus and advanced south toward Dublin. James's armies, which by now had reached Drogheda en route to the Irish capital, wheeled around to block Schomberg's movements. In September the two forces took up camp on opposite sides of Dundalk, a town in the south of Ulster province. They remained there through the winter.

During this lull in fighting, James's envoys in France were able to secure reinforcements from the mainland. Some 6,000 French musketeers landed in southern Ireland in March 1690. In London, William convinced Parliament to grant him more funds for the duration of the war. He also announced his intention to personally bring an end to the Jacobite rising. At the head of 15,000 reinforcements, William landed at Carrickfergus on June 14, 1690.

James deduced that protecting Dublin was of paramount importance. It was both the Irish seat of power and unacceptably unfortified. With Dublin's poor position as a defence point itself, his advisers were split regarding the best location to halt

William's advance. Some thought he should create a bottleneck at Moyry Pass, while others were wary of being flanked and slaughtered. James settled on a defensive position on the southern banks of the Boyne River, 25 miles (40 kilometres) north of Dublin and the ancient city's largest natural defence. He set up camp on June 29. William established his headquarters across the river shortly thereafter.

South of the Boyne, James II commanded an army of roughly 23,000 men. The overwhelming majority were Irish Catholics trained under Tyrconnell's supervision, in addition to the 6,000 French soldiers from Louis XIV. While the French had seen combat, the Irish troops were far less experienced and bore outdated muskets. Furthermore, James had a speckled military past that painted him as a poor commander. At the Boyne, James decided to position the bulk of his forces along the river, deployed such that they could make immediate contact with William's army upon their crossing. This would hold their centre in place and prevent William's artillery from firing, without killing their fellow soldiers. The remainder of his men were tasked with destroying bridges and guarding potential fords. To this end, James set a small force east to the crossing at Drogheda and dispatched dragoons to the southwestern ford near the village of Rosnaree.

North of the Boyne, William III's army numbered some 37,000 men. Roughly half were British. The remainder were mostly Dutch, with a few thousand Danes and a smattering of French Huguenots. His Dutch soldiers were seasoned fighters from the war against France, and all were armed with modern flintlock muskets. William also possessed an estimated eight times the number of James's artillery pieces.

Unlike his opponent, William had proven his military acumen, in his defence of the Netherlands. He was determined to bring his skills to the Boyne as well. After much internal debate, William settled on a three-pronged strategy. On his right flank, a troop of cavalry and several thousand infantrymen would move to cross the river at Slane.

In the centre, the Duke of Schomberg would concentrate roughly 20,000 men on James's core army and simultaneously bombard them with artillery. On the left, William himself would lead some 8,000 men to a third river crossing and force James's right flank to meet him. All three parts were to be executed simultaneously to deny James the opportunity to respond.

In the early hours of July 1, William's right wing began to mobilize. They marched south to cross north of Rosnaree but were met by a number of Jacobite dragoons, who held up the crossing until mid-morning. Although the Williamite forces successfully crossed, James's commanders were now aware of their enemy's movements, and they sent a sizable detachment to stop any further advance.

In the centre, William split his forces into three groups, which forded at Drybridge, Yellow Island, and Oldbridge. William himself stayed with the reserves, awaiting further developments. James had ordered his men to fall back a bit to give battle on slightly more favourable ground, but upon seeing the Williamite centre's movements, he ordered his commanders to mount a counterattack. Over the course of a few hours, they were able to slow enemy advances, even killing Schomberg, William's lieutenant. However, the Jacobites could not stop the vastly more powerful army. Perceiving the overall success of his centre's manoeuvre, William prepared to cross the Boyne himself, reaching the southern banks at Mill's Ford. With the tide of the battle now firmly in William's favour, James ordered a measured withdrawal south to Duleek. He and his army escaped mostly intact.

The Battle of the Boyne may have been a victory for William III, but it was far from decisive. William's failure to destroy the Jacobites or adequately pursue the retreating army only made it more difficult to quell the rebellion in Ireland. The scattered remains of James's army fell back to Dublin and then southwest to Limerick, on the other end of the island. James himself fled to France. On July 6 William entered Dublin with little resistance. He then issued the Declaration of Finglas, which demanded total Irish repentance or the forfeit of their lands. Rather than surrender, the remaining Jacobites fortified Limerick and held out under siege until the following year. The 1691 Treaty of Limerick brought a formal end to this rising. But with James II still alive in France, William III's reign would suffer periodic challenges through the end of the century.

The Battle of the Boyne also had an impact on the continental balance of power. The League of Augsburg was rightfully fearful of France's rising power, and Louis XIV's repeated attacks on the Dutch Republic were of particular concern. The Franco-Irish defeat at the Boyne reassured William's allies that Louis would not go unchecked. Britain could be counted on to resist French expansionism. With the crown now in Protestant hands, Britain was both politically and religiously opposed to French Catholic domination. William's ascent helped bring an end to the War of the Grand Alliance by 1697.

Chapter four

The Irish Rebellion 1798

The Irish Rebellion of 1798 (Irish: *Éirí Amach 1798*; Ulster-Scots: *The Hurries*[106]) was a major uprising against British rule in Ireland. The main organising force was the Society of United Irishmen, a republican revolutionary group influenced by the ideas of the American and French revolutions: originally formed by Presbyterian radicals angry at being shut out of power by the Anglican establishment, they were joined by many from the majority Catholic population.

Following some initial successes, particularly in County Wexford, the uprising was suppressed by government militia and yeomanry forces, reinforced by units of the British Army, with a civilian and combatant death toll estimated between 10,000 and 50,000. A French expeditionary force landed in County Mayo in August in support of the rebels: despite victory at Castlebar, they were also eventually defeated. The aftermath of the Rebellion led to the passing of the Acts of Union 1800, merging the Parliament of Ireland into the Parliament of the United Kingdom.

Despite its rapid suppression the 1798 Rebellion remains a significant event in Irish history. Centenary celebrations in 1898 were instrumental in the development of modern Irish nationalism, while several of the Rebellion's key figures, such as Wolfe Tone, became important reference points for later republicanism. Debates over the significance of 1798, the motivation and ideology of its participants, and acts committed during the Rebellion continue to the present day.

Since 1691 and the end of the Williamite War, the government of Ireland had been dominated by an Anglican minority establishment. Membership of the Irish Parliament became restricted to members of the established church, who were expected to identify closely with the economic and political interests of England. The support of the Catholic gentry for the Jacobite side during the war had led to Parliament passing a series of Penal Laws, barring them from holding government or military positions and restricting Catholics' ability to purchase or inherit land. The proportion of land owned by Catholics, already reduced following earlier 17th century conflicts, continued to decline.

[106] Patterson, William Hugh (1880). "Glossary of Words in the Counties of Antrim and Down". *www.ulsterscotsacademy.com.*

The effect of the Penal Laws was to destroy the political influence of the Catholic gentry, many of whom sought alternative opportunities in the European military. The same laws, however, also discriminated against Presbyterians and other Protestant Dissenters, who were increasingly important in trade and commerce and were particularly strongly represented in Ulster.

By the middle of the 18th century, several factors combined to increase demands for political reform. Despite Ireland nominally being a sovereign kingdom governed by the monarch and its own Parliament, legislation such as the Declaratory Act 1719 meant it, in reality, had less independence than most of Britain's North American colonies. Merchants grew increasingly frustrated by commercial restrictions favouring England at Ireland's expense, adding to the list of grievances; it was claimed that Ireland was "debarred from the common and natural benefits of trade" while still being "obliged to support a large national and military establishment".[107] Financial controversies such as "Wood's halfpence" in 1724 and the "Money Bill Dispute" of 1753, over the appropriation of an Irish treasury surplus by the Crown, alienated sections of the Protestant professional class, leading to riots in Cork and Dublin.[108]

This developing national consciousness led some members of the "Protestant Ascendancy" to advocate greater political autonomy from Great Britain. The movement was led by figures like Charles Lucas, a Dublin apothecary exiled in 1749 for promoting the so-called "patriot" cause: Lucas returned 10 years later and was elected as an MP, beginning a period of increased "patriot" influence in Parliament.[109] Some of the "patriots" also began seeking support from the growing Catholic middle class: in 1749 George Berkeley, Bishop of Cloyne issued an address to the Catholic clergy, urging cooperation in the Irish national interest. In 1757 John Curry formed the Catholic Committee, which campaigned for repeal of the Penal Laws from a position of loyalty to the regime.[110]

From 1778 onwards a number of local militias known as the Irish Volunteers were raised in response to the withdrawal of regular forces to fight in the American Revolutionary War. Thousands of middle and upper-class Anglicans, along with a few Presbyterians and Catholics, joined the Volunteers, who became central to the growing sense of a distinct Irish political identity. Although the Volunteers were formed to defend Ireland against possible French invasion, many of their members and others in the "patriot" movement became strongly influenced by American efforts to secure independence, which were widely discussed in the Irish press.[111] Cl

---

[107] Morley 2002, p. 43.
[108] Stanbridge 2003, p. 165.
[109] Stanbridge 2003, p. 166.
[110] Morley 2002, p. 45.

ose links with recent emigrants meant that northern Presbyterians were particularly sympathetic to the Americans, who they felt were subject to the same injustices.[112]

In 1782 the Volunteers held a Convention at Dungannon which demanded greater legislative independence; this heavily influenced the British executive to amend legislation restricting the Irish Parliament, confirmed by the Irish Appeals Act 1783. With increased legislative independence secured, "Patriot" MPs such as Henry Grattan continued to press for greater enfranchisement, although the campaign quickly foundered on the issue of Catholic emancipation: although Grattan supported it, many "patriots" did not, and even the Presbyterians were "bitterly divided" on whether it should be immediate or gradual.[113]

Against this background actual reform proceeded slowly. The Papists Act 1778 began to dismantle some earlier restrictions by allowing Catholics to join the army and to purchase land if they took an oath of allegiance to the Crown. In 1793 Parliament passed laws allowing Catholics meeting the property qualification to vote, but they could still neither be elected nor appointed as state officials.

Catholic opposition to the government.

Since the early 18th century, the remains of the Catholic landowning class, once strongly Jacobite, had protected their position by adopting an "obsequious" attitude to the regime, cultivating the favour of the Hanoverian monarchs directly rather than that of a hostile Irish Parliament.[114] The death of the Old Pretender in 1766, and Pope Clement XIII's subsequent recognition of the Hanoverians, reduced government suspicions of Jacobite sympathies among Catholics. Most senior Catholic churchmen also expressed loyalty to the government, hoping to secure increased tolerance. These attitudes however "barely impinged on the mass of the population".[115]

19th century historiography assumed that the rural, Catholic Ireland of the majority was largely quiet during the 18th century and unaffected by urban demands for reform. Outbreaks of rural violence by "Whiteboys" from the 1760s onwards, directed against landlords and tithe proctors, were assumed by historians such as Lecky to have been driven by local, agrarian issues such as tenant farmers' rents rather than wider political consciousness.[116]

---

[111] Dickinson 2008, pp. xx-xxi.
[112] Stewart 1995, p. 9.
[113] Stewart 1995, p. 10.
[114] Morley 2002, p. 45.
[115] Morley 2002, p. 46.
[116] Morley 2002, pp. 48-9.

More recently it has been argued that the persistence of Jacobite imagery among Whiteboy and other groups suggests that strong opposition to Protestant and British rule remained widespread in Gaelic-speaking rural Ireland.[117] A further dimension was provided by a younger generation of Catholic gentry and "middlemen" in counties like Wexford, some of whom were radicalised by time spent in Revolutionary France, and who often emerged as local leaders in 1798.[118]

Unrest had also grown in County Armagh in the decade prior to the Rebellion involving clashes between groups of "Defenders", a Catholic secret society, and Protestant gangs of "Break of Day Men" or "Peep o' Day Boys". Originating as non-sectarian "fleets" of young men, the groups emerged in north Armagh in the 1780s before spreading southwards. Like "White boyism" this activity is often depicted as economic in origin, triggered by competition between Protestants and Catholics in the lucrative linen industry of the area.[119] However, there is evidence that as time went on the Defenders developed an Increasing political consciousness.[120]

The 1789 French Revolution provided further inspiration to more radical members of the Volunteer movement, who saw it as an example of the common people cooperating to remove a corrupt regime.[121] In early 1791, wool merchant Samuel Neilson, a former Volunteer who had attended the Dungannon convention, made plans to set up a pro-French newspaper, the *Northern Star*. He was joined from spring 1791 by a group from the Belfast Volunteers led by doctor William Drennan, who formed a secret political club called the "Irish Brotherhood".[122] Inspired by events in France and the publication of Thomas Paine's *Rights of Man*, they drew up a programme including the independence of Ireland on a republican model, parliamentary reform, and the restoration of all civic rights to Catholics.[123]

While Neilson, Drennan and the other Belfast radicals were Presbyterian, a second club set up the following month in Dublin included a more representative mix of Anglicans, Presbyterians, and Catholics from the city's professional classes. One member, barrister Theobald Wolfe Tone, suggested the name "Society of United Irishmen", which was adopted by the whole organisation.[124] The Society initially took a constitutional approach, but the 1793 outbreak of war with France forced the organisation underground when Pitt's government acted to suppress the political clubs. Tone fled to America, and Drennan was arrested and charged with seditious

---

[117] Dunne 2010, 3845.
[118] Dunne 2010, 2306.
[119] Miller 1990, p. 4.
[120] Stewart 1995, pp. 20-21.
[121] Stewart 1995, p. 10.
[122] Stewart 1995, p. 10.
[123] Stewart 1995, p. 10.
[124] Stewart 1995, pp. 10-12.

libel; although acquitted, he took little further part in events.[125] In response Neilson and others in the Belfast group began restructuring the United Irishmen on revolutionary lines.[126]

In May 1795 the Belfast delegates approved a "New System" of organisation: this was based on cells or 'societies' of 20-35 men, with a tiered structure of baronial, county, and provincial committees reporting to a single national committee, mirroring the structure of the Presbyterian church.[127] In 1796 the New System was transformed into a military structure, each group of three 'societies' forming one company. Numbers grew rapidly; many Presbyterian shopkeepers and farmers joined in the North, while recruitment efforts among the Defenders resulted in the admission of many new Catholic members across the country.[128]

In the same period a group of new leaders were elected to the United "Directory" in Dublin, notably two radicals from the aristocracy, Arthur O'Connor and MP Lord Edward FitzGerald. Other members of the committee included lawyer Thomas Addis Emmet, physician William McNevin, and Catholic Committee secretary Richard McCormick.[129] To augment their growing strength, the United Irish leadership decided to seek military help from the current French XXXevolutionary government, the Directory. Tone travelled from the United States to France to press the case for intervention, landing at Le Havre in February 1796 following a stormy winter crossing.[130]

Tone had arrived in France without either instructions or accreditation from the United Irishmen, but almost single-handedly convinced the French Directory to alter its policy.[131] His written "memorials" on the situation in Ireland came to the attention of Director Lazare Carnot, who, seeing an opportunity to destabilise Great Britain, asked for a formal invasion plan to be developed. By May, General Henry Clarke, head of the War Ministry's *Bureau Topographique*, had drawn up an initial plan offering the Irish 10,000 troops and arms for 20,000 more men, with strict insistence that the United Irishmen attempt no rising until the French had landed.[132] I n June Carnot wrote to the experienced general Lazare Hoche asking him to act as commander and describing the plan as "the downfall of the most dangerous of our enemies. I see in it the safety of France for centuries to come."[133]

---

[125] Stewart 1995, pp. 19-20.
[126] Stewart 1995, pp. 19-20.
[127] Stewart 1995, p. 20.
[128] Stewart 1995, pp. 20-21.
[129] Madden 1860, p. 14
[130] Elliott 2012, p. 271.
[131] Elliott 2012, p. 271.
[132] Elliott 2012, p. 286.
[133] Elliott 2012, p. 287.

A force of 15,000 veteran troops was assembled at Brest under Hoche. Sailing on 16 December, accompanied by Tone, the French arrived off the coast of Ireland at Bantry Bay on 22 December 1796 after eluding the Royal Navy; however, unremitting storms, bad luck and poor seamanship all combined to prevent a landing.[134] Tone remarked that "England had its luckiest escape since the Armada;"[135] the fleet was forced to return home and the army intended to spearhead the invasion of Ireland was split up and sent to fight in other theatres of the French Revolutionary Wars.

By 1797 reports began to reach Britain that a secret revolutionary army was being prepared in Ireland by Tone's associates.[136] Naval mutinies at Spithead and the Nore suggested that French-inspired agitators were trying to spread the revolution to England; the crisis however appeared to pass, and in October the Navy defeated an invasion fleet of France's client state, the Batavian Republic, at Camperdown.[137]

Tone had attempted to convince the increasingly influential general Napoleon Bonaparte, who had recently mounted a successful campaign in Italy that another landing in Ireland was feasible. Bonaparte initially showed little interest: he was largely unfamiliar with the Irish situation and needed a war of conquest, not of liberation, to pay his army. However, by February 1798 British spies reported he was preparing a fleet in the Channel ports ready for the embarkation of up to 50,000 men. Their destination remained unknown, but the reports were immediately passed to the Irish government under the Viceroy, Lord Camden.[138]

In early 1798 a series of violent attacks on magistrates in County Tipperary, County Kildare and King's County alarmed the authorities. They also received information that a faction of the United Irish leadership, led by Fitzgerald and O'Connor, felt they were "sufficiently well organised and equipped" to begin an insurgency without French aid; they were opposed by Emmet, McCormick and NcNevin, who favoured an approach protecting life and property and wanted to wait for a French landing.[139] Camden came under increasing pressure from hard-line Irish MPs, led by Speaker John Foster, to crack down on the disorder in the south and midlands and arrest the Dublin leadership.

---

[134] Stewart 1995, p. 31.
[135] *The Writings of Theobald Wolfe Tone 1763–98, Volume Two: America, France and Bantry Bay – August 1795 to December 1796* (Journal entry 26 December 1796) – eds. T W Moody, R B MacDowel and C J Woods, Clarendon Press (USA) ISBN 0-19-822383-8
[136] Pakenham 1997, 387.
[137] Pakenham 1997, 406.
[138] Pakenham 1997, 475.
[139] Pakenham 1997, 637.

Camden prevaricated for some time, partly as he feared a crackdown would itself provoke an insurrection: the British Home Secretary Lord Portland agreed, describing the proposals as "dangerous and inconvenient".[140] The situation changed when United Irish documents on manpower were leaked by an informer, silk merchant Thomas Reynolds, suggesting nearly 280,000 men across Ulster, Leinster and Munster were preparing to join the "revolutionary army".[141] The Irish government learned from Reynolds that a meeting of the Leinster "Directory" had been set for 10 March in the Dublin house of wool merchant Oliver Bond, where a motion for an immediate rising would be voted on. Camden decided to move to arrest the leadership, arguing to London that he otherwise risked having the Irish Parliament turn against him.[142] On the 10th most of the moderates among the leadership such as Emmett, McNevin and Dublin City delegate Thomas Traynor were taken several of the 'country' delegates arrived late to the meeting and escaped, as did McCormick. The only other senior member to escape was Fitzgerald himself, who went into hiding; the incident had the effect of strengthening Fitzgerald's faction and pushing the leadership towards rebellion.

The Irish government effectively imposed martial law on 30 March, although civil courts continued sitting. Overall command of the army was transferred from Ralph Abercromby to Gerard Lake, who supported an aggressive approach against suspected rebels.[143]

A rising in Cahir, County Tipperary broke out in response, but was quickly crushed by the High Sheriff, Col. Thomas Judkin-Fitzgerald. Militants led by Samuel Neilson and Lord Edward FitzGerald with the help of co-conspirator Edmund Gallagher dominated the rump United Irish leadership and planned to rise without French aid, fixing the date for 23 May.

The initial plan was to take Dublin, with the counties bordering Dublin to rise in support and prevent the arrival of reinforcements followed by the rest of the country who were to tie down other garrisons.[144] The signal to rise was to be spread by the interception of the mail coaches from Dublin. However, last-minute intelligence from informants provided the Government with details of rebel assembly points in Dublin and a huge force of military occupied them barely one hour before rebels were to assemble. The Army then arrested most of the rebel leaders in the city. Deterred by the military, the gathering groups of rebels quickly dispersed, abandoning the intended rallying points, and dumping their weapons in the

---

140 Pakenham 1997, 718.
141 Pakenham 1997, 748.
142 Pakenham 1997, 776.
143 Pakenham 1997, 1063.
144 R. B. McDowell, *Ireland in the Age of Imperialism and Revolution, 1760–1801* (1991) pp 612–36.

surrounding lanes. In addition, the plan to intercept the mail coaches miscarried, with only the Munster-bound coach halted at Johnstown, near Naas, on the first night of the rebellion.

Although the planned nucleus of the rebellion had imploded, the surrounding districts of Dublin rose as planned and were swiftly followed by most of the counties surrounding Dublin. The first clashes of the rebellion took place just after dawn on 24 May. Fighting quickly spread throughout Leinster, with the heaviest fighting taking place in County Kildare where, despite the Army successfully beating off almost every rebel attack, the rebels gained control of much of the county as military forces in Kildare were ordered to withdraw to Naas for fear of their isolation and destruction as at Prosperous. However, rebel defeats at Carlow and the hill of Tara, County Meath, effectively ended the rebellion in those counties. In County Wicklow, news of the rising spread panic and fear among loyalists; they responded by massacring rebel suspects held in custody at Dunlavin Green and in Carnew. A baronet, Sir Edward Crosbie, was found guilty of leading the rebellion in Carlow and executed for treason.

In County Wicklow, large numbers rose but chiefly engaged in a bloody rural guerrilla war with the military and loyalist forces. General Joseph Holt led up to 1,000 men in the Wicklow Mountains and forced the British to commit substantial forces to the area until his capitulation in October.

In the north-east, mostly Presbyterian rebels led by Henry Joy McCracken[145] rose in County Antrim on 6 June. They briefly held most of the county, but the rising there collapsed following defeat at Antrim town. In County Down, after initial success at Saintfield, rebels led by Henry Munro were defeated in the longest battle of the rebellion at Ballynahinch.[146]

The rebels had most success in the south-eastern county of Wexford where they seized control of the county, but a series of bloody defeats at the Battle of New Ross, Battle of Arklow, and the Battle of Bunclody prevented the effective spread of the rebellion beyond the county borders. 20,000 troops eventually poured into Wexford and defeated the rebels at the Battle of Vinegar Hill on 21 June. The dispersed rebels spread in two columns through the midlands, Kilkenny, and finally towards Ulster. The last remnants of these forces fought on until their final defeat on 14 July at the battles of Knightstown Bog, County Meath and Ballyboughal, County Dublin.[147]

---

[145] "Henry Joy McCracken – United Irishman". Ulsterhistory.co.uk. Archived from the original on 4 February 2012. Retrieved 7 March 2012.

[146] Guy Beiner (2018). *Forgetful Remembrance: Social Forgetting and Vernacular Historiography of a Rebellion in Ulster*. Oxford University Press. ISBN 9780198749356.

[147] Daniel Gahan (1995). *The People's Rising: The Great Wexford Rebellion of 1798*. Gill

On 22 August, nearly two months after the main uprisings had been defeated, about 1,000 French soldiers under General Humbert landed in the north-west of the country, at Kilcummin in County Mayo. Joined by up to 5,000 local rebels, they had some initial success, inflicting a humiliating defeat on the British in Castlebar (also known as the *Castlebar races* to commemorate the speed of the retreat) and setting up a short-lived "Irish Republic" with John Moore as president of one of its provinces, Connacht. This sparked some supportive uprisings in Longford and Westmeath which were quickly defeated. The Franco-Irish force won another minor engagement at the battle of Collooney before the main force was defeated at the battle of Ballinamuck, in County Longford, on 8 September 1798. The Irish Republic had only lasted twelve days from its declaration of independence to its collapse. The French troops who surrendered were repatriated to France in exchange for British prisoners of war, but hundreds of the captured Irish rebels were executed. This episode of the 1798 Rebellion became a major event in the heritage and collective memory of the West of Ireland and was commonly known in Irish as *Bliain na bhFrancach* and in English as "The Year of the French".[148]

On 12 October 1798, a larger French force consisting of 3,000 men, and including Wolfe Tone himself, attempted to land in County Donegal near Lough Swilly. They were intercepted by a larger Royal Navy squadron, and finally surrendered after a three-hour battle without ever landing in Ireland. Wolfe Tone was tried by court-martial in Dublin and found guilty. He asked for death by firing squad, but when this was refused, Tone cheated the hangman by slitting his own throat in prison on 12 November and died a week later.

Small fragments of the great rebel armies of the Summer of 1798 survived for a number of years and waged a form of guerrilla or "fugitive" warfare in several counties. In County Wicklow, General Joseph Holt fought on until his negotiated surrender in Autumn 1798. It was not until the failure of Robert Emmet's rebellion in 1803 that the last organised rebel forces under Captain Michael Dwyer capitulated. Small pockets of rebel resistance had also survived within Wexford and the last rebel group under James Corcoran was not vanquished until February 1804.

The Act of Union, having been passed in August 1800, came into effect on 1 January 1801 and took away the measure of autonomy granted to Ireland's Protestant Ascendancy.[149] It was passed largely in response to the rebellion and was

---

Books. ISBN 9780717159154.
[148] Guy Beiner, *Remembering the Year of the French: Irish Folk History and Social Memory* (University of Wisconsin Press, 2007).
[149] Nevin, Seamus (2012). "History Repeating: Georgian Ireland's Property Bubble". *History Ireland*. 20 (1): 22–24. JSTOR 41331440.

underpinned by the perception that the rebellion was provoked by the brutish misrule of the Ascendancy as much as the efforts of the United Irishmen.

Religious, if not economic, discrimination against the Catholic majority was gradually abolished after the Act of Union but not before widespread mobilisation of the Catholic population under Daniel O'Connell. Discontent at grievances and resentment persisted but resistance to British rule now largely manifested itself along anti-taxation lines, as in the Tithe War of 1831–36.

Presbyterian radicalism was effectively tamed or reconciled to British rule by inclusion in a new Protestant Ascendancy, as opposed to a merely Anglican one. By mid-1798 a schism between the Presbyterians and Catholics had developed, with radical Presbyterians starting to waver in their support for revolution.[150] The government capitalised on this by acting against the Catholics in the radical movement instead of the northern Presbyterians.[151] Prior to the rebellion, anyone who admitted to being a member of the United Irishmen was expelled from the Yeomanry, however former Presbyterian radicals were now able to enlist in it, and those radicals that wavered in support saw it as their chance to reintegrate themselves into society.[152] The government also had news of the sectarian massacre of Protestants at Scullabogue spread to increase Protestant fears and enhance the growing division.[153] Anglican clergyman Edward Hudson claimed that "the brotherhood of affection is over", as he enlisted former radicals into his Portglenone Yeomanry corps.[154] On 1 July 1798 in Belfast, the birthplace of the United Irishmen movement, it is claimed that everyman had the red coat of the Yeomanry on.[155] How ever, the Protestant contribution to the United Irish cause was not yet entirely finished as several of the leaders of the 1803 rebellion were Anglican or Presbyterian.

Nevertheless, this fostering or resurgence of religious division meant that Irish politics was largely, until the Young Ireland movement in the mid-19th century, steered away from the unifying vision of the egalitarian United Irishmen and based on sectarian fault lines with Unionist and Dublin Castle individuals at the helm of power in Ireland. After Robert Emmets rebellion of 1803 and the Act of Union Ulster Presbyterians and other dissenters were likely bought off by British/English Anglican ruling elites with industry ship building, woollen mill and as the 19th

[150] Blackstock, Alan: *A Forgotten Army: The Irish Yeomanry.* History Ireland, Vol 4. 1996
[151] Blackstock, Alan: *A Forgotten Army: The Irish Yeomanry.* History Ireland, Vol 4. 1996
[152] Blackstock, Alan: *A Forgotten Army: The Irish Yeomanry.* History Ireland, Vol 4. 1996
[153] Blackstock, Alan: *A Forgotten Army: The Irish Yeomanry.* History Ireland, Vol 4. 1996
[154] Blackstock, Alan: *A Forgotten Army: The Irish Yeomanry.* History Ireland, Vol 4. 1996
[155] Blackstock, Alan: *A Forgotten Army: The Irish Yeomanry.* History Ireland, Vol 4. 1996

century progressed, they become less and less radical and Republican/Nationalist in outlook.

The intimate nature of the conflict meant that the rebellion at times took on the worst characteristics of a civil war, especially in Leinster. Sectarian resentment was fuelled by the remaining Penal Laws still in force. Rumours of planned massacres by both sides were common in the days before the rising and led to a widespread climate of fear.

The aftermath of almost every British victory in the rising was marked by the massacre of captured and wounded rebels with some on a large scale such as at Carlow, New Ross, Ballinamuck and Killala.[156] The British were responsible for particularly gruesome massacres at Gibbet Rath, New Ross and Enniscorthy, burning rebels alive in the latter two.[157] For those rebels who were taken alive in the aftermath of battle, being regarded as traitors to the Crown, they were not treated as prisoners of war but were executed, usually by hanging. Local forces publicly executed suspected members of the United Irishmen without trial in Dunlavin in what is known as the Dunlavin Green executions and in Carnew days after the outbreak of the rebellion.[158]

In addition, non-combatant civilians were murdered by the military, who also carried out many instances of rape, particularly in County Wexford.[159] Many individual instances of murder were also unofficially carried out by local Yeomanry units before, during and after the rebellion as their local knowledge led them to attack suspected rebels. "Pardoned" rebels were a particular target.[160]

According to the historian Guy Beiner, the Presbyterian insurgents in Ulster suffered more executions than any other arena of the 1798 rebellion, and the brutality with which the insurrection was quelled in counties Antrim and Down was long remembered in local folk traditions.[161]

---

[156] Stock, Joseph. *A Narrative of what passed at Killalla, in the County of Mayo, and the parts adjacent, during the French invasion in the summer of 1798.* Dublin & London, 1800
[157] p. 146 "*Fr. John Murphy of Boolavogue 1753–98*" (Dublin, 1991) Nicholas Furlong ISBN 0-906602-18-1
[158] Bartlett, Thomas (1997). *A Military History of Ireland.* Cambridge University Press. p. 279. ISBN 978-0-521-62989-8.
[159] p. 28, "*The Mighty Wave: The 1798 Rebellion in Wexford*" (Four Courts Press 1996) Daire Keogh (Editor), Nicholas Furlong (Editor) ISBN 1-85182-254-2
[160] p. 113 "*Revolution, Counter-Revolution and Union*" (Cambridge University Press, 2000) Ed. Jim Smyth ISBN 0-521-66109-9
[161] Guy Beiner, "Severed Heads and Floggings: The Undermining of Oblivion in Ulster in the Aftermath of 1798" in *The Body in Pain in Irish Literature and Culture*, edited by Fionnuala Dillane, Naomi McAreavey and Emilie Pine (Palgrave Macmillan, 2016), pp. 77–97.

County Wexford was the only area which saw widespread atrocities by the rebels during the Wexford Rebellion. Massacres of loyalist prisoners took place at the Vinegar Hill camp and on Wexford bridge. After the defeat of a rebel attack at New Ross, the Scullabogue Barn massacre occurred where between 80[162] and 200[163] mostly Protestant men, women, and children were imprisoned in a barn which was then set alight.[164] In Wexford town, on 20 June some 70 loyalist prisoners were marched to the bridge (first stripped naked, according to an unsourced claim by historian James Lydon[165]) and piked to death.[166]

Contemporary estimates put the death toll from 20,000 (Dublin Castle) to as many as 50,000[167] of which 2,000 were military and 1,000 loyalist civilians.[168] Some modern research argues that these figures may be too high. Firstly, a list of British soldiers killed, compiled for a fund to aid the families of dead soldiers, listed just 530 names. Secondly, Professor Louis Cullen, through an examination of depletion of the population in County Wexford between 1798 and 1820, put the fatalities in that county due to the rebellion at 6,000. Historian Thomas Bartlett therefore argues, "a death toll of 10,000 for the entire island would seem to be in order".[169] Other modern historians believe that the death toll may be even higher than contemporary estimates suggest as the widespread fear of repression among relatives of slain rebels led to mass concealment of casualties.[170]

By the centenary of the Rebellion in 1898, conservative Irish nationalists and the Catholic Church would both claim that the United Irishmen had been fighting for "Faith and Fatherland", and this version of events is still, to some extent, the lasting popular memory of the rebellion. A series of popular "98 Clubs" were formed. At the bicentenary in 1998, the non-sectarian and democratic ideals of the Rebellion were emphasised in official commemorations, reflecting the desire for reconciliation at the time of the Good Friday Agreement which was hoped would end "The Troubles" in Northern Ireland.

According to R. F. Foster, the 1798 rebellion was "probably the most concentrated episode of violence in Irish history".

---

[162] Edward Hay, *History of the Insurrection of the County of Wexford, A. D. 1798*, (Dublin, 1803), p. 204
[163] Lydon, James F. *The making of Ireland: from ancient times to the present* pg 274
[164] Dunne, Tom; *Rebellions: Memoir, Memory and 1798*. The Lilliput Press, 2004. ISBN 978-1-84351-039-0
[165] Lydon, James F. *The making of Ireland: from ancient times to the present* pg 274
[166] Musgrave, Sir Richard (1802). *Memoirs of the different rebellions in Ireland* (third ed.)..
[167] Thomas Pakenham, P.392 The Year of Liberty (1969) ISBN 0-586-03709-8
[168] Marianne Elliott, "*Rebellion, a Television history of 1798*" (RTÉ 1998)
[169] Bartlett in Smyth, ed, p100
[170] Marianne Elliott, "*Rebellion, a Television history of 1798*" (RTÉ 1998)

In the aftermath of these riots, any sign of insurrection would again see the perpetrators being shipped off to Australia or to the "New World" and used as slaves.

Chapter five

Captain Boycott

Well, if you ever wondered where the term to "boycott" comes from, then look and wonder no more.

Charles Cunningham Boycott was an English land agent whose ostracism by his local community in Ireland gave the English language the verb "to boycott". He had served in the British Army 39th Foot, which brought him to Ireland. After retiring from the army, Boycott worked as a land agent for Lord Erne, a landowner in the Lough Mask area of County Mayo.[171]

In 1880, as part of its campaign for the Three Fs (fair rent, fixity of tenure, and free sale) and specifically in resistance to proposed evictions on the estate, local activists of the Irish National Land League encouraged Boycott's employees (including the seasonal workers required to harvest the crops on Lord Erne's estate) to withdraw their labour, and began a campaign of isolation against Boycott in the local community. This campaign included shops in nearby Ballinrobe refusing to serve him, and the withdrawal of services. Some were threatened with violence to ensure compliance.

The campaign against Boycott became a *cause célèbre* in the British press after he wrote a letter to *The Times*. Newspapers sent correspondents to the West of Ireland to highlight what they viewed as the victimisation of a servant of a peer of the realm by Irish nationalists.

Fifty Orangemen from County Cavan and County Monaghan travelled to Lord Erne's estate to harvest the crops, while a regiment of the 19th Royal Hussars and more than 1,000 men of the Royal Irish Constabulary were deployed to protect the harvesters. The episode was estimated to have cost the British government and others at least £10,000 to harvest about £500 worth of crops.

Boycott left Ireland on 1 December 1880, and in 1886, became land agent for Hugh Adair's Flixton estate in Suffolk. He died at the age of 65 on 19 June 1897 in his home in Flixton, after an illness earlier that year.

Charles Cunningham Boycott was born in 1832 to Reverend William Boycatt and his wife Georgiana.[172] He grew up in the village of Burgh St Peter in Norfolk,

---

[171] "Captain Charles Boycott". *The Keep Military Museum.*
[172] Boycott, (1997) p. 4

England;[173] the Boycatt family had lived in Norfolk for almost 150 years.[174] They were of Huguenot origin, and had fled from France in 1685 when Louis XIV revoked civil and religious liberties to French Protestants.[175] Charle s Boycott was named Boycatt in his baptismal records. The family changed the spelling of its name from Boycatt to Boycott in 1841.[176]

Boycott was educated at a boarding school in Blackheath, London.[177] He was interested in the military—and in 1848, entered the Royal Military Academy, Woolwich, in hopes of serving in the Corps of Royal Sappers and Miners.[178] He was discharged from the academy in 1849 after failing a periodic exam,[179] and the following year his family bought him a commission in the 39th Foot regiment for £450.[180] [181]

Boycott's regiment transferred to Belfast shortly after his arrival.[182] Six months later, it was sent to Newry before marching to Dublin, where it remained for a year.[183] In 1852, Boycott married Anne Dunne in St Paul's Church, Arran Quay, Dublin.[184] He was ill between August 1851 and February 1852 and sold his commission the following year,[185] but decided to remain in Ireland. He leased a farm in County Tipperary, where he acted as a landlord on a small scale.[186]

After receiving an inheritance, Boycott was persuaded by his friend, Murray McGregor Blacker, a local magistrate, to move to Achill Island, a large island off the coast of County Mayo.[187] McGregor Blacker agreed to sublet 2,000 acres (809 ha) of land belonging to the Irish Church Mission Society on Achill to Boycott, who moved there in 1854.[188] According to Joyce Marlow in the book, *Captain Boycott and the Irish*, Boycott's life on

the island was difficult initially, and in Boycott's own words it was only after "a long struggle against adverse circumstances" that he became prosperous.[189] With

---

173 Boycott, (1997) p. 4
174 Marlow, (1973) pp. 13–14
175 Marlow, (1973) pp. 13–14
176 Marlow, (1973) pp. 13–14
177 Boycott, (1997) pp. 84–85
178 Boycott, (1997) pp. 84–85
179 Boycott, (1997) pp. 84–85
180 Boycott, (1997) pp. 84–85
181 Marlow, (1973) p. 18
182 Boycott, (1997) pp. 89–95
183 Boycott, (1997) pp. 89–95
184 Boycott, (1997) pp. 89–95
185 Boycott, (1997) pp. 89–95
186 Marlow, (1973) pp. 19–27
187 Marlow, (1973) pp. 29–43
188 Marlow, (1973) pp. 29–43
189 Marlow, (1973) pp. 29–43

money from another inheritance and profits from farming, he built a large house near Dooagh.[190] [191]

Boycott was involved in a number of disputes while on Achill.[192] Two years after his arrival, he was unsuccessfully sued for assault by Thomas Clarke, a local man.[193] Clarke said that he had gone to Boycott's house because Boycott owed him money.[194] He said that he had asked for repayment of the debt, and that Boycott had refused to pay him and told him to go away, which Clarke refused to do.[195] Clarke alleged that Boycott approached him and said: "If you do not be off, I will make you."[196] Clarke later withdrew his allegations, and said that Boycott did not actually owe him any money.[197]

Both Boycott and McGregor Blacker were involved in a protracted dispute with Mr Carr, the agent for the Achill Church Mission Estate, from whom McGregor Blacker leased the lands, and Mr O'Donnell, Carr's bailiff.[198] The dispute began when Boycott and Carr supported different sets of candidates in elections for the Board of Guardians to the Church Mission Estate, and Boycott's candidates won.[199] Carr was also the local receiver of wrecks, which meant that he was entitled to collect the salvage from all shipwrecks in the area, and guard it until it was sold in a public auction.[200] The local receiver had a right to a percentage of the sale and to keep whatever did not sell.[201] In 1860 Carr wrote a letter to the Official Receiver of Wrecks stating that Boycott and his men had illegally broken up a wreck and moved the salvage to Boycott's property.[202] In response to this accusation, Boycott sued Carr for libel and claimed £500 in damages.[203]

In 1873, Boycott moved to Lough Mask House, owned by Lord Erne, four miles (6 km) from Ballinrobe in County Mayo.[204] Lord Erne, the third Earl Erne, was a wealthy landowner who lived in Crom Castle in County Fermanagh.[205] He owned 40,386 acres (163.44 km^2) of land in Ireland, of which 31,389 were in County

---

[190] Marlow, (1973) pp. 29–43
[191] Boycott, (1997) p. 95
[192] Marlow, (1973) pp. 29–43
[193] Marlow, (1973) pp. 29–43
[194] Marlow, (1973) pp. 29–43
[195] Marlow, (1973) pp. 29–43
[196] Marlow, (1973) pp. 29–43
[197] Marlow, (1973) pp. 29–43
[198] Marlow, (1973) pp. 29–43
[199] Marlow, (1973) pp. 29–43
[200] Marlow, (1973) pp. 29–43
[201] Marlow, (1973) pp. 29–43
[202] Marlow, (1973) pp. 29–43
[203] Marlow, (1973) pp. 29–43
[204] Marlow, (1973) pp. 59–70
[205] Boycott, (1997) p. 212

Fermanagh, 4,826 in County Donegal, 1,996 in County Sligo, and 2,184 in County Mayo.[206] Lord Erne also owned properties in Dublin.[207]

Boycott agreed to be Lord Erne's agent for 1,500 acres (6.1 km^2) he owned in County Mayo. One of Boycott's responsibilities was to collect rents from tenant farmers on the land,[208] for which he earned ten per cent of the total rent due to Lord Erne, which was £500 each year.[209] In his roles as farmer and agent, Boycott employed numerous local people as labourers, grooms, coachmen, and house-servants.[210] Joyce Marlow wrote that Boycott had become set in his mode of thought, and that his twenty years on Achill had "...strengthened his innate belief in the divine right of the masters, and the tendency to behave as he saw fit, without regard to other people's point of view or feelings."[211]

During his time in Lough Mask before the controversy began, Boycott had become unpopular with the tenants.[212] He had become a magistrate and was an Englishman, which may have contributed to his unpopularity,[213] but according to Marlow it was due more to his personal temperament.[214] While Boycott himself maintained that he was on good terms with his tenants, they said that he had laid down many petty restrictions, such as not allowing gates to be left open and not allowing hens to trespass on his property, and that he fined anyone who transgressed these restrictions.[215] He had also withdrawn privileges from the tenants, such as collecting wood from the estate.[216] In August 1880, his labourers went on strike in a dispute over a wage increase.[217]

In the nineteenth century, agriculture was the biggest industry in Ireland.[218] In 1876, the government of the United Kingdom of Great Britain and Ireland commissioned a survey to find who owned the land in Ireland. The survey found that almost all land was the property of just 10,000 people, or 0.2% of the population.[219] The majority were small landlords, but the 750 richest landlords owned half of the country

---

[206] Boycott, (1997) p. 212
[207] Boycott, (1997) p. 212
[208] Marlow, (1973) pp. 59–70
[209] Marlow, (1973) pp. 59–70
[210] Marlow, (1973) pp. 59–70
[211] Marlow, (1973) pp. 59–70
[212] Marlow, (1973) pp. 59–70
[213] Marlow, (1973) pp. 59–70
[214] Marlow, (1973) pp. 59–70
[215] Marlow, (1973) pp. 59–70
[216] Marlow, (1973) pp. 59–70
[217] Marlow, (1973) pp. 133–142
[218] Collins, (1993) pp. 19–35
[219] Collins, (1993) pp. 19–35

between them.[220] Many of the richest were absentee landlords who lived in Britain or elsewhere in Ireland, and paid agents like Charles Boycott to manage their estates.[221]

Landlords generally divided their estates into smaller farms that they rented to tenant farmers.[222] Tenant farmers were generally on one-year leases, and could be evicted even if they paid their rents.[223] Some of the tenants were large farmers who farmed over 100 acres (0.40 km^2), but the majority were much smaller on average between 15 and 50 acres ($0.06–0.20 \text{ km}^2$).[224] Many small farmers worked as labourers on the larger farms.[225] The poorest agricultural workers were the landless labourers, who worked on the land of other farmers.[226] Farmers were an important group politically, having more votes than any other sector of society.[227]

In the 1850s, some tenant farmers formed associations to demand the three Fs: fair rent, fixity of tenure, and free sale.[228] In the 1870s, the Fenians tried to organise the tenant farmers in County Mayo to resist eviction.[229] They mounted a demonstration against a local landlord in Irishtown and succeeded in getting him to lower his rents.[230]

Michael Davitt was the son of a small tenant farmer in County Mayo who became a journalist and joined the Irish Republican Brotherhood. He was arrested and given a 15-year sentence for gunrunning.[231] Charles Stewart Parnell, then Member of Parliament for Meath and member of the Home Rule League, arranged to have Davitt released on probation. When Davitt returned to County Mayo, he was impressed by the Fenians' attempts to organise farmers. He thought that the "land question" was the best way to get the support of the farmers for Irish independence.[232]

In October 1879, after forming the Land League of Mayo, Davitt formed the Irish National Land League. The Land League's aims were to reduce rents and to stop evictions, and in the long term, to make tenant farmers owners of the land they farmed. Davitt asked Parnell to become the leader of the league. In 1880, Parnell was also elected leader of the Home Rule Party.[233]

---

[220] Collins, (1993) pp. 19–35
[221] Collins, (1993) pp. 19–35
[222] Collins, (1993) pp. 19–35
[223] Collins, (1993) pp. 19–35
[224] Collins, (1993) pp. 19–35
[225] Collins, (1993) pp. 19–35
[226] Collins, (1993) pp. 19–35
[227] Collins, (1993) pp. 19–35
[228] Collins, (1993) pp. 72–79
[229] Collins, (1993) pp. 72–79
[230] Collins, (1993) pp. 72–79
[231] Collins, (1993) pp. 72–79
[232] Collins, (1993) pp. 72–79
[233] Collins, (1993) pp. 72–79

On 19 September 1880, Parnell gave a speech in Ennis, County Clare to a crowd of Land League members.[234] He asked the crowd, "What do you do with a tenant who bids for a farm from which his neighbour has been evicted?"[235] The crowd responded, "kill him", "shoot him".[236] Parnell replied:[237]

I wish to point out to you a very much better way a more Christian and charitable way, which will give the lost man an opportunity of repenting. When a man takes a farm from which another has been evicted, you must shun him on the roadside when you meet him you must shun him in the streets of the town you must shun him in the shop you must shun him on the fair green and in the market place, and even in the place of worship, by leaving him alone, by putting him in moral Coventry, by isolating him from the rest of the country, as if he were the leper of old you must show him your detestation of the crime he committed.

This speech set out the Land League's powerful weapon of social ostracism, which was first used against Charles Boycott.[238]

The Land League was very active in the Lough Mask area, and one of the local leaders, Father John O'Malley, had been involved in the labourer's strike in August 1880.[239] The following month Lord Erne's tenants were due to pay their rents.[240] He had agreed to a 10 per cent reduction owing to a poor harvest, but all except two of his tenants demanded a 25 per cent reduction.[241] Boycott said that he had written to Lord Erne, and that Erne had refused to accede to the tenants' demands.[242] He then issued demands for the outstanding rents, and obtained eviction notices against eleven tenants.[243]

Three days after Parnell's speech in Ennis, a process server and seventeen members of the Royal Irish Constabulary began the attempt to serve Boycott's eviction notices.[244] Legally, they had to be delivered to the head of the household or his spouse within a certain time period. The process server successfully delivered notices to three of the tenants, but a fourth, Mrs Fitzmorris, refused to accept the notice and began waving a red flag to alert other tenants that the notices were being served.[245] The women of the area descended on the process server and the

---

[234] Collins, (1993) p. 81
[235] Collins, (1993) p. 81
[236] Collins, (1993) p. 81
[237] Hachey et al, (1996) pp. 119
[238] Collins, (1993) p. 81
[239] Marlow, (1973) pp. 133–142
[240] Marlow, (1973) pp. 133–142
[241] Marlow, (1973) pp. 133–142
[242] Marlow, (1973) pp. 133–142
[243] Marlow, (1973) pp. 133–142
[244] Marlow, (1973) pp. 133–142

constabulary, and began throwing stones, mud, and manure at them, succeeding in driving them away to seek refuge in Lough Mask House.[246]

The process server tried unsuccessfully to serve the notices the following day.[247] Ne ws soon spread to the nearby Ballinrobe, from where many people descended on Lough Mask House, where, according to journalist James Redpath, they advised Boycott's servants and labourers to leave his employment immediately.[248] Boycott said that many of his servants were forced to leave "under threat of ulterior consequences".[249] Martin Branigan, a labourer who subsequently sued Boycott for non-payment of wages, claimed he left because he was afraid of the people who came into the field where he was working.[250] Eventually, all Boycott's employees left, forcing him to run the estate without help.[251]

Within days, the blacksmith, postman, and laundress were persuaded or volunteered to stop serving Boycott.[252] Boycott's young nephew volunteered to act as postman, but he was intercepted en route between Ballinrobe and Lough Mask, and told that he would be in danger if he continued.[253] Soon, shopkeepers in Ballinrobe stopped serving Boycott, and he had to bring food and other provisions by boat from Cong.[254]

Before October 1880, Boycott's situation was little known outside County Mayo.[255] On 14 October of that year, Boycott wrote a letter to *The Times* about his situation:

Sir, the following detail may be interesting to your readers as exemplifying the power of the Land League. On the 22nd of September a process-server, escorted by a police force of seventeen men, retreated to my house for protection, followed by a howling mob of people, who yelled and hooted at the members of my family. On the ensuing day, September 23rd, the people collected in crowds upon my farm, and some hundred or so came up to my house and ordered off, under threats of ulterior consequences, all my farm labourers, workmen, and stablemen, commanding them never to work for me again. My herd has been frightened by them into giving up his employment, though he has refused to give up the house he held from me as part of his emolument. Another herd on an off farm has also been compelled to resign his situation. My blacksmith has received a letter threatening him with murder if he does

---

[245] Marlow, (1973) pp. 133–142
[246] Marlow, (1973) pp. 133–142
[247] Marlow, (1973) pp. 133–142
[248] Marlow, (1973) pp. 133–142
[249] Marlow, (1973) pp. 133–142
[250] Marlow, (1973) pp. 133–142
[251] Marlow, (1973) pp. 133–142
[252] Marlow, (1973) pp. 133–142
[253] Marlow, (1973) pp. 133–142
[254] Marlow, (1973) pp. 133–142
[255] Boycott, (1997) p. 232

any more work for me, and my laundress has also been ordered to give up my washing.

A little boy, twelve years of age, who carried my post-bag to and from the neighbouring town of Ballinrobe, was struck and threatened on 27th September, and ordered to desist from his work; since which time I have sent my little nephew for my letters and even he, on 2nd October, was stopped on the road and threatened if he continued to act as my messenger. The shopkeepers have been warned to stop all supplies to my house, and I have just received a message from the post mistress to say that the telegraph messenger was stopped and threatened on the road when bringing out a message to me and that she does not think it safe to send any telegrams which may come for me in the future for fear they should be abstracted, and the messenger injured. My farm is public property; the people wander over it with impunity. My crops are trampled upon, carried away in quantities, and destroyed wholesale. The locks on my gates are smashed, the gates thrown open, the walls thrown down, and the stock driven out on the roads. I can get no workmen to do anything, and my ruin is openly avowed as the object of the Land League unless I throw up everything and leave the country. I say nothing about the danger to my own life, which is apparent to anybody who knows the country.

After the publication of this letter, Bernard Becker, special correspondent of the *Daily News*, travelled to Ireland to cover Boycott's situation.[256] On 24 October, he wrote a dispatch from Westport that contained an interview with Boycott.[257] He reported that Boycott had £500 worth of crops that would rot if help could not be found to harvest them.[258] According to Becker, "Personally he is protected, but no woman in Ballinrobe would dream of washing him a cravat or making him a loaf. All the people have to say is that they are sorry, but that they 'dare not.'"[259] Boycott had been advised to leave, but he told Becker that "I can hardly desert Lord Erne, and, moreover, my own property is sunk in this "place."[260] Becker's report was reprinted in the *Belfast News-Letter* and the Dublin *Daily Express*.[261] On 29 October, the Dublin *Daily Express* published a letter proposing a fund to finance a party of men to go to County Mayo to save Boycott's crops.[262] Between them, the *Daily Express*, *The Daily Telegraph*, *Daily News*, and *News Letter* raised £2,000 to fund the relief expedition.[263]

---

[256] Marlow, (1973) pp. 143–155
[257] Marlow, (1973) pp. 143–155
[258] Marlow, (1973) pp. 143–155
[259] Becker (1881) p. 1–17
[260] Becker (1881) p. 1–17
[261] Marlow, (1973) pp. 143–155
[262] Marlow, (1973) pp. 143–155
[263] Hickey; Doherty, (2003) p. 40

In Belfast in early November 1880, The Boycott Relief Fund was established to arrange an armed expedition to Lough Mask.[264] Plans soon gained momentum, and within days, the fund had received many subscriptions.[265] The committee had arranged with the Midland Great Western Railway for special trains to transport the expedition from Ulster to County Mayo.[266] Many nationalists viewed the expedition as an invasion.[267] The *Freeman's Journal* denounced the organisers of the expedition, and asked, "How is it that this Government do not consider it necessary to prosecute the promoters of these warlike expeditions?"[268] [269]

William Edward Forster, Chief Secretary for Ireland made it clear in a communication with the proprietor of the Dublin *Daily Express* that he would not allow an armed expedition of hundreds of men, as the committee was planning, and that 50 unarmed men would be sufficient to harvest the crops.[270] He said that the government would consider it their duty to protect this group.[22] On 10 November 1880, the relief expedition consisting of one contingent from County Cavan and one from County Monaghan left for County Mayo.[271] Additional troops had already arrived in County Mayo to protect the expedition.[272] Boycott himself said that he did not want such a large number of Ulstermen, as he had saved the grain harvest himself, and that only ten or fifteen labourers were needed to save the root crops. He feared that a large number of Ulstermen would lead to sectarian violence.[273] While local Land League leaders said that there would be no trouble from them if the aim was simply to harvest the crops, more extreme sections of the local population did threaten violence against the expedition and the troops.[274]

The expedition experienced hostile protests on their route through County Mayo, but there was no violence, and they harvested the crops without incident.[275] Rumours spread amongst the Ulstermen that an attack was being planned on the farm, but none materialised.[276]

---

[264] Marlow, (1973) pp. 143–155
[265] Marlow, (1973) pp. 143–155
[266] Marlow, (1973) pp. 143–155
[267] Marlow, (1973) pp. 143–155
[268] Marlow, (1973) pp. 143–155
[269] *"The people of Ballinrobe and its neighbourhood..."Freeman's Journal. 5 November 1880. p. 4. Archived from the original on 30 April 2012. Retrieved 21 August 2012.*
[270] Marlow, (1973) pp. 157–173
[271] Marlow, (1973) pp. 157–173
[272] Marlow, (1973) pp. 157–173
[273] Marlow, (1973) pp. 157–173
[274] Marlow, (1973) pp. 157–173
[275] Marlow, (1973) pp. 157–173
[276] Marlow, (1973) pp. 157–173

On 27 November 1880, Boycott, his family and a local magistrate were escorted from Lough Mask House by members of the 19th Hussars.[277] A carriage had been hired for the family, but no driver could be found for it, and an army ambulance and driver had to be used.[278] The ambulance was escorted to Claremorris railway station, where Boycott and his family boarded a train to Dublin,[279] where Boycott was received with some hostility.[280] The hotel he stayed in received letters saying that it would be boycotted if Boycott remained.[281] He had intended to stay in Dublin for a week, but Boycott was advised to cut his stay short.[282] He left Dublin for England on the Holyhead mail boat on 1 December.[283]

The cost to the government of harvesting Boycott's crops was estimated at £10,000:[284] in Parnell's words, "one shilling for every turnip dug from Boycott's land".[285] In a letter requesting compensation to William Ewart Gladstone, then Prime Minister of the United Kingdom, Boycott said that he had lost £6,000 of his investment in the estate.[286]

Boycotting had strengthened the power of the peasants,[287] and by the end of 1880 there were reports of boycotting from all over Ireland.[288] The events at Lough Mask had also increased the power of the Land League, and the popularity of Parnell as a leader.[289]

On 28 December 1880, Parnell and other Land League leaders were put on trial on charges of conspiracy to prevent the payment of rent.[290] The trial attracted thousands of people onto the streets outside the court. A *Daily Express* reporter wrote that the court reminded him "more of the stalls of the theatre on opera night".[291] On 24 January 1881, the judge dismissed the jury, it having been hung ten to two in favour of acquittal.[292] Parnell and Davitt received this news as a victory.[293]

---

[277] Marlow, (1973) pp. 215–219
[278] Marlow, (1973) pp. 215–219
[279] Marlow, (1973) pp. 215–219
[280] Marlow, (1973) pp. 215–219
[281] Marlow, (1973) pp. 215–219
[282] Marlow, (1973) pp. 215–219
[283] Marlow, (1973) pp. 215–219
[284] Marlow, (1973) p 224
[285] Hickey; Doherty, (2003) p. 40
[286] Marlow, (1973) p. 234
[287] Marlow, (1973) pp. 228
[288] Marlow, (1973) pp. 221–231
[289] Marlow, (1973) pp. 221–231
[290] Marlow, (1973) pp. 221–231
[291] Marlow, (1973) pp. 221–231
[292] Marlow, (1973) pp. 221–231
[293] Marlow, (1973) pp. 221–231

After the boycotting, Gladstone discussed the issue of land reform, writing in an 1880 letter, "The subject of the land weighs greatly on my mind and I am working on it to the best of my ability."[294] In December 1880, the Bessborough Commission, headed by Frederick Ponsonby, 6th Earl of Bessborough, recommended major land reforms, including the three Fs.[295]

William Edward Forster argued that a Coercion Act which would punish those participated in events like those at Lough Mask, and would include the suspension of habeas corpus should be introduced before any Land Act. Gladstone eventually accepted this argument.[296] When Forster attempted to introduce the Protection of Person and Property Act 1881, Parnell and other Land League MPs attempted to obstruct its passage with tactics such as filibustering. One such filibuster lasted for 41 hours.[297] Eventually, the Speaker of the house intervened, and a measure was introduced whereby the Speaker could control the house if there was a three to one majority in favour of the business being urgent.[298] This was the first time that a check was placed on a debate in a British parliament.[299] The act was passed on 28 February 1881.[300] There was a negative reaction to the passing of the act in both England and Ireland.[301] In England, the Anti-Coercion Association was established, which was a precursor to the Labour Party.[302]

In April 1881 Gladstone introduced the Land Law (Ireland) Act 1881, in which the principle of the dual ownership of the land between landlords and tenants was established, and the three Fs introduced.[303] The act set up the Irish Land Commission, a judicial body that would fix rents for a period of 15 years and guarantee fixity of tenure.[304] According to *The Annual Register*, the act was "probably the most important measure introduced into the House of Commons since the passing of the Reform Bill".[305]

According to James Redpath, the verb "to boycott" was coined by Father O'Malley in a discussion between them on 23 September 1880.[306] The following is Redpath's account:[307]

---

294 Marlow, (1973) p. 225
295 Marlow, (1973) pp. 233–243
296 Marlow, (1973) pp. 233–243
297 Marlow, (1973) pp. 233–243
298 Marlow, (1973) pp. 233–243
299 Marlow, (1973) pp. 233–243
300 Marlow, (1973) pp. 233–243
301 Marlow, (1973) pp. 233–243
302 Marlow, (1973) pp. 233–243
303 Marlow, (1973) p. 249
304 Marlow, (1973) p. 249
305 Marlow, (1973) p. 249
306 Marlow, (1973) p. 249

I said, "I'm bothered about a word."

"What is it?" asked Father John.

"Well," I said, "When the people ostracise a land-grabber we call it social excommunication, but we ought to have an entirely different word to signify ostracism applied to a landlord or land-agent like Boycott. Ostracism won't do – the peasantry would not know the meaning of the word – and I can't think of any other."

"No," said Father John, "ostracism wouldn't do."

He looked down, tapped his big forehead, and said: "How would it do to call it to Boycott him?"

According to Joyce Marlow, the word was first used in print by Redpath in the *Inter-Ocean* on 12 October 1880.[308] The coining of the word, and its first use in print, came before Boycott and his situation was widely known outside County Mayo.[309] In November 1880, an article in the *Birmingham Daily Post* referred to the word as a local term in connection to the boycotting of a Ballinrobe merchant.[310] Still in 1880, *The Illustrated London News* described how "To 'Boycott' has already become a verb active, signifying to 'ratten', to intimidate, to 'send to Coventry', and to 'taboo'".[311] In 1888, the word was included in the first volume of *A New English Dictionary on Historical Principles* (later known as the Oxford English Dictionary).[312] According to Gary Minda in his book, *Boycott in America: how imagination and ideology shape the legal mind*, "Apparently there was no other word in the English language to describe this dispute."[313] The word also entered the lexicon of languages other than English, such as Dutch, French, German, Polish and Russian.[314]

After leaving Ireland, Boycott and his family visited the United States.[315] His arrival in New York generated a great deal of media interest; the *New York Tribune* said that, "The arrival of Captain Boycott, who has involuntarily added a new word to the language, is an event of something like international interest."[316] *The New York Times* said, "For private reasons the visitor made the voyage incognito, being registered simply as 'Charles Cunningham.'"[317] The purpose of the visit was to see

---

[307] Marlow, (1973) p. 249
[308] Marlow, (1973) p. 249
[309] Marlow, (1973) p. 249
[310] "The agitation in Ireland". *Birmingham Daily Post*. 13 November 1880. p. 5.
[311] Murray, (1888) p. 1040
[312] Murray, (1888) p. 1040
[313] Minda, (1999) pp. 27–28
[314] Minda, (1999) pp. 27–28
[315] Marlow, (1973) pp. 245–249
[316] Marlow, (1973) pp. 245–249
[317] "Arrival of capt. Boycott" (PDF). *The New York Times*. 6 April 1881. Retrieved 2 January 2012.

friends in Virginia, including Murray McGregor Blacker, a friend from his time on Achill Island who had settled in the United States.[318] Boycott returned to England after some months.[319]

In 1886, Boycott became a land agent for Hugh Adair's Flixton estate in Suffolk, England.[320] He had a passion for horses and racing, and became secretary of the Bungay race committee.[321] Boycott continued to spend holidays in Ireland, and according to Joyce Marlow, he left Ireland without bitterness.[322]

In early 1897, Boycott's health became very poor. In an attempt to improve his health, he and his wife went on a cruise to Malta.[323] In Brindisi, he became seriously ill, and had to return to England.[324] His health continued to deteriorate, and on 19 June 1897 he died at his home in Flixton, aged 65.[325] His funeral and burial took place at the church at Burgh St Peter, conducted by his nephew Arthur St John Boycott, who was at Lough Mask during the first boycott.[326] Charles Boycott's widow, Annie, was subsequently sued over the funeral expenses and other debts, and had to sell some assets.[327] A number of London newspapers, including *The Times*, published obituaries.[328]

---

[318] Marlow, (1973) pp. 245–249
[319] Marlow, (1973) pp. 245–249
[320] Marlow, (1973) pp. 264–276
[321] Marlow, (1973) pp. 264–276
[322] Marlow, (1973) pp. 264–276
[323] Marlow, (1973) pp. 264–276
[324] Marlow, (1973) pp. 264–276
[325] Marlow, (1973) pp. 264–276
[326] Marlow, (1973) pp. 264–276
[327] Marlow, (1973) pp. 264–276
[328] Marlow, (1973) pp. 264–276

Chapter six

The Irish Uprising – Easter 1916

The Easter Rising also known as the Easter Rebellion, was an armed insurrection in Ireland during Easter Week in April 1916. The Rising was launched by Irish republicans against British rule in Ireland with the aim of establishing an independent Irish Republic while the United Kingdom was fighting the First World War. It was the most significant uprising in Ireland since the rebellion of 1798 and the first armed conflict of the Irish revolutionary period. Sixteen of the Rising's leaders were executed from May 1916, but the insurrection, the nature of the executions, and subsequent political developments ultimately contributed to an increase in popular support for Irish independence.

Organised by a seven-man Military Council of the Irish Republican Brotherhood, the Rising began on Easter Monday, 24 April 1916 and lasted for six days. Members of the Irish Volunteers, led by schoolmaster and Irish language activist Patrick Pearse, joined by the smaller Irish Citizen Army of James Connolly and 200 women of Cumann na mBan, seized strategically important buildings in Dublin and proclaimed the Irish Republic. The British Army brought in thousands of reinforcements as well as artillery and a gunboat. There was street fighting on the routes into the city centre, where the rebels slowed the British advance and inflicted many casualties. Elsewhere in Dublin, the fighting mainly consisted of sniping and long-range gun battles. The main rebel positions were gradually surrounded and bombarded with artillery. There were isolated actions in other parts of Ireland; Volunteer leader Eoin MacNeill had issued a countermand in a bid to halt the Rising, which greatly reduced the number of rebels who mobilised.

With much greater numbers and heavier weapons, the British Army suppressed the Rising. Pearse agreed to an unconditional surrender on Saturday 29 April, although sporadic fighting continued briefly. After the surrender, the country remained under martial law. About 3,500 people were taken prisoner by the British and 1,800 of them were sent to internment camps or prisons in Britain. Most of the leaders of the Rising were executed following courts-martial. The Rising brought physical force republicanism back to the forefront of Irish politics, which for nearly fifty years had been dominated by constitutional nationalism.

Opposition to the British reaction to the Rising contributed to changes in public opinion and the move toward independence, as shown in the December 1918 election in Ireland which was won by the Sinn Féin party, which convened the First Dáil (Irish Parliament) and declared independence.

Of the 485 people killed, 260 were civilians, 143 were British military and police personnel, and 82 were Irish rebels, including 16 rebels executed for their roles in the Rising. More than 2,600 people were wounded. Many of the civilians were killed or wounded by British artillery fire or were mistaken for rebels. Others were caught in the crossfire during firefights between the British and the rebels. The shelling and resulting fires left parts of central Dublin in ruins.

The Acts of Union 1800 united the Kingdom of Great Britain and the Kingdom of Ireland as the United Kingdom of Great Britain and Ireland, abolishing the Irish Parliament and giving Ireland representation in the British Parliament. From early on, many Irish nationalists opposed the union and the continued lack of adequate political representation, along with the British government's handling of Ireland and Irish people, particularly the Great Irish Famine.[329] Opposition took various forms: constitutional (the Repeal Association; the Home Rule League), social (disestablishment of the Church of Ireland; the Land League) and revolutionary (Rebellion of 1848; Fenian Rising).[330] The Irish Home Rule movement sought to achieve self-government for Ireland, within the United Kingdom. In 1886, the Irish Parliamentary Party under Charles Stewart Parnell succeeded in having the First Home Rule Bill introduced in the British parliament, but it was defeated. The Second Home Rule Bill of 1893 was passed by the House of Commons but rejected by the House of Lords.

After the death of Parnell, younger and more radical nationalists became disillusioned with parliamentary politics and turned toward more extreme forms of separatism. The Gaelic Athletic Association, the Gaelic League and the cultural revival under W. B. Yeats and Augusta, Lady Gregory, together with the new political thinking of Arthur Griffith expressed in his newspaper *Sinn Féin* and organisations such as the National Council and the Sinn Féin League, led many Irish people to identify with the idea of an independent Gaelic Ireland.[331] [332] This was sometimes referred to by the generic term *Sinn Féin*,[333] with the British authorities using it as a collective noun for republicans and advanced nationalists.[334]

---

[329] MacDonagh, pp. 14–17
[330] Mansergh, Nicholas, *The Irish Question 1840–1921*, George Allen & Unwin, 1978, ISBN 0-04-901022-0 p. 244
[331] MacDonagh, Oliver, pp. 72–74
[332] Feeney, p. 22

The Third Home Rule Bill was introduced by British Liberal Prime Minister H. H. Asquith in 1912. Irish Unionists, who were overwhelmingly Protestants, opposed it, as they did not want to be ruled by a Catholic-dominated Irish government. Led by Sir Edward Carson and James Craig, they formed the Ulster Volunteers (UVF) in January 1913.[335] In response, Irish nationalists formed a rival paramilitary group, the Irish Volunteers, in November 1913. The Irish Republican Brotherhood (IRB) was a driving force behind the Irish Volunteers and attempted to control it. Its leader was Eoin MacNeill, who was not an IRB member.[336] The Irish Volunteers' stated goal was "to secure and to maintain the rights and liberties common to all the people of Ireland". It included people with a range of political views, and was open to "all able-bodied Irishmen without distinction of creed, politics or social group".[337] Anoth er militant group, the Irish Citizen Army, was formed by trade unionists as a result of the Dublin Lock-out of that year.[338] British Army officers threatened to resign if they were ordered to take action against the UVF. When the Irish Volunteers smuggled rifles into Dublin, the British Army attempted to stop them and shot into a crowd of civilians. By 1914, Ireland seemed to be on the brink of a civil war.[339] This seemed to be averted in August of that year by the outbreak of the First World War,[340] and Ir eland's involvement in it. Nevertheless, on 18 September 1914 the Government of Ireland Act 1914 was enacted and placed on the statute book, but the Suspensory Act was passed at the same time, which deferred Irish Home Rule for one year, with powers for it to be suspended for further periods of six months so long as the war continued.[341] It was widely believed at the time that the war would not last more than a few months.[342] On 14 September 1915 an Order in Council was made under the Suspensory Act to suspend the Government of Ireland Act until 18 March 1916. Another such Order was made on 29 February 1916, suspending the Act for another six months.[343]

The Supreme Council of the IRB met on 5 September 1914, just over a month after the British government had declared war on Germany. At this meeting, they decided to stage an uprising before the war ended and to secure help from Germany.[344] Respo

---

333 Feeney, p. 37
334 O'Leary, Brendan (2019). *A Treatise on Northern Ireland, Volume I: Colonialism.* Oxford University Press. p. 320. ISBN 978-0199243341.
335 Those who set the stage" (PDF). *The 1916 Rising: Personalities and Perspectives.* National Library of Ireland.
336 Foy and Barton, pp. 7–8
337 Macardle, pp. 90–92
338 Townshend, p. 49
339 Collins, M.E. *Sovereignty and partition, 1912–1949.* Edco Publishing, 2004. pp. 32–33
340 Townshend, pp. 59–60
341 Hennessey, Thomas (1998), p. 76
342 Jackson, Alvin: p. 164
343 Hennessey, Thomas (1998), p. 76

nsibility for the planning of the rising was given to Tom Clarke and Sean Mac Diarmada.[345] The Irish Volunteers the smaller of the two forces resulting from the September 1914 split over support for the British war effort[346] set up a "headquarters staff" that included Patrick Pearse[347] as Director of Military Organisation, Joseph Plunkett as Director of Military Operations and Thomas MacDonagh as Director of Training. Eamonn Ceannt was later added as Director of Communications.[348]

In May 1915, Clarke and Mac Diarmada established a Military Committee or Military Council within the IRB, consisting of Pearse, Plunkett and Ceannt, to draw up plans for a rising.[349] Clarke and Mac Diarmada joined it shortly after. The Military Council was able to promote its own policies and personnel independently of both the Volunteer Executive and the IRB Executive. Although the Volunteer and IRB leaders were not against a rising in principle, they were of the opinion that it was not opportune at that moment.[350] Volunteer Chief-of-Staff Eoin MacNeill supported a rising only if the British government attempted to suppress the Volunteers or introduce conscription in Ireland, and if such a rising had some chance of success. IRB President Denis McCullough and prominent IRB member Bulmer Hobson held similar views.[351] The Military Council kept its plans secret, so as to prevent the British authorities learning of the plans, and to thwart those within the organisation who might try to stop the rising. IRB members held officer rank in the Volunteers throughout the country and took their orders from the Military Council, not from MacNeill.[352]

Shortly after the outbreak of World War I, Roger Casement and Clan na Gael leader John Devoy met the German ambassador to the United States, Johann Heinrich von Bernstorff, to discuss German backing for an uprising. Casement went to Germany and began negotiations with the German government and military. He persuaded the Germans to announce their support for Irish independence in November 1914.[353] Casement also attempted to recruit an Irish Brigade, made up of Irish prisoners of war, which would be armed and sent to Ireland to join the uprising. However, only 56 men volunteered. Plunkett joined Casement in Germany

---

[344] Caulfield, Max, p. 18
[345] Foy and Barton, p. 16
[346] Foy and Barton, p. 13
[347] Sean Farrell Moran, *Patrick Pearse and the Politics of Redemption: The Mind of the Easter Rising,* (1994), Ruth Dudley Edwards, *Patrick Pearse and the Triumph of Failure,* (1977), Joost Augustin, *Patrick Pearse,* (2009)
[348] Townshend, p. 92
[349] Foy and Barton, pp. 16, 19
[350] McGarry, p. 116
[351] Townshend, p. 94
[352] Macardle, p. 119
[353] Foy and Barton, p. 25

the following year. Together, Plunkett and Casement presented a plan (the 'Ireland Report') in which a German expeditionary force would land on the west coast of Ireland, while a rising in Dublin diverted the British forces so that the Germans, with the help of local Volunteers, could secure the line of the River Shannon, before advancing on the capital.[354] The German military rejected the plan, but agreed to ship arms and ammunition to the Volunteers.[355]

James Connolly head of the Irish Citizen Army (ICA), a group of armed socialist trade union men and women was unaware of the IRB's plans, and threatened to start a rebellion on his own if other parties failed to act. If they had done it alone, the IRB and the Volunteers would possibly have come to their aid;[356] however, the IRB leaders met with Connolly in January 1916 and convinced him to join forces with them. They agreed that they would launch a rising together at Easter and made Connolly the sixth member of the Military Council. Thomas MacDonagh would later become the seventh and final member.

The death of the old Fenian leader Jeremiah O'Donovan Rossa in New York in August 1915 was an opportunity to mount a spectacular demonstration. His body was sent to Ireland for burial in Glasnevin Cemetery, with the Volunteers in charge of arrangements. Huge crowds lined the route and gathered at the graveside. Pearse made a dramatic funeral oration, a rallying call to republicans, which ended with the words "Ireland unfree shall never be at peace".[357]

In early April, Pearse issued orders to the Irish Volunteers for three days of "parades and manoeuvres" beginning on Easter Sunday. He had the authority to do this, as the Volunteers' Director of Organisation. The idea was that IRB members within the organisation would know these were orders to begin the rising, while men such as MacNeill and the British authorities would take it at face value.

On 9 April, the German Navy dispatched the SS *Libau* for County Kerry, disguised as the Norwegian ship *Aud*.[358] It was loaded with 20,000 rifles, one million rounds of ammunition, and explosives. Casement also left for Ireland aboard the German submarine *U-19*. He was disappointed with the level of support offered by the Germans, and he intended to stop or at least postpone the rising.[359]

On Wednesday 19 April, Alderman Tom Kelly, a Sinn Féin member of Dublin Corporation, read out at a meeting of the corporation a document purportedly leaked

---

[354] McNally and Dennis, p. 30
[355] Foy and Barton, pp. 25–28
[356] Eoin Neeson, *Myths from Easter 1916*
[357] Kennedy, pp. 199–200
[358] Caulfield, Max, p. 29
[359] Foy and Barton, p.56

from Dublin Castle, detailing plans by the British authorities to shortly arrest leaders of the Irish Volunteers, Sinn Féin and the Gaelic League, and occupy their premises.[360] Although the British authorities said the "Castle Document" was fake, MacNeill ordered the Volunteers to prepare to resist.[361] Unbeknownst to MacNeill, the document had been forged by the Military Council to persuade moderates of the need for their planned uprising. It was an edited version of a real document outlining British plans in the event of conscription.[362] That same day, the Military Council informed senior Volunteer officers that the rising would begin on Easter Sunday. However, it chose not to inform the rank-and-file, or moderates such as MacNeill, until the last minute.[363]

The following day, MacNeill got wind that a rising was about to be launched and threatened to do everything he could to prevent it, short of informing the British.[364] MacNeill was briefly persuaded to go along with some sort of action when Mac Diarmada revealed to him that a German arms shipment was about to land in County Kerry. MacNeill believed that when the British learned of the shipment, they would immediately suppress the Volunteers, thus the Volunteers would be justified in taking defensive action, including the planned manoeuvres.[365]

The *Aud* and the *U-19* reached the coast of Kerry on Good Friday, 21 April. This was earlier than the Volunteers expected and so none were there to meet the vessels. The Royal Navy had known about the arms shipment and intercepted the *Aud*, prompting the captain to scuttle the ship. Furthermore, Casement was captured shortly after he landed at Banna Strand.[366]

When MacNeill learned from Volunteer Patrick Whelan that the arms shipment had been lost, he reverted to his original position. With the support of other leaders of like mind, notably Bulmer Hobson and The O'Rahilly, he issued a countermand to all Volunteers, cancelling all actions for Sunday. This countermanding order was relayed to Volunteer officers and printed in the Sunday morning newspapers. It succeeded only in delaying the rising for a day, although it greatly reduced the number of Volunteers who turned out.

British Naval Intelligence had been aware of the arms shipment, Casement's return, and the Easter date for the rising through radio messages between Germany and its

[360] Townshend, pp. 131–132
[361] Foy and Barton, p. 47
[362] McGarry, p. 117
[363] Foy and Barton, p. 48
[363] Foy and Barton, p. 52
[364] Michael Tierney, *Eoin MacNeill*, pp. 199, 214
[365] Michael Tierney, *Eoin MacNeill*, pp. 199, 214
[366] Foy and Barton, pp. 57–58

embassy in the United States that were intercepted by the Royal Navy and deciphered in Room 40 of the Admiralty.[367] The information was passed to the Under-Secretary for Ireland, Sir Matthew Nathan, on 17 April, but without revealing its source and Nathan was doubtful about its accuracy.[368] When news reached Dublin of the capture of the *Aud* and the arrest of Casement, Nathan conferred with the Lord Lieutenant, Lord Wimborne. Nathan proposed to raid Liberty Hall, headquarters of the Citizen Army, and Volunteer properties at Father Matthew Park and at Kimmage, but Wimborne insisted on wholesale arrests of the leaders. It was decided to postpone action until after Easter Monday, and in the meantime, Nathan telegraphed the Chief Secretary, Augustine Birrell, in London seeking his approval.[369] By the time Birrell cabled his reply authorising the action, at noon on Monday 24 April 1916, the Rising had already begun.[370]

On the morning of Easter Sunday, 23 April, the Military Council met at Liberty Hall to discuss what to do considering MacNeill's countermanding order. They decided that the Rising would go ahead the following day, Easter Monday, and that the Irish Volunteers and Irish Citizen Army would go into action as the 'Army of the Irish Republic'. They elected Pearse as president of the Irish Republic, and as Commander-in-Chief of the army; Connolly became Commandant of the Dublin Brigade.[371] Messengers were then sent to all units informing them of the new orders.[372]

On the morning of Monday 24 April, about 1,200 members of the Irish Volunteers and Irish Citizen Army mustered at several locations in central Dublin. Among them were members of the all-female Cumann na mBan. Some wore Irish Volunteer and Citizen Army uniforms, while others wore civilian clothes with a yellow Irish Volunteer armband, military hats, and bandoliers.[373] [374] They were armed mostly with rifles (especially 1871 Mausers), but also with shotguns, revolvers, a few Mauser C96 semi-automatic pistols, and grenades.[375] The number of Volunteers who mobilised was much smaller than expected. This was due to MacNeill's countermanding order, and the fact that the new orders had been sent so soon beforehand. However, several hundred Volunteers joined the Rising after it began.[376]

---

[367] Ó Broin, p. 138
[368] Ó Broin, p. 79
[369] Ó Broin, pp. 81–87
[370] Ó Broin, p. 88
[371] Foy and Barton, p. 66
[372] Chronology of the Easter Rising. Century Ireland – RTÉ.
[373] Ward, Alan. *The Easter Rising: Revolution and Irish Nationalism*. Wiley, 2003. p. 5
[374] Cottrel, Peter. *The War for Ireland: 1913–1923*. Osprey, 2009. p. 41
[375] Dorney, John. The Weapons of 1916. *Irish Independent*. 3 March 2016.
[376] McGarry, p. 129

Shortly before midday, the rebels began to seize important sites in central Dublin. The rebels' plan was to hold Dublin city centre. This was a large, oval-shaped area bounded by two canals: the Grand to the south and the Royal to the north, with the River Liffey running through the middle. On the southern and western edges of this district were five British Army barracks. Most of the rebels' positions had been chosen to defend against counterattacks from these barracks.[377] The rebels took the positions with ease. Civilians were evacuated and policemen were ejected or taken prisoner.[378] Windows and doors were barricaded, food and supplies were secured, and first aid posts were set up. Barricades were erected on the streets to hinder British Army movement.[379]

A joint force of about 400 Volunteers and Citizen Army gathered at Liberty Hall under the command of Commandant James Connolly. This was the headquarters battalion, and it also included Commander-in-Chief Patrick Pearse, as well as Tom Clarke, Sean Mac Diarmada and Joseph Plunkett.[380] They marched to the General Post Office (GPO) on O'Connell Street, Dublin's main thoroughfare, occupied the building and hoisted two republican flags. Pearse stood outside and read the Proclamation of the Irish Republic.[381] Copies of the Proclamation were also pasted on walls and handed out to bystanders by Volunteers and newsboys.[382] The GPO would be the rebels' headquarters for most of the Rising. Volunteers from the GPO also occupied other buildings on the street, including buildings overlooking O'Connell Bridge. They took over a wireless telegraph station and sent out a radio broadcast in Morse code, announcing that an Irish Republic had been declared. This was the first radio broadcast in Ireland.[383]

Elsewhere, some of the Headquarters Battalion under Michael Mallin occupied St Stephen's Green, where they dug trenches and barricaded the surrounding roads. The 1st Battalion, under Edward 'Ned' Daly, occupied the Four Courts and surrounding buildings, while a company under Sean Heuston occupied the Mendicity Institution, across the River Liffey from the Four Courts. The 2nd Battalion, under Thomas MacDonagh, occupied Jacob's biscuit factory. The 3rd Battalion, under Eamonn de Valera, occupied Boland's Mill and surrounding buildings. The 4th Battalion, under Eamonn Ceannt, occupied the South Dublin Union and the distillery

---

[377] Dorney, John. *The Story of the Easter Rising, 1916.* Green Lamp, 2010. p. 33
[378] McGarry, p. 133
[379] McGarry, p. 135
[380] McNally and Dennis, p. 41
[381] Foy and Barton, pp. 192, 195
[382] McGarry, p. 134
[383] McGee, John. "Time to celebrate a centenary of Irish broadcast heroes". *Irish Independent*, 6 March 2016.

on Marrowbone Lane. From each of these garrisons, small units of rebels established outposts in the surrounding area.[384]

The rebels also attempted to cut transport and communication links. As well as erecting roadblocks, they took control of various bridges and cut telephone and telegraph wires. Westland Row and Street railway stations were occupied, though the latter only briefly. The railway line was cut at Fairview and the line was damaged by bombs at Amiens Street, Broadstone, Kingsbridge and Lansdowne Road.[385]

Around midday, a small team of Volunteers and Fianna Eireann members swiftly captured the Magazine Fort in the Phoenix Park and disarmed the guards. The goal was to seize weapons and blow up the ammunition store to signal that the Rising had begun. They seized weapons and planted explosives, but the blast was not loud enough to be heard across the city.[386] The 23-year-old son of the fort's commander was fatally shot when he ran to raise the alarm.[387]

A contingent under Sean Connolly occupied Dublin City Hall and adjacent buildings.[388] They attempted to seize neighbouring Dublin Castle, the heart of British rule in Ireland. As they approached the gate a lone and unarmed police sentry, James O'Brien, attempted to stop them and was shot dead by Connolly. According to some accounts, he was the first casualty of the Rising. The rebels overpowered the soldiers in the guardroom but failed to press further. The British Army's chief intelligence officer, Major Ivon Price, fired on the rebels while the Under-Secretary for Ireland, Sir Matthew Nathan, helped shut the castle gates. Unbeknownst to the rebels, the Castle was lightly guarded and could have been taken with ease.[389] The rebels instead laid siege to the Castle from City Hall. Fierce fighting erupted there after British reinforcements arrived. The rebels on the roof exchanged fire with soldiers on the street. Sean Connolly was shot dead by a sniper, becoming the first rebel casualty.[390] By the following morning, British forces had re-captured City Hall and taken the rebels prisoner.[391]

The rebels did not attempt to take some other key locations, notably Trinity College, in the heart of the city centre and defended by only a handful of armed unionist students.[392] Failure to capture the telephone exchange in Crown Alley left

384 McNally and Dennis, pp. 39–40
385 McKenna, Joseph. *Guerrilla Warfare in the Irish War of Independence*. McFarland, 2011. p. 19
386 Caulfield, Max, pp. 48–50
387 "Children of the Revolution". History Ireland. Volume 1, issue 23 (May/June 2013).
388 Foy and Barton, pp. 87–90
389 Foy and Barton, pp. 84–85
390 Chronology of the Easter Rising. Century Ireland – RTÉ.
391 Chronology of the Easter Rising. Century Ireland – RTÉ.
392 Townshend, pp. 163–164

communications in the hands of Government with GPO staff quickly repairing telephone wires that had been cut by the rebels.[393] The failure to occupy strategic locations was attributed to lack of manpower.[394] In at least two incidents, at Jacob's[395] and Stephen's Green,[396] the Volunteers and Citizen Army shot dead civilians trying to attack them or dismantle their barricades. Elsewhere, they hit civilians with their rifle butts to drive them off.[397]

The British military were caught totally unprepared by the Rising and their response of the first day was generally un-coordinated. Two squadrons [398] of British cavalry were sent to investigate what was happening. They took fire and casualties from rebel forces at the GPO and at the Four Courts.[399] [400] As one troop passed Nelson's Pillar, the rebels opened fire from the GPO, killing three cavalrymen and two horses[401] and fatally wounding a fourth man. The cavalrymen retreated and were withdrawn to barracks. On Mount Street, a group of Volunteer Training Corps men stumbled upon the rebel position and four were killed before they reached Beggars Bush Barracks.[402]

The only substantial combat of the first day of the Rising took place at the South Dublin Union where a piquet from the Royal Irish Regiment encountered an outpost of Eamonn Ceannt's force at the north-western corner of the South Dublin Union. The British troops, after taking some casualties, managed to regroup and launch several assaults on the position before they forced their way inside and the small rebel force in the tin huts at the eastern end of the Union surrendered.[403] However, the Union complex remained in rebel hands. A nurse in uniform, Margaret Keogh, was shot dead by British soldiers at the Union. She is believed to have been the first civilian killed in the Rising.[404]

Three unarmed Dublin Metropolitan Police were shot dead on the first day of the Rising and their Commissioner pulled them off the streets. Partly because of the police withdrawal, a wave of looting broke out in the city centre, especially in the area of O'Connell Street (still officially called "Sackville Street" at the time).[405]

[393] Ferguson, Stephen (2012). *Business as Usual – GPO Staff in 1916*. Mercier Press. p. 60. ISBN 9781856359948.
[394] McGarry, p. 129
[395] McGarry p. 142
[396] Stephens p. 18
[397] McGarry, pp. 142–143; Townshend, p. 174
[398] Townsend, Easter 1916, p.170
[399] Caulfield, Max, pp. 54–55
[400] Coffey, Thomas M. *Agony at Easter: The 1916 Irish Uprising*, pp. 38, 44, 155
[401] Coffey, Thomas M. *Agony at Easter: The 1916 Irish Uprising*, pp. 38, 44, 155
[402] O'Brien, *Blood on the Streets, the Battle for Mount Street*, pp. 22–23
[403] Caulfield, Max, pp. 76–80
[404] "Nurse Margaret Keogh, the first civilian fatality of the Rising". *Irish Independent*. 4 March 2016.
[405] Townshend, pp. 263–264

Lord Wimborne, the Lord Lieutenant, declared martial law on Tuesday evening and handed over civil power to Brigadier-General William Lowe. British forces initially put their efforts into securing the approaches to Dublin Castle and isolating the rebel headquarters, which they believed was in Liberty Hall. The British commander, Lowe, worked slowly, unsure of the size of the force he was up against, and with only 1,269 troops in the city when he arrived from the Curragh Camp in the early hours of Tuesday 25 April. City Hall was taken from the rebel unit that had attacked Dublin Castle on Tuesday morning.[406] [407]

In the early hours of Tuesday, 120 British soldiers, with machine-guns, occupied two buildings overlooking St Stephen's Green: the Shelbourne Hotel and United Services Club[408] At dawn they opened fire on the Citizen Army occupying the green. The rebels returned fire but were forced to retreat to the Royal College of Surgeons building. They remained there for the rest of the week, exchanging fire with British forces.[409]

Fighting erupted along the northern edge of the city centre on Tuesday afternoon. In the northeast, British troops left Amiens Street railway station in an armoured train, to secure and repair a section of damaged tracks. They were attacked by rebels who had taken up position at Annesley Bridge. After a two-hour battle, the British were forced to retreat and several soldiers were captured.[410] At Phibsborough, in the northwest, rebels had occupied buildings and erected barricades at junctions on the North Circular Road. The British summoned 18-pounder field artillery from Athlone and shelled the rebel positions, destroying the barricades. After a fierce firefight, the rebels withdrew.[411]

That afternoon Pearse walked out into O'Connell Street with a small escort and stood in front of Nelson's Pillar. As a large crowd gathered, he read out a 'manifesto to the citizens of Dublin,' calling on them to support the Rising.[412]

The rebels had failed to take either of Dublin's two main railway stations or either of its ports, at Dublin Port and Kingstown. As a result, during the following week, the British were able to bring in thousands of reinforcements from Britain and from their garrisons at the Curragh and Belfast. By the end of the week, British strength stood at over 16,000 men.[413] [414] Their firepower was provided by field artillery which they

[406] Coogan 2001, p. 107
[407] Townshend, p. 191
[408] Caulfield, p. 122
[409] Chronology of the Easter Rising. Century Ireland – RTÉ.
[410] Caulfield, pp. 145–146
[411] Caulfield, pp. 145–146
[412] Foy and Barton, p. 180

positioned on the Northside of the city at Phibsborough and at Trinity College, and by the patrol vessel *Helga*, which sailed up the Liffey, having been summoned from the port at Kingstown. On Wednesday, 26 April, the guns at Trinity College and *Helga* shelled Liberty Hall, and the Trinity College guns then began firing at rebel positions, first at Boland's Mill and then in O'Connell Street.[415] Some rebel commanders, particularly James Connolly, did not believe that the British would shell the 'second city' of the British Empire.[416] [417]

The principal rebel positions at the GPO, the Four Courts, Jacob's Factory and Boland's Mill saw little action. The British surrounded and bombarded them rather than assault them directly. One Volunteer in the GPO recalled, "we did practically no shooting as there was no target".[418] However, where the rebels dominated the routes by which the British tried to funnel reinforcements into the city, there was fierce fighting.

At 5:25PM Volunteers Eamon Martin, Garry Holohan, Robert Beggs, Sean Cody, Dinny O'Callaghan, Charles Shelley, Peadar Breslin and five others attempted to occupy Broadstone railway station on Church Street, the attack was unsuccessful and Martin was injured.[419] [420] [421] [422] [423]

On Wednesday morning, hundreds of British troops encircled the Mendicity Institution, which was occupied by 26 Volunteers under Sean Heuston. British troops advanced on the building, supported by snipers and machine-gun fire, but the Volunteers put up stiff resistance. Eventually, the troops got close enough to hurl grenades into the building, some of which the rebels threw back. Exhausted and almost out of ammunition, Heuston's men became the first rebel position to surrender. Heuston had been ordered to hold his position for a few hours, to delay the British, but had held on for three days.[424]

Reinforcements were sent to Dublin from Britain and disembarked at Kingstown on the morning of Wednesday 26 April. Heavy fighting occurred at the rebel-held positions around the Grand Canal as these troops advanced towards Dublin. More

---

[413] Townshend, p. 191
[414] McGarry, pp. 167–169
[415] Townshend, p. 191
[416] McGarry, p. 192
[417] Foy and Barton, p. 181
[418] McGarry, p. 175
[419] Chronology of the Easter Rising. Century Ireland – RTÉ.
[420] Witness Statement by Eamon Martin to Bureau of Military History, 1951
[421] Witness Statement of Sean Cody to Bureau of Military History, 1954
[422] Witness Statement of Nicholas Kaftan to Bureau of Military History
[423] Witness Statement of Charles Shelley to Bureau of Military History, 1953
[424] O'Brien, Paul. Heuston's Fort – The Battle for the Mendicity Institute, 1916. The Irish Story. 15 August 2012.

than 1,000 Sherwood Foresters were repeatedly caught in a crossfire trying to cross the canal at Mount Street Bridge. Seventeen Volunteers were able to severely disrupt the British advance, killing or wounding 240 men.[425] Despite there being alternative routes across the canal nearby, General Lowe ordered repeated frontal assaults on the Mount Street position.[426] The British eventually took the position, which had not been reinforced by the nearby rebel garrison at Boland's Mills, on Thursday,[427] but the fighting there inflicted up to two-thirds of their casualties for the entire week for a cost of just four dead Volunteers.[428] It had taken nearly nine hours for the British to advance 300 yd (270 m).[429]

On Wednesday Linenhall Barracks on Constitution Hill was burnt down under the orders of Commandant Edward Daly to prevent its reoccupation by the British.

The rebel position at the South Dublin Union (site of the present-day St. James's Hospital) and Marrowbone Lane, further west along the canal, also inflicted heavy losses on British troops. The South Dublin Union was a large complex of buildings and there was vicious fighting around and inside the buildings. Cathal Brugha, a rebel officer, distinguished himself in this action and was badly wounded. By the end of the week, the British had taken some of the buildings in the Union, but others remained in rebel hands.[430] British troops also took casualties in unsuccessful frontal assaults on the Marrowbone Lane Distillery.[431]

The third major scene of fighting during the week was in North King Street, north of the Four Courts. The rebels had established strong outposts in the area, occupying numerous small buildings and barricading the streets. From Thursday to Saturday, the British made repeated attempts to capture the area, in what was some of the fiercest fighting of the Rising. As the troops moved in, the rebels continually opened fire from windows and behind chimneys and barricades. At one point, a platoon led by Major Sheppard made a bayonet charge on one of the barricades but was cut down by rebel fire. The British employed machine guns and attempted to avoid direct fire by using makeshift armoured trucks, and by mouse-holing through the inside walls of terraced houses to get near the rebel positions.[432] By the time of the rebel headquarters' surrender on Saturday, the South Staffordshire Regiment under Colonel Taylor had advanced only 150 yd (140 m) down the street at a cost of 11 dead and 28 wounded.[433] The enraged troops broke into the houses along the street

[425] Coogan, p. 122
[426] Caulfield, p. 196
[427] O'Brien, p. 69
[428] McGarry, p. 173
[429] McGarry, p. 173
[430] Caulfield, pp. 225–228
[431] Ryan, pp. 128–133
[432] Dorney, John. "The North King Street Massacre, Dublin 1916". The Irish Story. 13 April 2012.

and shot or bayoneted fifteen unarmed male civilians whom they accused of being rebel fighters.[434]

Elsewhere, at Portobello Barracks, an officer named Bowen Colthurst summarily executed six civilians, including the pacifist nationalist activist, Francis Sheehy-Skeffington.[435] These instances of British troops killing Irish civilians would later be highly controversial in Ireland.

The headquarters garrison at the GPO was forced to evacuate after days of shelling when a fire caused by the shells spread to the GPO. Connolly had been incapacitated by a bullet wound to the ankle and had passed command on to Pearse. The O'Rahilly was killed in a sortie from the GPO. They tunnelled through the walls of the neighbouring buildings to evacuate the Post Office without coming under fire and took up a new position in 16 Moore Street. The young Sean McLoughlin was given military command and planned a breakout, but Pearse realised this plan would lead to further loss of civilian life.[436]

On Saturday 29 April, from this new headquarters, Pearse issued an order for all companies to surrender.[437] Pearse surrendered unconditionally to Brigadier-General Lowe. The surrender document read:

To prevent the further slaughter of Dublin citizens, and in the hope of saving the lives of our followers now surrounded and hopelessly outnumbered, the members of the Provisional Government present at headquarters have agreed to an unconditional surrender, and the commandants of the various districts in the City and County will order their commands to lay down arms.[438]

The other posts surrendered only after Pearse's surrender order, carried by nurse Elizabeth O'Farrell, reached them.[439] Sporadic fighting, therefore, continued until Sunday, when word of the surrender was got to the other rebel garrisons.[440] Command of British forces had passed from Lowe to General John Maxwell, who arrived in Dublin just in time to take the surrender. Maxwell was made temporary military governor of Ireland.[441]

Irish Volunteer units mobilised on Easter Sunday in several places outside of Dublin, but because of Eoin MacNeill's countermanding order, most of them returned home

---

[433] Coogan pp. 152–155
[434] Coogan p. 155, McGarry p. 187
[435] Coogan p. 155, McGarry p. 187
[436] Charlie McGuire, "Seán McLoughlin – the boy commandant of 1916", *History Ireland*, Vol. 14, No. 2
[437] Townshend, pp. 243–246
[438] "Dublin may seek surrender letter". *BBC News*. 9 January 2006.
[439] Townshend, pp. 246–247
[440] Townshend
[441] McGarry, pp. 203–204

without fighting. In addition, because of the interception of the German arms aboard the *Aud*, the provincial Volunteer units were very poorly armed.

In the south, around 1,200 Volunteers commanded by Tomás Mac Curtain mustered on the Sunday in Cork, but they dispersed on Wednesday after receiving nine contradictory orders by dispatch from the Volunteer leadership in Dublin. At their Sheares Street headquarters, some of the Volunteers engaged in a standoff with British forces. Much to the anger of many Volunteers, MacCurtain, under pressure from Catholic clergy, agreed to surrender his men's arms to the British.[442] The only violence in Cork occurred when the RIC attempted to raid the home of the Kent family. The Kent brothers, who were Volunteers, engaged in a three-hour firefight with the RIC. An RIC officer and one of the brothers were killed, while another brother was later executed.[443]

In the north, Volunteer companies were mobilised in County Tyrone at Coalisland (including 132 men from Belfast led by IRB President Dennis McCullough) and Carrickmore, under the leadership of Patrick McCartan. They also mobilised at Creeslough, County Donegal under Daniel Kelly and James McNulty.[444] However, in part because of the confusion caused by the countermanding order, the Volunteers in these locations dispersed without fighting.[445]

In Fingal (north County Dublin), about 60 Volunteers mobilised near Swords. They belonged to the 5th Battalion of the Dublin Brigade (also known as the Fingal Battalion), and were led by Thomas Ashe and his second in command, Richard Mulcahy. Unlike the rebels elsewhere, the Fingal Battalion successfully employed guerrilla tactics. They set up camp and Ashe split the battalion into four sections: three would undertake operations while the fourth was kept in reserve, guarding camp and foraging for food.[446] The Volunteers moved against the RIC barracks in Swords, Donabate and Garristown, forcing the RIC to surrender and seizing all the weapons.[447] They also damaged railway lines and cut telegraph wires. The railway line at Blanchardstown was bombed to prevent a troop train reaching Dublin.[448] This derailed a cattle train, which had been sent ahead of the troop train.[449]

---

[442] Townshend, p. 235
[443] Townshend, p. 238
[444] O'Duibhir, Liam (2009). *The Donegal Awakening*. Mercier Press. pp. 39, 45, 76, 104, 255, 289, 292.
[445] Townshend, p. 226
[446] Maguire, Paul. The Fingal Battalion: A Blueprint for the Future? Archived 6 May 2016 at the Wayback Machine. *The Irish Sword*. Military History Society of Ireland, 2011. pp. 9–13
[447] Maguire, Paul. The Fingal Battalion: A Blueprint for the Future? Archived 6 May 2016 at the Wayback Machine. *The Irish Sword*. Military History Society of Ireland, 2011. pp. 9–13
[448] Maguire, Paul. The Fingal Battalion: A Blueprint for the Future? Archived 6 May 2016 at the Wayback Machine. *The Irish Sword*. Military History Society of Ireland, 2011. pp. 9–13
[449] *The 1916 Rebellion Handbook p. 27*

The only large-scale engagement of the Rising, outside Dublin city, was at Ashbourne, County Meath.[450] [451] On Friday, about 35 Fingal Volunteers surrounded the Ashbourne RIC barracks and called on it to surrender, but the RIC responded with a volley of gunfire.[452] A firefight followed, and the RIC surrendered after the Volunteers attacked the building with a homemade grenade.[453] Before the surrender could be taken, up to sixty RIC men arrived in a convoy, sparking a five-hour gun battle, in which eight RIC men were killed and 18 wounded.[454] Two Volunteers were also killed and five wounded,[455] and a civilian was fatally shot.[456] The RIC surrendered and were disarmed. Ashe let them go after warning them not to fight against the Irish Republic again.[457] Ashe's men camped at Kilsalaghan near Dublin until they received orders to surrender on Saturday.[458] The Fingal Battalion's tactics during the Rising foreshadowed those of the IRA during the War of Independence that followed.[459]

Volunteer contingents also mobilised nearby in counties Meath and Louth but proved unable to link up with the North Dublin unit until after it had surrendered. In County Louth, Volunteers shot dead an RIC man near the village of Castle Bellingham on 24 April, in an incident in which 15 RIC men were also taken prisoner.[460] [461]

In County Wexford, 100-200 Volunteers-led by Robert Brennan, Seamus Doyle and Sean Etchingham-took over the town of Enniscorthy on Thursday 27 April until Sunday.[462] Volunteer officer Paul Galligan had cycled 200 km from rebel headquarters in Dublin with orders to mobilise.[463] They blocked all roads into the

---

[450] Boyle, John F. *The Irish Rebellion of 1916: a brief history of the revolt and its suppression* (Chapter IV: Outbreaks in the Country). Biblio Bazaar, 2009. pp. 127–152
[451] Townshend, pp. 215–216
[452] Maguire, Paul. The Fingal Battalion: A Blueprint for the Future? Archived 6 May 2016 at the Wayback Machine. *The Irish Sword*. Military History Society of Ireland, 2011. pp. 9–13
[453] Maguire, Paul. The Fingal Battalion: A Blueprint for the Future? Archived 6 May 2016 at the Wayback Machine. *The Irish Sword*. Military History Society of Ireland, 2011. pp. 9–13
[454] Maguire, Paul. The Fingal Battalion: A Blueprint for the Future? Archived 6 May 2016 at the Wayback Machine. *The Irish Sword*. Military History Society of Ireland, 2011. pp. 9–13
[455] Townshend, pp. 218–221
[456] McGarry, pp. 235–237
[457] Maguire, Paul. The Fingal Battalion: A Blueprint for the Future? Archived 6 May 2016 at the Wayback Machine. *The Irish Sword*. Military History Society of Ireland, 2011. pp. 9–13
[458] Townshend, p. 221
[459] Maguire, Paul. The Fingal Battalion: A Blueprint for the Future? Archived 6 May 2016 at the Wayback Machine. *The Irish Sword*. Military History Society of Ireland, 2011. pp. 9–13
[460] Boyle, John F. *The Irish Rebellion of 1916: a brief history of the revolt and its suppression* (Chapter IV: Outbreaks in the Country). Biblio Bazaar, 2009. pp. 127–152
[461] Dorney, John. The Easter Rising in County Wexford. The Irish Story. 10 April 2012.
[462] Boyle, John F. *The Irish Rebellion of 1916: a brief history of the revolt and its suppression* (Chapter IV: Outbreaks in the Country). Biblio Bazaar, 2009. pp. 127–152
[463] Dorney, John. The Easter Rising in County Wexford. The Irish Story. 10 April 2012.

town and made a brief attack on the RIC barracks, but chose to blockade it rather than attempt to capture it. They flew the tricolour over the Athenaeum building, which they had made their headquarters, and paraded uniformed in the streets.[464] The y also occupied Vinegar Hill, where the United Irishmen had made a last stand in the 1798 rebellion.[465] The public largely supported the rebels and many local men offered to join them.[466]

By Saturday, up to 1,000 rebels had been mobilised, and a detachment was sent to occupy the nearby village of Ferns.[467] In Wexford, the British assembled a column of 1,000 soldiers (including the Connaught Rangers[468]), two field guns and a 4.7 inch naval gun on a makeshift armoured train.[469] On Sunday, the British sent messengers to Enniscorthy, informing the rebels of Pearse's surrender order. However, the Volunteer officers were sceptical.[470] Two of them were escorted by the British to Arbour Hill Prison, where Pearse confirmed the surrender order.[471]

In County Galway, 600 to 700 Volunteers mobilised on Tuesday under Liam Mellows. His plan was to "bottle up the British garrison and divert the British from concentrating on Dublin".[472] However, his men were poorly armed, with only 25 rifles, 60 revolvers, 300 shotguns and some homemade grenades – many of them only had pikes.[473] Most of the action took place in a rural area to the east of Galway city. They made unsuccessful attacks on the RIC barracks at Caring Bridge and Oranmore, captured several officers, and bombed a bridge and railway line, before taking up position near Athenry.[474] There was also a skirmish between rebels and an RIC mobile patrol at Carnmore Crossroads. A constable, Patrick Whelan, was shot dead after he had called to the rebels: "Surrender, boys, I know ye all".[475]

On Wednesday, HMS *Laburnum* arrived in Galway Bay and shelled the countryside on the north-eastern edge of Galway.[476] The rebels retreated South-east to Moyode,

464 Townshend, p. 241
465 Dorney, John. The Easter Rising in County Wexford. The Irish Story. 10 April 2012.
466 Dorney, John. The Easter Rising in County Wexford. The Irish Story. 10 April 2012.
467 Dorney, John. The Easter Rising in County Wexford. The Irish Story. 10 April 2012.
468 Boyle, John F. *The Irish Rebellion of 1916: a brief history of the revolt and its suppression* (Chapter IV: Outbreaks in the Country). Biblio Bazaar, 2009. pp. 127–152
469 Dorney, John. The Easter Rising in County Wexford. The Irish Story. 10 April 2012.
470 Dorney, John. The Easter Rising in County Wexford. The Irish Story. 10 April 2012.
471 Townshend, pp. 241–242
472 Dorney, John. The Easter Rising in Galway, 1916. The Irish Story. 4 March 2016.
473 Mark McCarthy & Shirley Wrynn. *County Galway's 1916 Rising: A Short History*. Galway County Council.
474 Townshend, pp. 227–230
475 Dorney, John. The Easter Rising in Galway, 1916. The Irish Story. 4 March 2016.
476 Mark McCarthy & Shirley Wrynn. *County Galway's 1916 Rising: A Short History*. Galway County Council.

an abandoned country house and estate. From here they set up lookout posts and sent out scouting parties.[477] On Friday, HMS *Gloucester* landed 200 Royal Marines and began shelling the countryside near the rebel position.[478] [479] The rebels retreated further south to Limepark, another abandoned country house. Deeming the situation to be hopeless, they dispersed on Saturday morning. Many went home and were arrested following the Rising, while others, including Mellows, went "on the run". By the time British reinforcements arrived in the west, the Rising there had already disintegrated.[480]

In County Limerick, 300 Irish Volunteers assembled at Glenquin Castle near Killeedy, but they did not take any military action.[481] [482] [483]

In County Clare, Michael Brennan marched with 100 Volunteers (from Meelick, Oatfield, and Cratloe) to the River Shannon on Easter Monday to await orders from the Rising leaders in Dublin, and weapons from the expected Casement shipment. However, neither arrived and no actions were taken.[484]

The Easter Rising resulted in at least 485 deaths, according to the Glasnevin Trust.[485] Of those killed:

- 260 (about 54%) were civilians
- 126 (about 26%) were U.K. forces (120 U.K. military personnel, 5 Volunteer Training Corps members, and one Canadian soldier)

35 – Irish Regiments: -

- 11 – Royal Dublin Fusiliers
- 10 – Royal Irish Rifles
- 9 – Royal Irish Regiment
- 2 – Royal Inniskilling Fusiliers
- 2 – Royal Irish Fusiliers
- 1 – Leinster Regiment

[477] Mark McCarthy & Shirley Wrynn. *County Galway's 1916 Rising: A Short History*. Galway County Council.
[478] Dorney, John. The Easter Rising in Galway, 1916. The Irish Story. 4 March 2016.
[479] Townshend, pp. 227–230
[480] McGarry, p. 233
[481] 1916 legacy remembered and renewed at Glenquin Castle".
[482] O'Donnell, Ruan (1 January 2009). *Limerick's Fighting Story 1916–21: Told by the Men Who Made It*. Mercier Press Ltd. p. 249. ISBN 978-1-85635-642-8.
[483] "History to be relived at Limerick castle".
[484] Power, Joe (2015). *Clare and the Great War*. p. 135. ISBN 9780750965569.
[485] 1916 Necrology. Glasnevin Trust Archived 5 April 2017 at the Wayback Machine.

74 – British Regiments: -

- 29 – Sherwood Foresters
- 15 – South Staffordshire
- 2 – North Staffordshire
- 1 – Royal Field Artillery
- 4 – Royal Engineers
- 5 – Army Service Corps
- 10 – Lancers
- 7 – 8th Hussars
- 2 – 2nd King Edwards Horse
- 3 – Yeomanry

1 – Royal Navy

- 82 (about 16%) were Irish rebel forces (64 Irish Volunteers, 15 Irish Citizen Army and 3 Fianna Éireann)
- 17 (about 4%) were police[486]

14 – Royal Irish constabulary

3 – Dublin Metropolitan Police

More than 2,600 were wounded; including at least 2,200 civilians and rebels, at least 370 British soldiers and 29 policemen.[487] All 16 police fatalities and 22 of the British soldiers killed were Irishmen.[488] About 40 of those killed were children (under 17 years old),[489] four of whom were members of the rebel forces.[490] (See the list of names bibliography at the rear of this book).

The number of casualties each day steadily rose, with 55 killed on Monday and 78 killed on Saturday.[491] The British Army suffered their biggest losses in the Battle of Mount Street Bridge on Wednesday, when at least 30 soldiers were killed. The rebels

---

[486] 1916 Necrology. Glasnevin Trust
[487] Foy and Barton, page 325
[488] *1916 Rebellion Handbook*, pp. 50–55
[489] "40 children were killed in the 1916 Rising but they are barely mentioned in history". *TheJournal.ie*. 29 November 2015.
[490] Joe Duffy's list of children killed in the 1916 Rising.
[491] 1916 Necrology. Glasnevin Trust

also suffered their biggest losses on that day. The RIC suffered most of their casualties in the Battle of Ashbourne on Friday.[492]

Most of the casualties, both killed and wounded, were civilians. Most of the civilian casualties and most of the casualties overall were caused by the British Army.[493] This was due to the British using artillery, incendiary shells and heavy machine guns in built-up areas, as well as their "inability to discern rebels from civilians".[494] One Royal Irish Regiment officer recalled, "they regarded, not unreasonably, everyone they saw as an enemy, and fired at anything that moved".[495] Many other civilians were killed when caught in the crossfire. Both sides, British and rebel, also shot civilians deliberately on occasion; for not obeying orders (such as to stop at checkpoints), for assaulting or attempting to hinder them, and for looting.[496] There were also instances of British troops killing unarmed civilians out of revenge or frustration: notably in the North King Street Massacre, where fifteen were killed, and at Portobello Barracks, where six were shot.[497] Furthermore, there were incidents of friendly fire. On 29 April, the Royal Dublin Fusiliers under Company Quartermaster Sergeant Robert Flood shot dead two British officers and two Irish civilian employees of the Guinness Brewery after he decided they were rebels. Flood was court-martialled for murder but acquitted.[498]

According to historian Fearghal McGarry, the rebels attempted to avoid needless bloodshed. Desmond Ryan stated that Volunteers were told "no firing was to take place except under orders or to repel attack".[499] Aside from the engagement at Ashbourne, policemen and unarmed soldiers were not systematically targeted, and a large group of policemen was allowed to stand at Nelson's Pillar throughout Monday.[500] McGarry writes that the Irish Citizen Army "were more ruthless than Volunteers when it came to shooting policemen" and attributes this to the "acrimonious legacy" of the Dublin Lock-out.[501]

The vast majority of the Irish casualties were buried in Glasnevin Cemetery in the aftermath of the fighting.[502] British families came to Dublin Castle in May 1916 to reclaim the bodies of British soldiers, and funerals were arranged. Soldiers whose

---

[492] 1916 Necrology. Glasnevin Trust
[493] McGarry, pp. 184–185
[494] McGarry, pp. 184–185
[495] McGarry, pp. 184–185
[496] McGarry, pp. 184–185
[497] McGarry, pp. 186–187
[498] Royal Dublin Fusiliers website – 5th Battalion RDF during the Easter Rising
[499] McGarry, pp. 176–177
[500] McGarry, pp. 176–177
[501] McGarry, pp. 176–177
[502] Necrology. Glasnevin Trust Archived 5 April 2017 at the Wayback Machine.

bodies were not claimed were given military funerals in Grangegorman Military Cemetery.

General Maxwell quickly signalled his intention "to arrest all dangerous Sinn Feiners", including "those who have taken an active part in the movement although not in the present rebellion",[503] reflecting the popular belief that Sinn Féin, a separatist organisation that was neither militant nor republican, was behind the Rising.

A total of 3,430 men and 79 women were arrested, including 425 people for looting.[504] A series of courts-martial began on 2 May, in which 187 people were tried, most of them at Richmond Barracks. The president of the courts-martial was Charles Blackader. Controversially, Maxwell decided that the courts-martial would be held in secret and without a defence, which Crown law officers later ruled to have been illegal.[505] Some of those who conducted the trials had commanded British troops involved in suppressing the Rising, a conflict of interest that the Military Manual prohibited.[506] Only one of those tried by courts-martial was a woman, Constance Markievicz, who was also the only woman to be kept in solitary confinement.[507] Ninety were sentenced to death. Fifteen of those (including all seven signatories of the Proclamation) had their sentences confirmed by Maxwell and fourteen were executed by firing squad at Kilmainham Gaol between 3 and 12 May. Among them was the seriously wounded Connolly, who was shot while tied to a chair because of his shattered ankle. Maxwell stated that only the "ringleaders" and those proven to have committed "coldblooded murder" would be executed. However, the evidence presented was weak, and some of those executed were not leaders and did not kill anyone: Willie Pearse described himself as "a personal attaché to my brother, Patrick Pearse"; John MacBride had not even been aware of the Rising until it began, but had fought against the British in the Boer War fifteen years before; Thomas Kent did not come out at all—he was executed for the killing of a police officer during the raid on his house the week after the Rising. The most prominent leader to escape execution was Eammon de Valera, Commandant of the 3rd Battalion, who did so partly because of his American birth.[508]

Most of the executions took place over a ten-day period:

---

503 Townshend, p. 273
504 Townshend, pp. 263–264
505 Foy and Barton, pp. 294–295
506 Foy and Barton, pp. 294–295
507 Foy and Barton, pp. 294–295
508 *S. J. Connolly (2004). Oxford Companion to Irish History. Oxford University Press.
p. 607. ISBN 978-0-19-923483-7.*

- 3 May: Patrick Pearse, Thomas MacDonagh and Thomas Clarke
- 4 May: Joseph Plunkett, William Pearse, Edward Daly and Michael O'Hanrahan
- 5 May: John MacBride
- 8 May: Éamonn Ceannt, Michael Mallin, Seán Heuston and Con Colbert
- 12 May: James Connolly and Seán Mac Diarmada

As the executions went on, the Irish public grew increasingly hostile towards the British and sympathetic to the rebels. After the first three executions, John Redmond, leader of the moderate Irish Parliamentary Party, said in the British Parliament that the rising "happily, seems to be over. It has been dealt with firmness, which was not only right, but it was the duty of the Government to so deal with it".[509] However, he urged the Government "not to show undue hardship or severity to the great masses of those who are implicated".[510] As the executions continued, Redmond pleaded with Prime Minister H. H. Asquith to stop them, warning that "if more executions take place in Ireland, the position will become impossible for any constitutional party".[511] Ulster Unionist Party leader Edward Carson expressed similar views.[512] [513]Redmond 's deputy, John Dillon, made an impassioned speech in parliament, saying "thousands of people, who ten days ago were bitterly opposed to the whole of the Sinn Fein movement and to the rebellion, are now becoming infuriated against the Government on account of these executions". He said, "it is not murderers who are being executed; it is insurgents who have fought a clean fight, a brave fight, however misguided". Dillon was heckled by English MPs.[514] The British Government itself had also become concerned at the reaction to the executions, and at the way the courts-martial were being carried out. Asquith had warned Maxwell that "a large number of executions would sow the seeds of lasting trouble in Ireland".[515] After Connolly's execution, Maxwell bowed to pressure and had the other death sentences commuted to penal servitude.[516]

Most of the people arrested were subsequently released,[517] however under Regulation 14B of the Defence of the Realm Act 1914 1,836 men were interned at internment camps and prisons in England and Wales.[518] Many of them, like Arthur

---

[509] House of Commons debate, 3 May 1916: resignation of Mr. Birrell. Hansard
[510] House of Commons debate, 3 May 1916: resignation of Mr. Birrell. Hansard
[511] Finnan, Joseph. *John Redmond and Irish Unity: 1912 – 1918*. Syracuse University Press, 2004. p. 196
[512] House of Commons debate, 3 May 1916: resignation of Mr. Birrell. Hansard
[513] Lewis, Geoffrey. *Carson: The Man Who Divided Ireland*. Bloomsbury Publishing, 2006. p. 185
[514] House of Commons debate, 11 May 1916: Continuance of Martial Law. Hansard
[515] "Easter Rising 1916 – the aftermath: arrests and executions". *The Irish Times*, 24 March 2016.
[516] Foy and Barton, p. 325
[517] Foy and Barton, pp. 294–295
[518] Foy and Barton, pp. 294–295

Griffith, had little or nothing to do with the Rising. Camps such as Frongoch internment camp became "Universities of Revolution" where future leaders including Michael Collins, Terence McSwiney and J. J. O'Connell began to plan the coming struggle for independence.[519]

Sir Roger Casement was tried in London for high treason and hanged at Pentonville Prison on 3 August.[520]

After the Rising, claims of atrocities carried out by British troops began to emerge. Although they did not receive as much attention as the executions, they sparked outrage among the Irish public and were raised by Irish MPs in Parliament.

One incident was the 'Portobello killings. On Tuesday 25 April, Dubliner Francis Sheehy-Skeffington, a pacifist nationalist activist, had been arrested by British soldiers. Captain John Bowen-Colthurst then took him with a British raiding party as a hostage and human shield. On Rathmines Road he stopped a boy named James Coade, whom he shot dead. His troops then destroyed a tobacconist's shop with grenades and seized journalists Thomas Dickson and Patrick MacIntyre. The next morning, Colthurst had Skeffington and the two journalists shot by firing squad in Portobello Barracks.[521] The bodies were then buried there. Later that day he shot a Labour Party councillor, Richard O'Carroll. When Major Sir Francis Vane learned of the killings he telephoned his superiors in Dublin Castle, but no action was taken. Vane informed Herbert Kitchener, who told General John Maxwell to arrest Colthurst, but Maxwell refused. Colthurst was eventually arrested and court-martialled in June. He was found guilty of murder but insane and detained for twenty months at Broadmoor. Public and political pressure led to a public inquiry, which reached similar conclusions. Major Vane was discharged "owing to his action in the Skeffington murder case".[522] [523]

The other incident was the 'North King Street Massacre'. On the night of 28–29 April, British soldiers of the South Staffordshire Regiment, under Colonel Henry Taylor, had burst into houses on North King Street and killed fifteen male civilians whom they accused of being rebels. The soldiers shot or bayoneted the victims, then secretly buried some of them in cellars or back yards after robbing them. The area saw some of the fiercest fighting of the Rising and the British had taken heavy casualties for little gain. Maxwell attempted to excuse the killings and argued that

[519] "*The Green Dragon* No 4, Autumn 1997". Ballinagree.freeservers.com. 31 March 2005. Retrieved 13 November 2011.
[520] "Execution of Roger Casement". *Midland Daily Telegraph*. 3 August 1916. Retrieved – via British Newspaper Archive.
[521] Bacon, Bryan (2015). *A Terrible Duty: The Madness of Captain Bowen-Colthurst*. Thena Press.
[522] McGarry, p. 186
[523] Townshend, p. 193

the rebels were ultimately responsible. He claimed that "the rebels wore no uniform" and that the people of North King Street were rebel sympathisers. Maxwell concluded that such incidents "are absolutely unavoidable in such a business as this" and that "under the circumstance the troops behaved with the greatest restraint". A private brief, prepared for the Prime Minister, said the soldiers "had orders not to take any prisoners" but took it to mean they were to shoot any suspected rebel. The City Coroner's inquest found that soldiers had killed "unarmed and unoffending" residents. The military court of inquiry ruled that no specific soldiers could be held responsible, and no action was taken.[524] [525]

These killings, and the British response to them, helped sway Irish public opinion against the British.[526]

A Royal Commission was set up to enquire into the causes of the Rising. It began hearings on 18 May under the chairmanship of Lord Hardinge of Penshurst. The Commission heard evidence from Sir Matthew Nathan, Augustine Birrell, Lord Wimborne, Sir Neville Chamberlain (Inspector-General of the Royal Irish Constabulary), General Lovick Friend, Major Ivor Price of Military Intelligence and others.[527] The report, published on 26 June, was critical of the Dublin administration, saying that "Ireland for several years had been administered on the principle that it was safer and more expedient to leave the law in abeyance if collision with any faction of the Irish people could thereby be avoided."[528] Birrell and Nathan had resigned immediately after the Rising. Wimborne had also reluctantly resigned, recalled to London by Lloyd George, but was re-appointed in late 1917. Chamberlain resigned soon after.[529]

At first, many Dubliners were bewildered by the outbreak of the Rising.[530] James Stephens, who was in Dublin during the week, thought, "None of these people were prepared for Insurrection. The thing had been sprung on them so suddenly they were unable to take sides." [531] There was great hostility towards the Volunteers in some parts of the city. Historian Keith Jeffery noted that most of the opposition came from people whose relatives were in the British Army and who depended on their army allowances.[532] Those most openly hostile to the Volunteers were the "separation

---

[524] Coogan, pp. 152–155
[525] Townshend, pp. 293–294
[526] What was the Easter Rising?. Century Ireland – RTÉ.
[527] Ó Broin, Leon, *Dublin Castle & the 1916 Rising* pp. 153–159
[528] Townshend p. 297
[529] John Kendle, "Walter Long, Ireland, 1911–1924" (London 1992)
[530] "In many areas the reaction of civilians was puzzlement, they simply had no idea what was going on." Townshend
[531] Stephens p. 57
[532] Kennedy, p. 286

women" (so-called because they were paid "separation money" by the British government), whose husbands and sons were fighting in the British Army in the First World War. There was also hostility from unionists.[533] Supporters of the Irish Parliamentary Party also felt the rebellion was a betrayal of their party.[534] When occupying positions in the South Dublin Union and Jacob's factory, the rebels got involved in physical confrontations with civilians who tried to tear down the rebel barricades and prevent them taking over buildings. The Volunteers shot and clubbed several civilians who assaulted them or tried to dismantle their barricades.[535]

That the Rising resulted in a great deal of death and destruction, as well as disrupting food supplies, also contributed to the antagonism toward the rebels. After the surrender, the Volunteers were hissed at, pelted with refuse, and denounced as "murderers" and "starvers of the people".[536] Volunteer Robert Holland for example remembered being "subjected to very ugly remarks and cat-calls from the poorer classes" as they marched to surrender. He also reported being abused by people he knew as he was marched through the Kilmainham area into captivity and said the British troops saved them from being manhandled by the crowd.[537] [538]

However, some Dubliners expressed support for the rebels.[539] Canadian journalist and writer Frederick Arthur McKenzie wrote that in poorer areas, "there was a vast amount of sympathy with the rebels, particularly after the rebels were defeated".[540] He wrote of crowds cheering a column of rebel prisoners as it passed, with one woman remarking "Shure, we cheer them. Why shouldn't we? Aren't they our own flesh and blood?".[541] At Boland's Mill, the defeated rebels were met with a large crowd, "many weeping and expressing sympathy and sorrow, all of them friendly and kind".[542] Other onlookers were sympathetic but watched in silence.[543] Christoph er M. Kennedy notes that "those who sympathised with the rebels would, out of fear for their own safety, keep their opinions to themselves".[544] Áine Ceannt witnessed

---

[533] Foy and Barton, pp. 203–209
[534] "The loyalists spoke with an air of contempt, 'the troops will settle the matter in an hour or two, these pro-Germans will run away...' The Redmondites were more bitter, 'I hope they'll all be hanged' ... 'Shooting's too good for them. Trying to stir up trouble for us all.'" Ernie O'Malley, *On Another Man's Wound*, p. 60.
[535] Fearghal McGarry, *The Rising: Ireland Easter 1916*, p. 143
[536] McGarry, p. 252
[537] Ryan, p. 135
[538] "Witness statement of Robert Holland" (PDF). *Bureau of Military History*. Archived from the original (PDF) on 28 September 2013.
[539] McGarry, pp. 252–256
[540] Ellis, pp. 196–197
[541] Kennedy, p. 288
[542] McGarry, pp. 252–256
[543] McGarry, pp. 252–256
[544] Kennedy, p. 288

British soldiers arresting a woman who cheered the captured rebels.[545] An Royal Irish Constabulary District Inspector's report stated: "Martial law, of course, prevents any expression of it; but a strong undercurrent of disloyalty exists".[546] Thomas Johnson, the Labour Party leader, thought there was "no sign of sympathy for the rebels, but general admiration for their courage and strategy".[547]

The aftermath of the Rising, and in particular the British reaction to it, helped sway a large section of Irish nationalist opinion away from hostility or ambivalence and towards support for the rebels of Easter 1916. Dublin businessman and Quaker James G. Douglas, for example, hitherto a Home Ruler, wrote that his political outlook changed radically during the course of the Rising because of the British military occupation of the city and that he became convinced that parliamentary methods would not be enough to expel the British from Ireland.[548] A meeting called by Count Plunkett on 19 April 1917 led to the formation of a broad political movement under the banner of Sinn Féin[549] which was formalised at the Sinn Féin Ard Fheis of 25 October 1917. The Conscription Crisis of 1918 further intensified public support for Sinn Féin before the general elections to the British Parliament on 14 December 1918, which resulted in a landslide victory for Sinn Féin, winning 73 seats out of 105, whose Members of Parliament (MPs) gathered in Dublin on 21 January 1919 to form Dáil Éireann and adopt the Declaration of Independence.[550]

Shortly after the Easter Rising, poet Francis Ledwidge wrote *"O'Connell Street"* and *"Lament for the Poets of 1916"*, which both describe his sense of loss and an expression of holding the same "dreams,"[551] as the Easter Rising's Irish Republicans. He would also go on to write *lament for Thomas MacDonagh* for his fallen friend and fellow Irish Volunteer. A few months after the Easter Rising, W. B. Yeats commemorated some of the fallen figures of the Irish Republican movement, as well as his torn emotions regarding these events, in the poem *Easter, 1916.*

Some of the survivors of the Rising went on to become leaders of the independent Irish state. Those who were executed were venerated by many as martyrs; their graves in Dublin's former military prison of Arbour Hill became a national monument and the Proclamation text was taught in schools. An annual commemorative military parade was held each year on Easter Sunday. In

---

[545] McGarry, pp. 252–256
[546] Kennedy, p. 288
[547] Townshend, pp. 265–268
[548] J. Anthony Gaughan, ed. (1998). *Memoirs of Senator James G. Douglas; concerned citizen.* University College Dublin Press. pp. 52, 53. ISBN 978-1-900621-19-9.
[549] Bell, p. 27
[550] Robert Kee *The Green Flag: Ourselves Alone*
[551] Francis Ledwidge". *www.ricorso.net.*

1935, Éamon de Valera unveiled a statue of the mythical Irish hero Cú Chulainn, sculpted by Oliver Sheppard, at the General Post Office as part of the Rising commemorations that year – it is often seen to be an important symbol of martyrdom in remembrance of the 1916 rebels. Memorials to the heroes of the Rising are to be found in other Irish cities, such as Limerick. The 1916 Medal was issued in 1941 to people with recognised military service during the Rising.[552] (The medal was issued in 1941 and was awarded to anyone with recognised military service in Easter 1916.)

The parades culminated in a huge national celebration on the 50th anniversary of the Rising in 1966.[553] Medals were issued by the government to survivors who took part in the Rising at the event. RTÉ, the Irish national broadcaster, as one of its first major undertakings made a series of commemorative programmes for the 1966 anniversary of the Rising. Roibéárd Ó Faracháin, head of programming said, "While still seeking historical truth, the emphasis will be on homage, on salutation."[554] At the same time, CIÉ, the Republic of Ireland's railway operator, renamed several of its major stations after republicans who played key roles in the Easter Rising.[555]

Ireland's first commemorative coin was also issued in 1966 to pay tribute to the Easter Rising. It was valued at 10 shillings, therefore having the highest denomination of any pre-decimal coin issued by the country. The coin featured a bust of Patrick Pearse on the obverse and an image of the statue of Cú Chulainn in the GPO on the reverse. Its edge inscription reads, "Éirí Amach na Cásca 1916", which translates to, "1916 Easter Rising". Due to their 83.5% silver content, many of the coins were melted down shortly after issue.[556] A €2 coin (2 Euros) was also issued by Ireland in 2016, featuring the statue of Hibernia above the GPO, to commemorate the Rising's centenary.[557]

With the outbreak of the Troubles in Northern Ireland, government, academics and the media began to revise the country's militant past, and particularly the Easter Rising. The coalition government of 1973–77, in particular the Minister for Posts and Telegraphs, Conor Cruise O'Brien, began to promote the view that the violence of 1916 was essentially no different from the violence then taking place in the streets of Belfast and Derry. O'Brien and others asserted that the Rising was doomed to military defeat from the outset, and that it failed to account for the determination of Ulster Unionists to remain in the United Kingdom.[558]

---

[552] "THE 1916 MEDAL" *Military Archives*. Defence Forces Ireland.
[553] News Items Relating to the 1916 Easter Rising Commemorations". *RTÉ*. IE. 1966.
[554] *Brennan, Cathal. "A TV pageant, the Golden Jubilee Commemorations of the 1916 Rising".*
[555] *"Irish Station Names – Heroes of the Easter Uprising". www.sinfin.net.*
[556] "O'Brien Coin Guide: Irish Pre-Decimal Ten Shillings". *The Old Currency Exchange is a specialist dealer and valuer of coins, tokens and banknotes. 27 March 2016.*
[557] *"Commemorative €2 released to mark the 1916 Centenary"*
[558] O'Brien, Conor Cruise (1972). *States of Ireland*. Hutchinson. pp. 88, 99. ISBN 0-09-113100-6.

Irish republicans continue to venerate the Rising and its leaders with murals in republican areas of Belfast and other towns celebrating the actions of Pearse and his comrades, and annual parades in remembrance of the Rising. The Irish government, however, discontinued its annual parade in Dublin in the early 1970s, and in 1976 it took the unprecedented step of proscribing (under the Offences against the State Act) a 1916 commemoration ceremony at the GPO organised by Sinn Féin and the Republican Commemoration Committee.[559] A Labour Party TD, David Thornley, embarrassed the government (of which Labour was a member) by appearing on the platform at the ceremony, along with Máire Comerford, who had fought in the Rising, and Fiona Plunkett, sister of Joseph Plunkett.[560]

With the advent of a Provisional IRA ceasefire and the beginning of what became known as the Peace Process during the 1990s, the government's view of the Rising grew more positive and in 1996 an 80th anniversary commemoration at the Garden of Remembrance in Dublin was attended by the Taoiseach and leader of Fine Gael, John Bruton.[561] In 2005, the Taoiseach, Bertie Ahern, announced the government's intention to resume the military parade past the GPO from Easter 2006, and to form a committee to plan centenary celebrations in 2016.[562] The 90th anniversary was celebrated with a military parade in Dublin on Easter Sunday, 2006, attended by the President of Ireland, the Taoiseach and the Lord Mayor of Dublin.[563] There is now an annual ceremony at Easter attended by relatives of those who fought, by the President, the Taoiseach, ministers, senators and TDs, and by usually large and respectful crowds.

The Rising continues to attract debate and analysis. In 2016 *The Enemy Files*, a documentary presented by a former British Secretary of State for Defence, Michael Portillo, was shown on RTÉ One and the BBC, ahead of the centenary.[564] Portillo declared that the execution of the 16 leaders of the insurrection could be justified in its context – a military response, against the background of the appalling European war – but that the rebels had set a trap that the British fell into and that every possible response by the British would have been a mistake of some kind.[565] He commented on the role of Patrick Pearse, the martyrdom controversy and the Proclamation's reference to "our gallant German allies in Europe".[566]

---

[559] Irish Times, 22 April 1976
[560] Irish Times, 26 April 1976
[561] Reconstructing the Easter Rising, Colin Murphy, *The Village*, 16 February 2006
[562] Irish Times, 22 October 2005
[563] "In pictures: Easter Rising commemorations". *BBC News*. 16 April 2006.
[564] McGreevy, Ronan (19 March 2016). "How the British 'lost' the Easter Rising: In 'The Enemy Files', Michael Portillo shows how events in 1916 were dealt with by London". *The Irish Times*.
[565] McGreevy, Ronan (19 March 2016). "How the British 'lost' the Easter Rising: In 'The Enemy Files', Michael Portillo shows how events in 1916 were dealt with by London". *The Irish Times*.
[566] McGreevy, Ronan (19 March 2016). How the British "lost" the Easter Rising: in "The Enemy Files",

In December 2014 Dublin City[567] Council approved a proposal to create a historical path commemorating the Rising, similar to the Freedom Trail in Boston. Lord Mayor of Dublin Christy Burke announced that the council had committed to building the trail, marking it with a green line or bricks, with brass plates marking the related historic sites such as the Rotunda and the General Post Office.

A pedestrian staircase that runs along 53rd Avenue, from 65th Place to 64th Street in west Queens, New York City was named 'Easter Rising Way' in 2016. Sinn Féin leader, Gerry Adams spoke at the naming ceremony.[568]

Violence erupted between Catholics and Protestant again, this time in Northern Ireland, (Ulster). Once again, British troops were deployed, but this was terrorism on British soil, and I make no apology for saying that this terrorism (known Officially as the "Troubles", or by the U.K. Government as Operation Banner) was sponsored terrorism funding by citizens of the United States of American. The very Nation who rattles the sabre at any Nation involved in terrorism, turned a blind eye to the fact that Americans, albeit from the Northern States, were funding these terrorist acts. Officially the troubles lasted from 14th. August 1969 to 31st. July 2007 or, 37 years, 11 months, 2 weeks, and 3 days. When the troops were first re-deployed in Ulster, they were led to believe that they were there to protect the Catholics from the Protestants, but that was not the case. There were terrorists on both sides, but now the Catholics wanted the Protestant North to be re-affirmed with the Irish Republic and become a whole Island nation again.

Unofficially it has never really gone away.

I served in Northern Ireland with the British Army, during what is commonly referred to as "The Troubles".

Michael Portillo shows how events in 1916 were dealt with by London How the British 'lost' the Easter Rising: In 'The Enemy Files', Michael Portillo shows how events in 1916 were dealt with by London". *The Irish Times.*

[567] Hertz, Kayla (16 December 2014). "Dublin's 1916 Rising Freedom Trail will be based on Boston's". Irish Central.

[568] McGreevy, Ronan. *"New York's newest street name? Easter Rising Way". The Irish Times. Retrieved 19 July 2019.*

In my opinion, what is happening now under the guise of Terrorism is nothing more the thugs playing at being Gangsters. They are in reality, nothing more than cowards and bullies.

Chapter seven

Michael Collins

Michael "Mick" Collins was   an Irish revolutionary leader.   He   was   a Finance and Teachta Dála (TD *member of parliament*) for Cork South in the First Dáil of 1919. He was also the Director of Intelligence for the IRA, and member of the Irish delegation during the Anglo-Irish Treaty negotiations. After that he was both Chairman   of   the   Provisional   Government and Commander-in-chief of the National Army.[569] Throughout this time, at least as of 1919, he was also President of the Irish Republican Brotherhood. Under the rules of the Brotherhood this meant that he was President of the Irish Republic. Collins was shot and killed in August 1922, during the Irish Civil War.

He was born on his family farm named Woodfield in Sam's Cross near Clonakilty, West Cork. Michael Collins was the third son and youngest of eight children. Most biographies state his date of birth as 16 October 1890; however, his tombstone gives his date of birth as 12 October 1890. His father, also named Michael, was a member of the republican Fenian movement, but had left and settled down to farming. Collins was six years old when his father died.

After leaving school aged 15, Collins took the British Civil Service examination in Cork in February 1906,[570] In 1910, he moved to London where he became a messenger at a London firm of stock brokers, Horne and Company.[571] While in London he lived with his elder sister, and studied at King's College London. He joined the London GAA and, through this, the Irish Republican Brotherhood, a secret, oath-bound society dedicated to achieving Irish independence. In 1915, he moved to the Guaranty Trust Company of New York where he remained until his return to Ireland the following year.[572]

Michael Collins first became known during the Easter Rising in 1916. A skilled organiser and very intelligent, he was highly respected in the IRB. When the Rising itself took place on Easter Monday, 1916, he fought alongside Patrick Pearse and others in the General Post Office in Dublin.

---

[569] *Ryan, Meda (2006). Michael Collins and the Women Who Spied for Ireland (2nd ed.). Cork: Mercier Press. p. 71. ISBN 978-1856355131.*
[570] British Postal Service Appointment Books, 1737 -1969 – Michael Collins
[571] British Postal Service Appointment Books, 1737 -1969 – Michael Collins
[572] Coogan, Tim Pat (1990). *Michael Collins*. London: Arrow Books. pp. 15–17. ISBN 978-0099685807.

Collins, like many of the other participants, was arrested, almost executed.[573] He was imprisoned at Frongoch internment camp. Collins became one of the leading figures in Sinn Féinafter the Rising. This was a small nationalist party which the British government and the Irish media mistakenly accredited the Rising to. By October 1917, Collins had become a member of the executive of Sinn Féin and Director of Organisation of the Irish Volunteers. Éamon de Valera was president of both organisations.[574]

Collins was nominated in the 1918 general election to elect Irish MPs to the British House of Commons in London. Collins won for Sinn Féin, becoming MP for Cork South.[575] However, unlike their rivals in the Irish Parliamentary Party, Sinn Féin MPs had announced that they would not take their seats in Westminster, but instead would set up an Irish Parliament in Dublin.

That new parliament, called *Dáil Éireann* (meaning "Assembly of Ireland") met in the Mansion House, Dublin in January 1919, although De Valera and leading Sinn Féin MPs had been arrested.

In de Valera's absence, Cathal Brugha was elected Príomh Aire ('Main' or 'Prime', Minister', but often translated as 'President of Dáil Éireann'). He was replaced by de Valera, when Collins helped him escape from Lincoln Prison in April 1919.

The Irish War of Independence began on the same day that the First Dáil met on 21 January 1919. An ambush party of IRA volunteers acting without orders and led by Seán Treacy attacked a group of Royal Irish Constabulary men. They were escorting a shipment of gelignite to a quarry in Soloheadbeg, County Tipperary. Two policemen were shot dead during the fight. This incident is the first action taken in the Irish War of Independence.

In 1919, Collins had a few roles. In the summer he was elected president of the IRB, Director of Intelligence of the Irish Republican Army. He also became the Minister for Finance.[576] His ministry was able to organise a large bond issue in the form of a "National Loan" to fund the new Irish Republic. Collins and Richard Mulcahy were the two main organisers for the Irish Republican Army, in as far as it was possible to direct the actions of disorganised guerrilla units.

In 1920, the British offered a prize of £10,000 (equivalent to £500,000.00 in Sterling / or €628,430.00 in Euros by 2020 rates of exchange) for information leading to the

[573] Mackay, James (1996). *Michaél Collins – A Life*. Edinburgh: Mainstream Publishing. pp. 27–38. ISBN 978-1851588572.

[574] Hart, Peter (2005). *Mick – The Real Michael Collins*. London: Macmillan. pp. 26–29. ISBN 978-1405090209.

[575] 16th October 1890 – Birth of Michael Collins". *Civil Records on Irish Genealogy Site.*

[576] "17th July 1815 – Baptism of Michael Collins' father". *Church Records on Irish Genealogy Site.*

capture or death of Collins. His fame had so transcended the IRA movement that he was nicknamed "The Big Fellow".

In July 1921, the British suddenly offered a truce. Arrangements were made for a conference between the British government and the leaders of the as-yet unrecognised Irish Republic.

In August 1921, Eamonn de Valera made the Dáil upgrade his office from Prime Minister to President of the Irish Republic. This made him on the same level as George V in the negotiations. Eventually, however, he said that as the King would not attend, then neither would he. Instead, with the reluctant agreement of his cabinet, de Valera assembled a team of delegates to go in his place. The team was headed by Vice-President Arthur Griffith with Collins as Deputy.

The negotiations resulted in the Anglo-Irish Treaty which was signed on 6 December 1921. In it, a new state was agreed upon, called the "Irish Free State". The agreement made an all-Ireland state possible. The six-county region in the northeast could opt out of the Free State if they wanted to. If this happened, an Irish Boundary Commission was to redraw the Irish border. The Irish Free State was established in December 1922, and as expected, Northern Ireland opted to remain part of the United Kingdom proper.

Although it was not the republic he was fighting for, Collins concluded that the Treaty offered Ireland "the freedom to achieve freedom." He knew that the treaty, and in particular the issue of partition, would not be popular in Ireland. When he signed the treaty, he said "I have signed my own death warrant."

Sinn Féin split over the treaty, and the Dáil debated the matter bitterly for ten days until it was approved by a vote of 64 to 57.[577] The Supreme Council of the IRB, which was informed in detail about the Treaty negotiations voted unanimously (*without exceptions*) to accept the Treaty. The only exception was the later COS of the IRA Liam Lynch.[578]

As expected, the Treaty was extremely controversial in Ireland.

First, Éamon de Valera, President of the Irish Republic until 9 January, had been unhappy that Collins had signed any deal without his and his cabinet's authorisation.

Second, the contents of the Treaty were bitterly disputed. De Valera and many other members of the republican movement did not want Ireland to be a dominion of the

---

[577] 3rd August 1852 – Baptism of Michael Collins' mother". *Church Records on Irish Genealogy Site.*
[578] 26th February 1876 – Marriage of Michael Collins' parents" (PDF). *Church Records on Irish Genealogy Site.*

British Empire. They did not like the *symbolism* of having to give a statement of faithfulness to the British king.

The dividing of Ireland between the Irish Free State and Northern Ireland was not as controversial. One of the main reasons for this was that Collins was secretly planning to launch a guerrilla war against the Northern State. In the early months of 1922, he had sent IRA units to the border, and arms and money to the northern units. In May–June 1922, he and IRA Chief of Staff Liam Lynch organised an attack of both pro- and anti-treaty IRA units along the new border. This offensive was officially called off under British pressure on 3 June and Collins issued a statement that "no troops from the 26 counties, either those under official control, who were pro-treaty, or those attached to the Irish Republican Army, Executive, who were anti-treaty, should be permitted to invade the six-county area."[579]

The new Provisional Government was formed under Collins, who became "President of the Provisional Government of Southern Ireland" (i.e., Prime Minister). He also remained Minister for Finance of Griffith's republican administration after de Valera stepped down.

In the months leading up to the outbreak of civil war in June 1922, Collins tried to heal the split in the nationalist movement and prevent civil war. De Valera, having opposed the Treaty in the Dáil, withdrew from the assembly with his supporters. Collins secured a compromise, "The Collins/De Valera Pact", whereby the two factions of Sinn Féin, pro- and anti-Treaty, would fight the soon-to-be Free State's first election jointly and form a coalition government afterwards. This Pact was agreed without Griffith's knowledge, and he opposed it as a potential betrayal of the Treaty. For a time, it appeared that a split would occur in the pro-Treaty ranks but Griffith relented realizing that Collins held all the power. His friendship with Collins did not survive. (ANTHONY J. JORDAN IN "ARTHUR GRIFFITH with James Joyce & WB Yeats – Liberating Ireland". Westport Books. ISBN 978-0-9576229-0-6 pp. 173–5 & 188-189.)

To try and find a compromise, Collins proposed that the Free State would have a republican constitution, with no mention of the British king. However, the British did not sign the proposed republican constitution. They argued they had signed the Treaty in good faith and its terms could not be changed so quickly.

On 14 April 1922, a group of 200 anti-Treaty IRA men occupied the Four Courts in Dublin in defiance of the Provisional government. Collins, who wanted to avoid civil war at all costs, did not attack them until June 1922, when British pressure also forced his hand. After a final attempt to persuade the men to leave, Collins borrowed

---

[579] Coogan, T. P. *Michael Collins*, London; Arrow Books, 1991, ISBN 1851588574.

two 18 pounder artillery pieces from the British and bombarded the Four Courts until the men surrendered.[580]

This led to the Irish Civil War as fighting broke out in Dublin between the anti-Treaty IRA and the provisional government's troops.

Under Collins' supervision, the Free State rapidly took control of the capital. In July 1922, anti-Treaty forces held the southern province of Munster and several other areas of the country. De Valera and the other anti-Treaty TDs supported the anti-Treaty IRA.

By mid-1922, Collins no longer really worked as Chairman of the Provisional Government. He became the Commander-in-Chief of the National Army, a formal uniformed army that formed around the pro-Treaty IRA.[581]

Collins, along with Richard Mulcahy and Eoin O'Duffy decided on a series of seaborne landings into republican held areas. They re-took Munster and the west in July–August 1922. As part of this offensive, Collins travelled to his native Cork. This was against the advice of his companions, and despite suffering from stomach-ache, and depression. Collins is said to have told his comrades that "They wouldn't shoot me in my own county". He recorded his plan for peace in his diary: Republicans must "accept the People's Verdict" on the Treaty but could then "go home without their arms (*guns*). We don't ask for any surrender of their principles". "We want to avoid any possible unnecessary destruction and loss of life." But if Republicans did not accept his terms, "further blood is on their shoulders".[582]

On the road to Bandon, at the village of *Béal na mBláth* (Irish, "the Mouth of Flowers"), Collins stopped to ask directions. However, the man whom they asked, Dinny Long, was also a member of the local Anti-Treaty IRA. An ambush was then prepared for the convoy when it made its journey back to Cork city. They knew Collins would return by the same road as the two other roads from Bandon to Cork were destroyed by Republicans. The ambush party, commanded by Liam Deasy, opened fire on Collins' convoy.[583]

Collins was killed in the gun battle, which lasted about 20 minutes, from 8:00 p.m. to 8:20 p.m. He was the only fatality. He had ordered his convoy to stop and return fire, instead of choosing the safer option of driving on in his touring car or transferring to the safety of the accompanying armoured car, as his

---

[580] *Murphy, John F. (17 August 2010). "Michael Collins and the Craft of Intelligence". International Journal of Intelligence and Counterintelligence. 17 (2): 334.*

[581] *West Cork People*, 22 August 2002, p. 3

[582] Mackay, James. *Michael Collins: A Life*. p. 38

[583] Stewart, Anthony Terence Quincey. *Michael Collins: The Secret File*. p. 8

companion, Emmet Dalton, had wished.[584] They do not know who fired the fatal shot.

Collins' men brought his body back to Cork where it was then shipped to Dublin because it was feared the body might be stolen in an ambush if it were transported by road.[585] His body lay in state for three days in Dublin City Hall where tens of thousands of mourners walked past his coffin to pay their respects. His funeral mass took place at Dublin's Pro Cathedral where a number of foreign and Irish dignitaries were in attendance. Some 500,000 people attended his funeral, almost one fifth of the country's population.

Eamon de Valera is reported to have stated in 1966:

"I can't see my way to becoming Patron of the Michael Collins Foundation. It is my considered opinion that in the fullness of time, history will record the greatness of Collins and it will be recorded at my expense"

[584] James Alexander Mackay *Michael Collins: A Life* Mainstream Publishing, 1996. p. 46
[585] Clarke, Kathleen (2008). *Kathleen Clarke: Revolutionary Woman*. Dublin: O'Brien Press Ltd.

Chapter eight

The Rebellious Scots

William Wallace

As I said in my introduction, the movie "Braveheart" whilst stirring up Scotland's passion for independence, it was not historically accurate. He never slept with the Princess of Wales, even though it was hinted at in the movie. When Sir William Wallace was executed, the Princess who would go onto to be the Princess of Wales, was only three years old. Another misconception from the movie, was that he rebelled because his wife had been murdered by the English Garrison Commander. In fact, there is no record of Wallace ever being married and there is no record of him ever having fathered any children. Don't you just love Hollywood?

William Wallace, in full Sir William Wallace, (born c. 1270, probably near Paisley, Renfrew, Scotland and died August 23, 1305, London, England), one of Scotland's greatest national heroes and the chief inspiration for Scottish resistance to the English King Edward I. He served as guardian of the kingdom of Scotland during the first years of the long and ultimately successful struggle to free his country from English rule.

Wallace was the second son of Sir Malcolm Wallace of Elderslie in Renfrewshire. In 1296 King Edward I of England deposed and imprisoned the Scottish King John de Balliol and declared himself ruler of Scotland. Sporadic resistance had already occurred when, in May 1297, Wallace and a band of some 30 men burned Lanark and killed its English sheriff. Joined by Sir William Douglas ("the Hardy"), Wallace next marched on Scone, drove out the English justiciar, and attacked the English garrisons between the Rivers Forth and Tay. The Scottish steward, Robert the Bruce (later King Robert I), and others now gathered an army, but it was forced to surrender at Irvine by Sir Henry de Percy and Sir Robert de Clifford (July 1297). Wallace, however, remained in action "with a large company in the Forest of Selkirk," according to a contemporary report made to Edward. Wallace laid siege to Dundee but abandoned it to oppose, with Andrew de Moray, an English army that was advancing toward Stirling under John de Warenne, Earl of Surrey.

Surrey failed to bring Wallace to terms outside Stirling, and, on the morning of September 11, 1297, the English began to file across the narrow bridge over the

Forth. Wallace and Moray, in a position northwest of the Abbey Craig, held back their troops until about half the English had crossed. They then attacked with such sudden fury that almost all who had crossed were killed or driven into the river and drowned. Surrey, with the rest of his army, retreated hastily, having first destroyed the bridge, but the Scots crossed by a ford and pursued them. With only a small following, Surrey escaped to Berwick and York. For the moment Scotland was almost free of occupation. A letter long survived in which Moray and Wallace, writing from Haddington on October 11, urged the Hanseatic towns of Hamburg and Lübeck to resume trade with Scotland, now "recovered by war from the power of the English." Moray, who had been wounded at Stirling Bridge, died soon afterward. Wallace now ravaged Northumberland and Cumberland, burning Alnwick and besieging Carlisle. To the monks of Hexham, however, he granted special protection.

Upon returning to Scotland early in December 1297, Wallace was knighted (it is not known by whom) and was elected or assumed the title of guardian of the kingdom. In the name of King John de Balliol, then a prisoner in London, Wallace set himself to reorganize the army and regulate the affairs of the country. He seems to have acted wisely and vigorously and to have been supported by Bishop Robert Wishart of Glasgow, the steward's brother Sir John Stewart, Sir John Graham of Dundaff, Sir John Comyn ("the Red"), Robert the Bruce, and others. Some nobles, many of whom had English estates and hostages in Edward's hands, were only lukewarm to Wallace's leadership, and his position depended entirely upon his success on the battlefield.

Early in 1298 Surrey returned and relieved the English-held castles of Roxburgh and Berwick but by Edward's orders advanced no farther. Edward himself crossed the Tweed on July 3 and moved toward Stirling with a strong force of heavy cavalry, a body of archers, and Irish and Welsh auxiliaries. Wallace retreated slowly, wasting the country behind him so Edward's force could not resupply itself on the march. Edward, with his army half-starved and mutinous, was on the point of retreat when, early on July 21 near Kirkliston, he learned that Wallace was awaiting him near Falkirk.

Edward advanced and on the following day found Wallace on a carefully chosen sloping ground, his front protected by a small river. The English cavalry, having with some difficulty crossed the river and the adjacent marshy ground, launched repeated charges on the four schiltrons (circular battle formations) of Wallace's spearmen. They drove off the field the small body of Scottish horse under Comyn but made no impression on the schiltrons and suffered considerable losses. The archers, however, now advanced, and their deadly volleys soon broke up the spearmen's ranks, and further cavalry charges turned them to flight. Thousands of the Scots were slain in the pursuit, and among the dead were Sir John Stewart and Sir John de Graham. Wallace retired northward with the survivors, burning Stirling and Perth as he went. Edward, unable to maintain his forces in Scotland, returned south, reaching Carlisle on September 8. His military reputation ruined, Wallace resigned the guardianship in December 1298 and was succeeded by Bruce and Comyn.

There is some evidence that Wallace went to France in 1299 and thereafter returned to Scotland to act as a solitary guerrilla leader, but from the autumn of 1299 nothing is known of his activities for more than four years. The rebellion he had led nevertheless continued until 1304, at which point most Scottish nobles submitted to Edward. How much this continued resistance was due to Wallace's influence is uncertain, but Wallace was the one leader to whom Edward would never offer any terms of capitulation and whom he most persistently tried to capture. On August 5, 1305, Wallace was arrested near Glasgow by Sir John Menteith, and, according to two early chroniclers, by treachery. He was carried to Dumbarton Castle and then to London, having possibly been brought before King Edward along the way.

On August 23, 1305, Wallace was conveyed to Westminster Hall, where he was indicted and condemned to death. There was no trial because he was declared a traitor to the king; Wallace emphatically denied this charge, as he had never sworn allegiance to Edward. That same day he was hanged, disembowelled, and finally beheaded and quartered at Smithfield. His head was set on London Bridge and his limbs exposed at Newcastle, Berwick, Stirling, and Perth. In 1306 Bruce raised the rebellion that eventually won independence for Scotland.

Chapter nine

The Rebellious Scots

Robert The Bruce – the Outlaw King

There have been several films made in honour of Robert the Bruce, but they are made for entertainment and not necessarily based on fact.

Robert the Bruce, original name Robert VIII de Bruce, also called Robert I, (born July 11, 1274, and died June 7, 1329, Cardross, Dumbartonshire, Scotland, King of Scotland (1306–29), who freed Scotland from English rule, winning the decisive Battle of Bannockburn (1314) and ultimately confirming Scottish independence in the Treaty of Northampton (1328).

The Anglo-Norman family of Bruce, which had come to Scotland in the early 12th century, was related by marriage to the Scottish royal family, and hence the sixth Robert de Bruce (died 1295), grandfather of the future king, claimed the throne when it was left vacant in 1290. The English King Edward I claimed feudal superiority over the Scots and awarded the crown to Balliol instead.

The eighth Robert de Bruce was born in 1274. His father, the seventh Robert de Bruce (died 1304), resigned the title of earl of Carrick in his favour in 1292, but little else is known of his career until 1306. In the confused period of rebellions against English rule from 1295 to 1304 he appears at one time among the leading supporters of the rebel William Wallace, but later apparently regained Edward I's confidence. There is nothing at this period to suggest that he was soon to become the Scottish leader in a war of independence against Edward's attempt to govern Scotland directly.

The decisive event was the murder of John ("the Red") Comyn in the Franciscan church at Dumfries on February 10, 1306, either by Bruce or his followers. Comyn, a nephew of John de Balliol, was a possible rival for the crown, and Bruce's actions suggest that he had already decided to seize the throne. He hastened to Scone and was crowned on March 25.

The new King's position was very difficult. Edward I, whose garrisons held many of the important castles in Scotland, regarded him as a traitor and made every effort to crush a movement that he treated as a rebellion. King Robert was twice defeated in 1306, at Methven, near Perth, on June 19, and at Dalry, near Tyndrum, Perthshire, on August 11. His wife and many of his supporters were captured, and three of his brothers executed. Robert himself became a fugitive, hiding on the remote island of Rathlin off the north Irish coast. It was during this period, with his fortunes at low ebb, that he is supposed to have derived hope and patience from watching a spider perseveringly weaving its web.

In February 1307 he returned to Ayrshire. His main supporter at first was his only surviving brother, Edward, but in the next few years he attracted several others. Robert himself defeated John Comyn, earl of Buchan (a cousin of the slain John "the Red"), and in 1313 captured Perth, which had been in the hands of an English garrison. Much of the fighting, however, was done by Robert's supporters, notably James Douglas and Thomas Randolph, later earl of Moray, who progressively conquered Galloway, Douglasdale, the forest of Selkirk and most of the eastern borders, and finally, in 1314, Edinburgh. During these years the king was helped by the support of some of the leading Scottish churchmen and also by the death of Edward I in 1307 and the ineptness of his successor, Edward II. The test came in 1314 when a large English army attempted to relieve the garrison of Stirling. Its defeat at Bannockburn on June 24 marked the triumph of Robert I.

Almost the whole of the rest of his reign had passed before he forced the English government to recognize his position. Berwick was captured in 1318, and there were repeated raids into the north of England, which inflicted great damage. Eventually, after the deposition of Edward II (1327), Edward III's regency government decided to make peace by the Treaty of Northampton (1328) on terms that included the recognition of Robert I's title as king of Scots and the abandonment of all English claims to overlordship.

Robert's main energies in the years after 1314, however, were devoted to settling the affairs of his kingdom. Until the birth of the future king David II in 1324 he had no male heir, and two statutes, in 1315 and 1318, were concerned with the succession. In addition, a parliament in 1314 decreed that all who remained in the allegiance of the English should forfeit their lands; this decree provided the means to reward supporters, and there are many charters regranting the lands so forfeited. Sometimes these grants proved dangerous, for the king's chief supporters became enormously powerful. James Douglas, knighted at Bannockburn, acquired important lands in the counties of Selkirk and Roxburgh that became the nucleus of the later power of the Douglas family on the borders. Robert I also had to restart the processes of royal government, for administration had been in abeyance since 1296. By the end of the reign the system of exchequer audits was again functioning, and to this period belongs the earliest surviving roll of the register of the great seal.

In the last years of his life, Robert I suffered from ill health and spent most of this time at Cardross, Dumbartonshire, where he died, possibly of leprosy. His body was buried in Dunfermline Abbey, but the heart was removed on his instructions and taken by Sir James Douglas on crusade in Spain. Douglas was killed, but it appears that the heart was recovered and brought back for burial, as the king had intended, at Melrose Abbey. In 1921 a cone-shaped casket containing a heart was uncovered during excavations at the abbey, reburied at that time, and re-excavated in 1996. (Heart burial was relatively common among royalty and the aristocracy, however, there is no specific evidence that this casket is that of Robert the Bruce.) In later times Robert I came to be revered as one of the heroes of Scottish national sentiment and legend.

Chapter ten

The Battle of Bannockburn 1314

Battle of Bannockburn, (June 23–24, 1314), decisive battle in Scottish history whereby the Scots under Robert I (the Bruce) defeated the English under Edward II, expanding Robert's territory and influence.

By the time of the battle in 1314, all of Scotland had been cleared of strongholds loyal to Edward II with the exception of the besieged Stirling Castle, which the defenders had promised to surrender if they had not been relieved by June 24. Edward is estimated to have assembled an army of some 13,000-infantry bolstered by a contingent of Welsh archers and roughly 3,000 cavalry to aid those still loyal to him in Scotland. His primary objective was the raising of the siege of Stirling Castle. To meet Edward's army, Robert gathered his smaller force, consisting of perhaps 7,000 infantry(primarily pikemen) and several hundred light horse, at the New Park, a hunting preserve a mile or two (1.6 to 3.2 km) south of Stirling. Robert planned to use the trees there to funnel any attack into his heavy infantry and freshly dug anti-cavalry ditches. He had taken up his position there when the English vanguard appeared on June 23.

Edward attempted to circumvent the Scottish positions and possibly relieve Stirling Castle with a small unit of cavalry, but Scottish infantrymen rushed to meet them. After those two groups fought to a stalemate, Scottish reinforcements arrived to send the English cavalry fleeing. Meanwhile, a second unit of English cavalry charged the Scottish main position, interpreting their opponent's movements as a possible retreat. After being rebuffed by the main Scottish force at the New Park, the second English attack climaxed with Robert's engaging in personal combat with an English knight. The encounter was reportedly observed by both armies, and it ended with Robert's cleaving the knight's head with his battle axe. After that, all English troops retreated to the main army as night fell. That evening the two armies experienced very different situations. Scottish morale was high following the day's victory, and Robert sought to increase it with an encouraging speech. Meanwhile, the English, who feared a counterattack, spent much of the night awake and in formation; those who did rest dealt with poor camp conditions in a wet marsh.

Edward attempted to circumvent the Scottish positions and possibly relieve Stirling Castle with a small unit of cavalry, but Scottish infantrymen rushed to meet them. After those two groups fought to a stalemate, Scottish reinforcements arrived to send the English cavalry fleeing. Meanwhile, a second unit of English cavalry charged the Scottish main position, interpreting their opponent's movements as a possible retreat. After being rebuffed by the main Scottish force at the New Park, the second English attack climaxed with Robert's engaging in personal combat with an English knight. The encounter was reportedly observed by both armies, and it ended with Robert's cleaving the knight's head with his battle axe. After that, all English troops retreated to the main army as night fell. That evening the two armies experienced very different situations. Scottish morale was high following the day's victory, and Robert sought to increase it with an encouraging speech. Meanwhile, the English, who feared a counterattack, spent much of the night awake and in formation; those who did rest dealt with poor camp conditions in a wet marsh.

The Scots began the second day of the battle by holding mass. Edward supposedly delayed the engagement, initially confused by the disposition of Scottish infantrymen wielding long spears. Nevertheless, he still ordered an attack against the Scots with his cavalry. Upon the initial charge, the English avoided the anti-cavalry ditches, but they were unable to penetrate the Scottish lines. After multiple cavalry charges failed to break the Scottish defences, Robert began to move his infantry forward. As the English backed up, the ditches hindered them after multiple horsemen fell in and could not escape. The battle transformed into an all-out rout, with many of the English being slaughtered. Edward himself barely escaped.

English losses included 34 barons and knights as well as thousands of footmen killed or captured while fleeing from the battle. The Scots claimed to have lost only two knights but several hundred infantrymen. The battle is traditionally regarded as the culmination of the Scottish Wars of Independence, although Scottish independence would not be officially recognized until 1328, at the conclusion of the Treaty of Northampton with Edward's successor, Edward III.

Bannockburn has been credited with initiating a new form of warfare in Europe in which infantry, not cavalry, dominated the battlefield. The battle also marked the last major victory of the Scots over the English during the Middle Ages.

Chapter eleven

The Covenanters
(King James versus King Jesus)

*Some of the Script used in this chapter is seen in the way in
which things were said and written at this point in history.*

I have a special interest I the Covenanters, because when I was growing up, we lived
in a Southern suburb of the City of Aberdeen, Scotland. The suburb was known as
Kincorth, but it is also known as the Covenanters Hill. Some of the streets at the foot
of the hill have Covenanter in their name, such as Covenanters Row and
Covenanters Crescent. My last house in Kincorth, (1990-1993), my house was built
on what had been the Covenanters encampment before fight the King's Army at the
foot of the hill. It was more of a skirmish than a battle. The Covenanters won this
skirmish, and the Churches in Aberdeen were the last to put their names to the
National Covenant. It should be of no surprise therefore, that my own ministry today
is called *"Third Millennium Covenanters."*

The Covenanters were members of a 17th-century Scottish religious and political
movement, who supported a Presbyterian Church of Scotland, and the primacy of its
leaders in religious affairs. The name derived from *Covenant*, a biblical term for a
bond or agreement with God.

The origins of the movement lay in disputes with King James VI & I (he was King
James VI of Scotland, but he now sat on the English throne and was therefore King
James I in England), and his son Charles I of England over church structure
and doctrine. In 1638, thousands of Scots signed the National Covenant, pledging to
resist changes imposed by Charles on the kirk; following victory in the 1639 and
1640 Bishops' Wars, the Covenanters took control of Scotland.

The 1643 Solemn League and Covenant brought them into the First English Civil
War on the side of Parliament, but they supported Charles in the 1648 Second
English Civil War. After his execution in 1649, the Covenanter government agreed
to restore his son Charles II to the English throne; defeat in the 1651 Third English
Civil War led to Scotland's incorporation into the Commonwealth of England.

After the 1660 Restoration, the Covenanters lost control of the kirk and became a
persecuted minority, leading to several armed rebellions and a

The author standing at the gates to the Covenanter Prison

The Prison is in the grounds of the Greyfriars' Kirkyard (of Greyfriars' Bobby fame) This prison was an open courtyard where the prisoners died from the elements (weather) or they survived only to be taken down to Edinburgh's Grass Market to be executed. I had to ask permission to take photographs and was surprised to see that the sign stating that it was a prison had been removed, although it had still been there three days earlier. Perhaps the Church of Scotland were feeling guilty about no longer staying loyal to Bible.

Period from 1679 to 1688 known as "The Killing Time". Following the 1688 Glorious Revolution in Scotland, the Church of Scotland was re-established as a wholly Presbyterian structure and most Covenanters readmitted. This marked the end of their existence as a significant movement, although dissident minorities persisted in Scotland, Ireland, and North America.

In the mid-16th century, John Knox and other converts from Catholicism founded a reformed Church of Scotland, or Kirk, Presbyterian in structure, and Calvinist in doctrine. Members committed to maintain the kirk as the sole form of religion in Scotland, under a Godly bond, or 'Covenant', the first of which was signed by the Lords of the Congregation in December 1557. In 1560, the Parliament of Scotland adopted the Scots Confession, largely written in four days by Knox, which rejected many Catholic teachings and practices.[586] Scotland adopted the Scots Confession, largely written in four days by Knox, which rejected many Catholic teachings and practices.[587]

The Confession was adopted by James VI, enjoined on persons of all ranks and classes, and re-affirmed in 1590, then in 1596. However, James argued that as king

---

[586] Wormald 2018, pp. 120–121.
[587] Wormald 2018, pp. 120–121.

he was also head of the church, governing through bishops appointed by himself; very simply, 'No bishops, no king.'[588] The alternative view was best expressed by Andrew Melville as '...Thair is twa Kings and twa Kingdomes in Scotland... Chryst Jesus the King and this Kingdome the Kirk, whose subject King James the Saxt is';[589] the kirk was subject only to God, and its members, including James, ruled by presbyteries, consisting of ministers and elders.[590]

Although James successfully imposed bishops on the kirk, it remained Calvinist in doctrine; when he also became king of England in 1603, he saw a unified Church as the first step in creating a centralised, Unionist state.[591] Although both nominally Episcopalian in structure and Protestant in doctrine, even Scottish bishops rejected many Church of England practises as little better than Catholic.[592]

Opposition to Catholicism remained widespread in Scotland, even though by 1630 it was largely confined to the aristocracy and remote, Gaelic-speaking areas of the Highlands and Islands.[593] Many Scots fought in the Thirty Years' War, one of the most destructive religious conflicts in European history, while there were close links with the Protestant Dutch Republic, then fighting for independence from Catholic Spain. Lastly, the majority of kirk ministers had been educated in French Calvinist universities, most of which were suppressed in the 1620s.[594]

The result was a general perception Protestant Europe was under attack and increased sensitivity to changes in church practice; in 1636, the Book of Canons replaced John Knox's Book of Discipline and excommunicated anyone who denied the King's supremacy in church matters.[595] When followed by a new Book of Common Prayer in 1637, it caused anger and widespread rioting, traditionally sparked when Jenny Geddes threw a stool at the minister during a service in St Giles Cathedral.[596] More recently, historians like Mark Kishlansky have argued her protest was part of a series of planned and co-ordinated opposition to the Prayer book, whose origin was as much political as it was religious.[597]

Supervised by Archibald Johnston and Alexander Henderson, in February 1638 representatives from all sections of Scottish society agreed a National Covenant, pledging resistance to liturgical 'innovations.' An important factor in the political

---

[588] Lee 1974, pp. 50–51.
[589] Melville 1842, p. 370.
[590] Church of Scotland. "Our Structure".
[591] Stephen 2010, pp. 55–58.
[592] McDonald 1998, pp. 75–76.
[593] Fissel 1994, pp. 269, 278.
[594] Wilson 2009, pp. 787–778.
[595] Stevenson 1973, pp. 45–46.
[596] Mackie, Lenman & Parker 1986, p. 203.
[597] Mackie, Lenman & Parker 1986, p. 203.

contest with Charles was the Covenanter belief they were preserving an established and divinely ordained form of religion which he was seeking to alter.[598] Debate as to what that meant persisted until finally settled in 1690. For example, the Covenant made no reference to bishops; Murdoch MacKenzie, Bishop of Orkney from 1677 to 1688, viewed himself as a Covenanter and argued their expulsion interfered with that form. Nevertheless, when the General Assembly of the Church of Scotland met in Glasgow in December 1638, it abolished episcopacy and affirmed its right to meet annually.[599]

Support was widespread except in Aberdeenshire and Banff, heartland of Royalist and Episcopalian resistance for the next 60 years.[600] The Marquess of Argyll and six other members of the Scottish Privy Council had backed the Covenant;[601] Charles tried to impose his authority in the 1639 and 1640 Bishop's Wars, with his defeat leaving the Covenanters in control of Scotland.[602] When the First English Civil War began in 1642, the Scots remained neutral at first but sent troops to Ulster to support their co-religionists in the Irish Rebellion; the bitterness of this conflict radicalised views in Scotland and Ireland.[603]

Since Calvinists believed a 'well-ordered' monarchy was part of God's plan, the Covenanters committed to "defend the king's person and authority with our goods, bodies, and lives". The idea of government without a king was inconceivable.[604] This view was generally shared by English Parliamentarians, who wanted to control Charles, not remove him, but both they and their Royalist opponents were further divided over religious doctrine. In Scotland, near unanimous agreement on doctrine meant differences centred on who held ultimate authority in clerical affairs. Royalists tended to be 'traditionalist' in religion and politics but there were various factors, including nationalist allegiance to the kirk. Individual motives were very complex, and many fought on both sides, including Montrose, a Covenanter general in 1639 and 1640 who nearly restored Royalist rule in Scotland in 1645.[605]

The Covenanter faction led by Argyll saw religious union with England as the best way to preserve a Presbyterian Kirk and in October 1643, the Solemn League and Covenant agreed a Presbyterian Union in return for Scottish military support.[606] Royalists and moderates in both Scotland and England opposed this on nationalist

---

[598] Mackie, Lenman & Parker 1986, p. 204.
[599] Harris 2014, p. 372.
[600] Plant 2010
[601] Mackie, Lenman & Parker 1986, pp. 205–206.
[602] Mackie, Lenman & Parker 1986, pp. 209–210.
[603] Royle 2004, p. 142.
[604] Macleod 2009, pp. 5–19 passim.
[605] Harris 2014, pp. 53–54.
[606] Robertson 2014, p. 125.

grounds, while religious Independents like Oliver Cromwell claimed he would fight, rather than agree to it.[607]

The Covenanters and their English Presbyterian allies gradually came to see the Independents who dominated the New Model Army as a bigger threat than the Royalists and when Charles surrendered in 1646, they began negotiations to restore him to the English throne. In December 1647, Charles agreed to impose Presbyterianism in England for three years and suppress the Independents but his refusal to take the Covenant himself split the Covenanters into Engagers and Kirk Party fundamentalists or Whiggamores. Defeat in the Second English Civil War resulted in the execution of Charles in January 1649 and the Kirk Party taking control of the General Assembly.[608]

In February 1649, the Scots proclaimed Charles II King of Scotland and Great Britain; under the terms of the Treaty of Breda, the Kirk Party agreed to restore Charles to the English throne and in return he accepted the Covenant. Defeats at Dunbar and Worcester resulted with Scotland being incorporated into the Commonwealth of England, Scotland and Ireland in 1652.[609]

After defeat in 1651, the Covenanters split into two factions. Over two-thirds of the ministry supported the Resolution of December 1650 re-admitting Royalists and Engagers and were known as 'Resolutioners.' 'Protestors' were largely former Kirk Party fundamentalists or Whiggamores who blamed defeat on compromise with 'malignants.' Differences between the two were both religious and political, including church government, religious toleration, and the role of law in a godly society.[610]

Following the events of 1648–51, Cromwell decided the only way forward was to eliminate the power of the Scottish landed elite and the kirk. The Terms of Incorporation published on 12 February 1652 made a new Council of Scotland responsible for regulating church affairs and allowed freedom of worship for all Protestant sects. Since Presbyterianism was no longer the state religion, kirk sessions and synods functioned as before but its edicts were not enforced by civil penalties.[611]

Covenanters were hostile to sects like the Congregationalists or Quakers because they advocated separation of church and state. Apart from a small number of Protestors known as Separatists, the vast majority refused to accept these changes,

---

[607] Rees 2016, pp. 118–119.
[608] Mitchison, Fry & Fry 2002, pp. 223–224.
[609] Royle 2004, p. 612.
[610] Holfelder 1998, p. 9.
[611] Morrill 1990, p. 162.

and Scotland was incorporated into the Commonwealth without further consultation on 21 April 1652.[612]

Contests for control of individual presbyteries made the split increasingly bitter and in July 1653 each faction held its own General Assembly in Edinburgh. Robert Lilburne, English military commander in Scotland, used the excuse of Resolutioner church services praying for the success of Glencairn's rising to dissolve both sessions. The Assembly would not formally reconvene until 1690, the Resolutioner majority instead meeting in informal 'Consultations' and Protestors holding field assemblies or conventicles outside Resolutioner-controlled kirk structures.[613]

When the Protectorate was established in 1654, Lord Broghill, head of the Council of State for Scotland summarised his dilemma; 'the Resolutioners love Charles Stuart and hate us, while the Protesters love neither him nor us.'[614] Neither side was willing to co-operate with the Protectorate except in Glasgow, where Protestors led by Patrick Gillespie used the authorities in their contest with local Resolutioners.[615]

Since the Resolutioners controlled 750 of 900 parishes, Broghill recognised they could not be ignored; his policy was to isolate the 'extreme' elements of both factions, hoping to create a new, moderate majority.[616] He therefore encouraged internal divisions within the kirk, including appointing Gillespie Principal of the University of Glasgow, against the wishes of the James Guthrie and Warriston led Protestor majority. The Protectorate authorities effectively became arbitrators between the factions, each of whom appointed representatives to argue their case in London; the repercussions affected the kirk for decades to come.[617]

After the Restoration of the Monarchy in 1660, Scotland regained control of the kirk, but the Rescissory Act 1661 restored the legal position of 1633 and removing the Covenanter reforms of 1638–1639. The Privy Council of Scotland restored bishops on 6 September 1661. James Sharp, leader of the Resolutioners, became Archbishop of St Andrews; Robert Leighton was consecrated Bishop of Dunblane, and soon an entire bench of bishops had been appointed.[618]

In 1662, the kirk was restored as the national church, independent sects banned and all officeholders required to renounce the 1638 Covenant; about a third, or around 270 in total, refused to do so and lost their positions as a result.[619] Most occurred in

---

[612] Baker 2009, pp. 290–291.
[613] Holfelder 1998, pp. 190–192.
[614] Dow 1979, p. 192.
[615] Holfelder 1998, p. 196.
[616] Dow 1979, p. 204.
[617] Holfelder 1998, p. 213.
[618] Mackie, Lenman & Parker 1986, pp. 231–234.
[619] Mackie, Lenman & Parker 1986, pp. 231–234.

the south-west of Scotland, an area particularly strong in its Covenanting sympathies; the practice of holding conventicles outside the formal structure continued, often attracting thousands of worshippers.[620]

The government alternated between persecution and toleration; in 1663, dissenting ministers were declared 'seditious persons' and imposed heavy fines on those who failed to attend the parish churches of the "King's curates". In 1666 a group of men from Galloway captured the local military commander, marched on Edinburgh and were defeated at the Battle of Rullion Green. Around 50 prisoners were taken, while a number of others were arrested; 33 were executed and the rest transported to Barbados.[621]

The Rising led to the replacement of the Duke of Rothes as King's Commissioner by John Maitland, 1st Duke of Lauderdale who followed a more conciliatory policy. Letters of Indulgence were issued in 1669, 1672 and 1679, allowing evicted ministers to return to their parishes if they agreed to avoid politics. A number returned but over 150 refused the offer, while many Episcopalians were alienated by the compromise.[622]

The outcome was a return to persecution; preaching at a conventicle was made punishable by death, while attendance attracted severe sanctions. In 1674, heritors (a proprietor of a heritable object) and masters were made responsible for the 'good behaviour' of their tenants and servants; from 1677, this meant posting bonds for those living on their land. In 1678, 3,000 Lowland militia and 6,000 Highlanders, known as the "Highland Host", were billeted in the Covenanting shires, especially those in the South-West, as a form of punishment.[623]

The assassination of Archbishop Sharp by Covenanter radicals in May 1679 led to a revolt that ended at the Battle of Bothwell Bridge in June. Although battlefield casualties were relatively few, over 1,200 prisoners were sentenced to transportation, the chief prosecutor being Lord Advocate Rosehaugh.[624] Claims of undocumented, indiscriminate killing in the aftermath of the battle have also been made.[625]

Defeat split the movement split into moderates, and extremists headed by Donald Cargill and Richard Cameron who issued the Sanquhar Declaration in June 1680. While Covenanters previously claimed to object only to state religious policy, this renounced any allegiance to either Charles, or his Catholic brother James. Adherents

---

[620] Mitchison, Fry & Fry 2002, p. 253.
[621] Mackie, Lenman & Parker 1986, pp. 235–236.
[622] Mackie, Lenman & Parker 1986, p. 236.
[623] Mackie, Lenman & Parker 1986, pp. 237–238.
[624] Kennedy 2014, pp. 220–221.
[625] M'Crie 1875, p331

were known as Cameronians, and although a relatively small minority, the deaths of Cameron, his brother and Cargill gained them considerable sympathy.[626]

The 1681 Scottish Succession and Test Acts made obedience to the monarch a legal obligation, 'regardless of religion', but in return confirmed the primacy of the kirk "as currently constituted". This excluded the Covenanters, who wanted to restore it to the structure prevailing in 1640.[627] A number of government figures, including James Dalrymple, chief legal officer, and Archibald Campbell, 9th Earl of Argyll, objected to inconsistencies in the Act and refused to swear. Argyll was convicted of treason and sentenced to death, although he and Dalrymple escaped to the Dutch Republic.[628]

The Cameronians were now organised more formally as the 'United Societies'; estimates of their numbers vary from 6,000 to 7,000, mostly concentrated in Argyllshire.[629] Led by James Renwick, in 1684 copies of an *Apologetical Declaration* were posted in different locations, effectively declaring war on government officers.

This led to the period known in Protestant historiography as "the Killing Time"; the Scottish Privy Council authorised the extrajudicial execution of any Covenanters caught in arms, policies carried out by troops under John Graham, 1st Viscount Dundee.[630] At the same time, Lord Rosehaugh adopted the French practice of same day trial and execution for militants who refused to swear oaths of loyalty to the king.[631]

Despite his Catholicism, James VII became king in April 1685 with widespread support, largely due to fears of civil war if he were bypassed, and opposition to re-opening past divisions within the kirk.[632] These factors contributed to the rapid defeat of Argyll's Rising in June 1685; in a bid to widen its appeal, his manifesto omitted any mention of the 1638 Covenant. Renwick and his followers refused to support it as a result.[633]

A major factor in the defeat of Argyll's Rising was the desire for stability within the kirk. By issuing *Letters of Indulgence* to dissident Presbyterians in 1687, James now threatened to re-open this debate and undermine his own Episcopalian base. At the

---

[626] Christie 2008, p. 113.
[627] Harris 2007, pp. 153–157.
[628] Webb 1999, pp. 50–51.
[629] Christie 2008, p. 146.
[630] Mackie, Lenman & Parker 1986, pp. 240–245.
[631] Jardine
[632] Womersley 2015, p. 189.
[633] De Krey 2007, p. 227.

same time, he excluded the Society People, and created another Covenanter martyr with the execution of Renwick in February 1688.[634]

In June 1688, two events turned dissent into a crisis: the birth of James Francis Edward on 10 June created a Catholic heir, excluding James' Protestant daughter Mary and her husband William of Orange. Prosecuting the Bishops seemed to go beyond tolerance for Catholicism and into an assault on the Episcopalian establishment; their acquittal on 30 June destroyed James' political authority.[635] Representatives from the English political class invited William to assume the English throne; when he landed in Brixham on 5 November, James' army deserted him and he left for France on 23 December.[636]

The Scottish Convention elected in March to determine settlement of the Scottish throne was dominated by Covenanter sympathisers. On 4 April, it passed the Claim of Right and the 'Articles of Grievances', which held James forfeited the Crown by his actions; on 11 May, William and Mary became co-monarchs of Scotland. Although William wanted to retain bishops, the role played by Covenanters during the Jacobite rising of 1689, including the Cameronians' defence of Dunkeld in August, meant their views prevailed in the political settlement that followed. The General Assembly met in November 1690 for the first time since 1654; even before it convened, over 200 Episcopalian ministers had been removed from their livings.[637]

I discovered this stain glass window in a Glasgow church where my friend Rev. Tom Grieg, is now the Minister.

[634] Christie 2008, p. 160.
[635] Harris 2007, pp. 235–236.
[636] Harris 2007, pp. 3–5.
[637] Mackie, Lenman & Parker 1986, pp. 241–245.

The Assembly once again eliminated episcopacy and created two commissions for the south and north of the Tay, which over the next 25 years removed almost two-thirds of all ministers.[638] To offset this, nearly one hundred clergy returned to the kirk in the 1693 and 1695 Acts of Indulgence, while others were protected by the local gentry and retained their positions until death by natural causes.[639]

Following the 1690 Settlement, a small minority of the United Societies followed Cameronian leader Robert Hamilton in refusing to re-enter the kirk.[640] They continued as an informal grouping until 1706, when John McMillan was appointed minister; in 1743, he and Thomas Nairn set up the Reformed Presbyterian Church of Scotland.[641] Although the church still exists, the vast majority of its members joined the Free Church of Scotland in 1876.[642]

For more information on the Covenanters visit **www.3rdmc.org**

---

[638] Mackie, Lenman & Parker 1986, p. 246.
[639] Mackie, Lenman & Parker 1986, p. 253.
[640] Christie 2008, p. 250.
[641] McMillan 1950, pp. 141–153.
[642] Mackie, Lenman & Parker 1986, p. 253.

Chapter twelve

The Glencoe Massacre

The Massacre of Glencoe took place in Glen Coe in the Highlands of Scotland on 13 February 1692. An estimated 30 members and associates of Clan MacDonald of Glencoe were killed by Scottish government forces, allegedly for failing to pledge allegiance to the new monarchs, William III and Mary II.

Although the Jacobite rising of 1689 was no longer a serious threat by May 1690, unrest continued in the remote Highlands which consumed resources needed for the Nine Years War in Flanders. In late 1690, the Scottish government agreed to pay the Jacobite clans a total of £12,000 for swearing loyalty. However, arguments between the chiefs over how to divide the money meant by December 1691 they still had not done so.

Under pressure from William, Secretary of State Lord Stair decided to make an example as a warning of the consequences for further delay. The Glencoe MacDonalds were not the only ones who failed to meet the deadline, while the Keppoch MacDonalds did not swear until early February. The reason for their selection is still debated but appears to have been a combination of internal clan politics, and a reputation for lawlessness that made them an easy target.

While there are examples of similar events in Scottish history, the massacre was unusual in the context of late 17th century society and its brutality shocked contemporaries. It became a significant element in the persistence of Jacobitism in the Highlands during the first half of the 18th century and remains a powerful symbol for a variety of reasons.

The Background to the Massacre

Historians suggest the late 17th century Highlands were more peaceful than often suggested, in part because chiefs could be fined for crimes committed by their clansmen. The exception was Lochaber, identified as a refuge for cattle raiders and thieves by government officials, other chiefs, and Gaelic poets. Four Lochaber clans were consistently named in such accounts; the Glencoe and Keppoch MacDonalds, the MacGregors and the Camerons.[643]

---

[643] MacInnes 1986, pp. 174–176.

Levies from all four served in the Independent Companies used to suppress the Conventicles in 1678–80, and took part in the devastating Atholl raid that followed Argyll's Rising in 1685. Primarily directed against areas in Cowal and Kintyre settled by Lowland migrants, it destabilised large parts of the central and southern Highlands. As a result, the government had to use military force to restore order; before James VII and II was deposed by the November 1688 Glorious Revolution, he outlawed the Keppoch MacDonalds for attacking his troops.[644]

When James landed in Ireland to regain his kingdoms in March 1689, the Camerons and Keppoch MacDonalds joined a small force recruited by Viscount Dundee for a supporting campaign in Scotland. Dundee and 600 Highlanders died in the victory at Killiecrankie on 27 July; although organised Jacobite resistance ended after Cromdale in May 1690, much of the Highlands remained out of government hands.[645] Policing it used resources needed for the Nine Years' War in Flanders, while close links between Western Scotland and Ulster meant unrest in one country often spilled into the other.[646] As peace in the Highlands required control of Lochaber, the region had far wider strategic importance than it appears.[647]

After the Battle of Killiecrankie, the Scottish government held a series of meetings with the Jacobite chiefs, offering terms that varied based on events in Ireland and Scotland. In March 1690, the Secretary of State, Lord Stair, offered a total of £12,000 for swearing allegiance to William, which they accepted under the June 1691 Declaration of Achallader, the Earl of Breadalbane signing for the government. Crucially, Stair left its allocation up to Breadalbane and the chiefs; internal disputes delayed the actual taking of the oath, while the Battle of Aughrim in July ended the war in Ireland and any immediate prospect of a Stuart restoration.[648]

On 26 August, a Royal Proclamation offered a pardon to anyone taking the Oath prior to 1 January 1692, with severe reprisals for those who did not. Two days later, secret articles appeared, cancelling the agreement in the event of a Jacobite invasion, and signed by all the attendees, including Breadalbane, who claimed they had been manufactured by Glengarry, the MacDonald chief.[649] Stair's letters increasingly focused on enforcement, reflecting his belief forged or not, none of the signatories intended to keep their word.[650]

---

[644] MacInnes 1986, pp. 193–194.
[645] Lenman 1980, pp. 37–38.
[646] Lang 1912, pp. 284–286.
[647] MacInnes 1986, p. 195.
[648] Harris 2007, p. 439.
[649] Levine 1999, p. 139.
[650] Gordon 1845, pp. 44–47.

In early October, the chiefs asked James for permission to take the Oath unless he could mount an invasion before the deadline, a condition they knew to be impossible.[651] His approval was sent on 12 December, and received by Glengarry on the 23rd, who did not share it until the 28th. One suggestion for the delay was an internal power struggle between Protestant elements of the MacDonald clan, like Glencoe, and the Catholic minority, led by Glengarry.[652]

As a result, MacIain of Glencoe only left for Fort William on 30 December to take the Oath from the governor, Lieutenant Colonel John Hill. Since he was not authorised to accept it, Hill sent MacIain to Inverary with a letter for the local magistrate, Sir Colin Campbell confirming his arrival before the deadline. Sir Colin administered the Oath on 6 January, after which MacIain returned home.[653] Glengarry did not swear until 4 February, with others doing so by proxy, but only MacIain was excluded from the indemnity issued by the Scottish Privy Council.[654]

Stair's letter of 2 December to Breadalbane shows the intention of making an example was taken well before the deadline for the Oath but as a much bigger operation; *...the clan Donell must be rooted out and Lochiel. Leave the McLeans to Argyll...*[655] In January, he wrote three letters in quick succession to Sir Thomas Livingstone, military commander in Scotland; on 7[th], the intention was to *....destroy entirely the country of Lochaber, Locheal's lands, Kippochs, Glengarrie and Glenco...;* on 9[th] *...their chieftains all being papists, it is well the vengeance falls there; for my part, I regret the MacDonalds had not divi[de]d and...Kippoch and Glenco are safe.* The last on 11 January states; *...my lord Argile tells me Glenco hath not taken the oaths at which I rejoice....*[656]

Parliament passed a Decree of Forfeiture in 1690, depriving Glengarry of his lands, but he continued to hold Invergarry Castle, whose garrison included the senior Jacobite officers Alexander Cannon and Thomas Buchan. This suggests the Episcopalian Glencoe MacDonalds only replaced the Catholic Glengarry as the target on 11 January; MacIain's son John MacDonald told the 1695 Commission the soldiers came to Glencoe from the north '...Glengarry's house being reduced.'[657]

After two years of negotiations, Stair was under pressure to ensure the deal stuck, while Argyll was competing for political influence with his kinsman Breadalbane, who also found it expedient to concur with the plan.[658] Glengarry was pardoned and

---

[651] Szechi 1994, p. 45.
[652] Szechi 1994, p. 30.
[653] Buchan 1933, p. 59.
[654] Levine 1999, p. 140.
[655] Goring 2014, pp. 94–96.
[656] Goring 2014, pp. 97–100.
[657] Cobbett 1814, p. 904.

his lands returned, while maintaining his reputation at the Jacobite court by being the last to swear and ensuring Cannon and Buchan received safe conduct to France in March 1692.[659] In summary, the Glencoe MacDonalds were a small clan with few friends and powerful enemies.

Glenlyon, an impoverished local landowner whose niece was married to one of MacIain's sons. Campbell carried orders for 'free quarter', an established alternative to paying taxes in what was a largely non-cash society.[660] The Glencoe MacDonalds had themselves been similarly billeted on the Campbells when serving with the Highland levies used to police Argyll in 1678.[661]

Highland regiments were formed by first appointing Captains, each responsible for recruiting sixty men from his own estates. Muster rolls for the regiment from October 1691 show the vast majority came from areas in Argyll devastated by the 1685 and 1686 Atholl.[662] On 12 February, Hill ordered Lieutenant Colonel James Hamilton to take 400 men and block the northern exits from Glencoe at Kinlochleven. Meanwhile, another 400 men under Major Duncanson would join Glenlyon's detachment and sweep northwards up the glen, killing anyone they found, removing property and burning houses.[663]

On the evening of 12 February, Glenlyon received written orders from Duncanson carried by another Argyll officer, Captain Thomas Drummond; their tone shows doubts as to his ability or willingness to carry them out. *See that this be putt in execution without feud or favour, else you may expect to be dealt with as one not true to King nor Government, nor a man XXXro to carry Commissione in the Kings service.* As Captain of the Argylls' Grenadier company, Drummond was senior to Glenlyon; his presence appears to have been to ensure the orders were enforced, since witnesses gave evidence, he shot two people who asked Glenlyon for mercy.[664]

MacIain was killed, but his two sons escaped, and the 1695 Commission was given various figures for total deaths. The often quoted figure of 38 was based on hearsay evidence from Hamilton's men, while the MacDonalds claimed 'the number they knew to be slaine were about 25.'[665] Recent estimates put total deaths resulting from the Massacre as 'around 30', while claims others died of exposure have not been substantiated.[666]

---

[658] Levine 1999, p. 141.
[659] MacConechy 1843, p. 77.
[660] Kennedy 2014, p. 141.
[661] Lenman & Mackie 1991, pp. 238–239.
[662] Argyll Transcripts 1891, pp. 12–24.
[663] Somers 1843, p. 538.
[664] Somers 1843, p. 536.
[665] Cobbett 1814, pp. 902–903.
[666] Campsie

Casualties would have been higher, but, whether by accident or design, Hamilton and Duncanson arrived after the killings had finished. Duncanson was two hours late, only joining Glenlyon at the southern end at 7:00 am, after which they advanced up the glen burning houses and removing livestock. Hamilton was not in position at Kinlochleven until 11:00; his detachment included two lieutenants, Francis Farquhar and Gilbert Kennedy who often appear in anecdotes claiming they 'broke their swords rather than carry out their orders.' This differs from their testimony to the Commission and is unlikely, since they arrived hours after the killings, which were carried out at the opposite end of the glen.[667]

In his letters of 30 January to Lieutenant Colonel Hamilton and Colonel Hill, Stair expresses concern the MacDonalds would escape if warned, and emphasises the need for secrecy. This correlates with evidence from James Campbell, one of Glenlyon's company, stating they had no knowledge of the plan until the morning of 13 February.[668]

In May, fears of a French invasion meant the Argylls were posted to Brentford in England, then Flanders. The regiment remained here until the Nine Years' War ended in 1697; it was disbanded, and no action taken against those involved. Glenlyon died in Bruges in August 1696, Duncanson was killed in Spain in May 1705, Drummond survived to take part in another famous Scottish disaster of the period, the Darien Scheme.[669]

On 12 April 1692, the *Paris Gazette* published a copy of Glenlyon's orders, allegedly found in an Edinburgh coffee house and then taken to France.[670] Despite criticism of the government, there was little sympathy for the MacDonalds; the military commander in Scotland, Viscount Teviot wrote 'it's not that anyone thinks the thieving tribe did not deserve to be destroyed but that it should have been done by those quartered amongst them makes a great noise.'[671] The impetus behind an inquiry was political; as a former member of James' administration, who then became a supporter of the new regime, Stair was unpopular with both sides.[672]

In the debate that followed, Colonel Hill claimed most Highlanders were peaceful, and even in Lochaber, *a single person may travel safely where he will without harm.* He argued lawlessness was deliberately encouraged by leaders like Glengarry, while 'the middle sort of Gentry and Commons never got anything but hurt' from it. The 1693 Highland Judicial Commission tried to encourage use of the law to resolve

[667] Howell 2017, p. 903.
[668] Somers 1843, p. 537.
[669] Prebble 1968, p. 103.
[670] Levine 1999, p. 143.
[671] Prebble 1973, p. 198.
[672] Levine 1999, p. 141.

issues like cattle-theft, but it was undermined by the clan chiefs, as it reduced control over their tenants.[673]

The issue appeared to be settled until given fresh impetus in May 1695 when the English Licensing of the Press Act 1662 expired. It led to an explosion in the number of political pamphlets published in London, among them *Gallienus Redivivus, or Murther will out, &c. Being a true Account of the De Witting of Glencoe, Gaffney.* Written by Jacobite-activist Charles Leslie, the main focus was William's alleged complicity in the 1672 death of Johan de Witt, with Glencoe and other crimes included as secondary charges.[674]

A Commission was set up to determine XXXrocessr there was a case to answer'under 'Slaughter under trust', a 1587 act intended to reduce endemic feuding. The law applied specifically to murder committed in 'cold-blood', for example when articles of surrender had been agreed, or hospitality accepted.[675] It was first used in 1588 against Lachlan Mor Maclean, whose objections to his mother's second marriage led him to murder his new stepfather, John MacDonald, and 18 me'bers of the wedding party. It was subject to interpretation; James MacDonald, who locked his parents inside their house before setting fire to it in 1597, and the killing of prisoners after the 1647 Battle of Dunaverty, were deemed to have been committed in "hot blood" and excluded.[676]

As both a capital offence and treason, it was an awkward weapon with which to attack Stair, since William himself signed the orders and the intent was widely known in government circles. The Commission therefore focused on whether participants exceeded orders, not their legality; it concluded Stair and Hamilton had a case to answer but left the decision to William. [677] While Stair was dismissed as Secretary of State, he returned to government in 1700 and was made an earl by the last Stuart monarch, Queen Anne.[678] An application by the survivors for compensation was ignored; they rebuilt their houses, and participated in the 1715 and 1745 Jacobite risings.[679] An archaeological survey in 2019 showed Glencoe was occupied until the Highland Clearances of the mid-18th century.[680]

The brutality of the Massacre shocked Scottish society and became a Jacobite symbol of post-1688 oppression; in 1745, Prince Charles ordered Leslie's pamphlet and the

[673] Kennedy 2017, pp. 32–60.
[674] Frank 1983, pp. 103–115.
[675] Harris 2015, pp. 53–54.
[676] Levine 1999, p. 129.
[677] Somers 1843, p. 545.
[678] Hopkins 1998, p. 395.
[679] Prebble 1973 p. 214.
[680] MacDonald

1695 Parliamentary minutes reprinted in the Edinburgh *Caledonian Mercury*.[681] It was referenced by Whig historian, Thomas Macaulay, in his 1859 *History*.[682] He sought to exonerate William from every charge made by Leslie, including the Massacre, which he claimed was part of a Campbell–MacDonald clan feud.[683]

Victorian Scotland developed values that were pro-Union and pro-Empire, while also being uniquely Scottish.[684] Historical divisions meant this was largely expressed through a shared cultural identity, while the study of Scottish history itself virtually disappeared from universities.[685] Glencoe became part of a focus on 'the emotional trappings of the Scottish past...bonnie Scotland of the bens and glens and misty shieling, the Jacobites, Mary, Queen of Scots, tartan mania and the raising of historical statuary.'[686]

After the study of Scottish history re-emerged in the 1950s, Leslie's perspectives continued to shape views of William's reign as particularly disastrous for Scotland. The massacre was only one in a series of incidents deemed as such, including the Darien scheme, the famine of the late 1690s, and the Union of 1707.[687] It is still commemorated in an annual ceremony by the Clan Donald Society; initiated in 1930, this is held at the Upper Carnoch memorial, a tapering Celtic cross installed in 1883 at the eastern end of Glencoe village.[688]

Its continuing emotional power was demonstrated in 1998, when a plaque was installed at a granite boulder south of Carnach.[689] Originally known as the 'Soldier's Stone', [690] in the late 19th century, it was renamed *Clach Eanruig*, or 'Henry's Stone'; it is currently named the Henderson Stone, after the family reputed to be pipers to MacIain.[691]

Glencoe was a popular topic with 19th-century poets, the best-known work being Sir Walter Scott's "Massacre of Glencoe".[692] It was used as a subject by Thomas Campbell and George Gilfillan, whose main claim to modern literary fame is his sponsorship of William McGonagall, allegedly the worst poet in British history. Other poetic references include Letitia Elizabeth Landon's "Glencoe" (1823), T. S.

---

[681] Hopkins 1998, p. 1.
[682] Macaulay 1859, p. 277.
[683] Firth 1918, p. 287.
[684] Morris 1992, pp. 37–39.
[685] Kidd 1997, p. 100.
[686] Ash 1980, p. 10.
[687] Kennedy 2017, pp. 32–33.
[688] *"Site Record for Glencoe, Massacre of Glencoe Memorial; Macdonald's Monument; Glencoe Massacre"*. Royal Commission on the Ancient and Historical Monuments of Scotland.
[689] Pagan
[690] Dorson 1971, p. 156.
[691] Donaldson 1876, pp. 298, 301.
[692] Scott

Eliot's "Rannoch, by Glencoe" and "Two Poems from Glencoe" by Douglas Stewart.[693]

Examples in literature include "The Masks of Purpose" by Eric Linklater, and the novels *Fire Bringer* by David Clement-Davies, *Corrag* (known as *Witch Light* in paperback) by Susan Fletcher and *Lady of the Glen* by Jennifer Roberson. William Croft Dickinson references Glencoe in his 1963 short story "The Return of the Native". *A Song of Ice and Fire* author, George R. R. Martin, cites the Glencoe Massacre as one of two historical influences on the infamous "Red Wedding" in his 2000 book *A Storm of Swords*.[694]

It was"the subject of a popular folk song called The Massacre of Glencoe written by Jim Mclean in 1962.

---

[693] Stewart Douglas. Two Poems from Glencoe
[694] Hibberd, James (2 June 2013). "Game of Thrones author George R R Martin on why he wrote the red wedding". *Entertainment Weekly*.

Chapter thirteen

The Battle of Culloden Moor 1746

In the Eighteenth Century, there were two uprisings seeking to put Roman Catholic Scots, back onto the Scottish throne. In 1715 Prince James Stuart, the Old Pretender to the throne as he was dubbed, raised an army of loyal Scotsmen who wanted to see Scotland have its own Kings and Queens again. This was the first of two Jacobean Uprisings. He was defeated and so returned to France.

The second Jacobean uprising was in 1745 and ended in defeated at the Battle of Culloden Moor in April 1746. This second uprising was led by Prince Charles Edward Sturt, "Bonnie Prince Charlie", the eldest son of Prince James.

The Battle of Culloden was the final confrontation of the Jacobite rising of 1745. On 16 April 1746, the Jacobite army of Prince Charles Edward Stuart, was decisively defeated by a British government force under William Augustus, Duke of Cumberland, on Drummossie Moor near Inverness in the Scottish Highlands. It was the last pitched battle fought on British soil.

Charles was the eldest son of James Stuart, the exiled Stuart claimant to the British throne. Believing there was support for a Stuart restoration in both Scotland and England, he landed in Scotland in July 1745: raising an army of Scots Jacobite supporters, he took Edinburgh by September, and defeated a British government force at Prestonpans. The government recalled 12,000 troops from the Continent to deal with the rising: a Jacobite invasion of England reached as far as Derby before turning back, having attracted relatively few English recruits.

The Jacobites, with limited French military support, attempted to consolidate their control of Scotland, whereby early 1746, they were opposed by a substantial government army. A hollow Jacobite victory at Falkirk failed to change the strategic situation: with supplies and pay running short and with the government troops resupplied and reorganised under the Duke of Cumberland, son of British monarch George II, the Jacobite leadership had few options left other than to stand and fight. The two armies eventually met at Culloden, on terrain that gave Cumberland's larger, well-rested force the advantage. The battle lasted only an hour, with the Jacobites suffering a bloody defeat; between 1,500 and 2,000 Jacobites were killed or wounded,[695] [696] while about 300 government soldiers were killed or wounded.[697] While perhaps 5–6,000 Jacobites remained in arms in Scotland, the leadership took the decision to disperse, effectively ending the rising.[698]

Culloden and its aftermath continue to arouse strong feelings. The University of Glasgow awarded the Duke of Cumberland an honorary doctorate, but many modern commentators allege that the aftermath of the battle and subsequent crackdown on Jacobite sympathisers were brutal, earning Cumberland the sobriquet "Butcher". Efforts were subsequently made to further integrate the Scottish Highlands into the Kingdom of Great Britain; civil penalties were introduced to undermine the Scottish clan system, which had provided the Jacobites with the means to rapidly mobilise an army.

Queen Anne, the last monarch of the House of Stuart, died in 1714, with no living children. Under the terms of the Act of Settlement 1701, she was succeeded by her second cousin George I of the House of Hanover, who was a descendant of the Stuarts through his maternal grandmother, Elizabeth, a daughter of James VI and I. Many, however, particularly in Scotland and Ireland, continued to support the claim to the throne of Anne's exiled half-brother James, excluded from the succession under the Act of Settlement due to his Roman Catholic religion.

On 23 July 1745 James's son Charles Edward Stuart landed on Eriskay in the Western Islands in an attempt to reclaim the throne of Great Britain for his father, accompanied only by the "Seven Men of Moidart".[699] Most of his Scottish supporters advised he return to France, but his persuasion of Donald Cameron of Lochiel to back him encouraged others to commit, and the rebellion was launched at Glenfinnan on 19 August. The Jacobite army entered Edinburgh on 17 September, and Charles was proclaimed King of Scotland the next day.[700] Attracting more recruits, the Jacobites comprehensively defeated a government force at the Battle of Prestonpans on 21 September; the London government now recalled the Duke of Cumberland, the King's younger son and commander of the British army in Flanders, along with 12,000 troops.[701]

---

[695] Pittock 2016.
[696] Harrington 1991, p. 83.
[697] Pittock 2016.
[698] Zimmerman, Doron. 2003 *The Jacobite Movement in Scotland and in Exile, 1746-1759*, pp.23-25

[699] Graham, Roderick 2014. *Bonnie Prince Charlie: Truth or Lies*. St Andrew Press. p. 2. ISBN 978-0861537839.
[700] Duffy, Christopher 2003. *The '45: Bonnie Prince Charlie and the untold story of the Jacobite Rising* (First ed.). Orion. p. 198. ISBN 978-0304355259.
[701] Riding, Jacqueline (2016). *Jacobites; A New History of the 45 Rebellion*. Bloomsbury.

The Prince's Council, a committee formed of 15-20 senior leaders, met on 30 and 31 October to discuss plans to invade England. The Scots wanted to consolidate their position and although willing to assist an English rising or French landing, they would not do it on their own.[702] For Charles, the main prize was England; he argued removing the Hanoverians would guarantee an independent Scotland and assured the Scots that the French were planning to land in Southern England, while thousands of English supporters would join once across the border.[703]

Despite their doubts, the Council agreed to the invasion on condition the promised English and French support was forthcoming; the Jacobite army entered England on 8 November.[704] They captured Carlisle on 15 November, then continued south through Preston and Manchester, reaching Derby on 4 December. There had been no sign of a French landing or any significant number of English recruits, while they risked being caught between two armies, each one twice their size: Cumberland's, advancing north from London, and Wade's moving south from Newcastle upon Tyne. Despite Charles' opposition, the Council was overwhelmingly in favour of retreat and turned north the next day.[705]

Apart from a minor skirmish at Clifton Moor, the Jacobite army evaded pursuit and crossed back into Scotland on 20 December. Entering England and returning was a considerable military achievement and morale was high; Jacobite strength increased to over 8,000 with the addition of a substantial north-eastern contingent under Lord Lewis Gordon, as well as Scottish and Irish regulars in French service.[706] French-supplied artillery was used to besiege Stirling Castle, the strategic key to the Highlands. On 17 January, the Jacobites dispersed a relief force under Henry Hawley at the Battle of Falkirk Muir, although the siege made little progress.[707]

On 1 February, the siege of Stirling was abandoned and the Jacobites retreated to Inverness.[708] Cumberland's army advanced along the coast and entered Aberdeen on 27 February; both sides halted operations until the weather improved.[709] Several French shipments were received during the winter but the Royal Navy's blockade led to shortages of both money and food; when Cumberland left

p. 195. ISBN 978-1408819128.
[702] Riding, p.199.
[703] Stephen, Jeffrey (January 2010). "Scottish Nationalism and Stuart Unionism". *Journal of British Studies*. 49 (1, Scottish Special): 55–58. doi:10.1086/644534.
[704] Duffy, p.223
[705] Riding, pp. 304–305
[706] Home, Robert 2014. *The History of the Rebellion* (First published 1802 ed.). Nabu Publishing. pp. 329–333. ISBN 978-1295587384.
[707] Riding, pp. 209–216
[708] Home, pp. 353–354
[709] Riding, pp. 377–378

Aberdeen on 8 April, Charles and his officers agreed giving battle was their best option.[710]

The Jacobite Army is often assumed to have been largely composed of Gaelic-speaking Catholic Highlanders: in reality nearly a quarter of the rank and file were recruited in Aberdeenshire, Forfarshire and Banffshire, with another 20% from Perthshire.[711] [712] By 1745, Catholicism was the preserve of a small minority, and large numbers of those who joined the Rebellion were Non-juring Episcopalians.[713] Although the army was predominantly Scots, it contained a few English recruits plus significant numbers of Irish, Scottish and French professionals in French service with the Irish Brigade and *Royal Ecossais*.

To mobilise an army quickly, the Jacobites had relied heavily on the traditional right retained by many Scottish landowners to raise their tenants for military service. This assumed limited, short-term warfare: a long campaign demanded greater professionalism and training, and the colonels of some Highland regiments considered their men to be uncontrollable.[714] A typical 'clan' regiment was officered by the heavily-armed tacksmen, with their subtenants acting as common soldiers.[715] [716] The tacksmen served in the front rank, taking proportionately high casualties; the gentlemen of the Appin Regiment suffered one quarter of those killed, and one third of those wounded from their regiment.[717] Many Jacobite regiments, notably those from the north-east, were organised and drilled more conventionally, but as with the Highland regiments were inexperienced and hurriedly trained.

The Jacobites started the campaign relatively poorly armed. Although Highlanders are often pictured equipped with a broadsword, targe and pistol, this applied mainly to officers and most men seem to have been drilled in conventional fashion with muskets as their main weapon.[718] As the campaign progressed, supplies from France improved their equipment considerably and by the time of Culloden, many were equipped with 0.69 in (17.5 mm) calibre French and Spanish firelocks.[719]

[710] Pittock, Murray 2016. *Culloden: Great Battles*. OUP. pp. 58–98 passim. ISBN 978-0199664078.
[711] Pittock, Murray 1998. *Jacobitism*. Macmillan. p. 99.
[712] Aikman, Christian 2001. *No Quarter Given: The Muster Roll of Prince Charles Edward Stuart's Army, 1745-46*. Neil Wilson Publishing. p. 93. ISBN 978-1903238028.
[713] Szechi, Daniel, Sankey, Margaret (November 2001). "Elite Culture and the Decline of Scottish Jacobitism 1716-1745". *Past & Present*. (173): 90–128. doi:10.1093/past/173.1.90. JSTOR 3600841.
[714] Harrington 1991, pp. 35–40.
[715] Reid 1997, p. 58.
[716] Barthorp, Michael 1982. The Jacobite Rebellions 1689–1745. Man-at-arms' series. p 17-18. Osprey Publishing. ISBN 0-85045-432-8.
[717] Reid 1997, p. 58.
[718] Reid 2006, pp. 20–22.
[719] Reid 2006, pp. 20–22.

During the latter stage of the campaign, the Jacobites were reinforced by French regulars, mainly drawn from *Piquets* or detachments from regiments of the Irish Brigade along with a Franco-Irish cavalry unit, Fitz James's Horse. Around 500 men from the Irish Brigade fought in the battle, around 100 of whom were thought to have been recruited from 6th (Guise's) Foot taken prisoner at Fort Augustus. The *Royal Écossais* also contained British deserters; its commander attempted to raise a second battalion after the unit had arrived in Scotland.[720] Much of the Jacobite cavalry had been effectively disbanded due to a shortage of horses; Fitzjames', Strathallan's Horse, the Life Guards and the 'Scotch Hussars' retained a reduced presence at Culloden. The Jacobite artillery is generally regarded as playing little part in the battle, all but one of the cannons being a 3-pounders.[721]

Cumberland's army at Culloden comprised 16 infantry battalions, including four Scottish units and one Irish.[722] The bulk of the infantry units had already seen action at Falkirk, but had been further drilled, rested and resupplied since then.

Many of the infantry were experienced veterans of Continental service, but on the outbreak of the Jacobite rising, extra incentives were given to recruits to fill the ranks of depleted units. On 6 September 1745, every recruit who joined the Guards before 24 September was given £6, and those who joined in the last days of the month were given £4. In theory, a standard single-battalion British infantry regiment was 815 strong, including officers, but were often smaller in practice and at Culloden, the regiments were not much larger than about 400 men.[723]

The government cavalry arrived in Scotland in January 1746. Many were not combat experienced, having spent the preceding years on anti-smuggling duties. A standard cavalryman had a Land Service pistol and a carbine, but the main weapon used by the British cavalry was a sword with a 35-inch blade.[724]

The Royal Artillery vastly outperformed their Jacobite counterparts during the Battle of Culloden. However, up until this point in the campaign, the government artillery had performed dismally. The main weapon of the artillery was the 3-pounder. This weapon had a range of 500 yards (460 m) and fired two kinds of shot: round iron and canister. The other weapon used was the Coehorn mortar. These had a calibre of $4\frac{2}{5}$ inches (11 cm).[725]

---

[720] Reid 2006, pp. 22–23.
[721] Reid 2006, pp. 22–23.
[722] Reid 2002, p. *author's note*.
[723] Harrington 1991, pp. 25–29.
[724] Harrington 1991, pp. 29–33.
[725] Harrington 1991, pp. 29–33.

Following the defeat at Falkirk, Cumberland arrived in Scotland in January 1746 to take command of government forces. Deciding to wait out the winter, he moved his main army northwards to Aberdeen: 5,000 Hessian troops under Prince Frederick were stationed around Perth to suppress a possible Jacobite offensive in that area. The weather had improved to such an extent by 8 April that Cumberland resumed the campaign: his army reached Cullen on 11 April, where it was joined by six further battalions and two cavalry regiments.[726] On 12 April, Cumberland's force forded the Spey. This had been guarded by a 2000-strong Jacobite detachment under Lord John Drummond, but Drummond retreated towards Elgin and Nairn rather than offering resistance, for which he was sharply criticised after the rising by several Jacobite memoirists. By 14 April, the Jacobites had evacuated Nairn, and Cumberland's army camped at Balblair just west of the town.[727]

Several significant Jacobite units were still *en route* or engaged far to the north, but on learning of the government advance their main army of about 5,400 left its base at Inverness on 15 April and assembled in battle order at the estate of Culloden 5 miles (8 km) to the east.[728] The Jacobite leadership was divided on whether to give battle or abandon Inverness, but with most of their dwindling supplies stored in the town, there were few options left for holding their army together.[729] The Jacobite adjutant-general, John O'Sullivan, identified a suitable site for a defensive action at Drummossie Moor,[730] a stretch of open moorland between the walled enclosures of Culloden Parks[731] to the north and those of Culwhiniac to the south.[732]

Jacobite lieutenant-general Lord George Murray stated he "did not like the ground" at Drummossie Moor, which was relatively flat and open, and suggested an alternative, steeply sloping site near Daviot Castle. This was inspected by Brigadier Stapleton of the Irish Brigade and Colonel Ker on the morning of 15 April; they rejected it as the site was overlooked and the ground "mossy and soft". Murray's choice also failed to protect the road into Inverness, a key objective of giving battle.[733] The issue had not been fully resolved by the time of the battle and in the event, circumstances largely dictated the point at which the Jacobites formed line, some distance to the west of the site originally chosen by Sullivan.[734]

---

[726] Harrington 1991, p. 44.
[727] Reid 2002, pp. 51–56.
[728] "Map of Drummossie". MultiMap.
[729] Pittock 2016, p.58
[730] "Map of Drummossie Moor". MultiMap.
[731] Map of Culloden". MultiMap.
[732] Get map, *UK: Ordnance Survey*.
[733] Pittock 2016, p.60

On 15 April, the government army celebrated Cumberland's twenty-fifth birthday by issuing two gallons of brandy to each regiment.[735] At Murray's suggestion, the Jacobites tried that evening to repeat the success of Prestonpans by carrying out a night attack on the government encampment.

Murray proposed that they set off at dusk and march to Nairn; he planned to have the right wing of the first line attack Cumberland's rear, while the Duke of Perth with the left wing would attack the government's front. In support of Perth, Lord John Drummond and Charles would bring up the second line. The Jacobite force, however, started out well after dark, partly due to concerns they would be spotted by ships of the Royal Navy then in the Moray Firth. Murray led them across country with the intention of avoiding government outposts: Murray's one time *aide-de-camp*, James Chevalier de Johnstone later wrote, "this march across country in a dark night which did not allow us to follow any track was accompanied with confusion and disorder".[736]

By the time the leading troop had reached Culraick, still 2 miles (3.2 km) from where Murray's wing was to cross the River Nairn and encircle the town, there was only one hour left before dawn. After a heated council with other officers, Murray concluded that there was not enough time to mount a surprise attack and that the offensive should be aborted. Sullivan went to inform Charles Edward Stuart of the change of plan but missed him in the dark. Meanwhile, instead of retracing his path back, Murray led his men left, down the Inverness Road. In the darkness, while Murray led one-third of the Jacobite forces back to camp, the other two-thirds continued towards their original objective, unaware of the change in plan. One account of that night even records that Perth's men contacted government troops before realising the rest of the Jacobite force had turned home. A few historians, such as Jeremy Black and Christopher Duffy, have suggested that if Perth had carried on the night attack might have remained viable, though most have disagreed, as perhaps only 1200 of the Jacobite force accompanied him.[737] [738] [739]

Not long after the exhausted Jacobite forces had made it back to Culloden, an officer of Lochiel's regiment, who had been left behind after falling asleep in a wood, arrived with a report of advancing government troops.[740] By then, many Jacobite soldiers had dispersed in search of food or returned to Inverness, while others were

[734] Pittock 2016, p.58
[735] Harrington (1991), p. 44.
[736] Reid (2002), pp. 56–58.
[737] Britain as a military power 1688–1815 1999, p. 32
[738] Black, Jeremy, Culloden and the '45 (1990)
[739] Pittock 2016 p.67
[740] Reid 2002, pp. 56–58.

asleep in ditches and outbuildings; several hundred of their army may have missed the battle.

Following the abortive night attack, the Jacobites formed up in substantially the same battle order as the previous day, with the Highland regiments forming the first line. They faced north-east over common grazing land, with the Water of Nairn about 1 km to their right.[741] Their left wing, anchored on the Culloden Park walls, was under the command of the titular Duke of Perth, James Drummond; his brother John Drummond commanded the centre. The right wing, flanked by the Culwhiniac enclosure walls, was led by Murray. Behind them the 'Low Country' regiments were drawn up in column, in accordance with French practice. During the morning snow and hail "started falling very thick" onto the already wet ground, later turning to rain, though the weather turned fair as the battle started.[742]

Cumberland's army had struck camp and were underway by 5 am, leaving the main Inverness Road and marching across country. By 10 am the Jacobites finally saw them approaching at a distance of around 4 km; at 3 km from the Jacobite position Cumberland gave the order to form line, and the army marched forward in full battle order.[743] John Daniel, an Englishman serving with Charles's army, recorded that on seeing the government troops the Jacobites began to "huzza and bravado them", though without response: "on the contrary, they continued proceeding, like a deep sullen river".[744] Once within 500 metres, Cumberland moved his artillery up through the ranks.[745]

As Cumberland's forces formed into line of battle, it became clear that their right flank was in an exposed position and Cumberland moved up additional cavalry and other units to reinforce it.[746] In the Jacobite lines, Sullivan moved two battalions of Lord Lewis Gordon's regiment to cover the walls at Culwhiniac against a possible flank attack by government dragoons. Murray also moved the Jacobite right slightly forwards: this "change meant", as Sullivan called it, had the unintended result of skewing the Jacobite line and opening gaps, so Sullivan ordered Perth's, Glenbucket's and the Edinburgh Regiment from the second line to the first. While the Jacobite front rank now substantially outnumbered that of Cumberland, their reserve was further depleted, increasing their reliance on a successful initial attack.[747]

---

[741] Pittock 2016 p.69
[742] Pittock 2016 p.65
[743] Pittock 2016 p.79
[744] Blaikie, Walter 1916. *Origins of the Forty-Five*. Scottish History Society. p. 213.
[745] Pittock 2016 p.79
[746] Pittock 2016 p.83
[747] Pittock (2016) p.85

At approximately 1 p.m. Finlayson's Jacobite batteries opened fire, possibly in response to Cumberland sending forward Lord Bury to within 100 metres of the Jacobite lines to "ascertain the strength of their battery".[748] The government artillery responded shortly afterwards: while some later Jacobite memoirs suggest their troops were then subjected to artillery bombardment for 30 minutes or more while Charles delayed an advance, government accounts suggest a much shorter exchange before the Jacobites attacked. Campbell of Airds, in the rear, timed it at 9; Cumberland's aide-de-camp Yorke suggested only 2 or 3 minutes.[749]

The duration implies that the government artillery is unlikely to have fired more than thirty rounds at extreme range: statistical analysis concludes that this would have caused only 20-30 Jacobite casualties at this stage, rather than the hundreds suggested by some accounts. [750]

Shortly after 1 pm, Charles issued an order to advance, which Col. Harry Kerr of Graden first took to Perth's regiment, on the extreme left. He then rode down the Jacobite line giving orders to each regiment in turn; Sir John MacDonald and Brigadier Stapleton were also sent forward to repeat the order.[751] As the Jacobites left their lines, the government gunners switched to canister; this was augmented by fire from the coehorn mortars situated behind the government front line. As there was no need for careful aiming when using canister, the rate of fire increased dramatically, and the Jacobites found themselves advancing into heavy fire.

On the Jacobite right, the Atholl Brigade, Lochiel's and the Appin Regiment left their start positions and charged towards Barrell's and Munro's regiments. Within a few hundred yards, however, the centre regiments, Lady Mackintosh's and Lovat's, had begun to swerve rightwards, either trying to avoid canister fire or in order to follow the firmer ground along the road running diagonally across Drummossie Moor. The five regiments became entangled as a single mass, converging on the government left. The confusion was worsened when the three largest regiments lost their commanding officers, who were all at the front of the advance: MacGillivray and MacBean of Lady Mackintosh's both went down; Inverallochie of Lovat's fell, and Lochiel had his ankles broken by canister within a few yards of the government lines.

The Jacobite left, by contrast, advanced much more slowly, hampered by boggy ground and by having several hundred yards further to cover. According to the account of Andrew Henderson, Lord John Drummond walked across the front of the

[748] Pittock 2016 p.86
[749] Pollard, Tony 2009. *Culloden*. Pen and Sword (Kindle ed). p. loc. 2128.
[750] Pollard, Tony 2009. *Culloden*. Pen and Sword (Kindle ed). p. loc. 2128.
[751] Pittock 2016 p.87

Jacobite lines to try and tempt the government infantry into firing early, but they maintained their discipline. The three MacDonald regiments – Keppoch's, Clanranald's and Glengarry's – stalled before resorting to ineffectual long-range musket fire; they also lost senior officers, as Clanranald was wounded and Keppoch killed. The smaller units on their right – Maclachlan's Regiment and Chisholm's and Monaltrie's battalions – advanced into an area swept by artillery fire and suffered heavy losses before falling back.

The Jacobite right was particularly hard hit by a volley from the government regiments at nearly point blank range, but many of its men still reached the government lines and, for the first time, a battle was decided by a direct clash between charging Highlanders and formed infantry equipped with muskets and socket bayonets. The brunt of the Jacobite impact, led by Lochiel's regiment, was taken by just two government regiments – Barrell's 4th Foot and Dejean's 37th Foot. Barrell's lost 17 and suffered 108 wounded, out of a total of 373 officers and men. Dejean's lost 14 and had 68 wounded, with this unit's left wing taking a disproportionately higher number of casualties. Barrell's regiment temporarily lost one of its two colours. Major-General Huske, who was in command of the government's second line, quickly organised the counterattack. Huske ordered forward all of Lord Sempill's Fourth Brigade which had a combined total of 1,078 men (Sempill's 25th Foot, Conway's 59th Foot, and Wolfe's 8th Foot). Also sent forward to plug the gap was Bligh's 20th Foot, which took up position between Sempill's 25th and Dejean's 37th. Huske's counter formed a five battalion strong horseshoe-shaped formation which trapped the Jacobite right wing on three sides.[752]

Poor Barrell's regiment were sorely pressed by those desperadoes and outflanked. One stand of their colours was taken; Colonel Riches hand XXXis off in their defence ... We marched up to the enemy, and our left, outflanking them, wheeled in upon them; the whole then gave them 5 or 6 fires with vast execution, while their front had nothing left to oppose us, but their XXX pistols and broadswords; and fire from their centre and rear, (as, by this time, they were 20 or 30 deep) was vastly more fatal to themselves, than us.

With the Jacobite left under Perth failing to advance further, Cumberland ordered two troops of Cobham's 10th Dragoons to ride them down. The boggy ground, however, impeded the cavalry and they turned to engage the Irish Picquets whom Sullivan and Lord John Drummond had brought up to stabilise the deteriorating Jacobite left flank. Cumberland later wrote: "They came running on in their wild manner, and upon the right where I had place myself, imagining the greatest push

---

[752] Reid 2002, pp. 68–72.

would be there, they came down there several times within a hundred yards of our men, firing their pistols and brandishing their swords, but the Royal Scots and Pulteneys hardly took their fire-locks from their shoulders, so that after those faint attempts they made off; and the little squadrons on our right were sent to pursue them".[753]

With the collapse of the left wing, Murray brought up the *Royal Écossais* and Kilmarnock's Footguards who were still at this time unengaged, but by the time they had been brought into position, the Jacobite first line was in rout. The *Royal Écossais* exchanged musket fire with Campbell's 21st and commenced an orderly retreat, moving along the Culwhiniac enclosure in order to shield themselves from artillery fire. Immediately the half battalion of Highland militia, commanded by Captain Colin Campbell of Ballimore, which had stood inside the enclosure ambushed them. In the encounter Campbell of Ballimore was killed along with five of his men. The result was that the *Royal Écossais* and Kilmarnock's Footguards were forced out into the open moor and were engaged by three squadrons of Kerr's 11th Dragoons: the fleeing Jacobites must have put up a fight, for Kerr's 11th recorded at least 16 horses killed during the entirety of the battle.

The Irish Picquets under Stapleton bravely covered the Highlanders' retreat from the battlefield, preventing the fleeing Jacobites from suffering heavy casualties: this action cost half of the 100 casualties they suffered in the battle.[754] The *Royal Écossais* appear to have retired from the field in two wings; one part surrendered after suffering 50 killed or wounded, but their colours were not taken and a large number retired from the field with the Jacobite Lowland regiments.[755] A few Highland regiments also withdrew in good order, notably Lovat's first battalion who retired with colours flying; the government dragoons let them withdraw rather than risk a confrontation.[756]

The standby the French regulars gave Charles and other senior officers time to escape. Charles seems to have been rallying Perth's and Glenbucket's regiments when Sullivan rode up to Captain Shea, commander of his bodyguard: "You see all is going to pot. Yu can be of no great succour, so before a general deroute which will soon be, seize upon the Prince & take him off ...".[757] Contrary to government depictions of Charles as a coward, he yelled "they won't take me alive!" and called for a final charge into the government lines:[758] Shea however followed Sullivan's

[753] Roberts 2002, p. 173.
[754] McGarry, *Irish Brigades Abroad* p. 122
[755] Reid 2002, pp. 80–85.
[756] Pittock 2016 p.95
[757] Reid 2002, pp. 80–85.
[758] Pittock 2016 p.134

advice and led Charles from the field, accompanied by Perth and Glenbucket's regiments.

From this point on the fleeing Jacobite forces were split into several groups: the Lowland regiments retired in order southwards, making their way to Ruthven Barracks, while the remains of the Jacobite right wing also retired to the south. The MacDonald and other Highland left-wing regiments however were cut off by the government cavalry and forced to retreat down the road to Inverness. The result was that they were a clear target for government dragoons: Major-general Humphrey Bland led the pursuit of the fleeing Highlanders, giving "Quarter to None but about Fifty French Officers and Soldiers".[759]

Jacobite casualties are estimated at 1,500 – 2,000 killed or wounded, with many of these occurring in the pursuit after the battle.[760] [761] Cumberland's official list of prisoners taken includes 154 Jacobites and 222 "French" prisoners (men from the 'foreign units' in the French service). Added to the official list of those apprehended were 172 of the Earl of Cromartie's men, captured after a brief engagement the day before near Littleferry.

In striking contrast to the Jacobite losses, the government losses were reported as 50 dead and 259 wounded. Of the 438 men of Barrell's 4th Foot, 17 were killed and 104 were wounded. However, a large proportion of those recorded as wounded are likely to have died of their wounds: only 29 men out of the 104 wounded from Barrell's 4th Foot later survived to claim pensions, while all six of the artillerymen recorded as wounded died.[762]

Several senior Jacobite commanding officers were casualties including Keppoch, Viscount Strathallan, commissary-general Lachlan Maclachlan and Walter Stapleton, who died of wounds shortly after the battle. Others, including Kilmarnock, were captured. The only government officer casualty of high rank was Lord Robert Kerr, the son of William Kerr, 3rd Marquess of Lothian. Sir Robert Rich, 5th Baronet, who was a lieutenant-colonel and the senior officer commanding Barrell's 4th Foot, was badly wounded, losing his left hand and receiving several wounds to his head, and several captains and lieutenants had also been wounded.

As the first of the fleeing Highlanders approached Inverness they were met by the 2nd battalion of Lovat's regiment, led by the Master of Lovat. It has been suggested

---

[759] Reid 2002, pp. 80–85.
[760] Pittock 2016.
[761] Harrington 1991, p. 83
[762] Pittock 2016

that Lovat shrewdly switched sides and turned upon the retreating Jacobites, an act that would explain his remarkable rise in fortune in the years that followed.[763]

Following the battle, the Jacobites' Lowland regiments headed south, towards Corrybrough and made their way to Ruthven Barracks, while their Highland units made their way north, towards Inverness and on through to Fort Augustus. There they were joined by Barisdale's battalion of Glengarry's regiment and a small battalion of MacGregors.[764] At least two of those present at Ruthven, James Johnstone and John Daniel, recorded that the Highland troops remained in good spirits despite the defeat and eager to resume the campaign. At this point, continuing Jacobite resistance remained potentially viable in terms of manpower: at least a third of the army had either missed or slept through Culloden, which along with survivors from the battle gave a potential force of 5-6000 men.[765] However the roughly 1,500 men who assembled at Ruthven Barracks received orders from Charles to the effect that the army should disperse until he returned with French support.[766]

Similar orders must have been received by the Highland units at Fort Augustus, and by 18 April most of the Jacobite army was disbanded. Officers and men of the units in French service made for Inverness, where they surrendered as prisoners of war on 19 April. Most of the rest of the army broke up, with men heading for home or attempting to escape abroad,[767] although the Appin Regiment amongst others was still in arms as late as July.

Many senior Jacobites made their way to *Loch nan Uamh*, where Charles Edward Stuart had first landed at the outset of the campaign in 1745. Here on 30 April they were met by two French frigates – the *Mars* and *Bellone*. Two days later the French ships were spotted and attacked by three smaller Royal Navy sloops – the *Greyhound, Baltimore*, and *Terror*. The result was the last real engagement of the campaign; during the six hours in which the battle continued the Jacobites recovered cargo which had been landed by the French ships, including £35,000 of gold.[768]

With visible proof that the French had not deserted them, a group of Jacobite leaders attempted to prolong the campaign. On 8 May, nearby at Murlaggan, Lochiel, Lochgarry, Clanranald and Barisdale all agreed to rendezvous at Invermallie on 18 May, as did Lord Lovat and his son. The plan was that there they would be joined by what remained of Keppoch's men and Macpherson of Cluny's regiment, which had

---

[763] Reid 2002, pp. 88–90.
[764] Reid 2002, pp. 88–90.
[765] Zimmerman, Doron (2003) *The Jacobite Movement in Scotland and in Exile, 1746-1759*, p.25
[766] Roberts (2002), pp. 182–83.
[767] Reid 2002, pp. 88–90.
[768] Reid 2002, pp. 88–90.

not taken part in the battle at Culloden. However, things did not go as planned; after about a month of relative inactivity, Cumberland moved his army into the Highlands and on 17 May three battalions of regulars and eight Highland companies reoccupied Fort Augustus. The same day, the Macphersons surrendered. On the day of the planned rendezvous, Clanranald never appeared and Lochgarry and Barisdale only showed up with about 300 combined, most of whom immediately dispersed in search of food: Lochiel, who commanded possibly the strongest Jacobite regiment at Culloden, was only able to muster 300 men. The group dispersed, and the following week the Government launched punitive expeditions into the Highlands which continued throughout the summer. [769]

Following his flight from the battle, Charles Edward Stuart made his way towards the Hebrides, accompanied by a small group of supporters. By 20 April, Charles had reached *Arisaig* on the west coast of Scotland. After spending a few days with his close associates, he sailed for the island of Benbecula in the Outer Hebrides. From there he travelled to Scalpay, off the east coast of Harris, and from there made his way to Stornoway.[770] For five months Charles criss-crossed the Hebrides, constantly pursued by government supporters and under threat from local lairds who were tempted to betray him for the £30,000 upon his head.[771] During this time he met Flora Macdonald, who famously aided him in a narrow escape to Skye. Finally, on 19 September, Charles reached Borrodale on *Loch nan Uamh* in *Arisaig*, where his party boarded two small French ships, which ferried them to France.[772] He never returned to Scotland.

The morning following the Battle of Culloden, Cumberland issued a written order reminding his men that "the public orders of the rebels yesterday was to give us no quarter". Cumberland alluded to the belief that such orders had been found upon the bodies of fallen Jacobites. In the days and weeks that followed, versions of the alleged orders were published in the *Newcastle Journal* and the *Gentleman's Journal*. Today only one copy of the alleged order to "give no quarter" exists.[773] It is however considered to be nothing but a poor attempt at forgery, for it is neither written nor signed by Murray, and it appears on the bottom half of a copy of a declaration published in 1745. In any event, Cumberland's order was not carried out for two days, after which contemporary accounts report then that for the next two days the moor was searched, and all those wounded were put to death. On the other hand, the orders issued by Lord George Murray for the conduct of the aborted night

---

[769] Reid 2002, pp. 88–90.
[770] Harrington 1991, pp. 85–86.
[771] Prebble 1973, p. 301.
[772] Harrington 1991, pp. 85–86.
[773] Roberts 2002, pp. 177–80.

attack in the early hours of 16 April suggest that it would have been every bit as merciless. The instructions were to use only swords, dirks and bayonets, to overturn tents, and subsequently to locate "a swelling or bulge in the fallen tent, there to strike and push vigorously".[774] In total, over 20,000 head of livestock, sheep, and goats were driven off and sold at Fort Augustus, where the soldiers split the profits.[775]

While in Inverness, Cumberland emptied the jails that were full of people imprisoned by Jacobite supporters, replacing them with Jacobites themselves.[776] Prisoners were taken south to England to stand trial for high treason. Many were held on hulks on the Thames or in Tilbury Fort, and executions took place in Carlisle, York and Kennington Common.[777] The common Jacobite supporters fared better than the ranking individuals. In total, 120 common men were executed, one third of them being deserters from the British Army.[778] The common prisoners drew lots amongst themselves and only one out of twenty actually came to trial.

Although most of those who did stand trial were sentenced to death, almost all of these had their sentences commuted to penal transportation to the British colonies for life by the Traitors Transported Act 1746 (20 Geo. II, c. 46).[779] In all, 936 men were thus transported, and 222 more were banished. Even so, 905 prisoners were released under the Act of Indemnity which was passed in June 1747. Another 382 obtained their freedom by being exchanged for prisoners of war who were held by France. Of the total 3,471 prisoners recorded, nothing is known of the fate of 648.[780] The high ranking "rebel lords" were executed on Tower Hill in London.

Following up on the military success won by their forces, the British Government enacted laws further to integrate Scotland – specifically the Scottish Highlands – with the rest of Britain. Members of the Episcopal clergy were required to give oaths of allegiance to the reigning Hanoverian dynasty.[781] The Heritable Jurisdictions (Scotland) Act 1746 ended the hereditary right of landowners to govern justice upon their estates through barony courts.[782] Previous to this act, feudal lords (which

---

[774] Roberts 2002, pp. 177–80.

[775] Magnusson 2003, p. 623

[776] Reid 2002, pp. 88–90.

[777] Prebble (1973), p. 301.

[778] Prebble 1973, p. 301.

[779] "An act to prevent the return of such rebels and traitors concerned in the late rebellion, as have been, or shall be pardoned on condition of transportation; and also, to hinder their going into the enemy's country."

[780] Roberts 2002, pp. 196–97

[781] Britain from 1742 to 1754". *Encyclopædia Britannica.*

[782] Brown 1997, p. 133.

included clan chiefs) had considerable judicial and military power over their followers – such as the oft quoted power of "pit and gallows".[783] [784]Lords who were loyal to the Government were greatly compensated for the loss of these traditional powers, for example the Duke of Argyll was given £21,000.[785] Those lords and clan chiefs who had supported the Jacobite rebellion were stripped of their estates and these were then sold and the profits were used to further trade and agriculture in Scotland.[786] The forfeited estates were managed by factors. Anti-clothing measures were taken against the highland dress by an Act of Parliament in 1746. The result was that the wearing of <u>tartan</u> was banned except as a uniform for officers and soldiers in the British Army and later landed men and their sons.[787]

---

[783] Prebble 1973, p. 301.
[784] Britain from 1742 to 1754". *Encyclopædia Britannica*. Archived from the original on 20 March 2009. Retrieved
[785] Prebble 1973, p. 301.
[786] *"Britain from 1742 to 1754"*. *Encyclopædia Britannica.*
[787] Gibson 2002, pp. 27–28.

Chapter fourteen

THE ACT OF PROSCRIPTION

The first act to disarm the Highlands was introduced in 1716 after Charles' Father's abortive attempt the year before to depose King George I: the Old Pretender failed to arrive in Britain until it was over and French backing evaporated with the death of Louis XIV. Culloden brought about a third attempt to subdue to Highlands, this time with the Act of Proscription 1747 which was introduced in 1746 but gave the authorities a year to prise all arms from the Highland miscreants. August 1st 1747 was the 'crunch' day for the Highlanders and "no man or boy, within that part of Great Britain called Scotland will wear or put on the clothes commonly called Highland Clothes (that is to say) the plaid, philibeg, or little kilt, trews, shoulder belts, or any part whatsoever of what peculiarly belongs to the highland garb; and that no tartan, or party-coloured plaid or stuff shall be used for great coats, or for upper coats " For transgressing this new Act, which for the first time included Highland dress, the punishment was six months in prison or, if a second offender, "transportation to any of his Majesty's plantations beyond the seas and there to remain for a space of seven years."

There were many contemporary reports indicating that "it would take more than act of Parliament to stop the Highlander wearing his traditional clothes." Contrary to popular and oft cited belief, the Act did not ban tartan! Nor incidentally, did it ban playing bagpipes or Gaelic. However, whilst not banned per se, the removal of the principal use for tartan meant that the skills used for dyeing and particularly, the technicalities of weaving it, meant that much of the traditional know-how was lost within a generation. And with it, some ancient patterns undoubtedly disappeared.

During the period of the ban the raising of Highland Regiments for foreign service did much to promote the profile of the loyal Highlander and his dress, including tartan. By the early 1780s the Jacobite threat was no longer and Highland Regiments with their kilts and tartan had won renown in support of the Crown. This rehabilitation led to a move to restore Highland Dress to civilians in the Highlands.

Repeal of the Act of Proscription of the Highland Garb.
Given Royal Assent by King George III, on Monday 1st. July1782.

This copy of the text of the Act, is written in old Scots, so if a word looks wrong because it has an "f" where it should not be, that is because back then what we know as an "s" today was written as an "f" back then.

An Act to repeal fo much of an Act, made in the nineteenth Year of King George the Second (for the more effectual difarming the Highlands in Scotland, and for the other Purpofes therein mentioned), as reftrains the Ufe of the Highland Drefs.

WHEREAS by an Act, made in the nineteenth Year of the Reign of his late Majefty King George the Second, intituled, An Act for the more effectual difarming the Highlands in Scotland, and for more effectually fecuring the Peace of the faid Highlands; and for reftraining the Ufe of the Highland Drefs; and for further indemnifying fuch Perfons as have acted in Defence of his Majefty's Perfon and Government, during the unnatural Rebellion; and for indemnifying the Judges and other Officers of the Court of Justiciary in Scotland, for not performing the Northern Circuit in May, one thousand feven hundred and forty-fix; and for obliging the Mafters and Teachers of private Schools in Scotland, and Chaplains, Tutors, and Governors of Children or Youth, to take the Oaths to his Majefty, his Heirs and Succeffors, and to Register the fame; it was, among other Things, enacted, That, from and after the firft day of August, one thoufand feven hundred and forty feven, no Man or Boy, within that Part of Great Britain called Scotland, other than fuch as should be employed as Officers and Soldiers in his Majefty's Forces, fhould, on any Pretence whatfoever, wear or put on the Clothes, commonly called Highland Clothes; (that is to fay,) The Plaid, Philebeg or Little Kilt, Trowfe, Shoulder belts, or any Part whatfoever of what peculiarly belongs to the Highland Garb, and that no Tartan, or Party-coloured Plaid or Stuff, fhould be, ufed for Great Coats or for Upper Coats, under the Penalties therein mentioned; and the Time appointed for laying afide the faid Highland Drefs was, in certain Cafes therein mentioned, further prolonged by feveral Acts, one made in the twentieth, and the other in the twenty-firft Year of the Reign of his faid late Majefty King George the Second: And whereas it is judged expedient that fo much of the Acts above mentioned as reftrains the Ufe of the Highland Drefs fhould be repealed: Be it therefore enacted by the King's moft Excellent Majefty, by and with the Advice and Confent of the Lords Spiritual and Temporal, and Commons, in this prefent Parliament affembled, and by the Authority of the fame, That fo much of the Acts above-mentioned, or any other Act or Acts of Parliament, as reftrains the Ufe of the Highland Drefs, be, and the fame are hereby repealed.

That I hope explains why there were white Scots
sent to the New World, effectively as slaves.

Chapter fifteen

Native American Massacres

We know turn our attention to the many massacres of Native Americans not just at the hands of the Europeans and others that came to settle in the New World, but by other Native Americans long before Christopher Columbus arrived on the shores of America.

Definition of an Indian Massacre:

In the history of the European colonization of the Americas, an Indian massacre is any incident between European settlers and indigenous peoples wherein one group killed a significant number of the other group outside the confines of mutual combat in war.

"Indian massacre" is a phrase whose use and definition has evolved and expanded over time. The phrase was initially used by European colonists to describe attacks by indigenous Americans which resulted in mass colonial casualties. While similar attacks by colonists on Indian villages were called "raids" or "battles", successful Indian attacks on white settlements or military posts were routinely termed "massacres". Knowing very little about the native inhabitants of the American frontier, the colonists were deeply fearful, and often, European Americans who had rarely – or never – seen a Native American, read Indian atrocity stories in popular literature and newspapers. Emphasis was placed on the depredations of "murderous savages" in their information about Indians, and as the migrants headed further west, they frequently feared the Indians they would encounter.[788] [789]

The phrase eventually became commonly used to also describe mass killings of American Indians. Killings described as "massacres" often had an element of indiscriminate targeting, barbarism, or genocidal intent.[790] According to one historian, "Any discussion of genocide must, of course, eventually consider the so-called Indian Wars", the term commonly used for U.S. Army campaigns to subjugate

---

[788] *Conspiracy Theories in American History: An Encyclopedia*; Peter Knight; ABC-CLIO, 2003; Pg. 523

[789] *American Holocaust: The Conquest of the New World*; David E. Stannard; Oxford University Press, 1993; Pg. 130

[790] *Genocide and International Justice*; Rebecca Joyce Frey; InfoBase Publishing, 2009; Pgs. 7–12, 31–54

Indian nations of the American West beginning in the 1860s. In an older historiography, key events in this history were narrated as battles.

Since the late 20th century, it has become more common for scholars to refer to certain of these events as massacres, especially if there were large numbers of women and children as victims. This includes the Colorado territorial militia's slaughter of Cheyenne at Sand Creek (1864), and the US army's slaughter of Shoshone at Bear River (1863), Blackfeet on the Marias River (1870), and Lakota at Wounded Knee (1890). Some scholars have begun referring to these events as "genocidal massacres," defined as the annihilation of a portion of a larger group, sometimes to provide a lesson to the larger group.[791]

It is difficult to determine the total number of people who died because of "Indian massacres". In *The Wild Frontier: Atrocities during the American Indian War from Jamestown Colony to Wounded Knee*, lawyer William M. Osborn compiled a list of alleged and actual atrocities in what would eventually become the continental United States, from first contact in 1511 until 1890. His parameters for inclusion included the intentional and indiscriminate murder, torture, or mutilation of civilians, the wounded, and prisoners. His list included 7,193 people who died from atrocities perpetrated by those of European descent, and 9,156 people who died from atrocities perpetrated by Native Americans.[792]

In *An American Genocide, The United States and the California Catastrophe, 1846–1873*, historian Benjamin Madley recorded the numbers of killings of California Indians between 1846 and 1873. He found evidence that during this period, at least 9,400 to 16,000 California Indians were killed by non-Indians. Most of these killings occurred in what he said were more than 370 massacres (defined by him as the "intentional killing of five or more disarmed combatants or largely unarmed non-combatants, including women, children, and prisoners, whether in the context of a battle or otherwise").[793]

There are many recorded massacres of Native Americans from the pre-Columbian era when over 486 Native Americans died in 1325 at the Crow Creek Massacres, near what is now known as Chamberlain, South Dakota. With the last such massacre taking place on 19th. January 1911 in Nevada

The American Indian Wars, also known as the American Frontier Wars, the First

[791] *Genocide and American Indian History*; Jeffrey Ostler; University of Oregon, 2015
[792] Osborn, William M. (2001). *The Wild Frontier: Atrocities During The American-Indian War from Jamestown Colony to Wounded Knee*. Garden City, NY: Random House. ISBN 978-0-375-50374-0.
[793] Madley 2016, p.11, p.351

Nations Wars in Canada (French: *Guerres des Premières Nations*) and the Indian Wars were fought by European governments and colonists, and later by the United States and Canadian governments and American and Canadian settlers, against various American Indian and First Nation tribes. These conflicts occurred in North America from the time of the earliest colonial settlements in the 17th century until the early 20th century. The various wars resulted from a wide variety of factors. The European powers and their colonies also enlisted Indian tribes to help them conduct warfare against each other's colonial settlements. After the American Revolution, many conflicts were local to specific states or regions and frequently involved disputes over land use; some entailed cycles of violent reprisal.

As settlers spread westward across North America after 1780, armed conflicts increased in size, duration, and intensity between settlers and various Indian and First Nation tribes. The climax came in the War of 1812, when major Indian coalitions in the Midwest and the South fought against the United States and lost. Conflict with settlers became much less common and was usually resolved by treaty, often through sale or exchange of territory between the federal government and specific tribes. The Indian Removal Act of 1830 authorized the American government to enforce the Indian removal from east of the Mississippi River to the west on the American frontier, especially Oklahoma. The federal policy of removal was eventually refined in the West, as American settlers kept expanding their territories, to relocate Indian tribes to reservations.

- the Algonquians
- Anglo-Powhatan Wars (1610–14, 1622–32, 1644–46), including the 1622 Jamestown Massacre, between English colonists and the Powhatan Confederacy in the Colony of Virginia
- Pequot War of 1636–38 between the Pequot tribe and colonists from the Massachusetts Bay Colony and Connecticut Colony and allied tribes
- Kieft's War (1643–45) in the Dutch territory of New Netherland (New Jersey and New York) between colonists and the Lenape people
- Peach Tree War (1655), the large-scale attack by the Susquehannocks and allied tribes on several New Netherland settlements along the Hudson River
- Esopus Wars (1659–63), conflicts between the Esopus tribe of Lenape Indians and colonial New Netherlanders in Ulster County, New York
- King Philip's War (1675–78) in New England between colonists and the Wampanoags and the Narragansett people
- Tuscarora War (1711–15) in the Province of North Carolina

- Yamasee War (1715–17) in the Province of South Carolina
- Dummer's War (1722–25) in northern New England and French Acadia (New Brunswick and Nova Scotia)
- Pontiac's War (1763–66) in the Great Lakes region[794]
- Lord Dunmore's War (1774) in western Virginia (Kentucky and West Virginia)

In several instances, the conflicts reflected European rivalries, with Indian tribes splitting their alliances among the powers, generally siding with their trading partners. Various tribes fought on each side in King William's War, Queen Anne's War, Dummer's War, King George's War, and the French and Indian War, allying with British or French colonists according to their own self interests.[795]

British merchants and government agents began supplying weapons to Indians living in the United States following the Revolution (1783–1812) in the hope that, if a war broke out, they would fight on the British side. The British further planned to set up an Indian nation in the Ohio-Wisconsin area to block further American expansion.[796] The US protested and declared war in 1812. Most Indian tribes supported the British, especially those allied with Tecumseh, but they were ultimately defeated by General William Henry Harrison. The War of 1812 spread to Indian rivalries, as well.

Many refugees from defeated tribes went over the border to Canada; those in the South went to Florida while it was under Spanish control. During the early 19th century, the federal government was under pressure by settlers in many regions to expel Indians from their areas. The Indian Removal Act of 1830 offered Indians the choices of assimilating and giving up tribal membership, relocation to an Indian reservation with an exchange or payment for lands, or moving west. Some resisted fiercely, most notably the Seminoles in a series of wars in Florida. They were never defeated, although some Seminoles did remove to Indian Territory. The United States gave up on the remainder, by then living defensively deep in the swamps and Everglades. Others were moved to reservations west of the Mississippi River, most famously the Cherokee whose relocation was called the "Trail of Tears."

The American Revolutionary War was essentially two parallel wars for the American Patriots. The war in the east was a struggle against British rule, while the war in the west was an "Indian War". The newly proclaimed United States competed

[794] *Conspiracy Theories in American History: An Encyclopedia*; Peter Knight; ABC-CLIO, 2003; Pg. 523
[795] *American Holocaust: The Conquest of the New World*; David E. Stannard; Oxford University Press, 1993; Pg. 130
[796] *Genocide and International Justice*; Rebecca Joyce Frey; InfoBase Publishing, 2009; Pgs. 7–12, 31–54

with the British for control of the territory east of the Mississippi River. Some Indians sided with the British, as they hoped to reduce American settlement and expansion. In one writer's opinion, the Revolutionary War was "the most extensive and destructive" Indian war in United States history.[797]

Some Indian tribes were divided over which side to support in the war, such as the Iroquois Confederacy based in New York and Pennsylvania who split: the Oneida and Tuscarora sided with the American Patriots, and the Mohawk, Seneca, Cayuga, and Onondaga sided with the British. The Iroquois tried to avoid fighting directly against one another, but the Revolution eventually forced intra-Iroquois combat, and both sides lost territory following the war. The Crown aided the landless Iroquois by rewarding them with a reservation at Grand River in Ontario and some other lands. In the Southeast, the Cherokee split into a pro-patriot faction versus a pro-British faction that the Americans referred to as the Chickamauga Cherokee; they were led by Dragging Canoe. Many other tribes were similarly divided.

When the British made peace with the Americans in the Treaty of Paris (1783), they ceded a vast amount of Indian territory to the United States. Indian tribes who had sided with the British and had fought against the Americans were enemy combatants, as far as the United States was concerned; they were a conquered people who had lost their land.

The frontier conflicts were almost non-stop, beginning with Cherokee involvement in the American Revolutionary War and continuing through late 1794. The so-called "Chickamauga Cherokee", later called "Lower Cherokee," were from the Overhill Towns and later from the Lower Towns, Valley Towns, and Middle Towns. They followed war leader Dragging Canoe southwest, first to the Chickamauga Creek area near Chattanooga, Tennessee, then to the Five Lower Towns where they were joined by groups of Muskogee, white Tories, runaway slaves, and renegade Chickasaw, as well as by more than a hundred Shawnee. The primary targets of attack were the Washington District colonies along the Watauga, Holston, and Nolichucky Rivers, and in Carter's Valley in upper eastern Tennessee, as well as the settlements along the Cumberland River beginning with Fort Nashborough in 1780, even into Kentucky, plus against the Franklin settlements, and later states of Virginia, North Carolina, South Carolina, and Georgia. The scope of attacks by the Chickamauga and their allies ranged from quick raids by small war parties to large campaigns by four or five hundred warriors, and once more than a thousand. The Upper Muskogee under Dragging Canoe's close ally Alexander McGillivray frequently joined their campaigns and also operated separately, and the settlements on the Cumberland

---

[797] *Genocide and American Indian History*; Jeffrey Ostler; University of Oregon, 2015

came under attack from the Chickasaw, Shawnee from the north, and Delaware. Campaigns by Dragging Canoe and his successor John Watts were frequently conducted in conjunction with campaigns in the Northwest Territory. The colonists generally responded with attacks in which Cherokee settlements were completely destroyed, though usually without great loss of life on either side. The wars continued until the Treaty of Tellico Blockhouse in November 1794.[798]

In 1787, the Northwest Ordinance officially organized the Northwest Territory for settlement, and American settlers began pouring into the region. Violence erupted as Indian tribes resisted, and so the administration of President George Washington sent armed expeditions into the area. However, in the Northwest Indian War, a pan-tribal confederacy led by Blue Jacket (Shawnee), Little Turtle (Miami),[799] Buckongahelas (Lenape), and Egushawa (Ottawa) defeated armies led by Generals Josiah Harmar and Arthur St. Clair. General St. Clair's defeat was the most severe loss ever inflicted upon an American army by Indians. The Americans attempted to negotiate a settlement, but Blue Jacket and the Shawnee-led confederacy insisted on a boundary line that the Americans found unacceptable, and so a new expedition was dispatched led by General Anthony Wayne. Wayne's army defeated the Indian confederacy at the Battle of Fallen Timbers in 1794. The Indians had hoped for British assistance; when that was not forthcoming, they were compelled to sign the Treaty of Greenville in 1795, which ceded Ohio and part of Indiana to the United States.[800]

By 1800, the Indian population was approximately 600,000 in the continental United States. By 1890, their population had declined to about 250,000.[801] In 1800, William Henry Harrison became governor of the Indiana Territory, under the direction of President Thomas Jefferson, and he pursued an aggressive policy of obtaining titles to Indian lands.

Shawnee brothers Tecumseh and Tenskwatawa organized Tecumseh's War, another pan-tribal resistance to westward settlement.

Tecumseh was in the South attempting to recruit allies among the Creeks, Cherokees, and Choctaws when Harrison marched against the Indian confederacy, defeating Tenskwatawa and his followers at the Battle of Tippecanoe in 1811. The Americans hoped that the victory would end the militant resistance, but Tecumseh instead chose to ally openly with the British, who were soon at war with

---

[798] Osborn, William M. (2001). *The Wild Frontier: Atrocities During The American-Indian War from Jamestown Colony to Wounded Knee*. Garden City, NY: Random House. ISBN 978-0-375-50374-0.
[799] Madley 2016, p.11, p.351
[800] National Register Information System". *National Register of Historic Places*. National Park Service. January 23, 2007.
[801] *Genocide*. RW Press. p. 1963. ISBN 9781909284272.

the Americans in the War of 1812. The Creek War (1813–14) began as a tribal conflict within the Creek tribe, but it became part of the larger struggle against American expansion. Tecumseh was killed by Harrison's army at the Battle of the Thames, ending the resistance in the Old Northwest. The First Seminole War in 1818 resulted in the transfer of Florida from Spain to the United States in 1819.

American settlers began to push into Florida, which was now an American territory and had some of the most fertile lands in the nation. Paul Hoffman claims that covetousness, racism, and "self-defence" against Indian raids played a major part in the settlers' determination to "rid Florida of Indians once and for all". To compound the tension, runaway black slaves sometimes found refuge in Seminole camps, and the result was clashes between white settlers and the Indians residing there. Andrew Jackson sought to alleviate this problem by signing the Indian Removal Act, which stipulated the relocation of Indians out of Florida by force if necessary. The Seminoles were relatively new arrivals in Florida, led by such powerful leaders as Aripeka (Sam Jones), Micanopy, and Osceola, and they had no intention of leaving their new lands. they retaliated against the settlers, and this led to the Second Seminole War, the longest and most costly war that the Army ever waged against Indians.

In May 1830, the Indian Removal Act was passed by Congress which stipulated forced removal of Indians to Oklahoma. The Treaty of Paynes Landing was signed in May 1832 by a few Seminole chiefs who later recanted, claiming that they were tricked or forced to sign and making it clear that they would not consent to relocating to a reservation out west. The Seminoles' continued resistance to relocation led Florida to prepare for war. The St. Augustine Militia asked the US War Department for the loan of 500 muskets, and 500 volunteers were mobilized under Brig. Gen. Richard K. Call. Indian war parties raided farms and settlements, and families fled to forts or large towns, or out of the territory altogether. A war party led by Osceola captured a Florida militia supply train, killing eight of its guards and wounding six others; most of the goods taken were recovered by the militia in another fight a few days later. Sugar plantations were destroyed along the Atlantic coast south of St. Augustine, Florida, with many of the slaves on the plantations joining the Seminoles.

The US Army had 11 companies (about 550 soldiers) stationed in Florida. Fort King (Ocala) had only one company of soldiers, and it was feared that they might be overrun by the Seminoles. Three companies were stationed at Fort Brooke (Tampa), with another two expected imminently, so the army decided to send two companies to Fort King. On December 23, 1835, the two companies totalling 110 men left Fort Brooke under the command of Major Francis L. Dade. Seminoles shadowed the marching soldiers for five days, and they ambushed them and wiped out the command on December 28. Only three men survived, and one was hunted down and killed by a Seminole the next day. Survivors Ransome Clarke and Joseph Sprague returned to Fort Brooke. Clarke died of his wounds later, and he provided the only account of the battle from the army's perspective. The Seminoles lost three men and five wounded. On the same day as the massacre, Osceola and his followers shot and killed Agent Wiley Thompson and six others during an ambush outside of Fort King.

On December 29, General Clinch left Fort Drane with 750 soldiers, including 500 volunteers on an enlistment due to end January 1, 1836. The group was traveling to a Seminole stronghold called the Cove of the Withlacoochee, an area of many lakes on the southwest side of the Withlacoochee River. When they reached the river, the soldiers could not find the ford, so Clinch ferried his regular troops across the river in a single canoe. Once they were across and had relaxed, the Seminoles attacked. The troops fixed bayonets and charged them, at the cost of four dead and 59 wounded. The militia provided cover as the army troops then withdrew across the river.

In the Battle of Lake Okeechobee, Colonel Zachary Taylor saw the first major action of the campaign. He left Fort Gardiner on the upper Kissimmee River with 1,000 men on December 19 and headed towards Lake Okeechobee. In the first two days, 90 Seminoles surrendered. On the third day, Taylor stopped to build Fort Basinger where he left his sick and enough men to guard the Seminoles who had surrendered. Taylor's column caught up with the main body of the Seminoles on the north shore of Lake Okeechobee on December 25.

The Seminoles were led by "Alligator", Sam Jones, and the recently escaped Coacoochee, and they were positioned in a hammock surrounded by sawgrass. The ground was thick mud, and sawgrass easily cuts and burns the skin. Taylor had about 800 men, while the Seminoles numbered fewer than 400. Taylor sent in the Missouri volunteers first, moving his troops squarely into the centre of the swamp. His plan was to make a direct attack rather than encircle the Indians. All his men were on foot. As soon as they came within range, the Indians opened with heavy fire. The volunteers broke and their commander Colonel Gentry was fatally wounded, so they retreated across the swamp. The fighting in the sawgrass was deadliest for five companies of the Sixth Infantry; every officer but one was killed or wounded, along with most of their non-commissioned officers. The soldiers suffered 26 killed and 112 wounded, compared to 11 Seminoles killed and 14 wounded. No Seminoles were captured, although Taylor did capture 100 ponies and 600 head of cattle.

By 1842, the war was winding down and most Seminoles had left Florida for Oklahoma. The US Army officially recorded 1,466 deaths in the Second Seminole

War, mostly from disease. The number killed in action is less clear. Mahon reports 328 regular army killed in action, while Missall reports that Seminoles killed 269 officers and men. Almost half of those deaths occurred in the Dade Massacre, Battle of Lake Okeechobee, and Harney Massacre. Similarly, Mahon reports 69 deaths for the Navy, while Missal reports 41 for the Navy and Marine Corps. Mahon and the Florida Board of State Institutions agree that 55 volunteer officers and men were killed by the Seminoles, while Missall says that the number is unknown. A northern newspaper carried a report that more than 80 civilians were killed by Indians in Florida in 1839. By the end of 1843, 3,824 Indians had been shipped from Florida to the Indian Territory.

The series of conflicts in the western United States between indians, American settlers, and the United States Army are generally known as the Indian Wars. Many of these conflicts occurred during and after the Civil War until the closing of the frontier in about 1890. However, regions of the West that were settled before the Civil War saw significant conflicts prior to 1860, such as Texas, New Mexico, Utah, Oregon, California, and Washington state.

Various statistics have been developed concerning the devastation of these wars on the peoples involved. Gregory Michno used records dealing with figures "as a direct result of" engagements and concluded that "of the 21,586 total casualties tabulated in this survey, military personnel and civilians accounted for 6,596 (31%), while Indian casualties totalled about 14,990 (69%)" for the period of 1850–90. However, Michno says that he "used the army's estimates in almost every case" and "the number of casualties in this study are inherently biased toward army estimations". His work includes almost nothing on "Indian war parties", and he states that "army records are often incomplete".[802]

According to Michno, more conflicts with Indians occurred in the states bordering Mexico than in the interior states. Arizona ranked highest, with 310 known battles fought within the state's boundaries between Americans and Indians. Also, Arizona ranked highest of the states in deaths from the wars. At least 4,340 people were killed, including both the settlers and the Indians, over twice as many as occurred in Texas, the highest-ranking state. Most of the deaths in Arizona were caused by the Apaches. Michno also says that 51 percent of the battles took place in Arizona, Texas, and New Mexico between 1850 and 1890, as well as 37 percent of the casualties in the country west of the Mississippi River.[803]

American settlers and fur trappers had spread into the western United States territories and had established the Santa Fe Trail and the Oregon Trail. Relations

---

[802] Naimark, Norman M. (2017). *Genocide: A World History*. p. 41. ISBN 9780199765263.
[803] León Portilla: Cap. V

were generally peaceful between American settlers and Indians. The Bents of Bent's Fort on the Santa Fe Trail had friendly relations with the Cheyenne and Arapaho, and peace was established on the Oregon Trail by the Treaty of Fort Laramie signed in 1851 between the United States and the Plains Indians and the Indians of the northern Rocky Mountains. The treaty allowed passage by settlers, building roads, and stationing troops along the Oregon Trail.

The Pike's Peak Gold Rush of 1859 introduced a substantial white population into the Front Range of the Rockies, supported by a trading lifeline that crossed the central Great Plains. Advancing settlement following the passage of the Homestead Act and the growing transcontinental railways following the Civil War further destabilized the situation, placing white settlers into direct competition for the land and resources of the Great Plains and the Rocky Mountain West.[804] [805] Further factors included discovery of gold in the Black Hills resulting in the gold rush of 1875 – 1878, and in Montana during the Montana Gold Rush of 1862 – 1863 and the opening of the Bozeman Trail, which led to Red Cloud's War and later the Great Sioux War of 1876 -77.[806]

Miners, ranchers, and settlers expanded into the plain, and this led to increasing conflicts with the Indian populations of the West. Many tribes fought American settlers at one time or another, from the Utes of the Great Basin to the Nez Perce tribe of Idaho. But the Sioux of the Northern Plains and the Apaches of the Southwest waged the most aggressive warfare, led by resolute, militant leaders such as Red Cloud and Crazy Horse. The Sioux were relatively new arrivals on the Plains, as they had been sedentary farmers in the Great Lakes region previously. They moved west, displacing other Indian tribes, and becoming feared warriors. The Apaches supplemented their economy by raiding other tribes, and they practiced warfare to avenge the death of a kinsman.

During the American Civil War, Army units were withdrawn to fight the war in the east. They were replaced by the volunteer infantry and cavalry raised by the states of California and Oregon, by the western territorial governments, or by the local militias. These units fought the Indians and kept open communications with the east, holding the west for the Union and defeating the Confederate attempt to capture the New

Mexico Territory. After 1865, national policy called for all Indians either to ~~maintain their tribal ways as citizens, or to live~~ on

[804] Díaz del Castillo, Bernal (1963). Radice, Betty (ed.). The Conquest of New Spain. Translated by Cohen, J.M. London: Penguin Books. pp. 200–201. ISBN 0140441239.
[805] "Empires Past: Aztecs: Conquest". Library.thinkquest.org. Archived from the original on 2 February 2009". Archived from the original on February 2, 2009.
[806] El Calendario Mexica y la Cronografía. Rafael Tena 2008 INAH-CONACULTA p 48 108

reservations. Raids and wars between tribes were not allowed, and armed Indian bands off a reservation were the responsibility of the Army to round up and return.

In the 18ᵗʰ century, Spanish settlers in Texas came into conflict with the Apaches, Comanches, and Karankawas, among other tribes. Large numbers of American settlers reached Texas in the 1830s, and a series of armed confrontations broke out until the 1870s, mostly between Texans and Comanches. During the same period, the Comanches and their allies raided hundreds of miles deep into Mexico (see Comanche–Mexico Wars).

The first notable battle was the Fort Parker massacre in 1836, in which a huge war party of Comanches, Kiowas, Wichitas, and Delawares attacked the Texan outpost at Fort Parker. A small number of settlers were killed during the raid, and the abduction of Cynthia Ann Parker and two other children caused widespread outrage among Texans.

The Republic of Texas was declared and secured some sovereignty in their war with Mexico, and the Texas government under President Sam Houston pursued a policy of engagement with the Comanches and Kiowas. Houston had lived with the Cherokees, but the Cherokees joined with Mexican forces to fight against Texas. Houston resolved the conflict without resorting to arms, refusing to believe that the Cherokees would take up arms against his government. The administration of Mirabeau B. Lamar followed Houston's and took a very different policy towards the Indians. Lamar removed the Cherokees to the west and then sought to deport the Comanches and Kiowas. This led to a series of battles, including the Council House Fight, in which the Texas militia killed 33 Comanche chiefs at a peace parley. The Comanches retaliated with the Great Raid of 1840, and the Battle of Plum Creek followed several days later.

The Lamar Administration was known for its failed and expensive Indian policy; the cost of the war with the Indians exceeded the annual revenue of the government throughout his four-year term. It was followed by a second Houston administration, which resumed the previous policy of diplomacy. Texas signed treaties with all the tribes, including the Comanches. In the 1840s and 1850s, the Comanches and their allies shifted most of their raiding activities to Mexico, using Texas as a safe haven from Mexican retaliation.

Texas joined the Union in 1846, and the Federal government and Texas took up the struggle between the Plains Indians and the settlers.

The conflicts were particularly vicious and bloody on the Texas frontier in 1856 through 1858, as settlers continued to expand their settlements into the Comancheria.

The first Texan incursion into the heart of the Comancheria was in 1858, the so-called Antelope Hills Expedition marked by the Battle of Little Robe Creek.

The battles between settlers and Indians continued in 1860, and Texas militia destroyed an Indian camp at the Battle of Pease River. In the aftermath of the battle, the Texans learned that they had recaptured Cynthia Ann Parker, the little girl captured by the Comanches in 1836. She returned to live with her family, but she missed her children, including her son Quanah Parker. He was the son of Parker and Comanche Chief Peta Nocona, and he became a Comanche war chief at the Second Battle of Adobe Walls. He ultimately surrendered to the overwhelming force of the federal government and moved to a reservation in southwestern Oklahoma in 1875.

A number of wars occurred in the wake of the Oregon Treaty of 1846 and the creation of Oregon Territory and Washington Territory. Among the causes of conflict were a sudden immigration to the region and a series of gold rushes throughout the Pacific Northwest. The Whitman massacre of 1847 triggered the Cayuse War, which led to fighting from the Cascade Range to the Rocky Mountains. The Cayuse were defeated in 1855, but the conflict had expanded and continued in what became known as the Yakima War (1855–1858). Washington Territory Governor Isaac Stevens tried to compel Indian tribes to sign treaties ceding land and establishing reservations. The Yakama signed one of the treaties negotiated during the Walla Walla Council of 1855, establishing the Yakama Indian Reservation, but Stevens' attempts served mainly to intensify hostilities. Gold discoveries near Fort Colville resulted in many miners crossing Yakama lands via Naches Pass, and conflicts rapidly escalated into violence. It took several years for the Army to defeat the Yakama, during which time war spread to the Puget Sound region west of the Cascades. The Puget Sound War of 1855–1856 was triggered in part by the Yakima War and in part by the use of intimidation to compel tribes to sign land cession treaties. The Treaty of Medicine Creek of 1855 established an unrealistically small reservation on poor land for the Nisqually and Puyallup tribes. Violence broke out in the White River valley, along the route to Naches Pass and connecting nisqually and Yakama lands. The Puget Sound War is often remembered in connection with the Battle of Seattle (1856) and the execution of Nisqually Chief Leschi, a central figure of the war.[807]

In 1858, the fighting spread on the east side of the Cascades. This second phase of the Yakima War is known as the Coeur d'Alene War. The Yakama, Palouse, Spokane, and Coeur d'Alene tribes were defeated at the Battle of Four Lakes in late 1858.[808]

[807] Naimak, Norman M. (2017). *Genocide: A World History*. pp. 42–43. ISBN 9780199765263.
[808] Naimak, Norman M. (2017). *Genocide: A World History*. pp. 42–43. ISBN 9780199765263.

In southwest Oregon, tensions and skirmishes escalated between American settlers and the Rogue River peoples into the Rogue River Wars of 1855–1856. The California Gold Rush helped fuel a large increase in the number of people traveling south through the Rogue River Valley. Gold discoveries continued to trigger violent conflict between prospectors and Indians. Beginning in 1858, the Fraser Canyon Gold Rush in British Columbia drew large numbers of miners, many from Washington, Oregon, and California, culminating in the Fraser Canyon War. This conflict occurred in Canada, but the militias involved were formed mostly of Americans. The discovery of gold in Idaho and Oregon in the 1860s led to similar conflicts which culminated in the Bear River Massacre in 1863 and Snake War from 1864 to 1868.

In the late 1870s, another series of armed conflicts occurred in Oregon and Idaho, spreading east into Wyoming and Montana. The Nez Perce War of 1877 is known particularly for Chief Joseph and the four-month, 1,200-mile fighting retreat of a band of about 800 Nez Perce, including women and children. The Nez Perce War was caused by a large influx of settlers, the appropriation of Indian lands, and a gold rush—this time in Idaho. The Nez Perce engaged 2,000 American soldiers of different military units, as well as their Indian auxiliaries. They fought "eighteen engagements, including four major battles and at least four fiercely contested skirmishes", according to Alvin Josephy. Chief Joseph and the Nez Perce were much admired for their conduct in the war and their fighting ability.

The Bannock War broke out the following year for similar reasons. The Sheepeater Indian War in 1879 was the last conflict in the area.

Various wars between Spanish and Native Americans, mainly Comanches and Apaches, took place since the 17th century in the Southwest United States. Spanish governors made peace treaties with some tribes during this period. Several events stand out during the colonial period: On the one hand, the administration of Tomás Vélez Cachupín, the only colonial governor of New Mexico who managed to establish peace with the Comanches after having confronted them in the Battle of San Diego Pond, and learned how to relate to them without giving rise to misunderstandings that could lead to conflict with them. The Pueblo Revolt of 1680 was also highlighted, causing the Spanish province to be divided into two areas: one led by the Spanish governor and the other by the leader of the Pueblos. Several military conflicts happened between Spaniards and Pueblos in this period until Diego de Vargas made a peace treaty with them in 1691, which made them subjects of the Spanish governor again. Conflicts between Europeans and Amerindians continued following the acquisition of Alta California and Santa Fe de Nuevo México from Mexico at the end of the Mexican–American War in 1848, and the Gadsden Purchase in 1853. These spanned from 1846 to at least 1895. The first conflicts were in the New Mexico Territory, and later in California and the Utah Territory during and after the California Gold Rush.

Indian tribes in the southwest had been engaged in cycles of trading and fighting with one another and with settlers for centuries prior to the United States gaining control of the region. These conflicts with the United States involved every non-pueblo tribe in the region and often were a continuation of Mexican–Spanish conflicts. The Navajo Wars and Apache Wars are perhaps the best known. The last major campaign of the military against Indians in the Southwest involved 5,000 troops in the field, and resulted in the surrender of Chiricahua Apache Geronimo and his band of 24 warriors, women, and children in 1886.

The U.S. Army kept a small garrison west of the Rockies, but the California Gold Rush brought a great influx of miners and settlers into the area. The result was that most of the early conflicts with the California Indians involved local parties of miners or settlers. During the American Civil War, California volunteers replaced Federal troops and won the ongoing Bald Hills War and the Owens Valley Indian War and engaged in minor actions in northern California. California and Oregon volunteer garrisons in Nevada, Oregon, Idaho, Utah, New Mexico, and the Arizona Territories also engaged in conflicts with the Apache, Cheyenne, Goshute, Navajo, Paiute, Shoshone, Sioux, and Ute Indians from 1862 to 1866. Following the Civil War, California was mostly pacified, but federal troops replaced the volunteers and again took up the struggle against Indians in the remote regions of the Mojave Desert, and in the northeast against the Snakes (1864–1868) and Modocs (1872–1873).

The tribes of the Great Basin were mostly Shoshone, and they were greatly affected by the Oregon and California Trails and by Mormon pioneers to Utah. The Shoshone had friendly relations with American and British fur traders and trappers, beginning with their encounter with Lewis and Clark.

The traditional way of life of the Indians was disrupted, and they began raiding travellers along the trails and aggression toward Mormon settlers. During the American Civil War, the California Volunteers stationed in Utah responded to complaints, which resulted in the Bear River Massacre.[809] Following the massacre, various Shoshone tribes signed a series of treaties exchanging promises of peace for small annuities and reservations. One of these was the Box Elder Treaty which identified a land claim made by the North-western Shoshone. The Supreme Court declared this claim to be non-binding in a 1945 ruling,[810] [811] but the Indian Claims

---

[809] Karin Solveig Björnson, Kurt Jonassohn. *Genocide and Gross Human Rights Violations: In Comparative Perspective.* p. 202. ISBN 9781412824453.
[810] Victimario Histórico Militar: Capítulo IX" (in Spanish). Archived from the original on July 1, 2018.

Commission recognized it as binding in 1968. Descendants of the original group were compensated collectively at a rate of less than $0.50 per acre, minus legal fees.[812]

Most of the local groups were decimated by the war and faced continuing loss of hunting and fishing land caused by the steadily growing population. Some moved to the Fort Hall Indian Reservation when it was created in 1868. Some of the Shoshone populated the Mormon-sanctioned community of Washakie, Utah.[813]

From 1864 California and Oregon Volunteers also engaged in the early campaigns of the Snake War in the Great Basin areas of California, Nevada, Oregon and Idaho. From 1866 the U.S. Army replaced the Volunteers in that war which General George Crook ended in 1868 after a protracted campaign.[814]

Initially relations between participants in the Pike's Peak gold rush and the Native American tribes of the Front Range and the Platte valley were friendly.[815] [816]An attempt was made to resolve conflicts by negotiation of the Treaty of Fort Wise, which established a reservation in south-eastern Colorado, but the settlement was not agreed to by all of the roving warriors, particularly the Dog Soldiers. During the early 1860s tensions increased and culminated in the Colorado War and the Sand Creek Sand Creek Massacre, where Colorado volunteers fell on a peaceful Cheyenne village killing women and children,[817] which set the stage for further conflict.Massacre, where Colorado volunteers fell on a peaceful Cheyenne village killing women and children,[818] which set the stage for further conflict.

The peaceful relationship between settlers and the Indians of the colorado and Kansas plains was maintained faithfully by the tribes, but sentiment grew among the Colorado settlers for Indian removal. The savagery of the attacks on civilians during the Dakota War of 1862 contributed to these sentiments, as did the few minor incidents which occurred in the Platte Valley and in areas east of Denver. Regular

---

[811] Duncan, David Ewing (1997). *Hernando de Soto: A Savage Quest in the Americas*. University of Oklahoma Press. pp. 286–291, 376–384.

[812] Clayton, Lawrence A., "Hernando de Soto: A Brief" Archived February 10, 2008, at the Wayback Machine.

[813] Wilford, John Noble, "De Soto's Trail: Courage and Cruelty Come Alive", New York Times, May 19, 1987

[814] Steele, Ian Kenneth, *Warpaths: Invasions of North America*, Oxford University Press, 1994. pp. 15, 47, 116.

[815] Sauer, C., *Sixteenth Century North America; the land and the people as seen by the Europeans*, University of California Press, 1971, p. 141.

[816] Flint, R., *No settlement, no conquest: a history of the Coronado Entrada*, University of New Mexico Press, 2008, pp. 144–153.

[817] Brooke, James (February 9, 1998). "Conquistador Statue Stirs Hispanic Pride and Indian Rage". *The New York Times*.

[818] Brooke, James (February 9, 1998). "Conquistador Statue Stirs Hispanic Pride and Indian Rage". *The New York Times*.

army troops had been withdrawn for service in the Civil War and were replaced with the Colorado Volunteers, rough men who often favoured extermination of the Indians. They were commanded by John Chivington and George L. Shoup, who followed the lead of John Evans, territorial governor of Colorado. They adopted a policy of shooting on sight all Indians encountered, a policy which in short time ignited a general war on the Colorado and Kansas plains, the Colorado War.[819]

Raids by bands of plains Indians on isolated homesteads to the east of Denver, on the advancing settlements in Kansas, and on stage line stations along the South Platte, such as at Julesburg,[820] [821] and along the Smoky Hill Trail, resulted in settlers in both Colorado and Kansas adopting a murderous attitude towards Native Americans, with calls for extermination.[822] Likewise, the savagery shown by the Colorado Volunteers during the Sand Creek massacre resulted in Native Americans, particularly the Dog Soldiers, a band of the Cheyenne, engaging in savage retribution.

The Dakota War of 1862 (more commonly called the Sioux Uprising of 1862 in older authorities and popular texts) was the first major armed engagement between the U.S. and the Sioux (Dakota). After six weeks of fighting in Minnesota, led mostly by Chief Taoyateduta (aka, Little Crow), records conclusively show that more than 500 U.S. soldiers and settlers died in the conflict, though many more may have died in small raids or after being captured. The number of Sioux dead in the uprising is mostly undocumented. After the war, 303 Sioux warriors were convicted of murder and rape by U.S. military tribunals and sentenced to death. Most of the death sentences were commuted by President Lincoln, but on December 26, 1862, in Mankato, Minnesota, 38 Dakota Sioux men were hanged in what is still today the largest penal mass execution in U.S. history.[823]

After the expulsion of the Dakota, some refugees and warriors made their way to Lakota lands in what is now North Dakota. Battles continued between Minnesota regiments and combined Lakota and Dakota forces through 1864, as Colonel Henry Sibley pursued the Sioux into Dakota Territory. Sibley's army defeated the Lakota and Dakota in three major battles in 1863: the Battle of Dead Buffalo Lake on July 26, 1863, the Battle of Stony Lake on July 28, 1863, and the Battle of Whitestone Hill on September 3, 1863. The Sioux retreated further, but again faced an American army in 1864; this time, Gen. Alfred Sully led a force from near Fort Pierre, South

[819] Weber, David J., *The Spanish Frontier in North America*, Yale University Press, New Haven, 1992, pp. 85–86.

[820] Riley, Carroll, L., *Rio del Norte: People of the Upper Rio Grande from Earliest Times to the Pueblo Revolt*, University of Utah Press, 2007, p. 252, ISBN 978-0-87480-496-6

[821] *Staff, Times-Dispatch. "Highway marker dedicated for Paspahegh tribe".*

[822] Schlotterbeck, J., *Daily Life in the Colonial South*, Greenwood, 2013, p. 333, ISBN 978-0313340697

[823] *Research Jamestown: Legacy of the Massacre of 1622 – Americans at War. www.bookrags.com.*

Dakota, and decisively defeated the Sioux at the Battle of Killdeer Mountain on July 28, 1864.

On November 29, 1864, the Colorado territory militia responded to a series of Indian attacks on white settlements by attacking a Cheyenne and Arapaho encampment on Sand Creek in south-eastern Colorado, under orders to take no prisoners. The militia killed about 200 of the Indians, two-thirds of whom were women and children,[824] taking scalps and other grisly trophies of battle.[825]

Following the massacre, the survivors joined the camps of the Cheyenne on the Smokey Hill and Republican Rivers. They smoked the war pipe and passed it from camp to camp among the Sioux, Cheyenne, and Arapaho camped in the area, and they planned an attack on the stage station and fort at Julesburg which they carried out in the January 1865 Battle of Julesburg. This attack was followed up by numerous raids along the South Platte both east and west of Julesburg, and by a second raid on Julesburg in early February. The bulk of the Indians then moved north into Nebraska on their way to the Black Hills and the Powder River.[826] [827] In the spring of 1865, raids continued along the Oregon trail in Nebraska. Indians raided the Oregon Trail along the North Platte River and attacked the troops stationed at the bridge across the North Platte at Casper, Wyoming in the Battle of Platte Bridge.[828] [829]

After the Civil War, all the Indians were assigned to reservations, and the reservations were under the control of the Interior Department. Control of the Great Plains fell under the Army's Department of the Missouri, an administrative area of over 1,000,000 miles^2 encompassing all land between the Mississippi River and the Rocky Mountains. Maj. Gen. Winfield S. Hancock had led the department in 1866 but had mishandled his campaign, resulting in Sioux and Cheyenne raids that attacked mail stagecoaches, burned the stations, and killed the employees. They also raped, killed, and kidnapped many settlers on the frontier.[830]

---

[824] Spencer C. Tucker; James R. Arnold; Roberta Wiener (30 September 2011). 'The Encyclopedia of North American Indian Wars, 1607–1890: A Political, Social, and Military History. *ABC-CLIO. p. 332. ISBN 978-1-851096-97-8.*

[825] Miller, D.W. *The Forced Removal of American Indians from the Northeast: A History of Territorial Cessions and Relocations, 1620–1854*, McFarland, 2011, p. 14., ISBN 978-0-786464-96-8

[826] Adams, D. Jr., Charles F., *Wessagusset and Weymouth*, Nabu Press, pp. 24–26, ISBN 978-1-248636-92-3

[827] Jean-Baptiste Du Tertre, *Histoire Generale des Antilles...*, 2 vols. Paris: Jolly, 1667, I:5–6

[828] Hubbard, Vincent (2002). *A History of St. Kitts*. Macmillan Caribbean. pp. 17–18. ISBN 9780333747605.

[829] Muehlbauer, Matthew S.; Ulbrich, David J. (2013). *Ways of War: American Military History from the Colonial Era to the Twenty-First Century*. Routledge. p. 29. ISBN 9781136756047.

[830] Lucas, Beverly (2008). *Wethersfield*. Arcadia Publishing. p. 69. ISBN 9780738563459. Retrieved July 9, 2018.

Philip Sheridan was the military governor of Louisiana and Texas in 1866, but President Johnson removed him from that post, claiming that he was ruling over the area with absolute tyranny and insubordination. Shortly after, Hancock was removed as head of the Department of the Missouri and Sheridan replaced him in August 1867.[831] He was ordered to pacify the plains and take control of the Indians there, and he immediately called General Custer back to command of the 7th Cavalry; Hancock had suspended him.[832]

The Department of Missouri was in poor shape upon Sheridan's arrival. Commissioners from the government had signed a peace treaty in October 1867 with the Comanche, Kiowa, Kiowa Apache, Cheyenne, and Arapaho which offered them reservation land to live on along with food and supplies,[833] but Congress failed to pass it. The promised supplies from the government were not reaching the Indians and they were beginning to starve, numbering an estimated 6,000. Sheridan had only 2,600 men at the time to control them and to defend against any raids or attacks, and only 1,200 of his men were mounted.[834] These men were also under-supplied and stationed at forts that were in poor condition. They were also mostly unproven units that replaced retired veterans from the Civil War.

Sheridan attempted to improve the conditions of the military outpost and the Indians on the plains through a peace-oriented strategy. Toward the beginning of his command, members of the Cheyenne and Arapaho followed him on his travels from Fort Larned to Fort Dodge where he spoke to them. They brought their problems to him and explained how the promised supplies were not being delivered. In response, Sheridan gave them a generous supply of rations. Shortly after, the Saline Valley settlements were attacked, and that was followed by other violent raids and kidnappings in the region. Sheridan wanted to respond in force but was constrained by the government's peace policy and the lack of well-supplied mounted troops. He could not deploy official military units, so he commissioned a group of 47 frontiersmen and sharpshooters called Solomon's Avengers. They investigated the raids near Arickaree Creek and were attacked by Indians on September 17, 1868. The Avengers were under siege for eight days by some 700 Indian warriors, but they were able to keep them at bay until military units arrived to help. The Avengers lost six men and another 15 were wounded. Sherman finally gave Sheridan authority to respond in force to these threats.[835]

---

[831] Cave, Alfred A., *The Pequot War*, University of Massachusetts Press, 1996, pp. 144–154.
[832] Grumet, Robert S. *First Manhattans: A History of the Indians of Greater New York*, University of Oklahoma Press, 2011, p33-34, ISBN 978-0-806141-63-3
[833] Cave, Alfred A., *The Pequot War*, University of Massachusetts Press, 1996, pp. 144–154.
[834] *"William Keift"*. www.njcu.edu.
[835] *"William Keift"*. www.njcu.edu.

Sheridan believed that his soldiers would be unable to chase the horses of the Indians during the summer months, so he used them as a defensive force the remainder of September and October. His forces were better fed and clothed than the Indians and they could launch a campaign in the winter months. His winter campaign of 1868 started with the 19th Kansas Volunteers from Custer's 7th Cavalry, along with five battalions of infantry under Major John H. Page setting out from Fort Dodge on November 5. A few days later, a force moved from Fort Bascom to Fort Cobb consisting of units of the 5th Cavalry Regiment and two companies of infantry, where they met up with units from the 3rd Cavalry leaving from Fort Lyon. Sheridan directed the opening month of the campaign from Camp Supply. The Units from the 5th and 3rd Cavalry met at Fort Cobb without any sign of the 19th Kansas, but they had a lead on a band of Indians nearby and Custer led a force after them.[836]

Custer's force attacked the Cheyenne Indians and Black Kettle in the Battle of Washita River, and an estimated 100 Indians were killed and 50 taken prisoner. Custer lost 21 men killed and 13 men wounded, and a unit went missing under Major Elliott's command. Custer shot 675 ponies that were vital for the Indians' survival on the plains.[837] Immediately following the battle, Sheridan received backlash from Washington politicians who defended Black Kettle as a peace-loving Indian. This began the controversy as to whether the event was best described as a military victory or as a massacre, a discussion which endures among historians to this day.

Following Washita, Sheridan oversaw the refitting of the 19th Kansas and personally led them down the Washita River toward the Wichita Mountains. He met with Custer along the Washita River, and they searched for Major Elliott's missing unit. They found the bodies of the missing unit and the bodies of Mrs. Blynn and her child who had been taken by Indians the previous summer near Fort Lyon.[838] The defeat at Washita had scared many of the tribes and Sheridan was able to round up the majority of the Kiowa and Comanche people at Fort Cobb in December and get them to reservations. He began negotiations with Chief Little Robe of the Cheyennes and with Yellow Bear about living on the reservations.[839] Sheridan then began the construction of Camp Sill, later called Fort Sill, named after General Sill who died at Stone River.

Sheridan was called back to Washington following the election of President Grant. He was informed of his promotion to lieutenant general of the army and reassigned from the department. Sheridan protested and was allowed to stay in Missouri with the rank of lieutenant general. The last remnants of Indian resistance came from Tall

[836] *Winkler, David F. (1998). Revisiting the Attack on Pavonia. New Jersey Historical Society.*
[837] *Winkler, David F. (1998). Revisiting the Attack on Pavonia. New Jersey Historical Society.*
[838] *Winkler, David F. (1998). Revisiting the Attack on Pavonia. New Jersey Historical Society.*
[839] Beck, Sanderson (2006). "New Netherland and Stuyvesant 1642–64".

Bull Dog soldiers and elements of the Sioux and Northern Cheyenne tribes. The 5th Cavalry from Fort McPherson were sent to handle the situation on the Platte River in Nebraska. In May, the two forces collided at Summit Springs and the Indians were pursued out of the region. This brought an end to Sheridan's campaign, as the Indians had successfully been removed from the Platte and Arkansas and the majority of those in Kansas had been settled onto reservations. Sheridan left in 1869 to take command of the Army and was replaced by Major General Schofield.[840]

In 1875, the Great Sioux War of 1876–77 erupted when the Dakota gold rush penetrated the Black Hills. The government decided to stop evicting trespassers from the Black Hills and offered to buy the land from the Sioux. When they refused, the government decided instead to take the land and gave the Lakota until January 31, 1876, to return to reservations. The tribes did not return to the reservations by the deadline, and Lt. Colonel George Custer found the main encampment of the Lakota and their allies at the Battle of the Little Bighorn. Custer and his men were separated from their main body of troops, and they were all killed by the far more numerous Indians led by Crazy Horse and inspired by Sitting Bull's earlier vision of victory. The Anheuser-Busch brewing company made prints of a dramatic painting that depicted "Custer's Last Fight" and had them framed and hung in many American saloons as an advertising campaign, helping to create a popular image of this battle.[841]

The Lakotas conducted a Ghost Dance ritual on the reservation at Wounded Knee, South Dakota in 1890, and the Army attempted to subdue them. Gunfire erupted on December 29 during this attempt, and soldiers killed up to 300 Indians, mostly old men, women, and children in the Wounded Knee Massacre.[842] Following the massacre, author L. Frank Baum wrote: "The *Pioneer* has before declared that our only safety depends upon the total extermination of the Indians. Having wronged them for centuries, we had better, in order to protect our civilization, follow it up by one more wrong and wipe these untamed and untameable creatures from the face of the earth."[843]

The Last known conflicts

- October 5, 1898: Leech Lake, Minnesota: Battle of Sugar Point; last Medal of Honour given for Indian Wars campaigns was awarded to Private Oscar Burkard of the 3rd U.S. Infantry Regiment

[840] Beck, Sanderson (2006). "New Netherland and Stuyvesant 1642–64".
[841] Churchill 1997, p. 198
[842] Tucker, S.C. *The Encyclopaedia of North American Indian Wars, 1607–1890: A Political, Social, and Military History*, ABC-Clio, p. 414, ISBN 978-1-851096-97-8
[843] Major, D.C., Major, J.S. *A Huguenot on the Hackensack: David Demarest and His Legacy*, Fairleigh Dickinson University Press, 2007, p. 55, ISBN 978-1-611473-68-1

- 1907: Four Corners, Arizona: Two troops of the 5th Cavalry from Fort Wingate skirmish with armed Navajo men; one Navajo was killed and the rest escaped
- March 1909: Crazy Snake Rebellion, Oklahoma: Federal officials attack the Muscogee Creeks and allied Freedmen who had resisted forcible allotment and division of tribal lands by the federal government since 1901, headquartered at Hickory ceremonial grounds in Oklahoma; a two-day gun battle seriously wounded leader Chitto Harjo and quelled this rebellion[844]
- 1911: Chaco Canyon, New Mexico: A company of cavalry went from Fort Wingate to quell an alleged uprising by some Navajo.
- January 19, 1911: Washoe County, Nevada: The Last Massacre occurred; a group of Shoshones and Bannocks killed four ranchers; on February 26, 1911, eight of the Indians involved in the Last Massacre were killed by a posse in the Battle of Kelley Creek; the remaining four were captured
- March 1914 – March 15, 1915: Bluff War in Utah between Ute Indians and Mormon residents
- January 9, 1918: Santa Cruz County, Arizona: The Battle of Bear Valley was fought in Southern Arizona; Army forces of the 10th Cavalry engaged and captured a band of Yaquis, after a brief firefight[845]
- March 20–23, 1923: Posey War in Utah between Ute and Paiute Indians against Mormon residents.

Both the Renegade period and the Apache Wars ended in 1924 and brought the American Indian Wars to a close.

---

[844] Trelease, A., *Indian Affairs in Colonial New York; The Seventeenth Century*, pp. 79–80.
[845] Karnoutsos, Carmela (2007). "Peach Tree War". *Jersey City A to Z*. New Jersey City University..

Chapter sixteen

The Chinese Exclusion Act 1882

The Chinese Exclusion Act of 1882 was the first significant law restricting immigration into the United States. Many Americans on the West Coast attributed declining wages and economic ills to Chinese workers. Although the Chinese composed only 0.002 percent of the nation's population, Congress passed the exclusion act to placate worker demands and assuage prevalent concerns about maintaining white "racial purity."

This Act was meant to curb the influx of Chinese immigrants to the United States, particularly California, The Chinese Exclusion Act of 1882 was initially only meant suspended Chinese immigration for ten years and declared Chinese immigrant's ineligible for naturalization.

Chinese Immigration in America:

The Opium Wars (1839-42, 1856-60) of the mid-nineteenth century between Great Britain and China left China in debt. Floods and drought contributed to an exodus of peasants from their farms, and many left the country to find work. When gold was discovered in the Sacramento Valley of California in 1848, a large uptake in Chinese immigrants entered the United States to join the California Gold Rush.

Following an 1852 crop failure in China, over 20,000 Chinese immigrants came through San Francisco's customs house (up from 2,716 the previous year) looking for work. Violence soon broke out between white miners and the new arrivals, much of it racially charged. In May 1852, California imposed a Foreign Miners Tax of $3 month meant to target Chinese miners, and crime and violence escalated.

An 1854 Supreme Court Case, People v. Hall, ruled that the Chinese, like African Americans and Native Americans, were not allowed to testify in court, making it effectively impossible for Chinese immigrants to seek justice against the mounting violence. By 1870, Chinese miners had paid $5 million to the state of California via the Foreign Miners Tax, yet they faced continuing discrimination at work and in their camps.

Purpose of The Chinese Exclusion Act:

Meant to curb the influx of Chinese immigrants to the United States, particularly

California, The Chinese Exclusion Act of 1882 suspended Chinese immigration for ten years and declared Chinese immigrant's ineligible for naturalization. President Chester A. Arthur signed it into law on May 6, 1882. Chinese Americans already in the country challenged the constitutionality of the discriminatory acts, but their efforts failed.

Geary Act of 1892:

Proposed by California congressman Thomas J. Geary, The Geary Act went into effect on May 5, 1892. It reinforced and extended the Chinese Exclusion Act's ban on Chinese immigration for an additional ten years. It also required Chinese residents in the U.S. to carry special documentation certificates of residence from the Internal Revenue Service. Immigrants who were caught not carrying the certificates were sentenced to hard labour and deportation, and bail was only an option if the accused were vouched for by a "credible white witness."

Chinese Americans were finally allowed to testify in court after the 1882 trial of labourer Yee Shun, though it would take decades for the immigration ban to be lifted.

Impact of Chinese Exclusion Act:

The Supreme Court upheld the Geary Act in Fong Yue Ting v. United States in 1893, and in 1902 Chinese immigration was made permanently illegal. The legislation proved very effective, and the Chinese population in the United States sharply declined.

American experience with Chinese exclusion spurred later movements for immigration restriction against other "undesirable" groups such as Middle Easterners, Hindu and East Indians, and the Japanese with the passage of the Immigration Act of 1924. Chinese immigrants and their American-born families remained ineligible for citizenship until 1943 with the passage of the Magnuson Act. By then, the U.S. was embroiled in World War II and seeking to improve morale on the home front.

Chapter seventeen

The African Americans, their slavery and emancipation

Slavery in the U. K. was abolished in 1807, but it took
much longer for the United States to catch up.

The 13th Amendment, adopted on December 18, 1865, officially abolished slavery, but freed Black peoples' status in the post-war South remained precarious, and significant challenges awaited during the Reconstruction period.

Throughout the 17th and 18th centuries people were kidnapped from the continent of Africa, forced into slavery in the American colonies and exploited to work as indentured servants and labour in the production of crops such as tobacco and cotton. By the mid-19th century, America's westward expansion and the abolition movement provoked a great debate over slavery that would tear the nation apart in the bloody Civil War. Though the Union victory freed the nation's four million enslaved people, the legacy of slavery continued to influence American history, from the Reconstruction, to the civil rights movement that emerged a century after emancipation and beyond.

Hundreds of thousands of Africans, both free and enslaved, aided the establishment and survival of colonies in the Americas and the New World. However, many consider a significant starting point to slavery in America to be 1619, when the privateer The White Lion brought 20 African slaves ashore in the British colony of Jamestown, Virginia. The crew had seized the Africans from the Portuguese slave ship Sao Jao Bautista.

Throughout the 17th century, European settlers in North America turned to enslaved Africans as a cheaper, more plentiful labour source than indentured servants, who were mostly poor Europeans.

Though it is impossible to give accurate figures, some historians have estimated that 6 to 7 million enslaved people were imported to the New World during the 18th century alone, depriving the African continent of some of its healthiest and ablest men and women.

In the 17th and 18th centuries, enslaved Africans worked mainly on the tobacco, rice and indigo plantations of the southern coast, from the Chesapeake Bay colonies of Maryland and Virginia south to Georgia.

After the American Revolution, many colonists particularly in the North, where slavery was relatively unimportant to the agricultural economy began to link the oppression of enslaved Africans to their own oppression by the British, and to call for slavery's abolition.

Did you know? One of the first martyrs to the cause of American patriotism was Crispus Attucks, a former enslaved man who was killed by British soldiers during the Boston Massacre of 1770. Some 5,000 Black soldiers and sailors fought on the American side during the Revolutionary War.

But after the Revolutionary War, the new U.S. Constitution tacitly acknowledged the institution of slavery, counting each enslaved individual as three-fifths of a person for the purposes of taxation and representation in Congress and guaranteeing the right to repossess any "person held to service or labour" (an obvious euphemism for slavery).

In the late 18th century, with the land used to grow tobacco nearly exhausted, the South faced an economic crisis, and the continued growth of slavery in America seemed in doubt.

Around the same time, the mechanization of the textile industry in England led to a huge demand for American cotton, a southern crop whose production was limited by the difficulty of removing the seeds from raw cotton fibres by hand.

But in 1793, a young Yankee schoolteacher named Eli Whitney invented the cotton gin, a simple mechanized device that efficiently removed the seeds. His device was widely copied, and within a few years the South would transition from the large-scale production of tobacco to that of cotton, a switch that reinforced the region's dependence on enslaved labour.

Slavery itself was never widespread in the North, though many of the region's businessmen grew rich on the slave trade and investments in southern plantations. Between 1774 and 1804, all the northern states abolished slavery, but the institution of slavery remained vital to the South.

Though the U.S. Congress outlawed the African slave trade in 1808, the domestic trade flourished, and the enslaved population in the United States nearly tripled over the next 50 years. By 1860 it had reached nearly 4 million, with more than half living in the cotton-producing states of the South.

Enslaved people in the antebellum South constituted about one-third of the southern population. Most lived on large plantations or small farms; many masters owned fewer than 50 enslaved people.

Landowners sought to make their enslaved completely dependent on them through a system of restrictive codes. They were usually prohibited from learning to read and write, and their behaviour and movement was restricted.

Many masters raped enslaved women, and rewarded obedient behaviour with favours, while rebellious enslaved people were brutally punished. A strict hierarchy among the enslaved (from privileged house workers and skilled artisans down to lowly field hands) helped keep them divided and less likely to organize against their masters.

Marriages between enslaved men and women had no legal basis, but many did marry and raise large families; most slave owners encouraged this practice, but nonetheless did not usually hesitate to divide families by sale or removal.

Rebellions among enslaved people did occur notably ones led by Gabriel Prosser in Richmond in 1800 and by Denmark Vesey in Charleston in 1822 but few were successful.

The revolt that most terrified enslavers was that led by Nat Turner in Southampton County, Virginia, in August 1831. Turner's group, which eventually numbered around 75 Black men, murdered some 55-white people in two days before armed resistance from local white people and the arrival of state militia forces overwhelmed them.

Supporters of slavery pointed to Turner's rebellion as evidence that Black people were inherently inferior barbarians requiring an institution such as slavery to discipline them, and fears of similar insurrections led many southern states to further strengthen their slave codes to limit the education, movement, and assembly of enslaved people.

In the North, the increased repression of southern Black people only fanned the flames of the growing abolitionist movement.

From the 1830s to the 1860s, the movement to abolish slavery in America gained strength, led by free Black people such as Frederick Douglass and white supporters such as William Lloyd Garrison, founder of the radical newspaper *The Liberator*, and Harriet Beecher Stowe, who published the bestselling antislavery novel *Uncle Tom's Cabin*.

While many abolitionists based their activism on the belief that slaveholding was a sin, others were more inclined to the non-religious "free-labour" argument, which held that slaveholding was regressive, inefficient, and made little economic sense.

Free Black people and other antislavery northerners had begun helping enslaved people escape from southern plantations to the North via a loose network of safe houses as early as the 1780s. This practice, known as the Underground Railroad, gained real momentum in the 1830s. Conductors like Harriet Tubman guided escapees on their journey North, and "stationmasters" included such prominent figures as Frederick Douglass, Secretary of State William H. Seward and Pennsylvania congressman Thaddeus Stevens. Although estimates vary widely, it may have helped anywhere from 40,000 to 100,000 enslaved people reach freedom.

The success of the Underground Railroad helped spread abolitionist feelings in the North; it also undoubtedly increased sectional tensions, convincing pro-slavery southerners of their northern countrymen's determination to defeat the institution that sustained them.

America's explosive growth and its expansion westward in the first half of the 19th century—would provide a larger stage for the growing conflict over slavery in America and its future limitation or expansion.

In 1820, a bitter debate over the federal government's right to restrict slavery over Missouri's application for statehood ended in a compromise: Missouri was admitted to the Union as a slave state, Maine as a free state and all western territories north of Missouri's southern border were to be free soil.

Although the Missouri Compromise was designed to maintain an even balance between slave and free states, it was able to help quell the forces of sectionalism only temporarily.

In 1850, another tenuous compromise was negotiated to resolve the question of slavery in territories won during the Mexican American War.

Four years later, however, the Kansas-Nebraska Act opened all new territories to slavery by asserting the rule of popular sovereignty over congressional edict, leading pro and anti-slavery forces to battle it out with considerable bloodshed in the new state of Kansas.

Outrage in the North over the Kansas-Nebraska Act spelled the downfall of the old Whig Party and the birth of a new, all-northern Republican Party. In 1857, the Dred Scott decision by the Supreme Court (involving an enslaved man who sued for his freedom on the grounds that his master had taken him into free territory) effectively repealed the Missouri Compromise by ruling that all territories were open to slavery.

In 1859, two years after the Dred Scott decision, an event occurred that would ignite passions nationwide over the issue of slavery.

John Brown's raid on Harper's Ferry, Virginia in which the abolitionist and 22 men, including five Black men and three of Brown's sons raided and occupied a federal arsenal – resulted in the deaths of 10 people and Brown's hanging.

The insurrection exposed the growing national rift over slavery: Brown was hailed as a martyred hero by northern abolitionists but was vilified as a mass murderer in the South.

The South would reach the breaking point the following year when Republican candidate Abraham Lincoln was elected as president. Within three months, seven southern states had seceded to form the Confederate States of America; four more would follow after the Civil War began.

Though Lincoln's anti-slavery views were well established, the central Union war aim at first was not to abolish slavery, but to preserve the United States as a nation.

Abolition became a goal only later, due to military necessity, growing anti-slavery sentiment in the North and the self-emancipation of many people who fled enslavement as Union troops swept through the South.

On September 22, 1862, Lincoln issued a preliminary emancipation proclamation, and on January 1, 1863, he made it official that "slaves within any State, or designated part of a State in rebellion, shall be then, thenceforward, and forever free."

By freeing some 3 million enslaved people in the rebel states, the Emancipation Proclamation deprived the Confederacy of the bulk of its labour forces and put international public opinion strongly on the Union side.

Though the Emancipation Proclamation didn't officially end all slavery in America that would happen with the passage of the 13th Amendment after the Civil War's end in 1865 some 186,000 Black soldiers would join the Union Army, and about 38,000 lost their lives.

The 13th Amendment, adopted on December 18, 1865, officially abolished slavery, but freed Black peoples' status in the post-war South remained precarious, and significant challenges awaited during the Reconstruction period.

Previously enslaved men and women received the rights of citizenship and the "equal protection" of the Constitution in the 14th Amendment and the right to vote in the 15th Amendment, but these provisions of Constitution were often ignored or violated, and it was difficult for Black citizens to gain a foothold in the post-war economy thanks to restrictive Black codes and regressive contractual arrangements such as sharecropping.

Despite seeing an unprecedented degree of Black participation in American political life, Reconstruction was ultimately frustrating for African Americans, and the rebirth of white supremacy including the rise of racist organizations such as the Ku Klux Klan.

Almost a century later, resistance to the lingering racism and discrimination in America that began during the slavery era led to the civil rights movement of the 1960s, which achieved the greatest political and social gains for Black Americans since Reconstruction.

Whilst the Abolition of Slavery in the U. K. became Law in 1807,
you may be surprised to know that in it was not
illegal to own Slaves in the U. K. until 2004.

Chapter eighteen

Juneteenth

I had never heard about "Juneteenth", before, so when my wife and I were living with church family friends (the Francis Family) in Beaumont, Southeast Texas, during the first lockdown of 2020, they explained what it was and what it meant, I paid attention to every detail.

Juneteenth (short for "June Nineteenth") marks the day when federal troops arrived in Galveston, Texas in 1865 to take control of the state and ensure that all enslaved people be freed. The troops' arrival came a full two and a half years after the signing of the Emancipation Proclamation. Juneteenth honours the end to slavery in the United States and is considered the longest-running African American holiday.

Confederate General Robert E. Lee had surrendered at Appomattox Court House two months earlier in Virginia, but slavery had remained relatively unaffected in Texas, until U.S. General Gordon Granger stood on Texas soil and read General Orders No. 3: "The people of Texas are informed that, in accordance with a proclamation from the Executive of the United States, all slaves are free."

The Emancipation Proclamation issued by President Abraham Lincoln on January 1, 1863, had established that all enslaved people in Confederate states in rebellion against the Union "shall be then, thenceforward, and forever free."

But the Emancipation Proclamation didn't instantly free any enslaved people. The proclamation only applied to places under Confederate control and not to slave-holding border states or rebel areas already under Union control. However, as Northern troops advanced into the Confederate South, many enslaved people fled behind Union lines.

In Texas, slavery had continued as the state experienced no large-scale fighting or significant presence of Union troops. Many enslavers from outside the Lone Star State had moved there, as they viewed it as a haven for slavery.

After the war ended in the spring of 1865, General Granger's arrival in Galveston that June signalled freedom for Texas's 250,000 enslaved people. Although emancipation didn't happen overnight for everyone in some cases, enslavers withheld the information until after harvest season celebrations broke out among newly freed Black people, and Juneteenth was born. That December, slavery in America was formally abolished with the adoption of the 13ᵗʰ Amendment.

The year following 1865, freedmen in Texas organized the first of what became the annual celebration of "Jubilee Day" on June 19. In the ensuing decades, Juneteenth commemorations featured music, barbecues, prayer services and other activities, and as Black people migrated from Texas to other parts of the country the Juneteenth tradition spread.

In 1979, Texas became the first state to make Juneteenth an official holiday. Today, 47 states recognize Juneteenth as a state holiday, while efforts to make it a national holiday have so far stalled in Congress.

Chapter nineteen

The formation of the Klan

I want now to travel back in time to Christmas Eve, 1865, when a Social Fraternity was formed, that was to become like Black Lives Matter is today, it was highjacked by some of its members seeking to take the organisation down a path of hatred and destruction.

I refer of course to the Ku Klux Klan.

The Ku Klux Klan, the first Klan was founded immediately after the Civil War and lasted until the 1870s. The other began in 1915 and has continued to the present. They were both secretive and Racist groups. The Klan is a globally known White Supremacy Organisation infamous because of its hatred and intolerance of other non-white, non-Protestant groups.

The 19th-century Klan was originally organized as a social club by Confederate veterans in Pulaski, Tennessee, in December 1865. They apparently derived the name from the Greek word *kyklos*, from which comes the English "circle"; "Klan" was added for the sake of alliteration and Ku Klux Klan emerged. The organization quickly became a vehicle for Southern white underground resistance to Radical Reconstruction. Klan members sought the restoration of white supremacy through intimidation and violence aimed at the newly enfranchised Black freedmen. A similar organization, the Knights of the White Camelia, began in Louisiana in 1867.

In the summer of 1867, the Klan was structured into the "Invisible Empire of the South" at a convention in Nashville, Tennessee, attended by delegates from former Confederate states. The group was presided over by a grand wizard (Confederate cavalry general Nathan Bedford Forrest is believed to have been the first grand wizard) and a descending hierarchy of grand dragons, grand titans, and grand cyclopes. Dressed in robes and sheets designed to frighten superstitious Blacks and to prevent identification by the occupying federal troops, Klansmen whipped and killed freedmen and their white supporters in night-time raids.

The 19th-century Klan reached its peak between 1868 and 1870. A potent force, it was largely responsible for the restoration of white rule in North Carolina, Tennessee, and Georgia. But Forrest ordered it disbanded in 1869, largely because of the group's excessive violence. Local branches remained active for a time, however, prompting Congress to pass the Force Act in 1870 and the Ku Klux Klan Act in 1871.

The bills authorized the president to suspend the writ of habeas corpus, suppress disturbances by force, and impose heavy penalties upon terrorist organizations. Pres. Ulysses S. Grant was lax in utilizing this authority, although he did send federal troops to some areas, suspend habeas corpus in nine South Carolina counties, and appoint commissioners who arrested hundreds of Southerners for conspiracy. In United States v. Harris in 1882, the Supreme Court declared the Ku Klux Klan Act unconstitutional, but by that time the Klan had practically disappeared.

It disappeared because its original objective – the restoration of white supremacy throughout the South – had been largely achieved during the 1870s. The need for a secret antiblack organization diminished accordingly.

The 20th-century Klan had its roots more directly in the American nativist tradition. It was organized in 1915 near Atlanta, Georgia, by Col. William J. Simmons, a preacher and promoter of fraternal orders who had been inspired by Thomas Dixon's book The Clansman (1905) and D.W. Griffith's film The Birth of a Nation (1915). The new organization remained small until Edward Y. Clarke and Elizabeth Tyler brought to it their talents as publicity agents and fund raisers. The revived Klan was fuelled partly by patriotism and partly by a romantic nostalgia for the old South, but, more importantly, it expressed the defensive reaction of white Protestants in small-town America who felt threatened by the Bolshevik revolution in Russia and by the large-scale immigration of the previous decades that had changed the ethnic character of American society.

Chapter twenty

Atlanta Race Riots 1906

As I have researched into the Race riots that I knew about, I am amazed at the Violent attacks by armed mobs of White Americans against African Americans, in this chapter we look at the Race Riots in Atlanta, Georgia. These riots began on the evening of 22nd. September 1906, and continued through to the 24th. September.

The events were reported by newspapers around the world, including the French *Le Petit Journal* which described the "lynchings in the USA" and the "massacre of Negroes in Atlanta,"[846] the Scottish *Aberdeen Press & Journal* under the headline "Race Riots in Georgia,"[847] and the London *Evening Standard* under the headlines "Anti-Negro Riots" and "Outrages in Georgia."[848] The final death toll of the conflict is unknown and di"puted" but officially at least 25 African Americans[849] and two whites died.[850] Unofficial reports ranged from 10–100 black Americans killed during the massacre. According to the Atlanta History Centre, some black Americans were hanged from lampposts; others were shot, beaten or stabbed to death. They were pulled from street cars and attacked on the street; white mobs invaded black neighbourhoods, destroying homes and businesses.

The immediate catalyst was newspaper reports of four white women raped in separate incidents, allegedly by African American men. A grand jury later indicted two African Americans for raping Ethel Lawrence and her aunt. An underlying cause was the growing racial tension in a rapidly changing city and economy, competition for jobs, housing, and political power.

The violence did not end until after Governor Joseph M. Terrell called in the Georgia National Guard, and African Americans accused the Atlanta Police Department and some Guardsmen of participating in the violence against them. Local histories by whites ignored the massacre for decades. It was not until 2006 that the event was publicly marked – on its 100th anniversary. The next year, the Atlanta massacre was made part of the state's curriculum for public schools.[851]

---

846 Un lynchage monstre" (September 24, 1906) *Le Petit Journal*

847 THE RACE RIOTS IN GEORGIA". Aberdeenshire, Scotland. Aberdeen Press and Journal. September 25, 1906. p. 6.

848 "ANTI-NEGRO RIOTS". London, England. London Evening Standard. September 26, 1906. p. 7.

849 Burns, Rebecca (September 2006). "Four Days of Rage". *Atlanta Magazine*: 141–145.

850 "WHITES AND NEGROES KILLED AT ATLANTA; Mobs of Blacks Retaliate for Riots — Two Whites Killed; MANY NEGROES SURROUNDED; Two of Band That Killed an Officer Try to Escape but Are Captured and Lynched." (September 25, 1906) *New York Times*

After the end of the American Civil War and during the Reconstruction era, there was violence of whites against blacks throughout the South, as whites reacted to emancipation of blacks, subsequent black criminality, and political empowerment of freedmen. Increased tension also resulted from whites competing with blacks for wages, although the latter were usually restricted to lower-level jobs. Atlanta had developed rapidly, attracting workers for its rebuilding and, particularly from the 1880s as the "rail hub" of the South: workers from all over the country began to flood the city. This resulted in a dramatic increase in both the African American population (9,000 in 1880 to 35,000 in 1900) and the overall city population (from a population of 89,000 in 1900 to 150,000 in 1910)[852] as individuals from rural areas and small towns sought better economic opportunities.[853]

With this influx and the subsequent increase in the demand for resources, race relations in Atlanta became increasingly strained in the crowded city.[854] Whites expanded Jim Crow segregation in residential neighbourhoods and on public transportation.[855]

Freedmen and their descendants had gained the franchise during Reconstruction, and whites increasingly feared and resented their exercise of political power. African Americans had established prosperous businesses and developed an elite who distinguished themselves from working-class blacks. Some whites resented them. Among the successful black businessmen was Alonzo Herndon, who owned and operated a large, refined barber shop that served prominent white men. This new status brought increased competition between blacks and whites for jobs and heightened class distinctions.[856] [857] The police and fire department were still exclusively white, as were most employees in the city and county governments.

State requirements from 1877 limited black voting through poll taxes, record keeping and other devices to impede voter registration, but many freedmen and descendants could still vote. But both major candidates played on racial tensions during their campaigning for the gubernatorial election of 1906, in which M. Hoke

---

[851] SHAILA DEWAN, "100 Years Later, a Painful Episode Is Observed at Last", *New York Times*, 24 September 2006

[852] Mixon, Gregory, and Clifford Kuhn. "Atlanta Race Riot of 1906", *New Georgia Encyclopaedia*

[853] Steinberg, Arthur K. "Atlanta Race Riot (1906)." *Revolts, Protests, Demonstrations, and Rebellions in American History: An Encyclopaedia*, edited by Steven L. Danver, vol. 2, ABC-CLIO, 2011, pp. 681-684

[854] Steinberg, Arthur K. "Atlanta Race Riot (1906)." *Revolts, Protests, Demonstrations, and Rebellions in American History: An Encyclopaedia*, edited by Steven L. Danver, vol. 2, ABC-CLIO, 2011, pp. 681-684

[855] Mixon, Gregory, and Clifford Kuhn. "Atlanta Race Riot of 1906", *New Georgia Encyclopaedia*

[856] Burns 2006:4-5

[857] Walter C. Rucker, James N. Upton 2007. *Encyclopaedia of American Race Riots*. Greenwood Publishing Group pp. 14-20

Smith and Clark Howell competed for the Democratic primary nomination. Smith had explicitly "campaigned on a platform to disenfranchise black voters in Georgia."[858] Howell was also looking to exclude them from politics. Smith was a former publisher of the *Atlanta Journal* and Howell was the editor of the *Atlanta Constitution*. Both candidates used their influence to incite white voters and help spread the fear that whites may not maintain the current social order.[859] These papers and others attacked saloons and bars that were run and frequented by black citizens. These "dives", as whites called them, were said to have nude pictures of women. The *Atlanta Georgian* and the *Atlanta News* publicized police reports of white women who were allegedly sexually molested and raped by black men.[860]

Further information: The Clansman: A Historical Romance of the Ku Klux Klan

"Historians and contemporary commentators cite the stage production of *The Clansman* (by Thomas Dixon, Jr.) in Atlanta as a contributing factor to that city's race riot of 1906, in which white mobs rampaged through African American communities."[861] In Savannah, where it opened next, police and military were on high alert, and present on every streetcar going toward the theatre.[862] Authorities in Macon, where the play was next to open, asked for it not to be permitted, and it was not.[863]

On Saturday afternoon, September 22, 1906, Atlanta newspapers reported four sexual assaults on local white women, allegedly by black men. A grand jury later indicted two for the rape of Ethel Lawrence and her aunt. Following this report, several dozen white men and boys began gathering in gangs, and began to beat, stab, and shoot black people in retaliation, pulling them off or assaulting them on streetcars, beginning in the Points section of downtown. After extra editions of the paper were printed, by midnight estimates were that 10,000 to 15,000 white men and boys had gathered through downtown streets and were roaming to attack black people. By 10 pm, the first three blacks had been killed and more were being treated in the hospital (at least five of whom would die); among these were three women. Governor Joseph M. Terrell called out eight companies of the Fifth Infantry and one battery of light artillery.

---

[858] August 21, 1907: Literacy Test Proposed", This Day in Georgia History, Georgia Info, University Libraries
[859] Burns 2006:4-5
[860] Burns 2006:4-5
[861] Leiter, Andrew. "Thomas Dixon, Jr.: Conflicts in History and Literature". Documenting the American South.
[862] "Rioting Feared by Savannah". *Atlanta Constitution*. September 25, 1906. p. 3.
[863] "*The Clansman* Barred by Macon". *Atlanta Constitution*. September 25, 1906. p. 3.

By 2:30 am, some 25 to 30 blacks were reported dead, with many more injured. The trolley lines had been closed before midnight to reduce movement, in hopes of discouraging the mobs and offering some protection to the African American neighbourhoods, as whites were going there and attacking people in their houses or driving them outside.

Individual black men were killed on the steps of the US Post Office and inside the Marion Hotel, where a crowd chased one. During that night, a large mob attacked Decatur Street, the centre of black restaurants and saloons. It destroyed the businesses and assaulted any black people within sight. Mobs moved to Peters Street and related neighbourhoods to wreak more damage.[864] Heavy rain from 3 am to 5 am helped suppress the fever for rioting.[865]

The events were quickly publicized the next day, Sunday, as violence continued against black people, and the massacre was covered internationally. *Le Petit journal* of Paris reported, "Black men and women were thrown from trolley-cars, assaulted with clubs and pelted with stones."[866] By the next day, the *New York Times* reported that at least 25 to 30 black men and women were killed, with 90 injured. One white man was reported killed, and about 10 injured.[867]

An unknown and disputed number of black people were killed on the street and in their shops, and many were injured. In the centre of the city, the militia was seen by 1 am. But most were not armed and organized until 6 am when more were posted in the business district. Sporadic violence had continued in the late night in distant quarters of the city as small gangs operated. On Sunday hundreds of black people left the city by train and other means, seeking safety at a distance.[868]

On Sunday a group of African Americans met in the Brownsville community south of downtown and near Clark University to discuss actions; they had armed

---

[864] "ATLANTA MOBS KILL TEN NEGROES; Maybe 25 or 30 --- Assaults on Women the Cause; SLAIN WHEREVER FOUND; Cars Stopped in Streets, Victims Torn from Them; MILITIAMEN CALLED OUT; Trolley Systems Stopped to Keep the Mob from Reaching the Negro Quarter", *New York Times*, 23 September 1906
[865] "RIOTING GOES ON, DESPITE TROOPS; Negro Lynched, Another Shot, in Atlanta; SATURDAY'S DEAD ELEVEN; Exodus of Black Servants Troubles City; MAYOR BLAMES NEGROES; Leading Citizens Condemn the Rioters and Demand Cessation of Race Agitation -- Many Injured", *New York Times* (September 24, 1906)
[866] "Un lynchage monstre" (September 24, 1906) *Le Petit Journal*
[867] "RIOTING GOES ON, DESPITE TROOPS; Negro Lynched, Another Shot, in Atlanta; SATURDAY'S DEAD ELEVEN; Exodus of Black Servants Troubles City; MAYOR BLAMES NEGROES; Leading Citizens Condemn the Rioters and Demand Cessation of Race Agitation -- Many Injured", *New York Times* (September 24, 1906)
[868] "RIOTING GOES ON, DESPITE TROOPS; Negro Lynched, Another Shot, in Atlanta; SATURDAY'S DEAD ELEVEN; Exodus of Black Servants Troubles City; MAYOR BLAMES NEGROES; Leading Citizens Condemn the Rioters and Demand Cessation of Race Agitation -- Many Injured", *New York Times* (September 24, 1906)

themselves for defence. Fulton County police learned of the meeting and raided it; an officer was killed in an ensuing shootout. Three militia companies were sent to Brownsville, where they arrested and disarmed about 250 blacks, including university professors.[869] [870]

The New York Times reported that when Mayor James G. Woodward was asked as to the measures taken to prevent a race riot, he replied:

The best way to prevent a race riot depends entirely upon the cause. If your inquiry has anything to do with the present situation in Atlanta, then I would say the only remedy is to remove the cause. As long as the black brutes assault our white women, just so long will they be unceremoniously dealt with.[871]

He had gone around the city on Saturday night trying to calm the mobs but was generally ignored.

On September 28, *The New York Times* reported,

The Fulton County Grand Jury today made the following presentment: "Believing that the sensational manner in which the afternoon newspapers of Atlanta have presented to the people the news of the various criminal acts recently committed in this county has largely influenced the creation of the spirit animating the mob of last Saturday night; and that the editorial utterances of *The Atlanta News* for some time past have been calculated to create a disregard for the proper administration of the law and to promote the organization of citizens to act outside of the law in the punishment of crime."[872]

An unknown and disputed number of African Americans were killed in the conflict. At least two dozen African Americans were believed to have been killed. It was confirmed that there were two white deaths, one a woman who died of a heart attack after seeing mobs outside her house.

On the following Monday and Tuesday, leading citizens of the white community, including the mayor, met to discuss the events and prevent any additional violence.

---

[869] "3,000 GEORGIA TROOPS KEEP PEACE IN ATLANTA; Soldiers Disarming Negroes in All Parts of the City; HUNDREDS CAUGHT IN RAID; Clark University Professors Among Prisoners - Whites and Negroes Meet to Demand Peace", (September 26, 1906) *New York Times*

[870] "Georgia National Guard correspondence regarding the Atlanta Race Riot". *Incoming Correspondence, Adjutant General, Défense, RG 22-1-17, Georgia Archives.* Digital Library of Georgia. Retrieved June 19, 2016.

[871] "THE ATLANTA RIOTS" (September 25, 1906) *New York Times*

[872] "PAPER BLAMED FOR RIOTS.; Grand Jury Accuses Atlanta News of Stirring Up Race Feeling" (September 28, 1906) *New York Times*

The group included leaders of the black elite, helping establish a tradition of communication between these groups. But for decades the massacre was ignored or suppressed in the white community and left out of official histories of the city.

The New York Times noted on September 30 that a letter writer to the Charleston News and Courier wrote in response to the riots:

Separation of the races is the only radical solution of the negro problem in this country. There is nothing new about it. It was the Almighty who established the bounds of the habitation of the races. The negroes were brought here by compulsion; they should be induced to leave here by persuasion.[873]

The New York Times analysed the populations of the ten states in the South with the most African Americans, two of which were majority black, with two others nearly equal in populations, and African Americans totalling about 70% of the total white population. It noted practically the difficulties if so, many workers would be lost, in addition to their businesses.[874]

As an outcome of the massacre, the African American economy suffered, because of property losses, damage, and disruption. Some individual businesses were forced to close. The community made significant social changes,[875] pulling businesses from mixed areas, settling in majority-black neighbourhoods (some of which was enforced by discriminatory housing practices into the 1960s), and changing other social patterns. In the years after the massacre, African Americans were most likely to live in predominately black communities, including those that developed west of the city near Atlanta University or in eastern downtown. Many black businesses dispersed from the centre to the east, where the thriving black business district known as "Sweet Auburn" soon developed.[876]

Many African Americans rejected the accommodationist position of Booker T. Washington at Tuskegee Institute, believing that they had to be more forceful about protecting their communities and advancing their race. Some black Americans modified their opinions on the necessity of armed self-defence, even as many issued explicit warnings about the dangers of armed political struggle. Harvard – educated W. E. B. Du Bois, who was teaching at Atlanta University and supported leadership by the "Talented Tenth", purchased a shotgun after rioting broke out in the city. He said in response to the carnage, "I bought a Winchester double-barrelled

---

[873] "DEPORTING THE NEGROES" (September 30, 1906) *New York Times*
[874] "DEPORTING THE NEGROES" (September 30, 1906) *New York Times*
[875] Johnson, Nicholas (2014). *Negroes and The Gun: The Black Tradition of Arms*. Amherst, New York: Prometheus. pp. 151–157. ISBN 978-1-61614-839-3.
[876] Myrick-Harris, Clarissa (2006). "The Origins of the Civil Rights Movement in Atlanta, 1880-1910". *Perspectives*. 44 (8): 28.

shotgun and two dozen rounds of shells filled with buckshot. If a white mob had stepped on the campus where I lived I would without hesitation have sprayed their guts over the grass."[877] As his position solidified in later years, circa 1906 – 1920, Du Bois argued that organized political violence by black Americans was folly. Still, in response to real – world threats on black people, Du Bois "was adamant about the legitimacy and perhaps the duty of self-defence, even where there [might be a] danger of spill over into political violence."[878]

Elected in 1906, Governor Hoke Smith fulfilled a campaign promise by proposing legislation in August 1907 for a literacy test for voting, which would disenfranchise most blacks and many poor whites through subjective administration by whites. In addition, the legislature included provisions for grandfather clauses to ensure whites were not excluded because of lack of literacy or the required amount of property, and for the Democratic Party to have a white primary, another means of exclusion. These provisions were passed by constitutional amendment in 1908, effectively disfranchising most blacks.[879] Racial segregation was already established by law. Both systems under Jim Crow largely continued into the late 1960s.

After the Great War (World War I), Atlanta worked to promote racial reconciliation and understanding by creating the Commission on Interracial Cooperation in 1919; it later evolved into the Southern Regional Council.[880] But most institutions of the city remained closed to African Americans. For instance, no African American policemen were hired until 1948, after World War II.

The massacre was not covered in local histories and was ignored for decades. In 2006, on its 100th anniversary, the city and citizen groups marked the event with discussions, forums and related events such as "walking tours, public art, memorial services, numerous articles and three new books."[881] The next year, it was made part of the state's social studies curriculum for public schools.[882]

---

[877] Johnson, Nicholas (2014). *Negroes and The Gun: The Black Tradition of Arms*. Amherst, New York: Prometheus. pp. 151–157. ISBN 978-1-61614-839-3.
[878] Johnson, Nicholas (2014). *Negroes and The Gun: The Black Tradition of Arms*. Amherst, New York: Prometheus. pp. 151–157. ISBN 978-1-61614-839-3.
[879] August 21, 1907: Literacy Test Proposed", This Day in Georgia History, Georgia Info, University Libraries
[880] Newman, Harvey K.; Crunk, Glenda (2008). "Religious Leaders in the Aftermath of Atlanta's 1906 Race Riot". *Georgia Historical Quarterly*. 92 (4): 460–485.
[881] SHAILA DEWAN, "100 Years Later, a Painful Episode Is Observed at Last", *New York Times*, 24 September 2006
[882] SHAILA DEWAN, "100 Years Later, a Painful Episode Is Observed at Last", *New York Times*, 24 September 2006

Chapter twenty-one

The Birth of a Nation 1915 (Movie)

The Birth of a Nation, originally called *The Clansman*,[883] is a 1915 American silent drama film directed by D. W. Griffith and starring Lillian Gish. The screenplay is adapted from Thomas Dixon Jr.'s 1905 novel and play *The Clansman*. Griffith co-wrote the screenplay with Frank E. Woods and produced the film with Harry Aitken.

The Birth of a Nation is a landmark of film history.[884] [885] It was the first 12-reel film ever made and, at three hours, also the longest up to that point.[886] Its plot, part fiction and part history, chronicles the assassination of Abraham Lincoln by John Wilkes Booth and the relationship of two families in the Civil War and Reconstruction eras over the course of several years the pro-Union (Northern) Stonemans and the pro-Confederacy (Southern) Camerons. It was originally shown in two parts separated by an intermission, and it was the first to have a musical score for an orchestra. It pioneered close-ups, fade-outs, and a carefully staged battle sequence with hundreds of extras (another first) made to look like thousands.[887] It came with a 13-page "Souvenir Program".[888] It was the first American motion picture to be screened in the White House, viewed there by President Woodrow Wilson.

The film was cont"oversial even before its release and has remained so ever since; it has been called "the most controversial film ever made in the United States".[889] Linc oln is portrayed positively, unusual for a narrative that promotes the Lost Cause ideology. The film portrays African Americans (many of whom are played by white actors in blackface) as unintelligent and sexually aggressive toward white women. The film presents the Ku Klux Klan as a heroic force necessary to preserve American values and a white supremacist social order.[890] [891]presents the Ku Klux

---

[883] Thomas Dixon Dies, Wrote *Clansman*". *The New York Times*. April 4, 1946. p. 23.
[884] The Worst Thing About 'Birth of a Nation' Is How Good It Is". *The New Yorker*.
[885] "The Birth of a Nation (1915)". *filmsite.org*.
[886] Niderost, Eric (October 2005). "'The Birth of a Nation': When Hollywood Glorified the KKK". *HistoryNet*.
[887] Hubbert, Julie (2011). *Celluloid Symphonies: Texts and Contexts in Film Music History*. University of California Press. p. 12. ISBN 978-0-520-94743-6.
[888] Norton, Mary Beth (2015). *A People and a Nation, Volume II: Since 1865, Brief Edition*. Cengage Learning. p. 487. ISBN 978-1-305-14278-7.
[889] Souvenir. The Birth of a Nation". 1915.

Klan as a heroic force necessary to preserve American values and a white supremacist social order.[892] [893]

In response to the film's depictions of black people and Civil War history, African Americans across the nation organized and participated in protests against *The Birth of a Nation*. In places such as in Boston where thousands of white people viewed the film, black leaders tried to have it banned on the basis that it inflamed racial tensions and could incite violence.[894] The NAACP spearheaded an unsuccessful campaign to ban the film.[895] Griffith's indignation at efforts to censor or ban the film motivated him to produce *Intolerance* the following year.[896]

Despite its divisiveness, *The Birth of a Nation* was a huge commercial success and profoundly influenced both the film industry and American culture. The film has been acknowledged as an inspiration for the rebirth of the Ku Klux Klan, which took place only a few months after its release. In 1992, the Library of Congress deemed the film "culturally, historically, or aesthetically significant" and selected it for preservation in the National Film Registry.[897] [898]

The film consists of two parts of similar length. The f'rst part closes with the assassination of Abraham Lincoln, after which there is an intermission. At the New York premiere, Dixon spoke on stage between the parts, reminding the audience that the dramatic version of *The Clansman* appeared in that venue nine years previously. "Mr. Dixon also observed that he would have allowed none but the son of a Confederate soldier to direct the film version of *The Clansman*."[899]

Part 1: Civil War of United States:

---

[890] *Slide, Anthony (2004). American Racist: The Life and Films of Thomas Dixon. Also on Project Muse: http://muse.jhu.edu/book/10080. University Press of Kentucky. ISBN 978-0-8131-2328-8.*
[891] Rampell, Ed (March 3, 2015). "'The Birth of a Nation': The most racist movie ever made". *The Washington Post.*
[892] *Slide, Anthony (2004). American Racist: The Life and Films of Thomas Dixon. Also on Project Muse: http://muse.jhu.edu/book/10080. University Press of Kentucky. ISBN 978-0-8131-2328-8.*
[893] Rampell, Ed (March 3, 2015). "'The Birth of a Nation': The most racist movie ever made". *The Washington Post.*
[894] MJ Movie Reviews – Birth of a Nation, The (1915) by Dan DeVore".
[895] MJ Movie Reviews – Birth of a Nation, The (1915) by Dan DeVore".
[896] Armstrong, Eric M. (February 26, 2010). "Revered and Reviled: D.W. Griffith's 'The Birth of a Nation'". *The Moving Arts Film Journal.*
[897] The Birth of a Nation' Sparks Protest". Mass Moments. Archived from the original on May 12, 2013. Retrieved July 3, 2013.
[898] "Top Ten – Top 10 Banned Films of the 20th century – Top 10 – Top 10 List – Top 10 Banned Movies – Censored Movies – Censored Films". Alternativereel.com.
[899] "Complete National Film Registry Listing | Film Registry | National Film Preservation Board | Programs at the Library of Congress". *Library of Congress.*

The film follows two juxtaposed families. One is the Northern Stonemans: abolitionist U.S. Representative Austin Stoneman (based on the Reconstruction-era Representative Thaddeus Stevens of Pennsylvania),[900] [901] his daughter, and two sons. The other is the Southern Camerons: Dr. Cameron, his wife, their three sons and two daughters. Phil, the elder Stoneman son, falls in love with Margaret Cameron, during the brothers' visit to the Cameron estate in South Carolina, representing the Old South. Meanwhile, young Ben Cameron (modelled after Leroy McAfee)[902] idolizes a picture of Elsie Stoneman. When the Civil War arrives, the young men of both families enlist in their respective armies. The younger Stoneman and two of the Cameron brothers are killed in combat. Meanwhile, the Cameron women are rescued by Confederate soldiers who rout a black militia after an attack on the Cameron home. Ben Cameron leads a heroic final charge at the Siege of Petersburg, earning the nickname of "the Little Colonel", but he is also wounded and captured. He is then taken to a Union military hospital in Washington, D.C.

During his stay at the hospital, he is told that he will be hanged. Also at the hospital, he meets Elsie Stoneman, whose picture he has been carrying; she is working there as a nurse. Elsie takes Cameron's mother, who had travelled to Washington to tend her son, to see Abraham Lincoln, and Mrs. Cameron persuades the President to pardon Ben. When Lincoln is assassinated at Ford's Theatre, his conciliatory post-war policy expires with him. In the wake of the president's death, Austin Stoneman and other Radical Republicans are determined to punish the South, employing harsh measures that Griffith depicts as having been typical of the Reconstruction Era.[903]

Part 2: Reconstruction:

Stoneman and his protégé Silas Lynch, a psychopathic mulatto (modelled after Alonzo J. Ransier and Richard Howell Gleaves),[904] [905] head to South

---

[900] 'The Birth of a Nation' Documents History". *The Los Angeles Times*. January 4, 1993
[901] "The Birth of a Nation". *The New York Times*. March 4, 1915.
[902] .... the portrayal of "Austin Stoneman" (bald, clubfoot; mulatto mistress, etc.) made no mistaking that, of course, Stoneman was Thaddeus Stevens..." Robinson, Cedric J.; *Forgeries of Memory and Meaning*. University of North Carolina, 2007; p. 99.
[903] *Garsman, Ian (2011–2012). "The Tragic Era Exposed". Reel American History. Lehigh University Digital Library.*
[904] Corkin, Stanley (1996). *Realism and the birth of the modern United States: cinema, literature, and culture*. Athens: University of Georgia Press. p. 156. ISBN 0-8203-1730-6. OCLC 31610418.
[905] Griffith followed the then-dominant Dunning School or "Tragic Era" view of Reconstruction presented by early 20th-century historians such as William Archibald Dunning and Claude G.

Carolina to observe the implementation of Reconstruction policies first-hand. During the election, in which Lynch is elected lieutenant governor, blacks are observed stuffing the ballot boxes, while many whites are denied the vote. The newly elected, mostly black members of the South Carolina legislature are shown at their desks displaying extremely racist stereotypical behaviour, such as one member taking off his shoes and putting his feet up on his desk, and others drinking liquor and feasting on fried chicken.

Meanwhile, inspired by observing white children pretending to be ghosts to scare black children, Ben fights back by forming the Ku Klux Klan. As a result, Elsie, out of loyalty to her father, breaks off her relationship with Ben. Later, Flora Cameron goes off alone into the woods to fetch water and is followed by Gus, a freedman and soldier who is now a captain. He confronts Flora and tells her that he desires to get married. Frightened, she flees into the forest, pursued by Gus. Trapped on a precipice, Flora warns Gus she will jump if he comes any closer. When he does, she leaps to her death. Having run through the forest looking for her, Ben has seen her jump; he holds her as she dies, then carries her body back to the Cameron home. In response, the Klan hunts down Gus, tries him, finds him guilty, and lynches him.

Lynch then orders a crackdown on the Klan after discovering Gus's murder. He also secures the passing of legislation allowing mixed-race marriages. Dr. Cameron is arrested for possessing Ben's Klan regalia, now considered a capital crime. He is rescued by Phil Stoneman and a few of his black servants. Together with Margaret Cameron, they flee. When their wagon breaks down, they make their way through the woods to a small hut that is home to two sympathetic former Union soldiers who agree to hide them. An intertitle states, "The former enemies of North and South are united again in common defence of their Aryan birth right."[906]

Congressman Stoneman leaves to avoid being connected with Lt. Gov. Lynch's crackdown. Elsie, learning of Dr. Cameron's arrest, goes to Lynch to plead for his release. Lynch, who had been lusting after Elsie, tries to force her to marry him, which causes her to faint. Stoneman returns, causing Elsie to be placed in another room. At first Stoneman is happy when Lynch tells him he wants to marry a white woman, but he is then angered when Lynch tells him that it is Stoneman's daughter. Undercover Klansman spies go to get help when they discover Elsie's plight after

---

Bowers.Stokes 2007, pp. 190–191.
[906] Stokes 2007

she breaks a window and cries out for help. Elsie falls unconscious again and revives while gagged and being bound. The Klan gathered, with Ben leading them, ride in to gain control of the town. When news about Elsie reaches Ben, he and others go to her rescue. Elsie frees her mouth and screams for help. Lynch is captured. Victorious, the Klansmen celebrate in the streets. Meanwhile, Lynch's militia surrounds and attacks the hut where the Camerons are hiding. The Klansmen, with Ben at their head, race in to save them just in time. The next election day, blacks find a line of mounted and armed Klansmen just outside their homes and are intimidated into not voting.

The film concludes with a double wedding as Margaret Cameron marries Phil Stoneman and Elsie Stoneman marries Ben Cameron. The masses are shown oppressed by a giant warlike figure who gradually fades away. The scene shifts to another group finding peace under the image of Jesus Christ. The penultimate title is: "Dare we dream of a golden day when the bestial War shall rule no more. But instead, the gentle Prince in the Hall of Brotherly Love in the City of Peace."

The Klan was unable to stem the growth of a new racial tolerance in the South in the years that followed. Though the organization continued some of its surreptitious activities into the early 21st century, cases of Klan violence became more isolated, and its membership had declined to a few thousand. The Klan became a chronically fragmented mélange made up of several separate and competing groups, some of which occasionally entered alliances with neo-Nazi and other right-wing extremist groups.

Chapter twenty-two

The Red Summer of 1919

Red Summer is the period from late winter through early autumn of 1919 during which white supremacist terrorism and racial riots took place in more than three dozen cities across the United States, as well as in one rural county in Arkansas. The term "Red Summer" was coined by civil rights activist and author James Weldon Johnson, who had been employed as a field secretary by the National Association for the Advancement of Coloured People (NAACP) since 1916. In 1919, he organized peaceful protests against the racial violence which had occurred that summer.[907] [908]

In most instances, attacks consisted of white-on-black violence. However, numerous African Americans also fought back, notably in the Chicago and Washington, D.C. race riots, which resulted in 38 and 15 deaths, respectively, along with even more injuries, and extensive property damage in Chicago.[909] Still, the highest number of fatalities occurred in the rural area around Elaine, Arkansas, where an estimated 100 – 240 black people and five white people were killed, an event now known as the Elaine massacre.

The anti-black riots developed from a variety of post-World War I social tensions, generally related to the demobilization of both black and white members of the United States Armed Forces following World War I; an economic slump; and increased competition in the job and housing markets between ethnic European Americans and African Americans.[910] The time would also be marked by labour unrest, for which certain industrialists used black people as strike-breakers, further inflaming the resentment of white workers.

The riots and killings were extensively documented by the press, which, along with the federal government, feared socialist and communist influence on the black time following the 1917 Bolshevik Revolution in Russia. They also feared

---

907 Erickson, Alana J. 1960. "Red Summer." Pp. 2293–94 in *Encyclopaedia of African American Culture and History*. New York: Macmillan.
908 Cunningham, George P. 1960. "James Weldon Johnson." Pp. 1459–61 in *Encyclopaedia of African American Culture and History*. New York: Macmillan.
909 The New York Times 1919
910 Public Broadcasting Service (PBS) 2018, p. Part 3.

foreign anarchists, who had bombed the homes and businesses of prominent figures and government leaders.

With the mobilization of troops for World War I, and with immigration from Europe cut off, the industrial cities of the American Northeast and Midwest experienced severe labour shortages. As a result, northern manufacturers recruited throughout the South, from which an exodus of workers ensued.[911]

By 1919, an estimated 500,000 African Americans had emigrated from the Southern United States to the industrial cities of the Northeast and Midwest in the first wave of the Great Migration (which continued until 1940).[912] African-American workers filled new positions in expanding industries, such as the railroads, as well as many existing jobs formerly held by whites. In some cities, they were hired as strike-breakers, especially during the strikes of 1917.[913] This increased resentment against blacks among many working-class whites, immigrants, and first-generation Americans.

In the summer of 1917, violent racial riots against blacks due to labour tensions broke out in East St. Louis, Illinois and Houston, Texas.[914] Following the war, rapid demobilization of the military without a plan for absorbing veterans into the job market, and the removal of price controls, led to unemployment and inflation that increased competition for jobs. Jobs were very difficult for African Americans to get in the South due to racism and segregation.[915]

During the First Red Scare of 1919–20, following the 1917 Russian Revolution, anti-Bolshevik sentiment in the United States quickly followed on the anti-German sentiment arising in the war years. Many politicians and government officials, together with much of the press and the public, feared an imminent attempt to overthrow the U.S. government to create a new regime modelled on that of the Soviets. Authorities viewed with alarm African-Americans' advocacy of racial equality, labour rights, and the rights of victims of mobs to defend themselves.[916] In a private conversation in March 1919, President Woodrow Wilson said that "the American Negro returning from abroad would be our greatest medium in conveying Bolshevism to America."[917] Other whites expressed a wide range of opinions, some anticipating unsettled times and others seeing no signs of tension.[918]

---

[911] Kennedy 2004, pp. 279, 281–282.
[912] The New York Times 1919
[913] Kennedy 2004, pp. 279, 281–282.
[914] Barnes 2008, p. 4.
[915] The Great Migration
[916] Public Broadcasting Service (PBS) 2018, p. Part 3.
[917] McWhirter 2011, p. 56
[918] McWhirter 2011, pp. 19, 22–24

Early in 1919, Dr. George Edmund Haynes, an educator employed as director of Negro Economics for the U.S. Department of Labour, wrote: "The return of the Negro soldier to civil life is one of the most delicate and difficult questions confronting the Nation, north and south."[919] One black veteran wrote a letter to the editor of the *Chicago Daily News* saying the returning black veterans "are now new men and world men…and their possibilities for direction, guidance, honest use, and power are limitless, only they must be instructed and led. They have awakened, but they have not yet the complete conception of what they have awakened to."[920] W. E. B. Du Bois, an official of the NAACP and editor of its monthly magazine, saw an opportunity:[921]

By the God of Heaven, we are cowards and jackasses if now that the war is over, we do not marshal every ounce of our brain and brawn to fight a sterner, longer, more unbending battle against the forces of hell in our own land.

In the autumn of 1919, following the violence-filled summer, George Edmund Haynes reported on the events as a prelude to an investigation by the U.S. Senate Committee on the Judiciary. He identified 38 separate racial riots against blacks in widely scattered cities, in which whites attacked black people.[922] Unlike earlier racial riots against blacks in U.S. history, the 1919 events were among the first in which black people in number resisted white attacks and fought back.[923] A. Philip Randolph, a civil rights activist and leader of the Brotherhood of Sleeping Car Porters, publicly defended the right of black people to self-defence.[924]

In addition, Haynes reported that between January 1 and September 14, 1919, white mobs lynched at least 43 African Americans, with 16 hanged and others shot; while another 8 men were burned at the stake. The states were unwilling to interfere or prosecute such mob murders.[925] In May, following the first serious racial incidents, W. E. B. Du Bois published his essay "Returning Soldiers":[926]

We return from the slavery of uniform which the world's madness demanded us to don to the freedom of civil garb. We stand again to look America squarely in the face and call a spade a spade. We sing: This country of ours, despite all its better souls have done and dreamed, is yet a shameful land.…

---

[919] McWhirter 2011, p. 13
[920] McWhirter 2011, p. 15
[921] McWhirter 2011, p. 14
[922] McWhirter 2011, p. 14
[923] Maxouris 2019
[924] Erickson, Alana J. 1960. "Red Summer." Pp. 2293–94 in *Encyclopaedia of African American Culture an*
[925] The New York Times 1919
[926] McWhirter 2011, pp. 31–32, emphasis in original

We *return*.

We *return from fighting*.

We return *fighting*.

- April 13: In rural Georgia, the riot of Jenkins County led to 6 deaths, as well as the destruction of various property by arson, including the Carswell Grove Baptist Church, and 3 black Masonic lodges in Millen, Georgia.
- May 10: The Charleston riot resulted in the injury of 5 white and 18 black men, along with the death of 3 others: Isaac Doctor, William Brown, and James Talbot, all black. Following the riot, the city of Charleston, South Carolina imposed martial law.[927] A Naval investigation found that four U.S. sailors and one civilian all white men initiated the riot.[928]
- Early July: A white race riot in Longview, Texas led to the deaths of at least 4 men and destroyed the African-American housing district in the town.[929]
- July 3: Local police in Bisbee, Arizona attacked the 10th U.S. Cavalry, an African-American unit known as the "Buffalo Soldiers," formed in 1866.[930]
- July 14: The Garfield Park riot took place in Garfield Park, Indianapolis, where multiple people, including a 7-year-old girl, were wounded when gunfire broke out.

Beginning on July 19, Washington, D.C. saw four days of mob violence against black individuals and businesses perpetrated by white men many of whom in the military and in uniforms of all three services in response to the rumoured arrest of a black man for rape of a white woman. The men rioted, randomly beat black people on the street, and pulled others off streetcars for attacks.

When police refused to intervene, the black population fought back. The city closed saloons and theatres to discourage assemblies. Meanwhile, the four white-owned local papers, including the *Washington Post*, "ginned up...weeks of hysteria",[931] fanning the violence with incendiary headlines, calling in at least one instance for a mobilization of a "clean-up" operation.[932] After four days of police inaction,

---

[927] The New York Times
[928] Rucker & Upton 2007, pp. 92-93.
[929] The New York Times
[930] Rucker & Upton 2007, p. 554.
[931] Brockell, Gillian (July 15, 2019). "The deadly race riot 'aided and abetted' by The Washington Post a century ago". *Washington Post*.
[932] Perl 1999, p. A1

President Woodrow Wilson mobilized the National Guard to restore order.[933] When the violence ended, " total o" 15 people had died: 10 white people, including two police officers; and 5 black people. Fifty people were seriously wounded, while another 100 less severely wounded. It would be one of the few times in 20th-century white-on-black riots that white fatalities outnumbered those of black people.[934]

The NAACP sent a telegram of protest to President Woodrow Wilson:[935]

The shame put upon the country by the mobs, including United States soldiers, sailors, and marines, which have assaulted innocent and unoffending negroes in the national capital. Men in uniform have attacked negroes on the streets and pulled them from streetcars to beat them. Crowds are reported ...to have directed attacks against any passing negro.... The effect of such riots in the national capital upon race antagonism will be to increase bitterness and danger of outbreaks elsewhere. National Association for the Advancement of Coloured People calls upon you as President and Commander in Chief of the Armed Forces of the nation to make statement condemning mob violence and to enforce such military law as situation demands....

July 21: In Norfolk, Virginia, a white mob attacked a homecoming celebration for African-American veterans of World War I. At least 6 people were shot, and the local police called in Marines and Navy personnel to restore order.[936]

Beginning on July 27, the Chicago race riot marked the greatest massacre of Red Summer. Chicago's beaches along Lake Michigan were segregated by custom. When Eugene Williams, a black youth, swam into an area on the South Side customarily used by whites, he was stoned and drowned. Chicago police refused to take action against the attackers, thus young black men responded with violence, lasting for 13 days, with the white mobs led by the ethnic Irish.

White mobs destroyed hundreds of mostly black homes and businesses on the South Side of Chicago. The State of Illinois called in a militia force of 7 regiments: several thousand men, to restore order.[937] The resulting casualties of the riots include: 38 fatalities (23 blacks and 15 whites); 527 injured; and 1,000 black families left homeless.[938] Other accounts reported 50 people were killed, with unofficial numbers and rumours reporting even more.

---

[933] Mills 2006
[934] Ackerman 2008, pp. 60–62.
[935] The New York Times
[936] The New York Times
[937] The New York Times
[938] The Editors of Encyclopaedia 2019

On August 12, at their annual convention, the North-eastern Federation of Coloured Women's Clubs (NFCWC) denounced the rioting and burning of negroes' homes, asking President Wilson "to use every means within your power to stop the rioting in Chicago and the propaganda used to incite such."[939]

At the end of August, the NAACP protested again to the White House, noting the attack on the organization's secretary in Austin, Texas the previous week. Their telegram read: "The National Association for the Advancement of coloured People respectfully enquires how long the Federal Government under your administration intends to tolerate anarchy in the United States?"[940]

August 30–31, the Knoxville Riot in Tennessee broke out after the arrest of a black suspect on suspicion of murdering a white woman. Searching for the prisoner, a lynch mob stormed the county jail, where they liberated 16 white prisoners, including suspected murderers.[941] The mob attacked the African-American business district, where they fought against the district's black business owners, leaving at least 7 dead and wounding more than 20 people.[942] [943] [944]

10,000 ethnic whites from South Omaha attacked and burned the county courthouse to force the release of a black prisoner accused of raping a white woman. The mob lynched the suspect, Will Brown, hanging him and burning his body. The group then spread out, attacking black neighbourhoods and stores on the north side, destroying property valued at more than a million dollars.

Once the mayor and governor appealed for help, the federal government sent U.S. Army troops from nearby forts, who were commanded by Major General Leonard Wood, a friend of Theodore Roosevelt, and a leading candidate for the Republican nomination for President in 1920.[945]

On September 30, a massacre broke out against blacks in Elaine, Phillips County, Arkansas,[946] being distinct for having occurred in the rural South rather than a city.

The event erupted from the resistance of the white minority against the organization of labour by black sharecroppers, along with the fear of socialism. Planters opposed such efforts to organize and thus tried to disrupt their meetings in the local chapter of

939 The New York Times
940 The New York Times 1919
941 The New York Times 1919
942 Wheeler 2017
943 Whitaker 2009, p. 53.
944 Lakin 2000, pp. 1–29.
945 Pietrusza 2009, pp. 167–172.
946 Public Broadcasting Service (PBS) 2018, p. Part 3.

the Progressive Farmers and Household Union of America. In a confrontation, a white man was fatally shot and another wounded. The planters formed a militia to arrest the African-American farmers, and hundreds of whites came from the region. They acted as a mob, attacking black people over two days at random. During the riot, the mob killed an estimated 100 to 237 black people, while 5 whites also died in the violence.

Arkansas Governor Charles Hillman Brough appointed a Committee of Seven, composed of prominent local white businessmen, to investigate. The Committee would conclude that the Sharecroppers' Union was a Socialist enterprise and "established for the purpose of banding negroes together for the killing of white people."[947] The report generated such headlines as the following in the *Dallas Morning News*: "Negroes Seized in Arkansas Riots Confess to Widespread Plot; Planned Massacre of Whites Today." Several agents of the Justice Department's Bureau of Investigation spent a week interviewing participants, though speaking to no sharecroppers. The Bureau also reviewed documents, filing a total of nine reports stating there was no evidence of a conspiracy of the sharecroppers to murder anyone.

The local government tried 79 black people, who were all convicted by all-white juries, and 12 were sentenced to death for murder. As Arkansas and other southern states had disenfranchised most black people at the turn of the 20th century, they could not vote, run for political office, or serve on juries. The remainder of the defendants were sentenced to prison terms of up to 21 years. Appeals of the convictions of 6 of the defendants went to the U.S. Supreme Court, which reversed the verdicts due to failure of the court to provide due process. This was a precedent for heightened Federal oversight of defendants' rights in the conduct of state criminal cases.[948]

November 13: The Wilmington race riot was a violent riot between white and black residents of Wilmington, Delaware.

[947] Freedman 2001, p. 68.
[948] Whitaker 2009, pp. 131–142

Chapter twenty-three

The Tulsa Race Massacre

30th. May – 1st. June 1921

Tulsa race massacre of 1921, also called Tulsa race riot of 1921, one of the most severe incidents of racial violence in U.S. history. It occurred in Tulsa, Oklahoma, beginning on May 31, 1921, and lasting for two days. The massacre left somewhere between 30 and 300 people dead, mostly African Americans, and destroyed Tulsa's prosperous Black neighbourhood of Greenwood, known as the "Black Wall Street." More than 1,400 homes and businesses were burned, and nearly 10,000 people were left homeless. Despite its severity and destructiveness, the Tulsa race massacre was barely mentioned in history books until the late 1990s, when a state commission was formed to document the incident.

The Tulsa race massacre took place on May 31 and June 1, 1921. Alternatively known as the Black Wall Street massacre[949] or the Tulsa race riot,[950] Mobs of White residents, many of them deputized and given weapons by city officials, attacked Black residents and burned businesses of the Greenwood District in Tulsa, Oklahoma, US, in response to a pretended sexual assault against a 17-year-old white girl and killings of 10 white men.[951] It marks one of "the single worst incidents of racial violence in American history".[952] The attack, carried out on the ground and from private aircraft, destroyed more than 35 square blocks of the district at that time the wealthiest Black community in the United States, known as "Black Wall Street".[953]

More than 800 people were admitted to hospitals, and as many as 6,000 Black residents were interned in large facilities, many of them for several days.[954] [955] The

---

[949] Franklin 1931, pp. 8, 10.
[950] Oklahoma Commission 2001, pp. 193, 196.
[951] Brown, DeNeen L. (October 22, 2019). "HBO's 'Watchmen' depicts a deadly Tulsa race massacre that was all too real". *Washington Post*. Retrieved July 3, 2020. White city police officer "deputized" members of the lynch mob and "instructed them to get a gun and get a n-----," according to the Oklahoma Historical Society.
[952] White, Walter F. (August 23, 2001). "Tulsa, 1921". *The Nation*.
[953] Nearly 100 Years Later, Tulsa Begins Search for Mass Graves From 1921 Black Wall Street Massacre". *The Root*.

Oklahoma Bureau of Vital Statistics officially recorded 36 dead.[956] A 2001 state commission examination of events was able to confirm 39 dead, 26 Black and 13 White, based on contemporary autopsy reports, death certificates and other records.[957] The commission gave several estimates ranging from 75 to 300 dead.[958] [959]

The massacre began during the Memorial Day weekend after 19-year-old Dick Rowland, a Black shoe shine boy, was accused of assaulting Sarah Page, the 17-year-old White elevator operator of the nearby Drexel Building. He was taken into custody. After the arrest, rumours spread through the city that Rowland was to be lynched. Upon hearing reports that a mob of hundreds of White men had gathered around the jail where Rowland was being kept, a group of 75 Black men, some of whom were armed, arrived at the jail to ensure that Rowland would not be lynched. The sheriff persuaded the group to leave the jail, assuring them that he had the situation under control. A shot was fired, and then, according to the reports of the sheriff, "all hell broke loose." At the end of the exchange of fire, 12 people were dead, 10 White and 2 Black. As news of these deaths spread throughout the city, mob violence exploded. White rioters rampaged through the Black neighbourhood that night and the next morning, killing men and burning and looting stores and homes. Around noon on June 1, the Oklahoma National Guard imposed martial law, ending the massacre.

About 10,000 Black people were left homeless and property damage amounted to more than $1.5 million in real estate and $750,000 in personal property (equivalent to $32.65 million in 2020). Many survivors left Tulsa, while Black and White residents who stayed in the city kept silent about the terror, violence and resulting losses for decades. The massacre was largely omitted from local, state, and national histories.

In 1996, 75 years after the massacre, a bipartisan group in the state legislature authorized the formation of the Oklahoma Commission to Study the Tulsa Race Riot of 1921. The commission's final report, published in 2001, states that the city had conspired with the mob of White citizens against Black citizens; it

[954] Ellsworth, Scott (2009). "Tulsa Race Riot". *The Encyclopaedia of Oklahoma History and Culture.*
[955] Huddleston Jr, Tom (July 4, 2020). "'Black Wall Street': The history of the wealthy black community and the massacre perpetrated there". *CNBC.*
[956] Messer, Chris M.; Bell, Patricia A. (July 31, 2008). "Mass Media and Governmental Framing of Riots". *Journal of Black Studies.* 40 (5): 851–870. doi:10.1177/0021934708318607. JSTOR 40648610. S2CID 146678313.
[957] Messer, Chris M.; Beamon, Krystal; Bell, Patricia A. (2013). "The Tulsa Riot of 1921: Collective Violence and Racial Frames". *The Western Journal of Black Studies.* 37 (1): 50–59.
[958] *Various (February 21, 2001). Report on Tulsa Race Riot of 1921. Oklahoma Commission to Study the Tulsa Race Riot of 1921. p. 123. Archived from the original on June 21, 2020. Retrieved June 22, 2020.*
[959] Oklahoma Commission 2001, p. 114.

recommended a program of reparations to survivors and their descendants.[960] The state passed legislation to establish scholarships for the descendants of survivors, encourage the economic development of Greenwood, and develop a park in memory of the victims of the massacre in Tulsa. The Park was dedicated in 2010. In 2020, the massacre became a part of the Oklahoma school curriculum.[961]

I n 1921, Oklahoma had a racially, socially, and politically tense atmosphere. The territory of northern Oklahoma had been established for the resettlement of Native Americans from the southeast, some of whom had owned slaves.[962] Other areas had received many settlers from the South whose families had been slaveholders before the Civil War. Oklahoma was admitted as a state on November 16, 1907. The newly created state legislature passed racial segregation laws, commonly known as Jim Crow laws, as its first order of business. The 1907 Oklahoma Constitution did not call for strict segregation; delegates feared that, should they include such restrictions, U.S. President Theodore Roosevelt would veto the document. Still, the first law passed by the new legislature segregated all rail travel, and voter registration rules effectively disenfranchised most Black Americans. That meant they were also barred from serving on juries or in local office. These laws were enforced until after passage of the federal Voting Rights Act of 1965. Major cities passed additional restrictions.[963]

On August 4, 1916, Tulsa passed an ordinance that mandated residential segregation by forbidding Black or White people from residing on any block where three-fourths or more of the residents were members of the other race. Although the United States Supreme Court declared such an ordinance unconstitutional the following year, Tulsa and many other cities continued to establish and enforce segregation for the next three decades.[964]

Many servicemen returned to Tulsa following the end of the First World War in 1918, and as they tried to re-enter the labour market, social tensions and anti-Black sentiment increased in cities where job competition was high. North-eastern Oklahoma was in an economic slump that increased unemployment. The American Civil War, which ended in 1865, was still in living memory; civil rights for African Americans were lacking, and the Ku Klux Klan was resurgent (primarily through the

[960] *Brown, DeNeen L. (October 22, 2019). "HBO's 'Watchmen' depicts a deadly Tulsa race massacre that was all too real". Washington Post. Retrieved July 3, 2020. White city police officer "deputized" members of the lynch mob and "instructed them to get a gun and get a n-----," according to the Oklahoma Historical Society.*

[961] Oklahoma Commission 2001, pp. 13, 23.

[962] *White, Walter F. (August 23, 2001). "Tulsa, 1921". The Nation. ISSN 0027-8378.*

[963] Madigan, Tim. 2001. *The Burning: Massacre, Destruction, and the Tulsa Race Riot of 1921.* New York: St. Martin's Press. pp. 4, 131–32, 144, 159, 164, 183–184, 249. ISBN 0-312-27283-9

[964] Oklahoma Commission 2001,

wildly popular 1915 film *The Birth of a Nation*).[965] Since 1915, the Ku Klux Klan had been growing in urban chapters across the country. Its first significant appearance in Oklahoma occurred on August 12, 1921.[966] By the end of 1921, 3,200 of Tulsa's 72,000 residents were Klan members according to one estimate.[967] In the early 20th century, lynching's were common in Oklahoma as part of a continuing effort to assert and maintain white supremacy.[968] By 1921, at least 31 people, mostly men and boys, had been lynched in the newly formed state; 26 were Black.

At the same time, Black veterans pushed to have their civil rights enforced, believing they had earned full citizenship by military service. In what became known as the "Red Summer" of 1919, industrial cities across the Midwest and Northeast experienced severe race riots in which Whites, sometimes including local authorities, attacked Black communities. In Chicago and some other cities, Blacks defended themselves for the first time with force but were often outnumbered.

Tulsa, as a booming oil city, also supported many affluent, educated, and professional African American people. Greenwood was a district in Tulsa which was organized in 1906 following Booker T. Washington's 1905 tour of Arkansas, Indian Territory and Oklahoma. It was a namesake of the Greenwood District that Washington had established as his own demonstration in Tuskegee, Alabama, five years earlier. Greenwood became so prosperous that it came to be known as "the Negro Wall Street" (now commonly referred to as "the Black Wall Street").[969] Most Black people lived together in the district. Black Americans had created their own businesses and services in this enclave, including several grocers, two newspapers, two movie theatres, nightclubs, and numerous churches. Black professionals, including doctors, dentists, lawyers, and clergy, served their peers. During his trip to Tulsa in 1905, Washington encouraged the co-operation, economic independence and excellence being demonstrated there. Greenwood residents selected their own leaders and raised capital there to support economic growth. In the surrounding areas of north-eastern Oklahoma, they also enjoyed relative prosperity and participated in the oil boom.[970]

[965] Connor, Jay (2020). "The 1921 Tulsa Race Massacre Will Officially Become a Part of the Oklahoma School Curriculum Beginning in the Fall". *The Root*.

[966] Smith, Ryan (2018). "How Native American Slaveholders Complicate the Trail of Tears Narrative". *Smithsonian Magazine*. Archived from the original on October 16, 2019. Retrieved October 28, 2019.

[967] Hirsch 2002, p. 36.

[968] Smith, Ryan (2018). "How Native American Slaveholders Complicate the Trail of Tears Narrative". *Smithsonian Magazine*.

[969] *Clark, Alexis. "How 'The Birth of a Nation' Revived the Ku Klux Klan". HISTORY.*

[970] *Clark, Alexis. "How 'The Birth of a Nation' Revived the Ku Klux Klan". HISTORY. Retrieved March 1, 2021.*

On May 30, 1921, 19-year-old Dick Rowland, a Black shoe shine boy employed at a Main Street shine parlour, entered the only elevator of the nearby Drexel Building at 319 South Main Street to use the top-floor 'coloured' restroom, which his employer had arranged for use by his Black employees. There, he encountered Sarah Page, the 17-year-old White elevator operator on duty. Whether – and to what extent – Dick Rowland and Sarah Page knew each other has long been a matter of speculation. The two likely knew each other at least by sight as Rowland would have regularly rode in Page's elevator on his way to and from the restroom. Others have speculated that the pair might have been interracial lovers, a dangerous and deadly taboo then. What happened in the elevator is anyone's best guess. A clerk at Renberg's, a clothing store on the first floor of the Drexel, heard what sounded like a woman's scream and saw a young Black man rushing from the building. The clerk went to the elevator and found Page in a distraught state. Thinking she had been sexually assaulted; he summoned the authorities. Apart from the cl'rk's interpretation that Rowland'attempted to rape Page, many explanations have been given for the incident, with the most common being that that Dick Rowland tripped as he got onto the elevator and, as he tried to catch his fall, he grabbed onto the arm of Sarah Page, who then screamed. Others suggested that Rowland and Page had a lover's quarrel.[971]

The 2001 Oklahoma Commission Final Report notes that it was unusual for both Rowland and Page to be working downtown on Memorial Day, when most stores and businesses were closed, but has also speculated that Roland was there because the shine parlour he worked at may have been open, to draw in some of the parade traffic, while Page had been required to work in order to transport Drexel Building employees and their families to choice parade viewing spots on the building's upper floors.[972]

Although the police questioned Page, no written account of her statement has been found. However, the police determined that what happened between the two teenagers was something less than an assault. The authorities conducted a low-key investigation rather than launching a manhunt for her alleged assailant. Page told the police that Rowland had grabbed her arm but nothing more and that she would not press charges.[973] [974]

Regardless of whether assault had occurred, Rowland had reason to be fearful. At the time, such an accusation alone put him at risk for attack by angry mobs of White

[971] *Alexander, Charles C (1965). The Ku Klux Klan in the southwest. OCLC 637673750.*

[972] *Alexander, Charles C (1965). The Ku Klux Klan in the southwest. OCLC 637673750.*

[973] "Tulsa History: Urban Development (1901–1945)". *Tulsa Preservation Commission.* May 19, 2015.

[974] Levy, David W. (2005). "XIII: The Struggle for Racial Justice". *The University of Oklahoma: A History.* II: 1917–1950. University of Oklahoma Press. ISBN 978-0-8061-5277-6.

people. Realizing the gravity of the situation, Rowland fled to his mother's house in the Greenwood neighbourhood.[975]

On the morning after the incident, Henry Carmichael, a White detective, and Henry C. Pack, a Black patrolman, located Rowland on Greenwood Avenue and detained him. Pack was one of two Black officers on the city's police force, which included about 45 officers. Rowland was initially taken to the Tulsa city jail at the corner of First Street and Main Street. Late that day, Police Commissioner J. M. Adkison said he had received an anonymous telephone call threatening Rowland's life. He ordered Rowland transferred to the more secure jail on the top floor of the Tulsa County Courthouse.[976] transferred to the more secure jail on the top floor of the Tulsa County Courthouse.[977]

Rowland was well known among attorneys and other legal professionals within the city, many of whom knew Rowland through his work as a shoeshine boy. Some witnesses later recounted hearing several attorneys defend Rowland in their conversations with one another. One of the men said, "Why, I know that boy, and have known him a good while. That's not in him."[978]

The *Tulsa Tribune*, owned, published, and edited by Richard Lloyd Jones, and one of two White owned papers published in Tulsa, broke the story in that afternoon's edition with the headline: "Nab Negro for Attacking Girl In an Elevator", describing the alleged incident. According to some witnesses, the same edition of the *Tribune* included an editorial warning of a potential lynching of Rowland, titled "To Lynch Negro Tonight".[979] The paper was known at the time to have a "sensationalist" style of news writing. All original copies of that issue of the paper have apparently been destroyed, and the relevant page is missing from the microfilm copy.[980] The Tulsa Race Riot Commission in 1997 offered a reward for a copy of the editorial, which went unclaimed.[981] Other newspapers of the time like *The Black Dispatch* and the World did not call attention to any such editorial after the event.[982]

---

975 Hirsch 2002, pp. 37, 51.
976 *A Find of a Lifetime".* Archived from the original on September 29, 2007.. Currie Ballard silent film of African American towns in Oklahoma, 1920s. Rev. S. S. Jones for the National Baptist Convention. *American Heritage* magazine, 2006.
977 *A Find of a Lifetime".* Archived from the original on September 29, 2007.. Currie Ballard silent film of African American towns in Oklahoma, 1920s. Rev. S. S. Jones for the National Baptist Convention. *American Heritage* magazine, 2006.
978 Oklahoma Commission to Study the Tulsa Race Riot of 1921 (February 28, 2001). "Tulsa Race Riot" (PDF). pp. 56–58
979 "Story of Attack on Woman Denied". The Tulsa Daily World. June 2, 1921.
980 Hirsch 2002, pp. 79–80, 82, 86.
981 Hirsch 2002, pp. 79–80, 82, 86.
982 Hirsch 2002, pp. 79–80, 82, 86.

So, the exact content of the column, and whether it existed at all, remains in dispute. However, Chief of Detectives James Patton attributed the cause of the riots entirely to the newspaper account and stated, "If the facts in the story as told the police had only been printed, I do not think there would have been any riot whatsoever." [983]

The afternoon edition of the *Tribune* hit the streets shortly after 3 p.m., and soon news spread of a potential lynching. By 4 p.m., local authorities were on alert. White residents began congregating at and near the Tulsa County Courthouse. By sunset around 7:30 p.m., the several hundred White residents assembled outside the courthouse appeared to have the makings of a lynch mob. Willard M. McCullough, the newly elected sheriff of Tulsa County, was determined to avoid events such as the 1920 lynching of White murder suspect Roy Belton in Tulsa, which had occurred during the term of his predecessor.[984] The sheriff took steps to ensure the safety of Rowland. McCullough organized his deputies into a defensive formation around Rowland, who was terrified. The *Guthrie Daily Leader* reported that Rowland had been taken to the county jail before crowds started to gather.[985] The sheriff positioned six of his men, armed with rifles and shotguns, on the roof of the courthouse. He disabled the building's elevator and had his remaining men barricade themselves at the top of the stairs with orders to shoot any intruders on sight. The sheriff went outside and tried to talk the crowd into going home but to no avail. According to an account by Scott Ellsworth, the sheriff was "hooted down".[986] At about 8:20 p.m., three White men entered the courthouse, demanding that Rowland be turned over to them. Although vastly outnumbered by the growing crowd out on the street, Sheriff McCullough turned the men away.[987]

A few blocks away on Greenwood Avenue, members of the Black community gathered to discuss the situation at Gurley's Hotel.[988] [989] [990] Given the recent lynching of Belton, a White man accused of murder, they believed that Rowland was greatly at risk. Many Black residents were determined to prevent the crowd from

---

[983] *"Tulsa History: Urban Development (1901–1945)"*. Tulsa Preservation Commission. May 19, 2015.
[984] Franklin, Buck Colbert (2000). Franklin, John Hope; Franklin, John Whittington (eds.). *My Life and An Era: The Autobiography of Buck Colbert Franklin*. Louisiana State University Press. pp. 195–196.
[985] *Hendrickson, Paul (2019). Plagued by Fire: The Dreams and Furies of Frank Lloyd Wright. Knopf. p. 253. ISBN 978-0-3853-5365-6."* A *second* article is said to have appeared in the ... early edition, possibly on the editorial page, which far more blatantly race-baited the citizenry to come to the courthouse for an evening lynching. It was supposedly headlined: TO LYNCH NEGRO TONIGHT. But that alleged article.... too, got ripped out and disposed of."
[986] 1921 Race Riot: Tribune mystery unsolved". Randy Krehbiel, Tulsa World, May 31, 2002.
[987] Ellsworth 1992, 47–48.
[988] Oklahoma Commission 2001, p. 124.
[989] Willows 1921,
[990] "Negro Deputy Sheriff Blames Black Dope-Head for Inciting His Race Into Rioting Here". The Morning Tulsa Daily World. June 3, 1921.

lynching Rowland, but they were divided about tactics. Young World War I veterans prepared for a battle by collecting guns and ammunition. Older, more prosperous men feared a destructive confrontation that likely would cost them dearly.[991] O. W. Gurley stated that he had tried to convince the men that there would be no lynching, but the crowd responded that Sheriff McCullough had personally told them their presence was required.[992] About 9:30 p.m., a group of approximately 50–60 Black men, armed with rifles and shotguns, arrived at the jail to support the sheriff and his deputies in defending Rowland from the mob. Corroborated by ten witnesses, attorney James Luther submitted to the grand jury that they were following the orders of Sheriff McCullough who publicly denied he gave any orders:

I saw a car full of negroes driving through the streets with guns; I saw Bill McCullough and told him those negroes would cause trouble; McCullough tried to talk to them, and they got out and stood in single file. W. G. Daggs was killed near Boulder and Sixth street. I was under the impression that a man with authority could have stopped and disarmed them. I saw Chief of Police on south side of court house on top step, talking; I did not see any officer except the Chief; I walked in the court house and met McCullough in about 15 feet of his door; I told him these negroes were going to make trouble, and he said he had told them to go home; he went out and told the Whites to go home, and one said "they said you told them to come up here." McCullough said, "I did not" and a negro said you did tell us to come.[993] [994]

Having seen the armed Black men, some of the more than 1,000 Whites who had been at the courthouse went home for their own guns. Others headed for the National Guard armoury at the corner of Sixth Street and Norfolk Avenue, where they planned to arm themselves. The armoury contained a supply of small arms and ammunition. Major James Bell of the 180th Infantry Regiment learned of the mounting situation downtown and the possibility of a break-in, and he consequently took measures to prevent. He called the commanders of the three National Guard units in Tulsa, who ordered all the Guard members to put on their uniforms and report quickly to the armoury. When a group of Whites arrived and began pulling at the grating over a window, Bell went outside to confront the crowd of 300 to 400 men. Bell told them that the Guard members inside were armed and prepared to shoot anyone who tried to enter. After this show of force, the crowd withdrew from the armoury.[995]

[991] Brophy, Alfred L. (2007). "Tulsa (Oklahoma) Riot of 1921". In Rucker, Walter C.; Upton, James N. (eds.). *Encyclopaedia of American Race Riots*. Greenwood Publishing Group. p. 654. ISBN 978-0-313-33302-6.
[992] Willows 1921,
[993] Willows 1921,
[994] Negro Deputy Sheriff Blames Black Dope-Head for Inciting His Race Into Rioting Here". The Morning Tulsa Daily World. June 3, 1921.

At the courthouse, the crowd had swollen to nearly 2,000, many of them now armed. Several local leaders, including Reverend Charles W. Kerr, pastor of the First Presbyterian Church, tried to dissuade mob action. Chief of Police Gustafson later claimed that he tried to talk the crowd into going home.[996]

Anxiety on Greenwood Avenue was rising. Many Black residents worried about the safety of Rowland. Small groups of armed Black men ventured toward the courthouse in automobiles, partly for reconnaissance and to demonstrate they were prepared to take necessary action to protect Rowland.[997] Many White men interpreted these actions as a "Negro uprising" and became concerned. Eyewitnesses reported gunshots, presumably fired into the air, increasing in frequency during the evening.[998]

In Greenwood, rumours began to fly – in particular, a report that Whites were storming the courthouse. Shortly after 10 p.m., a second, larger group of approximately 75 armed Black men decided to go to the courthouse. They offered their support to the sheriff, who declined their help. According to witnesses, a White man is alleged to have told one of the armed Black men to surrender his pistol. The man refused, and a shot was fired. That first shot might have been accidental, or meant as a warning; it was a catalyst for an exchange of gunfire.[999]

The gunshots triggered an almost immediate response, with both sides firing on the other. The first "battle" was said to last a few seconds or so, but took a toll, as ten Whites and two Black men lay dead or dying in the street.[1000] The Black men who had offered to provide security retreated toward Greenwood. A rolling gunfight ensued. The armed White mob pursued the Black contingent toward Greenwood, with many stopping to loot local stores for additional weapons and ammunition. Along the way, bystanders, many of whom were leaving a movie theatre after a show, were caught off-guard by the mobs, and fled. Panic set in as the White mob began firing on any Black people in the crowd. The White mob also shot and killed at least one White man in the confusion.[1001] According to the Oklahoma Historical Society some in the mob were deputized by police and instructed to "get a gun and get a nigger".[1002]

---

[995] Oklahoma Commission 2001, pp. 58–59.

[996] White, Walter F. (June 29, 1921). "The Eruption of Tulsa". *The Nation*.

[997] White, Walter F. (June 29, 1921). "The Eruption of Tulsa". *The Nation*. Archived from the original on May 18, 2015. Retrieved May 18, 2015 – via Digital Prairie.

[998] White, Walter F. (August 23, 2001). "Tulsa, 1921". *The Nation*.

[999] White, Walter F. (August 23, 2001). "Tulsa, 1921". *The Nation*.

[1000] Franklin, Buck Colbert (2000). Franklin, John Hope; Franklin, John Whittington (eds.). *My Life and An Era: The Autobiography of Buck Colbert Franklin*. Louisiana State University Press. pp. 195–196.

[1001] "How The Big Fight In Tulsa Started". *The Guthrie Daily Leader*. June 1, 1921. pp. 1, 4.

[1002] Oklahoma Commission 2001, p. 60.

At around 11 p.m., members of the National Guard unit began to assemble at the armoury to organize a plan to subdue the rioters. Several groups were deployed downtown to set up guard at the courthouse, police station, and other public facilities. Members of the local chapter of the American Legion joined in on patrols of the streets. The forces appeared to have been deployed to protect the White districts adjacent to Greenwood. The National Guard rounded up numerous Black people and took them to the Convention Hall on Brady Street for detention.[1003]

At around midnight, a small crowd of Whites assembled outside the courthouse. They shouted in support of a lynching, but they did not rush the building, and nothing happened.[1004]

Throughout the early morning hours, groups of armed White and Black people squared off in gunfights. The fighting was concentrated along sections of the Frisco tracks, a dividing line between the Black and White commercial districts. A rumour circulated that more Black people were coming by train from Muskogee to help with an invasion of Tulsa. At one point, passengers on an incoming train were forced to take cover on the floor of the train cars, as they had arrived during crossfire, with the train taking hits on both sides. Small groups of Whites made brief forays by car into Greenwood, indiscriminately firing into businesses and residences. They often received return fire. Meanwhile, White rioters threw lighted oil rags into several buildings along Archer Street, igniting them.[1005]

As unrest spread to other parts of the city, many middle class White families who employed Black people in their homes as live-in cooks and servants were accosted by White rioters. They demanded the families turn over their employees to be taken to detention centres around the city. Many White families complied, but those who refused were subjected to attacks and vandalism in turn.[1006]

At around 1 a.m., the White mob began setting fires, mainly in businesses on commercial Archer Street at the southern edge of the Greenwood district. As news travelled among Greenwood residents in the early morning hours, many began to take up arms in defence of their neighbourhood, while others began a mass exodus from the city.[1007] Throughout the night both sides continued fighting, sometimes only sporadically.

As crews from the Tulsa Fire Department arrived to put out fires, they were turned away at gunpoint.[1008] Scott Ellsworth makes the same claim,[1009] but his reference

---

[1003] Hirsch 2002, p. 83.
[1004] Oklahoma Commission 2001, p. 60.
[1005] Hirsch 2002, pp. 87–88.
[1006] Oklahoma Commission 2001, p. 62.
[1007] Oklahoma Commission 2001, pp. 62, 67.

makes no mention of firefighters.[1010] Parrish gave only praise for the National Guard.[1011] Another reference Ellsworth gives to support the claim of holding firefighters at gunpoint is only a summary of events in which they suppressed the firing of guns by the rioters and disarmed them of their firearms.[1012] Yet another of his references states that they were fired upon by the White mob, "It would mean a fireman's life to turn a stream of water on one of those negro buildings. They shot at us all morning when we were trying to do something but none of my men were hit. There is not a chance in the world to get through that mob into the negro district."[1013] By 4 a.m., an estimated two dozen Black-owned businesses had been set ablaze.

Tulsa founder and Ku Klux Klan member W. Tate Brady participated in the riot as a night watchman.[1014] *This Land Press* reported that previously, Brady led the Tulsa Outrage, the November 7, 1917 tarring and feathering of members of the Industrial Workers of the World , an incident understood to be economically and politically, rather than racially, motivated.[1015] Previous reports regarding Brady's character seem favourable, and he hired Black employees in his businesses.[1016]

Upon sunrise, around 5 a.m., a train whistle sounded (Hirsch said it was a siren). Some rioters believed this sound to be a signal for the rioters to launch an all-out assault on Greenwood. A White man stepped out from behind the Frisco depot and was fatally shot by a sniper in Greenwood. Crowds of rioters poured from their shelter, on foot and by car, into the streets of the Black neighbourhood. Five White men in a car led the charge but were killed by a fusillade of gunfire before they had travelled one block.[1017]

Overwhelmed by the sheer number of White attackers, the Black residents retreated north on Greenwood Avenue to the edge of town. Chaos ensued as terrified residents fled. The rioters shot indiscriminately and killed many residents along the way. Splitting into small groups, they began breaking into houses and buildings, looting.

[1008] Oklahoma Commission 2001, p. 65.
[1009] Oklahoma Commission 2001, pp. 66–67.
[1010] Hirsch 2002, pp. 96–97.
[1011] Oklahoma Commission 2001, p. 80.
[1012] Jones, F. "96 Years Later The Greenwood Cultural Centre 1921 Race Riot Massacre Facts with Video".
[1013] *Hendrickson, Paul (2019). Plagued by Fire: The Dreams and Furies of Frank Lloyd Wright. Knopf. p. 253. ISBN 978-0-3853-5365-6.*"[A] *second* article is said to have appeared in the ... early edition, possibly on the editorial page, which far more blatantly race-baited the citizenry to come to the courthouse for an evening lynching. It was supposedly headlined: TO LYNCH NEGRO TONIGHT. But that alleged article.... too, got ripped out and disposed of."
[1014] Hirsch 2002, p. 103.
[1015] Oklahoma Commission 2001, p. 66.
[1016] Parrish 1922, p. 19.
[1017] Parrish 1922, p. 20.

Several residents later testified the rioters broke into occupied homes and ordered the residents out to the street, where they could be driven or forced to walk to detention centres.[1018] A rumour spread among the rioters that the new Mount Zion Baptist Church was being used as a fortress and armoury. Purportedly twenty caskets full of rifles had been delivered to the church, though no evidence was found.[1019]

Numerous eyewitnesses described airplanes carrying White assailants, who fired rifles and dropped firebombs on buildings, homes, and fleeing families. The privately owned aircraft had been dispatched from the nearby Curtiss-Southwest Field outside Tulsa.[1020] Law enforcement officials later said that the planes were to provide reconnaissance and protect against a "Negro uprising".[1021] Law enforcement personnel were thought to be aboard at least some flights.[1022] Eyewitness accounts, such as testimony from the survivors during Commission hearings and a manuscript by eyewitness and attorney Buck Colbert Franklin, discovered in 2015, said that on the morning of June 1, at least "a do"en or more" pl"nes circled the neighbourhood and dropped "burning turpentine balls" on an office building, a hotel, a filling station and multiple other buildings. Men also fired rifles at Black residents, gunning them down in the street.[1023] [1024]

Richard S. Warner concluded in his submission to The Oklahoma Commission that contrary to later reports by claimed eyewitnesses of seeing explosions, there was no reliable evidence to support such attacks.[1025] Warner noted that while a number of newspapers targeted at Black readers heavily reported the use of nitro-glycerine, turpentine and rifles from the planes, many cited anonymous sources or second-hand accounts.[1026] Beryl Ford, one of the pre-eminent historians of the disaster, concluded from his large collection of photographs that there was no evidence of any building damaged by explosions.[1027] Danney Goble commended Warner on his efforts and supported his conclusions.[1028] State representative Don Ross (born in Tulsa in 1941),

[1018] Letter Captain Frank Van Voorhis to Lieut. Col. L. J. F. Rooney". *digitalprairie.com*. July 30, 1921. pp. 1–3.
[1019] *Tulsa Daily World*, June 1, 1921
[1020] "Modern Ku Klux Klan Comes Into Being: Seventeen First Victims". *Tulsa Daily World*. November 10, 1917.
[1021] "Modern Ku Klux Klan Comes Into Being: Seventeen First Victims". *Tulsa Daily World*. November 10, 1917.
[1022] Myers, Jeffrey (November 5, 2014). "Examining the legacy of Tate Brady". *Tulsa World*.
[1023] Hirsch 2002, pp. 98–99.
[1024] "Modern Ku Klux Klan Comes Into Being: Seventeen First Victims". *Tulsa Daily World*. November 10, 1917.
[1025] Hirsch 2002, pp. 97–105, 108.
[1026] Hirsch 2002, pp. 97–105, 108.
[1027] Hirsch 2002, p. 107.
[1028] Oklahoma Commission 2001, pp. 73–74.

however, dissented from the evidence presented in the report concluding that bombs were in fact dropped from planes during the violence.[1029]

In 2015, a previously unknown written eyewitness account of the events of May 31, 1921, was discovered and subsequently obtained by the Smithsonian National Museum of African American History and Culture. The 10-page typewritten letter was authored by Buck Colbert Franklin, noted Oklahoma attorney and father of John Hope Franklin.[1030] [1031]

Notable quotes include:

Lurid flames roared and belched and licked their forked tongues into the air. Smoke ascended the sky in thick, black volumes and amid it all, the planes – now a dozen or more in number – still hummed and darted here and there with the agility of natural birds of the air.

Planes circling in mid-air: They grew in number and hummed, darted, and dipped low. I could hear something like hail falling upon the top of my office building. Down East Archer, I saw the old Mid-Way hotel on fire, burning from its top, and then another and another and another building began to burn from their top.

The sidewalks were literally covered with burning turpentine balls. I knew all too well where they came from, and I knew all too well why every burning building first caught fire from the top.

I paused and waited for an opportune time to escape. 'Where oh where is our splendid fire department with its half dozen stations?' I asked myself, 'Is the city in conspiracy with the mob?'

Franklin states that every time he saw a White man shot, he "felt happy"[1032] and he "swelled with pride and hope for the race."[1033] Franklin reports seeing multiple machine guns firing at night and hearing "thousands and thousands of guns" being fired simultaneously from all directions.[1034] He states that he was arrested by "a thousand boys, it seemed, firing their guns every step they took."[1035]

Adjutant General Charles Barrett of the Oklahoma National Guard arrived by special train at about 9:15 a.m., with 109 troops from Oklahoma City. Ordered in by the governor, he could not legally act until he had contacted all the appropriate local

---

[1029] Franklin 1931,
[1030] Hirsch 2002, pp. 98–99.
[1031] Oklahoma Commission 2001, p. 107.
[1032] Oklahoma Commission 2001, p. 106.
[1033] Oklahoma Commission 2001, p. 6.
[1034] Oklahoma Commission 2001, p. viii, prologue.
[1035] Oklahoma Commission 2001, p. 106.

authorities, including Mayor T. D. Evans, the sheriff, and the police chief. Meanwhile, his troops paused to eat breakfast. Barrett summoned reinforcements from several other Oklahoma cities. Barrett declared martial law at 11:49 a.m.,[1036] an d by noon the troops had managed to suppress most of the remaining violence.

Thousands of Black residents had fled the city; another 4,000 people had been rounded up and detained at various centres. Under martial law, the detainees were required to carry identification cards.[1037] As many as 6,000 Black Greenwood residents were interned at three local facilities: Convention Hall (now known as the Tulsa Theatre), the Tulsa County Fairgrounds (then located about a mile northeast of Greenwood) and McNulty Park (a baseball stadium at Tenth Street and Elgin Avenue).[1038] [1039] [1040]

A 1921 letter from an officer of the Service Company, Third Infantry, Oklahoma National Guard, who arrived on May 31, 1921, reported numerous events related to suppression of the riot:

- taking about 30–40 Black residents into custody.
- putting a machine gun on a truck and taking it on patrol, although it was not functioning and much less useful than "an ordinary rifle".
- being fired on from Black snipers from the "church" and returning fire.
- being fired on by White men.
- turning the prisoners over to deputies to take them to police headquarters.
- being fired upon again by armed Black residents and having two NCOs slightly wounded.
- searching for Black snipers and firearms.
- detailing an NCO to take 170 Black residents to the civil authorities: and
- delivering an additional 150 Black residents to the Convention Hall.[1041]

Captain John W. McCune reported that stockpiled ammunition within the burning structures began to explode which might have further contributed to casualties.[1042] Martial law was withdrawn on June 4, under Field Order No. 7.[1043]

[1036] *Tulsa Daily World*, June 1, 1921
[1037] Keyes, Allison (May 27, 2016). "A Long-Lost Manuscript Contains a Searing Eyewitness Account of the Tulsa Race Massacre of 1921". *Smithsonian Magazine*.
[1038] Ellsworth, Scott (2009). "Tulsa Race Riot". *The Encyclopaedia of Oklahoma History and Culture*.
[1039] Franklin 1931, p. 8.
[1040] Franklin 1931, p. 6.
[1041] Jones, F. "96 Years Later The Greenwood Cultural Centre 1921 Race Riot Massacre Facts with Video".
[1042] Franklin 1931, p. 4.
[1043] Oklahoma Commission 2001, pp. 123–132.

The massacre was covered by national newspapers, and the reported number of deaths varies widely. On June 1, 1921, the *Tulsa Tribune* reported that 9 White people and 68 Black people had died in the riot, but shortly afterwards it changed this number to a total of 176 dead. The next day, the same paper reported the count as 9 White people and 21 Black people. The *Los Angeles Express* headline said "175 Killed, Many Wounded".[1044] The *New York Times* said that 77 people had been killed, including 68 Black people, but it later lowered the total to 33. The *Richmond Times Dispatch* of Virginia reported that 85 people (including 25 White people) were killed; it also reported that the police chief had reported to Governor Robertson that the total was 75; and that a police major put the figure at 175.[1045] The Oklahoma Department of Vital Statistics put the number of deaths at 36 (26 Black and 10 White).[1046] Very few people, if any, died as a direct result of the fire. Official state records show 5 deaths by conflagration for the entire state in 1921.[1047]

Walter Francis White of the NAACP travelled to Tulsa from New York and reported that, although officials and undertakers said that the fatalities numbered 10 White and 21 Black, he estimated the number of the dead to be 50 Whites and between 150 and 200 Blacks;[1048] he also reported that 10 White men were killed on Tuesday; 6 White men drove into the Black section and never came out, and 13 Whites were killed on Wednesday; he reported that Major O.T. Johnson of the Salvation Army in Tulsa, said that 37 Blacks were employed as gravediggers to bury 120 Blacks in individual graves without coffins on Friday and Saturday.[1049] The Oklahoma Commission described Johnson's statement being that his crew was over three dozen grave diggers who dug "about" 150 graves.[1050] Ground-penetrating radar was used to investigate the sites purported to contain these mass graves. Multiple eyewitness reports and "oral histories" suggested the graves could have been dug at three different cemeteries across the city. The sites were examined, and no evidence of ground disturbance indicative of mass graves was found. However, at one site, ground disturbance was found in a five-meter square area, but cemetery records indicate that three graves had been dug and bodies buried within this envelope before the riot.[1051]

[1044] Oklahoma Commission 2001, pp. 83, 177.
[1045] Letter Chas F. Barrett, Adjutant General to Lieut. Col. L. J. F. Rooney, 1921 June 1".
[1046] *"Barrett Commends Tulsa for Co-operation With the State Military Authorities".* The Morning Tulsa Daily World. June 4, 1921. p. 2.
[1047] "Tulsa Dead Total 85 / Nine of Them White". *The Boston Daily Globe.* June 2, 1921.
[1048] *"Tulsa-race-riot". greenwoodculturalcenter.com.*
[1049] "Richmond Times-Dispatch". Richmond, VA. June 2, 1921. – via chroniclingamerica.loc.gov.
[1050] Hirsch 2002, p. 118.
[1051] "Sixth and Seventh Annual Report for the State Department of Health of Oklahoma, for the year ending June 30, 1922, and for the year ending June 30, 1923". State Department of Health of

Oklahoma's 2001 Commission into the riot provides multiple contradicting estimates. Goble estimates 100 – 300 deaths (also stating right after that no one was prosecuted even though nearly a hundred were indicted),[1052] and Franklin and Ellsworth estimate 75 – 100 deaths and describe some of the higher estimates as dubious as the low estimates.[1053] C. Snow was able to confirm 39 casualties, all listed as male although 4 were unidentifiable; 26 were Black and 13 were White.[1054] The 13 White fatalities were all taken to hospitals.[1055] Eleven of them had come from outside of Oklahoma, and possibly as many as half were petroleum industry workers. Only 8 of the confirmed 26 Black fatalities were brought to hospitals,[1056] an d as hospitals were segregated, and with the Black Frissell Memorial Hospital having burned down, the only place where the injured Black people were treated was at the basement of Morningside Hospital.[1057] Several hundred were injured.[1058]

The Red Cross, in their preliminary overview, mentioned wide-ranging external estimates of 55 to 300 dead; however, because of the hurried nature of undocumented burials, they declined to submit an official estimate, stating, "The number of dead is a matter of conjecture."[1059] The Red Cross registered 8,624 persons; 183 people were hospitalized, mostly for gunshot wounds or burns (they differentiate in their records on the basis of triage category not the type of wound), while a further 531 required first aid or surgical treatment; 8 miscarriages were attributed to be a result of the tragedy; 19 died in care between June December 1 and 30.[1060]

The commercial section of Greenwood was destroyed. Losses included 191 businesses, a junior high school, several churches, and the only hospital in the district. The Red Cross reported that 1,256 houses were burned and another 215 were looted but not burned.[1061] The Tulsa Real Estate Exchange estimated property losses amounted to US$1.5 million in real estate and $750,000 in personal property[1062] (equ ivalent to a total of $33 million in 2020).

Oklahoma. p. 64.

[1052] Walter Whites total estimate of about 250 White and Black fatalities is apparently confirmed in Tim Madigan, *The Burning: Massacre, Destruction, and the Tulsa Race Riot of 1921* (2013), p. 224

[1053] White, Walter F. (August 20, 2001). "Tulsa, 1921 (reprint of article "The Eruption of Tulsa", first published June 15, 1921)". *The Nation*. Archived from the original on February 4, 2015. Retrieved January 30, 2015.

[1054] Messer, Chris M.; Beamon, Krystal; Bell, Patricia A. (2013). "The Tulsa Riot of 1921: Collective Violence and Racial Frames". *The Western Journal of Black Studies*. 37 (1): 50–59.

[1055] Oklahoma Commission 2001, p. 121.

[1056] Oklahoma Commission 2001, p. 121.

[1057] Oklahoma Commission 2001, p. 13.

[1058] Oklahoma Commission 2001, p. 13.

[1059] Oklahoma Commission 2001, p. 23.

[1060] Oklahoma Commission 2001, p. 117.

[1061] Oklahoma Commission 2001, pp. 115–116.

The Red Cross report on December 1921 estimated that 10,000 people were made homeless by the destruction.[1063] Over the next year, local citizens filed more than US$1.8 million (equivalent to $26 million in 2020) in riot-related claims against the city.[1064]

On June 3, the *Morning Tulsa Daily World* reported major points of their interview with Deputy Sheriff Barney Cleaver concerning the events leading up to the Tulsa riot. Cleaver was deputy sheriff for Okmulgee County and not under the supervision of the city police department; his duties mainly involved enforcing law among the "coloured people" of Greenwood, but he also operated a business as a private investigator. He had pr"viously been dismissed as a city police investigator for assisting county officers with a"drug raid at Gurley's Hotel but not reporting his involvement to his superiors.[1065] He had considerable land holdings and suffered tremendous financial damages because of the riot. Among his holdings were several residential properties and Cleaver Hall, a large community gathering place and function hall. He reported personally evicting several armed criminals who had taken to barricading themselves within properties he owned. Upon eviction, they merely moved to Cleaver Hall. Cleaver reported that most of the violence started at Cleaver Hall along with the rioters barricaded inside. Charles Page offered to build him a new home.[1066]

The *Morning Tulsa Daily World* stated, "Cleaver named Will Robinson, a dope peddler and all-around bad negro, as the leader of the armed Blacks. He has also the names of three others who were in the armed gang at the courthouse. The rest of the negroes participating in the fight, he says, were former servicemen who had an exaggerated idea of their own importance... They did not belong here, had no regular employment and were simply a floating element with seemingly no ambition in life but to foment trouble."[4] O.W. Gurley, owner of Gurley's Hotel, identified the following men by name as arming themselves and gathering in his hotel: Will Robinson, Peg Leg Taylor, Bud Bassett, Henry Van Dyke, Chester Ross, Jake Mayes, O. B. Mann, John Suplesox, Fatty, Jack Scott, Lee Mable, John Bowman and W. S. Weaver.[1067]

By June 6, the Associated Press reported that a citizens' Public Safety Committee had been established, made up of 250 White men who vowed to protect the city and

---

[1062] Willows 1921, p. 3.
[1063] Willows 1921, p. 20, Condensed Report.
[1064] Willows 1921, pp. 4, 12, Condensed Report.
[1065] Oklahoma Commission 2001, p. 189.
[1066] Oklahoma Commission 2001, p. 124.
[1067] Willows 1921,

put down any more disturbance. A White man was shot and killed that day after he failed to stop as ordered by a National Guardsman.[1068]

Governor James B. A. Robertson had gone to Tulsa during the riot to ensure order was restored. Before returning to the capital, he ordered an inquiry of events, especially of the City and Sheriff's Office. He called for a Grand Jury to be empanelled, and Judge Valjean Biddison said that its investigation would begin June 8. The jury was selected by June 9. Judge Biddison expected that the state attorney general would call numerous witnesses, both Black and White, given the large scale of the riot.[1069]

State Attorney General S.P. Freeling initiated the investigation, and witnesses were heard over 12 days. In the end, the all-White jury attributed the riot to the Black mobs, while noting that law enforcement officials had failed in preventing the riot. A total of 27 cases were brought before the court, and the jury indicted more than 85 individuals. In the end, no one was convicted of charges for the deaths, injuries, or property damage.[1070]

On June 3, a group of over 1,000 businessmen and civic leaders met, resolving to form a committee to raise funds and aid in rebuilding Greenwood. Judge J. Martin, a former mayor of Tulsa, was chosen as the chairman of the group. He said at the mass meeting:

Tulsa can only redeem herself from the country-wide shame and humiliation into which she is today plunged by complete restitution and rehabilitation of the destroyed black belt. The rest of the United States must know that the real citizenship of Tulsa weeps at this unspeakable crime and will make good the damage, so far as it can be done, to the last penny.[1071]

Many Black families spent the winter of 1921 – 1922 in tents as they worked to rebuild. Charles Page was commended for his philanthropic efforts in the wake of the riot in the assistance of 'destitute Blacks'.[1072]

A group of influential White developers persuaded the city to pass a fire ordinance that would have prohibited many Black people from rebuilding in Greenwood. Their intention was to redevelop Greenwood for more business and industrial use and force Black people further to the edge of the city for residences. The case was

---

[1068] Willows 1921, p. 66.
[1069] Hirsch 2002, p. 119.
[1070] "Statement Barney Cleaver, Attorney General Civil Case No. 1062". 1921. Archived from the original on December 4, 2018. Retrieved December 4, 2018.
[1071] Hirsch 2002, p. 119.
[1072] "Tulsa Guard Kills Man". *Evening Public Ledger*. Philadelphia, Pennsylvania: Library of Congress; accessed December 31, 2016. June 6, 1921. p. 2.

litigated and appealed to the Oklahoma Supreme Court by Buck Colbert Franklin, where the ordinance was ruled as unconstitutional. Most of the promised funding was never raised for the Black residents, and they struggled to rebuild after the violence. Willows, the regional director of the Red Cross, noted this in his report, explaining his slow initial progress to facilitate the rehabilitation of the refugees. The fire code was officially intended to prevent another tragedy by banning wooden frame construction houses in place of previously burnt homes. A concession was granted to allow temporary wooden frame dwellings while a new building, which would meet the more restrictive fire code, was being constructed. This was quickly halted as residents within two weeks had started to erect full sized wooden frame dwellings in contravention of the agreement. It took a further two-month delay securing the court decision to reinstate the previous fire code. Willows heavily criticized the Tulsa city officials for interfering with his efforts, for their role in the Public Welfare Committee which first sought to rezone the "burned area" as industrial, and for constructing a union station in its place with no consideration for the refugees. Then he criticized them again for the dissolution of the Public Welfare Committee in favour of the formation of the Reconstruction Committee which failed to formulate a single plan, leaving the displaced residents prohibited from beginning reconstruction efforts for several months.[1073] Despite the Red Cross's best efforts to assist with reconstruction of Greenwood's residential area, the considerably altered present-day layout of the district and its surrounding neighbourhoods, as well as the extensive redevelopment of Greenwood by people unaffiliated with the neighbourhood prior to the riot, stand as proof that the Red Cross relief efforts had limited success.[1074]

Tulsa's main industries at the time of the riot were banking (BOK Financial Corporation), administrative (PennWell, Oklahoma Natural Gas Company), and petroleum engineering services (Skelly Oil), earning Tulsa the title of "Oil Capital of the World". Joshua Cosden is also regarded as a founder of the city, having constructed the tallest building in Tulsa, the Cosden Building. The construction of the Cosden Building and Union Depot were overseen by the Manhattan Construction Company, which was based in Tulsa. Francis Rooney is the great grandson and beneficiary of the estate of Laurence H. Rooney, founder of the Manhattan Construction Company.

City planners immediately saw the fire that destroyed homes and businesses across Greenwood as a fortunate event for advancing their objectives, meanwhile showing a disregard for the welfare of affected residents. Plans were made to rezone 'The Burned Area' for industrial use.[1075] The *Tulsa Daily World* reported that the mayor

---

[1073] Tulsa In Remorse to Rebuild Homes; Dead Now Put at 30". *The New York Times*. June 3, 1921.
[1074] Ellsworth 1992, pp. 94–96.

and city commissioners expressed that, "a large industrial section will be found desirable in causing a wider separation between negroes and whites."[1076] The reconstruction committee organized a forum to discuss their proposal with community leaders and stakeholders. Naming, among others, O.W. Gurley, Rev. H.T.F. Johnson, and Barney Cleaver as participants in the forum, it was reported that all members were in agreement with the plan to redevelop the burned district as an industrial section and agreed that the proposed union station project was desirable. "... not a note of dissension was expressed." The article states that these community leaders would again meet at the First Baptist Church in the following days.[1077] *The Black Dispatch* describes the content of the following meeting at the First Baptist Church. The reconstruction committee had intended to have the Black landholders sign over their property to a holding company managed by Black representatives on behalf of the city. The properties were then to be turned over to a White appraisal committee which would pay residents for the residential zoned land at the lower industrial zoned value in advance of the rezoning. Professor J.W. Hughes addressed the White reconstruction committee members in opposition to their proposition, coining a slogan which would come to galvanize the community, "I'm going to hold what I have until I get What I've lost."[1078]

Construction of the Tulsa Union Depot, a large central rail hub connecting three major railroads, began in Greenwood less than two years after the riot. Prior to the riot, construction had already been underway for a smaller rail hub nearby. However, in the aftermath of the riot, land on which homes and businesses had been destroyed by the fires suddenly became available, allowing for a larger train depot near the heart of the city to be built in Greenwood instead.[1079] [1080]

1921 Grand Jury investigation:

Allegations of corruption

Chief Chuck Jordan described the conduct of the 1921 Tulsa Police as, "... the police department did not do their job then, y'know, they just didn't."[1081] Parrish, an African-American citizen of Tulsa, summarized the lawlessness in Oklahoma as a contributing factor in 1922 as, "if...it were not for the profitable alliance of politics

[1075] Ellsworth 1992, pp. 94–96.
[1076] "No Trace of Girl". *The Black Dispatch*. June 17, 1921. 2018.
[1077] Willows 1921, pp. 22–25.
[1078] Willows 1921, pp. 22–23.
[1079] Ellsworth 1992, pp. 94–96.
[1080] "Burned District In Fire Limits, The Morning Tulsa daily world". June 9, 1921. p. 2.
[1081] "Leading Negroes Meet with Committee – to sanction Program". Tulsa Daily World. June 19, 1921. p. 2.

and vice or professional crime, the tiny spark which is the beginning of all these outrages would be promptly extinguished."[1082] Clark, a prominent Oklahoma historian and law professor, completed his doctoral dissertation in law on the subject of lawlessness in Oklahoma specifically on this period of time and how lawlessness had led to the rise of the second KKK, in order to illustrate the need for effective law enforcement and a functional judiciary.[1083]

Chief of Police John A. Gustafson was the subject of an investigation. Official proceedings began on June 6, 1921. He was prosecuted on multiple counts: refusing to enforce prohibition, refusing to enforce anti-prostitution laws; operating a stolen automobile-laundering racket and allowing known automobile thieves to escape justice, for the purpose of extorting the citizens of Tulsa for rewards relating to their return; repurposing vehicles for his own use or sale; operating a fake detective agency for the purpose of billing the city of Tulsa for investigative duties he was already being paid for as chief of police; failing to enforce gun laws; and failure to take action during the riots.[1084]

The attorney general of Oklahoma received numerous letters alleging members of the police force had conspired with members of the justice system to threaten witnesses in corruption trials stemming from the Grand Jury investigations. In the letters, various members of the public requested the presence of the state attorney general at the trial.[1085] An assistant of the attorney general replied to one such letter by stating that their budget was too stretched to respond and recommending instead that the citizens of Tulsa simply vote for new officers.[1086]

Gustafson was found to have a long history of fraud pre-dating his membership of the Tulsa Police Department. His previous partner in his detective agency, Phil Kirk, had been convicted of blackmail.[1087] Gustafson's fake detective agency ran up high billings on the police account. Investigators noted that many blackmail letters had been sent to members of the community from the agency. One particularly disturbing case involved the frequent rape, by her father, of an 11-year-old girl who had since become pregnant. Instead of prosecuting, they sent a "Black hand letter."[1088] On July 30, 1921, out of five counts of an indictment, Gustafson was found guilty of two counts: negligence for failing to stop the riot (which resulted in dismissal from police

[1082] *"Unbroken Faith Shown In Rehabilitation Program"*. *The Black Dispatch*. June 29, 1921. p. 1.
[1083] Oklahoma Commission 2001, pp. 38, 40, 168.
[1084] "Police Chief Donates Rare Picture Of Tulsa's First African-American Officer". May 31, 2016.
[1085] Parrish 1922, p. 87.
[1086] "Accusation District Court State of Oklahoma v. John A. Gustafson, Attorney General Civil Case No. 1062".
[1087] "Letter C. J. Seeber to S. P. Freeling, Attorney General". July 8, 1921
[1088] "Letter Archie A. Kinion to S. P. Freeling, Attorney General". July 7, 1921.

force), and conspiracy for freeing automobile thieves and collecting rewards (which resulted in a jail sentence).[1089]

Three days after the massacre, President Warren G. Harding spoke at the all-Black Lincoln University in Pennsylvania. He declared, "Despite the demagogues, the idea of our oneness as Americans has risen superior to every appeal to mere class and group. And so, I wish it might be in this matter of our national problem of races." Speaking directly about the events in Tulsa, he said, "God grant that, in the soberness, the fairness, and the justice of this country, we neve" see another spectacle like it."[1090]

There were no convictions for any of the charges related to violence.[1091] There were decades of silence about the terror, violence, and losses of this event. The riot was largely omitted from local, state and national histories: "The Tulsa race riot of 1921 was rarely mentioned in history books, classrooms or even in private. Black and White people alike grew into middle age unaware of what had taken place".[1092] It was not recognized in the *Tulsa Tribune* feature of "Fifteen Years Ago Today" or "Twenty-five Years Ago Today".[1093] A 2017 report detailing the history of the Tulsa Fire Department from 1897 until the date of publication makes no mention of the 1921 massacre.[1094] [1095]

Several people tried to document the events, gather photographs, and record the names of the dead and injured. Mary E. Jones Parrish, a young Black teacher and journalist from Rochester, New York, was hired by the Inter-racial Commission to write an account of the riot. Parrish was a survivor, and she wrote about her experiences, collected other accounts, gathered photographs, and compiled "a partial roster of property losses in the African American community." She published these in *Events of the Tulsa Disaster*.[1096] It was the first book to be published about the riot.[1097] The first academic account was a master's thesis written in 1946 by Loren L. Gill, a veteran of World War II, but the thesis did not circulate beyond the University of Tulsa.[1098]

[1089] "Letter Assistant Attorney General to R. J. Churchill". July 27, 1921
[1090] "Local Findings on John A. Gustafson, Attorney General Civil Case No. 1062; Page 1".
[1091] "Statement Barney Cleaver, Attorney General Civil Case No. 1062". 1921.
[1092] *"Witness Statements taken by R. E. Maxey, Attorney General Civil Case No. 1062". pp. 2–3.*
[1093] Humanities, National Endowment for the (July 30, 1921). "The Chicago whip. (Chicago, Ill.) 1919-19??, July 30, 1921, Image 1" – via chroniclingamerica.loc.gov.
[1094] Robenalt, James D. (June 21, 2020). "The Republican president who called for racial justice in America after Tulsa massacre". *The Washington Post*.
[1095] Sulzberger, A. G. (June 19, 2011). "As Survivors Dwindle, Tulsa Confronts Past". *The New York Times*.
[1096] Oklahoma Commission 2001, p. 26.
[1097] Goforth, Jill (2017). "History of Tulsa Fire Department" (PDF). Tulsa Fire Department.
[1098] Goforth, Jill (2017). "History of Tulsa Fire Department" (PDF). Tulsa Fire Department.

In 1971, a small group of survivors gathered for a memorial service at Mount Zion Baptist Church with Black and White people in attendance.[1099] That same year, the Tulsa Chamber of Commerce decided to commemorate the riot, but when they read the accounts and saw photos gathered by Ed Wheeler, host of a radio history program, detailing the specifics of the riot, they refused to publish them. He then took his information to the two major newspapers in Tulsa, both of which also refused to run his story. His article, "Profile of a Race Riot"[1100] was published in *Impact Magazine*, a publication aimed at Black audiences, but most of Tulsa's White residents never knew about it.[1101]

In the early 1970s, along with Henry C. Whitlow, Jr., a history teacher at Booker T. Washington High School, Mozella Franklin Jones helped to desegregate the Tulsa Historical Society by mounting the first major exhibition on the history of African Americans in Tulsa. Jones also created, at the Tulsa Historical Society, the first collection of massacre photographs available to the public.[1102] While researching and sharing the history of the riot, Jones collaborated with a White woman named Ruth Sigler Avery, who was also trying to publicize accounts of the riot. The two women, however, encountered pressure, particularly among Whites, to keep silent.[1103]

[1099] Parrish 1922,
[1100] Oklahoma Commission 2001, p. 28.
[1101] Oklahoma Commission 2001, pp. 28–29.
[1102] Oklahoma Commission 2001, p. 29.
[1103] Oklahoma Commission 2001, p. 29.

Chapter twenty-four

The Detroit Race Riots of 1943

The 1943 Detroit race riot took place in Detroit, Michigan, of the United States, from the evening of June 20 through to the early morning of June 22. It occurred in a period of dramatic population increase and social tensions associated with the military build-up of U.S. participation in World War II, as Detroit's automotive industry was converted to the war effort. Existing social tensions and housing shortages were exacerbated by racist feelings about the arrival of nearly 400,000 migrants, both African-American and White Southerners, from the South-eastern United States between 1941 and 1943. The new migrants competed for space and jobs, as well as against European immigrants and their descendants.

The Detroit riots were one of five that summer; it followed ones in Beaumont, TX, Harlem, NY, Los Angeles, CA (the Zoot Suit Riot), and Mobile, AL.

The rioting in Detroit began among youths at Belle Isle Park on June 20, 1943; the unrest moved into the city proper and was exacerbated by false rumours of racial attacks in both the black and white communities. It continued until June 22. It was suppressed after 6,000 federal troops were ordered into the city to restore peace. A total of 34 people were killed, 25 of them black and most at the hands of the white police force, while 433 were wounded (75 percent of them black), and property valued at $2 million ($30.4 million in 2020 US dollars) was destroyed. Most of the riot took place in the black area of Paradise Valley, the poorest neighbourhood of the city.[1104]

At the time, white commissions attributed the cause of the riot to black people and youths. But the NAACP claimed deeper causes: a shortage of affordable housing, discrimination in employment, lack of minority representation in the police, and white police brutality. A late 20th-century analysis of the rioters showed that the white rioters were younger and often unemployed (characteristics that the riot commissions had falsely attributed to blacks, despite evidence in front of them). If working, the whites often held semi-skilled or skilled positions. Whites travelled long distances across the city to join the first stage of the riot near the bridge to Belle Isle Park, and later some travelled in armed groups explicitly to attack the black neighbourhood in Paradise Valley. The black participants were often older,

---

[1104] Dominic J. Capeci, Jr., and Martha Wilkerson, "The Detroit Rioters of 1943: A Reinterpretation", *Michigan Historical Review,* Jan 1990, Vol. 16 Issue 1, pp. 49-72.

established city residents, who in many cases had lived in the city for more than a decade. Many were married working men and were defending their homes and neighbourhood against police and white rioters. They also looted and destroyed white-owned property in their neighbourhood.[1105]

By 1920, Detroit had become the fourth-largest city in the United States, with an industrial and population boom driven by the rapid expansion of the automobile industry.[1106] In this era of continuing high immigration from southern and eastern Europe, the Ku Klux Klan in the 1920s established a substantial presence in Detroit during its early 20th-century revival.[1107] The KKK became concentrated in midwestern cities rather than exclusively in the South.[1108] It was primarily anti-Catholic and anti-Jewish in this period, but it also supported white supremacy.

The KKK contributed to Detroit's reputation for racial antagonism, and there were violent incidents dating from 1915.[1109] Its lesser-known offshoot, Black Legion, was also active in the Detroit area. In 1936 and 1937, some 48 members were convicted of numerous murders and attempted murder, thus ending Black Legion's run. Both organizations stood for white supremacy. Detroit was unique among northern cities by the 1940s for its exceptionally high percentage of Southern-born residents, both black and white.[1110]

Soon after the U.S. entry into World War II, the automotive industry was converted to military production; high wages were offered, attracting large numbers of workers and their families from outside of Michigan. The new workers found little available housing, and competition among ethnic groups was fierce for both jobs and housing. With Executive Order 8802, President Roosevelt on June 25, 1941, had prohibited racial discrimination in the national defence industry. Roosevelt called upon all groups to support the war effort. The Executive Order was applied irregularly, and blacks were often excluded from numerous industrial jobs, especially more skilled and supervisory positions.

In 1941 at the beginning of the war, blacks numbered nearly 150,000 in Detroit, which had a total population of 1,623,452. Many of the blacks had migrated from the

---

[1105] Dominic J. Capeci, Jr., and Martha Wilkerson, "The Detroit Rioters of 1943: A Reinterpretation", *Michigan Historical Review*, Jan 1990, Vol. 16 Issue 1, pp. 49-72.
[1106] Kenneth Jackson, *The Ku Klux Klan in the City, 1915-1930*, Rowman & Littlefield, 1967, pp.127-129
[1107] General Article: "Detroit Riots 1943", *Eleanor Roosevelt, American Experience*, PBS
[1108] Kenneth Jackson, *The Ku Klux Klan in the City, 1915-1930*, Rowman & Littlefield, 1967, pp.127-129
[1109] Dominic J. Capeci, Jr., and Martha Wilkerson, "The Detroit Rioters of 1943: A Reinterpretation", *Michigan Historical Review*, Jan 1990, Vol. 16 Issue 1, pp. 49-72.
[1110] Gunnar Myrdal, *An American Dilemma: The Negro Problem and American Democracy*, New York: 1941, p. 568

South in 1915 to 1930 during the Great Migration, as the auto industry opened up many new jobs. By summer 1943, after the United States had entered World War II, tensions between whites and blacks in Detroit were escalating; blacks resisted discrimination, as well as oppression and violence by the Detroit Police Department. The police force of the city was overwhelmingly white, and the black population resented this.

In the early 1940s, Detroit's population reached more than 2 million, absorbing more than 400,000 whites and some 50,000 black migrants, mostly from the American South, where racial segregation was enforced by law.[1111] The more recent African American arrivals were part of the second wave of the black Great Migration, joining 150,000 blacks already in the city. The early residents had been restricted by informal segregation and their limited finances to the poor and overcrowded East Side of the city. A 60-block area east of Woodward Avenue was known as Paradise Valley, and it had aging and substandard housing.

White American migrants came largely from agricultural areas and especially rural Appalachia, carrying with them southern prejudices.[1112] Rumours circulated among ethnic white groups to fear African Americans as competitors for housing and jobs. Blacks had continued to seek to escape the limited opportunities in the South, exacerbated by the Great Depression and second-class social status under Jim Crow laws. After arriving in Detroit, the new migrants found racial bigotry there, too. They had to compete for low-level jobs with numerous European immigrants or their descendants, in addition to rural southern whites. Blacks were excluded from all of the limited public housing except the Brewster Housing Projects. They were exploited by landlords and forced to pay rents that were two to three times higher than families paid in the less densely populated white districts. Like other poor migrants, they were generally limited to the oldest, substandard housing.[1113]

After the Civil War, slavery became illegal. Former slaves and their descendants still faced severe discrimination. As a result, many former slaves could only find low paying work in agriculture or domestic service. Southern blacks migrated north in the 20th Century in hopes of leaving the oppressive culture in the South. Many considered Detroit to be the place of paradise, calling Detroit the "New Canaan." During the Civil War, Detroit was an important stop on the Underground Railroad, as many settled in the northern city or used it as a means to get to Canada."During Worl" War II, it was sought out as a refuge for blacks seeking to escape the lingering

---

[1111] Dominic J. Capeci, Jr., and Martha Wilkerson, "The Detroit Rioters of 1943: A Reinterpretation", *Michigan Historical Review,* Jan 1990, Vol. 16 Issue 1, pp. 49-72.
[1112] Sitkoff, "The Detroit Race Riot 1943"
[1113] The 1943 Detroit race riots". Detroit News. February 11, 1999. Archived from the original on May 26, 2012.

effects of the Jim Crow era. The promise of employment and escape from the violent racial tensions in the South drew in many African American workers to the North. Before the war, black workers in Detroit were scarce: even in 1942, 119 of 197 Detroit manufacturers surveyed did not have any black employees. However, by 1943, Detroit's labour shortage had become so severe that companies finally began employing African Americans. A report in 1944 showed that with the 44% increase of wartime employment, black employment increased by 103%. Company was the leading manufacturer in black employment: half of all blacks in the auto industry in the U.S. were employed by Ford, and 12% of all Ford workers were black. Ford made sure to develop close ties with African Americans, being in contact with leading clergy at major black churches and using ministers as a screening process to obtain recommendations for the best potential workers. This ensured that Ford only employed reliable long-term workers who would be willing to do the most labour-intensive jobs. Around 1910, Ford gave a salary of $5 a day to its workers, which translates to over $120 today. Because of the city's growth in population and employment opportunities, Detroit became a symbol of cultural rebirth. The statement "when I die, bury me in Detroit" became popular among the black community for these reasons.[1114]

The effect of World War II in E"rope and Asia was felt heavily in the U.S. even before the attack on Pearl Harbour. The defence industry was growing rapidly because the country was immersed in a military build-up to provide assistance to their European and Asian allies.[1115] On the home front, African-Americans were subjected to low-level jobs with little security or protection against the discrimination and prejudice they faced in the work place. A. Philip Randolph and other civil rights leaders took this opportunity to speak with President Roosevelt about expanding opportunities for African Americans by outlawing discrimination in the defence industry. At first, the president was hesitant to agree due to his political alignments but changed his mind when Randolph threatened a large march on the nation's capital.[1116] After President Roosevelt signed Executive Order 8802 which prohibited racial discrimination within the defence industry, he was then preoccupied with p'oviding adequate housing for the new additions to the workforce. Housing in many cities was substandard, especially for people of colour. Housing in Detroit was strained as both blacks and whites moved from southern states to Detroit to work in the booming manufacturing industry in the city. African-Americans were unable to buy houses in the suburbs during the majority of the 20th century due to racially biased practices, such as redlining and restrictive covenants. They had no choice but

---

[1114] Sugrue, Thomas (2014). *The Origins of the Urban Crisis* (First Princeton Classics ed.). Princeton University Press. pp. 25–27. ISBN 978-0-691-16255-3.
[1115] "Executive Order 8802 | United States history". *Encyclopaedia Britannica*.
[1116] "Executive Order 8802 | United States history". *Encyclopaedia Britannica*.

to live in substandard housing in downtown Detroit in an area more commonly known as Black Bottom. Properties in the city had high values for what residents were getting: single-family apartments crowded with multiple families, outstanding maintenance and, in many cases, no indoor plumbing.[1117] The influx of African Americans to Detroit exacerbated racial tensions already present in the city and culminated at the introduction of the Sojourner Truth Housing Project.

In 1941, in an attempt to lessen the severity of the housing crisis, the federal government and the Detroit Housing Commission (DHC) approved the construction of the Sojourner Truth Housing Project with 200 units for black defence workers. The original location for this housing project was chosen by the DHC to be in the Seven Mile-Fenelon neighbourhood in northeast Detroit. They believed that this location would be uncontroversial due to its proximity to an already existing African American neighbourhood.[1118] However, this decision was met with immense backlash.

White residents in the surrounding area formed an improvement association, the Seven Mile-Fenelon Improvement Association, and they were soon joined by the residents of the middle-class African American neighbourhood, Conant Gardens.[1119] These two groups formed an alliance and organized the resistance to the Sojourner Truth Project. These groups protested by meeting with city officials, sending thousands of angry letters to the government, and lobbying with their congressmen against the project, among other things.[1120] Since the Federal Housing Administration (FHA) refused to insure any mortgage loans in the area after the announcement of the project, many of the residents in the area believed that this project would decrease nearby property value and reduce their ability to build on nearby vacant lots.[1121] These beliefs were not unjustified due to the history of decreased property values in other integrated parts of the city. On the other side, civil rights groups and pro-public housing groups rallied for the federal government to keep its promise to allow black residents in Sojourner Truth housing and address the housing shortage. There was only one other housing project in the city for African Americans at this time.[1122]

[1117] Vivian M. Baulch; Patricia Zacharias. "The 1943 Detroit race riots". *www.mtholyoke.edu*. The Detroit News.

[1118] Sugrue, Thomas J. (2005). *The Origins of the Urban Crisis* (First Princeton Classic ed.). Princeton New Jersey: Princeton University Press. pp. 73–75. ISBN 978-0-691-12186-4.

[1119] Sugrue, Thomas J. (2005). *The Origins of the Urban Crisis* (First Princeton Classic ed.). Princeton New Jersey: Princeton University Press. pp. 73–75. ISBN 978-0-691-12186-4.

[1120] Sugrue, Thomas J. (2005). *The Origins of the Urban Crisis* (First Princeton Classic ed.). Princeton New Jersey: Princeton University Press. pp. 73–75. ISBN 978-0-691-12186-4.

[1121] Sugrue, Thomas J. (2005). *The Origins of the Urban Crisis* (First Princeton Classic ed.). Princeton New Jersey: Princeton University Press. pp. 73–75. ISBN 978-0-691-12186-4.

[1122] Sugrue, Thomas J. (2005). *The Origins of the Urban Crisis* (First Princeton Classic ed.). Princeton

In response to the uproar in the local community, the federal government changed its decision on the racial occupancy of the housing project multiple times. In January 1941, the DHC and federal officials declared that Sojourner Truth would have white occupants, but quickly decided instead that it would be occupied by black war workers just two weeks later. Ultimately, it was decided that the Sojourner Truth project would house black residents as originally promised, much to the frustration of the local white community.[1123]

February 1942 saw the culmination of these intense feelings about racial heterogeneity. As the first African Americans workers and their families attempted to move into their new homes, large crowds of both black supporters and white opponents surrounded the area.[1124] A billboard announcing "We Want White Tenants in our White Community" with American flags attached was put up just before the families were to move in. White residents protested the project in the name of "protecting" their neighbourhoods and property value.[1125] These efforts continued throughout the day as more people attempted to move in and tensions continued to rise. More than a thousand people showed up that day and, eventually, fighting erupted between the supporters and opponents. Over a dozen police came onto the scene, but the situation worsened. The fighting resulted in over 40 injured and 220 arrested. Of those arrested, 109 were held for trial, only three of whom were white.[1126]

Detroit officials postponed the movement of African Americans defence workers into the housing project to keep the peace.[1127] This created a problem for the workers who did not have any place to live. The one other public housing that housed black was able to take up some of the residents, but many others had to find housing in other places. After about 2 months, protesting had reduced and Detroit Mayor Edward Jeffries called the Detroit police and Michigan National Guard to escort and protect the African-American workers and their families as they moved into their new homes. The riot led the DHC to establish a new policy mandating racial segregation in all future public housing projects and promised that future housing projects would not "change the racial patterns of a neighbourhood."[1128] It

New Jersey: Princeton University Press. pp. 73–75. ISBN 978-0-691-12186-4.

[1123] Sugrue, Thomas (2014). *The Origins of the Urban Crisis*. Princeton University Press. pp. 73–74. ISBN 978-0-691-16255-3.

[1124] Sugrue, Thomas J. (2005). *The Origins of the Urban Crisis* (First Princeton Classic ed.). Princeton New Jersey: Princeton University Press. pp. 73–75. ISBN 978-0-691-12186-4.

[1125] Vivian M. Baulch; Patricia Zacharias (2000). "Rearview Mirror: The 1943 Detroit race riots".

[1126]Sugrue, Thomas J. (2005). *The Origins of the Urban Crisis* (First Princeton Classic ed.). Princeton New Jersey: Princeton University Press. pp. 73–75. ISBN 978-0-691-12186-4.

[1127] Vivian M. Baulch; Patricia Zacharias. "The 1943 Detroit race riots". *www.mtholyoke.edu*. The Detroit News.

[1128] Sugrue, Thomas J. (2005). *The Origins of the Urban Crisis* (First Princeton Classic ed.). Princeton

also established the precedent that white community groups could utilize the threat of violence to their advantage in future housing debates.[1129]

In June 1943, Packard Motor Car Company finally promoted three blacks to work next to whites in the assembly lines, in keeping with the anti-segregation policy required for the defence industry. In response, 25,000 whites walked off the job in a "hate" or wildcat strike at Packard, effectively slowing down the critical war production. Although whites had long worked with blacks in the same plant, many wanted control of certain jobs, and did not want to work right next to blacks. Harold Zeck remembers seeing a group of white women workers coming into the assembly line to convince the white men workers to walk out of work to protest black women using the white women's bathroom. Harold remembers one of the women saying, "They think their fannies are as good as ours." The protest ended when the men refused to leave work. There was a physical confrontation at Edgewood Park. In this period, racial riots also broke out in Los Angeles, Mobile, Alabama and Beaumont, Texas, mostly over similar job issues at defence shipyard facilities.[1130]

Altercations between youths started on June 20, 1943, on a warm Sunday evening on Belle Isle, an island in the Detroit River off Detroit's mainland. In what is considered a communal disorder,[1131] youths fought intermittently through the afternoon. The brawl eventually grew into a confrontation between groups of whites and blacks on the long Belle Isle Bridge, crowded with more than 100,000-day trippers returning to the city from the park. From there the riot spread into the city. Sailors joined fights against blacks. The riot escalated in the city after a false rumour spread that a mob of whites had thrown a black mother and her baby into the Detroit River. Blacks looted and destroyed white property as retaliation. Whites overran Woodward to Veron where they proceeded to tip over 20 cars that belonged to black families. The whites also started to loot stores while rioting.

Historian Marilyn S. Johnson argues that this rumour reflected black male fears about historical white violence against black women and children.[1132] An equally false rumour that blacks had raped and murdered a white woman on the Belle Isle Bridge swept through white neighbourhoods. Angry mobs of whites spilled onto Woodward Avenue near the Roxy Theatre around 4 a.m., beating blacks as they

New Jersey: Princeton University Press. pp. 73–75. ISBN 978-0-691-12186-4.

[1129] Sugrue, Thomas J. (2005). *The Origins of the Urban Crisis* (First Princeton Classic ed.). Princeton New Jersey: Princeton University Press. pp. 73–75. ISBN 978-0-691-12186-4.

[1130] Dominic J. Capeci, Jr., and Martha Wilkerson, "The Detroit Rioters of 1943: A Reinterpretation", *Michigan Historical Review,* Jan 1990, Vol. 16 Issue 1, pp. 49-72.

[1131] Marilynn S. Johnson, "Gender, Race, and Rumours: Re-Examining the 1943 Race Riots," *Gender and History* (1998): 10:252-77.

[1132] Marilynn S. Johnson, "Gender, Race, and Rumours: Re-Examining the 1943 Race Riots," *Gender and History* (1998): 10:252-77.

were getting off street cars on their way to work.[1133] They also went to the black neighbourhood of Paradise Valley, one of the oldest and poorest neighbourhoods in Detroit, attacking blacks who were trying to defend their homes. Blacks attacked white-owned businesses.

The clashes soon escalated to the point where mobs of whites and blacks were "assaulting one another, beating innocent motorists, pedestrians and streetcar passengers, burning cars, destroying storefronts and looting businesses."[1134] Both sides were said to have encouraged others to join in the riots with false claims that one of "their own" had been attacked unjustly.[1135] Blacks were outnumbered by a large margin, and suffered many more deaths, personal injuries and property damage. Out of the 34 people killed, 24 of them were black.[1136]

The riots lasted three days and ended only after Mayor Jeffries and Governor Harry Kelly asked President Franklin Roosevelt to intervene. He invoked the Insurrection Act of 1807 and ordered in federal troops. A total of 6,000 troops imposed a curfew, restored peace, and occupied the streets of Detroit. Over the course of three days of rioting, 34 people had been killed; 25 were African Americans, of which 17 were killed by the police (their forces were predominantly white and dominated by ethnic whites). 13 deaths remain unsolved. Nine deaths reported were white, and out of the 1,800 arrests made, 85% of them were black, and 15% were white.[1137] Of the approximately 600 persons injured, more than 75 percent were black people.

The first casualty was a white civilian who was struck by a taxi. Later, four young white males shot and killed a 58-year-old black civilian, Moses Kiska, who was sitting at the bus stop. Later, a white doctor ignored police warnings to avoid black neighbourhoods. The doctor then went to a house call in a black neighbourhood. He then was hit in the back of the head with a rock and beaten to death by black rioters. A couple years after the riot, a monument was dedicated to this doctor at the streets of East Grand and Gratiot.

After the riot, leaders on both sides had explanations for the violence, effectively blaming the other side. White city leaders, including the mayor, blamed young black hoodlums and persisted in framing the events as being caused by outsiders, people who were unemployed and marginal.[1138] Mayor Jeffries said, "Negro hoodlums started it, but the conduct of the police department, by and large, was magnificent."[1139]

[1133] "The 1943 Race Riots", *Detroit News*, February 10, 1999
[1134] Sitkoff, "The Detroit Race Riot 1943"
[1135] Sitkoff, "The Detroit Race Riot 1943"
[1136] *White, Walter. "What Caused the Detroit Riot?". Archives. National Association for the Advancement of Coloured People.*
[1137] Sitkoff, "The Detroit Race Riot 1943"
[1138] Sitkoff, "The Detroit Race Riot 1943"

The Wayne County prosecutor believed that leaders of the NAACP were to blame as instigators of the riots.[1140] Governor Kelly called together a Fact Finding Commission to investigate and report on the causes of the riot. Its mostly white members blamed black youths, "unattached, uprooted, and unskilled misfits within an otherwise law-abiding black community," and regarded the events as an unfortunate incident. They made these judgments without interviewing any of the rioters, basing their conclusions on police reports, which were limited.[1141]

Other officials drew similar conclusions, despite discovering and citing facts that disproved their thesis. Dr. Lowell S. Selling of the Recorder's Court Psychiatric Clinic conducted interviews with 100 black offenders. He found them to be "employed, well-paid, longstanding (of at least 10 years) residents of the city", with some education and a history of being law abiding. He attributed their violence to their Southern heritage. This view was repeated in a separate study by Elmer R. Akers and Vernon Fox, sociologist, and psychologist, respectively, at the State Prison of Southern Michigan. Although most of the black men they studied had jobs and had been in Detroit an average of more than 10 years, Akers and Fox characterized them as unskilled and unsettled; they stressed the men's Southern heritage as predisposing them to violence.[1142] Additionally, a commission was established to determine the cause of the riot, despite the unequal amount of violence toward blacks, the commission blamed the riot on blacks and their community leaders.[1143]

Detroit's black leaders identified numerous other substantive causes, including persistent racial discrimination in jobs and housing, frequent police brutality against blacks and the lack of black representation on the force, and the daily animosity directed at their people by much of Detroit's white population.[1144]

Following the violence, Japanese propaganda officials incorporated the event into its materials that encouraged black soldiers not to fight for the United States. They distributed a flyer titled "Fight Between Two Races".[1145] The Axis Powers

---

[1139] Babson, Steve (May 1, 1986). *Working Detroit: The Making of a Union Town*. Wayne State University Press. p. 119.

[1140] Sitkoff, "The Detroit Race Riot 1943"

[1141] Dominic J. Capeci, Jr., and Martha Wilkerson, "The Detroit Rioters of 1943: A Reinterpretation", *Michigan Historical Review,* Jan 1990, Vol. 16 Issue 1, pp. 49-72.

[1142] Dominic J. Capeci, Jr., and Martha Wilkerson, "The Detroit Rioters of 1943: A Reinterpretation", *Michigan Historical Review,* Jan 1990, Vol. 16 Issue 1, pp. 49-72.

[1143] Woodford, Arthur (2012). "Detroit Riot of 1943". *The Michigan Companion: A Guide to the Arts, Entertainment, Festivals, Food, Geography, Geology, Government, History, Holidays, Industry, Institutions, Media, People, Philanthropy, Religion, and Sports of the Great State of Michigan*: 168–169.

[1144] Sitkoff, "The Detroit Race Riot 1943"

[1145] "Japanese Pamphlet -- "A Fight Between Two Races"". *Pinterest.*

publicized the riot as a sign of Western decline. Racial segregation in the United States Armed Forces was ongoing, and the response to the riots hurt morale in African-American units – most significantly the 1511th Quartermaster Truck regiment, which mutinied against white officers and military police on June 24 in the Battle of Bamber Bridge.[1146] [1147]

Walter White, head of the NAACP, noted that there was no rioting at the Packard and Hudson plants, where leaders of the UAW and CIO had been incorporating blacks as part of the rank and file. These changes in the defence industry were directed by Executive Order by President Roosevelt and had begun to open opportunities for blacks.[1148]

Future Supreme Court Justice, Thurgood Marshall, then with the NAACP, assailed the city's handling of the riot. He charged that police unfairly targeted blacks while turning their backs on white atrocities. He said 85 percent of those arrested were black while whites overturned and burned cars in front of the Roxy Theatre with impunity as police watched. "This weak-kneed policy of the police commissioner coupled with the anti-Negro attitude of many members of the force helped to make a riot inevitable."[1149]

[1146] *"When the American military said sorry to Bamber Bridge". Lancashire Evening Post. April 12, 2012.*

[1147] Pollins, Harold. "WW2 People's War – The Battle of Bamber Bridge". BBC. Retrieved April 4, 2017.

[1148] Detroit Riots of 1943, *Encyclopaedia of African American History, 1896 to the Present: From the Age of Segregation to the Twenty-first Century,* Five-volume Set, ed. Paul Finkelman, Oxford University Press, USA, 2009, pp. 59-60

[1149] The 1943 Race Riots", *Detroit News,* February 10, 1999

Chapter twenty-five

Harlem Race Riots of 1943

(The contents of this Chapter is gleaned mostly from the Encyclopaedia Britannica)

Harlem race riot of 1943, riot that occurred in the Manhattan neighbourhood of Harlem on August 1–2, 1943. It was set off when a white police officer shot an African American soldier after he attempted to intervene in the police officer's arrest of an African American woman for disturbing the peace. The spark was ignited in the lobby of the Braddock Hotel, a seven-story hotel on the southeast corner of 126th Street and Eighth Avenue.

After the 1943 Detroit riots had left 30 people dead, mayors across the country attempted to quell the racial unrest simmering beneath the surface in their cities. New York City was suffering from spiralling cost increases because of the wartime economy, and Harlem, with its predominantly Black population, was hit especially hard. Tensions were high because of the high cost of living resulting from shortages of food and other essentials. Further, African Americans throughout the country continued to suffer from racial discrimination, and the Black residents of Harlem felt that the New York City police were harassing the African American community.

On August 1, 1943, an African American soldier tried to intervene when a white police officer tried to arrest an African American woman in Harlem for disorderly conduct. Bullets were fired, and the soldier was shot and wounded. As in the noted 1935 riot, rumours swirled through Harlem that the Black soldier was dead, and another riot began.

Rioters looted stores, smashed windows, and battled with police. On August 2 Mayor Fiorello La Guardia requested that U.S. Army troops help contain the violence. The mayor went on the radio, asking Harlem residents to remain in their homes, and he put a 10:30 PM curfew into effect. Meanwhile, army troops were posted on many street corners throughout Harlem.

During the riot, which ended on August 2, 6 people died, 495 were injured, and more than 500 were arrested. As in 1935, several stores and shops in Harlem suffered.

In the aftermath of the riot, the federal Office of Price Administration (OPA) agreed to open an office on 135th Street in Harlem to investigate complaints about price gouging. The office was soon flooded with complaints. Mayor La Guardia was warned that when lease renewals came due, the landlords would violate voluntary price restraints. The mayor thus increased pressure on the city agencies involved, which forced the landlords to comply with price controls, a circumstance that may have prevented another riot. The event was recalled by several African American writers, including James Baldwin, Langston Hughes, Claude Brown, and Malcolm X (then Malcolm Little).

Chapter twenty-six

Beaumont Race Riots of 1943

When I started to write this chapter, my friend, Bishop August Francis, who lives in Beaumont, urged me to be careful what I used as my source materials, because not everyone reports incidents truthfully. So, I am hoping that he is okay with what I have written here.

The 1943 race riot in Beaumont, Texas, erupted on June 15 and ended two days later. It related to wartime tensions in the overcrowded city, which had been flooded by workers from across the South. The immediate catalyst to white workers from the Pennsylvania Shipyard in Beaumont attacking black people and their property was a rumour that a white woman had been raped by a black man. This was one of several riots in the summer of 1943 in which black people suffered disproportionately as victims and had the greatest losses in property damage.[1150] [1151] The first took place in the largest shipyard in Mobile, Alabama in late May; others took place in Detroit and Los Angeles in June (the latter was a different situation, in which white servicemen attacked Latinos in the Zoot Suit Riots), and Harlem in August.

Beaumont had become a destination for tens of thousands of workers in the defence industry; from 1940 to 1943 the city had grown from 59,000 to 80,000 persons, with African Americans maintaining a proportion of roughly one third of the total.[1152] Workers were attracted to the build-up of high-paying jobs in the defence industry, concentrated at the shipyard, as Beaumont was located on the Neches River northeast of Houston on the Gulf Coast. A presidential Executive Order 8802 was issued to prohibit racial and religious discrimination among defence contractors, and African Americans sought a share of opportunities in the high-paying jobs. New residents in Beaumont competed for jobs and housing in the crowded town, where whites had imposed segregated facilities, as was common across the South. Racial riots erupted that summer in Detroit, Michigan; Mobile, Alabama; Los Angeles, California; and Harlem, New York. They were related to social competition and tensions arising from the wartime build-up. Some cities were struggling to accommodate the influx of black and white defence workers, dealing with shortages in housing and strained services.

[1150] James A. Burran, "Violence in an 'Arsenal of Democracy': The Beaumont Race Riot, 1943", *East Texas Historical Journal*, 1976 Vol. 14, Issue 1, Article 8, available at Scholar Works,
[1151] James S. Olson, "Beaumont Riot of 1943", *Handbook of Texas Online*
[1152] James S. Olson, "Beaumont Riot of 1943", *Handbook of Texas Online*

In 1942, socioeconomic conditions worsened as wartime shortages affected more people. This aggravated interracial tensions in Beaumont. Economic restrictions limited the availability of consumer goods, but defence workers were making good money and were ready for some goods after the privations of the Great Depression President Franklin D. Roosevelt announced a policy to end discrimination in employment in the defence industries through his Executive Order 8802 of 1941; he wanted to encourage all American citizens to support the war effort. From 1940 to 1943, Beaumont had grown more than 33% from 59,000 to 80,000 persons; both African Americans and whites flocked to the city for the industrial jobs. As the population grew, African Americans maintained their proportion of roughly one third of the total population.[1153]

Although public facilities were racially segregated under state law and African Americans had been disenfranchised by Southern states since the turn of the century, they sought the high-paying defence jobs at the shipyards, as had thousands of white workers. The yards employed thousands of workers; Pennsylvania Shipyard was one of the largest, with 8500 workers.[1154] [1155]

Racial animosity and friction during the Jim Crow era were not unusual, but wartime conditions made matters worse. More serious than the economic restrictions were service problems in the city caused by the huge increase in population. The city transportation could not keep up, and crowds added to the tensions between passengers on the segregated system. On June 30, 1942, there were confrontations on four separate buses: blacks were forced to stand or take inferior seats under Jim Crow practices. In one altercation on July 27, Charles J. Reco, a black military policeman, was shot four times and clubbed by Beaumont police as they removed him from a bus following a minor complaint of his knees sticking into the 'white section.'[1156] His military unit protested to the United States Department of War over the trea'ment by local police.[1157]

Four unrelated events amplified the mounting racial tensions in Beaumont. In the months before the riot, numerous atrocities were exacted upon African Americans in Houston, Texas, and the surrounding counties.[1158]

[1153] James S. Olson, "Beaumont Riot of 1943", *Handbook of Texas Online*

[1154] James A. Burran, "Violence in an 'Arsenal of Democracy': The Beaumont Race Riot, 1943", *East Texas Historical Journal,* 1976 Vol. 14, Issue 1, Article 8, available at Scholar Works

[1155] James S. Olson, "Beaumont Riot of 1943", *Handbook of Texas Online*

[1156] James S. Olson, "Beaumont Riot of 1943", *Handbook of Texas Online*

[1157] James A. Burran, "Violence in an 'Arsenal of Democracy': The Beaumont Race Riot, 1943", *East Texas Historical Journal,* 1976 Vol. 14, Issue 1, Article 8, available at Scholar Works

[1158] James A. Burran, "Violence in an 'Arsenal of Democracy': The Beaumont Race Riot, 1943", *East Texas Historical Journal,* 1976 Vol. 14, Issue 1, Article 8, available at Scholar Works

In the immediate event, starting June 15, 1943, a white woman in Beaumont said she had been raped by a black man.[1159] Learning of the charge, white workers confronted blacks at the Pennsylvania Shipyard and violence erupted. About 2,000 white workers, joined by 1,000 more whites, advanced on the jail where suspects were held. By the time they reached the jail, the mob numbered 4,000. The woman was unable to identify any prisoner as her alleged assailant. Breaking into small groups, white mobs attacked and terrorized black neighbourhoods near the jail in the central and north parts of the city and destroyed 100 homes.[1160]

The mayor requested assistance from the Texas Défense Guard (Later known as Texas State Guard). Adjutant General A. B. Knickerbocker of Texas sent one battalion of Texas Défense Guard from Beaumont and two battalions from Port Arthur,[1161] and acting governor A. M. Aikin Jr., speaker *pro tem* of the State House, established a curfew and martial law. A total of about 1,800 guardsmen, 100 state highway police, and 75 Texas Rangers were ordered into the city. The state highway police closed it off to prevent whites from outside entering the city to join the violence. The armed forces declared the city off limits for all military personnel.[1162] Black workers were banned from going to work, although the curfew was lifted by the end of June 16. Mayor Gary closed liquor stores, parks, and playgrounds to prevent any gathering of large crowds. After the mayor ended the curfew on June 16, the guardsmen left town.[1163]

Martial law was maintained by state units until June 20, during which more violence took place. By the end of the violence, one black man and one white man were dead, 50 persons were injured, and more than 200 were arrested. Another black man died from his injury's months later.[1164]

By June 20, a military tribunal had reviewed the cases of the 206 arrested. Twenty-nine cases were turned over to police authorities on charges of assault and battery, unlawful assembly, and arson. The remainder of suspects were released. No one was

---

[1159] One Dead, 11 Hurt In Beaumont Riots". *The Paris News*. June 16, 1943 – via Newspapers.com.
[1160] James S. Olson, "Beaumont Riot of 1943", *Handbook of Texas Online*
[1161] Beaumont Race Riot, 1943, Black Past website.
[1162] James S. Olson, "Beaumont Riot of 1943", *Handbook of Texas Online*
[1163] James S. Olson, "Beaumont Riot of 1943", *Handbook of Texas Online*
[1164] James A. Burran, "Violence in an 'Arsenal of Democracy': The Beaumont Race Riot, 1943", *East Texas Historical Journal,* 1976 Vol. 14, Issue 1, Article 8, available at Scholar Works
[1165] James A. Burran, "Violence in an 'Arsenal of Democracy': The Beaumont Race Riot, 1943", *East Texas Historical Journal,* 1976 Vol. 14, Issue 1, Article 8, available at Scholar Works

prosecuted for the deaths that occurred during the riots. Gradually blacks were allowed to return to work and defence production was resumed.[1165]

Chapter twenty-seven

The Battle of Bamber Bridge

(American Racial battle on English Soil in 1943)

The Battle of Bamber Bridge was an outbreak of racial violence between Black and White American servicemen stationed in the British village of Bamber Bridge, Lancashire in June 1943. The incident, which occurred a few days after the 1943 Detroit race riot, was started when white Military Police (MPs) attempted to arrest several African American soldiers from the racially segregated 1511th Quartermaster Truck Regiment at the Ye Old Hob Inn public house in Bamber Bridge.

After the arrival of more military police armed with machine guns, black soldiers armed themselves with rifles from their base armoury. Both sides exchanged fire through the night. One Black soldier was killed, and several MPs and soldiers injured. Although a court martial convicted 32 African American soldiers of mutiny and related crimes, poor leadership and racist attitudes among the MPs was blamed as the cause.[1166]

During the Second World War, Bamber Bridge hosted American servicemen from the 1511th Quartermaster Truck regiment, part of the Eighth Air Force. Their base, Air Force Station 569 (nicknamed "Adam Hall"), was on Mounsey Road, part of which still exists now as home to 2376 (Bamber Bridge) Squadron of the Royal Air Force Air Cadets. The 1511th Quartermaster Truck was a logistics unit, and its duty was to deliver materiel to other Eighth Air Forces bases in Lancashire.[1167] The 234th US Military Police Company were also in the town, on its north side. [1168]

The US Armed Forces were still racially segregated, and the soldiers of 1511 Quartermaster Truck were almost entirely black, and all but one of the officers were white, as were the MPs. Military commanders tended to treat the service units as "dumping grounds" for less competent officers, and the leadership in the unit was poor.[1169] Racial tensions were exacerbated by the Detroit earlier that week, which

---

[1166] Werrell, Ken (1978). Ramsey, Winston G. (ed.). "The Mutiny at Bamber Bridge". *After the Battle*. No. 22. pp. 1–11. ISBN 9780900913150.

[1167] Miller, Donald L. (2007). *Masters of the Air: America's Bomber Boys Who Fought the Air War Against Nazi Germany*. New York: Simon and Schuster. pp. 227–229. ISBN 9780743235457.

[1168] Werrell, Ken (1978). Ramsey, Winston G. (ed.). "The Mutiny at Bamber Bridge". *After the Battle*. No. 22. pp. 1–11. ISBN 9780900913150.

[1169] Nalty, Bernard C. (1 January 1986). *Strength for the Fight: A History of Black Americans in the*

had led to 34 deaths, including 25 black casualties.[1170] The people of Bamber Bridge supported the black troops, and when US commanders demanded a colour bar in the town, all three pubs in the town reportedly posted "Black Troops Only" signs.[1171]

On the evening of 24 June 1943, some soldiers from the 1511th Quartermaster Truck regiment were drinking with the English townsfolk in Ye Old Hob Inn. Two passing MPs, Corporal Roy A. Windsor and Private First Class Ralph F. Ridgeway, entered the pub and attempted to arrest one soldier (Private Eugene Nunn) upon seeing that he was improperly dressed (in a field jacket, rather than class A uniform). An argument ensued between the black soldier and the white MPs, with local people and British servicewomen of the Auxiliary Territorial Service siding with Nunn.[1172]

Even a white British soldier challenged the MPs by saying, "Why do you want to arrest them? They're not doing anything or bothering anybody."[1173]

Staff Sergeant William Byrd, who was black, defused the situation but as the MPs left, a beer was thrown at their jeep. After the MPs picked up two reinforcements, they spoke to Captain Julius F. Hirst and Lieutenant Gerald C. Windsor, who told the MPs to do their duty and to arrest the black soldiers. A group of MPs intercepted the soldiers on Station Road as they returned to their base at Mounsey Road. A fight broke out in the road, which led to shots being fired. One struck Private William Crossland in the back and killed him.[1174]

Some of the injured black soldiers returned to their base, but the killing caused panic as rumours began to spread that the MPs were out to shoot black soldiers. Although the colonel was absent, acting CO Major George C. Heris did his best to calm the situation. Lieutenant Edwin D. Jones, the unit's only black officer, managed to persuade the soldiers that Heris would be able to round up the MPs and see that justice was done.[1175]

However, at midnight, several jeeps full of MPs arrived at the camp, including one improvised armoured car armed with a large machine gun. That prompted black soldiers to arm themselves with weapons. Around two thirds of the rifles were taken, and a large group left the base in pursuit of the MPs.[1176] British police officers claimed that the MPs set up a roadblock and ambushed the soldiers.[1177]

Military. Simon and Schuster, Free Press. pp. 154–157, 228. ISBN 9780029224113.
[1170] When the American military said sorry to Bamber Bridge". *Lancashire Evening Post*. 12 April 2012.
[1171] *Pollins, Harold. "WW2 People's War – The Battle of Bamber Bridge". BBC.*
[1172] Werrell, Ken (1978). Ramsey, Winston G. (ed.). "The Mutiny at Bamber Bridge". *After the Battle*. No. 22. pp. 1–11. ISBN 9780900913150.
[1173] Warrell1975, p. 203.
[1174] Warrell1975, p. 203.
[1175] Werrell, Ken (1978). Ramsey, Winston G. (ed.). "The Mutiny at Bamber Bridge". *After the Battle*. No. 22. pp. 1–11. ISBN 9780900913150.

The black soldiers warned the townsfolk to stay inside when a firefight broke out between them and the MPs, which resulted in seven wounded. The shooting stopped around 04:00 the next morning. Eventually, the soldiers returned to the base, and by the afternoon, all but four rifles had been recovered.[1178] The violence left one man dead and seven people (five soldiers and two MPs) injured.[1179] Although a court martial convicted 32 black soldiers of mutiny and related crimes, poor leadership and racist attitudes among the MPs was blamed as the cause.[1180]

General Ira C. Eaker, commander of the Eighth Air Force, placed most of the blame for the violence on the white officers and MPs because of their poor leadership and the use of racial slurs by MPs. To prevent similar incidents happening again, he combined the black trucking units into a single special command. The ranks of that command were purged of inexperienced and racist officers, and the MP patrols were racially integrated. Morale among black troops stationed in England improved, and the rates of courts-martial fell. Although there were several more racial incidents between black and white American troops in Britain during the war, none was on the scale of that of Bamber Bridge.[1181] [1182]

Reports of the mutiny were heavily censored, with newspapers disclosing only that violence had occurred in a town somewhere in North West England.[1183] The author Anthony Burgess, who lived in the Bamber Bridge area after the war, wrote about the event briefly in *The New York Times* in 1973 and in his autobiography, *Little Wilson and Big God*.[1184] [1185]

Popular interest in the event increased in the late 1980s after a maintenance worker discovered bullet holes from the battle in the walls of a Bamber Bridge bank.[1186]

In June 2013, to commemorate the 70th anniversary of the incident, the University of Central Lancashire held a symposium.[1187] It included a screening of the 2009

[1176] Werrell, Ken (1978). Ramsey, Winston G. (ed.). "The Mutiny at Bamber Bridge". *After the Battle*. No. 22. pp. 1–11. ISBN 9780900913150.

[1177] When the American military said sorry to Bamber Bridge". *Lancashire Evening Post*. 12 April 2012.

[1178] Werrell, Ken (1978). Ramsey, Winston G. (ed.). "The Mutiny at Bamber Bridge". *After the Battle*. No. 22. pp. 1–11. ISBN 9780900913150.

[1179] Nalty, Bernard C. (1 January 1986). *Strength for the Fight: A History of Black Americans in the Military*. Simon and Schuster, Free Press. pp. 154–157, 228. ISBN 9780029224113.

[1180] Werrell, Ken (1978). Ramsey, Winston G. (ed.). "The Mutiny at Bamber Bridge". *After the Battle*. No. 22. pp. 1–11. ISBN 9780900913150.

[1181] *Miller, Donald L. (2007). Masters of the Air: America's Bomber Boys Who Fought the Air War Against Nazi Germany. New York: Simon and Schuster. pp. 227–229. ISBN 9780743235457.*

[1182] *Pollins, Harold. "WW2 People's War – The Battle of Bamber Bridge". BBC.*

[1183] *Rice, Alan (22 June 2018). "Black troops were welcome in Britain, but Jim Crow wasn't. The race riot of one night in June 1943". The Conversation.*

[1184] Pollins, Harold. "WW2 People's War – The Battle of Bamber Bridge". BBC

[1185] Warrell1975, p. 207.

[1186] Warrell1975, p. 203.

documentary *Choc'late Soldiers from the USA*[1188] [1189]which was produced by Gregory Cooke, and a performance of *Lie Back and Think of America*, a play written by Natalie Penn of Front Room, which had played at the Edinburgh Fringe Festival.[1190]

[1187] Rogerson, Derek (24 June 2018). "When race riots sparked a gun battle on streets of Bamber Bridge". *Lancashire Evening Post*

[1188] "A landmark documentary explores how African American soldiers and British civilians formed an unexpected bond during World War II", which had its world premiere at the Smithsonian Institution's National Museum of African American History and Culture on 10 November 2009. American History and Culture

[1189] "Choc'late Soldiers from the USA: Love, War and Change"(PDF). *Journal of African American History*.

[1190] Rogerson, Derek (24 June 2018). "When race riots sparked a gun battle on streets of Bamber Bridge". *Lancashire Evening Post*. Retrieved 5 April 2019.

Chapter twenty-eight

The Holocaust

This chapter covers the Holocaust a period of German history that they would rather we ALL forgot about. Then as now, there are many that deny that the Holocaust never actually happened. These people are referred to as Holocaust deniers. But when these "Death Camps" were liberated at the end of WWII, there were too many witnesses to uphold the truth that 6 million Jews were exterminated under the guise ethnic cleansing. Some say that the Jews had to die for what they did to Jesus, clearly those who believe this have never read the Bible, Jesus was always going to be put to death. It was all part of GOD's bigger picture for the future of mankind. The Holocaust lasted for four years, and despite the many photographs and the personal stories from the survivors as well as from Military personnel that liberated these death camps, there are still those who refuse to believe that the Germans could possibly have been so atrocious.

I saw a brilliant movie starring Timothy Spall as David Irvine who took Professor Deborah Lippstadt to court because he denied that the Holocaust ever took place, and she had written books to the contrary. The movie is called "Denial" it came out in 2016. You can find a promotional clip of the movie at the following link:

https://youtu.be/yH7ktvUWaYo

When one thinks of the Holocaust, one naturally has images of the 6 million Jews that perished in these death camps, but the true figure of those who died is more likely to be around 7,440,000 Jews. The Nazis rounded up more than 10 million Jews, 3,500,00 from Poland alone, and this was done pre-war, gleaned from a book by David M. Crowe, "The Holocaust: Roots, and Aftermath" published in 2008, *ISBN: 978-0-8133-4235-9.*[1191]

The Nazis did not stop at killing Jews only, they also rounded up anyone who was either a Romani (Gypsy) or Communist or Gay.

Below is a short introduction into what happened and when, but rather than fill page after page of the results of the mass killings of Jews in World War II, they say that a picture paints a thousand words, then the rest of this chapter will have pictures taken at Auschwitz and other Extermination Camps, this leaves you the reader to decide

---

[1191] Crowe 2008, p. 447.

for yourself if you are a Holocaust denier or not. There is no way so many people, both Jewish survivors and Military liberators could have staged the scenes from these death camps.

The Holocaust, also known as the Shoah,[1192] was the genocide of European Jews during World War II.[1193] Between 1941 and 1945, Nazi Germany and its collaborators systematically murdered some six million Jews across German occupied Europe,[1194] around two-thirds of Europe's Jewish population.[1195] The murders were carried out in pogroms (*A pogrom is a violent riot aimed at the massacre or expulsion of an ethnic or religious group, particularly one aimed at Jews. The Slavic term originally entered the English language to describe 19th- and 20th-century attacks on Jews in the Russian Empire.*) and mass shootings; by a policy of extermination through labour in concentration camps; and in chambers gas in German extermination camps, chiefly Auschwitz, Bełżec, Auschwitz, Bełżec, Chełmno, Majdanek, Sobibór, and Treblinka in occupied Poland.[1196]

Germany implemented the persecution in stages. Following Adolf Hitler's appointment as Chancellor on 30 January 1933, the regime built a network of concentration camps in Germany for political opponents and those deemed "undesirable", starting with Dachau on 22 March 1933.[1197] After the passing of the Enabling Act on 24 March,[1198] which gave Hitler plenary powers, the government began isolating Jews from civil society; this included boycotting Jewish businesses in April 1933 and enacting the Nuremberg Laws in September 1935. On 9 – 10 November 1938, eight months after Germany annexed Austria, Jewish businesses and other buildings were ransacked or set on fire throughout Germany and Austria on what became known as *Kristallnacht* (the "Night of Broken Glass"). After Germany invaded Poland in September 1939, triggering World War II, the regime set up ghettos to segregate Jews. Eventually thousands of camps and other detention sites were established across German-occupied Europe.

The segregation of Jews in ghettos culminated in the policy of extermination the Nazis called the Final Solution to the Jewish Question, discussed by senior

---

[1192] Hebrew: השואה, *HaShoah*, "the catastrophe"
[1193] Bloxham 2009, p. 1.
[1194] Matt Brosnan (Imperial War Museum, 2018): "The Holocaust was the systematic murder of Europe's Jews by the Nazis and their collaborators during the Second World War."
[1195] United States Holocaust Memorial Museum: "According to the *American Jewish Yearbook*, the Jewish population of Europe was about 9.5 million in 1933. By 1945, most European Jews - two out of every three - had been killed."
[1196] "Killing Centres: An Overview". *Holocaust Encyclopaedia*. United States Holocaust Memorial Museum.
[1197] For the date, see Marcuse 2001, p. 21.
[1198] Stackelberg & Winkle 2002, pp. 141–143.

government officials at the Wannsee Conference in Berlin in January 1942. As German forces captured territories in the East, all anti-Jewish measures were radicalized. Under the coordination of the SS, with directions from the highest leadership of the Nazi Party, killings were committed within Germany itself, throughout occupied Europe, and within territories controlled by Germany's allies. Paramilitary death squads called *Einsatzgruppen*, in cooperation with the German Army and local collaborators, murdered around 1.3 million Jews in mass shootings and pogroms from the summer of 1941. By mid-1942, victims were being deported from ghettos across Europe in sealed freight trains to extermination camps where, if they survived the journey, they were gassed, worked or beaten to death, or killed by disease, medical experiments, or during death marches. The killing continued until the end of World War II in Europe in May 1945.

The European Jews were targeted for extermination as part of a larger event during the Holocaust era (1933 – 1945),[1199] in which Germany and its collaborators persecuted and murdered millions of others, including ethnic Poles, Soviet civilians and prisoners of war, the Roma, the disabled, political and religious dissidents, and gay men.[1200]

The first recorded use of the term *holocaust* in its modern sense was in 1895 by *The New York Times* to describe the massacre of Armenian Christians by Ottoman Muslims.[1201]

The term comes from the Greek: ὁλόκαυστος, romanized: *holókaustos*; ὅλος *hólos*, "whole" + καυστός *kaustós*, "burnt offering".[1202]

The biblical term *shoah* (Hebrew: שׁוֹאָה), meaning "destruction", became the standard Hebrew term for the murder of the European Jews. According to *Haaretz*, the writer Yehuda Erez may have been the first to describe events in Germany as the *shoah*. *Davar* and later *Haaretz* both used the term in September 1939.[1203] Yom HaShoah became Israel's Holocaust Remembrance Day in 1951.[1204]

On 3 October 1941 the *American Hebrew* used the phrase "before the Holocaust", apparently to refer to the situation in France,[1205] and in May 1943 the *New York Times*, discussing the Bermuda Conference, referred to the "hundreds of thousands

---

[1199] Gray 2015, p. 5.
[1200] Stone 2010, pp. 2–3.
[1201] Crowe 2008, p. 1.
[1202] *Oxford Dictionaries* (2017): "from Old French holocauste, via late Latin from Greek holokauston, from holos 'whole' + kaustos 'burnt' (from kaiein 'burn')".
[1203] *Gilad, Elon (1 May 2019). "Shoah: How a Biblical Term Became the Hebrew Word for Holocaust". Haaretz.*
[1204] Cohen 2010, p. 580.
[1205] Fischel 2020, p. 151.

of European Jews still surviving the Nazi Holocaust".[1206] In 1968 the Library of Congress created a new category, "Holocaust, Jewish (1939 – 1945)".[1207] The term was popularised in the United States by the NBC mini-series *Holocaust* (1978) about a fictional family of German Jews,[1208] and in November that year the President's Commission on the Holocaust was established.[1209] As non-Jewish groups began to include themselves as Holocaust victims, many Jews chose to use the Hebrew terms *Shoah* or *Churban*.[1210] The Nazis used the phrase "Final Solution to the Jewish Question" (German: *die Endlösung der Judenfrage*).[1211]

Holocaust historians commonly define the Holocaust as the genocide of the European Jews by Nazi Germany and its collaborators between 1941 and 1945.[1212] Donald Niewyk and Francis Nicosia, in *The Columbia Guide to the Holocaust* (2000), favour a definition that includes the Jews, Roma, and the disabled: "the systematic, state-sponsored murder of entire groups determined by heredity."[1213]

Other groups targeted after Hitler became Chancellor of Germany in January 1933[1214] include those whom the Nazis viewed as inherently inferior (some Slavic people, particularly Poles and Russians,[1215] the Roma, and the disabled), and those targeted because of their beliefs or behaviour (such as Jehovah's Witnesses, communists, and homosexuals).[1216] Peter Hayes writes that the persecution of these groups was less uniform than that of the Jews. For example, the Nazis' treatment of the Slavs consisted of "enslavement and gradual attrition", while some Slavs were favoured; Hayes lists Bulgarians, Croats, Slovaks, and some Ukrainians.[1217] In contrast, Hitler regarded the Jews as what Dan Stone calls "a *Gegenrasse*: a 'counter-race' ... not really human at all."[1218]

[1206] Meltzer, Julian (23 May 1943). "Palestine Zionists Find Outlook Dark". *The New York Times.*
[1207] Lustigman & Lustigman 1994, p. 111.
[1208] Black 2016, p. 201.
[1209] Hilberg 2003, p. 1133 (vol. III).
[1210] Fischel 2020, p. 152.
[1211] Berenbaum 2006, p. xix.
[1212] Fischel 2020, p. 151.
[1213] *"What was the Holocaust?". Yad Vashem.*
[1214] Gray 2015, pp. 4–5; "What was the Holocaust?". Yad Vashem; "Documenting Numbers of Victims of the Holocaust and Nazi Persecution". *Holocaust Encyclopedia.* United States Holocaust Memorial Museum.
[1215] "Documenting Numbers of Victims of the Holocaust and Nazi Persecution". https://*encyclopedia.ushmm.org*. During the era of the Holocaust, German authorities also targeted and killed other groups, including at times their children, because of their perceived racial and biological inferiority: Roma (Gypsies), Germans with disabilities, and some of the Slavic peoples (especially Poles and Russians).
[1216] Gray 2015, p. 4.
[1217] Hayes 2015, pp. xiii–xiv.
[1218] Stone 2010, pp. 2–3.

The logistics of the mass murder turned Germany into what Michael Berenbaum called a "genocidal state".[1219] Eberhard Jäckel wrote in 1986 that it was the first time a state had thrown its power behind the idea that an entire people should be wiped out.[1220] In total, 165,200 German Jews were murdered.[1221] Anyone with three or four Jewish grandparents was to be exterminated,[1222] and complex rules were devised to deal with *Mischlinge* ("mixed breeds").[1223] Bureaucrats identified who was a Jew, confiscated property, and scheduled trains to deport them. Companies fired Jews and later used them as slave labour. Universities dismissed Jewish faculty and students. German pharmaceutical companies tested drugs on camp prisoners; other companies built the crematoria.[1224] As prisoners entered the death camps, they surrendered all personal property,[1225] which was catalogued and tagged before being sent to Germany for reuse or recycling.[1226] Through a concealed account, the German National Bank helped launder valuables stolen from the victims.[1227]

At least 7,000 camp inmates were subjected to medical experiments; most died during them or as a result.[1228]

The experiments, which took place at Auschwitz, Buchenwald, Dachau, Natzweiler – Struthof, Neuengamme, Ravensbrück, and Sachsenhausen, involved the sterilization of men and women, treatment of war wounds, ways to counteract chemical weapons, research into new vaccines and drugs, and survival of harsh conditions.[1229]

After the war, 23 senior physicians and other medical personnel were charged at Nuremberg with crimes against humanity. They included the head of the German Red Cross, tenured professors, clinic directors, and biomedical researchers.[1230] The most notorious physician was Josef Mengele, an SS officer who became the

---

[1219] Berenbaum 2006, p. 103.
[1220] Eberhard Jäckel (*Die Zeit*, 12 September 1986): "I maintain ... that the National Socialist killing of the Jews was unique in that never before had a state with the authority of its leader decided and announced that a specific group of humans, including the elderly, the women, the children and the infants, would be killed as quickly as possible, and then carried out this resolution using every possible means of state power."
[1221] https://encyclopedia.ushmm.org/content/en/article/jewish-losses-during-the-holocaust-by-country
[1222] Bauer 2002, p. 49.
[1223] Friedländer 2007, pp. 51–52.
[1224] Berenbaum 2006, p. 103.
[1225] Dwork & van Pelt 2003, pp. 287–288.
[1226] Arad 1999, pp. 154–159.
[1227] Fischel 1998, p. 167.
[1228] Fisher 2001, pp. 410–414.
[1229] Fisher 2001, pp. 410–414.
[1230] Hanauske-Abel 1996, p. 1453; Fisher 2001, pp. 410–414.

Auschwitz camp doctor on 30 May 1943.[1231] Interested in genetics,[1232] and keen to experiment on twins, he would pick out subjects on the ramp from the new arrivals during "selection" (to decide who would be gassed immediately and who would be used as slave labour), shouting *"Zwillinge heraus!"* (Twins step forward!).[1233] The twins would be measured, killed, and dissected. One of Mengele's assistants said in 1946 that he was told to send organs of interest to the directors of the "Anthropological Institute in Berlin-Dahlem". This is thought to refer to Mengele's academic supervisor, Otmar Freiherr von Verschuer, director from October 1942 of the Kaiser Wilhelm Institute of Anthropology, Human Heredity, and Eugenics in Berlin-Dahlem.[1234]

Throughout the Middle Ages in Europe, Jews were subjected to antisemitism based on Christian theology, which blamed them for killing Jesus. Even after the Reformation, Catholicism and Lutheranism continued to persecute Jews, accusing them of blood libels and subjecting them to pogroms and expulsions.[1235] The second half of the 19th century saw the emergence, in the German empire and Austria-Hungary, of the *völkisch* movement, developed by such thinkers as Houston Stewart Chamberlain and Paul de Lagarde. The movement embraced a pseudo-scientific racism that viewed Jews as a race whose members were locked in mortal combat with the Aryan race for world domination.[1236] These ideas became commonplace throughout Germany; the professional classes adopted an ideology that did not see humans as racial equals with equal hereditary value.[1237] The Nazi Party (the *Nationalsozialistische Deutsche Arbeiterpartei* or National Socialist German Workers' Party) originated as an offshoot of the *völkisch* movement, and it adopted that movement's antisemitism.[1238]

After World War I (1914–1918), many Germans did not accept that their country had been defeated. A stab-in-the-back myth developed, insinuating that disloyal politicians, chiefly Jews and communists, had orchestrated Germany's surrender. Inflaming the anti-Jewish sentiment was the apparent over-representation of Jews in the leadership of communist revolutionary governments in Europe, such as Ernst Toller, head of a short-lived revolutionary government in Bavaria. This perception contributed to the canard of Jewish Bolshevism.[1239]

[1231] Müller-Hill 1999, p. 338.
[1232] Müller-Hill 1999, p. 338.
[1233] Friedländer 2007, p. 505.
[1234] Müller-Hill 1999, pp. 340–342; Friedländer 2007, p. 505.
[1235] Jones 2006, p. 148; Bergen 2016, pp. 14–17.
[1236] Jones 2006, p. 148; Bergen 2016, pp. 14–17.
[1237] Friedlander 1994, pp. 495–496.
[1238] Fischer 2002, p. 47.
[1239] "Antisemitism in History: World War I". *Holocaust Encyclopedia*. United States Holocaust Memorial Museum.

Early anti-Semites in the Nazi Party included Dietrich Eckart, publisher of the *Völkischer Beobachter*, the party's newspaper, and Alfred Rosenberg, who wrote antisemitic articles for it in the 1920s. Rosenberg's vision of a secretive Jewish conspiracy ruling the world would influence Hitler's views of Jews by making them the driving force behind communism.[1240] Central to Hitler's world view was the idea of expansion and *Lebensraum* (living space) in Eastern Europe for German Aryans, a policy of what Doris Bergen called "race and space". Open about his hatred of Jews, he subscribed to common antisemitic stereotypes.[1241] From the early 1920s onwards, he compared the Jews to germs and said they should be'dealt with in the same way. He viewed Marxism as a Jewish doctrine, said he was fighting against "Jewish Marxism", and believed that Jews had created communism as part of a conspiracy to destroy Germany.[1242]

With the appointment in January 1933 of Adolf Hitler as Chancellor of Germany and the Nazi's seizure of power, German leaders proclaimed the rebirth of the *Volksgemeinschaft* ("people's community").[1243] Nazi policies divided the population into two groups: the *Volksgenossen* ("national comrades") who belonged to the *Volksgemeinschaft*, and the *Gemeinschaftsfremde* ("community aliens") who did not. Enemies were divided into three groups: the "racial" or "blood" enemies, such as the Jews and Roma; political opponents of Nazism, such as Marxists, liberals, Christians, and the "reactionaries" viewed as wayward "national comrades"; and moral opponents, such as gay men, the work-shy, and habitual criminals. The latter two groups were to be sent to concentration camps for "re-education", with the aim of eventual absorption into the *Volksgemeinschaft*. "Racial" enemies could never belong to the *Volksgemeinschaft*; they were to be removed from society.[1244]

Before and after the March 1933 Reichstag elections, the Nazis intensified their campaign of violence against opponents,[1245] setting up concentration camps for extrajudicial imprisonment.[1246] One of the first, at Dachau, opened on 22 March 1933.[1247] Initially the camp contained mostly Communists and Social Democrats.[1248] Other early prisons were consolidated by mid-1934 into purpose-built camps outside the cities, run exclusively by the SS.[1249] The camps served as a deterrent by terrorizing Germans who did not support the regime.[1250]

[1240] Yahil 1990, pp. 41–43.
[1241] Bergen 2016, pp. 52–54.
[1242] Bergen 2016, p. 56.
[1243] Fritzsche 2009, pp. 38–39.
[1244] Noakes & Pridham 1983, p. 499.
[1245] Wachsmann 2015, pp. 28–30
[1246] Wachsmann 2015, pp. 32–38.
[1247] Marcuse 2001, p. 21.
[1248] Longerich 2012, p. 155.
[1249] Wachsmann 2015, pp. 84–86.

Throughout the 1930s, the legal, economic, and social rights of Jews were steadily restricted.[1251] On 1 April 1933, there was a boycott of Jewish businesses.[1252] On 7 April 1933, the Law for the Restoration of the Professional Civil Service was passed, which excluded Jews and other "non-Aryans" from the civil service.[1253] Jews were disbarred from practicing law, being editors or proprietors of newspapers, joining the Journalists' Association, or owning farms.[1254] In Silesia, in March 1933, a group of men entered the courthouse and beat up Jewish lawyers; Friedländer writes that, in Dresden, Jewish lawyers and judges were dragged out of courtrooms during trials.[1255] Jewish students were restricted by quotas from attending schools and universities.[1256] Jewish businesses were targeted for closure or "Aryanization", the forcible sale to Germans; of the approximately 50,000 Jewish-owned businesses in Germany in 1933, about 7,000 were still Jewish-owned in April 1939. Works by Jewish composers,[1257] authors, and artists were excluded from publications, performances, and exhibitions.[1258] Jewish doctors were dismissed or urged to resign. The *Deutsches Ärzteblatt* (a medical journal) reported on 6 April 1933: "Germans are to be treated by Germans only."[1259]

The economic strain of the Great Depression led Protestant charities and some members of the German medical establishment to advocate compulsory sterilization of the "incurable" mentally and physically disabled,[1260] people the Nazis called *Lebensunwertes Leben* (life unworthy of life).[1261] On 14 July 1933, the Law for the Prevention of Hereditarily Diseased Offspring (*Gesetz zur Verhütung erbkranken Nachwuchses*), the Sterilization Law, was passed.[1262] *The New York Times* reported on 21 December that year: "400,000 Germans to be sterilized".[1263] T here were 84,525 applications from doctors in the first year. The courts reached a decision in 64,499 of those cases; 56,244 were in favour of sterilization.[1264] Estimate s for the number of involuntary sterilizations during the whole of the Third Reich range from 300,000 to 400,000.[1265]

[1250] Wachsmann 2015, p. 5.
[1251] Friedländer 1997, p. 33.
[1252] Friedländer 1997, pp. 19–20.
[1253] Burleigh & Wippermann 2003, p. 78.
[1254] Friedländer 1997, pp. 32–33.
[1255] Friedländer 1997, p. 29.
[1256] Burleigh & Wippermann 2003, p. 78.
[1257] Friedländer 1997, p. 134.
[1258] Evans 2005, pp. 158–159, 169.
[1259] Hanauske-Abel 1996, p. 1459.
[1260] Evans 2004, pp. 377–378.
[1261] Lifton 2000, p. 21.
[1262] Hanauske-Abel 1996, p. 1457.
[1263] Tolischus, Otto D. (21 December 1933). "400,000 Germans to be sterilized". *The New York Times*.
[1264] Hanauske-Abel 1996, p. 1458.
[1265] Proctor 1988, pp. 106–108.

In October 1939 Hitler signed a "euthanasia decree" backdated to 1 September 1939 that authorized *Reichsleiter* Philipp Bouhler, the chief of Hitler's Chancellery, and Karl Brandt, Hitler's personal physician, to carry out a program of involuntary euthanasia. After the war this program came to be known as *Aktion T4*,[1266] named after Tiergartenstraße 4, the address of a villa in the Berlin borough of Tiergarten,

where the various organizations involved were headquartered.[1267] T4 was mainly directed at adults, but the euthanasia of children was also carried out.[1268] Between 1939 and 1941, 80,000 to 100,000 mentally ill adults in institutions were killed, as were 5,000 children and 1,000 Jews, also in institutions. There were also dedicated killing centres, where the deaths were estimated at 20,000, according to Georg Renno, deputy director of Schloss Hartheim, one of the euthanasia centres, or 400,000, according to Frank Zeireis, commandant of the Mauthausen concentration camp.[1269] Overall, the number of mentally and physically disabled people murdered was about 150,000.[1270]

Although not ordered to take part, psychiatrists and many psychiatric institutions were involved in the planning and carrying out of *Aktion T4*.[1271] In August 1941, after protests from Germany's Catholic and Protestant churches, Hitler cancelled the T4 program,[1272] although disabled people continued to be killed until the end of the war.[1273] The medical community regularly received bodies for research; for example, the University of Tübingen received 1,077 bodies from executions between 1933 and 1945. The German neuroscientist Julius Hallervorden received 697 brains from one hospital between 1940 and 1944: "I accepted these brains of course. Where they came from and how they came to me was really none of my business."[1274]

On 15 September 1935, the Reichstag passed the Reich Citizenship Law and the Law for the Protection of German Blood and German Honour, known as the Nuremberg Laws. The former said that only those of "German or kindred blood" could be citizens. Anyone with three or more Jewish grandparents was classified as a Jew.[94] The second law said: "Marriages between Jews and subjects of the state of German or related blood are forbidden." Sexual relationships between them were also criminalized; Jews were not allowed to employ German women under the age of 45 in their homes.[1275] [1276] The laws referred to Jews but applied equally to the Roma

---

1266 Burleigh & Wippermann 2003, pp. 142–149.
1267 Kershaw 2000, pp. 252–261.
1268 Bloxham 2009, p. 171.
1269 Lifton 2000, p. 142.
1270 Niewyk & Nicosia 2000, p. 48.
1271 Strous 2007
1272 Lifton 2000, pp. 90–95.
1273 Niewyk & Nicosia 2000, p. 48
1274 Hanauske-Abel 1996, pp. 1458–1459.

and black Germans. Although other European countries – Bulgaria, Independent State of Croatia, Hungary, Italy, Romania, Slovakia, and Vichy France – passed similar legislation,[1277] Gerlach notes that "Nazi Germany adopted more nationwide anti-Jewish laws and regulations (about 1,500) than any other state."[1278]

By the end of 1934, 50,000 German Jews had left Germany,[1279] and by the end of 1938, approximately half the German Jewish population had left,[1280] among them the conductor Bruno Walter, who fled after being told that the hall of the Berlin Philharmonic would be burned down if he conducted a concert there.[1281] Albert Einstein, who was in the United States when Hitler came to power, never returned to Germany; his citizenship was revoked and he was expelled from the Kaiser Wilhelm Society and Prussian Academy of Sciences.[1282] Other Jewish scientists, including Gustav Hertz, lost their teaching positions and left the country.[1283]

On 12 March 1938, Germany annexed Austria. Ninety percent of Austria's 176,000 Jews lived in Vienna.[1284] The SS and SA smashed shops and stole cars belonging to Jews; Austrian police stood by, some already wearing swastika armbands.[1285] Jews were forced to perform humiliating acts such as scrubbing the streets or cleaning toilets while wearing tefillin.[1286] Around 7,000 Jewish businesses were "Aryanized", and all the legal restrictions on Jews in Germany were imposed in Austria.[1287] The Évian Conference was held in France in July 1938 by 32 countries, to help German and Austrian Jewish refugees, but little was accomplished and most countries did not increase the number of refugees they would accept.[1288] In August that year, Adolf Eichmann was appointed manager (under Franz Walter Stahlecker) of the Central Agency for Jewish Emigration in Vienna (*Zentralstelle für jüdische Auswanderung in Wien*).[1289] Sigmund Freud and his family arrived in London from Vienna in June 1938, thanks to what David Cesarani called "Herculean efforts" to get them out.[1290]

[1275] Nuremberg Race Laws". United States Holocaust Memorial Museum.
[1276] Arad, Gutman & Margaliot 2014, p. 78.
[1277] Nuremberg Race Laws". United States Holocaust Memorial Museum.
[1278] Gerlach 2016, p. 41.
[1279] Fischel 1998, p. 20.
[1280] Gilbert 2001, p. 285.
[1281] Friedländer 1997, p. 1.
[1282] Friedländer 1997, p. 12.
[1283] Evans 2005, p. 16.
[1284] Cesarani 2016, p. 152.
[1285] Cesarani 2016, p. 153.
[1286] Cesarani 2016, pp. 154–156.
[1287] Cesarani 2016, pp. 157–158.
[1288] Niewyk & Nicosia 2000, p. 200.
[1289] Cesarani 2016, p. 160.
[1290] Cesarani 2016, p. 162.

On 7 November 1938, Herschel Grynszpan, a Polish Jew, shot the German diplomat Ernst vom Rath in the German Embassy in Paris, in retaliation for the expulsion of his parents and siblings from Germany.[1291] When vom Rath died on 9 November, the synagogue and Jewish shops in Dessau were attacked. According to Joseph Goebbels' diary, Hitler decided that the police should be withdrawn: "For once the Jews should feel the rage of the people," Goebbels reported him as saying.[1292] The result, David Cesarani writes, was "murder, rape, looting, destruction of property, and terror on an unprecedented scale".[1293]

Known as *Kristallnacht* ("Night of Broken Glass"), the pogrom on 9 -10 November 1938 saw over 7,500 Jewish shops (out of 9,000) looted and attacked, and over 1,000 synagogues damaged or destroyed. Groups of Jews were forced by the crowd to watch their synagogues burn; in Bensheim they were made to dance around it and in Laupheim to kneel before it.[1294] At least 90 Jews died. The damage was estimated at 39 million Reichmarks.[1295] Contrary to Goebbel's statements in his diary, the police were not withdrawn; the regular police, Gestapo, SS and SA all took part, although Heinrich Himmler was angry that the SS had joined in.[1296] Attacks took place in Austria too.[1297] The extent of the violence shocked the rest of the world. *The Times* of London stated on 11 November 1938:

No foreign propagandist bent upon blackening germany before the world could outdo the tale of burnings and beatings, of blackguardly assaults upon defenceless and innocent people, which disgraced that country yesterday. Either the German authorities were a party to this outbreak or their powers over public order and a hooligan minority are not what they are proudly claimed to be.[1298]

Between 9 and 16 November, 30,000 Jews were sent to the Buchenwald, Dachau, and Sachsenhausen concentration camps.[1299] Many were released within weeks; by early 1939, 2,000 remained in the camps.[1300] German Jewry was held collectively responsible for restitution of the damage; they also had to pay an "atonement tax" of over a billion Reichmarks. Insurance payments for damage to their property were confiscated by the government. A decree on 12 November 1938 barred Jews from

---

[1291] Cesarani 2016, p. 181.
[1292] Cesarani 2016, p. 187.
[1293] Cesarani 2016, pp. 187–188.
[1294] Cesarani 2016, pp. 184–185.
[1295] Cesarani 2016, pp. 184, 187.
[1296] Cesarani 2016, pp. 188–189.
[1297] Cesarani 2016, pp. 194–195.
[1298] "A Black Day for Germany". *The Times* (48149). 11 November 1938. p. 15.
[1299] Evans 2005, p. 591.
[1300] Cesarani 2016, p. 200.

most remaining occupations.[1301] *Kristallnacht* marked the end of any sort of public Jewish activity and culture, and Jews stepped up their efforts to leave the country.[1302]

Before World War II, Germany considered mass deportation from Europe of German, and later European, Jewry.[1303] Among the areas considered for possible resettlement were British Palestine and, after the war began, French Madagascar,[1304] Siberia, and two reservations in Poland.[1305] Palestine was the only location to which any German resettlement plan produced results, via the Haavara Agreement between the Zionist Federation of Germany and the German government. Between November 1933 and December 1939, the agreement resulted in the emigration of about 53,000 German Jews, who were allowed to transfer RM 100 millions of their assets to Palestine by buying German goods, in violation of the Jewish-led anti-Nazi boycott of 1933.[1306]

Between 2.7 and 3 million Polish Jews died during the Holocaust out of a population of 3.3 – 3.5 million.[1307] More Jews lived in Poland in 1939 than anywhere else in the world; another 3 million lived in the Soviet Union. When the German Wehrmacht (armed forces) invaded Poland on 1 September 1939, triggering declarations of war from the UK and France, Germany gained control of about two million Jews in the territory it occupied. The rest of Poland was occupied by the Soviet Union, which invaded Poland from the east on 17 September 1939.[1308]

The Wehrmacht in Poland was accompanied by seven SS *Einsatzgruppen der Sicherheitspolitizei* ("special task forces of the Security Police") and an *Einsatzkommando*, numbering 3,000 men in all, whose role was to deal with "all anti-German elements in hostile country behind the troops in combat".[1309] German plans for Poland included expelling non-Jewish Poles from large areas, settling Germans on the emptied lands,[1310] sending the Polish leadership to camps, denying the lower classes an education, and confining Jews.[1311] The Germans sent Jews from all territories they had annexed (Austria, the Czech lands, and western Poland) to the central section of Poland, which was termed the General Government.[1312] Jews were

---

[1301] Evans 2005, pp. 595–596.
[1302] Ben-Rafael, Glöckner & Sternberg 2011, pp. 25–26.
[1303] Friedländer 1997, pp. 224–225.
[1304] Friedländer 1997, pp. 62–63, 219, 283, 310.
[1305] Cesarani 2016, p. 382; *Cesarani, David (17 February 2011). "From Persecution to Genocide". History: World Wars. BBC.*
[1306] Nicosia 2008, pp. 88–89.
[1307] Crowe 2008, p. 447; also see Polonsky 2001, p. 488.
[1308] "Total Jewish Population in the United States". *www.jewishvirtuallibrary.org.*
[1309] Crowe 2008, pp. 158–159.
[1310] Browning 2004, p. 16.
[1311] Bergen 2016, pp. 136–137.
[1312] Browning 2004, pp. 25–26.

eventually to be expelled to areas of Poland not annexed by Germany. Still, in the meantime, they would be concentrated in major cities ghettos to achieve, according to an order from Reinhard Heydrich dated 21 September 1939, "a better possibility of control and later deportation".[1313] From 1 December, Jews were required to wear Star of David armbands.[1314]

The Germans stipulated that each ghetto be led by a *Judenrat* of 24 male Jews, who would be responsible for carrying out German orders.[1315] These orders included, from 1942, facilitating deportations to extermination camps.[1316] The Warsaw Ghetto was established in November 1940, and by early 1941 it contained 445,000 people;[1317] the second largest, the Łódź Ghetto, held 160,000 as of May 1940.[1318] Th e inhabitants had to pay for food and other supplies by selling whatever goods they could produce.[1319] In the ghettos and forced-labour camps, at least half a million died of starvation, disease, and poor living conditions.[1320] Although the Warsaw Ghetto contained 30 percent of the city's population, it occupied only 2.4 percent of its area, averaging over nine people per room.[1321] Over 43,000 residents died there in 1941.[1322]

The Madagascar Plan:

With the fall of France, this gave rise to the "Madagascar Plan" in the summer of 1940, when French Madagascar in Southeast Africa became the focus of discussions about deporting all European Jews there; it was thought that the area's harsh living conditions would hasten deaths.[1323] Several Polish, French and British leaders had discussed the idea in the 1930s, as did German leaders from 1938.[1324] Adolf Eichmann's office was ordered to investigate the option, but no evidence of planning exists until after the defeat of France in June 1940.[1325] Germany's inability to defeat Britain, something that was obvious to the Germans by September 1940, prevented the movement of Jews across the seas,[1326] and the Foreign Ministry abandoned the plan in February 1942.[1327]

[1313] Black 2016, p. 29.
[1314] Browning 2004, pp. 25–26.
[1315] Black 2016, p. 31.
[1316] Browning 2004, p. 111
[1317] Hilberg 1993, p. 106.
[1318] Browning 2004, p. 124.
[1319] Hilberg 1993, p. 106.
[1320] Yahil 1990, p. 165.
[1321] Yahil 1990, p. 169; Browning 2004, p. 124.
[1322] Dwork & van Pelt 2003, p. 239.
[1323] Longerich 2010, pp. 161–164; for hastening deaths, also see Browning 2004, pp. 88–89.
[1324] Browning 2004, pp. 81–82.
[1325] Browning 2004, pp. 82–85.
[1326] Browning 2004, p. 88.

At first the *Einsatzgruppen* targeted the male Jewish intelligentsia, defined as male Jews aged 15–60 who had worked for the state and in certain professions. The commandos described them as "Bolshevist functionaries" and similar. From August 1941 they began to murder women and children too.[1328] Christopher Browning reports that on 1 August 1941, the SS Cavalry Brigade passed an order to its units: "Explicit order by RF-SS [Heinrich Himmler, Reichsführer-SS]. All Jews must be shot. Drive the female jews into the swamps."[1329]

Two years later, in a speech on 6 October 1943 to party leaders, Heinrich Himmler said he had ordered that women and children be shot, but according to Peter Longerich and Christian Gerlach, the murder of women and children began at different times in different areas, suggesting local influence.[1330]

Historians agree that there was a "gradual radicalization" between the spring and autumn of 1941 of what Longerich calls Germany's *Judenpolitik*, but they disagree about whether a decision – *Führerentscheidung* (Führer's decision) – to murder the European Jews had been made at this point.[1331] According to Browning, writing in 2004, most historians say there was no order, before the invasion of the Soviet Union, to kill all the Soviet Jews.[1332] Longerich wrote in 2010 that the gradual increase in brutality and numbers killed between July and September 1941 suggests there was "no particular order". Instead, it was a question of "a process of increasingly radical interpretations of orders".[1333]

Germany first used concentration camps as places of terror and unlawful incarceration of political opponents.[1334] Large numbers of Jews were not sent there until after *Kristallnacht* in November 1938.[1335] After war broke out in 1939, new camps were established, many outside Germany in occupied Europe.[1336] Most wartime prisoners of the camps were not Germans but belonged to countries under German occupation.[1337]

After 1942, the economic function of the camps, previously secondary to their penal and terror functions, came to the fore. Forced labour of camp prisoners became

---

[1327] Longerich 2010, p. 164.
[1328] "Einsatzgruppe member kills a Jewish woman and her child near Ivangorod, Ukraine, 1942". United States Holocaust Memorial Museum.
[1329] Longerich 2010, p. 207; Gerlach 2016, p. 70.
[1330] Browning 2004, p. 281.
[1331] Longerich 2010, p. 206; Gerlach 2016, pp. 71–72.
[1332] Wachsmann 2015, p. 300.
[1333] Browning 2004, p. 214.
[1334] Orth 2009, p. 181.
[1335] Fischel 2020, p. 77.
[1336] Baumel 2001, p. 135.
[1337] "Nazi Camps". *Holocaust Encyclopaedia*. United States Holocaust Memorial Museum.

commonplace.[1338] The guards became much more brutal, and the death rate increased as the guards not only beat and starved prisoners but killed them more frequently.[1339] *Vernichtung durch Arbeit* ("extermination through labour") was a policy; camp inmates would literally be worked to death, or to physical exhaustion, at which point they would be gassed or shot.[1340] The Germans estimated the average prisoner's lifespan in a concentration camp at three months, as a result of lack of food and clothing, constant epidemics, and frequent punishments for the most minor transgressions.[1341] The shifts were long and often involved exposure to dangerous materials.[1342]

Transportation to and between camps was often carried out in closed freight cars with little air or water, long delays and prisoners packed tightly.[1343] In mid – 1942 work camps began requiring newly arrived prisoners to be placed in quarantine for four weeks.[1344] Prisoners wore coloured triangles on their uniforms, the colour denoting the reason for their incarceration. Red signified a political prisoner, Jehovah's Witnesses had purple triangles, "asocials" ("asocial" was a word used by the Nazis to describe people who were unwilling to work, this category was also used to describe those who were work shy, beggars), they wore black triangles, criminals wore black and green, and gay men wore pink.[1345] Jews wore two yellow triangles, one over another to form a six-pointed star.[1346] Prisoners in Auschwitz were tattooed on arrival with an identification number.[1347]

At the end of 1941 in occupied Poland, the Germans began building additional camps or expanding existing ones. Auschwitz, for example, was expanded in October 1941 by building Auschwitz II-Birkenau a few kilometres away.[1348] By the spring or summer of 1942, gas chambers had been installed in these new facilities, except for Chełmno, which used gas vans.

Other camps that were sometimes described as extermination camps include Maly Trostinets near Minsk in the occupied Soviet Union, where 65,000 are thought to have died, mostly by shooting but also in gas vans;[1349] Mauthausen in Austria;[1350] St

---

[1338] Fischel 2020, p. 77.
[1339] "Nazi Camps". *Holocaust Encyclopaedia*. United States Holocaust Memorial Museum.
[1340] Wachsmann 2015, pp. 287–288.
[1341] Longerich 2010, pp. 314–320.
[1342] Black 2016, p. 76.
[1343] Black 2016, p. 104.
[1344] Friedländer 2007, p. 492–494.
[1345] Wachsmann 2015, p. 347.
[1346] Wachsmann 2015, pp. 125–127, 623.
[1347] Yahil 1990, p. 134; Wachsmann 2015, p. 119.
[1348] "Killing Centres: An Overview". *Holocaust Encyclopaedia*. United States Holocaust Memorial Museum.

utthof, near Gdańsk, Poland;[1351] as well as Sachsenhausen and Ravensbrück in Germany.[1352]

Chełmno, with gas vans only, had its roots in the Aktion T4 euthanasia program.[1353] In December 1939 and January 1940, gas vans equipped with gas cylinders and a sealed compartment had been used to kill disabled people in occupied Poland.[1354] As the mass shootings continued in Russia, Himmler and his subordinates in the field feared that the murders were causing psychological problems for the SS,[1355] and began searching for more efficient methods. In December 1941, similar vans, using exhaust fumes rather than bottled gas, were introduced into the camp at Chełmno,[1356] Victims were asphyxiated while being driven to prepared burial pits in the nearby forests.[1357] The vans were also used in the occupied Soviet Union, for example in smaller clearing actions in the Minsk ghetto,[1358] and in Yugoslavia.[1359] Apparently, as with the mass shootings, the vans caused emotional problems for the operators, and the small number of victims the vans could handle made them ineffective.[1360]

Christian Gerlach writes that over three million Jews were murdered in 1942, the year that "marked the peak" of the mass murder.[1361] At least 1.4 million of these were in the General Government area of Poland.[1362] Victims usually arrived at the extermination camps by freight train.[1363] Almost all arrivals at Bełżec, Sobibór and Treblinka were sent directly to the gas chambers,[1364] with individuals occasionally selected to replace dead workers.[1365] At Auschwitz, about 20 percent of Jews were selected to work.[1366] Those selected for death at all camps were told to undress and hand their valuables to camp workers.[1367] They were then herded naked into the gas

---

[1349] Gerlach 2016, p. 94; also see Cesarani 2016, p. 504.
[1350] "Maly Trostinets" (PDF). Yad Vashem, Heberer 2008, p. 131 and Lehnstaedt 2016, p. 30.
[1351] Fischel 2020, pp. 84, 210.
[1352] Fischel 1998, p. 81.
[1353] Didi-Huberman 2008, pp. 16–17.
[1354] Montague 2012, pp. 14–16, 64–65.
[1355] Bergen 2016, p. 160.
[1356] Czech 2000, p. 143; also see Piper 2000, p. 134, footnote 422, citing Danuta Czech, The Auschwitz Chronicle, p. 146.
[1357] Fischel 1998, pp. 42–43.
[1358] Montague 2012, pp. 76–85.
[1359] Cesarani 2016, p. 513.
[1360] Arad 2009, p. 138.
[1361] "Gas vans" (PDF). Yad Vashem.
[1362] Gerlach 2016, p. 99.
[1363] Gerlach 2016, p. 99, note 165.
[1364] Fischel 1998, pp. 81–85.
[1365] Black 2016, pp. 69–70.
[1366] Crowe 2008, p. 243.
[1367] Dwork & van Pelt 2003, pp. 287–288.

chambers. To prevent panic, they were told the gas chambers were showers or delousing chambers. [1368]

At Auschwitz, after the chambers were filled, the doors were shut and pellets of Zyklon-B were dropped into the chambers through vents,[1369] releasing toxic prussic acid.[1370] Those inside died within 20 minutes; the speed of death depended on how close the inmate was standing to a gas vent, according to the commandant Rudolf Höss, who estimated that about one-third of the victims died immediately.[1371] Johann Kremer, an SS doctor who oversaw the gassings, testified that: "Shouting and screaming of the victims could be heard through the opening and it was clear that they fought for their lives."[1372] The gas was then pumped out, and the Sonderkommando – work groups of mostly Jewish prisoners – carried out the bodies, extracted gold fillings, cut off women's hair, and removed jewellery, artificial limbs and glasses.[1373] At Auschwitz, the bodies were at first buried in deep pits and covered with lime, but between September and November 1942, on the orders of Himmler, 100,000 bodies were dug up and burned. In early 1943, new gas chambers and crematoria were built to accommodate the numbers.[1374]

Bełżec, Sobibór and Treblinka became known as the Operation Reinhard camps, named after the German plan to murder the Jews in the General Government area of occupied Poland.[1375] Between March 1942 and November 1943, around 1,526,500 Jews were gassed in these three camps in gas chambers using carbon monoxide from the exhaust fumes of stationary diesel engines.[1376] Gold fillings were pulled from the corpses before burial, but unlike in Auschwitz the women's hair was cut before death. At Treblinka, to calm the victims, the arrival platform was made to look like a train station, complete with a fake clock.[1377] Most of the victims at these three camps were buried in pits at first. From mid-1942, as part of *Sonderaktion 1005*, prisoners at Auschwitz, Chelmno, Bełżec, Sobibór, and Treblinka were forced to exhume and burn bodies that had been buried, in part to hide the evidence, and in part because of the terrible smell pervading the camps and a fear that the drinking water would become polluted.[1378] The corpses – 700,000 in Treblinka – were burned on wood in open fire pits and the remaining bones crushed into powder.[1379]

[1368] Piper 2000, pp. 219–220.
[1369] Piper 1998b, p. 173.
[1370] Piper 1998b, p. 162.
[1371] Piper 1998b, p. 157.
[1372] Piper 1998b, p. 170.
[1373] Piper 1998b, p. 163.
[1374] Piper 1998b, pp. 170–172.
[1375] Piper 1998b, pp. 163–164.
[1376] *"Killing Centres: An Overview"*. Holocaust Encyclopaedia. United States Holocaust Memorial Museum.
[1377] Cesarani 2016, pp. 479–480; for size compared to Auschwitz, Longerich 2010, p. 330.

The first major camp encountered by Allied troops, Majdanek, was discovered by the advancing Soviets soldiers, along with its gas chambers, on 25 July 1944.[1380] Treblinka, Sobibór, and Bełżec were never liberated, but were destroyed by the Germans in 1943.[1381] On 17 January 1945, 58,000 Auschwitz inmates were sent on a death march westwards;[1382] when the camp was liberated by the Soviets on 27 January, they found just 7,000 inmates in the three main camps and 500 in subcamps.[1383] Buchenwald was liberated by the Americans on 11 April;[1384] Bergen-Belsen by the British on 15 April;[1385] Dachau by the Americans on 29 April;[1386] Ravensbrück by the Soviets on 30 April;[1387] and Mauthausen by the Americans on 5 May.[1388] The Red Cross took control of Theresienstadt on 3 May, days before the Soviets arrived.[1389]

The British 11th Armoured Division found around 60,000 prisoners (90 percent Jews) when they liberated Bergen-Belsen,[1390] as well as 13,000 unburied corpses; another 10,000 people died from typhus or malnutrition over the following weeks.[1391] The BBC's war correspondent Richard Dimbleby described the scenes that greeted him and the British Army at Belsen, in a report so graphic the BBC declined to broadcast it for four days, and did so, on 19 April, only after Dimbleby threatened to resign.[1392] He said he had "never seen British soldiers so moved to cold fury":[1393]

"Here over an acre of ground lay dead and dying people. You could not see which was which. ... The living lay with their heads against the corpses and around them moved the awful, ghostly procession of emaciated, aimless people, with nothing to do and with no hope of life, unable to move out of your way, unable to look at the terrible sights around them ... Babies had been born here, tiny, wizened things that could not live. A mother, driven mad, screamed at a British sentry to give her milk for her child, and thrust the tiny mite into his arms. ... He opened the bundle and

[1378] Fischel 1998, pp. 83–85.
[1379] Arad 1999, pp. 170–171; also see Arad 2018, pp. 212–219.
[1380] Friedländer 2007, pp. 648–650; for trucks or wagons, Blatman 2011, p. 11.
[1381] Niewyk & Nicosia 2000, p. 165; for gas chambers, see Friedländer 2007, p. 627 and Longerich 2010, p. 411.
[1382] Longerich 2010, p. 411.
[1383] Strzelecki 2000, p. 27.
[1384] Stone 2015, p. 41.
[1385] Stone 2015, pp. 72–73.
[1386] Longerich 2010, p. 417.
[1387] Marcuse 2001, p. 50.
[1388] Wachsmann 2015, p. 577.
[1389] Gilbert 1985, pp. 808–809.
[1390] Stone 2015, pp. 72–73.
[1391] "The 11th Armoured Division (Great Britain)". *Holocaust Encyclopaedia*. United States Holocaust Memorial Museum.
[1392] "Bergen-Belsen". *Holocaust Encyclopaedia*. United States Holocaust Memorial Museum.
[1393] Bell 2017, p. 100.

found the baby had been dead for days. This day at Belsen was the most horrible of my life."

— Richard Dimbleby, 15 April 1945[1394]

The Jews killed represented around one third of world Jewry[1395] and about two-thirds of European Jewry, based on a pre-war figure of 9.7 million Jews in Europe.[1396] Most heavily concentrated in the east, the pre-war Jewish population in Europe was 3.5 million in Poland; 3 million in the Soviet Union; nearly 800,000 in Romania, and 700,000 in Hungary. Germany had over 500,000.[1397]

The most commonly cited death toll is the six million given by Adolf Eichmann to SS member Wilhelm Höttl, who signed an affidavit mentioning this figure in 1945.[1398] Historians' estimates range from 4,204,000 to 7,000,000.[1399] According to Yad Vashem, "all the serious research" confirms that between five and six million Jews died.[1400]

[1394] Reynolds 2014, pp. 277–278.

[1395] Crowe 2008, p. 447.

[1396] Gilbert 2001, p. 291.

[1397] *Lyall Grant, Mark (2 May 2011). "Introductory remarks at the screening of the film The Relief of Belsen". The Holocaust and the United Nations Outreach Programme. Archived from the original on 2 May 2019. "Dimbleby: My father's Belsen report sends 'shivers up my spine'". BBC. 15 April 2015. "Audio slideshow: Liberation of Belsen". BBC News. 15 April 2005. Archived from the original on 13 February 2009.*

[1398] Yad Vashem: "There is no precise figure for the number of Jews killed in the Holocaust. The figure commonly used is the six million quoted by Adolf Eichmann, a senior SS official. All the serious research confirms that the number of victims was between five and six million. Early calculations range from 5.1 million (Professor Raul Hilberg) to 5.95 million (Jacob Leschinsky). More recent research, by Professor Yisrael Gutman and Dr. Robert Rozett in the *Encyclopaedia of the Holocaust*, estimates the Jewish losses at 5.59–5.86 million, and a study headed by Dr. Wolfgang Benz presents a range from 5.29 million to 6.2 million.
"The main sources for these statistics are comparisons of pre-war censuses with post-war censuses and population estimates. Nazi documentation containing partial data on various deportations and murders is also used. We estimate that Yad Vashem currently has somewhat more than 4.2 million names of victims that are accessible."

[1399] Hilberg 2003, p. 1201.

[1400] Yad Vashem: "There is no precise figure for the number of Jews killed in the Holocaust. The figure commonly used is the six million quoted by Adolf Eichmann, a senior SS official. All the serious research confirms that the number of victims was between five and six million. Early calculations range from 5.1 million (Professor Raul Hilberg) to 5.95 million (Jacob Leschinsky). More recent research, by Professor Yisrael Gutman and Dr. Robert Rozett in the *Encyclopaedia of the Holocaust*, estimates the Jewish losses at 5.59–5.86 million, and a study headed by Dr. Wolfgang Benz presents a range from 5.29 million to 6.2 million.
"The main sources for these statistics are comparisons of pre-war censuses with post-war censuses and population estimates. Nazi documentation containing partial data on various deportations and murders is also used. We estimate that Yad Vashem currently has somewhat more than 4.2 million names of victims that are accessible."

Much of the uncertainty stems from the lack of a reliable figure for Jews in Europe in 1939, border changes that make double-counting of victims difficult to avoid, lack of accurate records from the perpetrators, and uncertainty about whether to include post-liberation deaths caused by the persecution.[1401] Early postwar calculations were 4.2–4.5 million from Gerald Reitlinger,[1402] 5.1 million from Raul Hilberg, and 5.95 million from Jacob Lestschinsky.[1403] In 1990, Yehuda Bauer and Robert Rozett estimated 5.59–5.86 million,[1404] and in 1991, Wolfgang Benz suggested 5.29 to just over 6 million.[1405] [1406]The figures include over one million children.[1407]

The death camps in occupied Poland accounted for half the Jews killed.

The Jewish death toll in these Polish Camps was as follows:

Auschwitz 960,000;[1408]
Treblinka 870,000;[1409]
Bełżec 600,000;[1410]
Chełmno 20,000; [1411]
Sobibór 250,000;[1412]
Majdanek 79,000.[1413]

Death rates were heavily dependent on the survival of European states willing to protect their Jewish citizens.[1414] In countries allied to Germany, the state's control

---

[1401] Fischel 2020, p. 10.
[1402] Fischel 2020, p. 10.
[1403] Michman 2012, p. 197.
[1404] Bauer & Rozett 1990, p. 1797.
[1405] Bauer & Rozett 1990, p. 1799.
[1406] Yad Vashem: "There is no precise figure for the number of Jews killed in the Holocaust. The figure commonly used is the six million quoted by Adolf Eichmann, a senior SS official. All the serious research confirms that the number of victims was between five and six million. Early calculations range from 5.1 million (Professor Raul Hilberg) to 5.95 million (Jacob Leschinsky). More recent research, by Professor Yisrael Gutman and Dr. Robert Rozett in the *Encyclopaedia of the Holocaust*, estimates the Jewish losses at 5.59–5.86 million, and a study headed by Dr. Wolfgang Benz presents a range from 5.29 million to 6.2 million.
"The main sources for these statistics are comparisons of pre-war censuses with post-war censuses and population estimates. Nazi documentation containing partial data on various deportations and murders is also used. We estimate that Yad Vashem currently has somewhat more than 4.2 million names of victims that are accessible."
[1407] "FAQ: How many Jews were murdered in the Holocaust?". Yad Vashem.
[1408] "Children during the Holocaust". United States Holocaust Memorial Museum.
[1409] Sobibor" (PDF). Yad Vashem.
[1410] "Auschwitz-Birkenau Extermination Camp". Yad Vashem.
[1411] "Belzec" (PDF). Yad Vashem.
[1412] "Majdanek" (PDF). Yad Vashem.
[1413] "Chelmno" (PDF). Yad Vashem.
[1414] Piper 2000, pp. 230–231; Piper 1998a, p. 62.

over its citizens, including the Jews, was seen as a matter of sovereignty. The continuous presence of state institutions thereby prevented the Jewish communities' complete destruction.[1415] In occupied countries, the survival of the state was likewise correlated with lower Jewish death rates: 75 percent of Jews survived in France and 99 percent in Denmark, but 75 percent died in the Netherlands, as did 99 percent of Jews who were in Estonia when the Germans arrived—the Nazis declared Estonia *Judenfrei* ("free of Jews") in January 1942 at the Wannsee Conference.[1416]

The survival of Jews in countries where states were not destroyed demonstrates the "crucial" influence of non-Germans (governments and others), according to Christian Gerlach.[1417] Jews who lived where pre-war statehood was destroyed (Poland and the Baltic states) or displaced (western USSR) were at the mercy of sometimes-hostile local populations, in addition to the Germans. Almost all Jews in German-occupied Poland, the Baltic states and the USSR were killed, with a 5 percent chance of survival on average.[1418] Of Poland's 3.3 million Jews, about 90 percent were killed.[1419]

The Nuremberg trials were a series of military tribunals held after the war by the Allies in Nuremberg, Germany, to prosecute the German leadership. The first was the 1945–1946 trial of 22 political and military leaders before the International Military Tribunal.[1420] Adolf Hitler, Heinrich Himmler, and Joseph Goebbels had committed suicide months earlier.[1421] The prosecution entered indictments against 24 men (two were dropped before the end of the trial)[1422] and seven organizations: the Reich Cabinet, Schutzstaffel (SS), Sicherheitsdienst (SD), Gestapo, Sturmabteilung (SA), and the "General Staff and High Command".[1423]

The indictments were for participation in a common plan or conspiracy for the accomplishment of a crime against peace; planning, initiating and waging wars of aggression and other crimes against peace; war crimes; and crimes against humanity. The tribunal passed judgements ranging from acquittal to death by hanging.[1424] Eleven defendants were executed, including Joachim von Ribbentrop, Wilhelm Keitel, Alfred

---

[1415] Piper 2000, pp. 230–231; Piper 1998a, p. 62.

[1416] Snyder 2012, pp. 164–165.

[1417] For Netherlands, "The Netherlands". Yad Vashem.
For France, Gerlach 2016, p. 14; for Denmark and Estonia, Snyder 2015, p. 212; for Estonia (Estland) and the Wannsee Conference, *"Besprechungsprotokoll" (PDF)*. *Haus der Wannsee-Konferenz.* p. 171.

[1418] Piper 2000, pp. 230–231; Piper 1998a, p. 62.

[1419] Gerlach 2016, p. 13.

[1420] Lusane 2003, pp. 97 - 98.

[1421] Blacks during the Holocaust". *Holocaust Encyclopaedia.* United States Holocaust Memorial Museum.

[1422] Robert Ley committed suicide in prison and Gustav Krupp was judged unfit for trial.[467]

[1423] Zweig 2001, pp. 531 - 532.

[1424] "International Military Tribunal: The Defendants". United States Holocaust Memorial Museum.

Rosenberg, and Alfred Jodl. Ribbentrop, the judgement declared, "played an important part in Hitler's 'final solution of the Jewish question'."[1425]

The subsequent Nuremberg trials, 1946–1949, tried another 185 defendants.[1426] West Germany initially tried few ex-Nazis, but after the 1958 Ulm Einsatzkommando trial, the government set up a dedicated agency.[1427] Other trials of Nazis and collaborators took place in Western and Eastern Europe. In 1960 Mossad agents captured Adolf Eichmann in Argentina and brought him to Israel to stand trial on 15 indictments, including war crimes, crimes against humanity, and crimes against the Jewish people. He was convicted in December 1961 and executed on 1st. June 1962 in the Ayalon Prison in Ramla, Israel. Eichmann's trial and death was televised globally and it revived interest in war criminals and the Holocaust in general.[1428]

Eichmann is the only person to be executed in Israel, as I discovered when I watched the movie **"Eichmann"** starring British actor, presenter, and comedian Stephen Fry. Fry himself a Jew, lost family members during the Holocaust. The movie was released in September 2007, it is available to watch on Amazon Prime.

More recently found another movie about Adolf Eichmann, it was called **"Operation Finale"**. This movie starred British actor Ben Kingsley as Eichmann. The film was released on 29th. August 2018, and is currently available on Netflix.

[1425] Biddiss 2001, p. 643.
[1426] Biddiss 2001, pp. 643 - 644.
[1427] Conot 1984, p. 495.
[1428] Biddiss 2001, p. 646.

Chapter twenty-nine

Whose idea was the Holocaust?

Many would be forgiven for thinking that Hitler or one of his top Nazi Officials came up with the idea of extermination as an answer to the Jewish question. But in actual fact it was the top Muslim, the Grand Mufti of Jerusalem, that made the suggestion to Hitler when they met in 1941. Hitler needed the support of the Grand Mufti, to help in his war effort. The Grand Mufti suggested that if Hitler were to exterminate the Jews that lived in Europe, then after Hitler had won the war, the Muslims would assist in exterminating the Jews globally. Hitler lost the war, but Muslims are still hell bent on exterminating the Jewish Race, and of course, they do so, whilst telling you that Islam is a Religion of Peace.

Full official record: What the mufti said to Hitler

The Arabs were Germany's natural friends, Haj Amin al-Husseini told the Nazi leader in 1941, because they had the same enemies, namely the English, the Jews, and the Communists

GRAND MUFTI:
The Grand Mufti began by thanking the Fuhrer for the great honour he had bestowed by receiving him. He wished to seize the opportunity to convey to the Fuhrer of the Greater German Reich, admired by the entire Arab world, his thanks of the sympathy which he had always shown for the Arab and especially the Palestinian cause, and to which he had given clear expression in his public speeches.

The Arab countries were firmly convinced that Germany would win the war and that the Arab cause would then prosper. The Arabs were Germany's natural friends because they had the same enemies as had Germany, namely the English, the Jews, and the Communists. Therefore, they were prepared to cooperate with Germany with all their hearts and stood ready to participate in the war, not only negatively by the commission of acts of sabotage and the instigation of revolutions, but also positively by the formation of an Arab Legion.

The Arabs could be more useful to Germany as allies than might be apparent at first glance, both for geographical reasons and because of the suffering inflicted upon them by the English and the Jews. Furthermore, they had had close relations with all Muslim nations, of which they could make use on behalf of the common cause. The Arab Legion would be quite easy to raise. An appeal by the Mufti to the Arab countries and the prisoners of Arab, Algerian, Tunisian and Moroccan nationality in Germany would produce a great number of volunteers eager to fight. Of Germany's victory the Arab world was firmly convinced, not only because the Reich possessed a large army, brave soldiers, and military leaders of genius, but also because the Almighty could never award the victory to an unjust cause.

'The Arabs could be more useful to Germany as allies than might be apparent at first glance, both for geographical reasons and because of the suffering inflicted upon them by the English and the Jews'

In this struggle, the Arabs were striving for the independence and unity of Palestine, Syria and Iraq. They had the fullest confidence in the Fuhrer and looked to his hand for the balm on their wounds, which had been inflicted upon them by the enemies of Germany.

The Mufti then mentioned the letter he had received from Germany, which stated that Germany was holding no Arab territories and understood and recognized the aspirations to independence and freedom of the Arabs, just as she supported the elimination of the Jewish national home.

A public declaration in this sense would be very useful for its propagandistic effect on the Arab peoples at this moment. It would rouse the Arabs from their momentary lethargy and give them new courage. It would also ease the Mufti's work of secretly organizing the Arabs against the moment when they could strike. At the same time, he could give the assurance that the Arabs would in strict discipline patiently wait for the right moment and only strike upon an order from Berlin.

With regard to the events in Iraq, the Mufti observed that the Arabs in that country certainly had by no means been incited by Germany to attack England, but solely had acted in reaction to a direct English assault upon their honour.

The Turks, he believed, would welcome the establishment of an Arab government in the neighbouring territories because they would prefer weaker Arab to strong European governments in the neighbouring countries and, being themselves a nation of 7 million, they had moreover nothing to fear from the 1,700,000 Arabs inhabiting Syria, Transjordan, Iraq, and Palestine.

France likewise would have no objections to the unification plan because it had conceded independence to Syria as early as 1936 and had given her approval to the unification of Iraq and Syria under King Faisal as early as 1933.

In these circumstances he was renewing his request that the Fuhrer make a public declaration so that the Arabs would not lose hope, which is so powerful a force in the life of nations. With such hope in their hearts the Arabs, as he had said, were willing to wait. They were not pressing for immediate realization for their aspirations; they could easily wait half a year or a whole year. But if they were not inspired with such a hope by a declaration of this sort, it could be expected that the English would be the gainers from it.

HITLER:

The Fuhrer replied that Germany's fundamental attitude on these questions, as the Mufti himself had already stated, was clear. Germany stood for uncompromising war against the Jews. That naturally included active opposition to the Jewish national home in Palestine, which was nothing other than a centre, in the form of a state, for the exercise of destructive influence by Jewish interests. Germany was also aware that the assertion that the Jews were carrying out the functions of economic pioneers in Palestine was a lie. The work there was done only by the Arabs, not by the Jews. Germany was resolved, step by step, to ask one European nation after the other to solve its Jewish problem, and at the proper time to direct a similar appeal to non-European nations as well.

Germany was at the present time engaged in a life and death struggle with two citadels of Jewish power: Great Britain and Soviet Russia. Theoretically there was a difference between England's capitalism and Soviet Russia's communism; actually, however, the Jews in both countries were pursuing a common goal. This was the decisive struggle; on the political plane, it presented itself in the main as a conflict between Germany and England, but ideologically it was a battle between National Socialism and the Jews. It went without saying that Germany would furnish positive and practical aid to the Arabs involved in the same struggle, because platonic promises were useless in a war for survival or destruction in which the Jews were able to mobilize all of England's power for their ends.

'Germany was resolved, step by step, to ask one European nation after the other to solve its Jewish problem, and at the proper time to direct a similar appeal to non-European nations as well'

The aid to the Arabs would have to be material aid. Of how little help sympathies alone were in such a battle had been demonstrated plainly by the operation in Iraq, where circumstances had not permitted the rendering of really effective, practical aid. In spite of all the sympathies, German aid had not been sufficient, and Iraq was overcome by the power of Britain, that is, the guardian of the Jews.

The Mufti could not but be aware, however, that the outcome of the struggle going on at present would also decide the fate of the Arab world. The Fuhrer therefore had to think and speak coolly and deliberately, as a rational man and primarily as a soldier, as the leader of the German and allied armies. Everything of a nature to help in this titanic battle for the common cause, and thus also for the Arabs, would have to be done. Anything however, that might contribute to weakening the military situation must be put aside, no matter how unpopular this move might be.

Germany was now engaged in very severe battles to force the gateway to the northern Caucasus region. The difficulties were mainly with regard to maintaining the supply, which was most difficult as a result of the destruction of railroads and highways as well as the oncoming winter. If at such a moment, the Fuhrer were to raise the problem of Syria in a declaration, those elements in France which were under de Gaulle's influence would receive new strength. They would interpret the Fuhrer's declaration as an intention to break up France's colonial empire and appeal to their fellow countrymen that they should rather make common cause with the English to try to save what still could be saved. A German declaration regarding Syria would in France be understood to refer to the French colonies in general, and that would at the present time create new troubles in western Europe, which means that a portion of the German armed forces would be immobilized in the west and no longer be available for the campaign in the east.

The Fuhrer then made the following statement to the Mufti, enjoining him to lock it in the uttermost depths of his heart:

1. He (the Fuhrer) would carry on the battle to the total destruction of the Judeo-Communist empire in Europe.

2. At some moment which was impossible to set exactly today but which in any event was not distant, the German armies would in the course of this struggle reach the southern exit from Caucasia.

3. As soon as this had happened, the Fuhrer would on his own give the Arab world the assurance that its hour of liberation had arrived. Germany's objective would then be solely the destruction of the Jewish element residing in the Arab sphere under the protection of British power. In that hour the Mufti would be the most authoritative spokesman for the Arab world. It would then be his task to set off the Arab operations, which he had secretly prepared. When that time had come, Germany could also be indifferent to French reaction to such a declaration.

Once Germany had forced open the road to Iran and Iraq through Rostov; it would be also the beginning of the end of the British World Empire. He (the Fuhrer) hoped that the coming year would make it possible for Germany to thrust open the Caucasian gate to the Middle East. For the good of their common cause, it would be better if the Arab proclamation were put off for a few more months than if Germany were to create difficulties for herself without being able thereby to help the Arabs.

He (the Fuhrer) fully appreciated the eagerness of the Arabs for a public declaration of the sort requested by the Grand Mufti. But he would beg him to consider that he (the Fuhrer) himself was the Chief of State of the German Reich for five long years during which he was unable to make to his own homeland the announcement of its liberation. He had to wait with that until the announcement could be made on the basis of a situation brought about by the force of arms that the Anschluss had been carried out.

The moment that Germany's tank divisions and air squadrons had made their appearance south of the Caucasus, the public appeal requested by the Grand Mufti could go out to the Arab world.

GRAND MUFTI:

The Grand Mufti replied that it was his view that everything would come to pass just as the Fuhrer had indicated. He was fully reassured and satisfied by the words which he had heard from the Chief of the German State. He asked, however, whether it would not be possible, secretly at least, to enter into an agreement with Germany of the kind he had just outlined for the Fuhrer.

HITLER:

The Fuhrer replied that he had just now given the Grand Mufti precisely that confidential declaration.

GRAND MUFTI:

The Grand Mufti thanked him for it and stated in conclusion that he was taking his leave from the Fuhrer in full confidence and with reiterated thanks for the interest shown in the Arab cause.

Chapter thirty

Japanese using Prisoners of War as slaves

The Japanese, to my knowledge have not yet apologised to the British and Commonwealth prisoners that suffered in their P. O. W. Camps during WWII.

Many people who have no relatives that suffered in the Japanese Camps, only know of the treatment of prisoners from movies such as the "Bridge over the River Kwai" or from the movie "To end all wars."

Both movies depict the atrocities suffered by the prisoners during their time in such camps. The latter movie was made in 2001 and consequently, the language is stronger than in the first movie. A more recent movie, "The Railway Man" also gives an account of this railway.

Burma Railway, also called Burma-Siam Railway, railway built during World War II connecting Bangkok and Moulmein (now Mawlamyine), Burma (Myanmar). The rail line was built along the Khwae Noi (Kwai) River valley to support the Japanese armed forces during the Burma Campaign. More than 12,000 Allied prisoners of war (POWs) and tens of thousands of forced labourers perished during its construction.

Early Japanese conquests:

In the opening months of the Pacific War, Japanese forces struck Allied bases throughout the western Pacific and Southeast Asia as part of the so-called Southern Operation. By late spring 1942, with the surrender of Allied strongholds in Singapore, Hong Kong, the Philippines, and the Dutch East Indies, an estimated 140,000 Allied prisoners of war had fallen into Japanese hands. In addition, approximately 130,000 civilians – including some 40,000 children – were captured by the Japanese. While civilians were generally treated better than military prisoners, conditions in Japanese captivity were almost universally deplorable. More than 11 percent of civilian internees and 27 percent of Allied POWs died or were killed while in Japanese custody; by contrast, the death rate for Allied POWs in German camps was around 4 percent.

In World War II the Japanese military forces quickly took advantage of their success at Pearl Harbour to expand their holdings throughout the Pacific and westward toward India. This expansion continued relatively unchecked until mid-1942. Then, after losing the Battle of Midway, Japan slowly went on the defensive and began losing island after island. This rapid turnabout was a surprise even to the American military forces.

The overwhelming majority of Allied POWs were from Commonwealth countries; they included approximately 22,000 Australians (of whom 21,000 were from the Australian Army, 354 from the Royal Australian Navy, and 373 from the Royal Australian Air Force), more than 50,000 British troops, and at least 25,000 Indian troops. The bulk of these forces were captured with the fall of Singapore, an event widely characterized as the worst military defeat in British history. The prisoners were sent to various destinations throughout the Pacific and Southeast Asia to provide forced labour for the Japanese army, journeys that carried with them a taste of the nightmare to come. Tens of thousands of POWs were packed onto vessels that came to be known as "Hell ships"; one in five prisoners did not survive the cramped, disease-ridden journey.

Many the British and Australian captives were sent to Burma (Myanmar). Burma was a key strategic objective for the Japanese for two reasons. First, the Burmese city of Lashio was the southern terminus of the Burma Road, the main resupply route for Chinese during the Sino-Japanese War. The Japanese assumed that if Chiang Kai-shek's Nationalist forces were deprived of this key logistical resource, their conquest of China could be easily completed. Second, the occupation of Burma would also put Japanese armies on the doorstep of British India. The Japanese hoped to capture the Indian region of Assam, with the intention of using it as the base for an insurrection under the Japanese-backed Indian revolutionary leader Subhas Chandra Bose. To pursue those ends and to support their continued offensives in the Burma theatre, the Japanese began construction of what came to be known as the Burma Railway.

After the Japanese were defeated in the Battles of the Coral Sea (May 4–8, 1942) and Midway (June 3–6, 1942), the sea-lanes between the Japanese home islands and Burma were no longer secure. New options were needed to support the Japanese forces in the Burma Campaign, and an overland route offered the most direct alternative. With an enormous pool of captive labour at their disposal, the Japanese forced approximately 200,000 Asian conscripts and over 60,000 Allied POWs to construct the Burma Railway. Among the Allied POWs were some 30,000 British, 13,000 Australians, 18,000 Dutch, and 700 Americans. Between June 1942 and October 1943 the POWs and forced labourers laid some 258 miles (415 km) of track from Ban Pong, Thailand (roughly 45 miles [72 km] west of Bangkok), to Thanbyuzayat, Burma (roughly 35 miles [56 km] south of Mawlamyine). During this time, prisoners suffered from disease, malnutrition, and cruel forms of punishment and torture inflicted by the Japanese.

The Japanese wanted the railway completed as quickly as possible, and working units were comprised of massive numbers of prisoners scattered over the entire length of the proposed route. Construction was extremely difficult, with the route crossing through thick, mosquito – infested jungle and uneven terrain while monsoon conditions prevailed. Rivers and canyons had to be bridged and sections of mountains had to be cut away to create a bed that was straight and level enough to accommodate the narrow-gauge track. The longest and deepest cuttings in the railway occurred at Konyu, some 45 miles (72 km) northwest of Kanchanaburi, Thailand. The first cut at Konyu was approximately 1,500 feet (450 metres) long and 23 feet (7 metres) deep, and the second was approximately 250 feet (75 metres) long and 80 feet (25 metres) deep. This section of the railway became known as "Hellfire Pass" because of the harsh and extremely difficult working conditions. Much of the excavation was carried out with inadequate hand tools, and, because work on the railway had fallen behind schedule, the pace of work was increased. Prisoners were made to work around the clock, with individual shifts lasting as long as 18 hours. The cuttings at Hellfire Pass became known as the "speedo" period, after a solecist command shouted by Japanese guards and engineers to their English-speaking prisoners. When the Japanese were not satisfied with the pace of work, prisoners were forced to endure atrocious physical punishment, and some 700 Allied prisoners died or were killed at Hellfire Pass.

Allied POWs experienced inhumane treatment and endured torture by Japanese forces. Not only were the long days of the POWs filled with harsh labour and punctuated by physical abuse, but also the prisoners were provided with grossly inadequate food. The daily food allotment typically included small portions of boiled rice and spoiled meat or fish; rations were routinely contaminated with rat droppings and infested with maggots. In addition, there was a lack of potable water. Consequently, the prisoners were malnourished, dehydrated, and predisposed to illness. These factors, compounded by the unsanitary conditions in the work camps and the tropical environment, meant that disease was rampant. Dysentery and diarrhoea were responsible for more than one-third of all deaths on the railway. Other diseases included cholera, malaria, and tropical ulcers.

With limited and unsatisfactory medicine and equipment, treating the sick was difficult. In this environment, Australian Army surgeon Ernest "Weary" Dunlop became renowned for his tireless effort in treating and saving many wounded and ill prisoners. Dunlop was captured in March 1942 when the Japanese took control of Java, and in January 1943 he was sent to work as a medical officer on the Burma Railway. Dunlop risked his life by standing up to the Japanese on behalf of the men in his care; the compassion and bravery that he displayed in the face of danger were the epitome of the ANZAC spirit of "mate ship."

The horrendous experiences endured by the thousands of POWs has made the Burma Railway a place of pilgrimage and commemoration. This is particularly true on Anzac Day (April 25), when Australians pay tribute to those who served and lost their lives during war. Memorial sites along the route of the railway include the Kanchanaburi War Cemetery, where nearly 7,000 Allied dead are interred, and the Hellfire Pass Memorial Museum, a museum and walking trail that draws an estimated 100,000 visitors annually. Artistic examinations of the Burma Railway include Pierre Boulle's novel *Le Pont de la rivière Kwaï* (1952; *The Bridge on the River Kwai*) and the David Lean-directed motion picture of the same name (1957). British POW Eric Lomax's memoir *The Railway Man* (1995; film 2013) recounts both his experience on the railway and the emotional scars that it left.

Chapter thirty-one

To end all wars

This movie is based on the true story of Captain Ernest Gordon, who stopped his degree studies in History to join up to fight in World War II. He never finished his studies in History at Edinburgh University, instead he became a Minister.

Who was Captain Ernest Gordon?

Captain (War Substantive Lieutenant) Ernest Gordon was captured in Singapore and came within inches of death, surviving only thanks to the care of two fellow prisoners.

Ernest Gordon was born in Scotland on 31st May 1916. He joined the 2nd Battalion of the Argyll and Sutherland Highlanders before the Second World War as a Territorial Army officer. 2nd Battalion was deployed to the Far East on the outbreak of war to protect British colonial possessions like India, Burma and the very important naval base in Singapore from Japanese attack.

Unfortunately for the British, Dominion and Colonial troops around Singapore, the numerically inferior Imperial Japanese Army harried and outwitted them, forcing the British surrender on 15th February 1942. Ernest Gordon was amongst the 60,000 soldiers captured.

Demonstrating their British pluck, Gordon and several other prisoners escaped their Japanese captors and successfully made their way to Java, Indonesia. They then took a native fishing boat from Padang and attempted to sail across the Indian Ocean for Sri Lanka. Once again fate got the better of them as Imperial Japanese Navy warships picked them up and ferried them back to Singapore.

Along with hundreds of other prisoners, Gordon was force marched from Singapore to the Jungles of Siam, where they would all participate in the construction of the Death Railway and the Bridge on the River Kwai.

It was not just the brutal treatment inflicted by Japanese soldiers that the POWs were forced to contend with. Gordon suffered the effects of numerous illnesses and disease including malnutrition, malaria, diphtheria, typhoid, beriberi, jungle ulcers, and an operation to remove a kidney, performed without pain relief. Gordon was so close to death that the Japanese soldiers placed him in what was called the "Death Ward", a barracks specifically set aside for prisoners who had no hope of survival.

Here however, he found salvation in the form of two fellow prisoners, who cared for him and treated his wounds and illnesses to the best of their abilities. "Dusty Miller", a Methodist, and "Dinty" Moore, a Roman Catholic, spent 24 hours a day with him. Gordon, an agnostic, was impressed and inspired by the selfless faith of these two soldiers which gave him a renewed hope and a sense of purpose. His miraculous recovery would go on to inspire the other men of the camp.

As Gordon recovered, he set up a university for the men to continue driving them and add purpose and direction to their lives in turn. Initially it was carried out in secret, however the Japanese guards eventually allowed it.

This would not be the end of Gordon's trauma, however. He was witness to one incident, according to *Real Heroes*, wherein a work party apparently lost a shovel. A Japanese guard threatened the entire party with execution unless the culprit came forward. One soldier stepped forward and stood to attention. He was beaten to death by the guard, the folly being that it was later discovered that the guard had miscounted the inventory, and thus there had never been a missing shovel.

Gordon ultimately survived the war and his internment. It is hard to believe a man could suffer all the above and come out alive, but what happened next must have deeply affected him. On liberation he sought news of his friends who had cared for him in the Death Ward. He found that, two weeks before the war's end, "Dusty Miller" had been crucified by a Japanese soldier who was frustrated with Dusty's sense of calm in the face of hardship. "Dinty" had sadly been killed when the Allies sunk his, unmarked, Prisoner Transport Ship.

After the war, Gordon moved to America where he became the Dean of the chapel at Princeton University; quite the turnaround for someone who used to describe themselves as agnostic. "Dusty" and "Dinty" clearly played a huge role in influencing the rest of Gordon's life, as he wrote his autobiography eventually titled "To End All Wars". His biography was adapted into the screenplay for the movie of the same name, released in 2001, starring Robert Carlyle and Keiffer Sutherland.

Chapter thirty-two

Dr Vernon Johns
Alabama – and the Deep South

If you have followed my previous works under the theme "Yesterday's Man", you will recall that the subject in book two of the series, "Billy Sunday" was a man that I had never heard of until I came across him whilst researching for "God's Generals" to add to our website.

As for Dr. Vernon Johns, again this is a Man of God that I had never heard of until one morning at the turn of the last century, when being unable to sleep, I got up and switched on the TV, and started flicking through the channels.

Eventually I came across a movie that starred James Earl Jones, as I had never seen Jones in a bad movie, I decided to watch the rest of this movie. When it finished, as I had missed the first 30 minutes or so, I took a note of the name of the movie and vowed to look out for it again and watch the whole movie. The movie was called "The Road to Freedom" but by the time I found the movie again the name had been changed to "The Vernon Johns Story".

It was a few years later before I found the movie and set up the satellite TV top set to record the movie as I was going out.

What follows is taken from a book that was a joint effort between both myself and Patrick L. Cooney PhD. Dr Cooney tried to write a book about Johns, nothing strange about except that Dr Cooney was unable to publish his book about an African American preacher because Dr Cooney himself was an African American, and his book was deemed to be racist, yet I was able to publish our joint venture, and as you know, I am white.

Our book is entitled "Vernon Johns – It's safe to murder negros."
ISBN: 9-781-53482-498-0

The movie "The Vernon Johns Story" can now be found in full on YouTube
https://youtu.be/CJH4e8cXlFw

Johns' true spirit would come out most clearly in Montgomery, Alabama. Virginia and Alabama were not the same, as Vernon Johns was to find out. Alabama was of the "deep South" with its more restrictive and cruel agricultural economy based on cotton, compared to the less severe economy of tobacco growing. The next three chapters will give the reader overviews of the nation in general and Alabama and Montgomery in particular.

Alabama Physical History:

Alabama's physical layout created one of the basic political divisions in the state (WPA 1959:77). The fall line, which marks the limit of seaward erosion of the land surface when sea level was much higher than now, runs from the halfway point on the eastern border of Alabama up to the northwest corner of the state. At the fall line the rivers flowing from the southern Appalachians run over the edge of the piedmont terrain of rolling hills. Here there are rock-strewn rapids and waterfalls that mark the limits of navigation for the rivers. Montgomery lies just south of the fall line in the central Black Belt, the wealthiest farm region in the state with its large cotton plantations and great number of slaves.

In the wiregrass region, the area of southeast Alabama, hay and grain crops and cattle were raised for export to the Black Belt. The area got its nickname from the very tough grass, known as wiregrass, eaten by the grazing cattle. Wiregrass has the reputation of being the kinkiest, thickest, and hardest grass to get rid of than any grass in the United States. On the Gulf Coast, the gulf and coastal plain, truck farming and citrus fruit cultivation was the rule. This section supplied much of the food consumed on the Black Belt plantations.

Early Alabama History:

Three different countries fought over the territory that later became the state of Alabama: Spain, France, and England (WPA 1959:35&41). The first white visitors to Alabama were the conquistador Hernando De Soto and his party looking for gold. They travelled into Creek Indian areas, passing near the future site of Montgomery in the autumn of 1540. Almost half a century before the first English settlement in what later became the United States, the first white colony in Alabama was founded in 1559 by Tristan De Luna, with authority from the Viceroy of Mexico to settle near Mobile Bay. The settlement, however, did not last long.

In 1629 English King Charles I made a Carolina grant to Sir Robert Heath which overlapped Spanish claimed land in Alabama territory. This was followed in 1663 by a second Carolina grant from Charles II to Carteret and others. In 1702 Jean Baptiste Le Moyne, Sieur de Bienville set up a settlement at Fort Louis de la Mobile (WPA 1959:42). The French moved up the Alabama River, hoping to check any progress by the English. North of Montgomery, they built Fort Toulouse near the site of present Wetumpka in 1714. Situated at the confluence of the Coosa and Tallapoosa Rivers, the fort served as a trading post and frontier defence against the English. A great trade war began.

Even before the arrival of English settlers in Alabama, slaves arrived in Mobile. In 1719 the ship Marechal de Villars landed the first shipload of slaves on Dauphin Island.

In 1756 the decaying government of France was drawn into still another war with England, the French and Indian War. The English, by winning this war, also won the fur trade war. In 1763 the French ceded Mobile to Great Britain by the Treaty of Paris. In 1783 the Floridas were returned to Spain by Great Britain.

The War of 1812 with England gave the Americans the long-awaited pretext for taking West Florida from Spain. Ostensibly to stop the use of the Spanish Gulf ports by the British fleet, General James Wilkinson and 600 Americans surprised a garrison of sixty Spaniards and thus captured Mobile from Spain (WPA 1959:46). When the War of 1812 erupted, the warlike Creeks, with the support of the British, initiated clashes with the Americans which resulted in full-scale combat (Tebbel 1966:118-121). A massacre of 200 troops by Creeks at Fort Mims, north of Mobile and north of Florida on the Alabama River was so horrible that it roused the United States government to action. The news rolled on to the Nashville sickbed of General Andrew Jackson, still ailing from wounds sustained in a duel with Colonel Thomas Hart Benton. "Jackson was the right man for the job of putting the Creeks in their place. He had no sympathy for the Indians, no understanding of their problems, and could not have cared less about the justice of their claims."

By November 3 the American troops reached the town of Tallassahatchee. Attacking it, the General employed a favourite formation, deploying his troops in a crescent which was intended to fold in upon the Indians (Tebbel 1966:119-121). As Davy Crockett, one of Jackson's soldiers, put it: "We shot them like dogs." They killed 186 Creeks. Only five Americans had been lost, with forty-one wounded. Jackson followed up this victory with another at a heavily fortified fort located at Horseshoe

Bend, a peninsula on the Tallapoosa River about fifty miles from the future site of Montgomery.

The Battle of Horseshoe Bend opened central Alabama to peaceful settlement. With three-fourths of the state open for settlement, whites flocked in to take up the rich farmland. In 1816 Montgomery County formed from Monroe County. In 1817 the United States government created the Alabama Territory with its capital at St. Stephens. The end result of these victories was that it opened Alabama to white settlement.

Layout of Montgomery:

The capitol district of Montgomery lies just southeast of a bend in the Alabama River. Its main street is Dexter Avenue, which runs from east to west. At the eastern end of the Dexter Avenue is the state capitol on Goat Hill. It was designed by George Nichols, Philadelphia architect with Stephen Button supervising the construction. The building, constructed of brick covered with stucco and patterned after the National Capitol in Washington D.C., ranks among the most beautiful of the Greek Revival capitols built during ante bellum days.

On the north lawn is the Confederate Monument, the cornerstone of which was laid by Jefferson Davis, April 26, 1886. The completed monument, unveiled December 7, 1898, was designed by Gordan C. Doud, a Montgomery artist, and executed by Alexander Doyle. There is also a statute of Jeff Davis presented November 19, 1940.

Just south of the capitol building is the First White House of the Confederacy. This was the Montgomery home of Confederate President Jefferson Davis and his family during their brief stay in the city. This two-story, white frame house with green shutters was built about 1852. It was formerly located on the southwest corner of Bibb and Lee Streets but, through an appropriation of the legislature, was moved to the present location in 1921.

One block west from the capitol, at the northeast corner of Dexter Avenue and Decatur Street is the black Dexter Avenue Baptist Church. It is across the street from the Judicial Department. The church is now a National Historic Landmark. It is a brick church with a tin roof and wooden steeple at the corner of Dexter and South Decatur. Just a couple blocks west of Dexter Avenue Baptist Church is the church of Edgar Gardner Murphy, the conservative white minister who worked with white and black liberals in mostly futile attempts to improve race relations in Alabama.

Dexter Avenue descends west to Court Square in the heart of the downtown business district, the former site of the County Courthouse. Built in 1822, this structure was on the road between the communities of Philadelphia and East Alabama. Before the Civil War, slaves were auctioned from a platform in the square. This was the main slave block; others were erected on either side of Dexter Avenue. In Court Square the McMonnies Fountain, with twenty-five jets and a life-size female figure, was erected in 1886 after it was exhibited at the Atlanta Exposition.

The parsonage of Dexter Avenue Baptist Church, where both Vernon Johns and Martin Luther King, Jr. once lived, is located on Jackson Street in the Centennial Hill neighborhood, southeast of the capitol. Developed in the late 1870s, Centennial Hill was the first substantial black residential neighbourhood in Montgomery. Teachers, ministers, doctors and businessmen made their homes along Jackson, Union, and High Streets. Descendants of many of the original owners still own and occupy these homes. Alabama State University is at the southern end of Jackson Street.

The Settlement of Montgomery:

The geography of the region was certainly the principal reason for its settlement and growth. To the south and southeast, fertile lands continued for twenty-six miles. The soil of the plains was "perfectly black, soapy, and rich," wrote naturalist and traveller William Bartram in 1776. The landscape had attracted and impressed travellers even before the signing of the Declaration of Independence. Alibamu Indians had established two towns along the banks of the Alabama River just north of present-day Montgomery. Walling the waters throughout the area were high bluffs, upon which downtown Montgomery now rests.

When the Alabama lands were offered for sale in 1817, two groups of speculators made their initial payments. A company of Georgians led by General John Scott first built the town of Alabama. A company of almost penniless New Englanders and Eastern adventurers, under the leadership of Massachusetts lawyer Andrew Dexter, then founded the town of New Philadelphia. The Georgians abandoned the town of Alabama and built the town of East Alabama in competition with the nearby town of New Philadelphia.

Because the cotton gin solved a major problem connected with the growing of cotton, it helped spur settlement. A contagion known as "Alabama Fever" spread through the seaboard states and more settlers came to Alabama.

A bitter rivalry between the two towns developed and was not terminated until the two towns were merged under the name of Montgomery, named in honor of Revolutionary War hero Major General Richard Montgomery, who lost his life in the Arnold expedition against Quebec. Montgomery County had been named three years earlier in honor of Major Lemuel P. Montgomery, killed at the Battle of Horseshoe Bend while serving with Andrew Jackson in the Creek War.

Montgomery became the foremost town in the demographic and geographic center of the state of Alabama. Having had ambitions from the beginning of becoming the capital city of Alabama, Montgomery now actively sought to wrest this prize from Tuscaloosa which had become the capital in the 1820s.

Montgomery became Alabama's capital in 1846. Several things influenced the legislature in its decision. Andrew Dexter had deeded the hill at the head of Market Street (Dexter Avenue) to the city with instructions that it be reserved for the capitol building. In addition, local businessmen, inspired by editor and lawyer John Jacob Seibels, proposed a bond issue for the construction of a fine building. How could the legislature refuse such generosity?

The Growth of the Cotton Industry

During the second decade of the nineteenth century, as market prices continued to rise, cotton was planted as rapidly as new land could be cleared (WPA 1959:75-76). The slave trade flourished because the cultivation and harvesting of the huge fields required a large and constant supply of labour. So much land was planted in cotton that corn, other staple farm products, and work animals had to be imported.

Compared to tobacco growing, the growing of cotton was very labour-intensive. In Virginia, with its infinite waterways, every planter could sell his goods at his own dockside, or one not very far away, and so there was little need for the rise of towns or marketplaces (Kluger 1975:456). But the greater need for slaves in the cotton growing areas meant larger plantations and a greater need for strict social control of the greater number of slaves.

Of the 565,000-white people in Alabama at the beginning of the War between the States, 33,730 were slave owners (WPA 1959:77). The large slaveholder, considered typical of the South before the war, was in reality a rarity. Most of the 435,000 slaves were held in small groups of 5 or 6 to an owner and only 34 planters in the state owned more than 200 slaves each.

Cotton planting season extended from the first of April until the middle of May, and picking was usually completed soon after the first killing frost in October or November (WPA 1959:79). During the spring and summer growing season, the fields were dark green with the foliage of the plants and studded with a profusion of blossoms that changed from a newly bloomed white through several shades of pink to a light red.

September and October were the months of greatest activity in cotton picking (WPA 1959:79). The cotton, gathered by hand, was placed in a bag dragged along by the worker, then emptied into large wagons which hauled it to the gin. Here huge suction pipes snatched the cotton from the high-walled wagon beds to the ginning machinery, in which lint and seed were separated by cylindrical "saws" revolving at tremendous speed. The lint was placed in great presses that squeezed it into oblong bales with an average weight of 500 pounds. From 1,300 to 1,500 pound of cotton was required for these 500-pound bales. The seed was usually sold to the ginnery for ultimate pressing and separation into cotton-seed oil, meal and hulls.

The financial base upon which the Deep-Southern society rested was a vast credit structure universally known as the factorage system (Nuermberger 1958:16). The factor performed many services. On the cotton itself these included weighing, sampling, draying, mending, storage, and finally sale to a larger factor or broker. The charge for all this, plus the factor's 2.5 percent commission for selling, made a total levy on the planter's crop of 8 to 12 percent. Whether the planter sold his crop to a local factor or shipped it directly to a well-known firm, his cotton ultimately had to reach large markets such as Memphis, Mobile, or New Orleans in the west, and Savannah or Charleston in the east.

Montgomery: Capital of the Confederacy

In 1860 the people of the United States elected Abraham Lincoln to the presidency. Alabama left the union on January 11, 1861. Also in January, South Carolina suggested that representatives of the six secessionist states meet in Montgomery to form a new government. Duly elected congressmen and senators boarded trains for Montgomery. They convened on February 4 and adopted a constitution four days later based on state's rights and slavery. The next day they elected two reluctant moderates to the highest offices: former Secretary of War Jefferson Davis of Mississippi as president and Alexander Stephens of Georgia as vice president.

It was nearly ten o'clock at night, February 16, when Jefferson Davis reached Montgomery (Strode 1955:406). En-route he had given twenty-five speeches to well-wishers. When the president-elect's train pulled into Montgomery, artillery salutes announced his approach. A mass of local citizens and important figures from all the seceded states were at the station to greet him. When he appeared, he was hailed with tremendous cheering. In returning thanks, he said the time for compromise had passed.

The fatigued and hoarse president-elect was taken to the Exchange Hotel where he was introduced by firebrand secessionist William Lowndes Yancy of Alabama with the assertion that "the man and the hour have met." Davis addressed a cheering throng from a balcony of the hotel. Davis initially used one of the parlours of the Exchange Hotel as his office and held cabinet meetings in his home only a couple of blocks behind the hotel.

On February 18, Jefferson Davis of Mississippi and Alexander H. Stephens, of Georgia, were inaugurated as president and vice-president of the confederate states (Strode 1955:408-9). As the President's carriage swung into position, Herman Arnold led his musicians up Dexter Avenue in a tune that had never been played anywhere before by a band, for he had orchestrated it himself only a week before. It was a minstrel piece called "I Wish I Was in Dixie's Land" just published the preceding June as sheet music arranged for pianoforte and came to be known as "Dixie". It proved to be stirring, as well as catchy and helped to excite the crowd to rousing cheers.

On May 21, 1861, the Confederate government moved from Montgomery to Richmond. Montgomery did not fall to federal forces until April 1865 when Major General James Wilson's raiders reached Montgomery ten days after their conquest of Selma. Apart from destroying five steamboats and the railroad machine shops, little damage was caused by the Yankees. One newspaper editor attributed their good behaviour to the fact that the local supply of liquor had been carefully hidden. Federal troops withdrew from Montgomery in 1874 and from Alabama in 1876. Dexter Avenue Baptist Church:

In 1867 in Montgomery the first independent black Baptist church was started with an exodus. Nearly seven hundred blacks followed the white preacher out of the First Baptist Church north through town to Columbus Street, then east up the muddy hill to Ripley Street. A former slave named Nathan Ashby became the first minister of the First Baptist Church (Coloured).

In 1877 a dissident faction of the First Baptist Church (Coloured) marched away in a second exodus forming the Second Baptist Church (Coloured). It was really a class division. The "higher elements" wanted to remodel the church to face the drier Ripley Street instead of the sloping Columbus, where they were obliged to muddy their shoes on Sundays after a rain. The "lower elements" thought this was unseemly and even un-Christian in its preoccupation with personal finery.

In January 1879, the new church paid $250 dollars for a lot and a building that stood proudly in the centre of town on Dexter Avenue diagonally across from the grand entrance of the Alabama state capitol. It was located on the city square. The new church became known as the Dexter Avenue Baptist Church. Its first minister was a former slave named Charles Octavius Boothe.

From the beginning, Dexter Avenue operated as a "deacons' church," that is the lay officers were free to hire any preacher they wanted without regard to bishops or other church hierarchy. Nearly a dozen preachers came and went in its first decade.

Alabama State College:

Alabama State University is now a publicly assisted, coeducational institution. It began in 1866 as Lincoln Normal School in Marion, Alabama. It was reorganized as a state-supported institution in 1874. On October 3, 1887, the university opened in Montgomery with a faculty of nine. Classes were held in Beulah Baptist Church.

The campus of the university was dominated by Bibb Graves Hall, which stood at the top of the hill, its steeple lifted high above the landscape. The segregationist governor Bibb Graves had been committed to black education and had done a great deal for Alabama State University.

William Burns Paterson was named president in 1878 and is recognized for his thirty-seven years of leadership during which time he kept the university alive despite nearly insurmountable odds. The first class of six students was graduated from the normal department during his administration.

George Washington Trenholm (Yeakey 1979:65), after one year as acting president, served as president from 1921 until his death in 1925. During his term, the school was organized on the 6-3-3 plan, a junior college department was created, operations began on the annual four-semester system and the departments of commerce and home economics were created. President Trenholm was succeeded in 1925 by his son, Harper Councill Trenholm. The school was raised to the status of a four-year college in 1928 and the first baccalaureate degrees were conferred in 1931.

Trenholm did not leave office until 1961. Among the important teachers and scholars at the school were John Hope Franklin and Horace Mann Bond. Alabama State was the meeting place for the only interracial organization in the city, the Alabama Council of Human Relations, which discussed mutual problems of the races.

Chapter thirty-three

The Backlash

Vernon Johns came to Alabama at a time of rising conservatism and reaction against the New Deal. This is all the more to his credit, showing he was a true prophet and not just responding to current movements.

Some observers thought that Alabama became one of the most liberal states in the union for a brief moment in time during the start of the period of the Great Depression. Southern politics can be very confusing unless one is quite clear on the difference between populism and liberalism. Alabama "liberalism" was really Alabama populism and populism is not a liberal movement. It is a right-wing movement based on the common man's resentment against big business (and blacks). The economic rhetoric about helping the common man fooled some observers into thinking that Alabama populism was liberal. It was not. Even the great Jim Folsom, governor of Alabama, was not a true liberal, but rather an Alabama populist with nice liberal-sounding rhetoric.

Southern Reaction against the New Deal:

The South at first liked Roosevelt's New Deal because it helped them economically (Hamilton 1987:115). But as the New Deal proceeded, the South felt threatened because to them it looked as though the blacks would be substantially helped and this might upset the system of segregation. Southerners were especially upset about the racial activities of Mrs. Roosevelt. Roosevelt's 1941 executive order creating a Fair Employment Practices Committee (FEPC), coupled with the threat of federal laws against lynching and poll taxes, provided anti-New Dealers with the ammunition they wanted.

It pained Roosevelt to realize that the Southe'ners, more than any other group, had done him in (Egerton 1994:221&228). They dismantled one New Deal program after another. The election of 1944 was Roosevelt's last hurrah for even the most moderate of the Southern politicians, Pepper of Florida and Hill of Alabama, "resorted to public affirmations of white supremacy in order to get themselves re-elected."

The 1946 off-year elections resulted in a drubbing for President Harry Truman. The Republicans now controlled both houses of Congress for the first time in almost twenty years. On December 5, 1946, Truman announced the formation of a fifteen-member Committee on Civil Rights to study and recommend new legislation aimed at protecting all segments of the population from discrimination and intolerance. In 1947 on the steps of the Lincoln Memorial, Truman addressed ten thousand people assembled for the annual conference of the NAACP the first such appearance a U.S. president had ever made – and said forthrightly that full civil rights and freedom must be guaranteed to all Americans. The historian David McCullough said the speech was "the strongest statement on civil rights heard in Washington since the time of Lincoln" (Egerton 1994:386,414,415-416). Symbolizing the progress in civil rights, April 11, 1947, marked the debut of Jackie Robinson with the Brooklyn Dodgers. It was trends and events such as these that so upset the South.

In Jackson, Mississippi on May 10, 1948, the States' Rights Party met in formal convocation. Reading the Montgomery Advertiser during those years one finds constant references to States' Rights and Dixiecrat supporters. For instance, October 1, 1948 (p. 18) the paper carried a story about Frank Dixon, former governor of Alabama and States Rights Democrat. He said the fight "is not against the Negro," but added that dire results would follow the setting up of the FEPC (Fair Employment Practices Commission). "I have never been one of those who fomented hatred between the two races. There's room for both, separate and apa"t." Blacks virtually did "ot exist in the pages of the montgomery Advertiser. The few art"cles on blacks in the newspaper were negative or were complaints about the NAACP.

There was a brief period of optimism in liberal camps with Truman's election in 1948. But opposition from the South helped to ensure that it was indeed very brief.

Reactionism Delayed in Alabama by Populism: Big Jim Folsom Egerton (1994:219-220) writes that "Some of the Southern states that historically had been rated as inferior frontier regions – Alabama, Tennessee, Arkansas – had managed by the 1940s to send some fairly progressive people to Congress." In May 1940 Alabama Democrats elected a convention delegation dominated by New Deal loyalists. These included Hill, Steagall, John Bankhead Jr., and Lt. Gov. Carmichael. (Hamilton 1987:91)

Liberalism in Alabama crested in 1938 when politicians like Hill, Bibb Graves, John Bankhead Jr., and Congressman Luther Patrick of Birmingham, sponsored the Southern Conference for Human Welfare (SCHW) (Hamilton 1987:107). The SCHW leaders attacked old southern bugaboos like the poll tax, lynching, freight-rate differentials, tenancy, and even referred obliquely to racial injustice. When this assemblage of New Dealers, idealists, labour leaders, prominent blacks, a few Socialists, a handful of Communists, and perhaps a dozen fellow travellers met in Birmingham that year, its open challenge to segregated seating provided the conservatives with a great deal of ammunition. Frightened by the ensuing row, prominent politicians like Hill, Patrick, Bankhead, and even Claude Pepper dissociated themselves officially from the SCHW. With the threat of changing racial customs, in the South the designation "liberal" became a real political liability.

To the surprise of Hill and fellow progressives and the consternation of right-wing Alabama Democrats, a "wild card," seemingly out of nowhere, seized their party's nomination for governor in the spring of 1946 (Hamilton 1987:141). Jim Folsom's emergence in 1946 was a surprise even to the progressive New Deal faction of the Democratic party. Folsom represented the persistence of populism in the politics of the South. (Barnard 1974:8)

Folsom was six-feet-eight inches tall with a size sixteen shoe. He left college in the pit of the Depression and wound up in Washington, D.C. with the WPA (Frady 1968:100). Folsom was every town's overgrown boy, a little bashful, but full of mischief that was easy to forgive. He had an aura of sincerity and integrity that widely appealed to Alabamians (Barnard 1974:20). Compared to other Southern politicians, Folsom (Elliott 1992:81) was colour-blind. "This is the one thing that set him apart from even some of his most otherwise faithful followers, and it eventually proved his ultimate undoing."

For decades before Folsom, Alabama had been dominated by a succession of governors representing the state's power structure of Black Belt plantation owners and large industrialists, which Folsom (Frady 1968:99) designated "the big mules." Campaigns for governor were insular and sedate affairs, largely conducted in back offices. Candidates rarely engaged in handshaking, baby-kissing popular campaigning.

When Folsom (Frady 1968:100) emerged as the front-runner in the first primary, a general state of alarm sounded among the establishment. Folsom planned to reapportion the state legislature, rewrite the state constitution, put at least one paved road in every county, distribute free textbooks, and repeal the poll tax.

Big Jim Folsom took to stumping the state in 1942 attacking the "Big Mules" of industry and agriculture and courting the votes of the little men. He was populism incarnate. To Alabama politician Carl Eliott (1992:79-80), Folsom represented everything he believed in. "He knew how to speak the people's language better than just about anybody I'd ever heard. To him, everyone was just 'fokes.'" He won the election.

Not really surprising, Folsom's administration (Frady 1968:101) was "essentially a disappointment. In most of his larger hopes, including reapportionment and the repeal of the poll tax, he was frustrated by a legislature still dominated by the Black Belt." After less than two years in office in January 1948 Folsom (Elliott 1992:80) announced his candidacy for the United States presidency. That dream, however, was short-lived. The electorate soon discovered that Folsom had fathered an illegitimate son during the 1946 gubernatorial campaign. The presidency was out and so was Folsom as governor in 1950.

George Wallace (Frady 1968: 74, 81, 83) was born in August 1919 in a small house just outside Clio, Barbour County, in south-eastern Alabama. From early adolescence he became intensely interested in politics. In 1935 when George was sixteen his father took him to Montgomery to run for page in the state senate. In the autumn of 1937, he arrived on the campus of the University of Alabama with eventual ambitions to be governor of Alabama. He graduated in 1942 and was handed a blank sheet of paper instead of a diploma on commencement night because he was still financially unable to pay some old student fees.

Back from the war, in 1946 he (Frady 1968:92-93, 96-99) ran for the state legislature in Barbour County and won. Folsom was Wallace's patron saint. When Wallace first came to Montgomery as a freshman legislator, he was simply a part of the Folsom phenomenon in Alabama. Wallace was so young and naive that as soon as he arrived in the capital city, he asked Folsom to appoint him speaker of the house.

Wallace had a real sense of identification with the less fortunate whites of Alabama and was genuinely concerned about their welfare. But Wallace's genuine involvement with populism represents the dangers faced by liberal thinkers when they romanticize the sufferings of common white folk.

Chapter thirty-four

Life in Montgomery

In Montgomery, most blacks were afraid. Rosa Parks (1992:72) wrote that "Those who were in good favour with the white folks didn't want to lose their privileged position. The rest didn't think anything could be done. There really wasn't any activist, public civil-rights movement that masses of people participated in until the Montgomery bus boycott in 1955. Until then only a few people were activists, and of course they were not in good favour with the whites." Parks (p. 136) added that "So many influential blacks in the South were so conservative. They had accepted favours from the white people and didn't want to offend them. We found that over and over in our voter-registration drives. Some of the biggest names in the African American community were not registered to vote."

Political activist Jo Ann Robinson (1987:39) seconded this observation. There were some sixty-eight black organizations in Montgomery, but "Nobody came forth with a 'time-to-act' suggestion. People had everything to lose and nothing to gain, some of them felt. And 'fighting City Hall' was a task nobody had done before, especially fighting to integrate city transportation lines."

On the eve of the Montgomery bus boycott there were only 500 members in the local NAACP (Yeakey 1979:62). And the regular attendees only numbered between ten and fifteen. In other words, the NAACP was weak, impotent, and ineffective. As Parks (1992:115) said "Membership was kind of small, and you could hardly get people to join."

The City of Montgomery did not provide a black high school until 1938, and it was not until 1946 that the school had its own building (Yeakey 1979:53). There was no black newspaper in Montgomery. But between the network of churches and social clubs, almost every black in the city had a vehicle for keeping abreast of important events.

Unlike some large southern cities, Montgomery maintained a rigid pattern of bus segregation. The bus drivers carried guns and even had police power to rearrange seating. In 1945, Alabama passed a law requiring that all bus companies under its jurisdiction actually enforce segregation.

On several occasions Rosa Parks (1992:136) resisted getting off the bus after violating various segregation rules. She would almost always hear mumbling from her fellow blacks: "How come she don't go around and get in the back?" "I remember having discussions about how a boycott of the city buses would really hurt the bus company in its pocketbook. But I also remember asking a few people if they would be willing to stay off the buses to make things better for us, and them saying that they had too far to go to work. So, it didn't seem as if there would be much support for a boycott."

Montgomery black leadership was dominated, as always in the Jim Crow era from the late 1890s to 1954, by conservative black leaders. What little liberal showing there was came from such Northern-based organizations as the NAACP, but in the South even the NAACP was small and limited in impact.

In Montgomery for three decades H. C. Trenholm was the "token leader." A moderate in politics, Trenholm was the black selected most often by whites to represent the black community. He preferred a low profile and worked behind the scenes in meetings with white leaders. Through years of experience, he had learned to humble himself before white men, many of whom were his intellectual inferiors. He could even "beg".

P. M. Blair (Yeakey 1979:81- 82) was the "prestige leader." He tended to avoid controversy. He had many contacts with white organizations, but he stuck to noncontroversial areas of business or welfare. There were black "yes" men who did "favours" for whites and got favours back. Blair was known to Montgomery whites as the city's "black mayor." Many of the yes men were black businessmen whose businesses could be closed at any time by the whites, and they often cooperated with whites in order to keep their businesses open (Robinson 1987:85).

Edgar Nixon was born in 1899, the fifth of eight children to Reverend Wesley M. Nixon, an untrained Baptist preacher (Baldwin and Woodson 1992:2). His wife died and Edgar's father had to be away for long periods at a time and so the children would often live with their father's sister, Pinky, who lived in Autauga County, Alabama.

Their father remarried and had nine more children (Baldwin and Woodson 1992:2). They were forced to live with their Aunt Pinky full-time. Formally, Edgar obtained

300

only a third-grade education because he had to work, but he was able to teach himself a great deal. He went to work for himself at age fourteen. In 1923 he became a baggage porter for a railroad station and in 1924 at the age of twenty-five became a Pullman Porter.

In 1925 a black man named A. Philip Randolph began to help organize black Pullman Porters (Pfeffer 1990:23). The first meeting of the BSCP in New York was held on August 25, 1925. In 1928 Nixon heard Randolph speak, joined the brotherhood, and became a Randolph disciple. Nixon himself, like Randolph was very influenced by the ideas of socialism. He called Randolph "the greatest black man in history." Nixon said "When I heard Randolph speak it was like a light. He done more to bring me in the fight for civil rights than anybody. Before that time, I figure that a Negro would be kicked around and accept whatever the white man did. I never knew the Negro had a right to enjoy freedom like everyone else. When Randolph stood there and talked that day, it made a different man of me. From that day on, I was determined that I was gonna fight for freedom until I was able to get some of it myself."

Nixon became convinced that the BSCP could become one of the principal civil rights organizations in the country (Baldwin and Woodson 1992:30-31&36-37). In 1938 Nixon founded the Montgomery Division of the BSCP and served as its president for the next twenty-five years. The BSCP became Alabama's first successful black union. It was largely due to the backing of BSCP that Nixon had the freedom and independence to become a somewhat forceful leader. The influence of the BSCP declined, however, as the continuing advance of the automobile and the continuing decline of the railroads was led to a decline of BSCP membership. By the end of 1952, the Montgomery BSCP was nearly bankrupt and by 1955 the organization was down to only nine members. In November 1955 the BSCP combined the Montgomery and Birmingham chapters.

In the 1930s Nixon joined Myles Horton of Tennessee's Highlander Folk School in an attempt to organize Alabama's cucumber pickers in a union (Egerton 1994:159). Horton's ambition, when he returned to the South early in the fall of 1932, was to establish an institution of education and social activism for working-class adults in the mountains of Appalachia. The Highlander Folk School emphasized unionism, democracy, and Christian socialism (Baldwin and Woodson 1992:29). The Higlander Folk School got its start when Horton and Don West leased a house and two hundred acres near Monteagle, Tennessee. Horton had picked up the support of such men as Abram Nightingale, theologian Reinhold Niebuhr, Harry F. Ward, sociologist Robert E. Park, socialist Norman Thomas, and Sherwood Eddy.

Highlander, however, did not aggressively challenge racial segregation in the thirties since their main customers were mostly white labouring people (Egerton 1994:158-159 & 160-161).

When violations of human rights occurred, the victims involved would telephone Mr. Nixon, and he would go to their rescue (Robinson 1987:28). In fact, anytime a black citizen was arrested in the city and had no one to bail them out they could call Mr. Nixon. Later Vernon Johns was to accompany Nixon on some of these emergency runs.

Rosa Parks

Rosa Parks went to Miss White's school which is now part of Booker T. Washington High School. For grades ten and eleven she went to the laboratory school at Alabama Normal School part of what was then called Alabama State Teachers' College for Negroes (later Alabama State University).

Her family moved from Huffman Street to South Union Street, where they stayed with King Kelly, who was a deacon of the Dexter Avenue Baptist Church. Mr. Kelly and his wife were very much against the type of thing Parks was doing (organizing), because Kelly worked for a men's clothing store in Montgomery as what was called a man of all work and was afraid of losing his job.

Rosa Parks made only twenty-three dollars a week as a seamstress at the men's alteration department of the Montgomery Fair, a large department store in downtown Montgomery (Durr 1985:278). Mrs. Parks's husband worked as a barber, and he was sometimes sick and unemployed. They lived in a housing project with her mother, who kept house for them.

Rosa Parks met Edgar Nixon in 1943 and was very impressed. Before Rosa Parks' arrest, Nixon had tried to desegregate Montgomery's buses, but had lacked the proper candidate to set the campaign in motion.

Disunity of Leadership

When Matin Luther King, Jr. (1958:34) came to Montgomery he found several problems as regards black organizations and leadership:

2 The community was crippled by the indifference of the educated group. This indifference expressed itself in a lack of participation in any move toward better

racial conditions, and a sort of tacit acceptance of things as they were. "Some of this lack of concern had its basis in fear. Many of the educated group were employed in vulnerable positions, and a forthright stand in the area of racial justice might result in the loss of a job. So rather than jeopardize their economic security, many steered clear of any move toward altering the status quo. But too much of the inaction was due to sheer apathy. Even in areas – such as voting – where they would not really be accused of tampering with the established order, the educated group had an indifference that for a period appeared incurable." The apparent apathy of the Negro ministers presented a special problem. Far too many had remained aloof from the area of social responsibility.

Events in the White Liberal Community in Montgomery

Clifford Durr moved to Birmingham about 1924 and got a job with Martin, Thompson, and Stern, the firm that represented the Alabama Power Company. The Durr family were originally from Montgomery. The family was Presbyterian, and they would invite Rev. Foster of Birmingham to stay with them when he came to Montgomery to preach and attend to church business. Rev. Foster's daughter, Virginia Foster, married Clifford Durr in 1926. At that time her brother-in-law Hugo Black was running for the Senate. He won. Virginia Durr led the life of a young married woman in Birmingham. She was active in the Junior League and in the church and belonged to a bridge club and a sewing circle and made clothes for her daughter. But she began little by little to wake up to the world. Slowly she became aware of how bad conditions were for so many people in Birmingham.

In 1933 the Durr family moved to Washington, D.C., where they lived throughout the New Deal years. A series of personal calamities (especially tied to suspicions that they were communists) forced the family to move back to Montgomery in 1951, on the eve of the civil rights struggle.

Aubrey Williams had made quite a name for himself in Washington, particularly for his work on the National Youth Administration, and he was very well thought of by the New Dealers (Durr 1985:246). He had been nominated for appointment by President Roosevelt to the Rural Electrification Administration. He was opposed and did not get the job. Williams came to Montgomery and bought a farm paper called the Southern Farmer. Williams was soon to become one of the foremost liberal advocates of social change in his native region (Egerton 1994:100). Williams lent E. D. Nixon the money to keep the NAACP going (Durr 1985:250). He was also trying to organize an integrated farmers' union. He was also a great friend of Jim Folsom.

After leaving Washington, Clifford Durr opened his law office in Montgomery. Through E. D. Nixon and Aubrey Williams, Durr began getting cases of blacks who had been beaten up in jail or who had been charged 500 percent interest on loans. Durr had a noblesse oblige attitude towards blacks. Virginia Durr (1985: 243 & 251) wrote that Cliff was brought up to believe that a Southern gentleman never took advantage of a black man. The black man had his place, and the white man had his place. But to cheat a black man or to take advantage of his ignorance was "common". Virginia wrote that it shocked the naive Cliff when he found that white men in Montgomery were taking advantage of poor, ignorant blacks who couldn't even sign their names. "It made him ashamed that they acted the way they did, and he felt a slight contempt for them."

The Durrs liked Edgar Nixon (Durr 1985:252). Once in the post office Virginia Durr said hello to Nixon and tried to shake his hand. Nixon told her not to call him Ed. He said it could get him lynched. "You ought to have better sense than to come up to a black man in the public post office and say 'Hello, Ed' and put out your hand."

Around the time that King started working with the NAACP the Alabama Council on Human Relations also caught his attention. This interracial group was concerned with human relations in Alabama. Its basic philosophy recognized that all men are created equal under God. The president of the Council was Rev. Ray Wadley, the young white minister of St. Mark's Methodist Church. A native Southerner, he was later shifted to a small, backwoods c'mmunity after his congregation protested his activities in the field of race relations. Two other prominent white members of the Council were Revs. Thomas P. Thrasher and Robert Graetz, both of whom were to be prominent in the subsequent bus boycott struggle.

Rev. Graetz (1991:3) worked with blacks in Montgomery. He said that "The police force represented the front line of the white segregationist army. In earlier times, business and professional men put on their white robes and hoods and rode out as the KKK, using whatever violence. But that kind of illegal activity was no longer tolerated, at least not officially. Nowadays the task of controlling Negroes was entrusted to the legally constituted constabulary."

Graetz (1991:21) described how the segregation laws were not only a burden to the blacks, but also to the whites for the whites themselves were forced to live by the rules of segregation. He also noted that there was an underground network of "liberals" who maintained close contact with each other.

He pointed that the North cooperated with Southern segregation. "Church officials stressed that my primary tasks were to proclaim the Gospel of Jesus Christ and to serve my people. 'The South is not receptive to intruders from the North,' they explained. 'You will bring harm to yourself and your family, not to mention the congregation and the church at large, if you go to Montgomery crusading for racial justice.'" He had to assure them that he would not start any trouble. As soon as the congregation realized a minister was a "liberal,'" a truly pejorative term, the minister was ask'" to move on."

Chapter thirty-five

The early years in Montgomery

Vernon Johns, a man who did not accept racist ways of thinking, was about to step into a thoroughly racist society, both black and white, and where even in the black community the conservatives dominated. There was going to be trouble for everyone involved. (And thank goodness for that!)

Dexter Avenue Baptist Church

R.D. Nesbitt, the church clerk of light tan skin at Dexter, "was one of the most widely known and highly respected men in the black community" (Yeakey 1979:50-51). He was an agent-salesman that worked his way up to become an executive of the Pilgrim Life and Health Insurance Company. He dressed well and conducted himself professionally and was reserved with strangers and even some of his friends.

Looking for a new minister for his church, in the late summer of 1945, Nesbitt travelled for the first and only time in his life to the annual meeting of the National Baptist Convention, its five million members making up the largest association of blacks in the world. His candidate was Alfred Charles Livingston Arbouin, a Jamaican and a Benedict graduate, who began his duties six months later. Almost immediately, Arbouin became involved in scandal. While her husband was away at the 1946 National Baptist Convention, Arbouin's wife caused a scandal by taking up with a soldier from the nearby Maxwell Air Force Base (Branch 1988:5-6). When criticized, she declared that she was a victim of spousal abuse and showed her bruises to the deacons who called her in for a private meeting. The deacons called for Arbouin's resignation. He refused to resign, but the court decided in favor of the deacons. R. D. Nesbitt was again looking for a minister, but the church waited nearly a year before seeking a new minister.

Dexter Avenue Baptist Church:

Alabama State College had hired a new music professor: Altona Trent Johns. She had taught music at R. R. Moton high school in Farmville, Virginia. Nesbitt knew about her husband Vernon Johns, considered one of the three great black preachers, the others being Mordecai Johnson and Howard Thurman. Through Mrs. Johns, Nesbitt invited the eminent preacher to deliver a trial sermon. Johns did so, reciting a long passage of scripture without looking at the Bible. They were so impressed that they suspended precedent for the first time in Nesbitt's memory and offered Johns their pulpit without an investigation or a second trial sermon. On the television program "Saturday Night with Connie Chung" (1989) Nesbitt remarked that "During his trial period at the church he was very professional. He displayed that type of intelligence that would fit the congregation. We had a silk-stocking church so to speak. We had a different Vernon Johns to start with, but after having been there for a period of time, the real Vernon Johns came up. And, of course, we were stuck with him then."

In October 1948 Vernon Johns moved into the parsonage at 309 South Jackson Street between Key and High – the home of Dexter Avenue Baptist Church ministers since 1919. Built around 1912, it is the last house of a row of houses. It is a rather long house; in fact, seven windows long. The roof has black roof tiles. It has a porch supported by four columns. The front door has two sidelights and a transom light over the door. Coretta Scott King (1969:100) said the parsonage was sixteen blocks from the church –in a segregated neighbourhood. "Our house was basically very nice but was run-down. It was a white frame structure with seven big rooms and a porch that later became rather famous. The furniture was of varied style, but very comfortable, and anything we thought we needed, the congregation gave us."

Ever the firebrand and traveller, Vernon Johns travelled up to Princess Anne County, Maryland to give an address to the faculty and students at Maryland State College Eastern Shore (J&G December 18, 1948:17), attended by one of Vernon Johns' sons, John Johns. He characterized educated Negroes as "economically, socially and philosophically illiterate." Obviously, his long absence from a regular job did not slow him down. He paid tribute t" the idea of education and scholarship, but roundly assailed Negro education and educated blacks, declaring, "I know what the white man gets out of Negro education, but I have never been able to learn exactly what it is that Negroes are supposed to get out of it." "Negroes have mastered the subject matter but have somehow missed the matter of the subject. They have made B – in civics and D – in citizenship."

He charged that educated blacks are economically illiterate beca–se they have not seen the wisdom of participating in any of the fundamental economic processes of the nation; they are socially illiterate because their "see-saw philosophy" has precluded any widespread dedication to effective community action; and they are philosophically illiterate because they have not demonstrated the courage of men who have found something for which they are willing to die. The speaker charged that blacks have wasted their economic strength. He declared succinctly, "The Negro has a wheelbarrow income and Cadillac ambitions." Dr. Johns asserted that the race has never pledged itself to concerted action for social betterment. Moreover, he was scornful of the Negroes' fears asserting, "No man is fit to be alive until he has something for which he would die." "We Negroes need to resolve," Dr. Johns concluded, "that we will not be forever hired out and forever sold out and forever bought out."

Vernon Johns was an expert on the Civil War (Powell 1995:24). He said "Black people should know about the Civil War because, in the final analysis, black people were the only beneficiaries of the cataclysmic bloodletting." At the start of 1949, Vernon Johns spoke before the Richmond Civil Council at Fifth Street Baptist Church. His subject for the occasion was "The Downfall of Dr. Douglas S. Freeman's Idol." (J&G January 1, 1949:15) Dr. Johns laid bare the uncanny military genius of General Robert E. Lee as contrasted with "Lee's bad judgment, which until the day of his death, found him believing that God was on his side." The speaker declared that Lee "always thought that God was a Mississippi planter who was humane to animals and his slaves, never realizing the truth that God was a fighting New England Abolitionist" (J&G January 8, 1949:4). After giving an historical background to the battles which led to the defeat of Lee with an emphasis on the rise of General U. S. Grant in the battles on Lookout Mountain, at Vicksburg and Chattanooga, Dr. Johns related the struggle between Grant and Lee from May 1864 to the close of the war as an object lesson for the "spirit of battle Negroes must wage against un-American discriminations."

Johns described the position of Grant on May 5th after the first day of the Battle of the Wilderness as one of "defeat in the eyes of lesser men." "But unlike McClellan, Burnside, Pope, and Hooker, who had retreated in the face of Lee's assaults, Grant ordered a moved around Lee's flanks and wired Washington that he was sending his wagons back for new supplies and planned to fight it out there in the Wilderness 'if it takes all summer.'" "It took all summer, and all winter, too, but Grant pursued Lee until he had defeated one of the great geniuses of all military history. And here in our struggle against the evils of discriminations in American life for our people we must fight 'if it takes all summer;' we must fight until we finish the job as Grant did."

The liberties we now enjoy were "purchased at a frightful cost in lives and treasure and when white people look at the irresponsible way many of us are exercising those liberties, they have a right to curse our memory when they remember what it cost. As part of our duty to repay what we cost the American nation, we must be able to discover what is unworthy in us by adverse self-analysis."

The speaker expressed the view that the full integration "f Negroes in America is "up to us." He warned that "we recognize that we live in the midst of people who are determined to fix upon us a contemptuous and contemptible estimate of ourselves" and admonished against the present state of affairs in which "we are leaving entirely to the other race the management of our existence." Dr. Johns concluded with a hopeful plea that "with courage and industry we complete our emancipation."

In June of 1949, President Elisha G. Hall (interview November 3, 1997) of Virginia Seminary, heard Vernon Johns speak at Virginia Seminary at the time of his graduation. Johns had on a white coat, what was supposed to be white for it was quite dirty, and he said "Well, I was out shuckin' corn and since I didn't have any more corn to shuck, I thought I would come over here to see what you all were doing" just as if shucking corn was more important than the commencement address. Dr. Hall remembered the students enjoying the speech very much and clapping heartily. Later, President Hall took a course in music education from Mrs. Johns at Virginia State. He said that she was a very nice person. Altona said to him, "My husband is going to speak at Virginia State." When he saw Johns, he said who the heck is this guy anyway, all trampified like this. But when Johns began to speak, Hall said "Great day! He could speak." Vernon Johns liked to draw out his words for effect. He said Vernon Johns liked sermons with some thought in them. He hated "light" sermons. He would say "That sermon was so light; I could have stayed at home. You (the audience) could have done as well."

Davis (July 15, 1949, West Virginia State College archives) wrote Mr. Rutherford a note asking "Will you be kind enough to get permission to pay Dr. Vernon Johns one hundred dollars ($100.00) in connection with his acceptance of my invitation to deliver the commencement address here at five o'clock in the afternoon of August 19, 1949? I will appreciate your prompt attention to this matter."

On July 16, 1949 (WVSC archives) Davis wrote Johns: "It was stimulating for me to see you at Virginia State College a few days ago. Naturally all of us regret exceedingly the cause which brought so many sad people to Virginia State College on July 8, for Dr. Foster's funeral. I am again inviting you to deliver a thirty-minute commencement address here at five o'clock in the afternoon on Friday, August 19, 1949. We will be able to take care of your expenses in coming to us and in addition provide a modest honorarium. You are familiar with our situation here. The people in this State hold you in high esteem and will welcome the opportunity to hear you on the occasion of our Summer Commencement Exercises."

Johns was the speaker at the summer session graduation exercises at West Virginia State College in August 1949 (Yellow Jacket, August 12, 1949:1). President Davis (WVSC archives) gave the introduction: "Ladies and Gentlemen: It is stimulating to be in contact with a person of brilliant mind. It is uplifting to listen to a man who can think independently, clearly, and creatively. Such are the known traits of our Convocation Speaker today. He is a preacher and a farmer. His success at farming has in some instances and with some people dulled the acoustic reception of his gospel message but not the power of the message. It is difficult to find in the pulpit of the church today the thinking and preaching equal of our speaker. I am happy to present now as our Summer Convocation Speaker a student, writer, scholar, teacher, farmer and preacher Dr. Vernon Johns."

Constant Fighter for Civil Rights

Vernon Johns (Yeakey 1979:103&105) "preached practically all the time on social conditions. His overriding concern: fight for civil rights." And Johns pretty much acted alone for he did not get much help from the other ministers. Rufus Lewis said that "He was the most outstanding man for preaching in our city; and many of the other preachers came to hear him preach." He, however, had little to do with the other ministers. Why should he, he reasons, since "they were not doing anything"

In an interview with the youngest of the Johns' children, Jeanne Johns Adkins said her father had no patience with upper class blacks. They weren't giving him anything back. In Montgomery the professors would be driving Lincolns and Cadillacs and be so proud. But at the department of motor vehicles the black professors at college were standing against the wall filling out their forms. He sat down, and someone told him that "Blacks don't sit." He replied " "Well, this black is going to sit."

We asked Jeanne if this kind of confrontation tickled her? "When his wrath was pointed at us, we were not too tickled, but when his wrath was pointed at others, we were tickled." She also added that Deacon Nesbitt tried to apologize to her and her sister Enid when they visited Montgomery recently.

Lee Thaxton told us that Dr. Trent, Vernon John's father-in-law and president of Livingstone College, asked Vernon Johns "Vernon, maybe I reckon you'll behave yourself now. You going to stay down there?' Vernon replied 'If they don't mess with me I will. But if they do, I'm going to raise hell.' (laughter) Johns was something else. I used to love to hear that guy preach."

There was an announcement that Vernon Johns would preach the following Sunday on the topic "Segregation After Death." The whites became nervous, and the police chief invited the minister down to the station to explain himself. Taylor Branch (1988:12) relates how the police chief asked Rev. Johns to come down to the station to explain himself. Instead of explaining, Johns started spouting the sermon from memory. It sounds somewhat doubtful to the authors of this book knowing the deep racism of southern whites, but Johns later boasted that after his sermon there was not "a dry eye in the station house."

In the actual sermon Johns reiterated an idea he had often preached about previously. He told the story of Christ's parable of the beggar Lazarus who went to heaven and the rich man Dives who went to hell, but the arrogant Dives stilled called out to Father Abraham to have Lazarus bring him some cool water to ease his torment in hell. But Abraham spoke of the "great gulf" that separated them. Johns likened this great gulf to segregation. What sent the rich man to hell was his insistence on segregation, not his wealth. In the sermon before his congregation Vernon Johns said that the segregationist attitudes of the white church goers made them as Christian as "sun worshipers." But what was so wonderful about Johns was that he saw segregation not just as a white problem, but a black one also. He saw the cooperation of blacks with segregation. He asked his own congregation on the day of the sermon, "What preacher wouldn't love to have a church full of members like Dives?" These types of remarks must have scandalized many of the well-dressed congregation.

He made the congregation feel uncomfortable as he said that the blacks, like Dives, were segregating themselves off through their wealth (Branch 1988:12). Off the pulpit, he often said the black middle-class congregation were "spinksterinkdum Negroes" who paraded in the "fashion show" that was their church.

Other controversial sermon topics were "Constructive (or Creative) Homicide" and "When the Rapist is White". Vernon was not a believer in nonviolence. He believed in taking whatever measures were necessary to achieve our God-given or constitutional rights (Abernathy 1989:120). His text was from Genesis, the story of how Moses was first chosen to lead his people, and Vernon began by summarizing it as follows: "God saw Moses when Moses slew the Egyptian and buried him in the sand, and he turned to an angel and said "Write that man's name down. Later on I can use him in my program.'" Then Johns said to the young men assembled before him: "If I were to summarize in a single phrase my remarks to you today, I would title them 'Constructive Homicide.'"

Johns was also socially outspoken (Branch 1988:15). One Sunday Dr. H. Councill Trenholm, president of Alabama State College, the largest employer of Montgomery Negroes generally and of Dexter members in particular, came to church. Johns growled "I want to pause here in the service, until Dr. Trenholm can get himself seated here on his semi-annual visit to the church." Trenholm never returned to Dexter while Johns was in Montgomery.

June 10, 1950 (p. 1) the Journal and Guide carried the story of the NAACP victory in the Sweatt Case that admitted a coloured student to the law school of the University of Texas. President Truman was asked to speak at Tuskegee by, among others, President F. D. Patterson of the institution. Segregation's end is near, Thurgood Marshall naively declared (J&G June 17, 1950:1).

"Johns called meetings with community leaders and worked to change the discriminatory treatment blacks received in the downtown stores and businesses in hiring and employment practices (Yeakey 1979:100-101). Few blacks in Montgomery could forget his efforts on their behalf." One instructor at Alabama State College, Mrs. O. B. Underwood, remembered that "Reverend Johns refused to be pushed back at any place, and he was very vehement with whites. He used to block doors, he used to stand on corners and sort of bless them out." His reputation as someone who stood up against the whites brought him black wome" who came to him with stories of being raped and beaten by white men. Each time he drove the girl to the Tuskegee hospital in the dead of the night for a medical examination. He went with the victim to file charges at the police station. The first case ended in an acquittal and the second went nowhere, as local authorities refused to order the accused, all policemen, to stand in a line-up.

In 1948, President Truman's executive order of July 26, 1948, ended segregation in the armed forces. This had an obvious effect on Montgomery since the city was heavily dependent on Maxwell and Gunter air force bases (J&G July 9, 1949:18). Colored airmen, boarding Montgomery City Lines buses at Maxwell Field would take the first vacant seat on buses. The drivers, however, compelled them to move to the rear seats or take a refund of their fare. Twice last week coloured airmen have been forced to vacate seats reserved for white persons. The first incident occurred when four coloured airmen in uniform boarded a bus at Maxwell Field and took seats toward the front. The driver ordered them to move to the rear or accept a refund of their fares. One of the airmen replied that they were on government property, and, therefore, permitted to occupy seats of their choice. The driver admitted that they were on a government reservation, but said they were riding on the bus company's property and, therefore, were governed by city and state segregation laws. Two of the coloured airmen elected to move to the rear and two accepted refunds and got off the bus.

There was considerable talk of banning bus segregation in Virginia. Even Governor Battle of Virginia heard a plea for an end to bus segregation. The bus lines favoured the end of Virginia travel segregation as did the white pastors. The Boothe anti-segregation bill would have banned segregation on the buses. On March 4, 1950:1 the paper reported that "Secret Killing of Boothe Measures Stuns Virginians." The bill was shelved by the Courts of Justice Committee of the Virginia House of Delegates (J&G Jan 28, 1950:11; Feb 11, 1950:1; February 25, 1950:1).

In 1952 in Montgomery a white bus driver and a black named Brooks, who had been drinking, exchanged words over the dime the passenger put into the slot of the meter box (Robinson 1987:21). The driver accused Brooks of not putting the money into the box. The driver called the police, and when the police came, they shot and killed Brooks as he got off the bus. Some blacks even argued that Brooks had gotten "out of his place" with the white bus driver.

Vernon Johns got into the act, protesting bus segregation. One day he decided not to move from his seat as requested by the bus driver. The bus driver stormed to the rear, shouting "Nigger! Didn't you hear me tell you to get the hell out of that seat?" "And didn't you hear me tell you that I'm going to sit right goddamned here?" Johns replied. The driver, stunned by the forceful vocabulary of the well-known minister, retreated in confusion (Bailey 1994:42; originally in Bennett 1976:49-50). Johns told the blacks on the bus to follow him off in protest, but no one followed. One Dexter church member on the bus remarked that he "should knowed better" than to try something like that.

One day Johns walked into a white restaurant and ordered a sandwich and a drink to take home with him (Branch 1988:14-15). His entrance into the all-white establishment immediately brought an end to the customers' conversations. They stared as Johns sat waiting for his sandwich. The attendant fixed the sandwich but poured the drink slowly onto the counter in front of Johns. Vernon simply ordered another drink saying, "There is something in me that doesn't like being pushed around, and it's starting to work." In the Connie Chung program (September 23, 19) they show Vernon Johns grabbing the attendant by his shirt collar and pulling him down to the point where the two men's faces were inches apart. This seems consistent with Johns' temper and reports of his use of violence. This challenge brought an immediate response from some of the white customers, who ran out of the restaurant heading for their pickup trucks and cars for their guns. Confronted with this show of force, Vernon later said "I pronounced the shortest blessing of my life over than sandwich. I said, 'Goddamn it" and hurriedly left the restaurant.

Relating this story from his pulpit the following Sunday (Bailey 1994:42; originally in Bennett 1976:49-50), the Rev. Johns said that he did not believe that God was offended by the unauthorized use of his name. He told his congregation that God probably said, "I'd better keep an eye on that boy; he's going to do a lot for Christianity down South."

"It's Safe to Murder Negroes"

The television program Saturday Night with Connie Chung (1989) brought out that in the bloody spring of 1949 a series of murders infuriated Johns. For instance, a white man on his porch saw a black man running down the street. The white man went in to get his double-barrelled shotgun. He shot the black man dead. The killer's explanation: "If he was running, he must have done something." It was the second week of May in 1949.

Toni Johns said "As I recall, a black girl had been raped. I think it was by six white police officers. We took her in our car to the hospital at Tuskegee Institute. I knew something bad was going to happen. I didn't know what. He was so agitated. He was talking under his breath. He said: I'm going to change the subject of my sermon to 'It's Safe to Murder Negroes.' I knew that that was a volatile subject."

Abernathy (1989:120) remembered it somewhat differently: "There was a period of particularly harsh repression, with almost every week the police were killing blacks, particularly on Saturday nights. A poor black man was shot down in the street just below Vernon Johns' church one Saturday evening. Everyone in Montgomery knew that he had been killed by a white man, and everyone was reasonably certain who the murderer was. But there was no serious investigation by local authorities, and it was clear that the killing was to be swept under the rug like so many other such killings over the years. The black leadership in the community grumbled behind closed doors no public protest was voiced with one exception. The following week Vernon posted on the bulletin board outside his church this sermon topic: It is safe to kill Negroes in Montgomery."

The newspapers reported that Johns was going to preach this sermon on Sunday morning and the white community was up in arms (Abernathy 1989:121). As it happened the all-white grand jury was then in session. When word reached them of the sign in front of Vernon's church, they charged that Vernon Johns was inciting people to riot and subpoenaed him to show why he should not be indicted. So the police department sent an officer to pick him up and bring him into the station. Vernon Johns called the sheriff's office and told them he would be happy to come in and testify before the grand jury and agreed to appear at ten a.m. the next morning."

Wyatt T. Walker on the program Saturday Night with Connie Chung (1989) said that "Just after he put it out on the church bulletin board, the commonwealth attorney came down. And Johns did not dress up much." In fact, Johns in overalls looked more like the church janitor than the church minister. The program had the following dialogue: "Hey, boy come here." Johns kept sweeping the sidewalk by the church bulletin board. "Make it light on yourself and get on over here before I got to cause you some problems." Johns came over. "Who's the pastor of this church?" Johns said "Can't you read? Vernon Johns. Reverend Vernon Johns." "Don't sass me boy. You think this 'John' actually means to preach this sermon?" Johns replied "Well, knowing the Reverend as I do, he will either preach it in heaven or he will preach it in hell." The white man responded "Well, we'll see about that. You tell Vernon I said be at the police station at three o'clock. And don't make me have to come back after him."

Johns went to the police station. "Boy, didn't I tell you to send the parson down here?" Johns replied, "I am the minister of the church." "Well, why didn't you tell me who you were when I talked to you a while ago?" Johns slyly responded: "Am I obliged to identify myself to every chance stranger I meet on the public thoroughfare?"

The judge asked Johns why he would want to preach such an inflammatory sermon dealing with the murder of one race by another. "Well, judge, the truth is always inflammatory," Johns answered and added: "Because everywhere I go in the South the Negro is forced to choose between his hide and his soul. Mostly he chooses his hide. I'm going to tell him that his hide is not worth it."

Abernathy (1989:121) reported that Johns "sat down and answered all the questions put to him, carefully pointing out that a black man had indeed been shot and killed in broad daylight, that nothing had thus far been done to bring his murderer to justice, and that until such time as an arrest had been made, the words on the board outside his church were no more than a statement of fact."

Vernon Johns (Yeakey 1979:104) was considered one of those "crazy Negroes, who the white folks didn't mess with." On one visit to the local police station an officer told him what might happen to him if he continued his inflammatory sermons. According to James Pierce (quoted in Yeakey 1979:104), a political science professor at Alabama State, Vernon replied "Two days from now my son's going to Korea, to fight, so many thousand miles away and yet he's fighting for those people for those things which he has been denied here. I just as soon for him to die here as to die over there, and by dying here he will be dying for his own cause."

The judge merely issued a warning to Johns. The judge decided to let Johns deliver the sermon as is, because he thought it would be the lesser evil (Branch 1988:23), saying "The whites of Montgomery would pay more attention if I stopped you." Vernon Johns sent letters to the city commissioners inviting them to send twelve of their best policemen to worship with his congregation the Sunday when the sermon was to be preached.

Toni Johns (Chung 1989) remembered that "There was a little telephone table in the hall right by my parents' bedroom. I picked it up. We're going to lynch you, you niggers." Saturday night a cross was burned at the church and cracked the glass on the church bulletin. This did not deter Vernon Johns.

We asked Jeanne Johns Adkins if she was upset by the burning of the cross? She said: "We accepted the fact that it goes with the territory." Probed on this topic, she admitted: "We were tense."

Toni Johns (Chung) said "I was never frightened when I was with my father. I was frightened for my father. Well, I used to be afraid all the time that he was going to be killed or get hit or beat or whatever because he was always doing things that were outside the proscribed behaviour for blacks. I thought white people might beat him or kill him. Those are things I never really talked about. I used to wonder if he was ever going to come home."

On the day of the sermon, Johns raised all the church windows in order that people could hear if they were standing outside (Yeakey 1979:103-104). The service was well attended. The police were infuriated, but they stayed in cars parked across the street from the church. In the sermon he predicted that violence against Negroes would continue if they "let it happen."

Johns' sermon had to compete with the sound of the policemen constantly revving their motorcycle engines. The atmosphere was highly charged. On the Connie Chung program Rufus Lewis commented that "I think people were a little afraid because they were so close to the capitol. And Vernon Johns didn't give a rap about that. He was so forthright in his speech, so forthright in the type of things he said that it frightened some people. They were just afraid. They didn't know what would happen to him nor to them."

Quoting from the program (Chung 1989), Vernon Johns said:

I just want to remind you what the clearest and simplest of these great Ten Commandments is: Thou shalt not kill. The Birmingham paper says that you have a better chance in 1948 of being murdered in Alabama than anywhere in the U S. A lot of the people doing the killing are the police officers who should know the law as well as anybody.

The officer Orris Thrash killed Amos Star for resisting arrest. Shot him in the back. So, I guess he was resisting while running away. And right here in Montgomery two police officers took a man, handcuffed him to a tree and beat him. Didn't kill him though. They got charged with assault. Just two weeks ago another Montgomery policeman got it right. He shot and killed one Henry Lee for resisting arrest. The coroner ruled it justifiable homicide. All these cases were justifiable homicide.

But you know there is no justifiable homicide. God never spoke about justifiable homicide. He said "Thou shalt not kill". He didn't say thou shalt not kill unless you've got an excuse. He didn't say thou shalt not kill unless you are a police officer. And he most assuredly did not say thou shalt not kill, unless you're white.

Last week, a white man was fined for shooting a rabbit out of season. But of course, it's safe to murder Negroes.

A rabbit is better off than a Negro because in Alabama niggers are always in season.

What would God have said if he had looked down upon us last week here in Montgomery? A Negro man was stopped by a trooper for speeding and brutally beaten with a tire iron while other Negroes stood by and did nothing. What would God have said when he looked down and saw an enraged police officer take up a young coloured boy and use his head as a battering ram when the boy's father said nothing, did nothing?

I'll tell you why it's safe to murder Negroes. Because Negroes stand by and let it happen. Do you know what occurred to me as I watched that cross burning in front of the church? When the Klan burns a cross it's a message. The next step is lynching. As I watched that cross it occurred to me that what we call the crucifixion is just that a lynching. Isn't it ironic? Everything we worship was made possible by a lynching. Because at that ultimate moment of death Jesus spoke the words that transformed a lynching into the crucifixion. That made Jesus the redeemer, not the condemner. Jesus said Father forgive them for they know not what they do. But you know what you do. And the white police officers who are free day after day to murder Negroes know what they do. And when you stand by and watch your brothers and sisters being lynched it's as if you stood by while Christ was being crucified.

In the program one of the congregants stood up to protest saying "We don't need this. And we don't need you to come here talking to us like this."

Johns responded "Woe unto you, scribes and Pharisees! Hypocrites! And that's you! Because you sit here Sunday morning and sing hymns while you know that every Saturday night your brother's been shot down in the streets and you know nothing except fear.

Are you afraid of trouble? Are you afraid of death? Are you afraid that if you speak too loudly, protest too strongly, you will become one of those lynched? Well, you may well be. He who takes not this cross and follows me is not worthy of me. So there you have the question. Are you worthy of Jesus or are you only worthy of the state of Alabama?"

Whether he actually spoke every one of these words is not known. But the words do, however, express the courage and spirit of the prophet Vernon Johns speaking from the pulpit mountain top.

Premonitions of Termination

As feelings hardened on both sides, Johns became shriller. He continued to sell his fish and vegetables to members of the community. Branch (1988:18) writes that "It was the fish that first got him hauled before the board of deacons. He abruptly resigned and walked out the door. Nesbitt was detailed to seek him out and arrange a truce. Nesbitt was actually more of a man in the middle. He was one of the few who was not a teacher." One-time Johns walked out of church in anger when the organist continued to refuse to play anything but the most conservative hymns. Nesbitt had to chase him several blocks down Dexter Avenue, begging him to return to the service. (Branch 1988:19) Still another resignation was tendered and refused in 1950.

Other Activities

During the following summer, Johns taught at the Virginia State College summer school for ministers at Petersburg (J&G July 16, 1949:14). There was an announcement in the paper that summer school for ministers would begin at Virginia State. It would last three weeks. The school was sponsored by the recently organized conference of Negro Colleges on Rural Life,

including Hampton Institute, Bishop Payne Divinity School, Virginia Union University, St. Paul Polytechnic Institute, and Virginia State College. Virginia Seminary had been invited to cooperate. (J&G June 19, 1943:7) Other members of the school faculty were Dr. W. H. R. Powell, pastor of Shiloh Baptist Church, Philadelphia; Dr. Harry W. Roberts, director; and Miss Selena B. Robinson, instructor in English. Harry Roberts, head of the sociology department at Virginia State, received his Ph.D. in 1943 from Yale upon acceptance of his thesis The Life and Labour of Rural Negroes in Virginia. (J&G March 6, 1943:1 and Mar 7, 1945:4) Johns also served as acting director of religious activities at Virginia State College.

"For the past three weeks Dr. Johns brought to the ministers attending the summer school his profound scholarship, deep religious insight, courageous creative thinking and boundless enthusiasm and inspiration. He is the preacher at the Sunday morning chapel service. He is now in the process of preparing a book for publication entitled 'Preaching the Parables.' Dr. Johns is pursuing the study of philosophy at the University of Chicago." (J&G July 16, 1949:14)

Dr. Vernon Johns delivered the convocation address of the summer session at West Virginia State College August 19 (J&G August 27, 1949:17). Eighty-three students graduated at the summer session.

News that Altona Trent Johns (along with co-author Vivian Flagg McBrier) had written a music book came out in the Journal and Guide on October 15 (1949:6). The two teachers published Finger Fun with Songs to be Sung for elementary school children.

The words and music were based on themes of special interest to children providing opportunity for fun while learning the elemental principles and techniques of music both oral and instrumental. All the illustrations in the book were of coloured children. The paper said that Mrs. Johns taught music at Virginia Theological Seminary and College. Mrs. McBrier headed the music department at Miner Teachers College in Washington, D.C., and was formerly music teacher at Dunbar High School in Lynchburg, Virginia. The book sells for $1.50 and may be secured from the publishers, Handy Brothers, New York City.

"Choir members of Alabama State back from tour", announced the Journal and Guide (December 7, 1949:16). Forty students chosen from the Symphonic Choir of the Alabama State College at Montgomery have returned to the campus after a tour which took them into Frankfort, Kentucky, Dayton, Yellow Springs, Wilberforce, and Cleveland, Ohio, and to Detroit, Michigan. Under the direction of Frederick D. Hall, well-known conductor and arranger, the group received wide acclaim for its performances in all of the cities where it appeared. The choir will present its annual program of Christmas music in two performances at the college December 11. Director Hall will be assisted at the piano by Mrs. Mildred Greenwood Hall and by Mrs. Altona Trent Johns.

August 31, 1951 (WVSC archives) President Davis of West Virginia State College wired Rev. Johns in Montgomery. "Have secured Reverend Moses Newsome's permission to invite you to address our faculty and students here at seven o'clock on Sunday evening, September 16th. Wire collect if you will accept this invitation to speak for us."

Chapter thirty-six

A fight for desegregation in Farmville

We have already shown how Vernon Johns influenced one of the main thrusts toward civil rights with his association with Rev. Adam Clayton Powell, Jr. This chapter will show his influence on another major thrust for civil rights the 1954 Supreme Court decision Brown vs. The Board of Education, which was a conglomerate of several cases handled together. At this time, Vernon Johns was preaching in Montgomery, Alabama.

Background

It was not until the late 1930's and early 1940's that blacks in the South – encouraged by the 1938 decision of the Supreme Court in the "Gaines Case" on the university level – turned to the Federal courts as a major resort in their fight for better elementary and secondary schools for their children. Thereafter, protests against and appeals for the correction of inequalities between white and black schools were increasingly followed by litigation. According to Wilkerson (1969:260&269), in Virginia, there were three successive trends in this developing fight. The first stage was asking for equal teachers' salaries. The Journal and Guide (January 22, 1938:1) carried a story about the equal pay campaign being backed by Virginia teachers. The second phase was for equal school physical facilities. The third phase was a demand for integration. It is important to understand that the school integration cases emerged directly out of organized efforts to equalize salaries and facilities in the separate white and Negro schools.

Willie Redd

Every Southern town, city and hamlet had one or more black leaders chosen by the whites. In Farmville this man was a relatively wealthy contractor named Willie Redd. He emphasized that the route to progress for blacks was cooperation with whites. And, of course, men like Willie Redd would have gotten a lot of support from the philosophies of men such as Booker T. Washington and Robert R. Moton of Tuskegee. (Kluger 1976:464)

The most influential white man in Farmville as regards race relations was J. Barrye Wall, Sr., editor of the Farmville Herald (Smith, Bob 1965:20). Wall consulted

Willie Redd when he wished to learn of the feelings of the Negro community on one subject or another. In the Farmville Herald they had a column by Basil Anderson entitled Coloured News. It was no bigger than the columns for the smallest of the white towns in the area.

Barbara Johns

Barbara Johns (1935-1991) grew up in Prince Edward County. Mary Spencer-Croner (1891-1972), Barbara Johns' maternal grandmother, had eight brothers and sisters. Apparently liking large families, she had nine children of her own following her marriage to Charles Spencer (1887 – 1927) (no relation to the Spencers of Lynchburg). Her husband lived in Sparrows Point, Maryland as a construction worker during the week, while Mary managed the household back home (Kluger 1976:452). Then suddenly Charles Spencer was killed in an accident on the job. The company sent barely enough compensation so she could pay $1,200 dollars for the 106-acre farm on which the family had been living. Mary decided that, with the help of her many children, she could work the farm for sustenance. The family grew tobacco as the cash crop and corn, wheat, and potatoes to eat.

In 1932 Mary Spencer married Robert Croner (1894-1987) (Kluger 1976:453). He share-cropped the big farm across the road from hers. Croner was a widower and he brought with him to the union five children. The total number of children was, hence, fourteen. They all had to live in the eight-room house, the boys, and girls in separate quarters. Robert added the raising of hogs to their vegetable farming.

Mary Croner's second child was Violet Spencer (sister of Jewel Spencer Clark who as a young girl worked for the Johns family). Violet married Robert Johns, the brother of Vernon Johns. They travelled north to Harlem in order to find work. In Harlem they had the first of their five children, Barbara Rose Johns, in 1935, to be followed by four other siblings. Violet Johns worked as a domestic, while her husband snatched what jobs he could. The family moved in with relatives in a rooming house on 129th Street. After a while, they gave up residence in the city and returned home to Prince Edward County.

In Prince Edward, both their parental families owned some land, but farming was brutal without proper equipment and paid very little, so Robert ran a little general store that older brother Vernon owned on The Road. The store was in a section of Darlington Heights, in which Negro farmers predominated. Despite this fact, the clientele was thoroughly mixed. White farmers were regular customers and white salesmen were regular visitors. But there was not much money in running the store.

In 1942 Violet found steady work with the government in Washington D.C. and the family lived in an apartment at Fourth and K Streets northeast not far from the Capitol, by which Barbara often would walk.

When the United States entered World War II, her father went into the Army, and the financial strain on her mother became even heavier, so the children were packed onto a train to live for the duration with their grandmother Mary Croner on her farmstead in Darlington Heights (Kluger 1976:453&455). In 1945 her father got out of the army and her mother left her job in Washington to return to the Prince Edward County. By the time the family was reunited after the war, Barbara had become an independent spirit, with a mind and tongue of her own, and a bit of a temper. Henry Powell said about Barbara: "She was something else. Barbara had three brothers and her mother was sick and finally died. She was the head-knocker. When she spoke even her old man, Robert Johns, jumped." She went to school at the Robert R. Moton High School in Farmville.

Barbara's family moved into Vernon's store for a time while her father built their new home down The Road half a mile to the east of Vernon's place. The store and the mill attached to it had a big sign painted on its side saying, "WE CHOP WHEAT AS FINE AS FLOUR." But their biggest job was grinding cornmeal for the hogs. They were a social centre for that outlying sector of the county, and whites and blacks alike, customers and salesmen, came to shoot the breeze or play cards and talk crops. Barbara would wait on customers after school and came to hold the white man in no special awe (Kluger 1976:454-455). Barbara's father was on good terms with all the whites around. Some would come and sit around and play cards. They were all poor dirt farmers. Mrs. Robert Johns remembers having difficulty adjusting back from the manners of Washington to rural Virginia: "People used to come in and I used to get so angry that they would . . . call you by your first name.' Violet, how about this' – and that kind of thing. I would tell them I thought only my personal friends called me by my first name. We used to have a verbal fight almost every day with some salesman or another" (Smith, Bob 1965:28-29 and Kluger 1976:455).

Barbara was a good student. She began to read and think and listen to her outspoken paternal grandmother, Sallie Johns (Kluger 1976:454). "She wasn't an easy person to get close to," Barbara remembers, "but I think she was more of an influence on me than Ma Croner. She had no fear and was not the slightest bit subservient to whites."

But it was Uncle Vernon who lifted Barbara's horizons. While her father was a quiet and kindly man, her uncle was a fire brand. Speaking of her uncle with fondness, Barbara (Kluger 1976:454) said "We'd always be on opposite sides in an argument.

I'm afraid we were both very antagonistic. He was beyond the intellectual scope of everyone around the county. I remember that white men would be at the store that he and my father ran together after the war and they'd listen to him speak and shake their heads, not understanding his language." No white man bested him in an argument, and Barbara Johns listened to his way with words and began to make it hers.

Barbara told Bob Smith (1965:28)"My uncle was always outspoken, and I used to admire the way he didn't care who you were if he thought that something was right. It used to be an admirable thing to me the way he would handle white men who would have an argument with him."

Vernon's wife, Altona, and their daughters brought another dimension of culture into Barbara's life. Bright and well-schooled, the daughters were frequent playmates of their cousin, and the girls wrote plays together that got staged at their grade school (Kluger 1976:455). Once they sold tickets to one of their plays and raised enough money to have electric lights installed in the school. Vernon's daughters studied music and used the resources of their father's library and of his mind to move far ahead of their classmates (Smith, Bob 1965: 29).

Reverend L. Francis Griffin

Vernon Johns preached in many communities, including Farmville, where the Reverend Charles Henry Dunstan Griffin occasionally invited him to the pulpit of the First Baptist Church on Farmville's Main Street, the oldest and largest black congregation in Prince Edward County (Kluger 1976:454). He was a graduate of Roanoke Collegiate Institute now a division of Shaw University. After his work at that school and other institutions of learning, he pastored at Cornerstone Baptist Church, Elizabeth City, North Carolina and at other churches in eastern North Carolina. He then went to Norfolk, Virginia.

Rev. Charles Griffin came to Farmville in 1927 after pastoring at Central Baptist, one of the biggest churches in Norfolk (Smith, Bob 1965:7). Fire destroyed it and the Reverend Griffin led his congregation of more than a thousand in a massive rebuilding drive that left him exhausted and in need of a less draining pastorate. Exhausted after the rebuilding, Rev. Griffin was ready to move on.

Leslie Francis Griffin was only ten years old when his father accepted the pastorate of the First Baptist Church in Farmville (Kluger 1976:462). Vernon Johns preached from time to time in Mr. Griffin's church. Leslie came to be influenced in part by

Johns who had a very different preaching message than that of Leslie's father. Like so many black preachers in the South, Charles Griffin preached a message that was a call to the brethren to keep the faith until a new day dawned on earth without oppression and poverty. His son said that he was impressed "by his father's ability to stay calm and not to call for retaliation against our tormentors." His father was a pacifist, nonviolence being a part of his nature. But he was an opponent of segregation even though he did not actively crusade against it. Like many another black theologian then, he would couch his message in terms of allegory to avoid being labelled a rabble-rouser.

Griffin's Church, Farmville

The elder Griffin liked the fiery preacher and thought he should be heard, even though they had little in common theologically and Rev. Johns often angered members of the Griffin congregation. Johns believed in preaching on the realities of life – on the kinds of sins that were tangible, on segregation, on the docility and ignorance of the Negro. Docility was his chief enemy. Johns would denounce the country Negroes who filled the churches where he spoke for their impenetrable docility, for not caring enough (Smith, Bob 1965:12, 27, 76). Those who had come to church to escape these realities were suitably offended. Mr. Johns believed this to be so much to the good. The younger Griffin said that Vernon was inconsiderate of those who were not up to his level in thinking.

While Johns and Rev. Griffin argued amiably, Leslie Griffin listened and was impressed (Smith, Bob 1965:10-11). He felt that "Johns was an advanced thinker. Nobody liked him. He could tell a person something and make him mad where somebody else could say the same thing and everything would be all right. Yes, he would arouse resentment. A prophet is not without honor except in his own country and Vernon was born in Prince Edward."

Once a month, Griffin would come by the general store and mill that Vernon and Robert Johns operated out on The Road and find a receptive audience there (Kluger 1976:463). Rev. Johns had a good library and he introduced young Leslie to his collection of books and his friends' books. Young Griffin liked Walter Rauschenbusch and the Social Gospel. But Vernon Johns made sure that the optimism of the Social Gospel was modified by the realism of Reinhold Niebuhr.

Johns' religion helped Leslie form a theology that was very different from his father's views. In telling of the kind of social gospel he first encountered from the lips of Vernon Johns, Leslie (Kluger 1976:463) said "I felt that all forms of worship should be related to a form of action." "Too many people do no more than pray and expect the world to change. I didn't and don't think that a church is meant to be housed inside a building. Everything abou' life is ' legitimate concern of my religion."

Leslie was somewhat of a rebel and very restless (Smith, Bob 1965:8). He was so far ahead of his classmates that he would become bored with school and would slip out and go out to Jesse Boland's place where Boland had an airplane that he would fly passengers about for a fee. His father would often decide to check on his son and would go out and get him and bring him back to school.

Mrs. Johns taught Leslie music and literature (Smith, Bob 1965:8&10). She wanted him to go on to Fisk University in the five-year program offered there by the Ford Foundation, as her daughters were to do.

Leslie did not finish high school, but rather went to New York for nearly a year to work as a shipping clerk (Smith, Bob 1965:11). In 1939 he went to Charlotte, North Carolina to work as a department store handyman. But it was the war that changed his life. He went into the service shortly after Pearl Harbour and became part of the first Negro tank outfit (758th Tank Battalion). He served under Generals George Patton and Mark Clark. He was in service for more than four years, and somewhere along the line he decided to become a minister.

Back from the war he finished his last year of high school in Rich Square, North Carolina, the home of his father's sister (Smith, Bob 1965:12). He then enrolled at Shaw University in North Carolina. Politics was a favourite subject of young Griffin at Shaw in 1948. The Henry Wallace campaign had touched a spark to the liberalism that had emerged from the war, and for a brief period there was ferment on the left. Griffin threw himself into it wholeheartedly.

In his second year at Shaw, he was married to a classmate, and a son, Skip, was born the next year (Smith, Bob 1965:12-13). Because of his poor financial condition, when Skip was born, he and his mother went to her parents' home in New Jersey. They later went to Farmville to stay with Leslie's parents.

Leslie finished college in 1949 (Smith, Bob 1965:11-12). During the summers he would preach at various locations. Vernon Johns was around, and he became an even greater influence on Griffin as time went on. Johns called Griffin a "disciple," and Griffin felt complimented.

Willie Reid of the Bland Reid Funeral home (1997) said that as a young man he would drive Vernon Johns and Griffin to various speaking engagements. He remembers the first time he met Vernon Johns. He drove Griffin down to Montgomery. When they got there, he found a church full of people being led by a big man with a Bible in his hand. He remembered how Johns would preach that "A man should live so his funeral won't be the biggest thing in his life." At Shaw University (Griffin's school), Vernon Johns preached to two or three hundred students at a time. He remembered how Johns would stop at the funeral home and take a bath and then get on the train to go speak somewhere. He remembered how there was nothing phony about Johns. He was very easy to talk to. When Johns would drive his own car, he would often carry pigs in the back. Henry Powell remembered that one time when Johns went up to Richmond to speak at Virginia Union, he carried two barrels of slop with him in the back seat. At the university there were flies everywhere and the stench was terrible. But that was Vernon Johns.

In October 1949 Leslie's father died. Members of the congregation asked young Griffin to take over the pulpit (Smith, Bob 1965:13 & Kluger 1976:463)). He accepted. He saw in the church an opportunity for the leadership he was now eager to exercise. At thirty-two, one term short of completing his studies at college, he was the new spiritual leader of the blacks of Prince Edward County.

In 1939 Farmville constructed a school for blacks, the R. R. Moton High School, named for Prince Edward County native Robert R. Moton, successor to Booker T. Washington at Tuskegee (Kluger 1976:459). The original brick structure contained seven classrooms, an auditorium, offices, lavatory facilities, and a classroom that had been converted to serve as a cafeteria. The school lacked a gymnasium, cafeteria, an auditorium with fixed seats, locker rooms, and an infirmary, all of which white Farmville High had. In addition, Moton's teachers were paid substantially less. Thanks to the efforts of Vernon Johns, school buses, even if old and rickety, picked up the black children of Darlington Heights to take them to the Farmville school.

In 1950, the Parent-Teachers Association appointed a committee to negotiate with the County School Board for a new high school. It was headed by Rev. L. Francis Griffin, and consisted of one representative from each school district. According to an anonymous leader (Wilkerson 1969:269), this committee "met with the School Board once a month for more than a year, presenting facts and figures, listing the needs of our schools. But we got nowhere. Constantly they told us there was no money. Finally, we got them to agree to secure land for a new high school – if we could find a suitable plot, they'd buy it. We found a place, up where the new high school is now located, 60 acres or more. But the Board then said they had no money to build with, and that we need not come back; they'd notify us through the press when they were in position to build."

This foot dragging was to challenge the patience of Barbara Johns (Kluger 1976:466). During her school day, Barbara joined the chorus and the drama group and the New Homemakers of America and was even elected to the student council. These activities would take her out of the country from time to time to other schools in other parts of Virginia and the more she saw of the outside world, the more dissatisfied she became with the facilities at Moton.

High on the list of complaints was overcrowding. The school, which had a capacity for handling of 300 pupils, had an enrolment of 455. In an earlier effort to relieve congestion three tarpaper covered frame house buildings were erected and cut up into thirteen classrooms of approximately fifteen by twenty feet each along with a manual arts shop, all of which are heated by small iron stoves. The average enrolment was thirty-three students per class, although some classes run as high as fifty-five.

Barbara Johns said that because the roofs leaked the pupils had to move from building to building in wet weather. Other problems such as poor ventilation and unevenness of heating often made it difficult and uncomfortable for the pupils to breathe, let alone concentrate upon their studies. Other school handicaps were the lack of a gymnasium and cafeteria facilities that would permit the serving of hot lunches.

Sometimes black leaders emerge when a crisis arises (Smith, Bob 1965:13,19-21 and Kluger 1976:463&464). But others are born rebels and look for an opportunity to protest. Leslie was the latter type. In talking to his parishioners, he found that the school situation was a hot issue. He saw his chance to make a difference here and so he decided to attend his first P.T.A. meeting. Long before the NAACP announced it policy of opposition to school segregation, Leslie was out there talking to whites and blacks about the evils of segregation. He contacted to Richmond lawyers Spottswood Robinson and Oliver Hill, who were roaming the state organizing a massive legal drive for equalized school facilities for blacks. In fact, he organized a chapter of the NAACP to help him in his efforts and was elected president of that organization. He also became head of the Moton PTA. The PTA was the principal black institution in the county. He took on as a supporter a boyhood friend, John Lancaster, the black county agricultural agent, who had similar ideas to those of Griffin's. The other ally of Griffin's was Moton High's principal, M. Boyd Jones. Together, the three men were a formidable triumvirate, though it was the minister, as the only one not dependent on whites for the bread on his dinner table, who carried the flag. Willie Reed resigned from the P.T.A. when Griffin and the new troublemakers came on the scene. Griffin hadXXXrocessf named chairman of the PTA committee that appeared before the school board. And he "waited for them to lose patience with the school board."

The School Strike

By her junior year Barbara Johns was fed up. It was late in the autumn of 1950 when Barbara broached the idea to the president of the Moton student body and her brother, John. She proposed that if things were not improved at the school that the entire Moton student body go out on strike until a new school was built.

Bob Smith (1965:76) wrote that "In the story of the strike that already has taken the shape of folklore on the lips of many white residents of Prince Edward County, the master devil is Mr. Vernon Johns. Mr. Griffin, who is the only principal in the strike still around, comes in for more than his share of tarring, and the names of John Lancaster and Boyd Jones are remembered. But only Mr. Johns is credited with the diabolical skills needed to 'invent' the strike. Talking about the school strike, Johns told journalist Carl Rowan 'It was a freak of nature, like a fixed star leaving its orbit'."

Barbara had kept a tight lid on her plans and the actual broaching of the idea of the strike came as a surprise to the student body. On a ruse they got Principal M. Boyd Jones to travel out to the Greyhound bus terminal in search of two students playing hooky, hoping, among other things, thereby to absolve him from blame for their contemplated action (Wilkerson 1969:269). While the principal was away, the student plotters went into action. She had all the students gather in the auditorium. When the approximately 450 students had been seated the stage curtains parted to reveal the secret student committee. A ripple of surprise went through the room. Barbara Johns was at the rostrum. According to reports, Barbara was very forceful in her determination to present her case to the students (Smith, Bob 1965:36-38). She asked that the teachers leave the room. In fact, according to her thirteen-year-old sister, Joanne, Barbara took off her shoe and hit it on a bench and said, "I want you all out of here." Most left voluntarily, but one had to be forcibly removed.

The principal returned in time to catch the student meeting. He was rather hysterical and pleaded with the students to go back to school. Barbara asked him to go back to his office, and he finally did. The students called Rev. Griffin to come to the school where he found student leaders behind locked doors. They asked him what to do about one boy who had dissented from the plan and wanted the students to get the consent of their parents. Griffins suggested that they simply take a vote among themselves (Smith, Bob 1965:38-40). On April 23, 1951, the black students of Moton High School walked out of class and refused to return for two weeks.

The students wrote to NAACP attorneys in Richmond, asking them to come to Farmville and start a suit for a new high school. Two attorneys did come; but they explained that, in view of the new policy of the N.A.A.C.P, they could not help with litigation unless a suit was filed to abolish school segregation. The P.T.A. met and unanimously voted to sue for integration, which they did in April 1951.

Students began picketing which they threatened to maintain until the school board set a definite date for the beginning of construction of a new school. The students paraded around the school carrying placards which urged the tearing down of "temporary" tar paper buildings and construction of "a new school now" (J&G May 5, 1951:1-2). The picketing ended when authorities informed everyone that the students along with their signs would have to get off of the school property.

On Wednesday afternoon representatives of the students' strike committee met with Superintendent McIlwaine, in an effort to determine when they might expect action on the construction of a 700-student, $800,000-dollar black high school which has been promised as part of the county's four-year school improvement program. Such a school had been promised for more than five years. The superintendent said that the matter would be referred to the school board.

On Thursday night, 950 patrons heard Barbara Johns, a junior and chairman of the student group, describe conditions which had led to the strike. W. Lester Banks, executive secretary of the Virginia Conference of Branches of the NAACP, who had been invited to the meeting by student leaders, outlined the present NAACP policy of seeking court action only toward the securing of full integration in public schools.

The student strike ended May 7. Principal M. Boyd Jones of R. R. Moton High School was fired from his position. Seeking to avert the dismissal of the principal, the parents made a formal request for a conference with the city-county school board (J&G June 30, 1951:1). (John Lancaster was also fired from his position as county agent. Luckily, he was able to get other jobs.) The parents were outspoken in their views that the impending dismissal of the principal is a retaliatory measure.

The NAACP lawyers filed suit on May 23, 1951, one month after the students had walked out of school. Thus began the case of Davis vs. County School Board of

Prince Edward County, Virginia, the only such case in a Southside rural area, and one of those decided by the United States Supreme Court on May 17, 1954 (Wilkerson 1969:269-270). Consolidated with four similar suits, it was destined to reach the U.S. Supreme Court as part of the historic Brown vs. The Board of Education of Topeka, Kansas.

Barbara's parents were scared that the whites might retaliate against their daughter, especially when a cross was burned on the yard of Robert Johns. When Vernon Johns heard the entire story, he was "tickled" by all the stir in his county (Smith, Bob 1965:75-76). Barbara returned with Uncle Vernon to Montgomery. Boyd Jones moved to Montgomery, too, to pursue his doctorate at Alabama State College. He promptly joined Mr. Johns' church.

Uncle Vernon drove Barbara to Montgomery in his green Buick (Branch 1988:22). He stopped on the side of the road to eat watermelon along with the cheese and milk he brought. This somewhat embarrassed Barbara. She also resented that her uncle did not mention her troubles at school.

March 9, 1952 the Lynchburg Branch of the NAACP held a mass meeting at Fifth Street Baptist Church. (J&G March 22, 1952:4) Guest speaker was the Rev. Leslie Francis Griffin, pastor of the First Baptist Church, Farmville, Virginia. He spoke on "The Wisdom of Dangerous and Reckless Living." (If that doesn't sound like a Vernon Johns type sermon we don't know what does.) Invocation was by the Reverend W. C. Butts, pastor of the Mt. Carmel Church. The purpose of the NAACP was given by the Rev. W. J. Hodge, pastor of the Diamond Hill Baptist Church, and president of the local branch.

Chapter thirty-seven

Montgomery the Latter years

Vernon Johns at Home:

Vernon Johns had started preaching in Montgomery, Alabama in 1948. This, however, did not stop him from frequently returning home to Darlington Heights.

In 1949 from Philadelphia the Rev. W. H. R. Powell family came to live in Farmville. His two sons were Henry and William. Henry Powell was born in Pittsburgh, but at two months of age the family moved to Philadelphia where his father became pastor of the Shiloh Baptist Church. Henry first learned of Vernon Johns when he attended a sermon given by Johns at his father's church. He remembered Johns saying that he had a family that included six children and they all lived on a farm that provided them with sufficient food and "almost enough" clothes. His father had wanted to send Henry away from Philadelphia and the troubles of the big city. Henry, living on campus, attended Virginia Seminary from 1941 to about 1945 (taking one year off). Henry then attended Virginia Union, graduating in 1950.

Shortly before his graduation from Virginia Union, Henry's father purchased a farm of 493 acres in Darlington Heights for $14,900 dollars. In the summer of 1949 Henry Powell's father and Vernon Johns attended a ministerial retreat and conference at Hampton Institute. Johns invited Reverend Powell down to his farm. While there, Rev. Powell immediately fell in love with a farm he saw for sale on the left side of Route 665 about a mile and a half west of Vernon's farm. He decided to buy the place. Rev. Powell set up a Bible camp there for summer residents, but it was never very successful. He should have involved people closer to Farmville, said his son William (William Powell interview). The farm had eighteen head of cattle and forty hogs, and they raised wheat and corn.

William Powell Jr. still has a pamphlet from the Seventh Annual Hol-Reba Bible Conference held August 6-18, 1963. The farmhouse pictured on the front of the brochure had a colourful awning over its porch was set on a wide lawn and looked very bucolic. There was a colourful awning over a porch. The address was Box 56, Cullen, Prince Edward County, Virginia. The programme offered a number of programs by different religious speakers on various parts of the Bible. W. H. R. Powell, Jr. was one of the devotional leaders. Lodging was $2 dollars a day, while board (of three meals) was only $3 dollars. The entire cost of a week at the conference was only $35.

We owe a lot of this information to Henry W. Powell (1995:9). He had a very special relationship with Vernon Johns. Johns was mentor, advisor, and confidant to Powell. Powell even came to think of Johns as a surrogate father. So, Powell got a special look into the life of Vernon Johns. Powell remembers Johns as being a gifted raconteur with a good sense of humour and a wide range of stories of unusual experiences and encounters (many of these engineered by Johns no doubt). Vernon was dividing his time between Montgomery and Farmville. Henry Powell estimated that Vernon may have even spent two weeks a month in Farmville during this period.

For about three years after graduation from Virginia Union Henry Powell worked on the farm in Darlington Heights where they grew tobacco, corn, and wheat. He did not like farm work very much, especially hating the terrible heat and the itching: "I couldn't wait to get into the shower after work." So, it is not surprising that Henry became a fifth-grade teacher. He taught in Farmville from 1956 to 1959 (when Prince Edward County closed its schools to prevent school integration).

He had quite a few neighbours including John Roebuck and his mother, Mrs. Hamilton, along with the Wheelers, the Berkeleys, and the Watkins. Henry always felt somewhat of an outsider in Darlington Heights for those in the small town considered him so. He also did not care much for the gossipy nature of the small town. One neighbour in particular was extremely nosey. Tiring of being constantly grilled about his private affairs, one-day Henry told the gossipy neighbour a tale about his brother, William. He said that William had gone crazy and that they had to take him to the hospital in Petersburg. Henry completely forgot about the incident, but it was to produce some ludicrous results. His brother came to him one day and said that when he was driving into Farmville, he passed two of the ladies of the neighbourhood who, upon seeing William, jumped into the bushes. William had also noticed that when he entered Vernon Johns' store, Anita Spencer (Tracy Spencer's wife), who ran the store, acted as if she was scared to death of him. Henry finally had to explain to William the ultimate cause of all this sudden fear.

Henry liked to hang out over at Hampden-Sydney College. One day some of the guys pledging in the fraternity told Henry that they had heard that he lived on a farm and also told him that they were in need of some ducks and pigs. Henry said that he could supply them with the pigs, but that they would have to go over to the two ponds on Vernon Johns' property to get the ducks. The fraternity pledges drove there and waded in the cold water to capture five or six ducks. The pledges later dyed the ducks and the pigs different colours. They then returned the pigs and ducks to their original owners. Henry forgot about the incident until one day Robert Johns,

Vernon's brother, came rushing up to him saying "Henry, you've got to come out with me to Vernon's place. There are ducks out there of all different colours." Robert explained that at first he saw this blood red duck, followed next by a blue one, and then an orange one. "Come on. You have got to see this!" Henry could barely contain himself. He told Robert he could not accompany him to Vernon's place. As far as Henry knows, Robert never found out what had really happened.

One day Henry Powell (1995:4) drove Vernon to Hampden-Sydney College where Vernon was to pick up some mail. While waiting for Vernon, Henry decided to enter a local store. Upon leaving the store, he found Vernon Johns surrounded by students for whom he was translating from Latin a plaque mounted on one of the buildings. "The expressions on the faces of the students showed surprise, and fascinated interest. Here was this black man in rough farm garb translating Latin. They both had a good laugh about the incident on the way home."

Vernon Johns' Last Stand in Montgomery:

When Vernon and Barbara Johns arrived in Montgomery, Jeanne Johns was the only year-round child in Montgomery. The others had gone off to college, Adelaide at 16 and Enid at 15. Jeanne said, "We all got full scholarships, so they did not have to pay for our education." She said of Barbara Johns: "She had fire in her too. She enjoyed the visit probably because youngest people enjoy the city (Montgomery) as compared to the country (Darlington Heights)."

Mrs. Altona Johns was honoured at a reception held in the lovely residence of Professor and Mrs. C. T. Smiley sponsored by the ladies of the Dexter Avenue Baptist Church. The affair was in celebration of Mrs. Johns having recently been awarded the M.A. degree in piano education by Teachers College of Columbia University the previous summer. (J&G October 27, 1951:3) There were one hundred guests which included members of the church, the Delta Sigma Theta Sorority, and the Anna M. Duncan Club, organizations with which Mrs. Johns was affiliated. In the receiving line were Professor and Mrs. Smiley, Dr. and Mrs. Johns, Professor T. H. Randall, Mrs. W. J. Reynolds, Miss Marguerite Moore, Dr. W. D. Pettus, C. C. Beverly, Robert D. Nesbitt, and Miss Olivette Dean. Julius Carroll, acting chairman of the music department of Alabama State College, where Mrs. Johns was a professor of piano, lauded her ability as a musician and her efficiency as a teacher. Miss Evelyn Wysinger presented the honouree with a lovely set of Eisenberg jewellery with pin and earring in the shape of the G-cleft. Other gifts were presented, including a cash token.

Vernon Johns continued with his economic message. He would refer to the congregation as a pack of educated fools because they produced nothing. And since they produced nothing, they were just consumers. And this made them nothing better than parasites. He (Chung 1989) would say "As far as I'm concerned, I will provide you with anything except whiskey and contraceptives." He would also hold up vegetables for all the congregation to see. "Now just to show you what can be produced on a small piece of land. I grew this in the back of the parsonage, and I left the roots on to prove that they are not store bought."

On the television program "Saturday Night with Connie Chung" (1989) Nesbitt said, "It wasn't nothing for Vernon Johns to bring stockings into church to sell." The program had a scene in which Nesbitt passed Vernon Johns on the street. Johns said "Deacon, can I sell you a fish?" Nesbitt replied, "Dr. Johns, don't you think that fish mongering is an undignified undertaking for a minister of the gospel?" Johns retorted "Deacon, do you think carpentry was an undignified undertaking for the saviour?"

One day Vernon Johns asked Dr. Sutherland (interview with the authors). "Why do you think the lord would tell me to get out of Alabama?" Evidently, Johns had a dream. Johns saw himself leaving Montgomery. They discussed the difference between a prophet and a pastor. Dr. Sutherland said that unlike the pastor, the prophet does not merge with his community. Asked if Johns saw himself as a prophet, Dr. Sutherland said "He didn't say it, but he acted it." He added that Johns was not a man to brag about himself. He didn't put himself into his sermons.

Taylor Branch (1988) writes that the last straw had come when Vernon Johns and Rufus Lewis drove onto the campus of Alabama State College with a truckload of watermelons. He says this really upset the women in particular. The deacons called Johns in, and Vernon walked out. Nesbitt later carried out his duty by informing Johns that the board of deacons had recommended that the church accept this latest resignation, his fifth. In a tense meeting, the Dexter congregation agreed by majority vote.

During an interview with Garnell Stamps and Lee Greene, Henry Powell asked "Do you know what his final words were?" Powell said that at Vernon Johns' last appearance before the congregation someone asked him: "Rev. Johns this is your last Sunday with us and we were wondering if you had something you would like to say." The controversial minister said "Yes, I believe there is something. " He stood up and said "Kiss my ass."

Garnel Stamps asked Alton Morton "Did you ever hear him (Johns) say anything about that church in Montgomery?" "He told me everything." "What did he say?" "He said the people there did not back him. He had a vision that things were going to happen, but the congregation was not with him."

Abernathy (1989) reported that Johns was stunned by the acceptance of his resignation. He decided to stay and fight for reinstatement. Altona resigned her position at Alabama State and left for Virginia State. Now alone Johns would often come over to the Abernathy's house, especially when the board turned off the electricity and gas at the parsonage. For a while he used the stove to cook his meals, burning back copies of the New York Times and the Washington Post, to which he subscribed and had saved for years. He wore two and three sweaters to bed and several pairs of socks, but he still shivered all night. He finally left Montgomery.

A few weeks later, he wrote Abernathy that he had been invited to speak at Religious Emphasis Week at Dillard University in New Orleans and would like to stay with Ralph and Juanita on Saturday night and preach at the First Baptist Church of Montgomery on Sunday of the next week.

If whites wanted to keep their social distance from blacks, middle class blacks wanted to keep their distance from lower class blacks. Johns constantly railed against class inequality among blacks. Johns' selling farm produce on the street scandalized the Dexter congregation. In this class conflict, Johns sided with the less privileged, hoping to get the more privileged to help set up businesses among the black community.

One of the class conflicts within the black community came over the playing of black spirituals. Dexter did not allow spirituals (Branch 1988:11). Johns loved Negro spirituals, such as "Go Down, Moses," "We'll Soon Be Free," and "I Got Shoes." He tried to schedule spirituals at numerous planning meetings, only to be told that it was "not done at Dexter." He tried to get the church organist, Edna King, to begin the spirituals, but she refused. He responded with lectures on the important differences between dignity, pride and vanity.

Another example of the upper-class attitude of the church was provided by Jeanne Johns Adkins (1993): "And once when my father preached, some lady shouted, and an usher went up to her and she said that she had shouted because she had been moved by what my father had said. He said 'Yes, but you don't get moved at Dexter.'"

Contrary to the desire of middle-class blacks, Johns constantly preached that blacks could work together to improve their lives (Yeakey 1979:101). He wanted blacks to be more independent of the whites. He said it was almost criminally short-sighted for educated Negroes to cling to titles and symbolic niches instead of building an economic base from which to deal more equally with whites as well as among themselves (Branch 1988:16). He tried to organize a cooperative food store in the Mobile Heights area in the southern part of Montgomery, but there was not enough community support and it failed. Many people lost money. He also tried to start a shoe store and sold fish in the basement of the church (Yeakey 1979:105).

Coretta Scott King (1969:95-96) related a story about Vernon Johns that her husband often told. She wrote that "Martin was a wonderful mimic, and when he would tell this story, you could just hear Dr. Johns' thick Virginia drawl." The story went thusly: "One-time Dr. Johns was performing a very staid and elegant wedding ceremony for one of the most outstanding Negro families in Montgomery. The church wedding had been proceeding, but just before the marriage was final, the minister stopped. He peered up and said, 'I would like to announce that right after the wedding there will be a watermelon cutting in the church basement. It will be twenty-five cents a slice, and for all you economical-minded people who order half a melon, the price will be a dollar fifty.' Then, without stopping for a minute, Dr. Johns continued, 'I now pronounce you man and wife.'

Taylor Branch (1988) makes a great deal of Vernon Johns' unorthodox selling methods and their impact on the congregation. The sermons attacking the authorities and the blacks themselves were one thing, but this was compounded by Johns' continued efforts at selling produce. But the authors would remind the reader of a saying often heard in relation to job employment: "If they like you, they will forgive every sin and keep you; if they don't like you, they will find every fault and fire you." It was much easier for the congregation to say they fired Johns because of his unorthodox habits rather than his preaching message. One of the worst sins for a social scientist to commit is to take as truth what his subjects say. The reference to the unorthodox social acts were largely rationalizations for the fact that Vernon Johns assaulted the professionals' and academics' sense of self. Johns challenged the social structure in which they led comfortable lives. He told them what was unforgivable: that they were not as smart as they thought and that they were cooperating with segregation. Johns would have eventually been fired even if he never committed any unorthodox social acts. The white community would have kept increasing the pressure on the black congregation until Johns would have had to go. But it is much easier to refer to his social behaviour than to his message as the real reason for his being let go from the congregation.

2) uncouth

On the television program Saturday Night with Connie Chung (1989), Andrew Young reported the story of a prominent family in the congregation of Dexter Avenue Baptist Church whose son was murdered. Vernon Johns felt that the son didn't amount to anything, never went to church, and hence did not deserve a funeral service in the church itself. The family persisted and the deacons forced Vernon Johns to have a service in the church. Andrew Young reported that on the day of the ceremony, Johns marched to the pulpit and quickly said "So and so lived a trifling and worthless life. He went around Montgomery daring someone to cut his throat. saturday night somebody obliged him. He lived like a dog; he died like a dog. Undertaker claim the body." Finished, Johns immediately turned around and left.

Vernon Johns was by temperament somewhat socially insensitive, but he was also deliberately insensitive as a way of fighting class prejudice in the black community. The charge of Johns being uncouth and socially insensitive is also related to class conflict within the black community. To the black middle class congregation (Yeakey 1979:109&110) "He seemed uncouth and backward, dressed poorly and seemed to care little for style and fashion." He would think nothing of walking into distinguished assemblies wearing mismatched socks, with farm mud on his shoes. In some respects, he appeared to"mock their stuck-up, affected self-images." Many thought he behaved eccentrically and acted beneath them.

This characteristic of Johns actually makes him more endearing as a prophet. Henry Powell often said that Vernon Johns was a regular guy with whom anyone could talk. He was not snobbish as were many of the black middle class. Powell says that Vernon Johns just did not care about material things. For instance, one-day Henry saw Vernon Johns at the store. Vernon told Henry that he just laid out $175 dollars for a new suit in order to attend some fancy ceremony. And $175 dollars in those days was a considerable amount. But two days after purchasing the suit, here was Vernon Johns in the pants of that expensive suit working in a muddy ditch. Henry reiterated that Vernon did this because he placed such little value on material things.

His sermons were often too "earthy" for his congregations (Yeakey 1979:110). In the early 1950s at Luther Foster's inauguration at Tuskegee as president of the school, Johns remarked that "When my grandfather was hanged for cutting his master in two with a scythe, they asked him on the gallows if he had anything to say. He said yes 'I'm just sorry I didn't do it thirty years before' and they dropped the trapdoor."

Bob Smith (1965:78) reported that Vernon Johns was not beyond changing a story a bit to make his point more forceful. For instance, after the Farmville school strike he told the slavery-day story of the white master whose slave turned on him in the fields and beheaded him with a scythe. According to the way Mr. Johns told the story, it all happened quite near the location of the old Moton High School.

Yeakey (1979:107, 108,110) says that Johns was curt and abrasive, always direct and to the point. "Whatever came into his mind he said it." "His ways drove people away, forced others to view him as a little crazy, and kept the few with whom he had to deal with regularly in constant contention with him." Moreover, "No one could predict what to expect from Vernon Johns when he went into the pulpit. He might say anything." But Yeakey does not understand the prophet. If only the prophet were not abrasive, so the saying goes. But then the prophet would not be a prophet.

Many authors seem to want to dismiss Johns' life by calling him an eccentric; that he would have been effective "if only" he was not so eccentric. Nobody would have been effective in Vernon Johns' day. Certainly not Martin Luther King, Jr. who was a relatively run-of- the-mill pastor before Rosa Parks and the Montgomery Bus Boycott. King would never have spoken out like Vernon Johns did. And wouldn't you have to be a little crazy to speak out in a Jim Crow society where not only the whites were telling you to shut up, but the blacks also?

3) social bluntness

Powell (1995:5) acknowledges that Vernon Johns was known for his social bluntness. He went to a church in Washington D.C. or Richmond where they said they would not pay him a fee for preaching but would pay for all his expenses. But no one met him when he arrived. Johns had to pay for his room and board and the taxi fare to the church. He told an officer of the church that he wanted to be paid. "Well, what will you do if we don't pay you?" "I will take you to court for breach of contract. Pay me now or pay me in court." Then he told the entire congregation off: "You thought that I wanted to be pastor of this fine, old church, and you thought that I wanted to live in your beautiful parsonage, and you thought that I wanted to bring my "amily here so that my children could go to the up-to-date schools in your city, rather than to the rude country schools where we live. You thought I wanted all these things so badly that I was going to submit to your dishonesty. If what we've seen here is indicative of the spirit of this church, then you are no different from the man who lurks in the alley waiting for someone to rob. There is no difference in intent, just in method." Needless to say, they never called him again.

Vernon Johns was riding the bus one day and noticed the terrible conditions of the "colored" area (Powell 1995:19). He went up to the bus driver and said, "Isn't separate but equal the damndest lie ever spawned in hell?" The driver evaded Johns by saying he was not responsible for the policy. Then Johns went to the manager of the station and repeated his question. The manager quickly took his leave of Johns.

When entering the post office in Farmville, a white man (Powell 1995:15-16) asked him "Say, do you know nigger so and so?" Vernon Johns said "I cursed him completely, told him about his miserable gutter origins, about the low lifestyle and revolting habits of the misbegotten clan that whelped him. I cussed him 'till leaves trembled on the trees and the sun shook in the heavens." The man turned out to be the mayor of Farmville. But even if Johns had known this, he still would have said the same to him.

Johns (Powell 1995:15) often used arrogance to counteract condescension. When he spoke at a program in Ohio where the main speaker was Senator Robert Taft, the hostess in a condescending tone asked, "In what order would you like to be presented?" Vernon responded "Oh, just put me wherever you want the best speech." Senator Taft was told of this and after the program he came up to Johns, shook his hand, and told Johns that he had indeed given the best speech.

4) bad temper and potential violence

Yeakey (1979:106) complained that Johns was very short tempered and would simply not tolerate simpleminded foolishness or allow an injustice to go unchallenged. Powell (1995:26) admitted Johns' short fuse and bad temper were legendary. Even his own parishioners were afraid to attack him directly because of his legendary temper.

That Johns was not a pacifist is related by the following tale (Boddie 1972:66). Johns was riding a slow train through Arkansas. The train stopped for refreshments. To a young white boy serving as a vendor, he shouted "Come here, boy." As the boy approached Johns a white man called to the boy, and he diverted towards the white man. Johns bellowed "Come here, boy" so loudly that it frightened the boy and he turned and went towards Johns. This so maddened the white man that he menacingly approached Johns. Johns, however, brought the man up short with the determined words: "Just crease your lips, and your brains will be mingled with the gravel!" Back in Montgomery, the absent-minded Johns drove through a red light and was apprehended. Appearing before the judge, Johns discovered him to be that white man from the Arkansas train platform.

Powell (1995:17-18) said that Vernon's wife was involved in an automobile accident in Farmville. They went to court. In court the lawyer referred to his wife by her first name "Altona." Vernon Johns roared from his seat in the audience "Don't you call my wife Altona. Her name to you is Mrs. Johns." After a short while the lawyer repeated "Altona" again. Vernon Johns jumped up brandishing a chair and advancing on the lawyer. "I told you not to call my wife Altona, and if you call her that again, I'll break your ne"k." A female lawyer replaced the male lawyer, and she was courteous during the rem"inder of the court session.

Jean Johns Adkins (1997 interview) says that her father was so bodacious that he scared white people. This is related to the traditional Southern fear of the "crazy Negro" (Dollard 1949:294). "The attitude seemed to be that they are enough to be feared when they are officially sane; when they are proved insane, special caution must be used."

Vernon Johns (Powell 1995:28) did not rule out violence. He taught the philosophy of "Fight back!" "One sensed that violence simmered in him, just below the surface."

5) too militant

Yeakey (1979:108&110) found that many in the Dexter Avenue congregation thought Johns put too much emphasis on the fight for civil rights for blacks. Some of the comments of the congregation were "We did not want to do those things he campaigned for; we were afraid of being criticized" and "He seemed too militant." They were scared and too adjusted to the system of segregation. What they were afraid of and thus did not want to do, they XXXrocessXXX "militant." It is amazing how thoroughly blacks become adjusted to the system of segregation and fail to support those who challenge the system (rather than merely take a radical-liberal or socialist approach within the system of segregation).

The only legitimate complaint against Vernon Johns was that he wrote very little, relying too heavily on the spoken word. Johns was a maverick who seldom wrote anything down. This made it harder for him to get his message across and harder for researchers to use his words in a recreation of his story. The tragedy is that he did not fully recognize his own role as prophet.

How Did Johns Cope with Rejection?

Why have we not heard more of Vernon Johns before? Why is Vernon Johns, even though he has had a television program and a movie done on his life, still an obscure figure? Henry W. Powell (1995:1) said that Vernon Johns laboured by choice in a self-imposed obscurity. He cared little for the plaudits of the crowd. Certainly, he understood the fickle, transient nature of public approval, and quite properly, he mistrusted it. He preferred a background role and anonymity to public acclaim.

There is no question that Johns was a tough cookie. He had a natural ability to be socially insensitive to people individually, at the same time, caring mightily for them as a group. This actually is a characteristic of many American politicians, including many presidents of the nations. Men like Calvin Coolidge and Richard Nixon were terribly difficult to talk to on a one-to-one basis, but they were absolutely at home with many people.

But we should not confuse a defensive attitude as an innate one. There is a good deal of isolation forced on the prophet, as almost everyone rejects the message in ways that are often harsh and nasty. This social rejection of the prophet is accompanied by a good deal of resentment and anger on the part of the prophet.

A prophet cannot be indifferent to the fate of his message. If he is being ignored, his message is also being ignored and that is unacceptable to the prophet. Indeed, it is the responsibility of the prophet to get the message out. It would be irresponsible for a prophet to take a background role. The prophet knows that he himself is not that important compared to the message. The message is everything and it has to be delivered no matter what it takes to get it out to the larger public.

Part of Johns' way of coping with rejection was that he had an amazing ability to close his mind on the problems of his past. This is seen in his sermon "What to do with What is Left" given as the closing sermon commemorating the eighty-third anniversary celebration of Montgomery, Alabama's First Baptist Church (colored) given Sunday at 7 p.m. July 30, 1950 (Bratcher 1950). It is a wonderful sermon that inspires one to go forward despite one's past, rather good, or bad.

Johns takes as his text the phrase "Strengthen the things that remain" from Revelation 3:2. He starts the sermon talking about some of the most general losses that individuals experience. These include the loss of goods, of time, of golden opportunities, and character. "But to stop with a review of our losses would be false to the text! It is to what is left that the text directs." He then gives many examples from sources such as the Bible and the Napoleonic Wars w"ere people accomplished wondrous things after seeming defeat. And they did so by focusing on the task at hand and not on the past.

"Let that which is lost become unimportant, lest the lost past causes us to lose also the present and future. 'Forgetting the things that are behind, I press forward to the mark.' It is tragic to lose what we yet may be by becoming engrossed either in how good we were or how bad we were as long as we are alive, we have something potentially significant left if we realize it. With all our material losses, our loss of time and opportunity and character we have something left. While life remains, we still have time." "There are instances of success where, but little remained. What wonders may be possible for this church to which so much is left" (Bratcher 1950:112-113). This is theXXXrocessXXXe that is needed if one is to be a prophet a single-minded devotedness to persevere against resistance from others.

Influence on Others:

The dismissal of a fighter for civil rights does not mean that a failure has occurred. Vernon Johns had a great influence on the black community of Montgomery. Yeakey (1979:110-111) was very critical of Johns, but even he admits "Regardless of his problems with the church, he did raise the congregation's political consciousness."

We will discuss his influence on Martin Luther King, Jr. in the next chapter. But there were several other prominent people that Johns affected including the Rev. Ralph Abernathy and several women of Montgomery.

Ralph Abernathy (1989:114-115) was drafted into the army in 1944 at the age of eighteen. By the time he got to Le Havre, France the war with Germany was almost over. He did arrive in time, however, to see the utter devastation of many of the German cities. Back in the United States, he attended and graduated from Alabama State University. He accepted a position at First Baptist Church, Montgomery. He talked about the differences between the old and new guard in Montgomery. The old guard were primarily preachers of the Gospel of "other worldliness." There would be equality after you died and were in heaven, but not on earth. They felt the idea of desegregation was either frivolous or threatening. They preached strict adherence to the law. They had a good relationship with the white leaders, and they did not want this threatened. These white leaders occasionally gave them minor posts of honour in the community. Behind doors they would denounce the whites, but in public they would say nothing controversial. The new guard consisted some of the younger preachers who wanted to do something about civil rights.

Consistent with Abernathy's comments on the old guard, this other-worldly emphasis seems always to be present. In a study of black clergymen in the 1920s Mays and Nicholson (1933:59, 122-123, 249) found that of the 100 sermons, 26 dealt with concrete life situations or were what may be called practical; and in a few instances they had social implications such as the relating of religion to the economic, racial, and international aspects of life; fifty-four were predominantly other-worldly; the other twenty were highly doctrinal or theological. Rural messages are more uniformly other-worldly. In a study of the activities of 609 urban churches, there were no events of an activist nature, although 590 engaged in poor relief.

Abernathy says one of the older pastors who agreed with the younger generation was Vernon Johns. When Abernathy assumed the pulpit of First Baptist Church, Johns became Abernathy's closest friend among the other Montgomery pastors. Abernathy referred to Johns as a "genius in the pulpit." Abernathy said he had first seen Johns in 1951 while Abernathy was a student at Atlanta University. Johns had been chosen by all-male Morehouse College as their speaker for Religious Emphasis Week. Vernon Johns encouraged Abernathy who became a disciple. Abernathy saw a new generation of black men and women coming along. They stressed courage, justice, and equality.

Mary Fair Burks (1990), chairman of the English department at Alabama State College, began the Women's Political Caucus in 1951 in response to the refusal of the local white League of Women Voters to integrate. The caucus grew to a membership of nearly two hundred. She wrote that her inspiration was a Vernon Johns sermon given in 1946.

Burks (1990:81), who had attended graduate school at the University of Michigan, became a faculty member at Alabama State College. She had suffered a terrible experience in Montgomery. After being cursed out by a white woman for coming too close to the higher caste member in her car, then being very roughly treated and arrested by the police. She wanted to do something about segregation. "But where to start?" She relates that she had no idea until Vernon Johns in 1946 mounted one of "his scathing attacks on the complacency of his affluent membership." Most of the members, she said, wore "masks of indifference or scorn" in reaction to his sermon.

Burks (1990:71) said that a trailblazer according to the dictionary is a pioneer in a field of endeavours, while a torchbearer indicates one who follows the trailblazer, imparting tested knowledge or truth provided originally by the pioneer in its rudimentary form. "Rosa Parks, Jo Anne Robinson, and members of the Women's

Political Council were trailblazers. Martin Luther King, Jr., was a torchbearer." But, of course, the greatest of the trail blazers was Vernon Johns. (This statement is a little too harsh toward Dr. King, but it does point out some of the difference between the prophet and the strategist.)

The Women's Political caucus benefited from the slight di"ferential in forbearance shown by Southern whites in their dealings with black women as opposed to black men (Lewis 1970: 49). The organization took the initiative in demanding fairer treatment for the city's black citizens. A handful of courageous men, such as Attorney Gray, Mr. Nixon, and Professor James Pierce, collaborated with the Council. This group had succeeded by 1955 in pressuring the white merchants to negotiate out of existence the separation of drinking fountains and the custom of not supplying titles of Mrs. and Miss when billing female customers.

A key member of the Women's Political caucus was Jo Ann Robinson, an English professor at Alabama State College (Parks 1992:110). Over the years she had her share of run-ins with bus drivers, but at first, she couldn't get the other women in the Council to get indignant. She was from Cleveland, Ohio, while most of the other members were natives of Montgomery. When she complained about the rudeness of the bus drivers, they said that was a fact of life in Montgomery. Later she often brought protests to the bus company on behalf of the Women's Political Council. Finally, she managed to get the company to agree that the buses would stop at every corner in black neighbourhoods, just as they did in the white neighbourhoods. But this was a very small victory. One of the other tasks that the Women's Political Caucus tried to accomplish was the opening of the parks to blacks. The only concession they won was permission for blacks to walk through the white parks on their way to work for the whites.

Another person active in the civil rights movement that Johns affected was Rufus Lewis. On the television program "Saturday Night with Connie Chung" (1989), Rufus Lewis said about Johns "If he had courage, it kind of gave you some courage too. So you were helped by his courage. It increased yours if you had any. And if you didn't have any, he'd give you a little."

Chapter thirty-eight

Vernon Johns and Martin Luther King Jr.

The Rev. Vernon Johns, of Montgomery, Alabama, and Miss Estell Thomas, dean of Women of Hampton Institute, were two of the speakers at the Homecoming and Farmers Day grandstand programs of the popular Suffolk Fair of October 21- 24, 1952. (J&G, October 18, 1952:3) The paper said that Johns is "well known in this state. He is a forceful speaker".

After Vernon was forced out at the Dexter Avenue Baptist Church in 1952, Altona Johns went to Virginia State University to be on the faculty of the Music Education Department. She had an A.B. from Atlanta University and an M.A. from Teacher's College, Columbia University, New York in musical education.

Virginia State University in Petersburg, Virginia is located in Chesterfield County in the town of Ettrick near Petersburg. Today it has around 1,300 men and 1,800 women students for an enrolment of around 3,000 students, 93% of whom are black. It has six undergraduate schools and one graduate school. The campus consists of 625 acres with fifty-two buildings in a suburban area twenty-five miles south of Richmond.

In the 1940s, the WPA guide (WPA 1940:282) noted that the Virginia State College for Negroes, located at the north end of Campbell's Bridge, covers 300 elevated acres above the Appomattox River. On the campus of thirty-seven acres are thirty-one brick buildings; the rest of the land is an experimental farm. Established in 1882 as the Virginia Normal and Collegiate Institute, it was created largely through the activities of public-spirited Negroes, particularly A. W. Harris, of Petersburg, who introduced the bill to establish the institution. Inadequate state support long retarded its progress. In 1902 the name was changed to Virginia Normal and Industrial Institute, and in 1920 the institute was made the Negro land-grant college of Virginia. The college steadily increased its enrolment and the standard of its twenty-three courses of instruction, which included liberal arts, agriculture, manual crafts, and a department of education. In 1930 the name of the institution was changed by the legislature to Virginia State College for Negroes. Enrolment in 1937-38 was 1,005, of which 576 were women.

John Manuel Gandy (1870-1947) was the third president of Virginia State College (Logan and Winston 1982:249-251). He was born in Mississippi to freed slaves and tenant farmers. He attended Jackson College 1886-1888 and went to Oberlin Academy in 1892. In 1898 he received a B.A. from Fisk in Nashville, followed by an M.A. In that same year he became a professor of Greek and Latin at the Virginia Normal and Collegiate Institute at Petersburg. He became the president in 1914, replacing James Hugo Johnston. In 1917 he married Carrie Senora Brown. Gandy Hall is named for him. He was friends with Booker T. Washington, R. R. Moton, Mary McLeod Bethune, Mary Church Terrell, E. R. Embree of the Rosenwald Fund, Jackson Davis of the General Education Board, and Maggie L. Walker.

After Johns re-joined his wife in Petersburg, he continued to go back and forth to his farm in Darlington Heights. One day Vernon came to Henry Powell (1995:18-19) and asked him to drive with him down to Montgomery to pick up Altona's grand piano that had been left behind. At that time Powell was afraid to drive with Vernon through the deep south. Given Vernon's temperament, wrote Henry, any situation could develop into a life-threatening predicament. Johns carried a loaded double-barrelled shotgun with him whenever he drove. At this time, he drove a white Mercury. Johns was not afraid of anything. He once said "We must not fear dying. There's a lot of things worse than dying, and one of them is being alive when you should be dead!" Luckily perhaps for Henry, he did not have to make that trip.

King (1958:38-39) wrote that in 1953 a few enterprising individuals came together under Johns' influence, and organized Farm and City Enterprises "A cooperative supermarket which has today developed into a thriving business. This was a tour de force in a community that had generally been abysmally slow to move."

Also, in 1953 Vernon Johns performed the marriage ceremony of his niece, Barbara Johns, to William H. R. Powell, Jr. He commented that the uniting of the Johns and Powell families would undoubtedly spell trouble for others. The couple had met in 1950. Powell took his new bride away from Darlington Heights to Philadelphia. She was to have six children in all and earn her M.S. in library science from Drexel, just north of the University of Pennsylvania in Philadelphia. Barbara was a school librarian for some twenty-two years and never became re-involved in politics. Her husband said she never thought what she did was that big of a deal, but that authors and reporters never let her forget as they periodically would contact her for her comments.

Back in Virginia, Johns started another cooperative economic venture. In Prince Edward County Rev. Johns in 1954 began to raise livestock. A 100-acre piece of land was deeded (Prince Edward County Courthouse) dated to October 1, 1954, to Virginia Farm and City Enterprises, Inc.

Vernon Johns came down to Norfolk, Virginia to speak at Dr. Sutherland's church there. Dr. Sutherland let Vernon be the orator of the day. He let Johns speak on his Farm and City Enterprises. He said Johns had worked on an economic cooperative in Alabama but couldn't get it started as he wanted it. He said quite a few of the pastors in Virginia let him present his economic proposition. He said Johns had a plan to sell farm goods directly to the consumer, cutting out the middleman.

At this time, he met and influenced a man that proved to be important to Martin Luther King, Jr. and the civil rights movement. Wyatt Tee Walker. Walker was born in 1929 in Brockton, Massachusetts. He received a B.S. (magna cum laude) from Virginia Union University in Richmond in 1950 and a Mdiv (summa cum laude) 1953. For eight years, 1953 to 1960, he was pastor of Historic Gilfield Baptist Church in Petersburg. Walker worked with Johns on the cooperative venture in Farmville. Walker was president of the NAACP of Virginia for five years. He was also state director of CORE, a national board member of the SCLC, and a trustee of Virginia Seminary. Later he would become chief of staff for Martin Luther King, Jr. He is now minister at Canaan Baptist Church, New York City.

Vernon Johns and the Virginia Farm and City Enterprises were sued by Leslie Davenport (1888-1970) for several trespasses of animals on his property. In September 1955 he recorded the possibility that he might be a creditor of Johns' assets if he won the pending case (Prince Edward County Courthouse).

A deed dated September 28, 1959 (Prince Edward County Courthouse) appointed James A. Overton liquidating receiver for the Virginia Farm and City Enterprise, Inc., a Virginia corporation. It dissolved the corporation by operation of law and Overton became empowered by the said order to sell, convey, and dispose of all or any parts of the assets of the dissolved corporation. A parcel of land of 100 acres was sold for $8,000 dollars to F. J. Boddie, the highest bid. The land had been given over to the Virginia Farm and City Enterprises as of October 1, 1954.

Sometime between 1950 and 1954 Dr. M. C. Sutherland (known as "Mac") (interview November 3, 1997), president of Virginia Seminary from 1966 to 1980, XXXrocessXXXs with Vernon Johns from Lynchburg, Virginia to Oberlin College where Johns was to give the annual alumni address. On Sunday Johns preached at the Rivermont in Lynchburg and Monday morning they took off for Ohio before having any breakfast. They decided to eat breakfast at Natural Bridge. They arrived at Natural Bridge around 8 or 9 a.m. Entering the restaurant the host had the two ministers follow him through the dining room to another dining area where the restaurant workers ate. They sat down in this secondary dining room. Dr. Sutherland didn't think anything about it. But Vernon Johns seemed perturbed. The waiter took their food order and then Johns took the pencil from the waiter and wrote a note on the back of the order form. The note asked the management if the cost of the meal was going to be adjusted for the convenience that they failed to get in service. The waiter asked Johns: "What should I do with this?" Johns replied, "Give it to the manager!" They brought the food. Dr. Johns said "Brother Sutherland, I cannot eat under these conditions. It disrupts me too much." He just couldn't eat he said. After a while the waiter came back with some written reply on the same piece of paper and left. Dr. Johns read it. He said to Dr. Sutherland "I just can't do it." And he went out to the car. What happened at breakfast, however, did not disrupt his thinking. He did not mention the incident again, but rather said to Dr. Sutherland (I want to run through my talk with you." He said the entire rest of the journey they talked about homiletics. Mac Sutherland added: "Vernon Johns was a man who could go and let go. If you can let go, you will help yourself. If you can't let go, you will hurt yourself."

Virginia Hughes (interview November 5, 1997) kept in contact with the Johns family for a while. She would go to a flower show in Petersburg and would often see them when they lived off campus. It was a little house separate but right across from the campus. One time she gave Altona three or four pictures of the Johns children because Altona said that all her pictures had burned in the fire.

In the mid-1950s, probably around 1955, Henry W. Powell (1995:9-10) drove Vernon Johns to Virginia Seminary to give the commencement address. Being dressed in farm garb Henry asked him about his attire. Vernon had his suit in a brown paper bag and said that "When we get to town, I'm going to bathe and dress at a friend's house." And sure enough he showered and shaved and dressed at Anne Spencer's house. On the way back from the commencement, Vernon said "You know I just thought of something." "What's that?" asked Henry. "I'll bet you that in the history of American education, this was the first graduating class that was ever addressed by a speaker who didn't have any underwear on." He had forgotten to pack underwear in his bag.

In December 1953 Deacon Nesbitt of the Dexter Avenue Baptist Church told W.C. Peden that he was having trouble searching for a new pastor. He said it was very difficult to satisfy the Dexter members. Peden arranged for Nesbitt to meet Martin L. King, Jr. Who was this Martin Luther King, Jr.?

Martin Luther King, Jr. was from Atlanta, the black "Athens" of the South. There was Atlanta University, Spelman College for girls, Morris Brown University, Clark College, Gammon Theological Seminary, and Atlanta Baptist College (later Morehouse College). Atlanta was the world's largest centre for Negro education and the colleges occupied an important place in municipal life.

According to the Works Projects Administration (WPA 1942:5) book on the city of Atlanta, perhaps no other Southern city showed so great a divergence, not only economic but educational and social, in the condition of its black citizens. This was reflected in the difference between Decatur Street and Auburn Avenue.

The less fortunate groups were largely concentrated in western Atlanta. The poorer Negroes live squalidly amid ramshackle wooden shanties and rooming houses crowded with many families and the cries of little children. The most populous business thoroughfare was Decatur Street, running eastward between rows of pawnshops with crowded windows, restaurants emitting the sharp smell of frying fish, and clothing stores with suits and overcoats hung over ropes along the pavements.

Auburn Avenue was a far quieter Negro business district of decorous hotels and office buildings. There was evidence of still greater refinement along Ashby Street and in the vicinity of Atlanta University, where many of the more prosperous blacks maintained attractive homes. The university set and their friends maintained a good living standard for themselves.

The early elite in Atlanta, with but few exceptions, lived in the then fashionable Auburn Avenue section of Northeast Atlanta. They originated from the mostly mulatto house-servant group, who were in a few cases aided by whites with whom they maintained close relationships. As compared to the field hands, most seized the advantage to pull improve their situation. Life for the mulatto aristocracy of old Atlanta (circa 1890-1910) cantered primarily on the respectable First Congregational Church, select Atlanta University, and perhaps half a dozen exclusive social clubs. Many of the elite had themselves been educated at Congregationalist Atlanta University (or its affiliated grammar and secondary school) and ordinarily sent their children there to be prepared for teaching and other white-collar occupations. However, a minority, connected with the A.M.E. church, the Methodist church, North, and its affiliated Clark University, or with the Atlanta Baptist, were accorded recognition in the highest social circles. (Meier 1992:105-106)

Martin Luther King, Jr.'s father, Mike King, of the Ebenezer Baptist Church was more like most Black Southern preachers of the times than he was like Vernon Johns. He was practical, organized, and intensely loyal to his people. His talents were harmonious with the theme of the most popular religious book of the 1920s, The Man Nobody Knows (1925), by advertising executive Bruce Barton (Branch 1988:41). This book was the decade's most popular work on Jesus (Ahlstrom 1972:905). Barton gave the Man from Nazareth front rank among the world's business organizers. Not only was President Coolidge declaring that America's business was business, but many also expounded the religious corollary equating being rich with being good.

In 1942 Martin entered Booker T. Washington High School as a thirteen-year-old tenth-grader. King Jr. soon decided to follow his father into the ministry. On a word from Rev King, Sr., Martin was quickly ordained as a full-fledged minister and made assistant pastor of his father's church. He took his first pulpit oration from "Life Is What You Make It," a published sermon by Harry Emerson Fosdick of New York's Riverside Church.

King had his first frank discussions about race on the Morehouse campus in Atlanta. Many of the countless theories about racism emanated from the sociology department and King decided to prepare himself for a legal career by majoring in sociology. By the end of his junior year, however, he had given up talk of becoming a lawyer and was noncommittal when asked about his future.

In 1948 King went to Crozer Theological Seminary in Chester, Pennsylvania. Here was an atmosphere of unorthodox freethinking. He fell under the influence of the Social Gospel movement. One of his heroes was Walter Rauschenbusch, a German Lutheran-turned Baptist preacher of the Social Gospel.

During his last year at Crozer, Martin read Reinhold Niebuhr. It changed his fundamental outlook on religion. The Social Gospel lost a good deal of its glow for him almost overnight. More of a realist than the Social Gospel thinkers, Niebuhr said, among other things, that whites would not admit the black to equal rights if not forced to do so. During his Christmas holidays in 1949 Martin Luther King, Jr. devoted himself exclusively to a study of the works of Marx. Reverend Barbour (Lewis 1970:36) reported that Martin was "economically a Marxist."

In June 1951 Martin graduated from Crozer with the highest-grade average in his class. He delivered the valedictory address and was awarded the Pearl M. Plafker citation for the most outstanding student and the J. Lewis Crozer fellowship of

$1,300 for graduate study. He went on to graduate school in divinity at Boston University.

On June 18, 1953, Martin married Coretta Scott shortly before he completed his residential requirements for his doctorate. He still had to write his thesis. His goal was to be placed in a ministerial position by September 1954.

First Meeting with Johns

Through the intercession of T. M. Alexander, Sr., of Atlanta, a friend of the King family, Martin was invited to preach at the Dexter Avenue Baptist Church in Montgomery. Johns learned that Dexter Avenue Baptist Church was planning to invite Martin to deliver a guest sermon. Vernon would be compromising the sermon of King by offering competition to King because both sermons would be on the same day. Johns, however, decided to take advantage of the situation anyway. Vernon made travel arrangements and hitchhiked from Petersburg to Atlanta. Let off at the bus station, he called the father of the young preacher and asked if he could ride down to Montgomery with his son. So, Martin Luther King, Jr. chauffeured Johns from the Atlanta bus station to Ralph Abernathy's house.

At dinner the three men (Abernathy 1989:126) sat in the living room and talked about the oppression of their people and the growing belief that a sea of change was taking place. They all agreed that Brown v. the Board of Education had altered forever the conditions on which the continuing struggle would be predicated. "No longer was the law unambiguously on the side of Jim Crow. It now appeared as if the law was on our side, that the federal government might eventually be pressed into service in our fight for freedom."

Abernathy (1989:126&129) rejected the idea that the civil rights movement was just a converging of chances. Abernathy had been greatly influenced by Vernon Johns and when King came to Montgomery, Abernathy worked on making King more interested in civil rights. King and Abernathy would meet to talk about various projects. Together Abernathy and King planned to turn Montgomery into a model of social justice and racial amity. "Martin provided the philosophic framework for the whole plan and we both insisted that its implementation be completely and militantly nonviolent. Martin and I had thoroughly read and absorbed the teaching of Henry David Thoreau and Mahatma Gandhi on this subject we knew in general what had to be done."

There might be a little bit of exaggeration by hindsight, but Abernathy (1989:126) wrote that King "was forthcoming in his advocacy of an active program to force the issue and to bring about freedom more rapidly. He was, he said, committed to the preaching of a Social Gospel that would awaken the Christian churches and mobilize them in the fight against segregation. He indicated that he had been working on plans to do just that and when the time came to do battle, he hoped the churches would be ready." King said it would take several years before he could put his plans into action.

At the dinner, Johns advised King "If you take my church and a nigra named Randall is still there on the Board, you'd better be very careful." (Branch 1988:106)

On January 24, 1954, while King delivered a trial sermon at Dexter, Vernon Johns preached "Segregation After Death" at Ebenezer. (Carson :29 & 42) King preached "The Three Dimensions of a Complete Life." "As the pulpit committee shepherded him around the church he heard stories about Vernon Johns, "a militant guy,' who had exhorted the congregation like a 'whirlwind' to get involved in social issues. But people at Dexter were 'scared people' who tended to accept the racial status quo." (Oates 1982:48)

The pulpit committee asked King t' accept a'position at Dexter. King flew back to Boston. He pondered the question: Why take the job when he knew that by returning to the South he would be returning to segregation? King in his book wrote that "We had the feeling that something remarkable was unfolding in the South, and we wanted to be on hand to witness it."

Coretta Scott King (1969:95) wrote that "My husband and Ralph Abernathy could sit for hours swapping stories about this outspoken minister who always gave his middle-class congregation a very hard time. According to Martin, Dr. Johns' main purpose was to rock the complacency of the refined members of the Dexter Avenue Baptist Church in whatever way he could." Johns' influence on King was most evident at the level of ideas. "Martin was just fascinated with Vernon Johns," according to Philip Lenud, King's friend at Morehouse College and his roommate at Boston University, because "Johns was such a theological genius." King felt that Johns "was complex, heavy, and funny," and he and his friend Ralph Abernathy spent many hours exchanging humorous stories about how the outspoken Johns used to rock the complacency of the middle-class, refined members at Montgomery's Dexter Avenue Baptist Church. Much of the humour brought to King's preaching was inspired by Johns. (Baldwin 1991:299-300)

Martin Luther King Jr. (1956:38) praised Johns in his book on the Montgomery bus boycott, Stride Toward Freedom: The Montgomery Story. "Vernon Johns was a brilliant preacher with a creative mind and an incredibly retentive memory. A fearless man, he never allowed an injustice to come to his attention without speaking out against it. When he was still pastor, hardly a Sunday passed that he did not lash out against complacency. He often chided the congregation for sitting up so proudly with their many academic degrees, and yet lacking the very thing the degrees should confer, that is, self- respect. One of his basic theses was that any individual who submitted willingly to injustice did not really deserve more justice."

In May 1954 King preached his first regular sermon at Dexter. He commuted for the next four months from Boston to Montgomery and back. Martin was very young looking. His wife said that Professor Mary Fair Burks, of Alabama State College, came to Dexter with Jo Ann Robinson, who was also a professor at the college. When she saw Martin, Professor Burks said, "You mean that little boy is my pastor? He looks like he ought to be home with his mamma." At first she thought he could not possibly have anything to say that would interest her, but after hearing him preach she was deeply impressed. (King, Coretta Scott 1969:100)

In September 1954 King moved into the parsonage on Jackson Street. He wrote his doctoral thesis and preached. He also formed a Social and Political Action Committee. Among the members were Mrs. Jo Ann Robinson and Rufus Lewis. He joined the NAACP and made several speeches for them. Rosa Parks met Dr. King when he was guest speaker at an NAACP meeting. She said that Dr. King was new to Montgomery, and Dr. Abernathy had been trying to get him active in civil-rights work. King found that the NAACP was not doing too much. Before King's arrival in Montgomery, and for several years after, most of the local NAACP's energies and funds were devoted to the defence of Jeremiah Reeves, a drummer in a black band, who had been arrested at the age of sixteen, accused of raping a white woman. The case dragged on for a total of seven years before he was put to death in 1958.

Montgomery Bus Boycott

On May 17, 1954, two weeks after King's first sermon as pastor-designate of Dexter, Chief Justice Earl Warren handed down the Court's decision in the Brown case, without advance notice. This decision raised considerably the hopes of blacks for defeating Jim Crow segregation. (When Vernon Johns heard the news, he was riding in a car with Wyatt Tee Walker. Walker stopped the car and both men got out, sank down on their knees, and gave thanks in prayer for the Supreme Court decision.)

Within the eighteen months preceding Rosa Parks' famous bus ride, at least four other black citizens of Montgomery – Claudette Colvin, Mrs. Amelia Browder, a Mrs. Smith, and the Reverend Vernon Johns – had indicated their displeasure with the system when they, too, on separate occasions refused to obey an order to give up their seats to white passengers. (Taylor 1976:236) Be that as it may, on December 1, 1955, Rosa Parks left the Montgomery Fair Department store late in the afternoon for her regular bus ride home. The Montgomery bus boycott and the civil rights movement started when she refused to relinquish her seat and move to the back of the bus.

Concerning Rosa Parks, Vernon Johns told Alton Morton, "It's only a few people that you can find that can get a glimpse of what you can imagine what is going to happen. And Rosa Parks was one of those rare people who could catch a vision."

In June 1953 the black community of Baton Rouge began a mass boycott against segregated buses. The official leader of the boycott was the Reverend T. J. Jemison, pastor of Mt. Zion Baptist Church. He held a bachelor's and a master's degree from two black universities, Alabama State and Virginia Union. Jemison was a "newcomer" to the city, and this was important as he was not associated with any of the factions in the community. The impact of the mass bus boycott went beyond Baton Rouge.

The news of it was disseminated through the black XXXrocessXXXsXXXal networks across the country. In 1956, Rev. Jemison would carry the blueprint of the Baton Rouge movement to the National Baptist Convention and make it available to activist clergy. Martin Luther King, Jr., and Ralph Abernathy, both ministers in Montgomery, Alabama, were aware of the Baton Rouge movement and consulted closely with Reverend Jemison when the famous Montgomery boycott was launched in 1955 (Morris 1984:43&25).

The advantage of having Dr. king as president of the boycott organization was that he was so new to Montgomery and to civil-rights work that he hadn't been there long enough to make any strong friends or enemies. King (Washington 1986:451) filed suit in the Unites States Federal District Court asking for an end to bus segregation. At the hearing on May 11, 1956, Vernon Johns (on a brief visit to Montgomery) was there. Ralph Abernathy sat on one side of King, Jr. and Johns on the other.

Events in Prince Edward County

In Farmville the whites reacted slowly to the black school strike started by Barbara Johns (Smith, Bob 1965:69). They hoped to be able to persuade the blacks to withdraw support for the suit in return for a new school. The new black high school building was constructed one year after suit was filed asking the court to direct the

Farmville school board to equalize facilities. Several years of petitioning by the black parents of Farmville prior to the suit had only led to promises, but no action (J&G, June 21, 1958:8)

A new Robert R. Moton High School was completed during the 1953-54 school term, at a cost of nearly $900,000 dollars (Wilkerson 1969:270). It was a fine structure, with separate auditorium, cafeteria, and gymnasium; an intercommunication system; a comprehensive program of studies; well-equipped laboratories and shops for science, art, commercial subjects, home economics, agriculture, and industrial arts; and an apparently able faculty of twenty-five teachers, all paid according to the same scale that applied in the white high schools.

Following the Brown decision, white resistance to school desegregation started to build in Prince Edward County. The whites organized the Defenders of State Sovereignty and Individual Liberties to prevent the integration of the schools in Virginia. J. Barrye Wall, editor and publisher of The Farmville Herald, and Robert B. Crawford, Farmville dry cleaner and civic leader, were two of the major founders of the group. the organization soon had 2,000 members and active chapters in twelve counties and in the city of Petersburg (Gates 1954:34-35, 38).

In June 1955 white citizens of the county formed a private education corporation to raise the money needed to pay the county's sixty-three white teachers their next year's salaries. There were 1,570 white children, but no plans were made for educating the 1,840 black children of the county.

The fourth circuit court sitting at Baltimore, Maryland ordered Prince Edward County to start desegregation (J&G November 16, 1957:1). But in 1959 Prince Edward County closed its schools rather than integrate them. The schools remained closed for the next four years.

Whites abandoned the public school system in Prince Edward County with the founding of the Prince Edward Education Foundation. The all-white Private schools opened September 1959. The Prince Edward Education Foundation opened two private high schools and six private grade schools in a score of miscellaneous buildings scattered over the country stores, churches, private homes, and other places. They used a motion-picture XXXrocess for assemblies. Henry Powell found himself without a job and had to move back to Philadelphia to make a living. Most of the black children received no more formal education until the Prince Edward Free School Association was established in the fall of 1963 (Gates 1964:211-212).

Henry Powell moved to Charlottesville, Virginia where he taught for two years. In 1961 he went back to Philadelphia to teach but could not stand the city after being in the country. He only stayed for two years and then in 1963 went to teach in Lynchburg. He stayed in the Lynchburg school system until his retirement sometime around 1987.

Reverend L. Francis Griffin

The story of the developments which followed the school strike and integration case in and around Farmville is a moving one – truly heroic leadership by the local minister in the face of varied threats and persecutions, including efforts (often successful) by the Defenders of State Sovereignty and Individual Liberties and other racist forces to intimidate black parents in the town (Smith, Bob 1965:72). Most of his congregation supported him.

For instance, he received solid support by independent black farmers in the countryside. But there was enough opposition to make his life very difficult. There was a minority in the congregation that was unhappy about his brand of social gospel and his role in the school strike. He heard from as far away as Washington of trouble in his church.

On the night of June 17, 1959, the Negro community of Prince Edward held a mass meeting at the New Hope Baptist Church near the Charlotte County line in response to the action of the board of supervisors cutting off all funds for public schools (Smith, Bob 1965:169-170). Rev. Griffin delivered a lecture on the injustices suffered by blacks and the necessity of standing up to them. The Rev. Wyatt T. Walker of Petersburg also emphasized this doctrine. To help some of the high school seniors, Rev. Griffin, through contacts arranged with Kittrell College, had that college offer high school as well as college courses. The college asked for half the normal tuition from each of the Prince Edward high school students but said that even those who could not raise the money should be sent. Some sixty-eight students took advantage of the opportunity.

At a meeting in Washington in January 1960, under the sponsorship of the National Council of Negro Women, representatives of twenty-one organizations named Griffin chairman of a project to set up "training centres" for the black children (Smith, Bob 1965:195). Churches, lodge halls, and other available private buildings were used. But the centres were not real schools. They were "morale builders" only.

On February 1, 1960, a group of North Carolina Agricultural and Technical College students in Greensboro, North Carolina, touched off a national wave of sit-ins when they attempted to be served at a downtown lunch counter. When black college students and others in Petersburg attempted to desegregate the library, Rev. Griffin was with them (Smith, Bob 1965:200-201).

The situation was not an easy one for Rev. Griffin. Carl Rowan of the Minneapolis Tribune had visited the Reverend back in 1953 and found him to be full of confidence. Returning to Prince Edward County in December 1955, Rowan (Smith, Bob 1965:133-134) found a far different picture. "Our rap on the door produced a far different figure from the confident leader I had met in 1953. Here was a sad-faced man, coughing, and wheezing, his eyes betraying a wish that we had not caught him in such circumstances." The house was bitterly cold, there were no rugs on the floor, and the furniture in the back bedroom was gone. "I looked at his children, their faces marked by what I was sure was ringworm. One child ran barefoot on the floor. The hair of the girls was uncombed. Their clothing bore holes that now showed a need for patches."

The whites had retaliated against the minister. The white merchants had come to a "gentleman's agreement" to freeze the reverend out of the community (Smith, Bob 1965:134). The merchants were suddenly demanding full payment instead of extending credit. This was especially true of the fuel company, which explains why Rowan found the house so bitterly cold in December. Other merchants demanded full payment of his credit debt. Some even had warrants issued against him for nonpayment of debt. They even repossessed his car.
Worst of all was the social ostracism the family had to endure from the whites and some blacks in the community. It was deemed "dangerous" to be seen with the Griffins (Smith, Bob 1965:138). The reverend's wife suffered the worse from this treatment. She had suffered mental distresses in the past, but she now plunged toward a complete breakdown. Rowan asked "What had happened to Mrs. Griffin? The charm, the attractiveness was gone. She seemed but a tired, distraught woman."

Willie Reid (1997) remembered that Griffin never had any money. If you gave him $50 dollars and on his way home, he met someone in need, that person was going to end up with a part of that $50 dollars. Reid and Griffin would often go on ambulance trips, sometimes all the way to Richmond, because of the difficulty of getting blacks accepted in the local white hospital.

Soon after Rowan's visit Griffin's five children were placed under the care of their grandmother (Smith, Bob 1965:138-139). Mrs. Griffin was in the hospital. The Reverend himself suffered from depression. He was so depressed, in fact, that he offered his resignation, saying he was going to take another job elsewhere. The job did not materialize, and the congregation asked him if he would be willing to stay and he did. He eventually took on the additional pastorates of two churches in small Virginia towns. His economic situation gradually improved somewhat.

As the Prince Edward case became better known, Griffin as the central local figure became something of a celebrity (Smith, Bob 1965:201&203-205). At the time, Griffin suffered from an ulcer on which the doctors eventually had to operate. His financial problems had cleared up with his joining the NAACP payroll as special consultant in the county. With the growing civil rights movement, Prince Edward became the target for civil rights activists. Griffin was so influential by now that nothing could be done in terms of civil rights without his cooperation. Dr. King came to view him as a "giant."

When some of the young preachers of the black community in Farmville asked if they could stage sit-ins and closed school demonstrations in Farmville in the spring of 1963, Griffin gave the idea his blessings (Smith, Bob 1965:207). He even brought in a youthful organizer from the Student Non-Violent Coordinating Committee (SNCC). All that summer pupils marched in the streets of Farmville carrying placards. Some of them were arrested. Griffin was by now president of the state NAACP.

In a decision handed down on May 25, 1964, the United States Supreme Court ordered that a decree be entered which would guarantee public education for blacks in Prince Edward County. Such a decree quickly followed, and, on June 23, the "Prince Edward County Board of Supervisors voted four to two to comply with the Federal Courts and reopen public schools. The public schools finally reopened in September 1964 (Gates 1964:213).

The job of opening the school was given to Dr. Neil V. Sullivan, a New Hampshireman who had pioneered in non-graded teaching and who had experience teaching various kinds of deprived students. At the time he was in charge of a Long Island, New York, school system. He agreed to serve in Prince Edward for a year and set about putting together a staff that would answer the board and various needs of the deprived Negro children of Prince Edward County. (Smith, Bob 1965:240)

One of the outstanding students going to the school at the time of Sullivan's tenure was Leslie "Skippy" Griffin, sixteen-year-old son of the Reverend L. Francis Griffin and possessor of the highest scholastic average at Moton High (Sullivan 1965:192-193). (He was later to be Director of Community Relations for the Boston Globe.) He accompanied Sullivan on a trip to Washington and to the Supreme Court building, March 30, 1964. The court was hearing Case 592, Griffin v. County School Board (Prince Edward). The children of two other Negro families, the original plaintiff (Davis v. County School Board) and his successor (Allen v. County School Board), had passed beyond school age and outgrown their roles in the case during the intervening years while the issues remained unresolved. Therefore, one of the children in whose name Prince Edward County was now being asked to provide integrated public schooling was none other than young Skippy Griffin, present to watch the proceedings even though, as it turned out, his father was unable to attend, forced back from Richmond by bad road conditions.

Today on the grounds of the former Robert R. Moton High School is a handsome new granite and bronze monument, dedicated to the Reverend L. Francis Griffin, who was called "the fighting preacher" and the "love preacher". It faces Griffin Boulevard, formerly Eli Street, in Farmville. The Town Council renamed the street after the 1980 death of Griffin, former minister of the First Baptist Church. Known as a man who "knew that democracy was not a spectator sport," he was a major participant in the civil rights arena.

"Dr Vernon Johns – Yesterdays' Man"
co-authored by Patrick L. Cooney PhD & William K. Mackie
available from Amazon Books

"The Vernon Johns Story – The Road to Freedom"
The full-length movie starring James Earl Jones
https://youtu.be/Koge3qy7xdo

"If you see a good fight, get in it."
Rev Dr Vernon Johns

Chapter thirty-nine

Dr Martin Luther King Jr.

Sadly, I do not know as much about Dr King as I do about Dr Johns, I do know about his protests, and his non-violent demonstrations. I was 14 years old when the news on the BBC reported on the assassination of Dr King.

Martin Luther King, Jr. was a social activist and Baptist minister who played a key role in the American civil rights movement from the mid-1950s until his assassination in 1968. King sought equality and human rights for African Americans, the economically disadvantaged and all victims of injustice through peaceful protest. He was the driving force behind watershed events such as the Montgomery Bus Boycott and the 1963 March on Washington, which helped bring about such landmark legislation as the Civil Rights Act and the Voting Rights Act. King was awarded the Nobel Peace Prize in 1964 and is remembered each year on Martin Luther King, Jr. Day, a U.S. federal holiday since 1986.

King was born Michael King Jr. on January 15, 1929, in Atlanta, Georgia, the second of three children to the Reverend Michael King and.[1429] [1430] [1431] King's mother named him Michael, which was entered onto the birth certificate by the attending physician.[1432] King's older sister is Christine King Farris and his younger brother was Alfred Daniel "A.D." King.[1433] King's maternal grandfather Adam

[1429] Olgletree, Charles J. (2004). All Deliberate Speed: Reflections on the First Half Century on Brown v. Board of Education. W. W. Norton & Co. page 138, ISBN 0-393-0587-2.
[1430] "Birth & Family". The King Centre. The Martin Luther King, Jr. Centre for Nonviolent Social Change.
[1431] "Martin Luther King Jr". Biography. A&E Television Networks, LLC. March 9, 2015.
[1432] Oates 1983, p. 4

Daniel Williams,[1434] who was a minister in rural Georgia, moved to Atlanta in 1893,[1435] and became pastor of the Ebenezer Baptist Church in the following year.[1436] William s was of African-Irish descent.[1437] [1438] [1439] Williams married Jennie Celeste Parks, who gave birth to King's mother, Alberta.[1440] King's father was born to sharecroppers, James Albert and Delia King of Stockbridge, Georgia.[1441] [1442] In his adolescent years, King Sr. left his parents' farm and walked to Atlanta where he attained a high school education.[1443] [1444] [1445] King Sr. then enrolled in Morehouse College and studied to enter the ministry.[1446] King Sr. and Alberta began dating in 1920, and married on November 25, 1926.[1447] [1448] Until Jennie's death in 1941, they lived together on the second floor of her parent's two-story Victorian house, where King was born.[1449] [1450] [1451] [1452]

Shortly after marrying Alberta, King Sr. became assistant pastor of the Ebenezer Baptist Church.[1453] Adam Daniel Williams died of a stroke in the spring of 1931.[1454] That fall, King's father took over the role of pastor at the church, where he would in time raise the attendance from six hundred to several thousand.[1455] [1456] In 1934, the church sent King Sr. on a multinational trip to Rome, Tunisia, Egypt, Jerusalem, Bethlehem, then Berlin for the meeting of the Baptist World Alliance (BWA).[1457] The trip ended with visits to sites in Berlin associated

[1433] King 1992, p. 76
[1434] "Upbringing & Studies". The King Centre.
[1435] "Martin Luther King Jr". *Biography*. A&E Television Networks, LLC. March 9, 2015.
[1436] Oates 1983, p. 6.
[1437] "King, James Albert".
[1438] Nsenga, Burton (January 13, 2011). "AfricanAncestry.com Reveals Roots of MLK and Marcus Garvey".
[1439] Nelson, Alondra (2016). *The Social Life of DNA*. pp. 160–61. ISBN 978-0-8070-2718-9.
[1440] "Martin Luther King Jr". *Biography*. A&E Television Networks, LLC. March 9, 2015.
[1441] "Birth & Family". *The King Centre*. The Martin Luther King, Jr. Centre for Nonviolent Social Change.
[1442] "Martin Luther King Jr". *Biography*. A&E Television Networks, LLC. March 9, 2015.
[1443] Frady 2002, p. 11.
[1444] Manheimer 2004, p. 10
[1445] Fleming 2008, p. 2.
[1446] Fleming 2008, p. 2.
[1447] Frady 2002, p. 12.
[1448] Oates 1983, p. 7.
[1449] Oates 1983, p. 4.
[1450] Frady 2002, p. 12.
[1451] Oates 1983, p. 7.
[1452] Oates 1983, p. 13.
[1453] Oates 1983, p. 7.
[1454] Oates 1983, p. 7.
[1455] "Martin Luther King Jr". *Biography*. A&E Television Networks, LLC. March 9, 2015.
[1456] Oates 1983, p. 7.
[1457] Brown, DeNeen L. (January 15, 2019). "The story of how Michael King Jr. became Martin Luther King Jr". *The Washington Post*.

with the Reformation leader, Martin Luther.[1458] While there, Michael King Sr. witnessed the rise of Nazism.[1459] In reaction, the BWA conference issued a resolution which stated, "This Congress deplores and condemns as a violation of the law of God the Heavenly Father, all racial animosity, and every form of oppression or unfair discrimination toward the Jews, toward coloured people, or toward subject races in any part of the world."[1460] He returned home in August 1934, and in that same year began referring to himself as Martin Luther King, and his son as Martin Luther King Jr.[1461] King's birth certificate was altered to read "Martin Luther King Jr." on July 23, 1957, when he was 28 years old.[1462]

King became friends with a white boy whose father owned a business across the street from his family's home.[1463] In September 1935, when the boys were about six years old, they started school.[1464] King had to attend a school for black children, Younge Street Elementary School,[1465] while his close playmate went to a separate school for white children only.[1466] Soon afterwards, the parents of the white boy stopped allowing King to play with their son, stating to him "we are white, and you are coloured".[1467] When King relayed the happenings to his parents, they had a long discussion with him about the history of slavery and racism in America.[1468] Upon learning of the hatred, violence and oppression that black people had faced in the U.S., King would later state that he was "determined to hate every white person".[1469]His parents instructed him that it was his Christian duty to love everyone.[1470]

King witnessed his father stand up against segregation and various forms of discrimination.[1471] Once, when stopped by a police officer who referred to King Sr. as "boy", King's father responded sharply that King was a boy but he was a man. When King's father took him into a shoe store in downtown Atlanta, the clerk

[1458] Brown, DeNeen L. (January 15, 2019). "The story of how Michael King Jr. became Martin Luther King Jr". *The Washington Post.*
[1459] Brown, DeNeen L. (January 15, 2019). "The story of how Michael King Jr. became Martin Luther King Jr". *The Washington Post.*
[1460] Nancy Clanton, The Atlanta Journal-Constitution (January 17, 2020). "Why Martin Luther King Jr.'s father changed their names". *The Atlanta Journal-Constitution.* Retrieved February 3, 2020.
[1461] Brown, DeNeen L. (January 15, 2019). "The story of how Michael King Jr. became Martin Luther King Jr". *The Washington Post.*
[1462] Brown, DeNeen L. (January 15, 2019). "The story of how Michael King Jr. became Martin Luther King Jr". *The Washington Post.*
[1463] Oates 1983, p. 10.
[1464] Oates 1983, p. 10.
[1465] Oates 1983, p. 10.
[1466] Oates 1983, p. 10.
[1467] Oates 1983, p. 10.
[1468] Oates 1983, p. 10.
[1469] Oates 1983, p. 10.
[1470] Manheimer 2004, p. 14
[1471] Frady 2002, p. 15.

told them they needed to sit in the back.[1472] King's father refused, stating "we'll either buy shoes sitting here or we won't buy any shoes at all", before taking King and leaving the store.[1473] He told King afterward, "I don't care how long I have to live with this system, I will never accept it."[1474] In 1936, King's father led hundreds of African Americans in a civil rights march to the city hall in Atlanta, to protest voting rights discrimination.[1475] King later remarked that King Sr. was "a real father" to him.[1476]

King memorized and sang hymns, and stated verses from the Bible, by the time he was five years old.[1477] Over the next year, he began to go to church events with his mother and sing hymns while she played piano.[1478] His favourite hymn to sing was *"I Want to Be More and More Like Jesus"*; he moved attendees with his singing.[1479] King later became a member of the junior choir in his church.[1480] King enjoyed opera, and played the piano.[1481] As he grew up, King garnered a large vocabulary from reading dictionaries and consistently used his expanding lexicon.[1482] He got into physical altercations with boys in his neighbourhood, but oftentimes used his knowledge of words to stymie fights.[1483] [1484] King showed a lack of interest in grammar and spelling, a trait which he carried throughout his life.[1485] In 1939, King sang as a member of his church choir in slave costume, for the all-white audience at the Atlanta premiere of the film *Gone with the Wind*.[1486] [1487] In September 1940, at the age of 12, King was enrolled at the Atlanta University Laboratory School for the seventh grade.[1488] [1489] While there, King took violin and piano lessons, and showed keen interest in his history and English classes.[1490]

[1472] Manheimer 2004, p. 9

[1473] Manheimer 2004, p. 10.

[1474] Manheimer 2004, p. 10.

[1475] Oates 1983, p. 8.

[1476] Oates 1983, p. 12.

[1477] Oates 1983, p. 9.

[1478] Oates 1983, p. 9.

[1479] Oates 1983, p. 9.

[1480] Millender, Dharathula H. (1986). *Martin Luther King Jr.: Young Man with a Dream*. Aladdin. pp. 45–46. ISBN 978-0-02-042010-1.

[1481] Frady 2002, p. 13.

[1482] Manheimer 2004, p. 15.

[1483] Manheimer 2004, p. 15.

[1484] Frady 2002, p. 13.

[1485] Frady 2002, p. 13.

[1486] Katznelson, Ira (2005). *When Affirmative Action was White: An Untold History of Racial Inequality in Twentieth Century America*. WW Norton & Co. p. 5. ISBN 0-393-05213-3.

[1487] Oates 1983, p. 11.

[1488] Boyd 1996, p. 23.

[1489] *"King enters seventh grade at Atlanta University Laboratory School"*. The Martin Luther King, Jr., Research and Education Institute. Stanford University. June 12, 2017. Retrieved September 17, 2020.

[1490] Boyd 1996, p. 23.

On May 18, 1941, when King had snuck away from studying at home to watch a parade, King was informed that something had happened to his maternal grandmother.[1491] Upon returning home, he found out that she had suffered a heart attack and died while being transported to a hospital.[1492] He took the death very hard and believed that his deception of going to see the parade may have been responsible for God taking her.[1493] His father instructed him in his bedroom that King shouldn't blame himself for her death, and that she had been called home to God as part of God's plan which could not be changed.[1494] [1495] King struggled with this, and could not fully believe that his parents knew where his grandmother had gone.[1496] Shortly thereafter, King's father decided to move the family to a two-story brick home on a hill that overlooked downtown Atlanta.[1497]

In his adolescent years, he initially felt resentment against whites due to the "racial humiliation" that he, his family, and his neighbours often had to endure in the segregated South.[1498] In 1942, when King was 13 years old, he became the youngest assistant manager of a newspaper delivery station for the *Atlanta Journal*.[1499] That year, King skipped the ninth grade and was enrolled in Booker T. Washington High School, where he maintained a B-plus average.[1500] [1501] The high school was the only one in the city for African-American students.[1502] It had been formed after local black leaders, including King's grandfather (Williams), urged the city government of Atlanta to create it.[1503]

While King was brought up in a Baptist home, King grew sceptical of some of Christianity's claims as he entered adolescence.[1504] He began to question the literalist teachings preached at his father's church.[1505] At the age of 13, he denied the bodily resurrection of Jesus during Sunday school.[1506] [1507] King has stated, he found himself unable to identify with the emotional displays and gestures from

---

[1491] Oates 1983, p. 12.
[1492] Oates 1983, p. 13.
[1493] Oates 1983, p. 13.
[1494] Oates 1983, p. 13.
[1495] Manheimer 2004, p. 16.
[1496] Oates 1983, p. 13.
[1497] Oates 1983, p. 13.
[1498] Blake, John (April 16, 2013). "How MLK became an angry black man". *CNN*.
[1499] King 1992, p. 82.
[1500] Manheimer 2004, p. 16.
[1501] Oates 1983, p. 15.
[1502] Oates 1983, p. 7.
[1503] Oates 1983, p. 7.
[1504] Manheimer 2005, p. 16.
[1505] Oates 1983, p. 14.
[1506] "An Autobiography of Religious Development". *The Martin Luther King Jr. Research and Education Institute*. Stanford University.
[1507] Oates 1983, p. 14.

congregants frequent at his church, and doubted if he would ever attain personal satisfaction from religion.[1508] [1509] He later stated of this point in his life, "doubts began to spring forth unrelentingly."[1510] [1511] [1512]

In high school, King became known for his public-speaking ability, with a voice which had grown into an orotund baritone.[1513] [1514] He proceeded to join the school's debate team.[1515] [1516] King continued to be most drawn to history and English,[1517] and choose English and sociology to be his main subjects while at the school.[1518] King maintained an abundant vocabulary.[1519] But, he relied on his sister, Christine, to help him with his spelling, while King assisted her with math.[1520] They studied in this manner routinely until Christine's graduation from high school.[1521] King also developed an interest in fashion, commonly adorning himself in well-polished patent leather shoes and tweed suits, which gained him the nickname "Tweed" or "Tweedie" among his friends.[1522] He further grew a liking for flirting with girls and dancing.[1523] His brother A. D. later remarked, "He kept flitting from chick to chick, and I decided I couldn't keep up with him. Especially since he was crazy about dances, and just about the best jitterbug in town."[1524]

On April 13, 1944, in his junior year, King gave his first public speech during an oratorical contest, sponsored by the Improved Benevolent and Protective Order of Elks of the World in Dublin, Georgia.[1525] In his speech he stated, "black America still wears chains. The finest negro is at the mercy of the meanest white man. Even winners of our highest honours face the class colour bar."[1526] [1527] King was selected

---

[1508] King 1998, p. 14.
[1509] Oates 1983, p. 14.
[1510] King 1998, p. 6.
[1511] "An Autobiography of Religious Development". *The Martin Luther King Jr. Research and Education Institute*. Stanford University.
[1512] Oates 1983, p. 14.
[1513] Fleming 2008, p. 8.
[1514] Oates 1983, p. 15.
[1515] Fleming 2008, p. 8.
[1516] Oates 1983, p. 15.
[1517] Oates 1983, p. 15.
[1518] Patterson 1969, p. 25.
[1519] Oates 1983, p. 15.
[1520] Oates 1983, p. 15.
[1521] Oates 1983, p. 15.
[1522] Frady 2002, p. 17.
[1523] Davis 2005, p. 18.
[1524] Oates 1983, p. 16.
[1525] "The Negro and the Constitution". *The Martin Luther King, Jr., Research and Education Institute*. Stanford University. December 9, 2014.
[1526] Manheimer 2004, p. 17.
[1527] "The Negro and the Constitution". *The Martin Luther King, Jr., Research and Education Institute*. Stanford University. December 9, 2014.

as the winner of the contest.[1528] [1529] On the ride home to Atlanta by bus, he and his teacher were ordered by the driver to stand so that white passengers could sit down. [1530] The driver of the bus called King a "black son-of-a-bitch".[1531] King initially refused but complied after his teacher told him that he would be breaking the law if he did not follow the directions of the driver.[1532] As all the seats were occupied, he and his teacher were forced to stand on the rest of the drive back to Atlanta.[1533] Later King wrote of the incident, saying "That night will never leave my memory. It was the angriest I have ever been in my life."[1534]

During King's junior year in high school, Morehouse College, an all-male historically black college which King's father and maternal grandfather had attended[1535] [1536] began accepting high school juniors who passed the school's entrance examination.[1537] As World War II was underway many black college students had been enlisted in the war, decreasing the numbers of students at Morehouse College.[1538] So, the university aimed to increase their student numbers by allowing junior high school students to apply.[1539] In 1944, at the age of 15, King passed the entrance examination and was enrolled at the university for the school season that autumn.[1540]

In the summer before King started his freshman year at Morehouse, he boarded a train with his friend Emmett "Weasel" Proctor and a group of other Morehouse College students to work in Simsbury, Connecticut at the tobacco farm of Cullman Brothers Tobacco (a cigar business).[1541] This was King's first trip outside of

---

[1528] "The Negro and the Constitution". *The Martin Luther King, Jr., Research and Education Institute*. Stanford University. December 9, 2014.
[1529] Oates 1983, p. 16.
[1530] Fleming 2008, p. 9.
[1531] Oates 1983, p. 16.
[1532] Fleming 2008, p. 9.
[1533] Oates 1983, p. 16.
[1534] Fleming 2008, p. 9.
[1535] Manhiemer 2005, p. 19.
[1536] Davis 2005, p. 10.
[1537] Oates 1983, p. 16.
[1538] Oates 1983, p. 16.
[1539] Oates 1983, p. 16.
[1540] There is some disagreement in sources regarding precisely when King took and passed the entrance exam in 1944. Oates (1993) and Schuman (2014) state that King passed the exam in the spring of 1944 before graduating from the eleventh grade and then being enrolled in Morehouse that fall. Manheimer (2005) states that King graduated from the eleventh grade, then applied and took the entrance exam before going to Connecticut but did not find out he had passed until August of 1944 when he was admitted. White (1974) states he took and passed the exam upon his return from Connecticut in 1944.
[1541] Tewa, Sophia (April 3, 2018). "How picking tobacco in Connecticut influenced MLK's life". *Connecticut Post*.

the segregated south into the integrated north.[1542] In a June 1944 letter to his father King wrote about the differences that struck him between the two parts of the country, "On our way here we saw some things I had never anticipated to see. After we passed Washington there was no discrimination at all. The white people here are very nice. We go to any place we want to and sit anywhere we want to."[1543] The students worked at the farm to be able to provide for their educational costs at Morehouse College, as the farm had partnered with the college to allot their salaries towards the university's tuition, housing, and other fees.[1544] [1545] On weekdays King and the other students worked in the fields, picking tobacco from 7:00am till at least 5:00pm, enduring temperatures above 100°F, to earn roughly $4 per day.[1546] [1547] On Friday evenings, King and the other students visited downtown Simsbury to get milkshakes and watch movies, and on Saturdays they would travel to Hartford, Connecticut to see theatre performances, shop and eat in restaurants.[1548] While each Sunday they would go to Hartford to attend church services, at a church filled with white congregants.[1549] King wrote to his parents about the lack of segregation in Connecticut, relaying how he was amazed they could go to the "one of the finest restaurants in Hartford" and that "Negroes and whites go to the same church".[1550]

He played freshm"n football there. The summer before his last year at Morehouse, in 1947, the 18-year-old King chose to enter the ministry. Throughout his time in college, King studied under the mentorship of its president, Baptist minister Benjamin Mays, who he would later credit with being his "spiritual mentor."[1551] King had concluded that the church offered the most assuring way to answer "an inner urge to serve humanity." His "inner urge" had begun developing, and he made peace with the Baptist Church, as he believed he would be a "rational" minister with sermons that were "a respectful force for ideas, even social

[1542] Christoffersen, John (January 17, 2011). "MLK Was Inspired by Time in Connecticut". NBC Connecticut.

[1543] Christoffersen, John (January 17, 2011). "MLK Was Inspired by Time in Connecticut". NBC Connecticut.

[1544] Tewa, Sophia (April 3, 2018). "How picking tobacco in Connecticut influenced MLK's life". Connecticut Post.

[1545] "MLK Worked Two Summers on Simsbury Tobacco Farm". NBC Connecticut. January 19, 2015.

[1546] "MLK Worked Two Summers on Simsbury Tobacco Farm". NBC Connecticut. January 19, 2015.

[1547] Christoffersen, John (January 17, 2011). "MLK Was Inspired by Time in Connecticut". NBC Connecticut.

[1548] "MLK Worked Two Summers on Simsbury Tobacco Farm". NBC Connecticut. January 19, 2015.

[1549] MLK Worked Two Summers on Simsbury Tobacco Farm". NBC Connecticut. January 19, 2015.

[1550] MLK Worked Two Summers on Simsbury Tobacco Farm". NBC Connecticut. January 19, 2015.

[1551] Kelly, Jason (January 1, 2013). "Benjamin Mays found a voice for civil rights". The University of Chicago.

protest."[1552] King graduated from Morehouse with a Bachelor of Arts (BA) in sociology in 1948, aged nineteen.[1553]

While studying at Boston University, he asked a friend from Atlanta named Mary Powell, who was a student at the New England Conservatory of Music, if she knew any nice Southern girls. Powell asked fellow student Coretta Scott if she was interested in meeting a Southern friend studying divinity. Scott was not interested in dating preachers but eventually agreed to allow Martin to telephone her based on Powell's description and vouching. On their first phone call, King told Scott "I am like Napoleon at Waterloo before your charms," to which she replied, "You haven't even met me." They went out for dates in his green Chevy. After the second date, King was certain Scott possessed the qualities he sought in a wife. She had been an activist at Antioch in undergrad, where Carol and Rod Serling were schoolmates.

King married Coretta Scott on June 18, 1953, on the lawn of her parents' house in her hometown of Heiberger, Alabama.[1554] They became the parents of four children: Yolanda King (1955–2007), Martin Luther King III (b. 1957), Dexter Scott King (b. 1961), and Bernice King (b. 1963).[1555] During their marriage, King limited Coretta's role in the civil rights movement, expecting her to be a housewife and mother.[1556]

In December 1959, after being based in Montgomery for five years, King announced his return to Atlanta at the request of the SCLC.[1557] In Atlanta, King served until his death as co-pastor with his father at the Ebenezer Baptist Church, and helped expand the Civil Rights Movement across the South.

Montgomery bus boycott, 1955
Montgomery bus boycott and Jim Crow laws

In March 1955, Claudette Colvin, a fifteen-year-old black schoolgirl in Montgomery refused to give up her bus seat to a white man in violation of Jim Crow laws, local laws in the Southern United States that enforced racial segregation. King was on the committee from the Birmingham African-American community that looked into the case; E. D. Nixon and Clifford Durr decided to wait for a better case to pursue because the Incident involved a minor.[1558]

[1552] Frady 2002, p. 18.
[1553] Finkelman, Paul (2013). Encyclopaedia of American Civil Liberties. Routledge. ISBN 978-1-135-94704-0.
[1554] "Coretta Scott King". The Daily Telegraph. February 1, 2006.
[1555] Warren, Mervyn A. (2001). King Came Preaching: The Pulpit Power of Dr. Martin Luther King, Jr. InterVarsity Press. p. 35. ISBN 0-8308-2658-0.
[1556] Civil Rights History from the Ground Up: Local Struggles, a National Movement. University of Georgia Press. 2011. p. 410. ISBN 978-0-8203-3865-1.
[1557] "SCLC Press Release". January 28, 2015.

Nine months later on December 1, 1955, a similar incident occurred when Rosa Parks was arrested for refusing to give up her seat on a city bus.[1559] (*See more about Rosa Parks in Chapter forty-one of this book*). Both incidents led to the Montgomery bus boycott, which was urged and planned by Nixon and led by King.[1560] King was in his twenties and had just taken up his clerical role. The other ministers asked him to take a leadership role simply because his relative newness to community leadership made it easier for him to speak out. King was hesitant about taking the role but decided to do so if no one else wanted the role.[1561]

The boycott lasted for 385 days,[1562] and the situation became so tense that King's house was bombed.[1563] King was arrested and jailed during this campaign, which overnight drew the attention of national media, and greatly increased King's public stature. The controversy ended when the United States District Court issued a ruling in *Browder v. Gayle* that prohibited racial segregation on all Montgomery public buses.[1564] Blacks resumed riding the buses again, and were able to sit in the front with full legal authorization. [1565] [1566]

King's role in the bus boycott transformed him into a national figure and the best-known spokesman of the civil rights movement.[1567]

Southern Christian Leadership Conference:

In 1957, King, Ralph Abernathy, Fred Shuttlesworth, Joseph Lowery, and other civil rights activists founded the Southern Christian Leadership Conference (SCLC). The group was created to harness the moral authority and organizing power of black churches to conduct nonviolent protests in the service of civil rights reform. The group was inspired by the crusades of evangelist Billy Graham, who befriended King,[1568] as well as the national organizing of the group In Friendship, founded by King allies Stanley Levison and Ella Baker.[1569] King led the SCLC until his death.[1570]

[1558] Manheimer 2004, p. 103.

[1559] "December 1, 1955: Rosa Parks arrested". *CNN*. March 11, 2003.

[1560] *Walsh, Frank (2003). The Montgomery Bus Boycott. Gareth Stevens. p. 24. ISBN 0-8368-5375-X.*

[1561] Interview with Coretta Scott King, Episode 1, PBS tv series Eyes on the Prize

[1562] *McMahon, Thomas F. (2004). Ethical Leadership Through Transforming Justice. University Press of America. p. 25. ISBN 0-7618-2908-3.*

[1563] *Fisk, Larry J.; Schellenberg, John (1999). Patterns of Conflict, Paths to Peace. Broadview Press. p. 115. ISBN 1-55111-154-3.*

[1564] King 1992, p. 9.

[1565] Jackson 2006, p. 53.

[1566] Interview with Coretta Scott King, Episode 1, PBS tv series Eyes on the Prize.

[1567] Frady 2002, p. 52.

[1568] Miller, Steven P. (2009). *Billy Graham and the Rise of the Republican South*. Philadelphia: University of Pennsylvania Press. p. 92. ISBN 978-0-8122-4151-8.

[1569] "Levison, Stanley David". *The Martin Luther King, Jr., Research and Education Institute*. May 17, 2017.

[1570] Marable, Manning; Mullings, Leith (2000). *Let Nobody Turn Us Around: Voices of Resistance,*

The SCLC's 1957 Prayer Pilgrimage for Freedom was the first time King addressed a national audience.[1571] Other civil rights leaders involved in the SCLC with King included: James Bevel, Allen Johnson, Curtis W. Harris, Walter E. Fauntroy, C. T. Vivian, Andrew Young, The Freedom Singers, Cleveland Robinson, Randolph Blackwell, Annie Bell Robinson Devine, Charles Kenzie Steele, Alfred Daniel Williams King, Benjamin Hooks, Aaron Henry and Bayard Rustin.[1572]

The Gandhi society:

Harry Wachtel joined King's legal advisor Clarence B. Jones in defending four ministers of the SCLC in the libel case *New York Times Co. v. Sullivan*; the case was litigated in reference to the newspaper advertisement "Heed Their Rising Voices". Wachtel founded a tax-exempt fund to cover the suit's expenses and assist the nonviolent civil rights movement through a more effective means of fundraising. This organization was named the "Gandhi Society for Human Rights." King served as honorary president for the group. He was displeased with the pace that President Kennedy was using to address the issue of segregation. In 1962, King and the Gandhi Society produced a document that called on the President to follow in the footsteps of Abraham Lincoln and issue an executive order to deliver a blow for civil rights as a kind of Second Emancipation Proclamation. Kennedy did not execute the order.[1573]

The FBI was underwritten directive from Attorney General Robert F. Kennedy when it began tapping King's telephone line in the fall of 1963.[1574] Kennedy was concerned that public allegations of communists in the SCLC would derail the administration's civil rights initiatives. He warned King to discontinue these associations and later felt compelled to issue the written directive that authorized the FBI to wiretap King and other SCLC leaders.[1575] FBI Director J. Edgar Hoover feared the civil rights movement and investigated the allegations of communist infiltration. When no evidence emerged to support this, the FBI used the incidental details caught on tape over the next five years in attempts to force King out of his leadership position in the COINTELPRO program.[1576]

Reform, and Renewal: an African American Anthology. Rowman & Littlefield. pp. 391–92. ISBN 0-8476-8346-X.

[1571] *"Prayer Pilgrimage for Freedom"*. Civil Rights Digital Library. Retrieved October 25, 2013.

[1572] "Program from the SCLC's Tenth Annual Convention". The King Centre.

[1573] "Martin Luther King Jr. and the Global Freedom Struggle: Gandhi Society for Human Rights". Stanford University. Retrieved August 30, 2013.

[1574] Theoharis, Athan G.; Poveda, Tony G.; Powers, Richard Gid; Rosenfeld, Susan (1999). *The FBI: A Comprehensive Reference Guide*. Greenwood Publishing. p. 148. ISBN 0-89774-991-X.

[1575] Herst 2007, pp. 372–74.

[1576] Theoharis, Athan G.; Poveda, Tony G.; Powers, Richard Gid; Rosenfeld, Susan (1999). *The FBI: A Comprehensive Reference Guide*. Greenwood Publishing Group. p. 123. ISBN 0-89774-991-X.

King believed that organized, nonviolent protest against the system of southern segregation known as Jim Crow laws would lead to extensive media coverage of the struggle for black equality and voting rights. Journalistic accounts and televised footage of the daily deprivation and indignities suffered by southern blacks, and of segregationist violence and harassment of civil rights workers and marchers, produced a wave of sympathetic public opinion that convinced most Americans that the civil rights movement was the most important issue in American politics in the early 1960s.[1577] [1578]

King organized and led marches for blacks' right to vote, desegregation, labour rights, and other basic civil rights.[1579] Most of these rights were successfully enacted into the law of the United States with the passage of the Civil Rights Act of 1964 and the 1965 Voting Rights Act.[1580] [1581]

The SCLC put into practice the tactics of nonviolent protest with great success by strategically choosing the methods and places in which protests were carried out. There were often dramatic stand-offs with segregationist authorities, who sometimes turned violent.[1582]

Survived knife attack, 1958

On September 20, 1958, King was signing copies of his book *Stride Toward Freedom* in Blumstein's department store in Harlem when he narrowly escaped death. Izola Curry, a mentally ill black woman who thought that King was conspiring against her with communists, stabbed him[1583] in the chest with a letter opener, which nearly impinged on the aorta. King received first aid by police officers Al Howard and Philip Romano.[1584] King underwent emergency surgery with three doctors: Aubre de Lambert Maynard, Emil Naclerio and John W. V. Cordice; he remained hospitalized for several weeks. Curry was later found mentally incompetent to stand trial.[1585] [1586]

[1577] Wilson, Joseph; Marable, Manning; Ness, Immanuel (2006). *Race and Labour Matters in the New U.S. Economy*. Rowman & Littlefield. p. 47. ISBN 0-7425-4691-8.

[1578] *Schofield, Norman (2006). Architects of Political Change: Constitutional Quandaries and Social Choice Theory. Cambridge University Press. p. 189. ISBN 0-521-83202-0.*

[1579] Jackson 2006, p. 53.

[1580] *Shafritz, Jay M. (1998). International Encyclopaedia of Public Policy and Administration. Westview Press. p. 1242. ISBN 0-8133-9974-2.*

[1581] *Loevy, Robert D.; Humphrey, Hubert H.; Stewart, John G. (1997). The Civil Rights Act of 1964: The Passage of the Law that Ended Racial Segregation. SUNY Press. p. 337. ISBN 0-7914-3361-7.*

[1582] Glisson 2006, p. 190.

[1583] Pearson, Hugh (2002). *When Harlem Nearly Killed King: The 1958 Stabbing of Dr. Martin Luther King, Jr.* Seven Stories Press. p. 37. ISBN 978-1-58322-614-8.

[1584] *Wilson, Michael (November 13, 2020). "Before 'I (We)Have a Dream,' Martin Luther King Almost Died. This Man Saved Him". The New York Times.*

[1585] Graham, Renee (February 4, 2002). "'King' is a Deft Exploration of the Civil Rights Leader's

Atlanta Sit-Ins, Prison Sentence, and the 1960 Elections

Georgia governor Ernest Vandiver expressed open hostility towards King's return to his hometown in late 1959. He claimed that "wherever M. L. King, Jr., has been there has followed in his wake a wave of crimes", and vowed to keep King under surveillance.[1587] On May 4, 1960, several months after his return, King drove writer Lillian Smith to Emory University when police stopped them. King was cited for "driving without a license" because he had not yet been issued a Georgia license. King's Alabama license was still valid, and Georgia law did not mandate any time limit for issuing a local license.[1588] King paid a fine but was apparently unaware that his lawyer agreed to a plea deal that also included a probationary sentence.

Meanwhile, the Atlanta Student Movement had been acting to desegregate businesses and public spaces in the city, organizing the Atlanta sit-ins from March 1960 onwards. In August the movement asked King to participate in a mass October sit-in, timed to highlight how 1960's Presidential election campaign had ignored civil rights. The coordinated day of action took place on October 19. King participated in a sit-in at the restaurant inside Rich's, Atlanta's largest department store, and was among the many arrested that day. The authorities released everyone over the next few days, except for King. Invoking his probationary plea deal, judge J. Oscar Mitchell sentenced King on October 25 to four months of hard labour. Before dawn the next day, King was taken from his county jail cell and transported to a maximum-security state prison. [1589]

The arrest and harsh sentence drew nationwide attention. Many feared for King's safety, as he started a prison sentence with people convicted of violent crimes, many of them White and hostile to his activism.[1590] Both Presidential candidates were asked to weigh in, at a time when both parties were courting the support of Southern Whites and their political leadership including Governor Vandiver. Nixon, with whom King had a closer relationship prior to the sit-in, declined to make a statement despite a personal visit from Jackie Robinson requesting his intervention. Nixon's opponent John F. Kennedy called the governor (a Democrat) directly, enlisted his brother Robert to exert more pressure on state authorities, and also, at the personal request of Sargent Shriver, made a phone call to King's wife to express his sympathy

---

Stabbing". *The Boston Globe.* – via HighBeam Research
[1586] "Today in History, September 20". – via HighBeam Research (subscription required). Associated Press. September 19, 2012.
[1587] *"Samuel Vandiver, in the MLK Encyclopaedia". July 6, 2017.*
[1588] *"Traffic stop 60 years ago spurred Martin Luther King Jr. into greater action". The Rome Sentinel. May 4, 2020.*
[1589] "Negro Integration Leader Sentenced to Four Months". Associated Press. October 25, 1960.
[1590] Levingston, Steven (June 20, 2017). "John F. Kennedy, Martin Luther King Jr., and the Phone Call That Changed History". Time.com.

and offer his help. The pressure from Kennedy and others proved effective, and King was released two days later. King's father decided to openly endorse Kennedy's candidacy for the November 8 election which he narrowly won.[1591]

After the October 19 sit-ins and following unrest, a 30-day truce was declared in Atlanta for desegregation negotiations. However, the negotiations failed, and sit-ins and boycotts resumed in full swing for several months. On March 7, 1961, a group of Black elders including King notified student leaders that a deal had been reached: the city's lunch counters would desegregate in fall 1961, in conjunction with the court-mandated desegregation of schools.[1592] [1593] Many students were disappointed at the compromise. In a large meeting March 10 at Warren Memorial Methodist Church, the audience was hostile and frustrated towards the elders and the compromise. King then gave an impassioned speech calling participants to resist the "cancerous disease of disunity," and helping to calm tensions.[1594]

Albany Movement, 1961:

The Albany Movement was a desegregation coalition formed in Albany, Georgia, in November 1961. In December, King and the SCLC became involved. The movement mobilized thousands of citizens for a broad-front nonviolent attack on every aspect of segregation within the city and attracted nationwide attention. When King first visited on December 15, 1961, he "had planned to stay a day or so and return home after giving counsel."[1595] The following day he was swept up in a mass arrest of peaceful demonstrators, and he declined bail until the city made concessions. According to King, "that agreement was dishonoured and violated by the city" after he left town.[1596]

King returned in July 1962 and was given the option of forty-five days in jail or a $178 fine (equivalent to $1,500 in 2020); he chose jail. Three days into his sentence, Police Chief Laurie Pritchett discreetly arranged for King's fine to be paid and ordered his release. "We had witnessed persons being kicked off lunch counter stools ... ejected from churches ... and thrown into jail ... But for the first time, we witnessed being kicked out of jail."[1597] It was later acknowledged by the King Centre that Billy Graham was the one who bailed King out of jail during this time.[1598]

[1591] King, Martin Luther Jr. "Chapter 15: Atlanta Arrest and Presidential Politics". *The Autobiography Of Martin Luther King, Jr.* Hatchette.
[1592] "Photos: How Atlanta Public Schools integrated in 1961". *Atlanta Journal-Constitution.*
[1593] Burns, Rebecca (August 1, 2011). "The integration of Atlanta Public Schools". Atlanta Magazine.
[1594] Hatfield, Edward A. "Atlanta Sit-ins". *New Georgia Encyclopaedia.*
[1595] King, Jr., Martin Luther (2001). *The Autobiography of Martin Luther King Jr.* Hatchette Digital. p. 147. ISBN 978-0-7595-2037-0.
[1596] King, Jr., Martin Luther (2001). *The Autobiography of Martin Luther King Jr.* Hatchette Digital. p. 147. ISBN 978-0-7595-2037-0.
[1597] King, Martin Luther Jr. (1990). *A Testament of Hope: The Essential Writings and Speeches of*

After nearly a year of intense activism with few tangible results, the movement began to deteriorate. King requested a halt to all demonstrations and a "Day of Penance" to promote nonviolence and maintain the moral high ground. Divisions within the black community and the canny, low-key response by local government defeated efforts.[1599] Though the Albany effort proved a key lesson in tactics for King and the national civil rights movement,[1600] the national media was highly critical of King's role in the defeat, and the SCLC's lack of results contributed to a growing gulf between the organization and the more radical SNCC. After Albany, King sought to choose engagements for the SCLC in which he could control the circumstances, rather than entering pre-existing situations.[1601]

In April 1963, the SCLC began a campaign against racial segregation and economic injustice in Birmingham, Alabama. The campaign used nonviolent but intentionally confrontational tactics, developed in part by Rev. Wyatt Tee Walker. Black people in Birmingham, organizing with the SCLC, occupied public spaces with marches and sit-ins, openly violating laws that they considered unjust.

King's intent was to provoke mass arrests and "create a situation so crisis-packed that it will inevitably open the door to negotiation."[1602] The campaign's early volunteers failed in shutting down the city, or in drawing media attention to the police's actions. Over the concerns of an uncertain King, SCLC strategist James Bevel changed the course of the campaign by recruiting children and young adults to join in the demonstrations.[1603] *Newsweek* called this strategy a Children's Crusade.[1604]

During the protests, the Birmingham Police Department, led by Eugene "Bull" Connor, used high-pressure water jets and police dogs against protesters, including children. Footage of the police response was broadcast on national television news and dominated the nation's attention, shocking many white Americans and consolidating black Americans behind the movement.[1605] Not all the demonstrators were peaceful, despite the avowed intentions of the SCLC. In some cases, bystanders attacked the police, who responded with force. King and the SCLC were criticized for putting children in harm's way. But the campaign was a success: Connor lost his

Martin Luther King Jr. Harper Collins. p. 105. ISBN 978-0-06-064691-2.
[1598] King Centre: Billy Graham
[1599] Glisson 2006, pp. 190–93.
[1600] *"Albany, GA Movement"*. Civil Rights Movement Archive.
[1601] Frady 2002, p. 96.
[1602] Garrow 1986, pp. 246.
[1603] McWhorter, Diane (2001). "Two Mayors and a King". *Carry Me Home: Birmingham, Alabama: The Climactic Battle of the Civil Rights Revolution.* Simon and Schuster. ISBN 978-0-7432-2648-6.
[1604] Harrell, David Edwin; Gaustad, Edwin S.; Miller, Randall M.; Boles, John B.; Woods, Randall Bennett; Griffith, Sally Foreman (2005). *Unto a Good Land: A History of the American People, Volume 2.* Wm B Eerdmans Publishing. p. 1055. ISBN 0-8028-2945-7.
[1605] Frady 2002, pp. 113–14.

job, the "Jim Crow" signs came down, and public places became more open to blacks. King's reputation improved immensely.[1606]

King was arrested and jailed early in the campaign his 13th arrest[1607] out of 29.[1608] From his cell, he composed the now-famous "Letter from Birmingham Jail" that responds to calls on the movement to pursue legal channels for social change. King argues that the crisis of racism is too urgent, and the current system too entrenched: "We know through painful experience that freedom is never voluntarily given by the oppressor; it must be demanded by the oppressed."[1609] He points out that the Boston Tea Party, a celebrated act of rebellion in the American colonies, was illegal civil disobedience, and that, conversely, "everything Adolf Hitler did in Germany was 'legal'."[1610] Walter Reuther, president of the United Auto Workers, arranged for $160,000 to bail out King and his fellow protestors.[1611]

King, representing the SCLC, was among the leaders of the "Big Six" civil rights organizations who were instrumental in the organization of the March on Washington for Jobs and Freedom, which took place on August 28, 1963. The other leaders and organizations comprising the Big Six were Roy Wilkins from the National Association for the Advancement of Coloured People; Whitney Young, National Urban League; A. Philip Randolph, Brotherhood of Sleeping Car Porters; John Lewis, SNCC; and James L. Farmer Jr., of the Congress of Racial Equality.[1612]

Bayard Rustin's open homosexuality, support of socialism, and his former ties to the Communist Party USA caused many white and African-American leaders to demand King distance himself from Rustin,[1613] which King agreed to do.[1614] However, he did collaborate in the 1963 March on Washington, for which Rustin was the primary logistical and strategic organizer.[1615] [1616] For King, this role was another

---

[1606] Harrell, David Edwin; Gaustad, Edwin S.; Miller, Randall M.; Boles, John B.; Woods, Randall Bennett; Griffith, Sally Foreman (2005). *Unto a Good Land: A History of the American People, Volume 2.* Wm B Eerdmans Publishing. p. 1055. ISBN 0-8028-2945-7.

[1607] "Integration: Connor and King". *Newsweek*: 28, 33. April 22, 1963.

[1608] King, Coretta Scott. "The Meaning of The King Holiday". The King Centre.

[1609] Greene, Helen Taylor; Gabbidon, Shaun L. (April 14, 2009). "Political Prisoners". *Encyclopaedia of Race and Crime*. SAGE Publications. pp. 636–639. ISBN 978-1-4522-6609-1.

[1610] Greene, Helen Taylor; Gabbidon, Shaun L. (April 14, 2009). "Political Prisoners". *Encyclopaedia of Race and Crime*. SAGE Publications. pp. 636–639. ISBN 978-1-4522-6609-1.

[1611] *King, Martin Luther Jr. "Letter from Birmingham Jail". The Martin Luther King Jr. Research and Education Institute. Archived from the original on January 7, 2013. Retrieved August 22, 2012.* King began writing the letter on newspaper margins and continued on bits of paper brought by friends.

[1612] "The Great Society: A New History with Amity Shlaes". *Hoover Institution*.

[1613] Gates, Henry Louis; Appiah, Anthony (1999). *Africana: The Encyclopaedia of the African and African American Experience*. Basic Civitas Books. p. 1251. ISBN 0-465-00071-1.

[1614] Arsenault, Raymond (2006). *Freedom Riders: 1961 and the Struggle for Racial Justice*. Oxford University Press. p. 62. ISBN 0-19-513674-8.

which courted controversy, since he was one of the key figures who acceded to the wishes of United States President John F. Kennedy in changing the focus of the march.[1617] [1618]

Kennedy initially opposed the march outright, because he was concerned it would negatively impact the drive for passage of civil rights legislation. However, the organizers were firm that the march would proceed.[1619] With the march going forward, the Kennedys decided it was important to work to ensure its success. President Kennedy was concerned the turnout would be less than 100,000. Therefore, he enlisted the aid of additional church leaders and Walter Reuther, president of the United Automobile Workers, to help mobilize demonstrators for the cause.[1620]

The march originally was conceived as an event to dramatize the desperate condition of blacks in the southern U.S. and an opportunity to place organizers' concerns and grievances squarely before the seat of power in the nation's capital. Organizers intended to denounce the federal government for its failure to safeguard the civil rights and physical safety of civil rights workers and blacks. The group acquiesced to presidential pressure and influence, and the event ultimately took on a far less strident tone.[1621] As a result, some civil rights activists felt it presented an inaccurate, sanitized pageant of racial harmony; Malcolm X called it the "Farce on Washington", and the Nation of Islam forbade its members from attending the march.[1622] [1623]

The march made specific demands: an end to racial segregation in public schools; meaningful civil rights legislation, including a law prohibiting racial discrimination in employment; protection of civil rights workers from police brutality; a $2 minimum wage for all workers (equivalent to $17 in 2020); and self-government

[1615] Frady 2002, p. 42.
[1616] De Leon, David (1994). Leaders from the 1960s: A biographical sourcebook of American activism. Greenwood Publishing. pp. 138–43. ISBN 0-313-27414-2.
[1617] Cashman, Sean Dennis (1991). African Americans and the Quest for Civil Rights, 1900–1990. NYU Press. p. 162. ISBN 0-8147-1441-2.
[1618] Schlesinger Jr., Arthur M. (2002) [1978]. Robert Kennedy and His Times. Houghton Mifflin Books. p. 351. ISBN 0-345-28344-9.
[1619] Marable, Manning (1991). Race, Reform, and Rebellion: The Second Reconstruction in Black America, 1945–1990. Univ. Press of Mississippi. p. 74. ISBN 0-87805-493-6.
[1620] Rosenberg, Jonathan; Karabell, Zachary (2003). Kennedy, Johnson, and the Quest for Justice: The Civil Rights Tapes. WW Norton & Co. p. 130. ISBN 0-393-05122-6.
[1621] Schlesinger Jr., Arthur M. (2002) [1978]. Robert Kennedy and His Times. Houghton Mifflin Books. pp. 350, 351. ISBN 0-345-28344-9.
[1622] Schlesinger Jr., Arthur M. (2002) [1978]. Robert Kennedy and His Times. Houghton Mifflin Books. pp. 350, 351. ISBN 0-345-28344-9.
[1623] Boggs, Grace Lee (1998). Living for Change: An Autobiography. U of Minnesota Press. p. 127. ISBN 0-8166-2955-2.

for Washington, D.C., then governed by congressional committee.[1624] Despite tensions, the march was a resounding success.[1625] More than a quarter of a million people of diverse ethnicities attended the event, sprawling from the steps of the Lincoln Memorial onto the National Mall and around the reflecting pool. At the time, it was the largest gathering of protesters in Washington, D.C.'s history.[1626]

On March 29, 1968, King went to Memphis, Tennessee, in support of the black sanitary public works employees, who were represented by AFSCME Local 1733. The workers had been on strike since March 12 for higher wages and better treatment. In one incident, black street repairmen received pay for two hours when they were sent home because of bad weather, but white employees were paid for the full day.[1627] [1628] [1629]

On April 3, King addressed a rally and delivered his "I've Been to the Mountaintop" address[1630] at Mason Temple, the world headquarters of the Church of God in Christ. King's flight to Memphis had been delayed by a bomb threat against his plane.[1631] In the prophetic peroration of the last speech of his life, in reference to the bomb threat, King said the following:

And then I got to Memphis. And some began to say the threats or talk about the threats that were out. What would happen to me from some of our sick white brothers? Well, I don't know what will happen now. We've got some difficult days ahead. But it doesn't matter with me now. Because I've been to the mountaintop. And I don't mind. Like anybody, I would like to live a long life. Longevity has its place. But I'm not concerned about that now. I just want to do God's will. And He's allowed me to go up to the mountain. And I've looked over. And I've seen the promised land. I may not get there with you. But I want you to know tonight, that we, as a people, will get to the promised land. So, I'm happy, tonight. I'm not worried about anything. I'm not fearing any man. Mine eyes have seen the glory of the coming of the Lord.[1632]

[1624] Aron, Paul (2005). *Mysteries in History: From Prehistory to the Present.* ABC-CLIO. pp. 398–99. ISBN 1-85109-899-2.
[1625] Davis, Danny (January 16, 2007). "Celebrating the Birthday and Public Holiday for Martin Luther King, Jr". *Congressional Record.* Library of Congress.
[1626] Davis, Danny (January 16, 2007). "Celebrating the Birthday and Public Holiday for Martin Luther King, Jr". *Congressional Record.* Library of Congress.
[1627] Isserman, Maurice (2001). *The Other American: The Life of Michael Harrington.* Public Affairs. p. 281. ISBN 1-58648-036-7.
[1628] *"1,300 Members Participate in Memphis Garbage Strike". AFSCME. February 1968.*
[1629] "Memphis Strikers Stand Firm". AFSCME. March 1968.
[1630] Davis, Townsend (1998). *Weary Feet, Rested Souls: A Guided History of the Civil Rights Movement.* W. W. Norton & Company. p. 364. ISBN 978-0-393-04592-5.
[1631] *Daina Ramey Berry (March 27, 2018). "Martin Luther King, Jr.'s Final Speech". History.com.*
[1632] *Thomas, Evan (November 19, 2007). "The Worst Week". Newsweek. p. 2.*

King was booked in Room 306 at the Lorraine Motel (owned by Walter Bailey) in Memphis. Ralph Abernathy, who was present at the assassination, testified to the United States House Select Committee on Assassinations that King and his entourage stayed at Room 306 so often that it was known as the "King-Abernathy suite."[1633] According to Jesse Jackson, who was present, King's last words on the balcony before his assassination were spoken to musician Ben Branch, who was scheduled to perform that night at an event King was attending: *"Ben, make sure you play 'Take My Hand, Precious Lord' in the meeting tonight. Play it real pretty."*[1634]

King was fatally shot by James Earl Ray at 6:01 p.m., Thursday, April 4, 1968, as he stood on the motel's second-floor balcony. The bullet entered through his right cheek, smashing his jaw, then travelled down his spinal cord before lodging in his shoulder.[1635] [1636]Abernathy heard the shot from inside the motel room and ran to the balcony to find King on the floor.[1637] Jackson stated after the shooting that he cradled King's head as King lay on the balcony, but this account was disputed by other colleagues of King; Jackson later changed his statement to say that he had "reached out" for King.[1638]

After emergency chest surgery, King died at St. Joseph's Hospital at 7:05 p.m.[1639] A ccording to biographer Taylor Branch, King's autopsy revealed that though only 39 years old, he "had the heart of a 60 year old", which Branch attributed to the stress of 13 years in the civil rights movement.[1640] King is buried within Martin Luther King Jr. National Historical Park.[1641]

The assassination of Dr King, led to a nationwide wave of race riots in Washington, D.C., Chicago, Baltimore, Louisville, Kansas City, and dozens of other cities. Presidential candidate Robert F. Kennedy was on his way to Indianapolis for a

---

[1633] *Montefiore, Simon Sebag (2006). Speeches that Changed the World: The Stories and Transcripts of the Moments that Made History. Quercus. p. 155. ISBN 1-84724-369-X.*

[1634] "King V. Jowers Conspiracy Allegations". *United States Department of Justice Investigation of Recent Allegations Regarding the Assassination of Dr. Martin Luther King, Jr.* U.S. Department of Justice. June 2000.

[1635] Pilkington, Ed (April 3, 2008). "40 years after King's death, Jackson hails first steps into promised land". *The Guardian.*

[1636] Garner, Joe; Cronkite, Walter; Kurtis, Bill (2002). *We Interrupt This Broadcast: The Events that Stopped Our Lives ... from the Hindenburg Explosion to the Attacks of September 11.* Sourcebooks. p. 62. ISBN 1-57071-974-8.

[1637] Pepper, William (2003). *An Act of State: The Execution of Martin Luther King.* Verso. p. 159. ISBN 1-85984-695-5.

[1638] Frady 2002, pp. 204–05.

[1639] Purnick, Joyce (April 18, 1988). "Koch Says Jackson Lied About Actions After Dr. King Was Slain". *The New York Times.*

[1640] Lokos, Lionel (1968). *House Divided: The Life and Legacy of Martin Luther King.* Arlington House. p. 48.

[1641] *"Citizen King Transcript".* PBS.

campaign rally when he was informed of King's death. He gave a short, improvised speech to the gathering of supporters informing them of the tragedy and urging them to continue King's ideal of nonviolence.[1642] The following day, he delivered a prepared response in Cleveland.[1643] James Farmer Jr. and other civil rights leaders also called for non-violent action, while the more militant Stokely Carmichael called for a more forceful response.[1644] The city of Memphis quickly settled the strike on terms favourable to the sanitation workers.[1645]

The plan to set up a shantytown in Washington, D.C., was carried out soon after the April 4 assassination. Criticism of King's plan was subdued in the wake of his death, and the SCLC received an unprecedented wave of donations for the purpose of carrying it out. The campaign officially began in Memphis, on May 2, at the hotel where King was murdered.[1646] Thousands of demonstrators arrived on the National Mall and stayed for six weeks, establishing a camp they called "Resurrection City."[1647]

President Lyndon B. Johnson tried to quell the riots by making several telephone calls to civil rights leaders, mayors and governors across the United States and told politicians that they should warn the police against the unwarranted use of force.[1648] But his efforts didn't work out: "I'm not getting through," Johnson told his aides. "They're all holing up like generals in a dugout getting ready to watch a war."[1649] Johnson declared April 7 a national day of mourning for the civil rights leader.[1650] Vice President Hubert Humphrey attended King's funeral on behalf of the President, as there were fears that Johnson's presence might incite protests and perhaps violence.[1651] At his widow's request, King's last sermon at Ebenezer Baptist Church was played at the funeral,[1652] a recording of his "Drum Major" sermon, given on February 4,

[1642] Risen, Clay. "The Unmaking of the President"(April 2008). Smithsonian Magazine.

[1643] Klein, Joe (2006). *Politics Lost: How American Democracy was Trivialized by People Who Think You're Stupid*. New York: Doubleday. p. 6. ISBN 978-0-385-51027-1

[1644] Newfield, Jack (1988). *Robert Kennedy: A Memoir* (3rd ed.). New York City: Plume. p. 248. ISBN 978-0-452-26064-1.

[1645] "1968 Year In Review". *United Press International*.

[1646] "AFSCME Wins in Memphis". AFSCME The Public Employee. April 1968.

[1647] McKnight, Gerald D. (1998). "'The Poor People Are Coming!' 'The Poor People Are Coming!'". *The last crusade: Martin Luther King Jr., the FBI, and the poor people's campaign*. Westview Press. ISBN 0-8133-3384-9.

[1648] Risen, Clay (2009). *A Nation on Fire: America in the Wake of the King Assassination*. John Wiley & Sons. ISBN 978-0-470-17710-5.

[1649] Risen, Clay (2009). *A Nation on Fire: America in the Wake of the King Assassination*. John Wiley & Sons. ISBN 978-0-470-17710-5.

[1650] Engler, Mark (January 15, 2010). "Dr. Martin Luther King's Economics: Through Jobs, Freedom". *The Nation*.

[1651] Manheimer, Ann S. (2004). *Martin Luther King Jr.: Dreaming of Equality*. Twenty-First Century Books. p. 97. ISBN 1-57505-627-5.

[1652] Dickerson, James (1998). *Dixie's Dirty Secret: The True Story of how the Government, the Media, and the Mob Conspired to Combat Immigration and the Vietnam Anti-war Movement*. ME Sharpe.

1968. In that sermon, King made a request that at his funeral no mention of his awards and honours be made, but that it be said that he tried to "feed the hungry", "clothe the naked", "be right on the Vietnam war question", and "love and serve humanity."[1653] His good friend Mahalia Jackson sang his favourite hymn, "Take My Hand, Precious Lord", at the funeral.[1654] The assassination helped to spur the enactment of the Civil Rights Act of 1968.[1655]

Two months after King's death, James Earl Ray who was on the loose from a previous prison escape was captured at London Heathrow Airport while trying to leave England on a false Canadian passport. He was using the alias Ramon George Sneyd on his way to white-ruled Rhodesia.[1656] Ray was quickly extradited to Tennessee and charged with King's murder. He confessed to the assassination on March 10, 1969, though he recanted this confession three days later.[1657] On the advice of his attorney Percy Foreman, Ray pleaded guilty to avoid a trial conviction and thus the possibility of receiving the death penalty. He was sentenced to a 99-year prison term.[1658] [1659] Ray later claimed a man he met in Montreal, Quebec, with the alias "Raoul" was involved and that the assassination was the result of a conspiracy. He spent the remainder of his life attempting, unsuccessfully, to withdraw his guilty plea and secure the trial he never had.[1660] Ray died in 1998 at age 70.[1661]

Ray's lawyers maintained he was a scapegoat similar to the way that President, John F. Kennedy's assassin Lee Harvey Oswald is seen by conspiracy theorists. [1662] Supp orters of this assertion said that Ray's confession was given under pressure and that he had been threatened with the death penalty.[1663][1664] They admitted that Ray was a

p. 169. ISBN 0-7656-0340-3.

[1653] Hatch, Jane M.; Douglas, George William (1978). *The American Book of Days*. Wilson. p. 321. ISBN 9780824205935.

[1654] King, Martin Luther, Jr. (2007). *Dream: The Words and Inspiration of Martin Luther King, Jr.* Blue Mountain Arts. p. 26. ISBN 978-1-59842-240-5.

[1655] Risen, Clay (2009). *A Nation on Fire: America in the Wake of the King Assassination*. John Wiley & Sons. ISBN 978-0-470-17710-5.

[1656] Werner, Craig (2006). *A Change is Gonna Come: Music, Race & the Soul of America*. University of Michigan Press. p. 9. ISBN 0-472-03147-3.

[1657] Ling, Peter J. (2002). *Martin Luther King, Jr.* Routledge. p. 296. ISBN 0-415-21664-8.

[1658] Ling, Peter J. (2002). *Martin Luther King, Jr.* Routledge. p. 296. ISBN 0-415-21664-8.

[1659] Flowers, R. Barri; Flowers, H. Loraine (2004). *Murders in the United States: Crimes, Killers And Victims Of The Twentieth Century*. McFarland. p. 38. ISBN 0-7864-2075-8.

[1660] Flowers, R. Barri; Flowers, H. Loraine (2004). *Murders in the United States: Crimes, Killers And Victims Of The Twentieth Century*. McFarland. p. 38. ISBN 0-7864-2075-8.

[1661] Davis, Lee (1995). *Assassination: 20 Assassinations that Changed the World*. JG Press. p. 105. ISBN 1-57215-235-4.

[1662] Gelder, Lawrence Van (April 24, 1998). "James Earl Ray, 70, Killer of Dr. King, Dies in Nashville". *NYTimes.com*.

[1663] Flowers, R. Barri; Flowers, H. Loraine (2004). *Murders in the United States: Crimes, Killers And*

thief and burglar, but claimed that he had no record of committing violent crimes with a weapon.[1665] However, prison records in different U.S. cities have shown that he was incarcerated on numerous occasions for charges of armed robbery.[1666] In a 2008 interview with CNN, Jerry Ray, the younger brother of James Earl Ray, claimed that James was smart and was sometimes able to get away with armed robbery. Jerry Ray said that he had assisted his brother on one such robbery. "I never been with nobody as bold as he is," Jerry said. "He just walked in and put that gun on somebody, it was just like it's an everyday thing."[1667]

Those suspecting a conspiracy in the assassination point to the two successive ballistics tests which proved that a rifle similar to Ray's Remington Gamemaster had been the murder weapon. Those tests did not implicate Ray's specific rifle.[1668] [1669] Witnesses near King at the moment of his death said that the shot came from another location. They said that it came from behind thick shrubbery near the boarding house which had been cut away in the days following the assassination and not from the boarding house window.[1670] However, Ray's fingerprints were found on various objects (a rifle, a pair of binoculars, articles of clothing, a newspaper) that were left in the bathroom where it was determined the gunfire came from.[1671] An examination of the rifle containing Ray's fingerprints determined that at least one shot was fired from the firearm at the time of the assassination.[1672]

In 1997, King's son Dexter Scott King met with Ray, and publicly supported Ray's efforts to obtain a new trial.[1673]

Victims Of The Twentieth Century. McFarland. p. 38. ISBN 0-7864-2075-8.

[1664] House Select Committee on Assassinations (2001). *Compilation of the Statements of James Earl Ray: Staff Report*. The Minerva Group. p. 17. ISBN 0-89875-297-3.

[1665] House Select Committee on Assassinations (2001). *Compilation of the Statements of James Earl Ray: Staff Report*. The Minerva Group. p. 17. ISBN 0-89875-297-3.

[1666] Knight, Peter (2003). *Conspiracy Theories in American History: An Encyclopaedia*. ABC-CLIO. p. 402. ISBN 1-57607-812-4.

[1667] Knight, Peter (2003). *Conspiracy Theories in American History: An Encyclopaedia*. ABC-CLIO. p. 402. ISBN 1-57607-812-4.

[1668] Flowers, R. Barri; Flowers, H. Loraine (2004). *Murders in the United States: Crimes, Killers And Victims Of The Twentieth Century*. McFarland. p. 38. ISBN 0-7864-2075-8.

[1669] Polk, James (December 29, 2008). "The case against James Earl Ray". CNN. Retrieved July 12, 2014.

[1670] "Questions left hanging by James Earl Ray's death". BBC. April 23, 1998.

[1671] Knight, Peter (2003). *Conspiracy Theories in American History: An Encyclopaedia*. ABC-CLIO. p. 402. ISBN 1-57607-812-4.

[1672] Knight, Peter (2003). *Conspiracy Theories in American History: An Encyclopaedia*. ABC-CLIO. p. 402. ISBN 1-57607-812-4.

[1673] Frank, Gerold (1972). *An American Death: The True Story of the Assassination of Dr. Martin Luther King Jr. and the Greatest Manhunt of our Time*. Doubleday. p. 283.

Two years later, King's widow Coretta Scott King and the couple's children won a wrongful death claim against Loyd Jowers and "other unknown co-conspirators." Jowers claimed to have received $100,000 to arrange King's assassination. The jury of six whites and six blacks found in favour of the King family, finding Jowers to be complicit in a conspiracy against King and that government agencies were party to the assassination.[1674][1675] William F. Pepper represented the King family in the trial.

In 2000, the U.S. Department of Justice completed the investigation into Jowers' claims but did not find evidence to support allegations about conspiracy. The investigation report recommended no further investigation unless some new reliable facts are presented.[1676] A sister of Jowers admitted that he had fabricated the story so he could make $300,000 from selling the story, and she in turn corroborated his story in order to get some money to pay her income tax.

In 2002, *The New York Times* reported that a church minister, Rev. Ronald Denton Wilson, claimed his father, Henry Clay Wilson—not James Earl Ray—assassinated King. He stated, "It wasn't a racist thing; he thought Martin Luther King was connected with communism, and he wanted to get him out of the way." Wilson provided no evidence to back up his claims.[1677]

King researchers David Garrow and Gerald Posner disagreed with William F. Pepper's claims that the government killed King.[1678] In 2003, Pepper published a book about the long investigation and trial, as well as his representation of James Earl Ray in his bid for a trial, laying out the evidence and criticizing other accounts.[1679][1680]

King's friend and colleague, James Bevel, also disputed the argument that Ray acted alone, stating, "There is no way a ten-cent white boy could develop a plan to kill a million-dollar black man."[1681] In 2004, Jesse Jackson stated: The fact is there were saboteurs to disrupt the march. And within our own organization, we found a very key person who was on the government payroll. So, infiltration within, saboteurs from without and the press attacks. ... I will never believe that James Earl Ray had

[1674] "James Earl Ray, convicted King assassin, dies". CNN. April 23, 1998.

[1675] "Trial Transcript Volume XIV". The King Centre.

[1676] Smith, Robert Charles; Seltzer, Richard (2000). *Contemporary Controversies and the American Racial Divide*. Rowman & Littlefield. p. 97. ISBN 0-7425-0025-X.

[1677] "Loyd Jowers, 73, Who Claimed A Role in the Killing of Dr. King". *The New York Times*. May 23, 2000.

[1678] Canedy, Dana (April 5, 2002). "A Minister Says His Father, Now Dead, Killed Dr. King". *The New York Times*.

[1679] Sargent, Frederic O. (2004). *The Civil Rights Revolution: Events and Leaders, 1955–1968*. McFarland. p. 129. ISBN 0-7864-1914-8.

[1680] Pepper, William (2003). *An Act of State: The Execution of Martin Luther King*. Verso. p. 182. ISBN 1-85984-695-5.

[1681] King, Desmond (March 14, 2003). "The colours of conspiracy". *Times Higher Education*.

the motive, the money, and the mobility to have done it himself. Our government was very involved in setting the stage for and I think the escape route for James Earl Ray.[1682]

Dr King has become a national icon in the history of American liberalism and American progressivism. His main legacy was to secure progress on civil rights in the U.S. Just days after King's assassination, Congress passed the Civil Rights Act of 1968.[1683] Title VIII of the Act, commonly known as the Fair Housing Act, prohibited discrimination in housing and housing-related transactions on the basis of race, religion, or national origin (later expanded to include sex, familial status, and disability). This legislation was seen as a tribute to King's struggle in his final years to combat residential discrimination in the U.S.[1684] The day following King's assassination, school teacher Jane Elliott conducted her first "Blue Eyes/Brown Eyes" exercise with her class of elementary school students in Riceville, Iowa. Her purpose was to help them understand King's death as it related to racism, something they little understood as they lived in a predominantly white community.[1685]

King's wife Coretta Scott King followed in her husband's footsteps and was active in matters of social justice and civil rights until her death in 2006. The same year that Martin Luther King was assassinated, she established the King Centre in Atlanta, Georgia, dedicated to preserving his legacy and the work of championing nonviolent conflict resolution and tolerance worldwide.[1686] Their son, Dexter King, serves as the centre's chairman.[1687] Daughter Yolanda King, who died in 2007, was a motivational speaker, author and founder of Higher Ground Productions, an organization specializing in diversity training.[1688]

Even within the King family, members disagree about his religious and political views about gay, lesbian, bisexual, and transgender people. King's widow Coretta publicly said that she believed her husband would have supported gay rights.[1689] However, his youngest child, Bernice King, has said publicly that he would have been opposed to gay marriage.[1690]

[1682] Branch, Taylor (2006). *At Canaan's Edge: America in the King Years, 1965–68.* Simon & Schuster. p. 770. ISBN 978-0-684-85712-1.
[1683] Krugman, Paul R. (2009). *The Conscience of a Liberal.* W. W. Norton & Company. p. 84. ISBN 978-0-393-33313-8.
[1684] Krugman, Paul R. (2009). *The Conscience of a Liberal.* W. W. Norton & Company. p. 84. ISBN 978-0-393-33313-8.
[1685] "The History of Fair Housing". U.S. Department of Housing and Urban Development.
[1686] Peters, William. "A Class Divided: One Friday in April, 1968". *Frontline.* PBS.
[1687] *"The King Center's Mission". The King Center.*
[1688] *"Chairman's Message: Introduction to the King Center and its Mission". The King Center.*
[1689] "Welcome". Higher Ground Productions.
[1690] "The Triple Evils". The King Center.

On February 4, 1968, at the Ebenezer Baptist Church, in speaking about how he wished to be remembered after his death, King stated:

I'd like somebody to mention that day that Martin Luther King Jr. tried to give his life serving others. I'd like for somebody to say that day that Martin Luther King Jr. tried to love somebody.

I want you to say that day that I tried to be right on the war question.

I want you to be able to say that day that I did try to feed the hungry. I want you to be able to say that day that I did try in my life to clothe those who were naked. I want you to say on that day that I did try in my life to visit those who were in prison. And I want you to say that I tried to love and serve humanity.

Yes, if you want to say that I was a drum major. Say that I was a drum major for justice. Say that I was a drum major for peace. I was a drum major for righteousness. And all the other shallow things will not matter. I won't have any money to leave behind. I won't have the fine and luxurious things of life to leave behind. But I just want to leave a committed life behind.[1691] [1692]

On June 25, 2019, *The New York Times Magazine* listed Martin Luther King Jr. among hundreds of artists whose material was reportedly destroyed in the 2008 Universal Studios fire.[1693]

FBI director J. Edgar Hoover personally ordered surveillance of King, with the intent to undermine his power as a civil rights leader.[1694] [1695] The Church Committee, a 1975 investigation by the U.S. Congress, found that "From December 1963 until his death in 1968, Martin Luther King Jr. was the target of an intensive campaign by the Federal Bureau of Investigation to 'neutralize' him as an effective civil rights leader."[1696]

In the fall of 1963, the FBI received authorization from Attorney General Robert F. Kennedy to proceed with wiretapping of King's phone lines, purportedly due to his association with Stanley Levison.[1697] The Bureau informed President John F.

[1691] Newfield, Jack (1988). *Robert Kennedy: A Memoir* (3rd ed.). New York City: Plume. p. 248. ISBN 978-0-452-26064-1.

[1692] *Williams, Brandt (January 16, 2005). "What would Martin Luther King do?". Minnesota Public Radio.*

[1693] "IBM advertisement". *The Dallas Morning News*. January 14, 1985. p. 13A.

[1694] Wurtz, Tom (June 16, 2014). "MLK agreed with Catholics on homosexuality". *The Cincinnati Enquirer.*

[1695] King, Martin Luther, Jr. (1992). "Advice for Living". *The papers of Martin Luther King, Jr.* Clayborne Carson, Peter Holloran, Ralph E. Luker, Penny A. Russell. Berkeley: University of California Press. ISBN 0-520-07950-7. OCLC 24847922.

[1696] Dyson, Michael Eric (2008). "Facing Death". *April 4, 1968: Martin Luther King Jr.'s death and how it changed America*. Basic Civitas Books. pp. 58–59. ISBN 978-0-465-00212-2.

Kennedy. He and his brother unsuccessfully tried to persuade King to dissociate himself from Levison, a New York lawyer who had been involved with Communist Party USA.[1698] [1699] Although Robert Kennedy only gave written approval for limited wiretapping of King's telephone lines "on a trial basis, for a month or so",[1700] Hoover extended the clearance, so his men were "unshackled" to look for evidence in any areas of King's life they deemed worthy.[1701]

The Bureau placed wiretaps on the home and office phone lines of both Levison and King, and bugged King's rooms in hotels as he travelled across the country.[1702] [1703] In 1967, Hoover listed the SCLC as a black nationalist hate group, with the instructions: "No opportunity should be missed to exploit through counterintelligence techniques the organizational and personal conflicts of the leaderships of the groups to insure the targeted group is disrupted, ridiculed, or discredited."[1704] [1705]

In a secret operation code-named "Minaret", the National Security Agency monitored the communications of leading Americans, including King, who were critical of the U.S. war in Vietnam.[1706] A review by the NSA itself concluded that Minaret was "disreputable if not outright illegal."[1707]

For years, Hoover had been suspicious of potential influence of communists in social movements such as labour unions and civil rights.[1708] Hoover directed the FBI to track King in 1957, and the SCLC when it was established.[1709]

[1697] Honey, Michael K. (2007). "Standing at the Crossroads". *Going down Jericho Road the Memphis strike, Martin Luther King's last campaign* (1 ed.). Norton. pp. 92–93. ISBN 978-0-393-04339-6. Hoover developed around-the-clock surveillance campaign aimed at destroying King.

[1698] Church, Frank (April 23, 1976), "Church Committee Book III", *Dr. Martin Luther King Jr., Case Study*, Church Committee

[1699] Garrow, David J. (July–August 2002). "The FBI and Martin Luther King". *The Atlantic Monthly.*

[1700] Ryskind, Allan H. (February 27, 2006). "JFK and RFK Were Right to Wiretap MLK". *Human Events.*

[1701] Herst 2007, pp. 372–74.

[1702] Church, Frank (April 23, 1976), "Church Committee Book III", *Dr. Martin Luther King Jr., Case Study*, Church Committee

[1703] Kotz 2005

[1704] King, Martin Luther, Jr. (1992). "Advice for Living". *The papers of Martin Luther King, Jr.* Clayborne Carson, Peter Holloran, Ralph E. Luker, Penny A. Russell. Berkeley: University of California Press. ISBN 0-520-07950-7. OCLC 24847922.

[1705] Herst 2007, p. 372.

[1706] Christensen, Jen (April 7, 2008). "FBI tracked King's every move". CNN.

[1707] Christensen, Jen (April 7, 2008). "FBI tracked King's every move". CNN.

[1708] Glick, Brian (1989). *War at Home: Covert Action Against U.S. Activists and What We Can Do About It.* South End Press. p. 77. ISBN 978-0-89608-349-3.

[1709] Theoharis, Athan G.; Poveda, Tony G.; Powers, Richard Gid; Rosenfeld, Susan (1999). *The FBI: A Comprehensive Reference Guide.* Greenwood Publishing Group. p. 123. ISBN 0-89774-991-X.

Due to the relationship between King and Stanley Levison, the FBI feared Levison was working as an "agent of influence" over King, in spite of its own reports in 1963 that Levison had left the Party and was no longer associated in business dealings with them.[1710] Another King lieutenant, Jack O'Dell, was also linked to the Communist Party by sworn testimony before the House Un-American Activities Committee (HUAC).[1711]

Despite the extensive surveillance conducted, by 1976 the FBI had acknowledged that it had not obtained any evidence that King himself or the SCLC were actually involved with any communist organizations.[1712]

For his part, King adamantly denied having any connections to communism. In a 1965 *Playboy* interview, he stated that "there are as many Communists in this freedom movement as there are Eskimos in Florida." He argued that Hoover was "following the path of appeasement of political powers in the South" and that his concern for communist infiltration of the civil rights movement was meant to "aid and abet the salacious claims of southern racists and the extreme right-wing elements."[1713] Hoover did not believe King's pledge of innocence and replied by saying that King was "the most notorious liar in the country."[1714] After King gave his "I Have A Dream" speech during the March on Washington on August 28, 1963, the FBI described King as "the most dangerous and effective Negro leader in the country."[1715] It alleged that he was "knowingly, willingly and regularly cooperating with and taking guidance from communists."[1716]

The attempts to prove that King was a communist was relat"d to the feeling of many"segregationists that blacks in the South were content with the status quo, but had been stirred up by "communists" and "outside agitators."[1717] As context, the civil rights movement in 1950s and '60s arose from activism within the black community dating back to before World War I. King said that "the Negro revolution

[1710] The Guardian, September 26, 2013, "Declassified NSA Files Show Agency Spied on Muhammad Ali and MLK Operation Minaret Set Up in 1960s to Monitor Anti-Vietnam Critics, Branded 'Disreputable If Not Outright Illegal' by NSA Itself," The Guardian

[1711] Downing, Frederick L. (1986). *To See the Promised Land: The Faith Pilgrimage of Martin Luther King, Jr.* Mercer University Press. pp. 246–47. ISBN 0-86554-207-4.

[1712] Dyson, Michael Eric (2008). "Facing Death". *April 4, 1968: Martin Luther King Jr.'s death and how it changed America*. Basic Civitas Books. pp. 58–59. ISBN 978-0-465-00212-2.

[1713] Dyson, Michael Eric (2008). "Facing Death". *April 4, 1968: Martin Luther King Jr.'s death and how it changed America*. Basic Civitas Books. pp. 58–59. ISBN 978-0-465-00212-2.

[1714] *Woods, Jeff (2004). Black Struggle, Red Scare: Segregation and Anti-communism in the South, 1948–1968. LSU Press. p. 126. ISBN 0-8071-2926-7. See also: Wannall, Ray (2000). The Real J. Edgar Hoover: For the Record. Turner Publishing. p. 87. ISBN 1-56311-553-0.*

[1715] Kotz 2005

[1716] Washington 1991, p. 362.

[1717] Bruns, Roger (2006). *Martin Luther King Jr.: A Biography*. Greenwood Publishing. p. 67. ISBN 0-313-33686-5.

is a genuine revolution, born from the same womb that produces all massive social upheavals the womb of intolerable conditions and unendurable situations."[1718]

CIA files declassified in 2017 revealed that the agency was investigating possible links between King and Communism after a Washington Post article dated November 4, 1964, claimed he was invited to the Soviet Union and that Ralph Abernathy, as spokesman for King, refused to comment on the source of the invitation.[1719] Mail belonging to King and other civil rights activists was intercepted by the CIA program HTLINGUAL.[1720]

The FBI having concluded that King was dangerous due to communist infiltration, attempts to discredit King began through revelations regarding his private life. FBI surveillance of King, some of it since made public, attempted to demonstrate that he also had numerous extramarital affairs.[1721] Lyndon B. Johnson once said that King was a "hypocritical preacher".[1722]

In his 1989 autobiography *And the Walls Came Tumbling Down*, Ralph Abernathy stated that King had a "weakness for women", although they "all understood and believed in the biblical prohibition against sex outside of marriage. It was just that he had a particularly difficult time with that temptation."[1723] In a later interview, Abernathy said that he only wrote the term "womanizing", that he did not specifically say King had extramarital sex and that the infidelities King had were emotional rather than sexual.[1724]

Abernathy criticized the media for sensationalizing the statements he wrote about King's affairs,[1725] such as the allegation that he admitted in his book that King had a sexual affair the night before he was assassinated.[1726] In his original wording, Abernathy had stated that he saw King coming out of his room with a woman when he awoke the next morning and later said that "he may have been in there discussing and debating and trying to get her to go along with the movement, I don't know...the Sanitation Worker's Strike."[1727]

[1718] Kotz 2005, p. 83.

[1719] Gilbert, Alan (1990). *Democratic Individuality: A Theory of Moral Progress*. Cambridge University Press. p. 435. ISBN 0-521-38709-4.

[1720] Washington 1991, p. 363.

[1721] Kotz 2005

[1722] Naftali, Timothy (December 19, 2005). "Bush and the NSA spying scandal". *HuffPost*.

[1723] Brown, DeNeen L. (January 18, 2014). "Martin Luther King Jr. met Malcolm X just once. The photo still haunts us with what was lost". *The Washington Post*. Retrieved October 31, 2020.

[1724] Sidey, Hugh (February 10, 1975). "L.B.J., Hoover and Domestic Spying". *Time*.

[1725] Sidey, Hugh (February 10, 1975). "L.B.J., Hoover and Domestic Spying". *Time*.

[1726] Sidey, Hugh (February 10, 1975). "L.B.J., Hoover and Domestic Spying". *Time*.

[1727] Sidey, Hugh (February 10, 1975). "L.B.J., Hoover and Domestic Spying". *Time*.

In his 1986 book *Bearing the Cross*, David Garrow wrote about a number of extramarital affairs, including one woman King saw almost daily. According to Garrow, "that relationship ... increasingly became the emotional centrepiece of King's life, but it did not eliminate the incidental couplings ... of King's travels." He alleged that King explained his extramarital affairs as "a form of anxiety reduction." Garrow asserted that King's supposed promiscuity caused him "painful and at times overwhelming guilt."[1728] King's wife Coretta appeared to have accepted his affairs with equanimity, saying once that "all that other business just doesn't have a place in the very high-level relationship we enjoyed."[1729] Shortly after *Bearing the Cross* was released, civil rights author Howell Raines gave the book a positive review but opined that Garrow's allegations about King's sex life were "sensational" and stated that Garrow was "amassing facts rather than analysing them."[1730]

The FBI distributed reports regarding such affairs to the executive branch, friendly reporters, potential coalition partners and funding sources of the SCLC, and King's family.[1731] The bureau also sent anonymous letters to King threatening to reveal information if he did not cease his civil rights work.[1732] The FBI – King suicide letter sent to King just before he received the Nobel Peace Prize read, in part:

The American public, the church organizations that have been helping Protestants, Catholics and Jews will know you for what you are an evil beast. So will others who have backed you. You are done. King, there is only one thing left for you to do. You know what it is. You have just 34 days in which to do (this exact number has been selected for a specific reason; it has definite practical significant). You are done. There is but one way out for you. You better take it before your filthy fraudulent self is bared to the nation.[1733]

TheXXXroer was XXXrocessXXXsied by a tape recording excerpted from FBI wiretaps of several of King's extramarital liaisons.[1734] King interpreted this package as an attempt to drive him to suicide,[1735] although William Sullivan, head of the Domestic Intelligence Division at the time, argued that it may have only been

[1728] Abernathy, Ralph (1989). *And the walls came tumbling down: an autobiography*. Harper & Row. p. 471. ISBN 978-0-06-016192-7.

[1729] Abernathy, Ralph David (October 29, 1989). "And the Walls Came Tumbling Down". Booknotes.

[1730] *Bearing the Cross: Martin Luther King Jr. and the Southern Christian Leadership Conference*. William Morrow & Co. 1986. pp. 375–76.

[1731] Frady 2002, p. 67.

[1732] Raines, Howell (November 30, 1986). "Driven to Martyrdom". *The New York Times*.

[1733] Spragens, William C. (1988). *Popular Images of American Presidents*. Greenwood Publishing. p. 532. ISBN 978-0-313-22899-5.

[1734] *Gage, Beverly (November 11, 2014). "What an Uncensored Letter to M.L.K. Reveals". The New York Times.*

[1735] Kotz 2005, p. 247.

intended to "convince Dr. King to resign from the SCLC."[1736] King refused to give in to the FBI's threats.[1737]

In 1977, Judge John Lewis Smith Jr. ordered all known copies of the recorded audiotapes and written transcripts resulting from the FBI's electronic surveillance of King between 1963 and 1968 to be held in the National Archives and sealed from public access until 2027.[1738]

In May 2019, FBI files emerged alleging that King "looked on, laughed and offered advice" as one of his friends raped a woman. His biographer, David Garrow, wrote that "the suggestion... that he either actively tolerated or personally employed violence against any woman, even while drunk, poses so fundamental a challenge to his historical stature as to require the most complete and extensive historical review possible".[1739] These allegations sparked a heated debate among historians.[1740] Claybo rne Carson, Martin Luther King biographer and overseer of the Dr. King records at Stanford University states that he came to the opposite conclusion of Garrow saying "None of this is new. Garrow is talking about a recently added summary of a transcript of a 1964 recording from the Willard Hotel that others, including Mrs. King, have said they did not hear Martin's voice on it. The added summary was four layers removed from the actual recording. This supposedly new information comes from an anonymous source in a single paragraph in an FBI report. You have to ask how anyone could conclude King looked at a rape from an audio recording in a room where he was not present."[1741] Carson bases his position of Coretta Scott King's memoirs where she states "I set up our reel-to-reel recorder and listened. I have read scores of reports talking about the scurrilous activities of my husband but once again, there was nothing at all incriminating on the tape. It was a social event with people laughing and telling dirty jokes. But I did not hear Martin's voice on it, and there was nothing about sex or anything else resembling the lies J. Edgar and the FBI were spreading." The tapes that could confirm or refute the allegation are scheduled to be declassified in 2027.[1742]

[1736] Dyson, Michael Eric (2008). "Facing Death". *April 4, 1968: Martin Luther King Jr.'s death and how it changed America*. Basic Civitas Books. pp. 58–59. ISBN 978-0-465-00212-2.

[1737] Kotz 2005

[1738] Frady 2002, pp. 158–59.

[1739] *Wilson, Sondra K. (1999). In Search of Democracy: The NAACP Writings of James Weldon Johnson, Walter White, and Roy Wilkins (1920–1977). Oxford University Press. p. 466. ISBN 0-19-511633-X.*

[1740] Phillips, Geraldine N. (Summer 1997). "Documenting the Struggle for Racial Equality in the Decade of the Sixties". *Prologue*. The National Archives and Records Administration. Retrieved June 15, 2008.

[1741] *Garrow, David J. (May 30, 2019). "The troubling legacy of Martin Luther King". Standpoint.*

[1742] Murch, Donna (June 8, 2019). "A historian's claims about Martin Luther King are shocking – and irresponsible". *The Guardian*.

A fire station was located across from the Lorraine Motel, next to the boarding house in which James Earl Ray was staying. Police officers were stationed in the fire station to keep King under surveillance.[1743] Agents were watching King at the time he was shot.[1744] Immediately following the shooting, officers rushed out of the station to the motel. Marrell McCollough, an undercover police officer, was the first person to administer first aid to King.

The antagonism between King and the FBI, the lack of an all-points bulletin to find the killer, and the police presence nearby led to speculation that the FBI was involved in the assassination.[1745]

Dr King's family did not believe that James Earl Ray was the killer. Ray died on the 23rd. April 1998.

[1743] Reynolds, Barbara Ann (July 3, 2019). "Salacious FBI information again attacks character of MLK". New York Amsterdam News

[1744] Griffey, Trevor. "J. Edgar Hoover's revenge: Information the FBI once hoped could destroy Rev. Martin Luther King Jr. has been declassified". *The Conversation*.

[1745] McKnight, Gerald (1998). *The Last Crusade: Martin Luther King Jr., the FBI, and the Poor People's Crusade*. Westview Press. p. 76. ISBN 0-8133-3384-9.

Chapter forty

I have a dream

Full text to the "I Have a Dream" speech by Dr Martin Luther King Junior

Five score years ago, a great American, in whose symbolic shadow we stand today, signed the Emancipation Proclamation. This momentous decree came as a great beacon light of hope to millions of Negro slaves who had been seared in the flames of withering injustice. It came as a joyous daybreak to end the long night of their captivity.

But one hundred years later, the Negro still is not free. One hundred years later, the life of the Negro is still sadly crippled by the manacles of segregation and the chains of discrimination. One hundred years later, the Negro lives on a lonely island of poverty in the midst of a vast ocean of material prosperity. One hundred years later, the Negro is still languishing in the corners of American society and finds himself an exile in his own land. So, we have come here today to dramatize a shameful condition.

In a sense we have come to our nation's capital to cash a check. When the architects of our republic wrote the magnificent words of the Constitution and the Declaration of Independence, they were signing a promissory note to which every American was to fall heir. This note was a promise that all men, yes, black men as well as white men, would be guaranteed the unalienable rights of life, liberty, and the pursuit of happiness.

It is obvious today that America has defaulted on this promissory note insofar as her citizens of colour are concerned. Instead of honouring this sacred obligation, America has given the Negro people a bad check, a check which has come back marked "insufficient funds." But we refuse to believe that the bank of justice is bankrupt. We refuse to believe that there are insufficient funds in the great vaults of opportunity of this nation. So, we have come to cash this check, a check that will give us upon demand the riches of freedom and the security of justice. We have also come to this hallowed spot to remind America of the fierce urgency of now. This is no time to engage in the luxury of cooling off or to take the tranquilizing drug of gradualism. Now is the time to make real the promises of democracy. Now is the time to rise from the dark and desolate valley of segregation to the sunlit path of racial justice. Now is the time to lift our nation from the quick sands of racial injustice to the solid rock of brotherhood. Now is the time to make justice a reality for all of God's children.

It would be fatal for the nation to overlook the urgency of the moment. This sweltering summer of the Negro's legitimate discontent will not pass until there is an invigorating autumn of freedom and equality. Nineteen sixty-three is not an end, but a beginning. Those who hope that the Negro needed to blow off steam and will now be content will have a rude awakening if the nation returns to business as usual. There will be neither rest nor tranquility in America until the Negro is granted his citizenship rights. The whirlwinds of revolt will continue to shake the foundations of our nation until the bright day of justice emerges.

But there is something that I must say to my people who stand on the warm threshold which leads into the palace of justice. In the process of gaining our rightful place we must not be guilty of wrongful deeds. Let us not seek to satisfy our thirst for freedom by drinking from the cup of bitterness and hatred.

I am happy to join with you today in what will go down in history as the greatest demonstration for freedom in the history of our nation.

We must forever conduct our struggle on the high plane of dignity and discipline. We must not allow our creative protest to degenerate into physical violence. Again and again we must rise to the majestic heights of meeting physical force with soul force. The marvelous new militancy which has engulfed the Negro community must not lead us to a distrust of all white people, for many of our white brothers, as evidenced by their presence here today, have come to realize that their destiny is tied up with our destiny. They have come to realize that their freedom is inextricably bound to our freedom. We cannot walk alone.

As we walk, we must make the pledge that we shall always march ahead. We cannot turn back. There are those who are asking the devotees of civil rights, "When will you be satisfied?" We can never be satisfied as long as the Negro is the victim of the unspeakable horrors of police brutality. We can never be satisfied, as long as our bodies, heavy with the fatigue of travel, cannot gain lodging in the motels of the highways and the hotels of the cities. We cannot be satisfied as long as the Negro's basic mobility is from a smaller ghetto to a larger one. We can never be satisfied as long as our children are stripped of their selfhood and robbed of their dignity by signs stating, "For Whites Only". We cannot be satisfied as long as a Negro in

Mississippi cannot vote, and a Negro in New York believes he has nothing for which to vote. No, no, we are not satisfied, and we will not be satisfied until justice rolls down like waters and righteousness like a mighty stream.

I am not unmindful that some of you have come here out of great trials and tribulations. Some of you have come fresh from narrow jail cells. Some of you have come from areas where your quest for freedom left you battered by the storms of persecution and staggered by the winds of police brutality. You have been the veterans of creative suffering. Continue to work with the faith that unearned suffering is redemptive.

Go back to Mississippi, go back to Alabama, go back to South Carolina, go back to Georgia, go back to Louisiana, go back to the slums and ghettos of our northern cities, knowing that somehow this situation can and will be changed. Let us not wallow in the valley of despair.

I say to you today, my friends, so even though we face the difficulties of today and tomorrow, I still have a dream. It is a dream deeply rooted in the American dream.

I have a dream that one day this nation will rise up and live out the true meaning of its creed: "We hold these truths to be self-evident: that all men are created equal."

I have a dream that one day on the red hills of Georgia the sons of former slaves and the sons of former slave owners will be able to sit down together at the table of brotherhood.

I have a dream that one day even the state of Mississippi, a state sweltering with the heat of injustice, sweltering with the heat of oppression, will be transformed into an oasis of freedom and justice.

I have a dream that my four little children will one day live in a nation where they will not be judged by the color of their skin but by the content of their character.

I have a dream today.

I have a dream that one day, down in Alabama, with its vicious racists, with its governor having his lips dripping with the words of interposition and nullification; one day right there in Alabama, little black boys and black girls will be able to join hands with little white boys and white girls as sisters and brothers.

I have a dream today.

I have a dream that one day every valley shall be exalted, every hill and mountain shall be made low, the rough places will be made plain, and the crooked places will be made straight, and the glory of the Lord shall be revealed, and all flesh shall see it together.

This is our hope. This is the faith that I go back to the South with. With this faith we will be able to hew out of the mountain of despair a stone of hope. With this faith we will be able to transform the jangling discords of our nation into a beautiful symphony of brotherhood. With this faith we will be able to work together, to pray together, to struggle together, to go to jail together, to stand up for freedom together, knowing that we will be free one day.

This will be the day when all of God's children will be able to sing with a new meaning, "My country, 'tis of thee, sweet land of liberty, of thee I sing. Land where my fathers died, land of the pilgrim's pride, from every mountainside, let freedom ring."

And if America is to be a great nation this must become true. So let freedom ring from the prodigious hilltops of New Hampshire. Let freedom ring from the mighty mountains of New York. Let freedom ring from the heightening Alleghenies of Pennsylvania!

Let freedom ring from the snow-capped Rockies of Colorado!
Let freedom ring from the curvaceous slopes of California!
But not only that; let freedom ring from Stone Mountain of Georgia!
Let freedom ring from Lookout Mountain of Tennessee!
Let freedom ring from every hill and molehill of Mississippi. From every mountainside, let freedom ring.

And when this happens, when we allow freedom to ring, when we let it ring from every village and every hamlet, from every state and every city, we will be able to speed up that day when all of God's children, black men and white men, Jews and Gentiles, Protestants and Catholics, will be able to join hands and sing in the words of the old Negro spiritual, "Free at last! Free at last! Thank God Almighty, we are free at last!"

Chapter forty-one

Rosa Parks

Rosa Parks, was an American civil rights activist whose refusal to relinquish her seat on a public bus precipitated the 1955–56 Montgomery bus boycott in Alabama, which became the spark that ignited the civil rights movement in the United States.

Born to parents James McCauley, a skilled stonemason and carpenter, and Leona Edwards McCauley, a teacher, in Tuskegee, Alabama, Rosa Louise McCauley spent much of her childhood and youth ill with chronic tonsillitis. When she was two years old, shortly after the birth of her younger brother, Sylvester, her parents chose to separate. Estranged from their father from then on, the children moved with their mother to live on their maternal grandparents' farm in Pine Level, Alabama, outside Montgomery. The children's great-grandfather, a former indentured servant, also lived there; he died when Rosa was six.

For much of her childhood, Rosa was educated at home by her mother, who also worked as a teacher at a nearby school. Rosa helped with chores on the farm and learned to cook and sew. Farm life, though, was less than idyllic. The Ku Klux Klan was a constant threat, as she later recalled, "burning Negro churches, schools, flogging and killing" Black families. Rosa's grandfather would often keep watch at night, rifle in hand, awaiting a mob of violent white men. The house's windows and doors were boarded shut with the family, frequently joined by Rosa's widowed aunt and her five children, inside. On nights thought to be especially dangerous, the children would have to go to bed with their clothes on so that they would be ready if the family needed to escape. Sometimes Rosa would choose to stay awake and keep watch with her grandfather.

Rosa and her family experienced racism in less violent ways, too. When Rosa entered school in Pine Level, she had to attend a segregated establishment where one teacher was put in charge of about 50 or 60 schoolchildren. Though white children in the area were bused to their schools, Black children had to walk. Public transportation, drinking fountains, restaurants, and schools were all segregated under Jim Crow laws. At age 11 Rosa entered the Montgomery Industrial School for Girls, where Black girls were taught regular school subjects alongside domestic skills. She went on to attend a Black junior high school for 9th grade and a Black teacher's college for 10th and part of 11th grade. At age 16, however, she was forced to leave school because of an illness in the family, and she began cleaning the houses of white people.

In 1932, at age 19, Rosa married Raymond Parks, a barber, and a civil rights activist, who encouraged her to return to high school and earn a diploma. She later made a living as a seamstress. In 1943 Rosa Parks became a member of the Montgomery chapter of the National Association for the Advancement of Coloured People (NAACP), and she served as its secretary until 1956.

On December 1, 1955, Parks was riding a crowded Montgomery city bus when the driver, upon noticing that there were white passengers standing in the aisle, asked Parks, and other Black passengers to surrender their seats and stand. Three of the passengers left their seats, but Parks refused. She was subsequently arrested and fined $10 for the offense and $4 for court costs, neither of which she paid. Instead, she accepted Montgomery NAACP chapter president E.D. Nixon's offer to help her appeal the conviction and thus challenge legal segregation in Alabama. Both Parks and Nixon knew that they were opening themselves to harassment and death threats, but they also knew that the case had the potential to spark national outrage. Under the aegis of the Montgomery Improvement Association—led by the young pastor of the Dexter Avenue Baptist Church, Martin Luther King, Jr., a boycott of the municipal bus company began on December 5. African Americans constituted some 70 percent of the ridership, and the absence of their bus fares cut deeply into revenue. The boycott lasted 381 days, and even people outside Montgomery embraced the cause: protests of segregated restaurants, pools, and other public facilities took place all over the United States. On November 13, 1956, the U.S. Supreme Court upheld a lower court's decision declaring Montgomery's segregated bus seating unconstitutional, and a court order to integrate the buses was served on December 20; the boycott ended the following day. For her role in igniting the successful campaign, Parks became known as the "mother of the civil rights movement."

Simplifications of Parks' story claimed that she had refused to give up her bus seat because she was tired rather than because she was protesting unfair treatment. But she was an accomplished activist by the time of her arrest, having worked with the NAACP on other civil rights cases, such as that of the Scottsboro Boys, nine Black youths falsely accused of sexually assaulting two white women. According to Parks' autobiography, "I was not tired physically, or no more tired than I usually was at the end of a working day. I was not old, although some people have an image of me as being old then. I was 42. No, the only tired I was, was tired of giving in." Parks was not the first Black woman to refuse to give up her bus seat for a white person 15-

year-old Claudette Colvin had been arrested for the same offense nine months earlier, and dozens of other Black women had preceded them in the history of segregated public transit. However, as secretary of the local NAACP, and with the Montgomery Improvement Association behind her, Parks had access to resources and publicity that those other women had not had. It was her case that forced the city of Montgomery to desegregate city buses permanently.

In 1957 Parks moved with her husband and mother to Detroit, where from 1965 to 1988 she worked on the staff of Michigan Congressman John Conyers, Jr. She remained active in the NAACP, and the Southern Christian Leadership Conference established an annual Rosa Parks Freedom Award in her honour. In 1987 she cofounded the Rosa and Raymond Parks Institute for Self-Development to provide career training for young people and offer teenagers the opportunity to learn about the history of the civil rights movement. She received numerous awards, including the Presidential Medal of Freedom(1996) and the Congressional Gold Medal (1999). Her autobiography, *Rosa Parks: My Story* (1992), was written with Jim Haskins.

Though achieving the desegregation of Montgomery's city buses was an incredible feat, Parks was not satisfied with that victory. She saw that the United States was still failing to respect and protect the lives of Black Americans. Martin Luther King, Jr., who had been brought to national attention by his organization of the Montgomery bus boycott, was assassinated less than a decade after Parks's case was won. Biographer Kathleen Tracy noted that Parks, in one of her last interviews, would not quite say that she was happy: "I do the very best I can to look upon life with optimism and hope and looking forward to a better day, but I don't think there is any such thing as complete happiness. It pains me that there is still a lot of Klan activity and racism. I think when you say you're happy, you have everything that you need and everything that you want, and nothing more to wish for. I haven't reached that stage yet."

After Parks died in 2005, her body lay in state in the rotunda of the U.S. Capitol, an honour reserved for private citizens who performed a great service for their country. For two days mourners visited her casket and gave thanks for her dedication to civil rights. Parks was the first woman and only the second Black person to receive the distinction.

Chapter forty-two

Watts Riots 1965

(Part of America's Forgotten History)

The Watts riots, sometimes referred to as the Watts Rebellion or Watts Uprising,[1746] took place in the Watts neighbourhood and its surrounding areas of Los Angeles from August 11 to 16, 1965.

On August 11, 1965, Marquette Frye, a 21-year-old African American man, was pulled over for drunken driving.[1747] After he failed a field sobriety test, officers attempted to arrest him. Marquette resisted arrest, with assistance from his mother, Rena Frye, and a physical confrontation ensued in which Marquette was struck in the face with a baton. Meanwhile, a crowd of onlookers had gathered.[1748] Rumours spread that the police had kicked a pregnant woman who was present at the scene. Six days of civil unrest followed, motivated in part by allegations of police abuse.[1749] Nearly 14,000 members of the California Army National Guard[1750] helped suppress the disturbance, which resulted in 34 deaths[1751] and over $40 million in property damage.[1752] It was the city's worst unrest until the Rodney King riots of 1992.

In the Great Migration of 1915 – 1940, major populations of African Americans moved to North-eastern and Midwestern cities such as Detroit, Chicago, St. Louis, Cincinnati, Philadelphia, Boston, and New York City to pursue jobs in newly established manufacturing industries; to cement better educational and social opportunities; and to flee racial segregation, Jim Crow laws, violence and racial bigotry in the Southern states. This wave of migration largely bypassed Los Angeles.

[1746] "Watts Rebellion (Los Angeles) | The Martin Luther King, Jr., Research and Education Institute". *kinginstitute.stanford.edu.* June 12, 2017.

[1747] Queally, James (July 29, 2015). "Watts Riots: Traffic stop was the spark that ignited days of destruction in L.A."*Los Angeles Times.*

[1748] *Queally, James (July 29, 2015). "Watts Riots: Traffic stop was the spark that ignited days of destruction in L.A."Los Angeles Times.*

[1749] "How Legacy Of The Watts Riot Consumed, Ruined Man's Life". *tribunedigital-orlandosentinel.*

[1750] *University, © Stanford; Stanford; California 94305 (June 12, 2017). "Watts Rebellion (Los Angeles)". The Martin Luther King Jr., Research and Education Institute.*

[1751] Hinton, Elizabeth (2016). *From the War on Poverty to the War on Crime: The Making of Mass Incarceration in America.* Harvard University Press. pp. 68–72. ISBN 9780674737235.

[1752] Joshua, Bloom; Martin, Waldo (2016). *Black Against Empire: The History And Politics Of The Black Panther Party.* University of California Press. p. 30.

In the 1940s, in the Second Great Migration, black workers and families migrated to the West Coast in large numbers, in response to defence industry recruitment efforts at the start of World War II. President Franklin D. Roosevelt issued Executive Order 8802 directing defence contractors not to discriminate in hiring or promotions, opening up new opportunities for minorities. The black population in Los Angeles dramatically rose from approximately 63,700 in 1940 to about 350,000 in 1965, rising from 4% of L.A.'s population to 14%.[1753]

Los Angeles had racially restrictive covenants that prevented specific minorities from renting and buying property in certain areas, even long after the courts ruled such practices illegal in 1948 and the Civil Rights Act of 1964 was passed. At the beginning of the 20th century, Los Angeles was geographically divided by ethnicity, as demographics were being altered by the rapid migration from the Philippines (U.S. unincorporated territory at the time) and immigration from Mexico, Japan, Korea, and Southern and Eastern Europe. In the 1910s, the city was already 80% covered by racially restrictive covenants in real estate.[1754] By the 1940s, 95% of Los Angeles and southern California housing was off-limits to certain minorities.[1755] Minorities who had served in World War II or worked in L.A.'s defence industries returned to face increasing patterns of discrimination in housing. In addition, they found themselves excluded from the suburbs and restricted to housing in East or South Los Angeles, which includes the Watts neighbourhood and Compton. Such real-estate practices severely restricted educational and economic opportunities available to the minority community.[1756]

Following the US entry into World War II after the attack on Pearl Harbor, the federal government removed and interned 70,000 Japanese-Americans from Los Angeles, leaving empty spaces in predominantly Japanese-owned areas. This further bolstered the migration of black residents into the city during the Second Great Migration to occupy the vacated spaces, such as Little Tokyo. As a result, housing in South Los Angeles became increasingly scarce, overwhelming the already established communities and providing opportunities for real estate developers. Davenport Builders, for example, was a large developer who responded to the demand, with an eye on undeveloped land in Compton. What was originally a mostly white neighbourhood in the 1940s increasingly became an African American,

---

[1753] The Great Migration: Creating a New Black Identity in Los Angeles", KCET
[1754] *Taylor, Dorceta (2014). Toxic Communities: Environmental Racism, Industrial Pollution, and Residential Mobility. NYU Press. p. 202. ISBN 9781479861620.*
[1755] Bernstein, Shana (2010). *Bridges of Reform: Interracial Civil Rights Activism in Twentieth Century Los Angeles.* Oxford University Press. pp. 107–109. ISBN 9780199715893.
[1756] Bernstein, Shana (2010). *Bridges of Reform: Interracial Civil Rights Activism in Twentieth Century Los Angeles.* Oxford University Press. pp. 107–109. ISBN 9780199715893.

middle-class dream in which blue-collar laborers could enjoy suburbia away from the slums.[1757]

In the post-World War II era, suburbs in the Los Angeles area grew explosively as black residents also wanted to live in peaceful white neighbourhoods. In a thinly veiled attempt to sustain their way of life and maintain the general peace and prosperity, most of these suburbs barred black people, using a variety of methods. White middle-class people in neighbourhoods bordering black districts moved en-masse to the suburbs, where newer housing was available. The spread of African Americans throughout urban Los Angeles was achieved in large part through blockbusting, a technique whereby real estate speculators would buy a home on an all-white street, sell or rent it to a black family, and then buy up the remaining homes from Caucasians at cut-rate prices, then sell them to housing-hungry black families at hefty profits.[1758]

The Rumford Fair Housing Act, designed to remedy residential segregation, was overturned by Proposition 14 in 1964, which was sponsored by the California real estate industry, and supported by a majority of white voters. Psychiatrist and civil rights activist Alvin Poussaint considered Proposition 14 to be one of the causes of black rebellion in Watts.[1759]

In 1950, William H. Parker was appointed and sworn in as Los Angeles Chief of Police. After a major scandal called Bloody Christmas of 1951, Parker pushed for more independence from political pressures that would enable him to create a more professionalized police force. The public supported him and voted for charter changes that isolated the police department from the rest of the city government. In the 1960s, the LAPD was promoted as one of the best police forces in the world·

Despite its reform and having a professionalized, military-like police force, William Parker's LAPD faced repeated criticism from the city's Latino and black residents for police brutality resulting from his recruiting of officers from the South with strong anti-black and anti-Latino attitudes. Chief Parker coined the term "Thin Blue Line", representing the police as holding down pervasive crime.[1760]

[1757] Bernstein, Shana (2010). Bridges of Reform: Interracial Civil Rights Activism in 20th Century Los Angeles - Oxford University Press. pp. 107–109. ISBN 9780199715893.
[1758] Gaspaire, Brent (January 7, 2013). "Blockbusting".
[1759] Theoharis, Jeanne (2006). The Black Power Movement: Rethinking the Civil Rights-Black Power Era. (New York: Routledge), p. 47-49.
[1760] Shaw, David (May 25, 2014). "Chief Parker Molded LAPD Image - Then Came the '60s: Police: Press treated officers as heroes until social upheaval prompted scepticism and confrontation". Los Angeles Times.

Resentment of such longstanding racial injustices is cited as reason why Watts' African American population exploded on August 11, 1965, in what would become the Watts Riots.[1761]

On the evening of Wednesday, August 11, 1965, 21-year-old Marquette Frye, an African-American man driving his mother's 1955 Buick while drunk, was pulled over by California Highway Patrol motorcycle officer Lee Minikus for alleged reckless driving.[1762] After Frye failed a field sobriety test, Minikus placed him under arrest and radioed for his vehicle to be impounded.[1763] Marquette's brother, Ronald, a passenger in the vehicle, walked to their house nearby, bringing their mother, Rena Price, back with him to the scene of the arrest.

When Rena Price reached the intersection of Avalon Boulevard and 116th Street that evening, she scolded Frye about drinking and driving as he recalled in a 1985 interview with the *Orlando Sentinel*.[1764] However, the situation quickly escalated: Someone shoved Price, Frye was struck, Price jumped an officer, and another officer pulled out a shotgun. Backup police officers attempted to arrest Frye by using physical force to subdue him. After community members reported that police had roughed up Frye and shared a rumour, they had kicked a pregnant woman, angry mobs formed.[1765] [1766] As the situation intensified, growing crowds of local residents watching the exchange began yelling and throwing objects at the police officers.[1767] Frye's mother and brother fought with the officers and eventually were arrested along with Marquette Frye.[1768] [1769] [1770]

After the arrests of Price and her sons the Frye brothers, the crowd continued to grow along Avalon Boulevard. Police came to the scene to break up the crowd

---

[1761] Watts Riots (August 1965) | The Black Past: Remembered and Reclaimed. The Black Past (August 11, 1965).

[1762] Dawsey, Darrell (August 19, 1990). "To CHP Officer Who Sparked Riots, It Was Just Another Arrest". *Los Angeles Times*.

[1763] Cohen, Jerry; Murphy, William S. (July 15, 1966). "Burn, Baby, Burn!" *Life*.

[1764] Szymanski, Michael (August 5, 1990). "How Legacy of the Watts Riot Consumed, Ruined Man's Life". *Orlando Sentinel*. Archived from the original on December 6, 2013. Retrieved June 22, 2013.

[1765] Dawsey, Darrell (August 19, 1990). "To CHP Officer Who Sparked Riots, It Was Just Another Arrest". *Los Angeles Times*.

[1766] Woo, Elaine (June 22, 2013). "Rena Price dies at 97; her and son's arrests sparked Watts riots". *Los Angeles Times*.

[1767] Abu-Lughod, Janet L. *Race, Space, and Riots in Chicago, New York, and Los Angeles*. New York: Oxford University Press, 2007.

[1768] Walker, Yvette (2008). *Encyclopaedia of African American History, 1896 to the Present: From the Age of Segregation to the Twenty-first Century*. Oxford University Press.

[1769] Alonso, Alex A. (1998). *Rebuilding Los Angeles: A Lesson of Community Reconstruction* (PDF). Los Angeles: University of Southern California.

[1770] Szymanski, Michael (August 5, 1990). "How Legacy of the Watts Riot Consumed, Ruined Man's Life". *Orlando Sentinel*. Retrieved June 22, 2013.

several times that night but were attacked when people threw rocks and chunks of concrete.[1771] A 46-square-mile (119 square kilometre) swath of Los Angeles was transformed into a combat zone during the ensuing six days.[1772]

After a night of increasing unrest, police and local black community leaders held a community meeting on Thursday, August 12, to discuss an action plan and to urge calm. The meeting failed. Later that day, Chief Parker called for the assistance of the California Army National Guard.[1773] Chief Parker believed the riots resembled an insurgency, compared it to fighting the Viet Cong, and decreed a "paramilitary" response to the disorder. Governor Pat Brown declared that law enforcement was confronting "guerrillas fighting with gangsters".[1774]

The rioting intensified, and on Friday, August 13, about 2,300 Na"ional Guards"en joined the police in trying to maintain order on the streets. Sergeant Ben Dunn said: "The streets of Watts resembled an all-out war zone in some far-off foreign country, it bore no resemblance to the United States of America."[1775] [1776] The first riot-related death occurred on the night of August 13, when a black civilian was killed in the crossfire during a shootout between the police and rioters. Over the next few days, rioting had then spread throughout other areas, including Pasadena, Pacoima, Monrovia, Long Beach, and even as far as San Diego, although they were very minor in comparison to Watts. About 200 Guardsmen and the LAPD were sent to assist the Long Beach Police Department (LBPD) in controlling the unruly crowd.

By nightfall on Saturday, 16,000 law enforcement personnel had been mobilized and patrolled the city.[1777] Blockades were established, and warning signs were posted throughout the riot zones threatening the use of deadly force (one sign warned residents to "Turn left or get shot"). Angered over the police response, residents of Watts engaged in a full-scale battle against the first responders. Rioters tore up sidewalks and bricks to hurl at Guardsmen and police, and to smash their vehicles.[1778]

[1771] Barnhill, John H. (2011). "Watts Riots (1965)". In Danver, Steven L. (ed.). Revolts, Protests, Demonstrations, and Rebellions in American History, Volume 3. ABC-CLIO.

[1772] Woo, Elaine (June 22, 2013). "Rena Price dies at 97; her and son's arrests sparked Watts riots". Los Angeles Times.

[1773] "Violence in the City: An End or a Beginning?".

[1774] Hinton, Elizabeth (2016). From the War on Poverty to the War on Crime: The Making of Mass Incarceration in America. Harvard University Press. pp. 68–72. ISBN 9780674737235.

[1775] Siegel, Fred (January 28, 2014). The Revolt Against the Masses: How Liberalism Has Undermined the Middle Class. Encounter Books. ISBN 9781594036989.

[1776] Troy, Tevi (2016). Shall We Wake the President? Two Centuries of Disaster Management from the Oval Office. Rowman and Littlefield. p. 156. ISBN 9781493024650.

[1777] Hinton, Elizabeth (2016). From the War on Poverty to the War on Crime: The Making of Mass Incarceration in America. Harvard University Press. pp. 68–72. ISBN 9780674737235.

[1778] Hinton, Elizabeth (2016). From the War on Poverty to the War on Crime: The Making of Mass

Those actively participating in the riots started physical fights with police, blocked Los Angeles Fire Department (LAFD) firefighters from using fire hoses on protesters and burning buildings, or stopped and beat white motorists while yelling racial slurs in the area. Arson and looting were largely confined to local white-owned stores and businesses that were said to have caused resentment in the neighbourhood due to low wages and high prices for local workers.[1779]

To quell the riots, Chief Parker initiated a policy of mass arrest.[1780] Following the deployment of National Guardsmen, a curfew was declared for a vast region of South Central Los Angeles.[1781] In addition to the Guardsmen, 934 LAPD officers and 718 officers from the Los Angeles County Sheriff's Department (LASD) were deployed during the rioting.[1782] Watts and all black-majority areas in Los Angeles were put under the curfew. All residents outside of their homes in the affected areas after 8:00 pm were subject to arrest. Eventually, nearly 3,500 people were arrested, primarily for curfew violations. By the morning of Sunday, August 15, the riots had largely been quelled.[1783]

Over the course of six days, between 31,000 and 35,000 adults participated in the riots. Around 70,000 people were "sympathetic, but not active."[1784] Over the six days, there were 34 deaths,[1785] [1786] 1,032 injuries,[1787] [1788] 3,438 arrests,[1789] [1790] and over $40 million in property damage.[1791] Many white Americans were fearful of the breakdown of social order in Watts, especially since white motorists were being

Incarceration in America. Harvard University Press. pp. 68–72. ISBN 9780674737235.
[1779] Oberschall, Anthony (1968). "The Los Angeles Riot of August 1965". *Social Problems*. **15** (3): 322–341. doi:10.2307/799788. JSTOR 799788.
[1780] Hinton, Elizabeth (2016). *From the War on Poverty to the War on Crime: The Making of Mass Incarceration in America*. Harvard University Press. pp. 68–72. ISBN 9780674737235.
[1781] "A Report Concerning the California National Guard's Part in Suppressing the Los Angeles Riot, August 1965" (PDF).
[1782] "Violence in the City: An End or a Beginning?".
[1783] Hinton, Elizabeth (2016). *From the War on Poverty to the War on Crime: The Making of Mass Incarceration in America*. Harvard University Press. pp. 68–72. ISBN 9780674737235.
[1784][1784] Barnhill, John H. (2011). "Watts Riots (1965)". In Danver, Steven L. (ed.). *Revolts, Protests, Demonstrations, and Rebellions in American History, Volume 3*. ABC-CLIO.
[1785] "The Watts Riots of 1965, in a Los Angeles newspaper... ". Timothy Hughes: Rare & Early Newspapers.
[1786] Reitman, Valerie; Landsberg, Mitchell (August 11, 2005). "Watts Riots, 40 Years Later". *Los Angeles Times*.
[1787] "The Watts Riots of 1965, in a Los Angeles newspaper... ". Timothy Hughes: Rare & Early Newspapers.
[1788] Watts Riot begins - August 11, 1965". This Day in History.
[1789] "The Watts Riots of 1965, in a Los Angeles newspaper... ". Timothy Hughes: Rare & Early Newspapers.
[1790] "Finding aid for the Watts Riots records 0084". Online Archive of California.
[1791] "The Watts Riots of 1965, in a Los Angeles newspaper... ". Timothy Hughes: Rare & Early Newspapers.

pulled over by rioters in nearby areas and assaulted.[1792] Many in the black community, however, believed the rioters were taking part in an "uprising against an oppressive system."[1793] In a 1966 essay, black civil rights activist Bayard Rustin wrote:

The whole point of the outbreak in Watts was that it marked the first major rebellion of Negroes against their own masochism and was carried on with the express purpose of asserting that they would no longer quietly submit to the deprivation of slum life.[1794]

Despite allegations that "criminal elements" were responsible for the riots, the vast majority of those arrested had no prior criminal record.[1795] Only three sworn personnel were killed in the riots: an LAFD firefighter was struck when a wall of a fire-weakened structure fell on him while fighting fires in a store,[1796] an LASD deputy was shot when another deputy's shotgun was discharged in a struggle with rioters,[1797] and an LBPD officer was shot by another police officer's gun that was discharged during a scuffle with rioters.[1798] 23 out of the 34 people killed in the riots were shot by LAPD officers or National Guardsmen.[1799]

Debate rose quickly over what had taken place in Watts, as the area was known to be under a great deal of racial and social tension. Reactions and reasoning about the riots greatly varied based on the perspectives of those affected by and participating in the riots' chaos.

National civil rights leader Rev. Dr. Martin Luther King Jr. spoke two days after the riots happened in Watts. The riots were partly a response to Proposition 14, a constitutional amendment sponsored by the California Real Estate Association and passed that had in effect repealed the Rumford Fair Housing Act.[1800] In 1966, the California Supreme Court reinstated the Rumford Fair Housing Act in the *Reitman v. Mulkey* case (a decision affirmed by the U.S. Supreme Court the following year), declaring the amendment to violate the US constitution and laws.

[1792] Queally, James (July 29, 2015). "Watts Riots: Traffic stop was the spark that ignited days of destruction in L.A.", *Los Angeles Times*.

[1793] Barnhill, John H. (2011). "Watts Riots (1965)". In Danver, Steven L. (ed.). *Revolts, Protests, Demonstrations, and Rebellions in American History, Volume 3*. ABC-CLIO.

[1794] Rustin, Bayard (March 1966). "The Watts". *Commentary Magazine*.

[1795] Hinton, Elizabeth (2016). *From the War on Poverty to the War on Crime: The Making of Mass Incarceration in America*. Harvard University Press. pp. 68–72. ISBN 9780674737235.

[1796] *"Fireman Warren E. Tilson, Los Angeles Fire Department"*. *Los Angeles Fire Department Historical Archive*.

[1797] "Deputy Sheriff Ronald E. Ludlow": Officer Down Memorial Page.

[1798] "Police Officer Richard R. LeFebvre": Officer Down Memorial Page.

[1799] Jerkins, Morgan (August 3, 2020). "A Haunting Story Behind the 1965 Watts Riots". *Time*.

[1800] Tracy Domingo, Miracle at Malibu Materialized, *Graphic*, November 14, 2002

A variety of opinions and explanations were published. Public opinion polls studied in the few years after the riot showed that a majority believed the riots were linked to communist groups who were active in the area protesting high unemployment rates and racial discrimination.[1801] Those opinions concerning racism and discrimination were expressed three years after hearings conducted by a committee of the U.S. Commission on Civil Rights took place in Los Angeles to assess the condition of relations between the police force and minorities. These hearings were also intended to make a ruling on the discrimination case against the police for their alleged mistreatment of members of the Nation of Islam.[1802] These different arguments and opinions are often cited in continuing debates over the underlying causes of the Watts riots.[1803]

After the Watts Riots, white families left surrounding nearby suburbs like Compton, Huntington Park, and South Gate in large numbers, leading to significant demographic and economic changes of these suburbs.[1804] Although the unrest did not reach these suburbs during the riots, many white residents in Huntington Park, for instance, left the area.[1805]

A commission under Governor Pat Brown investigated the riots, known as the McCone Commission, and headed by former CIA director John A. McCone. Other committee members included Warren Christopher, a Los Angeles attorney would be the committee's vice chairman, Earl C. Broady, Los Angeles Superior Court judge; Asa V. Call, former president of the State Chamber of Commerce; Rev. Charles Casassa, president of Loyola University of Los Angeles; the Rev. James E. Jones of Westminster Presbyterian Church and member of the Los Angeles Board of Education; Mrs. Robert G. Newmann, a League of Women Voters leader; and Dr. Sherman M. Mellinkoff, dean of the School of Medicine at UCLA. The only two African American members were Jones and Broady.[1806]

The commission released a 101-page report on December 2, 1965, entitled *Violence in the City – An End or a* [1807]*Beginning? A Report by the Governor's Commission on the Los Angeles Riots, 1965.*

[1801] Jeffries, Vincent & Ransford, H. Edward. "Interracial Social Contact and Middle-Class White Reaction to the Watts Riot". *Social Problems* 16.3 (1969): 312–324.

[1802] Jeffries, Vincent & Ransford, H. Edward. "Interracial Social Contact and Middle-Class White Reaction to the Watts Riot". *Social Problems* 16.3 (1969): 312–324.

[1803] Oberschall, Anthony (1968). "The Los Angeles Riot of August 1965". *Social Problems*. **15** (3): 322–341. doi:10.2307/799788. JSTOR 799788.

[1804] Ramirez, Aron (July 10, 2019). "On Race, Housing, and Confronting History". *The Downey Patriot.*

[1805] Holguin, Rick; Ramos, George (April 7, 1990). "Cultures Follow Separate Paths in Huntington Park". *Los Angeles Times.*

[1806] "King and Yorty Feud Over Causes of Rioting in LA". *Detroit Free Press at Newspapers.com.* August 20, 1965. p. 17.

[1807] *Violence in the City - An End or a Beginning? A Report by the Governor's Commission on the Los*

The McCone Commission identified the root causes of the riots to be high unemployment, poor schools, and related inferior living conditions that were endured by African Americans in Watts. Recommendations for addressing these problems included "emergency literacy and preschool programs, improved police-community ties, increased low-income housing, more job-training projects, upgraded health-care services, more efficient public transportation, and many more."

Most of these recommendations were never implemented.[1808]

Sadly, as you will discover as you continue to read this book, this was not to be the only time that riots broke out in the Watts district of Los Angles

---

Angeles Riots, 1965. University of Southern California.
[1808] *Dawsey, Darrell (July 8, 1990). "25 Years After the Watts Riots: McCone Commission's Recommendations Have Gone Unheeded". Los Angeles Times.*

Chapter forty-three

MOVE – Philadelphia – the city that bombed itself

MOVE, originally the Christian Movement for Life, is a militant black separatist group that advocates for nature laws and natural living, founded in 1972 in Philadelphia, Pennsylvania, United States, by John Africa (born Vincent Leaphart). The name, styled in all capital letters, is not an acronym. MOVE lived in a communal setting in West Philadelphia, abiding by philosophies of anarcho-primitivism.[1809] The group combined revolutionary ideology, similar to that of the Black Panthers, with work for animal rights.

MOVE is particularly known for two major conflicts with the Philadelphia Police Department (PPD). In 1978, a standoff resulted in the death of one police officer and injuries to 16 officers and firefighters. Nine members were convicted of killing the officer and received life sentences. In 1985, another firefight ended when a police helicopter dropped two bombs onto the roof of the MOVE compound, a townhouse located at 6221 Osage Avenue.[1810] [1811] The resulting fire killed six MOVE members and five of their children, and destroyed 65 houses in the neighbourhood.[1812]

The police bombing was strongly condemned. The MOVE survivors later filed a civil suit against the City of Philadelphia and the PPD and were awarded $1.5 million in a 1996 settlement.[1813] Other residents displaced by the destruction of the bombing filed a civil suit against the city and in 2005 were awarded $12.83 million in damages in a jury trial.

How things began:

[1809] "MOVE". *Encyclopedia of Greater Philadelphia.*

[1810] *Jackson, R (May 30, 2021). "A Racial Tragedy in Philadelphia: Part 1 - The MOVE 9 Versus American Jurisprudence". The Milwaukee Independent. Retrieved July 18, 2021. Nine members from Move, Eddie Africa, Janet Africa, Janine Africa, Mike Africa, Debbie Africa, Delbert Africa, Chuck Africa, Phil Africa and Merle Africa were charged with killing Officer Ramp. They refused to have a jury and would not cooperate with the court appointed attorney. The group of them became known as the MOVE 9. They were all found guilty of murder in the third degree and sentenced to 30 to 100 years in prison by Judge Edwin Malmed.*

[1811] "Let The Fire Burn". Kanopy.

[1812] "I'm From Philly. 30 Years Later, I'm Still Trying to Make Sense of the MOVE Bombing". Codeswitch. NPR.

[1813] Trippett, Frank (May 27, 1985). "It Looks Just Like a War Zone". *TIME.*

The group's name, MOVE, is not an acronym.[1814] Its founder, John Africa, chose this name to say what they intended to do. Members intend to be active because they say, "Everything that's alive moves. If it didn't, it would be stagnant, dead."[1815] Whe n members greet each other they say, "on the MOVE".[1816]

When the organization that would become MOVE was founded in 1972, John Africa was functionally illiterate.[1817] John Africa dictated his thoughts to Donald Glassey, a social worker from the University of Pennsylvania, and created what he called "The Guidelines" as the basis of his communal group.[1818] Africa and his mostly African-American followers wore their hair in dreadlocks, as popularized by the Caribbean Rastafari movement. MOVE advocated a radical form of green politics and a return to a hunter-gatherer society, while stating their opposition to science, medicine, and technology.[1819]

Members of MOVE identify as deeply religious and advocate for life. They believe that as all living beings are dependent, their lives should be treated as equally important. They advocate for justice that is not always based within institutions. MOVE members believe that for something to be just, it must be just for all living creatures.[1820] As John Africa had done, his followers changed their surnames to Africa to show reverence to what they regarded as their mother continent.[1821] [1822] [1823]

In a 2018 article about the group, Ed Pilkington of *The Guardian* described their political views as "a strange fusion of black power and flower power. The group that formed in the early 1970s melded the revolutionary ideology of the Black Panthers with the nature and animal-loving communalism of 1960s hippies. You might characterise them as black liberationists-cum-eco warriors."[1824] He noted the group also functioned as a rights advocacy organization. Pilkington quoted member Janine Africa, who wrote to him from prison: "We demonstrated against puppy mills, zoos, circuses, any form of enslavement of animals. We demonstrated against Three Mile Island and industrial pollution. We demonstrated against police

[1814] CNN – Philadelphia, city officials ordered to pay $1.5 million in MOVE case". *cnn.com*. June 24, 1996.
[1815] An account of the 1985 Incident from USA Today.
[1816] An account of the 1985 Incident from USA Today.
[1817] "About MOVE – On a Move". *onamove.com*.
[1818] "MOVE". *Encyclopedia of Greater Philadelphia*
[1819] *James, Louise Leaphart (September 26, 2013). John Africa. ISBN 9781483637884.*
[1820] An account of the 1985 Incident from USA Today.
[1821] Trippett, Frank (May 27, 1985). "It Looks Just Like a War Zone". *TIME*.
[1822] "An inauspicious beginning". *philly.com*. philly.com.
[1823] John Anderson and Hilary Hevenor, *Burning Down the House: MOVE and the tragedy of Philadelphia*, W.W. Norton & Co., 1987, ISBN 0-393-02460-1
[1824] 25 Years Ago: Philadelphia Police Bombs MOVE Headquarters Killing 11, Destroying 65 Homes, democracynow.org.

brutality. And we did so uncompromisingly. Slavery never ended, it was just disguised."[1825]

John Africa and his followers lived in a commune in a house owned by Glassey in the Powelton Village section of West Philadelphia. As activists, they staged bullhorn-amplified, profanity-laced demonstrations against institutions that they opposed, such as zoos, and speakers whose views they opposed. MOVE activities were scrutinized by law enforcement authorities,[1826] [1827] particularly under the administration of Mayor Frank Rizzo, a former police commissioner known for his hard line against activist groups.[1828]

In 1977, three MOVE members were jailed for inciting a riot, occasioning further tension, protests, and armed displays from the group.

In 1977, according to police accounts, the Philadelphia Police Department (PPD) obtained a court order for MOVE to vacate the Powelton Village property in response to a series of complaints made by neighbours. MOVE members agreed to vacate and surrender their weapons if the PPD released members of their group who were being held in city jails.[1829]

Nearly a year later, on August 8, 1978, the PPD came to a standoff with members of MOVE who had not left the Powelton Village property.[1830] When police attempted to enter the house, a shootout ensued. PPD officer James J. Ramp was killed by a shot to the back of the neck. 16 police officers and firefighters were also injured in the firefight.[1831] and denied that the group was responsible for his death, insisting that he was killed by fire from fellow police officers.[1832]

16 police officers and firefighters were also injured in the firefight.[1833] MOVE representatives claimed that Ramp was facing the house at the time and denied that the group was responsible for his death, insisting that he was killed by fire from

[1825] 25 Years Ago: Philadelphia Police Bombs MOVE Headquarters Killing 11, Destroying 65 Homes, democracynow.org.

[1826] Pilkington, Ed (July 31, 2018). "A siege. A bomb. 48 dogs. And the black commune that would not surrender". *The Guardian.*

[1827] 'Let The Fire Burn': A Philadelphia Community Forever Changed". *npr.org.* NPR.

[1828] 25 Years Ago: Philadelphia Police Bombs MOVE Headquarters Killing 11, Destroying 65 Homes, democracynow.org.

[1829] *"Survivor Remembers Bombing Of Philadelphia Headquarters". philadelphia.cbslocal.com. CBS Philly. May 13, 2013.*

[1830] Demby, Gene (May 13, 2015). "I'm from Philly 30 years later I'm still trying to make sense of the MOVE bombing". NPR.

[1831] *"Survivor Remembers Bombing Of Philadelphia Headquarters". philadelphia.cbslocal.com. CBS Philly. May 13, 2013.*

[1832] "Nose to Nose -". *TIME.* August 8, 1978.

[1833] *"Survivor Remembers Bombing Of Philadelphia Headquarters". philadelphia.cbslocal.com. CBS Philly. May 13, 2013.*

fellow police officers.[1834] Prosecutors alleged that MOVE members fired the fatal shot and charged Debbie Sims Africa and eight other MOVE members with collective responsibility for his death.

According to a 2018 article in *The Guardian*,

"Eyewitnesses, however, gave accounts suggesting that the shot may have come from the opposite direction to the basement, raising the possibility that Ramp was accidentally felled by police fire. MOVE members continue to insist that they had no workable guns in their house at the time of the siege. Several months earlier, in May 1978, several guns – most of them inoperative – had been handed over to police at the MOVE house; however, prosecutors at the trial of the MOVE Nine told the jury that at the time of the August siege there had been functioning firearms in the house."[1835]

The standoff lasted about an hour before MOVE members began to surrender.[1836]

The nine members of MOVE charged with third-degree murder for Ramp's death became known as the MOVE 9. Each was sentenced to a maximum of 100 years in prison. They were Chuck, Delbert, Eddie, Janet, Janine, Merle, Michael, Phil, and Debbie Sims Africa.

In 1998, at age 47, Merle Africa died in prison.[1837] Seven of the surviving eight members first became eligible for parole in the spring of 2008, but they were denied. Parole hearings for each of these prisoners were to be held yearly from that time.[1838] In 2015, at age 59, Phil Africa died in prison.[1839]

The first of the MOVE 9 to be released was Debbie Sims Africa on June 16, 2018.[1840] Debbie Sims Africa, who was 22 when sentenced, was released on parole and reunited with her 39-year-old son, Michael Davis Africa, Jr. She gave birth to him a month after she was imprisoned, and he was taken from her a week later.[1841] The

---

[1834] "Nose to Nose -". *TIME*. August 8, 1978.

[1835] Pilkington, Ed (May 25, 2019). "Move 9 women freed after 40 years in jail over Philadelphia police siege". *The Guardian*.

[1836] Pilkington, Ed (June 18, 2018). "'This is huge': black liberationist speaks out after her 40 years in prison". *The Guardian*.

[1837] Hornaday, Ann. "Review | HBO documentary about the 1978 MOVE standoff is a distressing look at the past — and the present". *Washington Post*. ISSN 0190-8286.

[1838] Move Death Merle Africa's Demise Labelled `Suspicious' *The Philadelphia Inquirer*, March 14, 1998

[1839] Lounsberry, Emilie (June 5, 2008). "MOVE members denied parole". *The Philadelphia Inquirer*. p. B06.

[1840] *Pilkington, Ed (May 25, 2019). "Move 9 women freed after 40 years in jail over Philadelphia police siege". The Guardian.*

[1841] *Pilkington, Ed (May 25, 2019). "Move 9 women freed after 40 years in jail over Philadelphia police siege". The Guardian.*

release of Debbie Sims Africa renewed attention on members of MOVE and the Black Panthers who remain imprisoned in the U.S. from the period of the 1960s and 1970s; there were at least 25 still in prison as of June 2018.[1842]

On October 23, 2018, Michael Davis Africa, the husband of Debbie Sims Africa, was released on parole.[1843] In May 2019, Janine and Janet Africa were released on parole after 41 years of imprisonment.[1844] On June 21, 2019, Eddie Goodman Africa was released on parole.[1845] Delbert Orr Africa was granted parole on December 20, 2019 and released January 18, 2020.[1846] The last of the MOVE 9 either to be paroled or to die behind bars was Chuck Sims Africa, who was released on parole on February 7, 2020 after 41 years of imprisonment.[1847] [1848]Delbert Orr Africa died of cancer at home on June 16, 2020.[1849]

In 1981, MOVE relocated to a row house at 6221 Osage Avenue in the Cobbs Creek area of West Philadelphia. Neighbours complained to the city for years about trash around their building, confrontations with neighbours, and bullhorn announcements of sometimes obscene political messages by MOVE members.[1850] T he bullhorn was broken and inoperable for the three weeks prior to the police bombing of the row house.[1851]

The police obtained arrest warrants in 1985 charging four MOVE occupants with crimes including parole violations, contempt of court, illegal possession of firearms,

---

[1842] Pilkington, Ed (May 25, 2019). "Move 9 women freed after 40 years in jail over Philadelphia police siege". The Guardian.

[1843] Roberts, Sam (January 14, 2015). "Phil Africa, of Black-Liberation Group Move, Long in Prison, Dies at 59". The New York Times. p. A21.

[1844] D'Onofrio, Michael (October 23, 2018). "Another MOVE 9 member tied to 1978 case leaves prison". The Philadelphia Tribune.

[1845] Pilkington, Ed (May 25, 2019). "Move 9 women freed after 40 years in jail over Philadelphia police siege". The Guardian. Guardian News & Media. ISSN 0261-3077.

[1846] Pilkington, Ed (June 23, 2019). "Move 9 member Eddie Goodman Africa released from prison after 41 years". The Guardian. Guardian News & Media. ISSN 0261-3077.

[1847] Pilkington, Ed (May 25, 2019). "Move 9 women freed after 40 years in jail over Philadelphia police siege". The Guardian. Guardian News & Media. ISSN 0261-3077. 26, 2019.

[1848] Pilkington, Ed (January 18, 2020). "Move 9 member Delbert Orr Africa freed after 42 years in prison". the Guardian.

[1849] Pilkington, Ed (February 7, 2020). "Chuck Sims Africa freed: final jailed Move 9 member released from prison". The Guardian. ISSN 0261-3077.

[1850] Dean, Mensah M. (June 16, 2020). "Delbert Africa, MOVE member released from prison in January after 41 years, has died".

[1851] Frank Trippett (May 27, 1985). "It Looks Just Like a War Zone". TIME magazine. Retrieved February 15, 2009. The Move property on Osage Avenue had become notorious for its abundant litter of garbage and human waste and for its scurrying rats and dozens of dogs. Bullhorns blared forth obscene tirades and harangues at all times of day and night. MOVE members customarily kept their children out of both clothes and school. They physically assaulted some neighbours and threatened others.

and making terrorist threats.[1852] The Mayor, Wilson Goode and the Police Commissioner Mr. Gregore J. Sambor, classified MOVE as a terrorist organization. Police evacuated residents of the area from the neighbourhood prior to their action. Residents were told that they would be able to return to their homes after a 24-hour period.

On Monday, May 13, 1985, nearly five hundred police officers, along with city manager Leo Brooks, arrived in force and attempted to clear the building and execute the arrest warrants.[1853] Nearby houses were evacuated.[1854] Water and electricity were shut off in order to force MOVE members out of the house. Commissioner Sambor read a long speech addressed to MOVE members that started with, "Attention MOVE: This is America. You have to abide by the laws of the United States." When the MOVE members did not respond, the police decided to forcibly remove the 13 members from the house,[1855] which consisted of seven adults and six children.

There was an armed standoff with police, who lobbed tear gas canisters at the building. The MOVE members fired at them, and a 90-minute gunfight ensued, in which one officer was bruised in the back by gunfire. Police used more than ten thousand rounds of ammunition before Commissioner Sambor ordered that the compound be bombed. From a Pennsylvania State Police helicopter, Philadelphia

Police Department Lt. Frank Powell proceeded to drop two one-pound bombs (which the police referred to as "entry devices") made of FBI-supplied Tovex, a dynamite substitute, targeting a cubicle on the roof of the house. The ensuing fire killed eleven of the people in the house (John Africa, five other adults, and five children aged 7 to 13). The fire spread and eventually destroyed approximately 65 nearby houses on Osage Avenue and nearby Pine Street. Although firefighters had earlier drenched the building prior to the bombing, after the fire broke out, officials said they feared that MOVE would shoot at the firefighters, so held them back.

Goode later testified at a 1996 trial that he had ordered the fire to be put out after the bunker had burned. Sambor said he received the order, but the fire commissioner testified that he did not receive the order.[1856] Ramona Africa, one of the two MOVE survivors from the house, said that police fired at those trying to escape.[1857]

[1852] "I'm From Philly. 30 Years Later, I'm Still Trying to Make Sense of the MOVE Bombing". Codeswitch. NPR.

[1853] "Survivor Remembers Bombing Of Philadelphia Headquarters". *philadelphia.cbslocal.com*. CBS Philly. May 13, 2013.

[1854] Let The Fire Burn". Kanopy.

[1855] "Survivor Remembers Bombing Of Philadelphia Headquarters". *philadelphia.cbslocal.com*. CBS Philly. May 13, 2013.

[1856] Brian Jenkins (April 2, 1996). "MOVE siege returns to haunt city". CNN.com.

[1857] Terry, Don (June 25, 1996). "Philadelphia Held Liable For Firebomb Fatal to 11". *The New York*

Goode appointed an investigative commission called the Philadelphia Special Investigation Commission (PSIC, aka MOVE Commission), chaired by William H. Brown, III. Sambor resigned in November 1985; in a speech the following year, he said that he was made a "surrogate" by Goode.[1858]

The MOVE Commission issued its report on March 6, 1986. The report denounced the actions of the city government, stating that "Dropping a bomb on an occupied row house was unconscionable."[1859] Following the release of the report, Goode made a formal public apology.[1860] No one from the city government was criminally charged in the attack. The only surviving adult MOVE member, Ramona Africa, was charged and convicted on charges of riot and conspiracy; she served seven years in prison.[1861]

In 1996 a federal jury ordered the city to pay a $1.5 million civil suit judgment to survivor Ramona Africa and relatives of two people killed in the bombing. The jury had found that the city used excessive force and violated the members' constitutional protections against unreasonable search and seizure.[1862] In 1985 Philadelphia was given the sobriquet "The City that Bombed Itself".[1863]

In 2005 federal judge Clarence Charles Newcomer presided over a civil trial brought by residents seeking damages for having been displaced by the widespread destruction following the 1985 police bombing of MOVE. A jury awarded them a $12.83 million verdict against the City of Philadelphia.[1864]

On November 12, 2020, the City Council of Philadelphia passed a resolution apologizing "for the decisions and events preceding and leading to the devastation that occurred on May 13, 1985."[1865] The Council established "an annual day of observation, reflection and recommitment" to remember the MOVE Bombing.[1866]

Times.

[1858] "Philadelphia MOVE Bombing Still Haunts Survivors". *NPR.org*. NPR.

[1859] Call, SCOTT J. HIGHAM, The Morning. "I WAS EXPENDABLE, SAMBOR LEARNED AFTER MOVE FIASCO". *mcall.com*.

[1860] "Philadelphia Special Investigation (MOVE) Commission Manuscript Collection".

[1861] Times, WILLIAM K. STEVENS, The New York. "GOODE OFFERS HIS APOLOGY FOR MOVE". *mcall.com*.

[1862] *Brian Jenkins (April 2, 1996). "MOVE siege returns to haunt city". CNN.com.*

[1863] Odom, Maida. "Ramona Africa Given Jail Term For Siege Role". *philly.com*.

[1864] Larry Eichel (May 8, 2005). "The MOVE Disaster: May 13, 1985". *The Philadelphia Inquirer*.

[1865] Douglas Martin (August 28, 2005). "CLARENCE NEWCOMER, 82, LONGTIME FEDERAL JUDGE," *South Florida Sun Sentinel*.

[1866] Douglas Martin (August 28, 2005). "CLARENCE NEWCOMER, 82, LONGTIME FEDERAL JUDGE," *South Florida Sun Sentinel*.

Chapter forty-four

The Watts Riots 1992

(Also known as the Rodney King Riots)

The 1992 Los Angeles riots were a series of riots and civil disturbances that occurred in Los Angeles County in April and May 1992. Unrest began in South Central Los Angeles on April 29, after a jury acquitted four officers of the Los Angeles Police Department (LAPD) charged with using excessive force in the arrest and beating of Rodney King. This incident had been videotaped and widely shown in television broadcasts. I doubt there will be anyone who reads this book, unless they were born after 1980, that has not seen the video tape of the King beating, that went viral.

The rioting took place in several areas in the Los Angeles metropolitan area, as thousands of people rioted over six days after the verdict's announcement but were concentrated in the South Central area. Widespread looting, assault, and arson occurred during the riots, which local police forces had difficulty controlling due to lack of personnel and resources. The situation in the Los Angeles area was resolved only after the California National Guard, United States military, and several federal law enforcement agencies were deployed to assist in ending the violence and unrest.

By the time the riots ended, 63 people had been killed,[1867] 2,383 had been injured, more than 12,000 had been arrested, and estimates of property damage were over $1 billion. Koreatown, where the bulk of the rioting in South Central Los Angeles occurred, received disproportionately more damage than surrounding areas. LAPD Chief of Police Daryl Gates, who had already announced his resignation by the time of the riots, was attributed with much of the blame for failure to de-escalate the situation and overall mismanagement.[1868] [1869]

Before the release of the Rodney King tape, minority community leaders in Los Angeles had repeatedly complained about harassment and use of excessive force against their residents by LAPD officers.[1870] Daryl Gates, Chief of the Los Angeles

---

[1867] Danver, Steven L., ed. (2011). "Los Angeles Uprising (1992)". *Revolts, Protests, Demonstrations, and Rebellions in American History: An Encyclopedia, Volume 3.* Santa Barbara, Calif.: ABC-CLIO. pp. 1095–1100. ISBN 978-1-59884-222-7.
[1868] *Bergesen, Albert; Herman, Max (1998). "Immigration, Race, and Riot: The 1992 Los Angeles Uprising". American Sociological Review. 63 (1): 39–54. doi:10.2307/2657476. JSTOR 2657476.*
[1869] Miranda, Carolina A. (April 28, 2017). "Of the 63 people killed during '92 riots, 23 deaths remain unsolved – artist Jeff Beall is mapping where they fell". *Los Angeles Times.*
[1870] *Mydans, Seth (October 22, 1992). "Failures of City Blamed for Riot In Los Angeles". The New York Times.*

Police Department (LAPD) from 1978 to 1992, has been attributed with much of the blame for the riots.[1871] [1872] According to one study, "scandalous racist violence... marked the LAPD under Gates's tempestuous leadership."[1873] Under Gates, the LAPD had begun Operation Hammer in April 1987, which was a large-scale attempt to crack down on gang violence in Los Angeles.

The origin of Operation Hammer can be traced t" the 1984 Olympic Games held in Los Angeles. Under Gates's direction, the LAPD expanded gang sweeps for the duration of the Olympics. These were implemented across wide areas of the city but especially in South Central and East Los Angeles, areas of predominately minority residents. After the games were over, the city began to revive the use of earlier anti-syndicalist laws to maintain the security policy started for the Olympic games. The police more frequently conducted mass arrests of African American youth, although the overwhelming number of them were never charged. Citizen complaints against police brutality increased 33 percent in the period 1984 to 1989.[1874]

By 1990 more than 50,000 people, mostly minority males, had been arrested in such raids.[1875] During this period, the LAPD arrested more young black men and women than at any period of time since the Watts riots of 1965. Critics have alleged that the operation was racist because it used racial profiling, targeting African-American and Mexican American youths.[1876] The perception that police had targeted non-White citizens likely contributed to the anger that erupted in the 1992 riots.[1877]

The Christopher Commission later concluded that a "significant number" of LAPD officers "repetitively use excessive force against the public and persistently ignore the written guidelines of the department regarding force." The biases related to race, gender, and sexual orientation were found to have regularly contributed to excessive force use.[1878] The commission's report called for the replacement of both Chief Daryl Gates and the civilian Police Commission.[1879]

[1871] "The Final Report: The L.A. Riots", *National Geographic Channel*, aired on October 4, 2006 10 pm EDT, approximately 38 minutes into the hour (including commercial breaks).

[1872] *"Violence and Racism Are Routine In Los Angeles Police, Study Says"*. www.nytimes.com. July 10, 1991.

[1873] Cannon, Lou; Lee, Gary (May 2, 1992). "Much Of Blame Is Laid On Chief Gates". *The Washington Post*.

[1874] Mydans, Seth (October 22, 1992). "Failures of City Blamed for Riot In Los Angeles". *The New York Times*.

[1875] Schrader, Stuart (2019). *Badges without Borders: How Global Counterinsurgency Transformed American Policing*. **56**. University of California Press. p. 216. ISBN 978-0-520-29561-2. JSTOR j.ctvp2n2kv.

[1876] Want to understand the 1992 LA riots – Start with the 1984 LA Olympics

[1877] Cockburn, Alexander; Jeffrey St. Clair (1998). *Whiteout: The CIA, Drugs, and the Press*. Verso. p. 77. ISBN 978-1-85984-139-6.

[1878] Moody, Mia Nodeen (2008). *Black and Mainstream Press' Framing of Racial Profiling: A Historical Perspective*. University Press of America. p. 14. ISBN 978-0-7618-4036-7.

In the year before the riots, 1991, there was growing resentment and violence between   the African-American and Korean-American communities.[1880] Racial tensions had been simmering for years between these groups. In 1989, the release of Spike Lee's film *Do the Right Thing* highlighted urban tensions between White Americans, Black Americans and Korean Americans over racism and economic inequality.[1881] Many Korean shopkeepers were upset because they suspected shoplifting from their black customers and neighbours. Many black customers were angry because they routinely felt disrespected and humiliated by Korean store owners. Neither group fully understood the extent or sheer enormity of the cultural differences and language barriers, which further fuelled tensions.[1882]

On March 16, 1991, a year before the Los Angeles riots, storekeeper Soon Ja Du shot and killed Latasha Harlins, a black ninth-grader after a physical altercation. Du was convicted of voluntary manslaughter and the jury recommended the maximum sentence of 16 years, but the judge, Joyce Karlin, decided against prison time and sentenced Du to five years of probation, 400 hours of community service, and a $500 fine instead.[1883] Relations between the Black- and Korean-American communities significantly worsened after this, and the former became increasingly mistrustful of the criminal justice system.[1884] A state appeals court later unanimously upheld Judge Karlin's sentencing decision in April 1992, a week before the riots.[1885]

The *Los Angeles Times* reported on several other significant incidents of violence between the communities at the time:

Other recent incidents include the May 25, 1991, shooting of two employees in a liquor store near 35th Street and Central Avenue. The victims, both recent emigrants from Korea, were killed after complying with robbery demands made by an assailant described by police as an African American. Last Thursday, an African American man suspected of committing a robbery in an auto parts store on Manchester Avenue was fatally wounded by his accomplice, who accidentally fired a shotgun round during a struggle with the shop's Korean American owner. "This violence is disturbing, too," store owner Park said. "But who cries for these victims?[1886]

[1879] Moody, Mia Nodeen (2008). *Black and Mainstream Press' Framing of Racial Profiling: A Historical Perspective*. University Press of America. p. 14. ISBN 978-0-7618-4036-7.

[1880] Kato, M. T. (2007). *From Kung Fu to Hip Hop: globalization, revolution, and popular culture*. SUNY Press. pp. 173–174. ISBN 978-0-7914-6991-0.

[1881] *Reinhold, Robert (May 3, 1992). "Riots in Los Angeles: The Overview; clean-up begins in Los Angeles; troops enforce surreal calm". The New York Times.*

[1882] Parvini, Sarah; Kim, Victoria (April 29, 2017). "25 years after racial tensions erupted, black and Korean communities reflect on L.A. riots". *Los Angeles Times*.

[1883] Bradshaw, Peter (August 2, 2019). "Do the Right Thing review – Spike Lee's towering, timeless tour de force". *The Guardian*.

[1884] "When LA Erupted In Anger: A Look Back At The Rodney King Riots". *NPR.org*.

[1885] *"How Koreatown Rose From The Ashes Of L.A. Riots". NPR. April 27, 2012.*

On the evening of March 3, 1991, Rodney King and two passengers were driving west on the Foothill Freeway (I-210) through the Sunland-Tujunga neighbourhood of the San Fernando Valley.[1887] The California Highway Patrol (CHP) attempted to initiate a traffic stop and a high-speed pursuit ensued with speeds estimated at up to 115 mph (185 km/h), before King eventually exited the freeway at Foothill Boulevard. The pursuit continued through residential neighbourhoods of Lake View Terrace in San Fernando Valley before King stopped in front of the Hanson Dam recreation centre. When King finally stopped, LAPD and CHP officers surrounded King's vehicle and married CHP officers Timothy and Melanie Singer arrested him and two other car occupants.[1888]

After the two passengers were placed in the patrol car, five Los Angeles Police Department (LAPD) officers – Stacey Koon, Laurence Powell, Timothy Wind, Theodore Briseno, and Rolando Solano – surrounded King, who came out of the car last. The officers involved were all White American, although Briseno and Solano were of Hispanic origin.[1889] They tasered him, struck him dozens of times with side-handled batons, kick stomped him in his back and tackled him to the ground before handcuffing him and hogtying his legs. Sergeant Koon later testified at trial that King resisted arrest and believed King was under the influence of PCP at the time of the arrest caused him to be very aggressive and violent toward the officers.[1890] Video footage of the arrest showed that King attempted to get up each time he was struck and that the police made no attempt to cuff him until he lay still.[1891] A subsequent test of King for the presence of PCP in his body at the time of the arrest was negative.[1892]

Unbeknownst to the police and King, the incident was captured on a camcorder by local civilian George Holliday from his nearby apartment across from Hansen Dam. The tape was roughly 12 minutes long. While the tape was presented during the trial, some clips of the incident were not released to the public.[1893] In a later interview, King, who was on parole for a robbery conviction and had past convictions for

---

[1886] "When LA Erupted In Anger: A Look Back At The Rodney King Riots". National Public Radio. April 26, 2017.

[1887] People v. Superior Court of Los Angeles County (Du), 5 Cal. App. 4th 822, 7 Cal.Rptr.2d 177 (1992), from Google Scholar.

[1888] Holguin, Rick; Lee, John H. (June 18, 1991). "Boycott of Store Where Man Was Killed Is Urged: Racial tensions: The African-American was slain while allegedly trying to rob the market owned by a Korean-American". *Los Angeles Times*.

[1889] Serrano, Richard A. (March 30, 1991). "Officers Claimed Self-Defence in Beating of King". *Los Angeles Times*.

[1890] *"Sergeant Says King Appeared to Be on Drugs". The New York Times. March 20, 1992.*

[1891] *Swift, David (July 10, 2020). "More than black and white". Standpoint.*

[1892] "Sergeant Says King Appeared to Be on Drugs". *The New York Times*. March 20, 1992.

[1893] Faragher, John. "Rodney King tape on national news". YouTube.

assault, battery and robbery,[1894] [1895] said that he had not surrendered earlier because he was driving while intoxicated under the influence of alcohol, which he knew violated the terms of his parole.

The footage of King being beaten by police became an instant focus of media attention and a rallying point for activists in Los Angeles and around the United States. Coverage was extensive during the first two weeks after the incident: the *Los Angeles Times* published 43 articles about it,[1896] *The New York Times* published 17 articles,[1897] and the *Chicago Tribune* published 11 articles.[1898] Eight stories appeared on ABC News, including a sixty-minute special on *Primetime Live.*[1899]

Upon watching the tape of the beating, LAPD chief of police Daryl Gates said:

I stared at the screen in disbelief. I played the one-minute-50-second tape again. Then again and again, until I had viewed it 25 times. And still I could not believe what I was looking at. To see my officers, engage in what appeared to be excessive use of force, possibly criminally excessive, to see them beat a man with their batons 56 times, to see a sergeant on the scene who did nothing to seize control, was something I never dreamed I would witness.[1900]

The Los Angeles County District Attorney subsequently charged four police officers, including one sergeant, with assault and use of excessive force.[1901] Due to the extensive media coverage of the arrest, the trial received a change of venue from Los Angeles County to Simi Valley in neighbouring Ventura County.[1902] The jury had no members who were entirely African-American.[1903] The jury was composed of nine white Americans (three women, six men), one bi-racial man,[1904] one Latin American

---

[1894] "Prosecution Rests Case in Rodney King Beating Trial". *tech.mit.edu – The Tech.*

[1895] Gonzalez, Juan (June 20, 2012). "George Holliday, the man with the camera who shot Rodney King while police subdued him, got burned, too. He got a quick thanks from King, but history-making video brought him peanuts and even the camera was finally yanked away". *Daily News.* New York.

[1896] *Doug Linder. "The Arrest Record of Rodney King". Law.umkc.edu.*

[1897] Official Negligence: How Rodney King and the Riots Changed Los Angeles and the LAPD pp. 41–42

[1898] *"Los Angeles Times: Archives". Pqasb.pqarchiver.com.*

[1899] *"The New York Times: Search for 'Rodney King'". The New York Times.*

[1900] "Archives: Chicago Tribune". Pqasb.pqarchiver.com.

[1901] *"Uprising: Hip Hop & The LA Riots".*

[1902] "Baltimore Is Everywhere: A Partial Culling of Unrest Across America", (Condensed from the *Encyclopedia of American Race Riots*, ed. Walter Rucker and James Nathaniel Upton), *New York* magazine, May 18–31, 2015, p. 33.

[1903] Mydans, Seth (March 6, 1992). "Police Beating Trial Opens With Replay of Videotape". *The New York Times.*

[1904] Abcarian, Robin (May 7, 2017). "An aggravating anniversary for Simi Valley, where a not-guilty verdict sparked the '92 L.A. riots". *Los Angeles Times.*

woman, and one American woman.[1905] The prosecutor, Terry White, was African American.[1906]

On April 29, 1992, the seventh day of jury deliberations, the jury acquitted all four officers of assault and acquitted three of the four of using excessive force. The jury could not agree on a verdict for the fourth officer charged with using excessive force.[1907] The verdicts were based in part on the first three seconds of a blurry, 13-second segment of the videotape that, according to journalist Lou Cannon, had not been aired by television news stations in their broadcasts. [1908] [1909]

The first two seconds of videotape, contrary to the claims made by the accused officers, show King attempting to flee past Laurence Powell. During the next one minute and 19 seconds, King is beaten continuously by the officers. The officers testified that they tried to restrain King before the videotape's starting point physically, but King could throw them off physically.[1910]

Afterward, the prosecution suggested that the jurors may have acquitted the officers because of becoming desensitized to the beating's violence, as the defence played the videotape repeatedly in slow motion, breaking it down until its emotional impact was lost.[1911]

Outside the Simi Valley courthouse where the acquittals were delivered, county sheriff's deputies protected Stacey Koon from angry protesters on the way to his car. Movie director John Singleton, who was in the crowd at the courthouse, predicted, "By having this verdict, what these people done, they lit the fuse to a bomb."[1912]

The riots began the day the verdicts were announced and peaked in intensity over the next two days. A dusk-to-dawn curfew and deployment by California National Guardsmen, U.S. troops, and Federal law enforcement personnel eventually controlled the situation.[1913]

[1905] Serrano, Richard (March 3, 1992). "Jury Picked for King Trial; No Blacks Chosen". *Los Angeles Times*.

[1906] *"Rodney King Juror Talks About His Black Father and Family For the First Time"*. LAist.web.archive.com April 28, 2012.

[1907] Serrano, Richard (March 3, 1992). "Jury Picked for King Trial; No Blacks Chosen". *Los Angeles Times*.

[1908] "Jurist – The Rodney King Beating Trials". Jurist.law.pitt.edu.

[1909] Law.umkc.edu

[1910] Serrano, Richard A. (April 30, 1992). "All 4 Acquitted in King Beating: Verdict Stirs Outrage; Bradley Calls It Senseless: Trial: Ventura County jury rejects charges of excessive force in episode captured on videotape. A mistrial is declared on one count against Officer Powell". *Los Angeles Times*.

[1911] *Doug Linder. "videotape". Law.umkc.edu.*

[1912] The American edition of the National Geographic Channel aired the program "The Final Report: The L.A. Riots" on October 4, 2006 10 pm EDT, approximately 27 minutes into the hour (including commercial breaks).

[1913] Cannon, Lou (1999). *Official Negligence: How Rodney King and the Riots Changed Los Angeles*

A total of 64 people died during the riots, including nine shots by law enforcement personnel and one by National Guardsmen.[1914] Of those killed during the riots, 2 were Asian, 28 were Black, 19 were Latino, and 15 were White. No law enforcement officials died during the riots.[1915] As many as 2,383 people were reported injured.[1916] Estimates of the material losses vary between about $800 million and $1 billion.[1917] Approximately 3,600 fires were set, destroying 1,100 buildings, with fire calls coming once every minute at some points. Widespread looting also occurred. Rioters targeted stores owned by Koreans and other ethnic Asians, reflecting tensions between them and the African American communities. [1918]

Many of the disturbances were concentrated in South Central Los Angeles, where the population was majority African American, and Hispanic. Fewer than half of all the riot arrests and a third of those killed during the violence were Hispanic.[1919] [1920]

The riots caused the Emergency Broadcast System and the National Oceanic and Atmospheric Administration to be activated on April 30, 1992, on KCAL-TV.

In the week before the Rodney King verdicts were reached, Los Angeles Police Chief Daryl Gates set aside $1 million for possible police overtime. Even so, on the last day of the trial, two-thirds of the LAPD's patrol captains were out of town in Ventura, California, on the first day of a three-day training seminar.[1921]

At 1 p.m. on April 29, Judge Stanley Weisberg announced that the jury had reached its verdict, which would be read in two hours' time. This was done to allow reporters and police and other emergency responders to prepare for the outcome, as unrest was feared if the officers were acquitted.[1922] The LAPD had activated its Emergency Operations Centre, which the Webster Commission described as "the doors were opened, the lights turned on and the coffee pot plugged in" but taken no other preparatory action. Specifically, the people intended to staff that Centre were not

and the LAPD (Reprint ed.). Basic Books. p. 284. ISBN 978-0813337258.
[1914] CNN Documentary Race + Rage: The Beating of Rodney King, aired originally on March 5, 2011; approximately 14 minutes into the hour (not including commercial breaks).
[1915] "Los Angeles Riots Fast Facts". CNN.
[1916] "Deaths during the L.A. riots". Los Angeles Times. April 25, 2012.
[1917] "Deaths during the L.A. riots". Los Angeles Times. April 25, 2012.
[1918] Sullivan, Meg (July 8, 2013). "New book by UCLA historian traces role of gender in 1992 Los Angeles riots". UCLA Newsroom.
[1919] Madison Gray (April 25, 2007). "The L.A. Riots: 15 Years After Rodney King". Time.
[1920] Daniel B. Wood (April 29, 2002). "L.A.'s darkest days". The Christian Science Monitor.
[1921] Pastor, M. (1995). "Economic Inequality, Latino Poverty, and the Civil Unrest in Los Angeles". Economic Development Quarterly. 9 (3): 238–258. doi:10.1177/089124249500900305. S2CID 153387638.
[1922] Pastor, M. (1995). "Economic Inequality, Latino Poverty, and the Civil Unrest in Los Angeles". Economic Development Quarterly. 9 (3): 238–258. doi:10.1177/089124249500900305. S2CID 153387638.

gathered until 4:45 p.m. In addition, no action was taken to retain extra personnel at the LAPD's shift change at 3 p.m., as the risk of trouble was deemed low.[1923]

When the Verdicts were announced:

The acquittals of the four accused Los Angeles Police Department officers came at 3:15 p.m. local time. By 3:45 p.m., a crowd of more than 300 people had appeared at the Los Angeles County Courthouse protesting the verdicts.

Meanwhile, at approximately 4:15 – 4:20 p.m., a group of people approached the Pay-Less Liquor and Deli on Florence Avenue just west of Normandie in South Central. In an interview, a member of the group said that the group "just decided they weren't going to pay for what they were getting." The store owner's son was hit with a bottle of beer, and two other youths smashed the store's glass front door. Two officers from the 77th Street Division of the LAPD responded to this incident and, finding that the instigators had already left, completed a report.[1924] [1925]

At 4:58 p.m.,[1926] Los Angeles Mayor Tom Bradley held a news conference to discuss the verdicts. He both expressed anger about the verdicts and appealed for calm.[1927]

"Today, this jury told the world that what we all saw with our own eyes wasn't a crime. Today, that jury asked us to accept the senseless and brutal beating of a helpless man. Today, that jury said we should tolerate such conduct by those sworn to protect and serve. My friends, I am here to tell this jury, "No. No, our eyes did not deceive us. We saw what we saw what we saw was a crime... We must not endanger the reforms we have achieved by resorting to mindless acts. We must not push back progress by striking back blindly."

Mayor Tom Bradley, post-verdict press conference:

Assistant Los Angeles police chief Bob Vernon later said he believed Bradley's remarks incited a riot and were perhaps taken as a signal by some citizens. Vernon said that the number of police incidents rose in the hour after the mayor's press conference.[1928]

[1923] Pastor, M. (1995). "Economic Inequality, Latino Poverty, and the Civil Unrest in Los Angeles". *Economic Development Quarterly*. **9** (3): 238–258. doi:10.1177/089124249500900305. S2CID 153387638.

[1924] Peter Kwong, "The First Multicultural Riots", in Don Hazen (ed.), *Inside the L.A. Riots: What Really Happened – and Why It Will Happen Again*, Institute for Alternative Journalism, 1992, p. 89.

[1925] Rosegrant, Susan (2000). *The Flawed Emergency Response to the 1992 Los Angeles Riots*. OCLC 50255450.

[1926] "LAPD Police Flee Angry Mob – begin of the La riots". YouTube. December 19, 2011.

[1927] Doug Linder. "videotape". Law.umkc.edu.

[1928] [1928] Doug Linder. "videotape". Law.umkc.edu.

At Florence and Halldale, two officers issued a plea for assistance in apprehending a young suspect who had thrown an object at their car and whom they were pursuing on foot.[1929] Approximately two dozen officers, commanded by 77th Street Division LAPD officer Lieutenant Michael Moulin, arrived and arrested the youth, 16-year-old Seandel Daniels, forcing him into the back of a car. The rough handling of the young man, a well-known minor in the community, further agitated an uneasy and growing crowd, who began taunting and berating the police.[1930] Among the crowd were Bart Bartholomew, a white freelance photographer for *The New York Times*, and Timothy Goldman, a black U.S. Air Force veteran in visit to his family,[1931] [1932] who began to record the events with his personal camcorder.[1933] [1934]

The police formed a perimeter around the arresting officers as the crowd grew more hostile, leading to further altercations and arrests (including that of Damian Williams' older brother, Mark Jackson). One member of the crowd stole the flashlight of an LAPD officer. Fearing police would resort to deadly force to repel the growing crowd, Lieutenant Moulin ordered officers out of the area altogether. Moulin later said that officers on the scene were outnumbered and unprepared to handle the situation because their riot equipment was stored at the police academy.

Hey, forget the flashlight, it's not worth it. It ain't worth it. It's not worth it. Forget the flashlight. Not worth it. Let's go.

Moulin made the call for reporting officers to retreat from the 71st and Normandie area entirely at approximately 5:50 p.m.[1935] [1936] They were sent to an RTD bus depot at 54th and Arlington[1937] and told to await further instructions. The command post formed at this location was set up at approximately 6 p.m. but had no cell phones or computers other than those in squad cars. It had insufficient numbers of telephone lines and handheld police radios to assess and respond to the situation.[1938] Finally,

[1929] Berry, LaVerle; Jones, Amanda; Powers, Terence (August 1999). *Media Interaction With the Public in Emergency Situations: Four Case Studies* (PDF). NCJ202329.

[1930] "Video: Part 1: Anatomy of a Riot (Index 10:41)". *ABC News*.

[1931] *"LAPPL – Los Angeles Police Protective League: Controversy over Rodney King beating, and L.A. riots reignites"*. lapd.com.

[1932] Cannon, Lou (January 26, 1998). "Worlds Collide at Florence and Normandie". *The Washington Post*.

[1933] "Witnesses reflect on LA's Rodney King riot 25 years later". *Associated Press*. April 26, 2017.

[1934] *"LAPPL – Los Angeles Police Protective League: Controversy over Rodney King beating, and L.A. riots reignites"*. lapd.com.

[1935] Cannon, Lou; Lee, Gary (May 2, 1992). "Much Of Blame Is Laid On Chief Gates". *The Washington Post*.

[1936] Peter Kwong, "The First Multicultural Riots", in Don Hazen (ed.), *Inside the L.A. Riots: What Really Happened – and Why It Will Happen Again*, Institute for Alternative Journalism, 1992, p. 89.

[1937] Mydans, Seth (July 31, 1992). "In Los Angeles Riots, a Witness With Videotapes". *The New York Times*

[1938] Mydans, Seth (July 31, 1992). "In Los Angeles Riots, a Witness With Videotapes". *The New York*

the site had no televisions, which meant that as live broadcasts of unrest began, command post officers could not see any of the coverage.[1939]

After the retreat of officers at 71st and Normandie, many proceeded one block south to the intersection of Florence and Normandie.[1940] As the crowd began to turn physically dangerous, Bartholomew managed to flee the scene with the help of Goldman. Someone hit Bartholomew with a wood plank, shattering his jaw, while others pounded him and grabbed his camera.[1941] Just after 6 p.m., a group of young men broke the padlock and windows to Tom's Liquor, allowing a group of more than 100 people to raid the store and loot it.[1942] Concurrently, the growing number of rioters in the street began attacking civilians of non-black appearance, throwing debris at their cars, pulling them from their vehicles when they stopped, smashing window shops, or assaulting them while they walked on the sidewalks. As Goldman continued to film the scene on the ground with his camcorder, the Los Angeles News Service team of Marika Gerrard and Zoey Tur arrived in a news helicopter, broadcasting from the air. The LANS feed appeared live on numerous Los Angeles television venues.[1943]

At approximately 6:15 p.m., as reports of vandalism, looting, and physical attacks continued to come in, Moulin elected to "take the information" but not respond personnel to restore order or rescue people in the area.[1944] Moulin was relieved by a captain, ordered only to assess the Florence and Normandie area, and, again, not to attempt to deploy officers there.[1945] Meanwhile, Tur continued to cover the events in progress live at the intersection. From overhead, Tur described the police presence at the scene around 6:30 p.m. as "none".[1946]

At 6:43 p.m., a white truck driver, Larry Tarvin, drove down Florence and stopped at a red light at Normandie in a large white delivery truck. With no radio in his truck, he did not know that he was driving into a riot.[1947] Tarvin was pulled from the

Times
[1939] Los Angeles Riots (Part I of V),
[1940] Rohrlich, Ted; Berger, Leslie (May 24, 1992). "Lack of Materiel Slowed Police Response to Riots: LAPD: Chronic shortage of radios, phones and cars forced command centre to scramble, records show". Los Angeles Times.
[1941] "LAPPL – Los Angeles Police Protective League: Controversy over Rodney King beating, and L.A. riots reignites". lapd.com.
[1942] "The Untold Story of the LA Riot". US News & World Report.
[1943] Cold motors (December 19, 2011), LAPD Police Flee Angry Mob – beginning of the La riots.
[1944] Berry, LaVerle; Jones, Amanda; Powers, Terence (August 1999). Media Interaction With the Public in Emergency Situations: Four Case Studies (PDF). NCJ202329.
[1945] "The Untold Story of the LA Riot", US News & World Report, May 23, 1993
[1946] DeLuca, Matthew (April 27, 2012). "Bob Tur, the L.A. Riots' Eye in the Sky, on Reginald Denny & More". The Daily Beast.
[1947] Mydans, Seth (May 22, 1992). "After the Riots; Reliving Riot Flash Point, Los Angeles Lieutenant Fights Chief". The New York Times.

vehicle by a group of men including Henry Watson, who proceeded to kick and beat him, before striking him unconscious with a fire extinguisher taken from his own vehicle.[1948] He lay unconscious for more than a minute[1949] as his truck was looted, before getting up and staggering back to his vehicle. With the help of an unknown African-American, Tarvin drove his truck out of further harm's way.[1950] [1951] Just before he did so, another truck, driven by Reginald Denny, entered the intersection.[1952] United Press International Radio Network reporter Bob Brill, who was filming the attack on Tarvin, was hit in the head with a bottle and stomped on.[1953] As noted, after the verdicts were announced, a crowd of protesters formed at the Los Angeles police headquarters at Parker Centre in Downtown Los Angeles. The crowd grew as the afternoon passed and became violent. The police formed a skirmish line to protect the building, sometimes moving back in the headquarters as protesters advanced, attempting to set the Parker Centre ablaze.[1954] In the midst of this, before 6:30 p.m., police chief Daryl Gates left Parker Centre, on his way to the neighbourhood of Brentwood. There, as the situation in Los Angeles deteriorated, Gates attended a political fundraiser against Los Angeles City Charter Amendment F,[1955] intended to "give City Hall more power over the police chief and provide more civilian review of officer misconduct".[1956] The amendment would limit the power and term length of his office.[1957]

The Parker Centre crowd grew riotous at approximately 9 p.m.,[1958] eventually making their way through the Civic Centre, attacking law enforcement, overturning vehicles, setting objects ablaze, vandalizing government buildings and blocking traffic on U.S. Route 101 going through other nearby districts in downtown Los Angeles looting and burning stores. Nearby Los Angeles Fire Department (LAFD)

[1948] LA News Archive (October 29, 2013), *LA Riots, Raw footage of Reginald Denny beatings – April 29, 1992,*

[1949] McMillan, Penelope (February 23, 1993). "'Other Trucker' Sues L.A. Over Beating at Outbreak of Riots: Violence: Larry Tarvin was assaulted at Florence and Normandie before Reginald Denny arrived. City claims immunity under state law". *Los Angeles Times.*

[1950] Mydans, Seth (May 22, 1992). "After the Riots; Reliving Riot Flash Point, Los Angeles Lieutenant Fights Chief". *The New York Times.*

[1951] *Los Angeles Riots (Part I of V),*

[1952] Mydans, Seth (May 22, 1992). "After the Riots; Reliving Riot Flash Point, Los Angeles Lieutenant Fights Chief". *The New York Times.*

[1953] *McMillan, Penelope (February 23, 1993). "'Other Trucker' Sues L.A. Over Beating at Outbreak of Riots: Violence: Larry Tarvin was assaulted at Florence and Normandie before Reginald Denny arrived. City claims immunity under state law". Los Angeles Times.*

[1954] Weather History for Los Angeles, CA". *www.wunderground.com.*

[1955] Weather History for Los Angeles, CA". *www.wunderground.com.*

[1956] "Charting the Hours of Chaos". *Los Angeles Fire Department Historical Archive.* Los Angeles Times (orig. archive pqasb.pqarchiver.com/latimes/doc/421691608.html). April 29, 2002.

[1957] Timothy Goldman (June 23, 2012), *Anatomy of the LA Riots (Part II),*

[1958] "The forgotten victim from Florence and Normandie". *Los Angeles Times*, May 6, 2012.

firefighters were shot at while trying to put out a blaze set by looters. The mayor had requested the California Army National Guard from Governor Pete Wilson; the first of these units, the 670th Military Police Company, had travelled almost 300 miles (480 km) from its main armoury and arrived in the afternoon to assist local police. They were first deployed to a police command centre, where they began handing out bulletproof vests to the firefighters after encountering the unit whose member had been shot. Later, after receiving ammunition from the L.A. Police Academy and a local gun store, the MPs deployed to hold the Martin Luther King Shopping Mall in Watts.[1959]

In the Lake View Terrace district of Los Angeles, 200 [1960] - 400 [1961] protesters gathered about 9:15 p.m. at the site where Rodney King was beaten in 1991, near the Hansen Dam Recreation Area. The group marched south on Osborne Street to the LAPD Foothill Division headquarters.[1962] There they began rock throwing, shooting into the air, and setting fires. The Foothill division police used riot-breaking techniques to disperse the crowd and arrest those responsible for rock throwing and the fires[1963] eventually leading to rioting and looting in the neighbouring area of Pacoima and its surrounding neighbourhoods in the San Fernando Valley.

Day 2 – Thursday, April 30

Mayor Bradley signed an order for a dusk-to-dawn curfew at 12:15 a.m. for the core area affected by the riots, as well as declaring a state of emergency for city of Los Angeles. At 10:15 a.m., he expanded the area under curfew.[1964] By mid – morning, violence appeared widespread and unchecked as extensive looting and arson were witnessed across Los Angeles County. Rioting moved from South Central Los Angeles, going north through Central Los Angeles decimating the neighbourhoods of Koreatown, Westlake, Pico – Union, Echo Park, Hancock Park, Fairfax, Mid – City and Mid-Wilshire before reaching Hollywood. The looting and fires engulfed Hollywood Boulevard, and simultaneously rioting moved West and South into the neighbouring independent cities of Inglewood, Hawthorne, Gardena, Compton, Carson and Long Beach, as well as moving East from South Central Los Angeles into the cities of Huntington Park, Walnut Park, Lynwood and Paramount. Looting and vandalism had also gone as far South as Los Angeles regions of

[1959] Sahagun, Louis; Schwada, John (June 3, 1992). "Measure to Reform LAPD Wins Decisively". *Los Angeles Times*.

[1960] "The forgotten victim from Florence and Normandie". *Los Angeles Times*, May 6, 2012.

[1961] *Los Angeles Riots (Part I of V)*,

[1962] Alexander, Von Hoffman (2003). *House by House, Block by Block: The Rebirth of America's Urban Neighbourhoods. Oxford University Press. p. 227. ISBN 0-19-514437-6.*

[1963] *Los Angeles Riots (Part I of V)*,

[1964] "The forgotten victim from Florence and Normandie". *Los Angeles Times*, May 6, 2012.

the Harbour Area in the neighbourhoods of San Pedro, Wilmington, and Harbour City.

Koreatown is a roughly 2.7 square-mile (7 square kilometre) neighbourhood between Hoover Street and Western Avenue, and 3rd Street and Olympic Boulevard, west of MacArthur Park and east of Hancock Park/Windsor Square.[1965] Korean immigrants had begun settling in the Mid-Wilshire area in the 1960s after the passage of the Immigration and Nationality Act of 1965. It was here that many opened successful businesses.[1966]

As the riots spread, roads between Koreatown and wealthy white neighbourhoods were blocked off by police and official defence lines were set up around the independent cities such as Beverly Hills and West Hollywood, as well as middle-upper class white neighbourhoods West of Robertson Boulevard in Los Angeles.[1967] A Korean-American resident later told reporters: "It was containment. The police cut off Koreatown traffic, while we were trapped on the other side without help. Those roads are a gateway to a richer neighbourhood. It can't be denied."[1968] Some Koreans later said they did not expect law enforcement to come to their aid.[1969]

The lack of law enforcement forced Koreatown ci"ilians to organize their own armed security teams, mainly composed of store owners, to defend their businesses from rioters.[1970] Many had military experience from serving in the Republic of Korea Armed Forces before emigrating to the United States.[1971] Open gun battles were televised, including an incident in which Korean shopkeepers armed with M1 carbines, Ruger Mini-14s, pump-action shotguns, and handguns exchanged gunfire with a group of armed looters, and forced their retreat.[1972] But there were casualties, such as 18-year-old Edward Song Lee, whose body can be seen lying in the street in images taken by photojournalist Hyungwon Kang.[1973]

[1965] Pike, John. "Operation Garden Plot / JTF-LAJoint Task Force Los Angeles". *www.globalsecurity.org.*
[1966] "Timeline", *LA Times*
[1967] Jorge, Rivas (April 29, 2013). "'Sa-I-Gu' Documentary Explores How Korean Women Remember the L.A. Riots". *Colour lines.*
[1968] Reyes-Velarde, Alejandra (March 22, 2019). "Hi Duk Lee, visionary who founded Los Angeles' Koreatown, dies at 79". *Los Angeles Times.*
[1969] "Strangers in Town". MTV. April 27, 2017.
[1970] *Lah, Kyung (April 29, 2017). "The LA riots were a rude awakening for Korean-Americans". CNN.*
[1971] Campbell, Andy; Ferner, Matt (April 28, 2017). "What Photographers Of The LA Riots Really Saw Behind The Lens". *Huffington Post.*
[1972] "The LA riots were a rude awakening for Korean - Americans". *www.cnn.com.* April 29, 2017.
[1973] *"Strangers in Town". MTV. April 27, 2017.*

After events in Koreatown, the 670th MP Company from National City, California were redeployed to reinforce police patrols guarding the Korean Cultural Centre and the Consulate – General of South Korea in Los Angeles.

Out of the $850 million worth of damage done in L.A., half of it was on Korean-owned businesses because most of Koreatown was looted and destroyed.[1974] The effects of the riots, which displaced Korean Americans and destroyed their sources of income, and the little aid given to those who suffered, still affected LA – based Koreans in 2017, as they struggled with economic hardship created by the riots.[1975]

The LAPD and the Los Angeles County Sheriff's Department (LASD) organized response began to come together by mid – day. The LAFD and Los Angeles County Fire Department (LACoFD) began to respond backed by police escort; California Highway Patrol reinforcements were airlifted to the city. U.S. President George H. W. Bush spoke out against the rioting, stating that "anarchy" would not be tolerated. The California Army National Guard, which had been advised not to expect civil disturbance and had, as a result, loaned its riot equipment out to other law enforcement agencies, responded quickly by calling up about 2,000 soldiers, but could not get them to the city until nearly 24 hours had passed. They lacked equipment and had to pick it up from the JFTB (Joint Forces Training Base), Los Alamitos, California, which at the time was mainly a mothballed former airbase.[1976]

Air traffic control procedures at Los Angeles International Airport were modified, with all departures and arrivals routed to and from the west, over the Pacific Ocean, avoiding overflights of neighbourhoods affected by the rioting.

Bill Cosby spoke on the local television station KNBC and asked people to stop the rioting and watch the final episode of his *The Cosby Show*.[1977] [1978] [1979] The U.S. Justice Department announced it would resume federal investigation of the Rodney King beating as a violation of federal civil rights law.[1980]

Los Angeles Dodgers manager Tommy Lasorda, who criticized rioters for burning down their own neighbourhoods, received death threats and was taken to the Los Angeles Police Academy for protection.

[1974] "Riot in Los Angeles: Pocket of Tension; A Target of Rioters, Koreatown Is Bitter, Armed and Determined". *www.nytimes.com*. May 3, 1992.
[1975] "Strangers in Town". MTV. April 27, 2017.
[1976] Peter Kivisto; Georganne Rundblad, eds. (2000). *Multiculturalism in the United States: Current Issues, Contemporary Voices*. Pine Forge Press (SAGE).
[1977] When LA Erupted In Anger: A Look Back At The Rodney King Riots". *NPR.org*.
[1978] "The 1992 Los Angeles Riots: Lessons in Command and Control from the Los Angeles Riots". *www.militarymuseum.org*.
[1979] "Bill Cosby". *IMDb*.
[1980] "The forgotten victim from Florence and Normandie". *Los Angeles Times*, May 6, 2012.

Day 3 – Friday, May 1

In the early morning hours of Friday, May 1, the major rioting was stopped.[1981] Rodn ey King gave an impromptu news conference in front of his lawyer's office, tearfully saying, "People, I just want to say, you know, can we all get along?"[1982] [1983] That morning, at 1:00 am, Governor Wilson had requested federal assistance. Upon request, Bush invoked the Insurrection Act with Executive Order 12804, federalizing the California Army National Guard and authorizing federal troops and federal law enforcement officers to help restore law and order.[1984] With Bush's authority, the Pentagon activated Operation Garden Plot, placing the California Army National Guard and federal troops under the newly formed Joint Task Force Los Angeles (JTF-LA). The deployment of federal troops was not ready until Saturday, by which time the rioting and looting were under control.

Meanwhile, the 40th Infantry Division (doubled to 4,000 troops) of the California Army National Guard continued to move into the city in Humvees; eventually 10,000 Army National Guard troops were activated. That same day, 1,000 federal tactical officers from different agencies across California were dispatched to L.A. to protect federal facilities and assist local police. This was the first federal law enforcement response to a civil disorder in any U.S. city since the Ole Miss riot of 1962. Later that evening, Bush addressed the country, denouncing "random terror and lawlessness". He summarized his discussions with Mayor Bradley and Governor Wilson and outlined the federal assistance he was making available to local authorities. Citing the "urgent need to restore order", he warned that the "brutality of a mob" would not be tole"ated, and he would "use what"ver force is necessar"". He referred to the Rodney King case, describing talking to his own grandchildren and noting the actions of "good and decent policemen" as well as civil rights leaders. He said he had directed the Justice Department to investigate the King case, and that "grand jury action is underway today", and justice would prevail. The Post Office announced that it was unsafe for their couriers to deliver mail. The public were instructed to pick up their mail at the main Post Office. The lines were approximately 40 blocks long, and the California National Guard were diverted to that location to ensure peace.[1985]

By this point, many entertainments and sports events were postponed or cancelled. The Los Angeles Lakers hosted the Portland Trail Blazers in an NBA

[1981] Bay Weekly: This Weeks Feature Stories". November 23, 2005.
[1982] "KNBC interrupts LA Riots Coverage, for Cosby Show Finale."
[1983] Delk, James. "MOUT: A Domestic Case Study – The 1982 Los Angeles Riots" (PDF). *rand.org*..
[1984] Keyes, Ralph (May 30, 2006). *The Quote Verifier: Who Said What, Where, and When. RalphKeyes.com*. ISBN 0-312-34004-4.
[1985] Mydans, Seth (December 9, 1993). "Jury Could Hear Rodney King Today". *The New York Times*.

playoff basketball game on the night the rioting started. The following game was still postponed until Sunday and moved to Las Vegas. The Los Angeles Clippers moved a playoff game against the Utah Jazz to nearby Anaheim. In baseball, the Los Angeles Dodgers postponed games for four straight days from Thursday to Sunday, including a whole three-game series against the Montreal Expos; all were made up as part of doubleheaders in July. In San Francisco, a city curfew due to unrest forced the postponement of a May 1, San Francisco Giants home game against the Philadelphia Phillies.[1986]

The horse racing venues Hollywood Park Racetrack and Los Alamitos Race Course were also shut down. L.A. Fiesta Broadway, a major event in the Latino community, was cancelled. In music, Van Halen cancelled two concert shows in Inglewood on Saturday and Sunday. Metallica and Guns N' Roses were forced to postpone and relocate their concert to the Rose Bowl as the LA Coliseum and its surrounding neighbourhood were still damaged. Michael Bolton cancelled his scheduled performance at the Hollywood Bowl Sunday. The World Wrestling Federation cancelled events on Friday and Saturday in the cities of Long Beach and Fresno.[1987] By the end of Friday night, the riots were completely quelled.[1988]

Day 4 – Saturday, May 2

On the fourth day, 3,500 federal troops – 2,000 soldiers of the 7th Infantry Division from Fort Ord and 1,500 Marines of the 1st Marine Division from Camp Pendleton – arrived to reinforce the National Guardsmen already in the city. The Marine Corps contingent included the 1st Light Armoured Reconnaissance Battalion, commanded by John F. Kelly. It was the first significant military occupation of Los Angeles by federal troops since the 1894 Pullman Strike,[1989] and also the first federal military intervention in an American city to quell a civil disorder since the 1968 King assassination riots, and the first deadliest modern unrest since the 1980 Miami riots at the time, only 12 years earlier.

These federal military forces took 24 hours to deploy to Huntington Park, about the same time it took for the National Guardsmen. This brought total troop strength to 13,500, making L.A. the largest military occupation of any U.S. city since the 1968 Washington, D.C. riots. Federal troops joined National Guardsmen to support local police in restoring order directly; the combined force contributed significantly to preventing violence.[1990] With most of the violence under control, 30,000 people

[1986] "Operation Garden Plot, JTF-LA Joint Task Force Los Angeles". GlobalSecurity.org.
[1987] Bush, George H.W. (May 1, 1992). "Address to the Nation on the Civil Disturbances in Los Angeles, California". George Bush Presidential Library.
[1988] "Bay Weekly: This Weeks Feature Stories". November 23, 2005.
[1989] "Baseball; 4 Doubleheaders For The Dodgers". The New York Times. May 19, 1992.
[1990] Keyes, Ralph (May 30, 2006). The Quote Verifier: Who Said What, Where, and

attended an 11 a.m. peace rally in Koreatown to support local merchants and racial healing.[1991]

Day 5 – Sunday, May 3

Mayor Bradley assured the public that the crisis was, more or less, under control as areas became quiet.[1992] Later that night, Army National Guardsmen shot and killed a motorist who tried to run them over at a barrier.[1993]

In another incident, the LAPD and Marines intervened in a domestic dispute in Compton, in which the suspect held his wife and children hostage. As the officers approached, the suspect fired two shotgun rounds through the door, injuring some of the officers. One of the officers yelled to the Marines, "Cover me," as per law enforcement training to be prepared to fire if necessary. However, per their military training, the Marines interpreted the wording as providing cover by establishing a base of firepower, resulting in a total of 200 rounds being sprayed into the house. Remarkably, neither the suspect nor the woman and children inside the house were harmed.[1994]

Aftermath:

Although Mayor Bradley lifted the curfew, signalling the riots' official end, sporadic violence and crime continued for a few days afterward. Schools, banks, and businesses reopened. Federal troops did not stand down until May 9. The Army National Guard remained until May 14. Some National Guardsmen remained as late as May 27.[1995]

When. RalphKeyes.com. ISBN 0-312-34004-4..

[1991] "The forgotten victim from Florence and Normandie". *Los Angeles Times*, May 6, 2012.

[1992] Cawthon, Graham. "1992 WWF results". The History of WWE.

[1993] "Past deployment of Military Troops, Los Angeles County.

[1994] Del Vecchio, Rick; Suzanne Espinosa & Carle Nolte (May 4, 1992). "Bradley Ready to Lift Curfew He Says L.A. is 'under control'". *San Francisco Chronicle*. p. A1.

[1995] Karen Ball (May 4, 1992). "Motorist Shooting shakes L.A. calm". *McCook Daily Gazette*. Associated Press. p. 1.

Chapter forty-five

The Spanish Inquisition

The Tribunal of the Holy Office of the Inquisition (Spanish: *Tribunal del Santo Oficio de la Inquisición*), commonly known as the Spanish Inquisition (Spanish: *Inquisición española*), was established in 1478 by Catholic Monarchs, King Ferdinand II of Aragon and Queen Isabella I of Castile. It was intended to maintain Catholic orthodoxy in their kingdoms and to replace the Medieval Inquisition, which was under Papal control. It became the most substantive of the three different manifestations of the wider Catholic Inquisition along with the Roman Inquisition and Portuguese Inquisition. The "Spanish Inquisition" may be defined broadly, operating in Spain and in all Spanish colonies and territories, which included the Canary Islands, the Kingdom of Naples, and all Spanish possessions in North, Central, and South America. According to modern estimates, around 150,000 people were prosecuted for various offenses during the three-century duration of the Spanish Inquisition, of which between 3,000 and 5,000 were executed (2.7% of all cases).[1996]

The Inquisition was originally intended primarily to identify heretics among those who converted from Judaism and Islam to Catholicism. The regulation of the faith of newly converted Catholics was intensified after the royal decrees issued in 1492 and 1502 ordering Muslims and Jews to convert to Catholicism or leave Castile.[1997] The Inquisition was not definitively abolished until 1834, during the reign of Isabella II, after a period of declining influence in the preceding century.

The Inquisition was created through papal bull, *Ad Abolendam*, issued at the end of the 12th century by Pope Lucius III to combat the Albigensian heresy in southern France. There were a large number of tribunals of the Papal Inquisition in various European kingdoms during the Middle Ages through different diplomatic and political means. In the Kingdom of Aragon, a tribunal of the Papal Inquisition was

---

[1996] Data for executions for witchcraft: Levack, Brian P. (1995). The Witch Hunt in Early Modern Europe (Second Edition). London and New York: Longman, and see Witch trials in Early Modern Europe for more detail.
[1997] Hans-Jürgen Prien (21 November 2012). *Christianity in Latin America: Revised and Expanded Edition*. BRILL. p. 11. ISBN 978-90-04-22262-5.

established by the statute of *Excommunicamus* of Pope Gregory IX, in 1232, during the era of the Albigensian heresy, as a condition for peace with Aragon.

The Inquisition was created through papal bull, *Ad Abolendam*, issued at the end of the 12th century by Pope Lucius III to combat the Albigensian heresy in southern France. There were a large number of tribunals of the Papal Inquisition in various European kingdoms during the Middle Ages through different diplomatic and political means. In the Kingdom of Aragon, a tribunal of the Papal Inquisition was established by the statute of *Excommunicamus* of Pope Gregory IX, in 1232, during the era of the Albigensian heresy, as a condition for peace with Aragon. The Inquisition was ill-received by the Aragonese, which led to prohibitions against insults or attacks on it. Rome was particularly concerned that the Iberian peninsula's large Muslim and Jewish population would have a 'heretical' influence on the Catholic population. Rome pressed the kingdoms to accept the Papal Inquisition after Aragon. Navarra conceded in the 13th century and Portugal by the end of the 14th, though its 'Roman Inquisition' was famously inactive. Castile refused steadily, trusting in its prominent position in Europe and its military power to keep the Pope's interventionism in check. By the end of the Middle Ages, England, due to distance and voluntary compliance, and the Castile (future part of Spain), due to resistance and power, were the only Western European kingdoms to successfully resist the establishment of the Inquisition in their realms.

Although Raymond of Penyafort was not an inquisitor, as a canon lawyer and king's advisor James I of Aragon had often consulted him on questions of law regarding the practices of the Inquisition in the king's domains. "The lawyer's deep sense of justice and equity, combined with the worthy Dominican's sense of compassion, allowed him to steer clear of the excesses that were found elsewhere in the formative years of the inquisitions into heresy."[1998]

Despite its early implantation, the Papal Inquisition was greatly resisted within the Crown of Aragon by both population and monarchs. With time, its importance was diluted, and, by the middle of the fifteenth century, it was almost forgotten although still there according to the law.

Regarding the living conditions of minorities, the kings of Aragon and other monarchies imposed some discriminatory taxation of religious minorities, so false conversions were a way of tax evasion.

In addition to the above discriminatory legislation, Aragon had laws specifically targeted at protecting minorities. For example, crusaders attacking Jewish or Muslim

---

[1998] Smith, Damien J., Heresy, and Inquisition in the lands of the Crown of Aragon, Brill 2010, ISBN 978-9-00418-289-9.

subjects of the King of Aragon while on their way to fight in the reconquest were punished with death by hanging. Up to the 14th century, the census and wedding records show an absolute lack of concern with avoiding intermarriage or blood mixture. Such laws were now common in most of central Europe. Both the Roman Inquisition and neighbouring Christian powers showed discomfort with Aragonese law and lack of concern with ethnicity, but to little effect. High-ranking officials of Jewish religion were not as common as in Castile, but were not unheard of either.[1999] Abraham Zacuto was a professor at the university of Cartagena. Vidal Astori was the royal silversmith for Ferdinand II of Aragon and conducted business in his name. And King Ferdinand himself was said to have Jewish ancestry on his mother's side.[2000]

There was never a tribunal of the Papal Inquisition in Castile, nor any inquisition during the Middle Ages. Members of the episcopate were charged with surveillance of the faithful and punishment of transgressors, always under the direction of the king.

During the Middle Ages in Castile, the Catholic ruling class and the population paid little or no attention to heresy. Castile did not have the proliferation of anti – Jewish pamphlets as England and France did during the 13th and 14th centuries – and those that have been found were modified, watered-down versions of the original stories.[2001] Jews and Muslims were tolerated and generally allowed to follow their traditional customs in domestic matters.[2002]

The legislation regarding Muslims and Jews in Castilian territory varied greatly, becoming more intolerant during the period of great instability and dynastic wars that occurred by the end of the 14th century. Castilian law is particularly difficult to summarize since, due to the model of the free Royal Villas, mayors and the population of border areas had the right to create their own fueros (law) that varied from one villa to the next. In general, the Castilian model was parallel to the initial model of Islamic Spain. Non-Catholics were subject to discriminatory legislation regarding taxation and some other specific discriminatory legislation such as a prohibition on wearing silk or "flashy clothes" [2003] that varied from county to county

[1999] Parrilla, Gonzalo Fernández, Miguel Hernando De Larramendi, and José Sangrador Gil. Pensamiento Y Circulación De Las Ideas En El Mediterráneo: El Papel De La Traducción. (Thought and Idea Propagation across the Mediterranean: The Role of Translators) Cuenca: Servicio De Publicaciones De La Universidad De Castilla-La Mancha, 1997

[2000] Cervera, César: "La ascendencia judía del Rey Fernando «El Católico» y su primo el II Duque de Alba" ABC, 3 June 2015 08:34h https://www.abc.es/espana/20150602/abci-ascendencia-judia-fernando-catolico-201506011949.html

[2001] Hassán, Iacob; Izquierdo Benito, Ricardo (2001). Universidad de Castilla La Mancha, ed. Judíos en la literatura Española (Jews in Spanish Literature). España

[2002] M.R. Menocal "The Ornament of the World: How Muslims, Jews, and Christians Created a Culture of Tolerance in Medieval Spain". Back Bay Books. New York, 2009

[2003] Suárez Fernández, Luis (2012). La expulsión de los judíos. Un problema europeo. Barcelona:

but were otherwise left alone. Forced conversion of minorities was against the law, and so was the belief in the existence of witchcraft, oracles, or similar superstitions. In general, all "people from the book" were permitted to practice their own customs and religions as far as they did not attempt proselytizing on the Christian population. Jews particularly had surprising freedoms and protections compared with other areas of Europe and were allowed to hold high public offices such as the counsellor, treasurer or secretary for the crown.[2004]

During most of the medieval period, intermarriage with converts was allowed and encouraged. Intellectual cooperation between religions was the norm in Castile. Some examples are the Toledo School of Translators from the 11th century. Jews and Moors were allowed to hold high offices in the administration (See Abrahám Seneor, Samuel HaLevi Abulafia, Isaac Abarbanel, López de Conchillos, Miguel Pérez de Almazán, Jaco Aben Nunnes and Fernando del Pulgar). [2005]

A tightening of the laws to protect the right of Jews to collect loans during the Medieval Crisis was one of the causes of the revolt against Peter the Cruel and catalyst of the anti-Semitic episodes of 1391 in Castile, a kingdom that had shown no significant antisemitic backlash to the black death and drought crisis of the early 14th century. Even after the sudden increase in hostility towards other religions that the kingdom experienced after the 14th-century crisis, which clearly worsened the living conditions of non-Catholics in Castile, it remained one of the most tolerant kingdoms in Europe.[2006]

The kingdom had serious problems with Rome regarding the Church's attempts to extend its authority into the kingdom. A focus of conflict was Castilian resistance to truly abandon the Mozarabic Rite, and the refusal to grant Papal control over Reconquest land (a request Aragon and Portugal conceded). These conflicts added to a strong resistance to allowing the creation of an Inquisition, and the kingdom's general willingness to accept heretics seeking refuge from prosecution in France.

The Spanish Inquisition is interpretable as a response to the multi-religious nature of Spanish society following the reconquest of the Iberian Peninsula from the Muslim Moors. After invading in 711, large areas of the Iberian Peninsula were ruled by Muslims until 1250, afterwards they were restricted to Granada, which fell in 1492. However, the Reconquista did not result in the total expulsion of Muslims

Ariel.

[2004] José María Zavala," Isabel Íntima" (Intimate Isabella), Planeta editorial. Madrid.

[2005] Suárez Fernández, Luis (2012). La expulsión de los judíos. Un problema europeo. Barcelona: Ariel.

[2006] Ortiz, César Mantilla. Derecho De Los Judíos De Castilla En La Época De Su Expulsión (Legal Rights of Jews in Castile at the Time of their Expulsion). Valladolid: Maxtor, 2015

from Spain, since they, along with Jews, were tolerated by the ruling Christian elite. Large cities, especially Seville, Valladolid and Barcelona, had significant Jewish populations cantered on Juderia, but in the coming years the Muslims became increasingly alienated and relegated from power centres.[2007]

Post-reconquest medieval Spain has been characterized by Americo Castro as a society of relatively peaceful co-existence punctuated by occasional conflict among the ruling Catholics and the Jews and Muslims. However, as historian Henry Kamen notes, this "was always a relationship between unequals."[2008] Despite their legal inequality, there was a long tradition of Jewish service to the Crown of Aragon, and Jews occupied many important posts, both religious and political. Castile itself had an unofficial rabbi. Ferdinand's father John II named the Jewish Abiathar Crescas Court Astronomer.

Anti-Semitic attitudes increased all over Europe during the late 13th century and throughout the 14th century. England and France expelled their Jewish populations in 1290 and 1306 respectively.[2009] At the same time, during the Reconquista, Spain's anti – Jewish sentiment steadily increased. This prejudice climaxed in the summer of 1391 when violent ant – Jewish riots broke out in Spanish cities like Barcelona[2010] T o linguistically distinguish them from non-converted or long-established Catholic families, new converts were called conversos, or New Catholics. This event though must be understood in the context of the fierce civil war and new politics that Peter the Cruel had brought to the land, and not be confused with spontaneous anti-Semitic reactions to the plague seen in northern Europe.

According to Don Hasdai Crescas, persecution against Jews began in earnest in Seville in 1391, on the 1st day of the lunar month Tammuz (June).[2011] From there the violence spread to Córdoba, and by the 17th day of the same lunar month, it had reached Toledo (called then by Jews after its Arabic name "Ṭulayṭulah") in the region of Castile.[2012] From there, the violence had spread to Majorca and by the 1st

[2007] Brian Catlos "Secundum suam zunam": Muslims in the Laws of the Aragonese "Reconquista", Mediterranean Studies Vol. 7 (1998), pp. 13–26 Published by: Penn State University Press
[2008] Kamen (1998), p. 4
[2009] Peters 1988, p. 79.
[2010] Peters 1988, p. 82.
[2011] Letter of Hasdai Crescas, *Shevaṭ Yehudah* by Solomon ibn Verga (ed. Dr. M. Wiener), Hannover 1855, pp. 128–130 (pp. 138–140 in PDF); Fritz Kobler, *Letters of the Jews through the Ages*, London 1952, pp. 272–75; *Mitre Fernández, Emilio (1994). Secretariado de Publicaciones e Intercambio Editorial (ed.). Los judíos de Castilla en tiempo de Enrique III: el pogrom de 1391 [The Castilian Jews at the time of Henry III: the 1391 pogrom] (in Spanish). Valladolid University. ISBN 978-84-7762-449-3.*; Solomon ibn Verga, *Shevaṭ Yehudah* (The Sceptre of Judah), Lvov 1846, p. 76 in PDF.
[2012] Letter from Hasdai Crescas to the congregations of Avignon, published as an appendix to Wiener's edition of *Shevaṭ Yehudah* of Solomon ibn Verga, in which he names the Jewish communities affected by the persecution of 1391. See pages 138 – 140 in PDF (Hebrew); Fritz Kobler, *Letters of the Jews*

day of the lunar month Elul it had also reached the Jews of Barcelona in Catalonia, where the slain were estimated at two-hundred and fifty. Indeed, many Jews who resided in the neighbouring provinces of Lérida and Gironda and in the kingdom of València had also been affected,[2013] as were also the Jews of Al – Andalus (Andalucía),[2014] while many died a martyr's death, others converted to save themselves.

Encouraged by the preaching of Ferrand Martínez, Archdeacon of Ecija, the general unrest affected nearly all of the Jews in Spain, during which time an estimated 200,000 Jews changed their religion or else concealed their religion, becoming known in Hebrew as Anusim,[2015] meaning, "those who are compelled [to hide their religion]." Only a handful of the more principal persons of the Jewish community, those who had found refuge among the viceroys in the outlying towns and districts, managed to escape.[2016]

Forced baptism was contrary to the law of the Catholic Church, and theoretically anybody who had been forcibly baptized could legally return to Judaism. Legal definitions of the time theoretically acknowledged that a forced baptism was not a valid sacrament, but confined this to cases where it was literally administered by physical force: a person who had consented to baptism under threat of death or serious injury was still regarded as a voluntary convert, and accordingly forbidden to revert to Judaism.[2017] After the public violence, many of the converted "felt it safer to remain in their new religion."[2018] Thus, after 1391, a new social group appeared and were referred to as *conversos* or *New Christians*. Many *conversos*, now freed from the anti-Semitic restrictions imposed on Jewish employment, attained important positions in fifteenth-century Spain, including positions in the government and in the Church. Among many others, physicians Andrés Laguna and Francisco López de Villalobos (Ferdinand's court physician), writers Juan del Enzina, Juan de

---

through the Ages, London 1952, pp. 272–75.

[2013] Solomon ibn Verga, Shevaṭ Yehudah (The Sceptre of Judah), Lvov 1846, pp. 41 (end) – 42 in PDF); Kamen (1998), p. 17. Kamen cites approximate numbers for Valencia (250) and Barcelona (400), but no solid data about Córdoba.

[2014] According to Gedaliah Ibn Yechia, these disturbances were caused by a malicious report spread about the Jews. See: Gedaliah Ibn Yechia, Shalshelet Ha-Kabbalah Jerusalem 1962, p. רנז, in PDF p. 277 (top) (Hebrew); Solomon ibn Verga, Shevat Yehudah, Lvov 1846 (p. 76 in PDF) (Hebrew).

[2015] Abraham Zacuto, Sefer Yuchasin, Cracow 1580 (q.v. Sefer Yuchasin, p. 266 in PDF) (Hebrew).

[2016] Letter of Hasdai Crescas, Shevaṭ Yehudah by Solomon ibn Verga (ed. Dr. M. Wiener), Hannover 1855, pp. 128–130 (pp. 138–140 in PDF); Fritz Kobler, Letters of the Jews through the Ages, London 1952, pp. 272–75; Mitre Fernández, Emilio (1994). Secretariado de Publicaciones e Intercambio Editorial (ed.). Los judíos de Castilla en tiempo de Enrique III: el pogrom de 1391 [The Castilian Jews at the time of Henry III: the 1391 pogrom] (in Spanish). Valladolid University. ISBN 978-84-7762-449-3.; Solomon ibn Verga, Shevaṭ Yehudah (The Sceptre of Judah), Lvov 1846, p. 76 in PDF.

[2017] Raymond of Peñafort, Summa, lib. 1 p.33, citing D.45 c.5.

[2018] Kamen (1998), p. 10

Mena, Diego de Valera and Alonso de Palencia, and bankers Luis de Santángel and Gabriel Sánchez (who financed the voyage of Christopher Columbus) were all *conversos*. *Conversos* – not without opposition – managed to attain high positions in the ecclesiastical hierarchy, at times becoming severe detractors of Judaism.[2019] So me even received titles of nobility and, as a result, during the following century some works attempted to demonstrate that virtually all of the nobles of Spain were descended from Israelites.[2020]

According to this hypothesis, the Inquisition was created to standardize the variety of laws and many jurisdictions Spain was divided into. It would be an administrative program analogous to the Santa Hermandad (the "Holy Brotherhood", a law enforcement body, answering to the crown, that prosecuted thieves and criminals across counties in a way local county authorities could not, ancestor to the Guardia Civil), an institution that would guarantee uniform prosecution of crimes against royal laws across all local jurisdictions.

The Kingdom of Castile had been prosperous and successful in Europe thanks in part to the unusual authority and control the king exerted over the nobility, which ensured political stability and kept the kingdom from being weakened by in-fighting (as was the case in England, for example). However, under the Trastámara dynasty, both kings of Castile and Aragon had lost power to the great nobles, who now formed dissenting and conspiratorial factions. Taxation and varying privileges differed from county to county, and powerful noble families constantly extorted the kings to attain further concessions, particularly in Aragon.

The main goals of the reign of the Catholic Monarchs were to unite their two kingdoms and strengthen royal influence to guarantee stability. In pursuit of this, they sought to further unify the laws of their realms and reduce the power of the nobility in certain local areas. They attained this partially by raw military strength by creating a combined army between the two of them that could outmatch the army of most noble coalitions in the Peninsula. However, it was impossible to change the entire laws of both realms by force alone, and due to reasonable suspicion of one another the monarchs kept their kingdoms separate during their lifetimes. The only way to unify both kingdoms and ensure that Isabella, Ferdinand, and their descendants maintained the power of both kingdoms without uniting them in life was to find, or create, an executive, legislative and judicial arm directly under the Crown

---

[2019] Notably Bishop Pablo de Santa Maria, author of *Scrutinium Scripturarum*, Jeronimo de Santa Fe (*Hebraomastix*) and Pedro de la Caballeria (*Zelus Christi contra Judaeos*). All three were *conversos*. (Kamen (1998), p. 39).
[2020] Notably the *Libro verde de Aragon* and *Tizón de la nobleza de España* (cited in Kamen (1998), p. 38).

empowered to act in both kingdoms. This goal, the hypothesis goes, might have given birth to the Spanish Inquisition.[2021]

The religious organization to oversee this role was obvious: Catholicism was the only institution common to both kingdoms, and the only one with enough popular support that the nobility could not easily attack it. Through the Spanish Inquisition, Isabella and Ferdinand created a personal police force and personal code of law that rested above the structure of their respective realms without altering or mixing them and could operate freely in both. As the Inquisition had the backing of both kingdoms, it would exist independent of both the nobility and local interests of either kingdom.[2022]

This is not true; the Inquisition always gave 30 days' notice before turning up. So, you were made aware in ample time to expect them.

According to this view, the prosecution of heretics would be secondary, or simply not considered different, from the prosecution of conspirators, traitors, or groups of any kind who planned to resist royal authority. At the time, royal authority rested on divine right and on oaths of loyalty held before God, so the connection between religious deviation and political disloyalty would appear obvious. This hypothesis is supported by the disproportionately high representation of the nobility and high clergy among those investigated by the Inquisition, as well as by the many administrative and civil crimes the Inquisition oversaw. The Inquisition prosecuted the counterfeiting of royal seals and currency, ensured the effective transmission of the orders of the kings, and verified the authenticity of official documents traveling through the kingdoms, especially from one kingdom to the other. See "Non-Religious Crimes".[2023]

[2021] Joseph Pérez, *The Spanish Inquisition: A History.* Yale University Press, 2005
[2022] Pérez, Joseph (2012) [2009]. Breve Historia de la Inquisición en España. Barcelona: Crítica. ISBN 978-84-08-00695-4.
[2023] Canessa De Sanguinetti, Marta. El Bien Nacer: Limpieza De Oficios Y Limpieza De Sangre: Raíces Ibéricas De Un Mal Latinoamericano. Taurus, Ediciones Santillana, 2000.

At a time when most of Europe had already expelled the Jews from the Christian kingdoms the "dirty blood" of Spaniards was met with open suspicion and contempt by the rest of Europe. As the world became smaller and foreign relations became more relevant to stay in power this foreign image of "being the seed of Jews and Moors" may have become a problem. In addition, the coup that allowed Isabella to take the throne from Joana of Avis and the Catholic Monarchs to marry had estranged Castile from Portugal, its historical ally, and created the need for new relationships. Similarly, Aragon's ambitions lay in control of the Mediterranean and the defence against France. As their policy of royal marriages proved, the Catholic Monarchs were deeply concerned about France's growing power and expected to create strong dynastic alliances across Europe. In this scenario, the Iberian reputation of being too tolerant was a problem.

Despite the prestige earned through the reconquest that foreign image on Spaniards coexisted with an almost universal image of heretics and "bad Christians" due to the long coexistence between the three religions, they had accepted in their lands. Anti-Jewish stereotypes created to justify or prompt the expulsion and expropriation of the European Jews were also applied to Spaniards in most European courts, and the idea of them being "greedy, gold – thirsty, cruel and violent", "like Jews", due to the "Jewish and Moorish blood" was prevalent in Europe before America was discovered by Europeans. Chronicles by foreign travellers circulated through Europe, describing the tolerant ambiance reigning in the court of Isabella and Ferdinand and how Moors and Jews were free to go about without anyone trying to convert them. Past and common clashes between the Pope and the kingdoms of the Iberian Peninsula, regarding the Inquisition in Castile's case and regarding South Italy in Aragon's case, also reinforced their image of heretics in the international courts. These accusations and images could have direct political and military consequences at the time, especially considering that the union of two powerful kingdoms was a particularly delicate moment that could prompt the fear and violent reactions from neighbours, even more if combined with the expansion of the Ottoman Turks on the Mediterranean.

The creation of the Inquisition and the expulsion of both Jews and Moriscos may have been part of a strategy to whitewash the image of Spain and ease international fears regarding Spain's allegiance. In this scenario, the creation of the Inquisition could have been part of the Catholic's Monarch strategy to "turn" away from African allies and "towards" Europe, a tool to turn both actual Spain and the Spanish image more European and improve relations with the Pope.[2024]

[2024] Elvira, Roca Barea María, and Arcadi Espada. Imperiofobia Y Leyenda Negra: Roma, Rusia, Estados Unidos Y El Imperio Español. Madrid: Siruela, 2017

The "Ottoman Scare" hypothesis:

No matter if any of the previous hypotheses were already operating in the minds of the monarchs, the alleged discovery of Morisco plots to support a possible Ottoman invasion were crucial factors in their decision to create the Inquisition.

At this time, the Ottoman Empire was in expansion and making its power noticeable in the Mediterranean and North Africa. At the same time, the Aragonese Mediterranean Empire was crumbling under debt and war exhaustion. Ferdinand reasonably feared that he would not be capable of repelling an Ottoman attack to Spain's shores, especially if the Ottomans had internal help. The regions with the highest concentration of Moriscos were those close to the common naval crossings between Spain and Africa. If the weakness of the Aragonese Naval Empire was combined with the resentment of the higher nobility against the monarchs, the dynastic claims of Portugal on Castile and the two monarch's exterior politic that turned away from Morocco and other African nations in favour of Europe, the fear of a second Muslim invasion, and thus the Muslim occupation was hardly unfounded. This fear may have been the base reason for the expulsion of those citizens who had either a religious reason to support the invasion of the Ottomans (Moriscos) or no particular religious reason to not do it (Jews). The Inquisition might have been part of the preparations to enforce these measures and ensure their effectiveness by rooting out false converts that would still pose a threat of foreign espionage.[2025]

In favour of this view there is the obvious military sense it makes, and the many early attempts of peaceful conversion and persuasion that the Monarchs used at the beginning of their reign, and the sudden turn towards the creation of the Inquisition and the edicts of expulsion when those initial attempts failed. The conquest of Naples by the Gran Capitan is also proof of an interest in Mediterranean expansion and re-establishment of Spanish power in that sea that was bound to generate frictions with the Ottoman Empire and other African nations. So, the Inquisition would have been created as a permanent body to prevent the existence of citizens with religious sympathies with African nations now that rivalry with them had been deemed unavoidable.[2026]

Philosophical and religious reasons:

The creation of the Spanish Inquisition would be consistent with the most important political philosophers of the Florentine School, with whom the kings were known to have contact (Guicciardini, Pico della Mirandola, Machiavelli, Segni, Pitti, Nardi, Varchi, etc.) Both Guicciardini and Machiavelli defended the importance of

---

[2025] Abou Al Fadl, K. (1994). Islamic law and Muslim minorities: the juristic discourse on Muslim minorities from the second/eight to the eleventh/seventeenth centuries. Islamic Law and Society, 1.
[2026] Boronat, P. (1901). Los moriscos españoles y su expulsión. 2 vols. Valencia.

centralization and unification to create a strong state capable of repelling foreign invasions and warned of the dangers of excessive social uniformity to the creativity and innovation of a nation. Machiavelli considered piety and morals desirable for the subjects but not so much for the ruler, who should use them to unify its population. He also warned of the nefarious influence of a corrupt church in the creation of a selfish population and middle nobility, which had fragmented the peninsula and made it unable to resist either France or Aragon. German philosophers at the time were spreading the importance of a vassal to share the religion of their lord.

The Inquisition may have just been the result of putting these ideas into practice. The use of religion as a unifying factor across a land that was allowed to stay diverse and maintain different laws in other respects, and the creation of the Inquisition to enforce laws across it, maintain said religious unity and control the local elites were consistent with most of those teachings.

Alternatively, the enforcement of Catholicism across the realm might indeed be the result of simple religious devotion by the monarchs. The recent scholarship on the expulsion of the Jews leans towards the belief of religious motivations being at the bottom of it.[2027] But considering the reports on Ferdinand's political persona, that is unlikely the only reason. Ferdinand was described, among others, by Machiavelli, as a man who didn't know the meaning of piety, but who made political use of it and would have achieved little if he had really known it. He was Machiavelli's main inspiration while writing The Prince.[2028]

The "Keeping the Pope in Check" hypothesis:

The hierarchy of the Catholic Church had made many attempts during the Middle Ages to take over Christian Spain politically, such as claiming the Church's ownership over all land reconquered from non – Christians (a claim that was rejected by Castille but accepted by Aragon and Portugal). In the past, the papacy had tried and partially succeeded, in forcing the Mozarabic Rite out of Iberia. Its meddling attempts had been pivotal for Aragon's loss of Rosellon. The meddling regarding Aragon's control over South Italy was even stronger historically. In their lifetime, the Catholic Monarchs had problems with Pope Paul II, a very strong proponent of absolute authority for the church over the kings. Carrillo actively opposed them both and often used Spain's "mixed blood" as an excuse to intervene. The papacy and the monarch of Europe had been involve" in a war for power all through the high Middle Ages that Rome had already won in other powerful kingdoms like France.

[2027] Stuart, Nancy Rubin. Isabella of Castile: The First Renaissance Queen. New York: ASJA Press, 2004.

[2028] Black, Robert. Machiavelli. Abigdon, Oxon: Routledge, Tylor &, 2013. pp83-120 (the quote is paraphrased)

Since the legitimacy granted by the church was necessary both, especially Isabella, to stay in power, the creation of the Spanish "inquisition may have been a way to apparently concede to the Pope's demands and criticism regarding Spain's mixed religious heritage, while at the same time ensuring that the Pope could hardly force the second inquisition of his own, and at the same time create a tool to control the power of the Roman Church in Spain. The Spanish Inquisition was unique at the time because it did not depend on the Pope in the slightest. Once the bull of creation was granted, the head of the Inquisition was the Monarch of Spain. It was in charge of enforcing the laws of the king regarding religion and other private-life matters, not of following orders from Rome, from which it was independent. This independence allowed the Inquisition to investigate, prosecute and convict clergy for both corruptions (paedophilia, forgery of documents, etc.) and possible charges of treason of conspiracy against the crown (on the Pope's behalf presumably) without the Pope's intervention. The inquisition was, despite its title of "Holy", not necessarily formed by the clergy and secular lawyers were equally welcome to it. If it was an attempt at keeping Rome out of Spain, it was an extremely successful and refined one. It was a bureaucratic body that had the nominal authority of the church and permission to prosecute members of the church, which the kings could not do, while answering only to the Spanish Crown. This did not prevent the Pope from having some influence on the decisions of Spanish monarchs, but it did force the influence to be through the kings, making direct influence very difficult.[2029]

Other hypotheses:

Other hypotheses that circulate regarding the Spanish Inquisition's creation include:

- Economic reasons: Since one of the penalties that the Inquisition could enforce on the convicts was the confiscation of their property, which became Crown property, it has been stated that the creation of the Inquisition was a way to finance the crown. There is no solid reason for this hypothesis to stand alone, nor for the Kings of Spain to need an institution to do this gradually instead of confiscating property through edicts, but it may be one of the reasons why the Inquisition stayed for so long. This hypothesis notes the tendency of the Inquisition to operate in large and wealthy cities and is favoured by those who consider that most of those prosecuted for practising Judaism and Islam in secret was actually innocent of it.[2030] Gustav Bergenroth editor and translator of the

---

[2029] Óscar González, *El Rey Y El Papa: Política Y Diplomacia En Los Albores Del Renacimiento (Castilla En El Siglo XV)*. Sílex, 2009

[2030] The Marranos of Spain. From the late XIVth to the early XVIth Century, 1966. Ithaca, 1999

Spanish state papers 1485–1509 believed that revenue was the incentive for Ferdinand and Isabella's decision to invite the Inquisition into Spain.[2031] Other authors point out that both monarchs were very aware of the economic consequences they would suffer from a decrease in population.

- Intolerance and racism: This argument is usually made regarding the expulsion of the Jews or the Moriscos,[2032] and since the Inquisition was so closely interconnected with those actions can be expanded to it. It varies between those who deny that Spain was really that different from the rest of Europe regarding tolerance and open – mindedness and those who argue that it used to be, but gradually the antisemitic and racist atmosphere of medieval Europe rubbed onto it. It explains the creation of the Inquisition as the result of the same forces than the creation of similar entities across Europe. This view may account for the similarities between the Spanish Inquisition and similar institutions but completely fails to account for its many unique characteristics, including its time of appearance and its duration through time, so even if accepted requires the addition of some of the other hypothesis to be complete.

- Purely religious reasons: essentially this view suggests that the Catholic Monarchs created the Inquisition to prosecute heretics and sodomites "because the Bible says so". A common criticism that this view receives is that the Bible also condemns greed, hypocrisy, and adultery, but the Inquisition was not in charge of prosecuting any of those things. It also did not prosecute those who did not go to mass on Sunday or otherwise broke the Catholic rituals as far as it was out of simple laziness. Considering this double standard, its role was probably more complex and specific.

Activity of the Inquisition:

Fray Alonso de Ojeda, a Dominican friar from Seville, convinced Queen Isabella of the existence of Crypto – Judaism among Andalusian *conversos* during her stay in Seville between 1477 and 1478.[2033] A report, produced by Pedro González de Mendoza, Archbishop of Seville, and by the Segovian Dominican Tomás de Torquemada – of converso family himself – corroborated this assertion.

[2031] "Introduction, Part 1 – British History Online *www.british-history.ac.uk.*
[2032] The Marranos of Spain. From the late XIVth to the early XVIth Century, 1966. Ithaca, 1999
[2033] The terms *converso* and crypto-Jew are somewhat vexed, and occasionally historians are not clear on how, precisely, they are intended to be understood. For the purpose of clarity, in this article *converso* will be taken to mean one who has sincerely renounced Judaism or Islam and embraced Catholicism. Crypto-Jew will be taken to mean one who accepts Christian baptism, yet continues to practice Judaism

Spanish monarchs Ferdinand and Isabella requested a papal bull establishing an inquisition in Spain in 1478. Pope Sixtus IV granted a bull permitting the monarchs to select and appoint two or three priests over forty years of age to act as inquisitors. In 1483, Ferdinand and Isabella established a state council to administer the inquisition with the Dominican Friar Tomás de Torquemada acting as its president, even though Sixtus IV protested the activities of the inquisition in Aragon and its treatment of the *conversos*. Torquemada eventually assumed the title of Inquisitor – General.[2034]

Thomas F. Madden describes the world that formed medieval politics: "The Inquisition was not born out of the desire to crush diversity or oppress people; it was rather an attempt to stop unjust executions. Yes, you read that correctly. Heresy was a crime against the state. Roman law in the Code of Justinian made it a capital offense. Rulers, whose authority was believed to come from God, had no patience for heretics".[2035]

Ferdinand II of Aragon pressured Pope Sixtus IV to agree to an Inquisition controlled by the monarchy by threatening to withdraw military support at a time when the Turks were a threat to Rome. The pope issued a bull to stop the Inquisition but was pressured into withdrawing it. On 1 November 1478, Sixtus published the Papal bull, *Exigit Sinceras Devotionis Affectus*, through which he gave the monarchs exclusive authority to name the inquisitors in their kingdoms. The first two inquisitors, Miguel de Morillo and Juan de San Martín, were not named, however, until two years later, on 27 September 1480 in Medina del Campo.

The first *auto – da – fé* was held in Seville on 6 February 1481: six people were burned alive. From there, the Inquisition grew rapidly in the Kingdom of Castile. By 1492, tribunals existed in eight Castilian cities: Ávila, Córdoba, Jaén, Medina del Campo, Segovia, Sigüenza, Toledo, and Valladolid. Sixtus IV promulgated a new bull categorically prohibiting the Inquisition's extension to Aragón, affirming that:[2036]... many true and faithful Christians, because of the testimony of enemies, rivals, slaves and other low people and still less appropriate without tests of any kind, have been locked up in secular prisons, tortured and condemned like relapsed heretics, deprived of their goods and properties, and given over to the secular arm to be executed, at great danger to their souls, giving a pernicious example and causing scandal to many.

Henry Kamen, The Spanish Inquisition:
According to the book A History of the Jewish People,[2037]

[2034] Peters 1988, p. 89.
[2035] Thomas Madden: The Real Inquisition. National Review 2004
[2036] Cited in Kamen (1998), p. 49

In 1482 the pope was still trying to maintain control over the Inquisition and to gain acceptance for his own attitude towards the New Christians, which was generally more moderate than that of the Inquisition and the local rulers.

A History of the Jewish People:

In 1483, Jews were expelled from all of Andalusia. Though the pope wanted to crack down on abuses, Ferdinand pressured him to promulgate a new bull, threatening that he would otherwise separate the Inquisition from Church authority.[2038]

Sixtus did so on 17 October 1483, naming Tomás de Torquemada Inquisidor General of Aragón, Valencia, and Catalonia.

Torquemada quickly established procedures for the Inquisition. A new court would be announced with a thirty-day grace period for confessions and the gathering of accusations by neighbours. Evidence that was used to identify a crypto – Jew included the absence of chimney smoke on Saturdays (a sign the family might secretly be honouring the Sabbath) or the buying of many vegetables before Passover or the purchase of meat from a converted butcher. The court could employ physical torture to extract confessions once the guilt of the accused had been established. Crypto – Jews were allowed to confess and do penance, although those who relapsed were executed.[2039]

In 1484, Pope Innocent VIII attempted to allow appeals to Rome against the Inquisition, which would weaken the function of the institution as protection against the pope, but Ferdinand in December 1484 and again in 1509 decreed death and confiscation for anyone trying to make use of such procedures without royal permission. With this, the Inquisition became the only institution that held authority across all the realms of the Spanish monarchy and, in all of them, a useful mechanism at the service of the crown. However, the cities of Aragón continued resisting, and even saw revolt, as in Teruel from 1484 to 1485. However, the murder of *Inquisidor* Pedro Arbués in Zaragoza on 15 September 1485, caused public opinion to turn against the *conversos* and in favour of the Inquisition. In Aragón, the Inquisitorial courts were focused specifically on members of the powerful *converso* minority, ending their influence in the Aragonese administration.

The Inquisition was extremely active between 1480 and 1530. Different sources give different estimates of the number of trials and executions in this period; some ~~estimate about 2,000 executions, based on the documentation of the *autos-da-fé*, the~~

[2037] Ben-Sasson, H.H., editor. 1976. p. 588.
[2038] Kamen (1998), pp. 49–50
[2039] Ben-Sasson, H.H., editor. A History of the Jewish People. Harvard University Press, 1976, pp. 588–590.

great majority being *conversos* of Jewish origin. He offers striking statistics: 91.6% of those judged in Valencia between 1484 and 1530 and 99.3% of those judged in Barcelona between 1484 and 1505 were of Jewish origin.[2040]

False conversions:

The Inquisition had jurisdiction only over Christians. It had no power to investigate, prosecute, or convict Jews, Muslims, or any open member of other religions. Anyone who was known to identify as either Jew or Muslim was outside of Inquisitorial jurisdiction and could be tried only by the King. All the inquisitions could do in some of those cases was to deport the individual according to the King's law, but usually, even that had to go through a civil tribunal. The Inquisition had the authority to try only those who self-identified as Christians (initially for taxation purposes, later to avoid deportation as well) while practicing another religion de facto. Even those were treated as Christians. If they confessed or identified not as "judeizantes" but as fully practicing Jews, they fell back into the previously explained category and could not be targeted, although they would have pleaded guilty to previously lying about being Christian.

Fray Alonso de Ojeda, a Dominican friar from Seville, convinced Queen Isabella of the existence of Crypto – Judaism among Andalusian *conversos* during her stay in Seville between 1477 and 1478.[2041] A report, produced by Pedro González de Mendoza, Archbishop of Seville, and by the Segovian Dominican Tomás de Torquemada – of converso family himself – corroborated this assertion.

Spanish monarchs Ferdinand and Isabella requested a papal bull establishing an inquisition in Spain in 1478. Pope Sixtus IV granted a bull permitting the monarchs to select and appoint two or three priests over forty years of age to act as inquisitors.[2042] In 1483, Ferdinand and Isabella established a state council to administer the inquisition with the Dominican Friar Tomás de Torquemada acting as its president, even though Sixtus IV protested the activities of the inquisition in Aragon and its treatment of the *conversos*. Torquemada eventually assumed the title of Inquisitor – General.[2043]

Thomas F. Madden describes the world that formed medieval politics: "The Inquisition was not born out of the desire to crush diversity or oppress people; it was

---

[2040] Kamen (1998), p. 60

[2041] The terms *converso* and crypto - Jew are somewhat vexed, and occasionally historians are not clear on how, precisely, they are intended to be understood. For the purpose of clarity, in this article *converso* will be taken to mean one who has sincerely renounced Judaism or Islam and embraced Catholicism. Crypto - Jew will be taken to mean one who accepts Christian baptism yet continues to practice Judaism.

[2042] Peters 1988, p. 85.

[2043] Peters 1988, p. 89.

rather an attempt to stop unjust executions. Yes, you read that correctly. Heresy was a crime against the state. Roman law in the Code of Justinian made it a capital offense. Rulers, whose authority was believed to come from God, had no patience for heretics".[2044]

Ferdinand II of Aragon pressured Pope Sixtus IV to agree to an Inquisition controlled by the monarchy by threatening to withdraw military support at a time when the Turks were a threat to Rome. The pope issued a bull to stop the Inquisition but was pressured into withdrawing it. On 1 November 1478, Sixtus published the Papal bull, *Exigit Sinceras Devotionis Affectus*, through which he gave the monarchs exclusive authority to name the inquisitors in their kingdoms. The first two inquisitors, Miguel de Morillo and Juan de San Martín, were not named, however, until two years later, on 27 September 1480 in Medina del Campo.

The first *auto – da – fé* was held in Seville on 6 February 1481: six people were burned alive. From there, the Inquisition grew rapidly in the Kingdom of Castile. By 1492, tribunals existed in eight Castilian cities: Ávila, Córdoba, Jaén, Medina del Campo, Segovia, Sigüenza, Toledo, and Valladolid. Sixtus IV promulgated a new bull categorically prohibiting the Inquisition's extension to Aragón, affirming that:[2045] ... many true and faithful Christians, because of the testimony of enemies, rivals, slaves and other low people and still less appropriate without tests of any kind, have been locked up in secular prisons, tortured and condemned like relapsed heretics, deprived of their goods and properties, and given over to the secular arm to be executed, at great danger to their souls, giving a pernicious example and causing scandal to many.

Crypto – Jews were allowed to confess and do penance, although those who relapsed were executed.[2046]

The Spanish Inquisition had been established in part to prevent *conversos* from engaging in Jewish practices, which, as Christians, they were supposed to have given up. However this remedy for securing the orthodoxy of *conversos* was eventually deemed inadequate since the main justification the monarchy gave for formally expelling all Jews from Spain was the "great harm suffered by Christians (i.e., *conversos*) from the contact, intercourse and communication which they have with the Jews, who always attempt in various ways to seduce faithful Christians from our Holy Catholic Faith", according to the 1492 edict.[2047]

[2044] Thomas Madden: The Real Inquisition. National Review 2004
[2045] Cited in Kamen (1998), p. 49
[2046] Ben-Sasson, H.H., editor. A History of the Jewish People. Harvard University Press, 1976, pp. 588–590.
[2047] quoted in Kamen (1998), p. 20

The Alhambra Decree, issued in January 1492, gave the choice between expulsion and conversion. It was among the few expulsion orders that allowed conversion as an alternative and is used as a proof of the religious, not racial, element of the measure. The enforcement of this decree was very unequal, however, with the focus mainly on coastal and southern regions, those at risk of Ottoman invasion and more gradual and ineffective enforcement towards the interior.[2048]

Historic accounts of the numbers of Jews who left Spain were based on speculation, and some aspects were exaggerated by early accounts and historians: Juan de Mariana speaks of 800,000 people, and Don Isaac Abravanel of 300,000. While few reliable statistics exist for the expulsion, modern estimates based on tax returns and population estimates of communities are much lower, with Kamen stating that of a population of approximately 80,000 Jews and 200,000 *conversos*, about 40,000 emigrated.[2049] The Jews of the kingdom of Castile emigrated mainly to Portugal (where the entire community was forcibly converted in 1497) and to North Africa. The Jews of the kingdom of Aragon fled to other Christian areas including Italy, rather than to Muslim lands as is often assumed.[2050] Although the vast majority of *conversos* simply assimilated into the Catholic dominant culture, a minority continued to practice Judaism in secret, gradually migrated throughout Europe, North Africa, and the Ottoman Empire, mainly to areas where Sephardic communities were already present as a result of the Alhambra Decree.[2051]

The most intense period of persecution of *conversos* lasted until 1530. From 1531 to 1560, however, the percentage of *conversos* among the Inquisition trials dropped to 3% of the total. There was a rebound of persecutions when a group of crypto-Jews was discovered in Quintanar de la Orden in 1588 and there was a rise in denunciations of *conversos* in the last decade of the sixteenth century. At the beginning of the seventeenth century, some *conversos* who had fled to Portugal began to return to Spain, fleeing the persecution of the Portuguese Inquisition, founded in 1536. This led to a rapid increase in the trials of crypto-Jews, among them a number of important financiers. In 1691, during a number of *autos – da – fé* in Majorca, 37 *chuetas*, or *conversos* of Majorca, were burned.[2052]

[2048] Suárez Fernández, Luis (2012). La expulsión de los judíos. Un problema europeo. Barcelona: Ariel.
[2049] Kamen (1998), pp. 29–31
[2050] Kamen (1998), p. 24
[2051] Murphy, Cullen (2012). *God's jury: the Inquisition and the making of the modern world*. Boston: Houghton Mifflin Harcourt. p. 75. ISBN 978-0-618-09156-0.
[2052] Murphy, Cullen (2012). *God's jury: the Inquisition and the making of the modern world*. Boston: Houghton Mifflin Harcourt. p. 75. ISBN 978-0-618-09156-0.

During the eighteenth century, the number of *conversos* accused by the Inquisition decreased significantly. Manuel Santiago Vivar, tried in Córdoba in 1818, was the last person tried for being a crypto-Jew.[2053]

The Inquisition searched for false or relapsed converts among the Moriscos, who had converted from Islam. Beginning with a decree on 14 February 1502, Muslims in Granada had to choose between conversion to Christianity or expulsion.[2054] In the Crown of Aragon, most Muslims had faced this choice after the Revolt of the Brotherhoods (1519 – 1523). It is important to note that the enforcement of the expulsion of the moriscos was enforced unevenly, especially in the lands of the interior and the north, where the coexistence had lasted for over five centuries and moriscos were protected by the population, and orders were partially or completely ignored.

The War of the Alpujarras (1568 – 71), a general Muslim/Morisco uprising in Granada that expected to aid Ottoman disembarkation in the peninsula, ended in a forced dispersal of about half of the region's Moriscos throughout Castile and Andalusia as well as increased suspicions by Spanish authorities against this community.

Many Moriscos were suspected of practising Islam in secret, and the jealousy with which they guarded the privacy of their domestic life prevented the verification of this suspicion. Initially, they were not severely persecuted by the Inquisition, experiencing instead a policy of evangelization[2055] a policy not followed with those *conversos* who were suspected of being crypto – Jews. There were various reasons for this. In the kingdoms of Valencia and Aragon, many of the Moriscos were under the jurisdiction of the nobility, and persecution would have been viewed as a frontal assault on the economic interests of this powerful social class. Most importantly, the moriscos had integrated into the Spanish society significantly better than the Jews, intermarrying with the population often, and were not seen as a foreign element, especially in rural areas.[2056] Still, fears ran high among the

---

[2053] Kamen (2014), p. 370

[2054] Hans-Jürgen Prien (21 November 2012). *Christianity in Latin America: Revised and Expanded Edition*. BRILL. p. 11. ISBN 978-90-04-22262-5.

[2055] Absent records, the Inquisition decreed that all Moors were to be regarded as baptized, and thus were Moriscos, subject to the Inquisition. Secular authorities then decreed (in 1526) that 40 years of religious instruction would precede any prosecution. Fifty Moriscos were burnt at the stake before the Crown clarified its position. Neither the Church nor the Moriscos utilized the years well. The Moriscos can be stereotyped as poor, rural, uneducated agricultural workers who spoke Arabic. The Church had limited willingness or ability to educate this now-hostile group. Green (2007), pp. 124–127

[2056] Trevor J. Dadson, The Assimilation of Spain's Moriscos: Fiction or Reality? Journal of Levantine Studies, Vol. 1, No. 2, Winter 2011, pp. 11–30

population that the Moriscos were traitorous, especially in Granada. The coast was regularly raided by Barbary pirates backed by Spain's enemy, the Ottoman Empire, and the Moriscos were suspected of aiding them.

In the second half of the century, late in the reign of Philip II, conditions worsened between Old Christians and Moriscos. The Morisco Revolt in Granada in 1568 – 1570 was harshly suppressed, and the Inquisition intensified its attention on the Moriscos. From 1570 Morisco cases became predominant in the tribunals of Zaragoza, Valencia and Granada; in the tribunal of Granada, between 1560 and 1571, 82% of those accused were Moriscos, who were a vast majority of the Kingdom's population at the time.[2057] Still, the Moriscos did not experience the same harshness as judaizing *conversos* and Protestants, and the number of capital punishments was proportionally less.[2058]

In 1609, King Philip III, upon the advice of his financial adviser the Duke of Lerma and Archbishop of Valencia Juan de Ribera, decreed the Expulsion of the Moriscos. Hundreds of thousands of Moriscos were expelled, some of them probably sincere Christians. This was further fuelled by the religious intolerance of Archbishop Ribera who quoted the Old Testament texts ordering the enemies of God to be slain without mercy and setting forth the duties of kings to extirpate them.[2059] T he edict required: 'The Moriscos to depart, under the pain of death and confiscation, without trial or sentence... to take with them no money, bullion, jewels or bills of exchange, just what they could carry.'[2060] Although initial estimates of the number expelled such as those of Henri Lapeyre reach 300,000 Moriscos (or 4% of the total Spanish population), the extent and severity of the expulsion in much of Spain has been increasingly challenged by modern historians such as Trevor J. Dadson.[2061] Nev ertheless, the eastern region of Valencia, where ethnic tensions were high, was particularly affected by the expulsion, suffering economic collapse and depopulation of much of its territory.

Of those permanently expelled, the majority finally settled in the Maghreb or the Barbary coast.[2062] Those who avoided expulsion or who managed to return were gradually absorbed by the dominant culture.[2063]

[2057] Kamen (1998), p. 217

[2058] Kamen (1998), p. 225

[2059] Lea (1901), p. 308

[2060] Lea (1901), p. 345

[2061] Trevor J. Dadson: *The Assimilation of Spain's Moriscos: Fiction or Reality?*. Journal of Levantine Studies, vol. 1, no. 2, Winter 2011, pp. 11–30

[2062] *Boase, Roger (4 April 2002). "The Muslim Expulsion from Spain". History Today. **52** (4). The majority of those permanently expelled settling in the Maghreb or Barbary Coast, especially in Oran, Tunis, Tlemcen, Tetuán, Rabat and Salé. Many travelled overland to France, but after the assassination of Henry of Navarre by Ravaillac in May 1610, they were forced to emigrate to Italy,*

The Inquisition pursued some trials against Moriscos who remained or returned after expulsion: at the height of the Inquisition, cases against Moriscos are estimated to have constituted less than 10 percent of those judged by the Inquisition. Upon the coronation of Philip IV in 1621, the new king gave the order to desist from attempting to impose measures on remaining Moriscos and returnees. In September 1628 the Council of the Supreme Inquisition ordered inquisitors in Seville not to prosecute expelled Moriscos "unless they cause significant commotion."[2064] The last mass prosecution against Moriscos for crypto – Islamic practices occurred in Granada in 1727, with most of those convicted receiving relatively light sentences. By the end of the 18th century, the indigenous practice of Islam is considered to have been effectively extinguished in Spain.[2065]

Christian heretics:

The Spanish Inquisition had jurisdiction only over Christians. Therefore, only those who self – identified as Christians could be investigated and trialled by it. Those in the group of "heretics" were all subject to investigation. All forms of heretic Christianity (Protestants, Orthodox, blaspheming Catholics, etc.) were considered under its jurisdiction.

Protestants and Anglicans:

Despite popular myths about the Spanish Inquisition relating to Protestants, it dealt with very few cases involving actual Protestants, as there were so few in Spain.[2066] T he Inquisition of the Netherlands is here not considered part of the Spanish Inquisition. Lutheran was a portmanteau accusation used by the Inquisition to act against all those who acted in a way that was offensive to the church. The first of the trials against those labelled by the Inquisition as "Lutheran" were those against the sect of mystics known as the "Alumbrados" of Guadalajara and Valladolid. The trials were long and ended with prison sentences of differing lengths, though none of the sect were executed. Nevertheless, the subject of the "Alumbrados" put the Inquisition on the trail of many intellectuals and clerics who, interested

---

Sicily or Constantinople.

[2063] Adams, Susan M.; Bosch, Elena; Balaresque, Patricia L.; Ballereau, Stéphane J.; Lee, Andrew C.; Arroyo, Eduardo; López-Parra, Ana M.; Aler, Mercedes; Grifo, Marina S. Gisbert; Brion, Maria; Carracedo, Angel; Lavinha, João; Martínez-Jarreta, Begoña; Quintana-Murci, Lluis; Picornell, Antònia; Ramon, Misericordia; Skorecki, Karl; Behar, Doron M.; Calafell, Francesc; Jobling, Mark A. (December 2008). "The Genetic Legacy of Religious Diversity and Intolerance: Paternal Lineages of Christians, Jews, and Muslims in the Iberian Peninsula". *The American Journal of Human Genetics*. **83** (6): 725–736. doi:10.1016/j.ajhg.2008.11.007. PMC 2668061. PMID 19061982.

[2064] Michel Boeglin: *La expulsión de los moriscos de Andalucía y sus límites. El caso de Sevilla (1610–1613)* (In Spanish

[2065] *Vínculos Historia: The Moriscos who remained. The permanence of Islamic origin population in Early Modern Spain: Kingdom of Granada, XVII-XVIII centuries* (In Spanish)

[2066] Kamen (2014), p. 100

in Erasmian ideas, had strayed from orthodoxy. This is striking because both Charles I and Philip II were confessed admirers of Erasmus.[2067] The humanist Juan de Valdés,[2068] fled to Italy to escape anti-Erasmian factions that came to power in the court,[2069] and the preacher, Juan de Ávila spent close to a year in prison after he was questioned about his prayer practices.[2070]

The first trials against Lutheran groups, as such, took place between 1558 and 1562, at the beginning of the reign of Philip II, against two communities of Protestants from the cities of Valladolid and Seville, numbering about 120.[2071] The trials signalled a notable intensification of the Inquisition's activities. A number of *autos – da – fé* were held, some of them presided over by members of the royal family, and around 100 executions took place.[2072] The *autos – da – fé* of the mid-century virtually put an end to Spanish Protestantism, which was, throughout, a small phenomenon to begin with.[2073]

After 1562, though the trials continued, the repression was much reduced. About 200 Spaniards were accused of being Protestants in the last decades of the 16th century.

Most of them were in no sense Protestants, Irreligious sentiments, drunken mockery, anticlerical expressions, were all captiously classified by the inquisitors (or by those who denounced the cases) as "Lutheran." Disrespect to church images, and eating meat on forbidden days, were taken as signs of heresy.[2074] It is estimated that a dozen Spaniards were burned alive.[2075] It is important to notice that Protestantism and Anglicanism were treated as a marker to identify agents of foreign powers and symptoms of political disloyalty as much as, if not more than a cause of prosecution. Religion, patriotism, obedience to the king and personal beliefs were not seen as separate aspects of life until the end of the Modern Age. Spain especially had a long tradition of using self-identified religion as a political and cultural marker, and expression of loyalty to a specific overlord, more than as an accurate description of

---

[2067] Kamen (2014), p. 94
[2068] Kamen (2014), p. 98
[2069] Daniel A. Crews (1 January 2008). *Twilight of the Renaissance: The Life of Juan de Valdés*. University of Toronto Press. pp. 42–. ISBN 978-0-8020-9867-2.
[2070] Rady Roldán-Figueroa (11 November 2010). *The Ascetic Spirituality of Juan de Ávila (1499–1569)*. BRILL. pp. 23–. ISBN 978-90-04-19204-1.
[2071] These trials, specifically those of Valladolid, form the basis of the plot of *The Heretic: A novel of the Inquisition* by Miguel Delibes (Overlook: 2006).
[2072] Kamen (1998), p. 99 gives the figure of about 100 executions for heresy of any kind between 1559 and 1566. He compares these figures with those condemned to death in other European countries during the same period, concluding that in similar periods England, under Mary Tudor, executed about twice as many for heresy: in France, three times the number, and ten times as many in the Low Countries.
[2073] Kamen (2014), pp. 102–108
[2074] Kamen (1998), p. 98
[2075] Kamen (1998), pp. 99–100

personal beliefs -here the common accusation of heretics they received from Rome. In that note, accusations, or prosecutions due to beliefs held by enemy countries must be seen as political accusations regarding political treason more than as religious ones. Other times the accusation of Protestantism was considered as an equivalent of blasphemy, just a general way of addressing insubordination.[2076]

Even though the Inquisition had theoretical permission to investigate Orthodox "heretics", it almost never did. There was no major war between Spain and any Orthodox nation, so there was no reason to do so. There was one casualty tortured by those "Jesuits" (though most likely, Franciscans) who administered the Spanish Inquisition in North America, according to authorities within the Eastern Orthodox Church: St. Peter the Aleut. Even that single report has various numbers of inaccuracies that make it problematic and has no confirmation in the Inquisitorial archives.

The "superstitions" includes trials related to witchcraft. The witch-hunt in Spain had much less intensity than in other European countries (particularly France, Scotland, and Germany). One remarkable case was that of Logroño, in which the witches of Zugarramurdi in Navarre were persecuted. During the *auto – da – fé* that took place
in Logroño on 7 and 8 November 1610, six people were burned and another five burned in effigy.[2077] The role of the Inquisition in cases of witchcraft was much more restricted than is commonly believed. Well after the foundation of the Inquisition, jurisdiction over sorcery and witchcraft remained in secular hands.[2078] In general the Inquisition maintained a sceptical attitude towards cases of witchcraft, considering it as a mere superstition without any basis. Alonso de Salazar Frías, who took the Edict of Faith to various parts of Navarre after the trials of Logroño, noted in his report to the Suprema that, "There were neither witches nor bewitched in a village until they were talked and written about".[2079]

Blasphemy:

Included under the rubric of *heretical propositions* were verbal offences, from outright blasphemy to questionable statements regarding religious beliefs, from

---

[2076] Rodriguez-Sala, Maria Luisa. Los PROTESTANTES Y LA INQUISICIÓN. UNAM. https://archivos.juridicas.unam.mx/www/bjv/libros/6/2905/6.pdf
[2077] These trials are the theme of the film *Akelarre*, by the Spanish director Pedro Olea.
[2078] Henry Kamen. *The Spanish Inquisition A Historical Revision.* 1999
[2079] Cited in Henningsen, Gustav, ed. "The Salazar Documents: Inquisitor Alonso de Salazar Frías and Others on the Basque Witch Persecution." *Cultures, Beliefs, and Traditions: Medieval and Early Modern Peoples,* Vol 21. Boston: Koninklijke Brill, 2004. "Second Report of Salazar to the Inquisitor General (Logroño, 24 March 1612): An account of the whole visitation and publication of the Edict with special reference to the witches' sect". p. 352.

issues of sexual morality to misbehaviour of the clergy. Many were brought to trial for affirming that *simple fornication* (sex between unmarried persons) was not a sin or for putting in doubt different aspects of Christian faith such as Transubstantiation or the virginity of Mary.[2080] Also, members of the clergy themselves were occasionally accused of heretical propositions. These offences rarely led to severe penalties.

Sodomy:

The first sodomite was burned by the Inquisition in Valencia in 1572, and those accused included 19% clergy, 6% nobles, 37% workers, 19% servants, and 18% soldiers and sailors.[2081]

Nearly all of almost 500 cases of sodomy between persons concerned the relationship between an older man and an adolescent, often by coercion, with only a few cases where the couple were consenting homosexual adults. About 100 of the total involved allegations of child abuse. Adolescents were generally punished more leniently than adults, but only when they were very young (under ca. 12 years) or when the case clearly concerned rape did, they have a chance to avoid punishment altogether. As a rule, the Inquisition condemned to death only those sodomites over the age of 25 years. As about half of those tried were under this age, it explains the relatively small percentage of death sentences.[2082]

Cases of sodomy did not receive the same treatment in all areas of Spain. In the Kingdom of Castile, crimes of sodomy were not investigated by the Inquisition unless they were associated with religious heresy. In other words, the sodomy itself was investigated only as, and when, considered a symptom of a heretic belief or practice. In any other area, cases were considered an issue for civil authorities, and even then were not very actively investigated. The Crown of Aragon was the only area in which cases of sodomy were considered under the Inquisitorial jurisdiction, probably due to the previous presence of the Pontifical Inquisition in that kingdom. Within the Crown of Aragon, the tribunal of the city of Zaragoza was famously harsh even at the time.[2083] The reason to group "sodomy" with heresies and not with "marriage and family" is that sodomy was strongly associated with Islam, Judaism, Catharism, and heresy in general. It was seen as a symptom more than as a condition or peculiarity.

Freemasonry:

Further information: Papal ban of Freemasonry and In eminenti apostolatus

---

[2080] Green (2007), pp. 223–224
[2081] Kamen (1998), p. 259
[2082] Monter, *Frontiers of Heresy*, pp. 276–299.
[2083] Kamen, Henry (2011). La Inquisición Española. Una revisión histórica. p. 192 pp259

The Roman Catholic Church has regarded Freemasonry as heretical since about 1738; the *suspicion* of Freemasonry was potentially a capital offense. Spanish Inquisition records reveal two prosecutions in Spain and only a few more throughout the Spanish Empire.[2084] In 1815, Francisco Javier de Mier y Campillo, the Inquisitor General of the Spanish Inquisition and the Bishop of Almería, suppressed Freemasonry and denounced the lodges as "societies which lead to atheism, to sedition and to all errors and crimes."[2085] He then instituted a purge during which Spaniards could be arrested on the charge of being "suspected of Freemasonry".[2086]

Censorship:

As one manifestation of the Counter-Reformation, the Spanish Inquisition worked actively to impede the diffusion of heretical ideas in Spain by producing "Indexes" of prohibited books. Such lists of prohibited books were common in Europe a decade before the Inquisition published its first. The first Index published in Spain in 1551 was, in reality, a reprinting of the Index published by the University of Leuven in 1550, with an appendix dedicated to Spanish texts. Subsequent Indexes were published in 1559, 1583, 1612, 1632, and 1640.

Included in the Indices, at one point, were some of the great works of Spanish literature, but most of the works were religious in nature and plays.[2087] A number of religious writers who are today considered saints by the Catholic Church saw their works appear in the Indexes. At first, this might seem counter – intuitive or even nonsensical, how were these Spanish authors published in the first place if their texts were then prohibited by the Inquisition and placed in the Index? The answer lies in the process of publication and censorship in Early Modern Spain. Books in Early Modern Spain faced prepublication licensing and approval (which could include modification) by both secular and religious authorities. However, once approved and published, the circulating text also faced the possibility of post – hoc censorship by being denounced to the Inquisition, sometimes decades later. Likewise, as Catholic theology evolved, once – prohibited texts might be removed from the Index.

At first, inclusion in the Index meant total prohibition of a text; however, this proved not only impractical and unworkable but also contrary to the goals of having a literate and well – educated clergy. Works with one line of suspect dogma would be prohibited in their entirety, despite the orthodoxy of the remainder of the text. In time, a compromise solution was adopted in which trusted Inquisition officials

2084 Green (2007), p. 320
2085 William R. Denslow, Harry S. Truman: *10,000 Famous Freemasons*, ISBN 1-4179-7579-2.
2086 William R. Denslow, Harry S. Truman: *10,000 Famous Freemasons*, ISBN 1-4179-7579-2.
2087 Germán Bleiberg; Maureen Ihrie; Janet Pérez (1993). *Dictionary of the Literature of the Iberian Peninsula*. Greenwood Publishing Group. pp. 374–. ISBN 978-0-313-28731-2.

blotted out words, lines, or whole passages of otherwise acceptable texts, thus allowing these expurgated editions to circulate. Although in theory, the Indexes imposed enormous restrictions on the diffusion of culture in Spain, some historians argue that such strict control was impossible in practice and that there was much more liberty in this respect than is often believed. And Irving Leonard has conclusively demonstrated that, despite repeated royal prohibitions, romances of chivalry, such as *Amadis of Gaul*, found their way to the New World with the blessing of the Inquisition. Moreover, with the coming of the Age of Enlightenment in the 18th century, increasing numbers of licenses to possess and read prohibited texts were granted.

Despite the repeated publication of the Indexes and a large bureaucracy of censors, the activities of the Inquisition did not impede the development of Spanish literature's "Siglo de Oro", although almost all its major authors crossed paths with the Holy Office at one point or another. Among the Spanish authors included in the Index are Bartolomé Torres Naharro, Juan del Enzina, Jorge de Montemayor, Juan de Valdés and Lope de Vega, as well as the anonymous *Lazarillo de Tormes* and the *Cancionero General* by Hernando del Castillo. *La Celestina*, which was not included in the Indexes of the 16th century, was expurgated in 1632 and prohibited in its entirety in 1790. Among the non-Spanish authors prohibited were Ovid, Dante, Rabelais, Ariosto, Machiavelli, Erasmus, Jean Bodin, Valentine Naibod and Thomas More (known in Spain as Tomás Moro). One of the most outstanding and best-known cases in which the Inquisition directly confronted literary activity is that of Fray Luis de León, noted humanist and religious writer of converso origin, who was imprisoned for four years (from 1572 to 1576) for having translated the Song of Songs directly from Hebrew.

Some scholars state that one of the main effects of the inquisition was to end free thought and scientific thought in Spain. As one contemporary Spaniard in exile put it: "Our country is a land of pride, envy and barbarism; down there one cannot produce any culture without being suspected of heresy, error and Judaism. Thus, silence was imposed on the learned."[2088] For the next few centuries, while the rest of Europe was slowly awakened by the influence of the Enlightenment, Spain stagnated.[2089] However, this conclusion is contested.

The censorship of books was very ineffective, and prohibited books circulated in Spain without significant problems. The Spanish Inquisition never persecuted scientists, and relatively few scientific books were placed on the Index. On the other

---

[2088] *Clive Walkley (2010). Juan Esquivel: A Master of Sacred Music During the Spanish Golden Age. Boydell & Brewer. pp. 7–. ISBN 978-1-84383-587-5.*
[2089] Johnson, Paul, *A History of Christianity*, Penguin, 1976.

hand, Spain was a state with more political freedom than in other absolute monarchies in the 16th to 18th centuries.[2090] The apparent paradox gets explained by both the hermeticism religious ideas of the Spanish church and monarchy, and the budding seed of what would become Enlightened absolutism taking shape in Spain. The list of banned books was not, as interpreted sometimes, a list of evil books but a list of books that lay people were very likely to misinterpret. The presence of highly symbolical and high-quality literature on the list was so explained. These metaphorical or parable sounding books were listed as not meant for free circulation, but there might be no objections to the book itself and the circulation among scholars was mostly free. Most of these books were carefully collected by the elite. The practical totality of the prohibited books can be found now as then in the library of the monasterio del Escorial, carefully collected by Philip II and Philip III. The collection was "public" after Philip II's death and members of universities, intellectuals, courtesans, clergy, and certain branches of the nobility didn't have too many problems to access them and commission authorised copies. The Inquisition has not been known to make any serious attempt to stop this for all the books, but there are some records of them "suggesting" the King of Spain to stop collecting grimoires or magic – related ones. This attitude was also not new. Translations of the Bible to Castillian and Provenzal (Catalan) had been made and allowed in Spain since the Middle Ages. The first preserved copy dates from the 13th century. However, like the bible of Cisneros they were mostly for scholarly use, and it was customary for laymen to ask religious or academic authorities to review the translation and supervise the use.

The Inquisition also pursued offenses against morals and general social order, at times in open conflict with the jurisdictions of civil tribunals. There were trials for bigamy, a relatively frequent offence[2091] in a society that only permitted divorce under the most extreme circumstances. In the case of men, the penalty was two hundred lashes and five to ten years of "service to the Crown". Said service could be whatever the court deemed most beneficial for the nation but it usually was either five years as an oarsman in a royal galley for those without any qualification[2092] (possibly a death sentence),[2093] or ten years working maintained but without salary in a public Hospital or charitable institution of the sort for those with some special skill,

---

[2090] Kamen (2005), pp. 126–130
[2091] Green (2007), p. 296
[2092] Green (2007), p. 298
[2093] Statistics are not available for Spanish oarsmen, but the general state of Mediterranean oared galleys circa 1570 was grim; cf. *Crowley, Roger (2009). Empires of the sea: The siege of Malta, the battle of Lepanto, and the contest for the canter of the world. New York: Random House Trade Paperbacks. pp. 77–78. ISBN 978-0-8129-77646.*: "… galley slaves led lives bitter and short. One way or another the oared galley consumed men like fuel. Each dying wretch dumped overboard had to be replaced – and there were never enough."

such as doctors, surgeons, or lawyers.[2094] The penalty was five to seven years as an oarsman in the case of Portugal.

Under the category of "unnatural marriage" fell any marriage or attempted marriage between two individuals who could not procreate. The Catholic Church in general, and a nation constantly at war like Spain,[2095] emphasised the reproductive goal of marriage.

The Spanish Inquisition's policy in this regard was restrictive but applied in a very egalitarian way. It considered unnatural any non-reproductive marriage, and natural any reproductive one, regardless of gender or sex involved. The two forms of obvious male sterility were either due to damage to the genitals through castration, or accidental wounding at war (capón), or to some genetic condition that might keep the man from completing puberty (lampiño). Female sterility was also a reason to declare a marriage unnatural but was harder to prove. One case that dealt with marriage, sex, and gender was the trial of Eleno de Céspedes.

Non-religious crimes:

Despite popular belief, the role of the Inquisition as a mainly religious institution, or religious in nature at all, is contested at best. Its main function was that of private police for the Crown with jurisdiction to enforce the law in those crimes that took place in the private sphere of life. The notion of religion and civil law being separate is a modern construction and made no sense in the 15th century, so there was no difference between breaking a law regarding religion and breaking a law regarding tax collection. The difference between them is a modern projection the institution itself did not have. As such, the Inquisition was the prosecutor (in some cases the only prosecutor) of any crimes that could be perpetrated without the public taking notice (mainly domestic crimes, crimes against the weakest members of society, administrative crimes and forgeries, organized crime, and crimes against the Crown).

Examples include crimes associated with sexual or family relations such as rape and sexual violence (the Inquisition was the first and only body who punished it across the nation), bestiality, paedophilia (quite often overlapping with sodomy), incest, child abuse or neglect and (as discussed) bigamy. Non-religious crimes also included procurement (not prostitution), human trafficking, smuggling, forgery or falsification of currency, documents or signatures, tax fraud (many

---

[2094] Lorenzo Arrazola, *Encyclopaedia Espanola De Derecho Y Administracion: Ciu-Col* (Enciclopedia of Spanish Penal and Administrative Law). Madrid: Saraswati Press, 2012, pp. 572
[2095] Cċeres, Fernando (2007). *Estudios Sobre Cultura, Guerra Y Poltica En La Corona De Castilla [Studies Over War Culture and Politics in the Kingdom of Castile]. Editorial Csic Consejo Superior de Investigaciones Cientflcas. siglos xiv–xvii.*

religious crimes were considered subdivisions of this one), illegal weapons, swindles, disrespect to the Crown or its institutions (the Inquisition included, but also the church, the guard, and the kings themselves), espionage for a foreign power, conspiracy, treason.[2096]

The non-religious crimes processed by the Inquisition accounted for a considerable percentage of its total investigations and are often hard to separate in the statistics, even when documentation is available. The line between religious and non-religious crimes did not exist in 15th century Spain as legal concept. Many of the crimes listed here and some of the religious crimes listed in previous sections were contemplated under the same article. For example, "sodomy" included paedophilia as a subtype. Often part of the data given for prosecution of male homosexuality corresponds to convictions for paedophilia, not adult homosexuality. In other cases, religious and non – religious crimes were seen as distinct but equivalent. The treatment of public blasphemy and street swindlers was similar (since in both cases you are "misleading in a harmful way). Making counterfeit currency and heretic proselytism was also treated similarly; both were punished by death and subdivided in similar ways since both were "spreading falsifications". In general heresy and falsifications of material documents were treated similarly by the Spanish Inquisition, indicating that they may have been thought of as equivalent actions.[2097]

Another difficulty to discriminate the inquisition's secular and religious activity is the common association of certain types of investigations. An accusation or suspicion on certain crime often launched an automatic investigation on many others. Anyone accused of espionage due to non-religious reasons would likely be investigated for heresy too, and anyone suspected of a heresy associated to a foreign power would be investigated for espionage too automatically. Likewise, some religious crimes were considered likely to be associated with non-religious crimes, like human trafficking, procurement, and child abuse was expected to be associated to sodomy, or sodomy was expected to be associated to heresy and false conversions. Which accusation started the investigation isn't always clear. Finally, trials were often further complicated by the attempts of witnesses or victims to add further charges, especially witchcraft. Like in the case of Eleno de Céspedes, charges for witchcraft done in this way, or in general, were quickly dismissed but they often show in the statistics as investigations made.

Organisation:
[2096] Online access to the Historical Archives of the Inquisition in Valencia, where the records of the trials and correspondence to officials can be found; you can find the corresponding ones to various other areas in Spain in the same webpage.
[2097] Elvira, Roca Barea María, and Arcadi Espada. Imperiofobia Y Leyenda Negra: Roma, Rusia, Estados Unidos Y El Imperio Español. Madrid: Siruela, 2017

Beyond its role in religious affairs, the Inquisition was also an institution at the service of the monarchy. The Inquisitor General, in charge of the Holy Office, was designated by the crown. The Inquisitor General was the only public office whose authority stretched to all the kingdoms of Spain (including the American viceroyalties), except for a brief period (1507–1518) during which there were two Inquisitors General, one in the kingdom of Castile, and the other in Aragon.

The Inquisitor General presided over the Council of the Supreme and General Inquisition (generally abbreviated as "Council of the Suprema"), created in 1483, which was made up of six members named directly by the crown (the number of members of the Suprema varied over the course of the Inquisition's history, but it was never more than 10). Over time, the authority of the Suprema grew at the expense of the power of the Inquisitor General.

The Suprema met every morning, except for holidays, and for two hours in the afternoon on Tuesdays, Thursdays, and Saturdays.

The morning sessions were devoted to questions of faith, while the afternoons were reserved for "minor heresies"[2098] cases of perceived unacceptable sexual behaviour, bigamy, witchcraft, etc.[2099]

Below the Suprema were the various tribunals of the Inquisition, which were originally itinerant, installing themselves where they were necessary to combat heresy, but later being established in fixed locations. During the first phase, numerous tribunals were established, but the period after 1495 saw a marked tendency towards centralization.

In the kingdom of Castile, the following permanent tribunals of the Inquisition were established:

- 1482 In Seville and in Córdoba.
- 1485 In Toledo and in Llerena.
- 1488 In Valladolid and in Murcia.
- 1489 In Cuenca.
- 1505 In Las Palmas (Canary Islands).
- 1512 In Logroño.
- 1526 In Granada.
- 1574 In Santiago de Compostela.

[2098] Henningsen, Gustav: The Spanish Inquisition and the Inquisitorial Mind, p. 220.
[2099] García Cárcel (1976), p. 21

There were only four tribunals in the kingdom of Aragon: Zaragoza and Valencia (1482), Barcelona (1484), and Majorca (1488). [2100]

Ferdinand the Catholic also established the Spanish Inquisition in Sicily (1513), housed in Palermo, and Sardinia, in the town of Sassari.[2101] In the Americas, tribunals were established in Lima and in Mexico City (1569) and, in 1610, in Cartagena de Indias (present day Colombia).

Initially, each of the tribunals included two inquisitors, *calificadors* (qualifiers), an *alguacil* (bailiff), and a *fiscal* (prosecutor); new positions were added as the institution matured. The inquisitors were preferably jurists more than theologians; in 1608 Philip III even stipulated that all inquisitors needed to have a background in law. The inquisitors did not typically remain in the position for a long time: for the Court of Valencia, for example, the average tenure in the position was about two years.[2102] Most of the inquisitors belonged to the secular clergy (priests who were not members of religious orders) and had a university education.

The *fiscal* oversaw presenting the accusation, investigating the denunciations, and interrogating the witnesses using physical and mental torture. The *calificadores* were generally theologians; it fell to them to determine whether the defendant's conduct added up to a crime against the faith. Consultants were expert jurists who advised the court in questions of procedure. The court had, in addition, three secretaries: the *notario de secuestros* (Notary of Property), who registered the goods of the accused at the moment of his detention; the *notario del secreto* (Notary of the Secret), who recorded the testimony of the defendant and the witnesses; and the *escribano general* (General Notary), secretary of the court. The *alguacil* was the executive arm of the court, responsible for detaining, jailing, and physically torturing the defendant. Other civil employees were the *nuncio*, ordered to spread official notices of the court, and the *alcaide*, the jailer in charge of feeding the prisoners.

In addition to the members of the court, two auxiliary figures existed that collaborated with the Holy Office: and the comissarios (commissioners). *Familiares* were lay collaborators of the Inquisition, who had to be permanently at the service of the Holy Office. To become a *familiar* was considered an honour, since it was a public recognition of *limpieza de sangre* - Old Christian status – and brought with it certain additional privileges. Although many nobles held the position, most of them came from the ranks of commoners. The commissioners,

---

[2100] Kamen (1998), p. 141
[2101] In Sicily, the Inquisition functioned until 30 March 1782, when it was abolished by King Ferdinand IV of Naples. It is estimated that 200 people were executed during this period.
[2102] García Cárcel (1976), p. 24

on the other hand, were members of the religious orders who collaborated occasionally with the Holy Office.

One of the most striking aspects of the organization of the Inquisition was its form of financing: devoid of its own budget, the Inquisition depended exclusively on the confiscation of the goods of the denounced. It is not surprising, therefore, that many of those prosecuted were rich men. That the situation was open to abuse is evident, as stands out in the memorandum that a *converso* from Toledo directed to Charles I:

Your Majesty must provide, before all else, that the expenses of the Holy Office do not come from the properties of the condemned, because if that is the case if they do not burn, they do not eat.[2103]

Accusations:

When the Inquisition arrived in a city, the first step was the *Edict of Grace*. Following the Sunday Mass, the Inquisitor would proceed to read the edict; it explained possible heresies and encouraged all the congregation to come to the tribunals of the Inquisition to "relieve their consciences". They were called *Edicts of Grace* because all of the self – incriminated who presented themselves within a *period of grace* (usually ranging from thirty to forty days) were offered the possibility of reconciliation with the Church without severe punishment.[2104] The promise of benevolence was effective, and many voluntarily presented themselves to the Inquisition and were often encouraged to denounce others who had also committed offenses, informants being the Inquisition's primary source of information. After about 1500, the Edicts of Grace were replaced by the *Edicts of Faith*, which left out the grace period and instead encouraged the denunciation of those guilty.[2105]

The denunciations were anonymous, and the defendants had no way of knowing the identities of their accusers.[2106] This was one of the points most criticized by those who opposed the Inquisition (for example, the Cortes of Castile, in 1518). In practice, false denunciations were frequent. Denunciations were made for a variety of reasons, from genuine concern to rivalries and personal jealousies.

Detention:

After a denunciation, the case was examined by the *calificadores*, who had to determine whether there was heresy involved, followed by the detention of the accused. In practice, however, many were detained in preventive custody, and many

---

[2103] Cited in Kamen (1998), p. 151
[2104] Kamen (1998), p. 57
[2105] Kamen (1998), p. 174
[2106] Though over the course of the trial, their identities likely became apparent.

cases of lengthy incarcerations occurred, lasting up to two years before the *calificadores* examined the case.[2107]

Detention of the accused entailed the preventive sequestration of their property by the Inquisition. The property of the prisoner was used to pay for procedural expenses and the accused's own maintenance and costs. Often the relatives of the defendant found themselves in outright misery. This situation was remedied only following instructions written in 1561.[2108]

Some authors, such as Thomas William Walsh, stated that the entire process was undertaken with the utmost secrecy, as much for the public as for the accused, who were not informed about the accusations that were levied against them. Months or even years could pass without the accused being informed about why they were imprisoned. The prisoners remained isolated, and, during this time, the prisoners were not allowed to attend Mass nor receive the sacraments. The jails of the Inquisition were no worse than those of secular authorities, and there are even certain testimonies that occasionally they were much better.[2109] There are few records of the time of the accused in prison, but the transcription of the trials repeatedly shows the accused being informed of every charge during the trial. They also show the accused's answers, in which they address each accusation specifically. Given that they would be informed anyway, it makes little sense that the accused would be kept in the dark prior to the trial, unless the investigation was still open.[2110]

Trial:

The inquisitorial process consisted of a series of hearings, in which both the denouncers and the defendant gave testimony. A defence counsel was assigned to the defendant, a member of the tribunal itself, whose role was simply to advise the defendant and to encourage them to speak the truth. The prosecution was directed by the *fiscal*. Interrogation of the defendant was done in the presence of the *Notary of the Secreto*, who meticulously wrote down the words of the accused. The archives of the Inquisition, in comparison to those of other judicial systems of the era, are striking in the completeness of their documentation. To defend themselves, the accused had two choices: *abonos* (to find favourable witnesses, akin to "substantive" evidence/testimony in Anglo-American law) or *tachas* (to demonstrate that the

---

[2107] In the tribunal of Valladolid, in 1699, various suspects (including a girl of 9 and a boy of 14) were jailed for up to two years with having had the least evaluation of the accusations presented against them" (Kamen (1998), p. 183).

[2108] Kamen (1998), p.184

[2109] Walsh, Thomas William, *Characters of the Inquisition*, P.J. Kennedy & Sons, 1940, p. 163.

[2110] https://www.mecd.gob.es/dam/jcr:7d0f0b12-1c0e-49f6-b437-23206a95086d/original-primera-parte.pdf preserved transcripts of a trial as sample

witnesses of accusers were not trustworthy, akin to Anglo-American "impeachment" evidence/testimony).

The documentation from the notary usually shows the following content, which gives us an idea of what the actual trial was likely to look like:[2111]

- A first page in which the notary wrote the date, the names, and charges of the members of the tribunal, the name of the accused and the accuser, the accusation, and the names of everyone present in the room during the trial.
- A second page with the accused's first statement about their innocence or culpability, and their general response and recollection of the facts. This part usually takes from a thick fluid paragraph to a couple of pages and are relatively formal, within the accused's education level, from which one

  can suspect that the accused had time to prepare it prior to either the trial or the declaration, and probably help from the defendant. This paragraph also shows the accused addressing every charge from the first page, by points, which shows that the accused must have been informed of the charges against them.

- A third section with the *fiscal*'s name and the transcription of a speech in which they address the accused's statement, also by points, and presents their case regarding each one separately.
- A fourth section, usually dated on the next day or a couple of days after the fiscal's intervention, with the name of the "procurador" (defendant) and the transcription of a speech in which they address the fiscal's arguments, again by points and separately, and defend the accused regarding each one.
- A fifth section with the tribunal's response to this. In the vast majority of cases, the response is to order the search and calling of certain individuals, as witnesses, or of some experts such as doctors to testify and ratify some parts of what has been said and giving a date for the tribunal to come together again and examine the evidence. Usually, the fiscal and procurator can ask for the presence of some witnesses here too, as it is inferred by them showing up later, but that is not always specifically stated in the transcripts and may be done outside of trial.

[2111] "redirigeme – Ministerio de Educación, Cultura y Deporte" (PDF). Mecd.gob.es. Retrieved 2 January 2019

- The next section is often dated sometime later. Each witness or expert is introduced by complete name, job, relationship to the victim if any, and relationship to the case. The witness's testimony is not transcribed word by word like in previous cases but summarized by the notary, probably because it was not prepared and does not follow a coherent, consistent order and writing implements were rather expensive to waste.
- A page in which the procurador (defendant) declared the questions he is going to make to (usually another) group of witnesses of his choice since he often states that "he has asked them to come "or "he has called them". The answers given by each witness follow, with each witness presented as in the previous section. These testimonies are also paraphrased and summarized but addressed by points, with the answer to each question paraphrased separately.
- The fiscal and the procurador require equal copies of the testimony of the witnesses and keep them, demanding that no copy is shown to anyone until the end of a period of usually six days in which the witnesses have the chance to call the tribunal again to change their mind or add something.
- A third meeting of the tribunal with a new date. The transcription of a new speech by the procurator stating his view of the declarations and wrapping the witnesses' testimony up from his perspective.
- A similar intervention, usually far shorter, from the fiscal.
- The response from the tribunal, paraphrased, which could be to dictate the sentence, but often was to require either further clarification from the witness (restarting the procedure from the second step) or call for another type of proof (restarting the procedure from the sixth step). These steps would repeat cyclically in the documentation of the trial, through different meetings of the tribunal and different weeks, until the tribunal has reached a conclusion.
- A literal transcription of the verdict and sentence. If the accused has been accused of more than one thing the sentence usually comes by points too. It is not uncommon for some of the accusations to be dismissed along with the process and said the process to continue taking into account the remaining ones. While sentences of innocence could be given at any point in a trial for multiple crimes, sentences of culpability only appear once the trial is over, and all investigations opened against the accused are closed.

Regarding the fairness of the trials, the structure of them was similar to modern trials and extremely advanced for the time. However, the Inquisition was dependent on the political power of the King. The lack of separation of powers allows assuming questionable fairness for certain scenarios. The fairness of the Inquisitorial tribunals seemed to be among the best in early modern Europe when it came to the trial of laymen.[2112] [2113] There are also testimonies by former prisoners that, if believed, suggest that said fairness was less than ideal when national or political interests were involved.[2114]

To obtain a confession or information relevant to an investigation, the Inquisition used torture, but not in a systematic way. It could only be applied when all other options, witnesses and experts had been used, the accused was found guilty or most likely guilty, and relevant information regarding accomplices or specific details were missing. It was applied mainly against those suspected of Judaizing and Protestantism beginning in the 16th century, in other words, "enemies of the state", since said crimes were usually thought to be associated with a larger organized network of either espionage or conspiracy with foreign powers. For example, Lea estimates that between 1575 and 1610 the court of Toledo tortured approximately a third of those processed for Protestant heresy.[2115] The recently opened Vatican Archives suggest even lower numbers.[2116] In other periods, the proportions varied remarkably. Torture was always a means to obtain the confession of the accused, not a punishment itself.

Torture:

Torture was employed in all civil and religious trials in Europe. The Spanish Inquisition used it more restrictively than was common at the time. Its main differentiation characteristic was that, as opposed to both civil trials and other inquisitions, it had very strict regulations regarding when, what, to whom, how many times, for how long and under what supervision it could be applied.[2117] The Spanish inquisition engaged in it far less often and with greater care than other courts.[2118] In the civil court, both Spanish and otherwise, there was no restriction regarding duration or any other point.

[2112] Thomas F. Madden. "The Truth about the Spanish Inquisition." Crisis (October 2003).

[2113] "LA INQUISICIÓN ESPAÑOLA".José Martínez MillánAlianza Editorial Bolsillo (2010)

[2114] Kamen, Henry (2011). La Inquisición Española. Una revisión histórica. pp. 191–192.

[2115] H. C. Lea, III, p. 33, Cited in Kamen (1998), p. 185. García Cárcel (1976), p. 43 finds the same statistics.

[2116] Thomas F. Madden. "The Truth about the Spanish Inquisition." Crisis (October 2003).

[2117] Bethencourt, Francisco. La Inquisición En La Época Moderna: España, Portugal E Italia, Siglos Xv-xix. Madrid: Akal, 1997.

[2118] Haliczer, Stephen, Inquisition and society in the kingdom of Valencia, 1478–1834, p. 79, University of California Press, 1990

- When: Torture was allowed only: *"when sufficient proofs to confirm the culpability of the accused have been gathered by other means, and every other method of negotiation have been tried and exhausted"*. It was stated by the inquisitorial rule that information obtained through torment was not reliable, and confession should only be extracted this way when all needed information was already known and proven. Confessions obtained through torture could not be used to convict or sentence anyone.

- What: The Spanish Inquisition was prohibited to *"maim, mutilate, draw blood or cause any sort of permanent damage"* to the prisoner. Ecclesiastical tribunals were prohibited by church law from shedding blood.[2119] There was a closed list of the allowed torture methods. These were all tried and used in the civil courts all through Europe, and therefore known to be "safe" in this regard. Any other method, regardless of whether it was legal in the country or practiced in civil courts, was not allowed.

- How many times: Each accusation allowed for a different number of torment sessions on the same person (once the "when" condition of the culpability being supported by the strong external evidence was fulfilled). The number was dependent on how "harmful to society" the crime was. Counterfeit currency allowed for a maximum of two. The most serious offenses allowed for a maximum of eight.

- For how long: "Torment" could be applied for a maximum of 15 minutes. The Roman Inquisition allowed for 30 minutes.

- Supervision: A Physician was usually available in case of emergency.[2120] It was also required for a doctor to certify that the prisoner was healthy enough to go through the torment without suffering harm.[2121]

Per contrast, European civil trials from England to Italy and from Spain to Russia could use, and did use, torture without justification and for as long as they considered. So much so that there were serious tensions between the Inquisition and Philip III, since the Inquisitors complained that "those people sent to the prisons of the King blasphemed and accused themselves of heresy just to be sent under the Inquisitorial jurisdiction instead of the King's" and that was collapsing the Inquisition's tribunals. During the reign of Philip IV there were registered complaints of the Inquisitors about people who "Blasphemed, mostly in winter, just to be detained and fed inside the prison". Despite some popular accounts, modern

---

[2119] Kamen (1998), p. 190
[2120] Kamen (1998), p. 189
[2121] Crespo Vargas, Pablo L. La Inquisición Española Y Las Supersticiones En El Caribe Hispano. Madrid: Palibrio, 2011. pp120-130

historians state that torture was only ever used to confirm information or a confession, not for punitive reasons.[2122]

Rafael Sabatinni states that among the methods of torture allowed, and common in other secular and ecclesiastical tribunals, were *garrucha, toca* and the *potro*,[2123] even though those claims contradict both the Inquisitorial law and the claims made by Kamen. The application of the *garrucha*, also known as the strappado, consisted of suspending the victim from the ceiling by the wrists, which are tied behind the back. Sometimes weights were tied to the ankles, with a series of lifts and drops, during which the arms and legs suffered violent pulls and were sometimes dislocated.[2124]

The use of te *toca* (cloth), also called *interrogatorio mejorado del agua* (improved waterboarding / improved water interrogation), is better documented. It consisted of introducing a cloth into the mouth of the victim, and forcing them to ingest water spilled from a jar so that they had the impression of drowning.[2125] The *potro*, the rack, in which the limbs were slowly pulled apart, was thought to be the instrument of torture used most frequently.[2126] Among them all, the "submarine / waterboarding" was by far the most commonly used, since it was cheap, and seen as "harmless and very safe" (safer for the victim than clothless waterboarding, hence the "improved" (*mejorado*) epithet).

The assertio that *confessionem esse veram, non factam vi tormentorum* (literally: 'a person's confession is truth, not made by way of torture') sometimes follows a description of how, after torture had ended, the subject freely confessed to the offenses. Thus, confessions following torture were deemed to be made of the confessor's free will, and hence valid.

Once the process concluded, the inquisidores met with a representative of the bishop and with the *consultores* (consultants), experts in theology or Canon Law (but not necessarily clergy themselves), which was called the *consulta de fe* (faith consultation/religion check). The case was voted, and sentence pronounced, which had to be unanimous. In case of discrepancies, the *Suprema* had to be informed.

Sentencing:

The results of the trial could be the following:

[2122] Kamen (1998), p. 189
[2123] Kamen (1998), p. 190
[2124] Sabatini, Rafael, *Torquemada and the Spanish Inquisition: A History*, p. 190, Kessinger Publishing (2003), ISBN 0-7661-3161-0.
[2125] Scott, George Ryley, *The History of Torture Throughout the Ages*, p. 172, Columbia University Press (2003) ISBN 0-7103-0837-X.
[2126] Carrol. James, *Constantine's Sword: The Church and the Jews: A History*, p. 356, Houghton Mifflin Books (2002), ISBN 0-618-21908-0.

1. Although quite rare in actual practice, the defendant could be acquitted. Inquisitors did not wish to terminate the proceedings. If they did, and new evidence turned up later, they would be forced into reopening and re – presenting the old evidence.

2. The trial could be suspended, in which case the defendant, although under suspicion, went free (with the threat that the process could be continued at any time) or was held in long-term imprisonment until a trial commenced. When set free after a suspended trial it was considered a form of acquittal without specifying that the accusation had been erroneous.

3. The defendant could be penanced. Since they were considered guilty, they had to publicly abjure their crimes (*de levi* if it was a misdemeanour, and *de vehementi* if the crime were serious), and accept a public punishment. Among these were *sanbenito*, exile, fines or even sentencing to service as oarsmen in royal galleys.

4. The defendant could be reconciled. In addition to the public ceremony in which the condemned was reconciled with the Catholic Church, more severe punishments were used, among them long sentences to jail or the galleys, plus the confiscation of all property. Physical punishments, such as whipping, were also used.

5. The most serious punishment was relaxation to the secular arm. The Inquisition had no power to kill the convict or determine the way they should die; that was a right of the King. Burning at the stake was a possibility, probably kept from the Papal Inquisition of Aragon, but a very uncommon one. This penalty was frequently applied to impenitent heretics and those who had relapsed. Execution was public. If the condemned repented, they were shown mercy by being garrotted before their corpse was burned; if not, they were burned alive.

Frequently, cases were judged *in absentia*, and when the accused died before the trial finished, the condemned were burned in effigy.

The distribution of the punishments varied considerably over time. It is believed that sentences of death were enforced in the first stages within the long history of the Inquisition. According to García Cárcel, the court of Valencia, one of the most active, employed the death penalty in 40% of the convicts before 1530, but later that percentage dropped to 3%.[2127]

[2127] García Cárcel (1976), p. 39

If the sentence was condemnatory, this implied that the condemned had to participate in the ceremony of an *auto de fe* (more commonly known in English as an *auto – da – fé*) that solemnized their return to the Church (in most cases), or punishment as an impenitent heretic. The *autos – da – fé* could be private (*auto particular*) or public (*auto publico* or *auto general*).

Although initially the public *autos* did not have any special solemnity nor sought a large attendance of spectators, with time they became solemn ceremonies, celebrated with large public crowds, amidst a festive atmosphere. The *auto-da-fé* eventually became a baroque spectacle, with staging meticulously calculated to cause the greatest effect among the spectators. The *autos* were conducted in a large public space (frequently in the largest plaza of the city), generally on holidays. The rituals related to the *auto* began the previous night (the "procession of the Green Cross") and sometimes lasted the whole day. The *auto – da – fé* frequently was taken to the canvas by painters: one of the better-known examples is the painting by Francesco Rizzi held by the Prado Museum in Madrid that represents the *auto* celebrated in the Plaza Mayor of Madrid on 30 June 1680. The last public *auto – da – fé* took place in 1691.

The *auto – da – fé* involved a Catholic Mass, prayer, a public procession of those found guilty, and a reading of their sentences.[2128] They took place in public squares or esplanades and lasted several hours; ecclesiastical and civil authorities attended. Artistic representations of the *auto – da – fé* usually depict torture and the burning at the stake. However, this type of activity never took place during an *auto – da – fé*, which was in essence a religious act. Torture was not administered after a trial concluded, and executions were always held after and separate from the *auto-da-fé*,[2129] though in the minds and experiences of observers and those undergoing the confession and execution, the separation of the two might be experienced as merely a technicality.

The first recorded *auto – da – fé* was held in Paris in 1242, during the reign of Louis IX.[2130] The first Spanish *auto – da – fé* did not take place until 1481 in Seville; six of the men and women subjected to this first religious ritual were later executed. The Inquisition had limited power in Portugal, having been established in 1536 and officially lasting until 1821, although its influence was much weakened with the government of the Marquis of Pombal in the second half of the 18th century. *Autos-da-fé* also took place in Mexico, Brazil, and Peru: contemporary historians of the Conquistadors such as Bernal Díaz del Castillo record them. They also took place in

---

[2128] Peters 1988: 93–94
[2129] Kamen (1998), pp. 192–213
[2130] Stavans 2005: xxxiv.

the Portuguese colony of Goa, India, following the establishment of Inquisition there in 1562 – 1563.

The arrival of the Enlightenment in Spain slowed inquisitorial activity. In the first half of the 18th century, 111 were condemned to be burned in person, and 117 in effigy, most of them for judaizing. In the reign of Philip V, there were 125 *autos-da-fé*, while in the reigns of Charles III and Charles IV only 44.

During the 18th century, the Inquisition changed: Enlightenment ideas were the closest threat that had to be fought. The main figures of the Spanish Enlightenment were in favour of the abolition of the Inquisition, and many were processed by the Holy Office, among them Olavide, in 1776; Iriarte, in 1779; and Jovellanos, in 1796; Jovellanos sent a report to Charles IV in which he indicated the inefficiency of the Inquisition's courts and the ignorance of those who operated them: "friars who take the position, only to obtain gossip and exemption from the choir; who are ignorant of foreign languages, who only know a little scholastic theology".[2131]

In its new role, the Inquisition tried to accentuate its function of censoring publications but found that Charles III had secularized censorship procedures, and, on many occasions, the authorization of the Council of Castile hit the more intransigent position of the Inquisition. Since the Inquisition itself was an arm of the state, being within the Council of Castile, civil rather than ecclesiastical censorship usually prevailed. This loss of influence can also be explained because the foreign Enlightenment texts entered the peninsula through prominent members of the nobility or government,[2132] influential people with whom it was very difficult to interfere. Thus, for example, Diderot's Encyclopaedia entered Spain thanks to special licenses granted by the king.

After the French Revolution, however, the Council of Castile, fearing that revolutionary ideas would penetrate Spain's borders, decided to reactivate the Holy Office that was directly charged with the persecution of French works. An Inquisition edict of December 1789, that received the full approval of Charles IV and Florida Blanca, stated that: having news that several books have been scattered and promoted in these kingdoms that, without being contented with the simple narration events of a seditious nature seem to form a theoretical and practical code of independence from the legitimate powers, destroying in this way the political and social order the reading of thirty and nine French works is prohibited, under fine.

[2131] Cited in Elorza, *La Inquisición y el pensamiento ilustrado.*Historia 16. Especial 10° Aniversario *La Inquisición*; p. 81.
[2132] Members of the government and the Council of Castile, as well as other members close to the court, obtained special authorization for books purchased in France, the Low Countries or Germany to cross the border without inspection by members of the Holy Office. This practice grew beginning with the reign of Charles III.

However, inquisitorial activity was impossible in the face of the information avalanche that crossed the border; in 1792, "the multitude of seditious papers... does not allow formalizing the files against those who introduce them".

The fight from within against the Inquisition was almost always clandestine. The first texts that questioned the Inquisition and praised the ideas of Voltaire or Montesquieu appeared in 1759. After the suspension of pre-publication censorship on the part of the Council of Castile in 1785, the newspaper *El Censor* began the publication of protests against the activities of the Holy Office by means of a rationalist critique. Valentin de Foronda published *Espíritu de los Mejores Diarios*, a plea in favour of freedom of expression that was avidly read in the salons. Also, in the same vein, Manuel de Aguirre wrote On Toleration in *El Censor*, *El Correo de los Ciegos* and *El Diario de Madrid*.[2133]

During the reign of Charles IV of Spain (1788–1808), in spite of the fears that the French Revolution provoked, several events accelerated the decline of the Inquisition. The state stopped being a mere social organizer and began to worry about the well-being of the public. As a result, the land-holding power of the Church was reconsidered, in the *señoríos* and more generally in the accumulated wealth that had prevented social progress.[2134] The power of the throne increased, under which Enlightenment thinkers found better protection for their ideas. Manuel Godoy and Antonio Alcalá Galiano were openly hostile to an institution whose only role had been reduced to censorship and was the very embodiment of the Spanish Black Legend, internationally, and was not suitable to the political interests of the moment:

The Inquisition? Its old power no longer exists: the horrible authority that this bloodthirsty court had exerted in other times was reduced the Holy Office had come to be a species of commission for book censorship, nothing more.[2135]

The Inquisition was first abolished during the domination of Napoleon and the reign of Joseph Bonaparte (1808 – 1812). In 1813, the liberal deputies of the Cortes of Cádiz also obtained its abolition,[2136] largely as a result of the Holy Office's condemnation of the popular revolt against French invasion. But the Inquisition was

---

[2133] The argument presented in the periodicals and other works circulating in Spain were virtually exact copies of the reflections of Montesquieu or Rousseau, translated into Spanish.

[2134] Church properties, in general, and those of the Holy Office in particular, occupied large tracts of today's Castile and León, Extremadura and Andalucia. The properties were given under feudal terms to farmers or to localities who used them as community property with many restrictions, owing a part of the rent, generally in cash, to the church.

[2135] Elorza, *La Inquisición y el Pensamiento Ilustrado*. Historia 16. Especial 10° Aniversario *La Inquisición*; pg. 88

[2136] See Antonio Puigblanch, *La Inquisición sin máscara*, Cádiz, 1811–1813.

reconstituted when Ferdinand VII recovered the throne on 1 July 1814. Juan Antonio Llorente, who had been the Inquisition's general secretary in 1789, became a Bonapartist and published a critical history in 1817 from his French exile, based on his privileged access to its archives.[2137]

Possibly as a result of Llorente's criticisms, the Inquisition was once again temporarily abolished during the three-year Liberal interlude known as the Trienio liberal, but still the old system had not yet had its last gasp. Later, during the period known as the Ominous Decade, the Inquisition was not formally re-established,[2138] al though, *de facto*, it returned under the so-called Congregation of the Meetings of Faith, tolerated in the dioceses by King Ferdinand. On 26 July 1826, the "Meetings of Faith" Congregation condemned and executed the school teacher Cayetano Ripoll, who thus became the last person known to be executed by the Inquisition.[2139]

On that day, Ripoll was hanged in Valencia, for having taught deist principles. This execution occurred against the backdrop of a European-wide scandal concerning the despotic attitudes still prevailing in Spain. Finally, on 15 July 1834, the Spanish Inquisition was definitively abolished by a Royal Decree signed by regent Maria Christina of the Two Sicilies, Ferdinand VII's liberal widow, during the minority of Isabella II and with the approval of the President of the Cabinet Francisco Martínez de la Rosa. (It is possible that something similar to the Inquisition acted during the 1833 – 1839 First Carlist War, in the zones dominated by the Carlists, since one of the government measures praised by Conde de Molina Carlos Maria Isidro de Borbon was the re – implementation of the Inquisition to protect the Church). During the Carlist Wars, it was the conservatives who fought the liberals who wanted to reduce the Church's power, amongst other reforms to liberalize the economy. It can be added that Franco during the Spanish Civil War is alleged to have stated that he would attempt to reintroduce it, possibly as a sop to Vatican approval of his coup.

The Alhambra Decree that had expelled the Jews was formally rescinded on 16 December 1968.[2140]

Outcomes:

Confiscations:

[2137] Kamen (2014), p. 382
[2138] Historians have different interpretations. One argument is that during the Ominous Decade, the Inquisition was re-established- because of a statement made by Alphonso upon a visit to the Vatican that he would reintroduce it if the occasion arose, but the Royal Decree that would have abolished the order of the Trienio Liberal was never approved, or at least, never published. The formal abolition under the regency of Maria Cristina was thus nothing more than a ratification of the abolition of 1820.
[2139] Kamen (2014), pp. 372–373
[2140] 1492 Ban on Jews Is Voided by Spain– *The New York Times*, 17 December 1968

It is unknown exactly how much wealth was confiscated from converted Jews and others tried by the Inquisition. Wealth confiscated in one year of persecution in the small town of Guadeloupe paid the costs of building a royal residence.[2141] There are numerous records of the opinion of ordinary Spaniards of the time that "the Inquisition was devised simply to rob people". "They were burnt only for the money they had", a resident of Cuenca averred. "They burn only the well – off", said another. In 1504 an accused stated, "only the rich were burnt". In 1484 Catalina de Zamora was accused of asserting that "this Inquisition that the fathers are carrying out is as much for taking property from the conversos as for defending the faith. It is the goods that are the heretics." This saying passed into common usage in Spain. In 1524 a treasurer informed Charles V that his predecessor had received ten million ducats from the conversos, but the figure is unverified. In 1592 an inquisitor admitted that most of the fifty women he arrested were rich. In 1676, the Suprema claimed it had confiscated over 700,000 ducats for the royal treasury (which was paid money only after the Inquisition's own budget, amounting in one known case to only 5%). The property on Mallorca alone in 1678 was worth "well over 2,500,000 ducats".[2142]

Death tolls and sentenced:

García Cárcel estimates that the total number prosecuted by the Inquisition throughout its history was approximately 150,000; applying the percentages of executions that appeared in the trials of 1560 – 1700 – about 2% - the approximate total would be about 3,000 put to death. Nevertheless, some authors consider that the toll may have been higher, keeping in mind the data provided by Dedieu and García Cárcel for the tribunals of Toledo and Valencia, respectively, and estimate between 3,000 and 5,000 were executed.[2143] Other authors disagree and estimate a max death toll between 1% and 5%, (depending on the time span used) combining all the processes the inquisition carried, both religious and non-religious ones.[2144] [2145] In either case, this is significantly lower than the number of people executed exclusively for witchcraft in other parts of Europe during about the same time span as the Spanish Inquisition (estimated at c. 40,000 – 60,000).[2146]

[2141] Anderson, James Maxwell. Daily Life during the Spanish Inquisition. Greenwood Press, 2002. ISBN 0-313-31667-8.

[2142] Kamen (1998), p. 150

[2143] Data for executions for witchcraft: Levack, Brian P. (1995). The Witch Hunt in Early Modern Europe (Second Edition). London and New York: Longman, and see Witch trials in Early Modern Europe for more detail.

[2144] Bethencourt, Francisco. La Inquisición En La Época Moderna: España, Portugal E Italia, Siglos Xv-xix. Madrid: Akal, 1997.

[2145] Eire, Carlos M. N. Reformations: The Early Modern World 1450–1650. New Haven: Yale University Press, 2016 pp 640

[2146] Data for executions for witchcraft: Levack, Brian P. (1995). The Witch Hunt in Early Modern

Modern historians have begun to study the documentary records of the Inquisition. The archives of the Suprema, today held by the National Historical Archive of Spain (Archivo Histórico Nacional), conserves the annual relations of all processes between 1540 and 1700. This material provides information for approximately 44,674 judgments. These 44,674 cases include 826 executions *in persona* and 778 *in effigie* (i.e., an effigy was burned). This material, however, is far from being complete, for example, the tribunal of Cuenca is entirely omitted, because no *relaciones de causas* from this tribunal have been found, and significant gaps concern some other tribunals (e.g., Valladolid). Many more cases not reported to the Suprema are known from the other sources (i.e., no *relaciones de causas* from Cuenca have been found, but its original records have been preserved), but were not included in Contreras – Henningsen's statistics for the methodological reasons.[2147] William Monter estimates 1000 executions between 1530 and 1630 and 250 between 1630 and 1730.[2148]

The archives of the Suprema only provide information prior to 1560. To study the processes themselves, it is necessary to examine the archives of the local tribunals; however, the majority have been lost to the devastation of war, the ravages of time or other events. Some archives have survived including those of Toledo, where 12,000 were judged for offences related to heresy, mainly minor "blasphemy", and those of Valencia.[2149] These indicate that the Inquisition was most active in the period between 1480 and 1530 and that during this period the percentage condemned to death was much more significant than in the years that followed. Modern estimates show approximately 2,000 executions *in persona* in the whole of Spain up to 1530.[2150]

Abuse of power:

Author Toby Green notes that the great unchecked power given to inquisitors meant that they were "widely seen as above the law"[2151] and sometimes had motives for imprisoning and sometimes executing alleged offenders other than for the purpose of punishing religious nonconformity, mainly in Hispano – America and Ibero – America.[2152]

Europe (Second Edition). London and New York: Longman, and see Witch trials in Early Modern Europe for more detail.

[2147] For full account see: Gustav Henningsen, *The Database of the Spanish Inquisition. The relaciones de causas project revisited*, in: Heinz Mohnhaupt, Dieter Simon, *Vorträge zur Justizforschung*, Vittorio Klostermann, 1992, pp. 43–85.

[2148] W. Monter, *Frontiers of Heresy: The Spanish Inquisition from the Basque Lands to Sicily*, Cambridge 2003, p. 53.

[2149] Jean-Pierre Dedieu, *Los Cuatro Tiempos*, in Bartolomé Benassar, *Inquisición Española: poder político y control social*, pp. 15–39.

[2150] Kamen (2005), p. 15

[2151] Green, Toby (2007). *Inquisition: The Reign of Fear*. New York: Thomas Dunne Books. pp. 4–5. ISBN 978-0-312-53724-1.

Green quotes a complaint by historian Manuel Barrios[2153] about one Inquisitor, Diego Rodriguez Lucero, who in Cordoba in 1506 burned to death the husbands of two different women he then kept as mistresses. According to Barrios,

the daughter of Diego Celemin was exceptionally beautiful, her parents and her husband did not want to give her to [Lucero], and so Lucero had the three of them burnt and now has a child by her, and he has kept for a long time in the alcazar as a mistress.[2154]

Data for executions for witchcraft: Levack, Brian P. (1995). *The Witch Hunt in Early Modern Europe* (Second Edition). London and New York: Longman and see "Witch trials in Early Modern Europe" for more detail.

Defenders of the Inquisition discrediting with Green are many and seem to be the growing trend in current scholarship.[2155] These authors don't necessarily deny the abuses of power but classify them as politically instigated and comparable to those of any other law enforcement body of the period. Criticisms, usually indirect, have gone from the suspiciously sexual overtones or similarities of these accounts with unrelated older antisemitic accounts of kidnap and torture,[2156] to the clear proofs of control that the king had over the institution, to the sources used by Green,[2157] or just by reaching completely different conclusions.[2158]

However, the context of Hispano America, that Green refers to often, was different from the Iberian context studied for many of those authors, due to the distance from the immediate executive power of the King and deserves to be examined separately. Among those who do, there are also discrediting voices regarding the nature and extent of the Inquisition's abuses.[2159]

[2152] Green, Toby (2007). *Inquisition: the Reign of Fear*. New York: Thomas Dunne Books. pp. 4–5. ISBN 978-0-312-53724-1.

[2153] Green, Toby (2007). *Inquisition: The Reign of Fear*. New York: Thomas Dunne Books. p. 65. ISBN 978-0-312-53724-1.

[2154] Barrios, Manuel (1991). *El Tribunal de la Inquisicion en Andalucia: Seleccion de Textos y Documentos*. Seville: J. Rodriguez Castillejo S.A. p. 58.

[2155] Elvira, Roca Barea María, and Arcadi Espada. Imperiofobia Y Leyenda Negra: Roma, Rusia, Estados Unidos Y El Imperio Español. Madrid: Siruela, 2017

[2156] Elvira, Roca Barea María, and Arcadi Espada. Imperiofobia Y Leyenda Negra: Roma, Rusia, Estados Unidos Y El Imperio Español. Madrid: Siruela, 2017

[2157] Contreras, Jaime y Gustav Henningsen (1986). "Forty-four thousand cases of the Spanish Inquisition (1540–1700): analysis of a historical data bank", en Henningsen G., J. A. Tedeschi et al. (comps.), The Inquisition in early modern Europe: studies on sources and methods. Dekalb: Northern Illinois University Press.

[2158] Pérez, Joseph (2006). The Spanish Inquisition: a history. New Haven, CT: Yale University Press; p. 173

[2159] *Las luchas por la memoria en América Latina. Historia reciente y memoria política.* Coordinadores Eugenia Allier Montaño y Emilio Crenzel. México: Bonilla Artigas. Editores: UNAM, Instituto de Investigaciones Sociales, 2015. 428 p.

Historiography:

How historians and commentators have viewed the Spanish Inquisition has changed over time and continues to be a source of controversy. Before and during the 19th – century historical interest focused on who was being persecuted. In the early and mid – 20th century, historians examined the specifics of what happened and how it influenced Spanish history. In the later 20th and 21st century, historians have re-examined how severe the Inquisition really was, calling into question some of the assumptions made in earlier periods.

19th to early 20th century scholarship:

Before the rise of professional historians in the 19th century, the Spanish Inquisition had largely been portrayed by Protestant scholars who saw it as the archetypal symbol of Catholic intolerance and ecclesiastical power.[2160] The Spanish Inquisition for them was largely associated with the persecution of Protestants, or inexplicably, of witches.[2161] William H. Prescott described the Inquisition as an "eye that never slumbered". Despite the existence of extensive documentation regarding the trials and procedures, and to the Inquisition's deep bureaucratization, none of these sources were studied outside of Spain, and Spanish scholars arguing against the predominant view were automatically dismissed. The 19th century professional historians, including the Spanish scholar Amador de los Ríos, were the first to successfully challenge this perception in the international sphere and get foreign scholars to make eco of their discoveries. Said scholars would obtain international recognition and start a period of revision on the Black Legend of the Spanish Inquisition.[2162]

At the start of the 20th century Henry Charles Lea published the ground - breaking *History of the Inquisition in Spain*. This influential work describes the Spanish Inquisition as "an engine of immense power, constantly applied for the furtherance of obscurantism, the repression of thought, the exclusion of foreign ideas and t Contreras, Jaime y Gustav Henningsen (1986). "Forty – four thousand cases of the Spanish Inquisition (1540 – 1700): analysis of a historical data bank", en Henningsen G., J. A. Tedeschi et al. The Inquisition in early modern Europe: studies on sources and methods. Dekalb: Northern Illinois University Press.

He obstruction of progress."[2163] Lea documented the Inquisition's methods and modes of operation in no uncertain terms, calling it "theocratic absolutism" at its worst.[2164] In the context of the polarization between Protestants and Catholics during

[2160] "A Kinder, Gentler Inquisition", by Richard Kagan in *The New York Times*, 19 April 1998.
[2161] "A Kinder, Gentler Inquisition", by Richard Kagan in *The New York Times*, 19 April 1998.
[2162] "A Kinder, Gentler Inquisition", by Richard Kagan in *The New York Times*, 19 April 1998.
[2163] "A Kinder, Gentler Inquisition", by Richard Kagan in *The New York Times*, 19 April 1998.
[2164] "A Kinder, Gentler Inquisition", by Richard Kagan in *The New York Times*, 19 April 1998.

the second half of the 19th century,[2165] some of Lea's contemporaries, as well as most modern scholars thought Lea's work had an anti-Catholic bias.[2166]

Starting in the 1920s, Jewish scholars picked up where Lea's work left off.[2167] They published Yitzhak Baer's *History of the Jews in Christian Spain*, Cecil Roth's *History of the Marranos* and, after World War II, the work of Haim Beinart, who for the first time published trial transcripts of cases involving conversos.

Contemporary historians who subscribe to the idea that the image of the Inquisition in historiography has been systematically deformed by the Black Legend include Edward Peters, Philip Wayne Powell, William S. Maltby, Richard Kagan, Margaret R. Greer, Helen Rawlings, Ronnie Hsia, Lu Ann Homza, Stanley G. Payne, Andrea Donofrio, Irene Silverblatt, Christopher Schmidt – Nowara, Charles Gibson, and Joseph Pérez. Contemporary historians who support the traditional view and deny the existence of a Black Legend include Toby Green. Contemporary historians who partially accept an impact of the Black Legend but deny other aspects of the hypothesis it includes Henry Kamen, David Nirenberg and Karen Armstrong.

Revision after 1960:
Historical revision of the Inquisition:

The works of Juderias in (1913) and other Spanish scholars prior to him were mostly ignored by international scholarship until 1960.

One of the first books to build on them and internationally challenge the classical view was *The Spanish Inquisition* (1965) by Henry Kamen. Kamen argued that the Inquisition was not nearly as cruel or as powerful as commonly believed. The book was very influential and largely responsible for subsequent studies in the 1970s to try to quantify (from archival records) the Inquisition's activities from 1480 to 1834.[2168] Those studies showed there was an initial burst of activity against conversos suspected of relapsing into Judaism, and a mid – 16th century pursuit of Protestants, but the Inquisition served principally as a forum Spaniards occasionally used to humiliate and punish people they did not like: blasphemers, bigamists, foreigners and, in Aragon, homosexuals, and horse smugglers.[2169] Kamen went on to publish two more books in 1985 and 2006 that incorporated new findings, further supporting

---

[2165] "Henry Charles Lea Papers – Biographical Sketch". *Univ. of Penn.-Penn Special Collections.* 11 January 2003. Retrieved 18 April 2007.

[2166] "Henry Charles Lea Papers – Biographical Sketch". *Univ. of Penn.-Penn Special Collections.* 11 January 2003. Retrieved 18 April 2007.

[2167] "A Kinder, Gentler inquisition", by Richard Kagan in *The New York Times*, 19 April 1998.

[2168] See for example Jean-Pierre Dedieu, Los Cuatro Tiempos, in Bartolomé Benassar, Inquiición Española: poder político y control social, pp. 15–39 and García Cárcel (1976)

[2169] A Kinder, Gentler Inquisition", by Richard Kagan in *The New York Times*, 19 April 1998.

the view that the Inquisition was not as bad as once described by Lea and others. Along similar lines is Edward Peters' *Inquisition* (1988).

One of the most important works about the inquisition's relation to the Jewish conversos or New Christians is *The Origins of the Inquisition in Fifteenth-Century Spain* (1995/2002) by Benzion Netanyahu. It challenges the view that most conversos were actually practicing Judaism in secret and were persecuted for their crypto-Judaism. Rather, according to Netanyahu, the persecution was fundamentally racial, and was a matter of envy of their success in Spanish society.[2170] This view has been challenged multiple times, and with some reasonable divergences the majority of historians either align with religious causes or with merely cultural ones, with no significant racial element.[2171]

Challenging some of the claims of revisionist historians is Toby Green in *Inquisition, the Reign of Fear*, who calls the claim by revisionists that torture was only rarely applied by inquisitors, a "worrying error of fact".[2172]

Historian Thomas F. Madden has written about popular myths of the Inquisition.[2173]

Literature:

The literature of the 18th century approaches the theme of the Inquisition from a critical point of view. In *Candide* by Voltaire, the Inquisition appears as the epitome of intolerance and arbitrary justice in Europe.

During the Romantic Period, the Gothic novel, which was primarily a genre developed in Protestant countries, frequently associated Catholicism with terror and repression. This vision of the Spanish Inquisition appears in, among other works, *The Monk* (1796) by Matthew Gregory Lewis (set in Madrid during the Inquisition, but can be seen as commenting on the French Revolution and the Terror); *Melmoth the Wanderer* (1820) by Charles Robert Maturin and *The Manuscript Found in Saragossa* by Polish author Jan Potocki.

The literature of the 19th century tends to focus on the element of torture employed by the Inquisition. In France, in the early 19th century, the epistolary novel *Cornelia Bororquia, or the Victim of the Inquisition*, which has been attributed to Spaniard ~~Luiz Gutiérrez, and is based~~ on the case of María de Bohórquez, ferociously

---

[2170] "Benzion Netanyahu's History". *Tablet Magazine*. 30 April 2012.

[2171] Vicente Ángel Álvarez Palenzuela. *Judíos y conversos en la España medieval. Estado de la cuestión* (Jews and converts in medieval Spain. Estate of the matter). Universidad Autónoma de Madrid) eHumanista/Converso 4 (2015):156–191

[2172] Green, Toby (2007). *Inquisition: The Reign of Fear*. New York: Thomas Dunne Books. p. 10. ISBN 978-0-312-53724-1.

[2173] *The Real Inquisition: investigating the popular myth* by Thomas F. Madden (National Review, 18 June 2004)

criticizes the Inquisition and its representatives. The Inquisition also appears in one of the chapters of the novel *The Brothers Karamazov* (1880) by Fyodor Dostoevsky, which imagines an encounter between Jesus and the Inquisitor General. One of the best-known stories of Edgar Allan Poe, "The Pit and the Pendulum", explores the use of torture by the Inquisition.

The Inquisition also appears in 20th century literature. *La Gesta del Marrano*, by the

Argentine author Marcos Aguinis, portrays the length of the Inquisition's arm to reach people in Argentina during the 16th and 17th centuries. The first book in Les Daniels' "Don Sebastian Vampire Chronicles", *The Black Castle* (1978), is set in 15th-century Spain and includes both descriptions of Inquisitorial questioning and an auto-da-fé, as well as Tomás de Torquemada, who is featured in one chapter. The Marvel Comics series *Marvel 1602* shows the Inquisition targeting Mutants for "blasphemy". The character Magneto also appears as the Grand Inquisitor. The Captain Alatriste novels by the Spanish writer Arturo Pérez-Reverte are set in the early 17th century. The second novel, *Purity of Blood*, has the narrator being tortured by the Inquisition and describes an auto – da – fé. Carme Riera's novella, published in 1994, *Dins el Darrer Blau* (*In the Last Blue*) is set during the repression of the *chuetas* (*conversos* from Majorca) at the end of the 17th century. In 1998, the Spanish writer Miguel Delibes published the historical novel *The Heretic*, about the Protestants of Valladolid and their repression by the Inquisition. Samuel Shellabarger's *Captain from Castile* deals directly with the Spanish Inquisition during the first part of the novel.

In the novel La Catedral del Mar by Ildefonso Falcones, published in 2006 and set in the 14th century, there are scenes of inquisition investigations in small towns and a great scene in Barcelona.

Film:

- The 1947 epic *Captain from Castile* by Darryl F. Zanuck, starring Tyrone Power, uses the Inquisition as the major plot point of the film. It tells how powerful families used their evils to ruin their rivals. The first part of the film shows this, and the reach of the Inquisition reoccurs throughout this movie following Pedro De Vargas (played by Power) even to the 'New World'.
- The Spanish Inquisition segment of the 1981 Mel Brooks movie *The History of the World Part 1* is a comedic musical performance based on the activities of the first Inquisitor General of Spain, Tomás de Torquemada.

- The film *The Fountain* (2006), by Darren Aronofsky, features the Spanish Inquisition as part of a plot in 1500 when the Grand Inquisitor threatens Queen Isabella's life.
- *Goya's Ghosts* (2006) by Miloš Forman is set in Spain between 1792 and 1809 and focuses realistically on the role of the Inquisition and its end under Napoleon's rule.
- The film *Assassin's Creed* (2016) by Justin Kurzel, starring Michael Fassbender, is set in both modern times and Spain during the Inquisition. The film follows Callum Lynch (played by Fassbender) as he is forced to relive the memories of his ancestor, Aguilar de Nerha (also played by Fassbender), an Assassin during the Spanish Inquisition.
- *The Pit and the Pendulum* (Roger Corman, 1961).
- *Akelarre* (Pedro Olea, 1984), a film, about the Logroño trial of the Zugarramurdi witches.
- Tomás de Torquemada is portrayed in *1492: The Conquest of Paradise* (1992)

Theatre, music, television, and video games:

- The Grand Inquisitor of Spain plays a part in *Don Carlos* (1867), a play by Friedrich Schiller (which was the basis for the opera *Don Carlos* in five acts by Giuseppe Verdi, in which the Inquisitor is also featured, and the third act is dedicated to an *auto – da – fé*).
- In the *Monty Python* comedy team's Spanish Inquisition sketches, an inept Inquisitor group repeatedly bursts into scenes after someone utters the words "I didn't expect to find a Spanish Inquisition", screaming "Nobody expects the Spanish Inquisition!" The Inquisition then uses ineffectual forms of torture, including a dish-drying rack, soft cushions and a comfy chair.
- The Spanish Inquisition features as a main plotline element of the 2009 video game *Assassin's Creed II: Discovery*.
- The Universe of *Warhammer 40,000* borrows several elements and concepts of the Catholic church Imaginarium, including the notion of the Black Legend's ideal of a fanatic Inquisitors, for some of its troops in *Warhammer 40,000: Inquisitor – Martyr*.
- The 1965 musical Man of La Mancha depicts a fictionalized account of the author Miguel de Cervantes' run-in with Spanish authorities. The character of Cervantes produces a play-within-a-play of his unfinished manuscript, Don Quixote, while he awaits sentencing by the Inquisition.

- The video game *Blasphemous* portrays a nightmarish version of the Spanish Inquisition, where the protagonist, named 'The Penitent one' wears a Sanbenito (cone-shaped) hat. The Penitent one battles twisted religious iconography and meets many characters attempting to atone for their sins along the way.

Contemporary politics:

The Spanish Inquisition is a recurring trope that makes an occasional appearance in the British parliament, like calling something "Nazi" to reject ideas seen as religiously authoritarian.

Chapter forty-six

Welsh Race Riots 1919

The 1919 South Wales race riots took place in the docks area of Newport and Barry, South Wales, as well as the Butetown district of Cardiff over a number of days in June 1919. Four men were killed during the disturbances. Similar riots took place in Glasgow, Liverpool and other parts of England.

The port towns of South Wales had attracted settlers from all over the world during the heyday of the docks in the latter decades of the 19th century. By 1911 the proportion of Cardiff's population that was black or Asian was second in the UK to London though, at around 700, the number was quite small and confined to the dock areas.[1] Wages in the docks could be undercut by employing foreign men at a lower rate. The Cardiff Seaman's Strike in June 1911 had become focused on Chinese sailors, with violence breaking out one afternoon resulting in all of Cardiff's Chinese laundries being smashed up.[2174]

The numbers of non-white settlers was augmented when soldiers and sailors were discharged from service in World War I, increasing the numbers of African, Arab and Asian residents even further. [2175] Trade on the docks picked up slowly, but not quickly enough to absorb everyone who had been demobbed from the war. Preference in employment was given to white men, though there were still many without work. There was also a housing shortage, compounded by resentment against non-whites who had bought houses and filled them with lodgers. There was also an antipathy towards non-whites who had married local white women (non-whites were almost entirely men at the time).[2176]

Tensions erupted into riots in Glasgow, Scotland in January 1919, followed by port towns and cities in England, such as London, South Shields, Hull, and Liverpool in the first half of the year.[2177]

[2174] *Evans, Neil (Spring 1980). "The South Wales Race Riots of 1919". Llafur. Society for the Study of Welsh Labour History. 3 (1): 5–7. via The National Library of Wales.*

[2175] Sutton, Shaheen (3 June 2020). "Remembering the Newport Race Riots of 1919". *Wales Arts Review.*

[2176] Evans, Neil. "The South Wales Race Riots of 1919". pp. 10–12. – via The National Library of Wales.

[2177] Sutton, Shaheen (3 June 2020). "Remembering the Newport Race Riots of 1919". *Wales Arts Review.*

Rioting initially broke out in Newport on 6 June 1919. A black man was attacked by a white soldier, because of an alleged remark made to a white woman. This rapidly escalated, with a mob of white men attacking anyone perceived to be non-white, or anything believed to be owned by non-whites. Houses and a restaurant owned by black people, Chinese laundries and a Greek-owned lodging house were attacked in Pillgwenlly and the town centre.[2178] Eight houses in the docks area were wrecked, with furniture from two of them being burnt in the street.[2179]

Clashes took place on 11 June 1919 between white soldiers returning from the Great War and local Butetown (Tiger Bay) men of mainly Yemeni, Somali and Afro-Caribbean backgrounds. [2180] Riots continued for three days, spreading out into Grangetown[2181] and parts of the city centre. Ethnic minority families armed themselves and hid in their houses, some of which were attacked and looted. The main road in Butetown, Bute Street, ended up covered with broken glass and the windows boarded up.[2182] By Saturday 14 June, things has quietened down, despite huge crowds being on the streets the day before, and the occupants of a Malay-owned shop having to escape attack by climbing on to their roof.[2183]

Threatening crowds gathered in Barry on the evening of 11 June 1919, following a fatal stabbing in Beverley Street, Cadoxton. Dock labourer, Frederick Longman, had been stabbed by Charles Emmanuel, who originated from the French West Indies.[2184] (it later transpired that Emanuel had been told by Longman to "go down your own street" and had been attacked with a poker before drawing his knife).[2185] A black shipwright who lived in the same street tried to escape when the mob broke into his lodging hou"e. The crowd caught up with him and pelted him with stones.[2186] The crowds didn't disperse until after midnight, but little damage was reported.[2187] On 12

[2178] Sutton, Shaheen (3 June 2020). "Remembering the Newport Race Riots of 1919". *Wales Arts Review*.

[2179] *"Black and White - Serious racial riot at Newport". South Wales Weekly Post. 14 June 1919. p. 2. – via Welsh Newspapers Online.*

[2180] Mohammed, Aamir (16 June 2019). "The notorious Race Riots of 1919 in Cardiff that shamed Wales". *Wales Online*.

[2181] "One thousand people came rioting down the street': Reliving a notorious chapter in Cardiff's past". *ITV News*. 3 November 2018.

[2182] Mohammed, Aamir (16 June 2019). "The notorious Race Riots of 1919 in Cardiff that shamed Wales". *Wales Online*.

[2183] "Race riots - Smart handling of dangerous affray - Cardiff looking quieter". *The Cambrian Daily Leader*. 14 June 1919. p. 1. – via Welsh Newspapers Online.

[2184] "Done to death at Cadoxton-Barry - Discharged soldier killed by negro seaman - Great excitement in the streets". *The Cambrian Daily Leader*. 13 June 1919. p. 5. – via Welsh Newspapers Online.

[2185] Evans, Neil. "The South Wales Race Riots of 1919". pp. 14–15. – via The National Library of Wales.

[2186] "Marking 100 years since Barry's race riots". *The Barry Gem*. 30 August 2019.

[2187] "Done to death at Cadoxton-Barry - Discharged soldier killed by negro seaman - Great excitement in the streets". *The Cambrian Daily Leader*. 13 June 1919. p. 5. – via Welsh Newspapers Online.

June the Fish & Chip shop owned by Mr Gillespie, a black man who'd lived in Barry for 20 years and married a local white woman, was smashed up by a mob.[2188]

Police were reported to have formed barricades on Thompson Street to prevent the attacking mobs reach Barry Docks. On 13 June, 300 soldiers arrived at Cadoxton and set up camp at Buttrills Fields.[2189]

Former soldier, Frederick Henry Longman, died after being stabbed in Barry. Three men died during the events in Cardiff: Mohammed Abdullah, a ship's fireman aged 21, died in hospital from a fractured skull, after being attacked in Butetown; John Donovan, aged 33, died after being shot at a city centre house in Millicent Street; Harold Smart aged 20 died after his throat was slit, though it was unclear whether this was directly related to the riots.[2190]

As well as the deaths of four men, hundreds of people were injured [2191] and dozens were arrested. The damage in Cardiff cost the city council £3000 to repair (equivalent to £138,881 in 2019).[2192]

Most people arrested were from the ethnic minority population. In Newport of the 30 people arrested, 27 were black.[2193] A total of 18 white people and ten non – white men appeared in court in Cardiff, with the non-white victims being initially dealt with far more harshly than their white counterparts.[2194] Nine black men from Cardiff were charged with murder and brought to trial in Swansea but, with the prosecution offering no evidence and reducing the charge to 'shooting with intent to murder', the jury did not even need to retire and discuss the case before finding all the men not guilty.[2195] Charles Emmanuel, who had killed a man in Barry, was sent to prison for five years for manslaughter, having been found not guilty of wilful murder.[2196]

[2188] "Terfysg yn Y Bae? Terfysg yn Y Barri! The history of the 1919 Race Riots goes beyond Cardiff". *Nation Cymru*. 18 May 2021.
[2189] "Terfysg yn Y Bae? Terfysg yn Y Barri! The history of the 1919 Race Riots goes beyond Cardiff". *Nation Cymru*. 18 May 2021.
[2190] Mohammed, Aamir (16 June 2019). "The notorious Race Riots of 1919 in Cardiff that shamed Wales". *Wales Online*.
[2191] Mohammed, Aamir (16 June 2019). "The notorious Race Riots of 1919 in Cardiff that shamed Wales". *Wales Online*.
[2192] Evans, Neil (Spring 1980). "The South Wales Race Riots of 1919". *Llafur*. Society for the Study of Welsh Labour History. **3** (1): 5–7. – via The National Library of Wales.
[2193] Sutton, Shaheen (3 June 2020). "Remembering the Newport Race Riots of 1919". *Wales Arts Review*.
[2194] Evans, Neil. "The South Wales Race Riots of 1919". pp. 18–19. – via The National Library of Wales.
[2195] "Racial riots - Coloured Men Discharged". *The Cambrian Daily Leader*. 16 July 1919. p. 1. – via Welsh Newspapers Online.
[2196] *Evans, Neil. "The South Wales Race Riots of 1919". pp. 14–15. – via The National Library of Wales.*

Though the riots were clearly remembered by the ethnic minority populations in South Wales, they were largely forgotten elsewhere. So much so, that when the Select Committee on Race and Immigration visited Cardiff in 1972, the police reported they had "no record of any serious disturbance involving the indigenous and immigrant population".[2197] Historians did not begin to record the history until the 1980s. There are still memorials or plaques in Cardiff, Newport or Barry remembering the riots.[2198]

At this time, there were other riots in Britain, but the Welsh Riots seems to be the least remembered, there were also riots in Glasgow and Liverpool.

[2197] Evans, Neil (Spring 1980). "The South Wales Race Riots of 1919". *Llafur*. Society for the Study of Welsh Labour History. **3** (1): 5–7. – via The National Library of Wales.
[2198] Sutton, Shaheen (3 June 2020). "Remembering the Newport Race Riots of 1919". *Wales Arts Review*.

Chapter forty-seven

The Notting Hill Riots 1958

Following the end of the Second World War, Afro-Caribbean immigration to Britain increased. By the 1950s, white working-class "Teddy Boys" were beginning to display hostility towards black families in the area, a situation exploited and inflamed by groups such as Oswald Mosley's Union Movement and other far-right groups such as the White Defence League, who urged disaffected white residents to keep Britain white.[2199]

There was an increase in violent attacks on black people throughout the summer. On 24 August 1958 a group of ten English youths committed serious assaults on six West Indian men in four separate incidents. At 5.40 a.m., the youths' car was spotted by two police officers who pursued them into the White City estate, where the gang abandoned their car. Using the car as a lead, investigating detectives arrested nine of the gang the next day, after working non-stop for twenty hours.[2200]

Just prior to the Notting Hill riots, there was racial unrest in the St Ann's neighbourhood in Nottingham which began on 23 August, and continued intermittently for two weeks.[2201]

The riot is often believed to have been triggered by an assault against Majbritt Morrison, a white Swedish woman,[2202] on 29 August 1958. Morrison had been arguing with her Jamaican husband Raymond Morrison at the Latimer Road Underground station. A group of various white people attempted to intervene in the argument, and a small fight broke out between the intervening people and some of Raymond Morrison's friends.[2203] The following day Majbritt Morrison was verbally and physically assaulted by a gang of white youths that had recalled seeing her the night before.[2204] According to one report, the youths threw milk bottles at Morrison

---

[2199] "Notting Hill Riots 1958". *The Exploring 20th century London Project*.
[2200] *Fido, Martin; Skinner, Keith (1999). The Official Encyclopaedia of Scotland Yard. London: Virgin Books. ISBN 0-7535-0515-0.*
[2201] Pressly, Linda (21 May 2007). "The 'forgotten' race riot". *BBC News*.
[2202] Travis, Alan (24 August 2002). "After 44 years secret papers reveal truth about five nights of violence in Notting Hill". *The Guardian*. London.
[2203] Olden, Mark (29 August 2008). "White riot: The week Notting Hill exploded". *The Independent*. London.
[2204] Dawson, Ashley (2007). *Mongrel Nation*. University of Michigan Press. pp. 27–29. ISBN 978-0-

and called her racial slurs such as "Black man's trollop",[2205] while a later report stated that she had also been struck in the back with an iron bar.[2206]

Later that night a mob of 300 to 400 white people were seen on Bramley Road attacking the houses of West Indian residents. The disturbances, rioting and attacks continued every night until 5 September.

The Metropolitan Police arrested more than 140 people during the two weeks of the disturbances, mostly white youths but also many black people found carrying weapons. A report to the Metropolitan Police Commissioner stated that of the 108 people charged with crimes such as grievous bodily harm, affray and riot and possessing offensive weapons, 72 were white and 36 were black.[2207]

The sentencing of the nine white youths by Mr Justice Salmon has been passed into judicial lore as an example of "exemplary sentencing" – a harsh punishment intended to act as a deterrent to others. Each of the youths received five years in prison and was ordered to pay £500.[2208]

A "Caribbean Carnival", precursor of the Notting Hill Carnival, was held on 30 January 1959 in St Pancras Town Hall. Activist Claudia Jones organized this carnival in response to the riots and to the state of race relations in Britain at the time.

The riots caused tension between the Metropolitan Police and the British African-Caribbean community which claimed that the police had not taken their reports of racial attacks seriously. In 2002, files were released that revealed that senior police officers at the time had assured the Home Secretary, Rab Butler, that there was little or no racial motivation behind the disturbance, despite testimony from individual police officers to the contrary.[2209]

The Windrush Scandal:

472-06991-0.
[2205] Dawson, Ashley (2007). *Mongrel Nation*. University of Michigan Press. pp. 27–29. ISBN 978-0-472-06991-0.
[2206] *Younge, Gary (17 August 2002). "The politics of partying". The Guardian. London.*
[2207] Travis, Alan (24 August 2002). "After 44 years secret papers reveal truth about five nights of violence in Notting Hill". *The Guardian*. London.
[2208] Ashworth, Andrew (2000). *Sentencing and Criminal Justice*. Cambridge University Press. p. 77. ISBN 0-521-67405-0.

[2209] Travis, Alan (24 August 2002). "After 44 years secret papers reveal truth about five nights of violence in Notting Hill". *The Guardian*. London.

The Windrush Scandal was a 2018 British political scandal concerning people who were wrongly detained, denied legal rights, threatened with deportation and in at least 83 cases[2210] [2211] wrongly deported from the UK by the Home Office. Many of those affected had been born British subjects and had arrived in the UK before 1973, particularly from Caribbean countries as members of the "Windrush generation"[2212] (so named after the *Empire Windrush*, the ship that brought one of the first groups of West Indian migrants to the UK in 1948).[2213]

As well as those who were deported, an unknown number were detained, lost their jobs or homes, had their passports confiscated or were denied benefits or medical care to which they were entitled.[2214] Several long – term UK residents were refused re – entry to the UK; a larger number were threatened with immediate deportation by the Home Office. Linked by commentators to the "hostile environment policy" instituted by Theresa May during her time as Home Secretary,[2215] [2216] [2217] the scandal led to the resignation of Amber Rudd as Home Secretary in April 2018 and the appointment of Sajid Javid as her successor.[2218] The scandal also prompted a wider debate about British immigration policy and Home Office practice.

The March 2020 independent *Windrush Lessons Learned Review* [2219] [2220] conducted by the inspector of constabulary concluded that May's Home Office showed "ignorance and thoughtlessness" and that what had happened had been "foreseeable and avoidable". It further found that immigration regulations were tightened "with

[2210] Rawlinson, Kevin (12 November 2018). "Windrush: 11 people wrongly deported from UK have died – Javid". *The Guardian*. Retrieved 25 March 2019. Javid … said there were 83 cases in which it had been confirmed people were wrongfully removed from the country and officials fear there may be a further 81
[2365] McCann, Kate (15 May 2018). "Home Secretary admits 63 Windrush migrants may have been deported and brands hostile environment 'un-British'". *The Telegraph*.
[2366] Agerholm, Harriet (3 July 2018). "Windrush generation: Home Office 'set them up to fail', say MPs". *The Independent*.
[2212] Stenhouse, Ann (30 April 2018). "What is the Windrush scandal – and how the Windrush generation got their name". *Daily Mirror*.
[2213] Rodgers, Lucy; Ahmed, Maryam (27 April 2018). "Windrush: Who exactly was on board?". BBC News.
[2214] Agerholm, Harriet (3 July 2018). "Windrush generation: Home Office 'set them up to fail', say MPs". *The Independent*.
[2215] "'It's inhumane': the Windrush victims who have lost jobs, homes and loved ones". *The Guardian*. 20 April 2018. ISSN 0261-3077.
[2216] "The human impact of Theresa May's hostile environment policies". *The Independent*. 21 April 2018.
[2217] Bush, Stephen (25 April 2018). "Why Amber Rudd Won't Suggest Real Solutions to the Worsening Windrush Scandal". *New Statesman*.
[2218] Wright, Oliver (30 April 2018). "Windrush scandal: Sajid Javid named home secretary after Amber Rudd resigns". *The Times*. ISSN 0140-0460.
[2219] Home Office; Patel, Priti. "Home Secretary's oral statement on the Windrush Lessons Learned Review by Wendy Williams".
[2220] Williams, Wendy (2020). *Windrush Lessons Learned Review* (PDF).

complete disregard for the Windrush generation" and that officials had made "irrational" demands for multiple documents to establish residency rights.[2221]

[2221] Gentleman, Amelia; Owen Bowcott (19 March 2020). "Windrush report condemns Home Office 'ignorance and thoughtlessness'". The Guardian.

Chapter forty-eight

The Brixton Riots 1981

The 1981 Brixton riot, or Brixton uprising,[2222] was a confrontation between the Metropolitan Police and protesters in Brixton, South London, England, between 10 and 12 April 1981. The main riot on 11 April, dubbed "Bloody Saturday" by *Time* magazine,[2223] resulted in 279 injuries to police and 45 injuries to members of the public;[2224] over a hundred vehicles were burned, including 56 police vehicles; almost 150 buildings were damaged, with thirty burned. There were 82 arrests. Reports suggested that up to 5,000 people were involved.[2225]

Brixton in South London was an area with serious social and economic problems.[2226] The whole United Kingdom was affected by a recession by 1981, but the local African-Caribbean community was suffering particularly high unemployment, poor housing, and a higher-than-average crime rate.[2227]

In the preceding months there had been growing unease between the police and the inhabitants of Lambeth, the Borough of London in which Brixton is located.[2228] On 18 January 1981 a number of black youths died in a fire during a house party in New Cross, in the nearby Borough of Lewisham. Although authorities stated that the fire started inside and was accidental, the public believed it was an arson attack and criticised the police investigation as inadequate. Black activists, including Darcus Howe, organised a march for the "Black People's Day of Action" on 2 March.[2229] Ac counts of turnout vary from 5,000[2230] to 20,000[2231] to 25,000.[2232]

[2222] Grover, Chris (13 September 2013). *Crime and Inequality*. Routledge. ISBN 9781134732999.

[2223] J. A. Cloake & M. R. Tudor. *Multicultural Britain*. Oxford University Press, 2001. pp.60-64

[2224] *"Britain: Bloody Saturday"*. Time. 20 April 1981.

[2225] "Battle 4 Brixton pt6 of 6". 22 April 2008. Retrieved 29 May 2009 – via YouTube.

[2226] "How smouldering tension erupted to set Brixton aflame". *The Guardian*. London. 13 April 1981.

[2227] Brain 2010, p. 65.

[2228] Kettle & Hodges 1982, pp. 100–101.

[2229] Weinreb, Ben; Weinreb, Matthew; Hibbert, Christopher; Keay, Julia; Keay, John (2008). *The London Encyclopaedia*. Pan Macmillan. p. 99. ISBN 978-1-405-04924-5.

[2230] Cornish, Winsome-Grace. "Honouring talent: The Black People's Day of Action". *Operation Black Vote: News,18 Feb 2011*.

[2231] Anim-Addo, Joan (1995). *Longest Journey: A History of Black Lewisham*. London: Deptford Forum Publishing Ltd. p. 137. ISBN 978-1-898536-21-5.

[2232] Szymanski, Jesse (19 August 2011). "Darcus Howe, the British Black Panther". *Vice Beta, Stuff, August 2011*. Vice Media, Inc.

The marchers walked 17 miles from Deptford to Hyde Park, passing the Houses of Parliament and Fleet Street.[2233] While the majority of the march finished in Hyde Park without incident, there was some confrontation with police at Blackfriars. According to Professor Les Back, "while the local press reported the march respectfully, the national papers unloaded the full weight of racial stereotyping."[2234] [2235] *The Evening Standard*'s front – page headline had displayed a photo of a policeman with a bloody face juxtaposed with Darcus Howe's quote about the march being "A good day". A few weeks later, the police arrested some of the march organizers and charged them with the offence of riot, but were later acquitted.[2236]

In 1980, the number of crimes recorded in the Lambeth borough was 30,805, with 10,626 of those taking place in the Brixton Division. Between 1976 and 1980, Brixton accounted for 35% of all crimes in the Borough, but 49% of all robbery and violent theft offences. The police recognised the rising crime: at the beginning of April, the Metropolitan Police began *Operation Swamp 81*, a plainclothes operation to reduce crime (named after prime minister Margaret Thatcher's 1978 assertion that the UK "might be rather swamped by people of a different culture"),[2237] and uniformed patrols were increased in the area. Officers from other Metropolitan police districts and the Special Patrol Group were dispatched into Brixton, and within five days, 943 people were stopped and searched, with 82 arrested, through the heavy use of what was colloquially known as the "Sus law."[2238] This referred to powers under the Vagrancy Act 1824, which allowed police to search and arrest members of the public when it was believed that they were acting suspiciously, and not necessarily committing a crime. The African- - Caribbean community accused the police of disproportionately using these powers against black people.

Public disfavour came to a head on Friday 10 April. At around 5:15 pm a police constable spotted a black youth named Michael Bailey running towards him, apparently away from three other black youths. Bailey was stopped and found to be badly bleeding but broke away from the constable. Stopped again on Atlantic Road, Bailey was found to have a four-inch stab wound.[2239] Bailey ran into a flat and was

[2233] Anim-Addo, Joan (1995). *Longest Journey: A History of Black Lewisham*. London: Deptford Forum Publishing Ltd. p. 137. ISBN 978-1-898536-21-5.

[2234] Kettle & Hodges 1982, pp. 100–101.

[2235] *Bowman, Andy. "A violent eruption of protest': Reflections on the 1981 Moss Side 'riots' (part one)". Manchester Mule, Monday, 15 August 2011.*

[2236] Anim-Addo, Joan (1995). *Longest Journey: A History of Black Lewisham*. London: Deptford Forum Publishing Ltd. p. 137. ISBN 978-1-898536-21-5.

[2237] Back, Les (2007). *Written in Stone: Black British Writing and Goldsmiths College* (PDF). London: Goldsmiths University of London. p. 7.

[2238] Petridis, Alexis (4 June 2020). "The 100 greatest UK No 1s: No 2, The Specials – Ghost Town". *The Guardian*.

[2239] Kettle & Hodges 1982, pp. 91–93.

helped by a family and the police constable there by putting kitchen roll on his wound. A crowd gathered and, as the police then tried to take the wounded boy to a waiting minicab on Railton Road, the crowd tried to intervene thinking the police did not appear to be providing or seeking the medical help Bailey needed quickly enough. As the minicab pulled away at speed a police car arrived and stopped the cab. When an officer from the police car realised Bailey was injured, he moved him into the back of the police car to take him to hospital more quickly and bound his wound more tightly to stop the bleeding. A group of 50 youths began to shout for Bailey's release, thinking the police were arresting him. "Look, they're killing him," claimed one. The crowd descended on the police car and pulled him out.

Rumours spread that a youth had been left to die by the police, or that the police looked on as the stabbed youth was lying on the street. Over 200 youths, black and white with predominantly Afro-Caribbean heritage reportedly turned on the police. In response the police decided to increase the number of police foot patrols in Railton Road, despite the tensions, and carry on with *Operation Swamp 81* throughout the night and into the following day.

It was believed by the local community that the stabbed youth died as a result of police brutality, fuelling tensions throughout the day as crowds slowly gathered. Tensions first erupted around 4 pm, as two police officers stopped and searched a mini cab in Railton Road. By this time Brixton Road (Brixton High Street) was reportedly filled with angry people and police cars were pelted with bricks. At around 5 pm the tension escalated and spread, and the 9 pm BBC News bulletin that evening reported 46 police officers injured, five seriously. Shops were looted on Railton Road, Mayall Road, Leeson Road, Acre Lane and Brixton Road. The looting in Brixton reportedly started at around 6 pm. At 6.15 pm the fire brigade received their first call, as a police van was set on fire by rioters in Railton Road, with the fire brigade being warned "riot in progress". As the fire brigade approached the police cordon, they were waved through without warning, driving down Railton Road towards 300 youths armed with bottles and bricks. The fire brigade met the crowd at the junction between Railton Road and Shakespeare Road and were attacked with stones and bottles.

The police put out emergency calls to police officers across London, asking for assistance. They had no strategy, and only had inadequate helmets and non-fireproof plastic shields to protect themselves with while clearing the streets of rioters. The police reportedly also had difficulties in radio communication. The police proceeded in clearing the Atlantic – Railton – Mayall area by pushing the rioters down the road, forming deep shield walls. The rioters responded with bricks, bottles, and petrol bombs.

At 5.30 pm the violence further escalated. Non-rioting members of the public attempted to mediate between the police and the rioters, calling for a de-escalation by withdrawing police out of the area. The destructive efforts of the rioters peaked at around 8 pm, as those attempts at mediation failed. Two pubs, 26 businesses, schools and other structures were set alight in the riots.

By 9.30 pm, over 1,000 police were dispatched into Brixton, squeezing out the rioters.[2240] By 1 am on 12 April 1981, the area was largely subdued, with no large groups – except the police – on the streets. The fire brigade refused to return until the following morning. Police numbers grew to over 2,500, and by the early hours of Sunday morning the rioting had fizzled out.[2241]

During the disturbances, 299 police were injured, along with at least 65 members of the public. 61 private vehicles and 56 police vehicles were destroyed. 28 premises were burned and another 117 damaged and looted. 82 arrests were made.[2242]

Between 3 and 11 July of that year, there was more unrest fuelled by racial and social discord, at Handsworth in Birmingham, Southall in London, Toxteth in Liverpool, Hyson Green in Nottingham and Moss Side in Manchester. There were also smaller pockets of unrest in Leeds, Leicester, Southampton, Halifax, Bedford, Gloucester, Wolverhampton, Coventry, Bristol, and Edinburgh.

Racial tension played a major part in most of these disturbances, although all of the riots took place in areas hit particularly hard by unemployment and recession.

The Home Secretary, William Whitelaw, commissioned a public inquiry into the riot headed by Lord Scarman. The Scarman report was published on 25 November 1981.

Scarman found unquestionable evidence of the disproportionate and indiscriminate use of 'stop and search' powers by the police against black people. As a consequence, a new code for police behaviour was put forward in the *Police and Criminal Evidence Act 1984*; and the act also created an independent Police Complaints Authority, established in 1985, to attempt to restore public confidence in the police.[2243] Scarman concluded that "complex political, social and economic factors created a disposition towards violent protest".[2244]

The 1999 MacPherson Report, an investigation into the murder of Stephen Lawrence and the failure of the police to establish sufficient evidence for the

---

[2240] "Battle 4 Brixton part 3 of 6". 13 April 2008. Retrieved 29 May 2009 – via YouTube.
[2241] "Britain: Bloody Saturday". *Time*. 20 April 1981.
[2242] *Petridis, Alexis (4 June 2020). "The 100 greatest UK No 1s: No 2, The Specials – Ghost Town". The Guardian.*
[2243] "Battle 4 Brixton part 5 of 6". 19 April 2008. YouTube.
[2244] *1981 riots timeline Untold History* (Channel Four Television)

prosecution of the charged suspects, found that recommendations of the 1981 Scarman Report had been ignored. The report concluded that the police force was "institutionally racist".[2245] This report, which did not cover the events of the Brixton Riots, disagreed with the conclusions made by Scarman.[2246]

On 25 March 2011, BBC Radio 4 broadcast *The Reunion*, a programme featuring reminiscences by participants, including police and black Brixton residents.[2247]

On 13 April, Margaret Thatcher dismissed the notion that unemployment and racism lay beneath the Brixton disturbances claiming "Nothing, but nothing, justifies what happened." Overall unemployment in Brixton stood at 13 percent, with 25.4 percent for ethnic minorities. Unemployment among black youths was estimated at 55 percent. Rejecting increased investment in Britain's inner cities, Thatcher added, "Money cannot buy either trust or racial harmony." Lambeth London Borough Council leader, Ted Knight, complained that the police presence "amounted to an army of occupation" that provoked the riots; Thatcher responded, "What absolute nonsense and what an appalling remark ... No one should condone violence. No one should condone the events ... They were criminal, criminal."

Small-scale disturbances continued to simmer throughout the summer. After four nights of rioting in Liverpool during the Toxteth riots, beginning 4 July, there were 150 buildings burnt and 781 police officers injured. CS gas was deployed for the first time on the British mainland to quell the rioting. On 10 July, there was fresh rioting in Brixton. It was not until the end of July that the disturbances began to subside.[2248]

The recommendations of the Scarman Report to tackle the problems of racial disadvantage and inner – city decline were not implemented.[2249] Rioting would break out again in the 1985 and 1995 Brixton riots.

[2245] *Q&A: The Scarman Report*, 27 April 2004 (BBC News)
[2246] "Q&A: Stephen Lawrence murder". *BBC News*. 5 May 2004.
[2247] "Q&A: The Scarman Report". *BBC News*. 27 April 2004.
[2248] "Battle 4 Brixton part 5 of 6". 19 April 2008. YouTube.
[2249] *1981 riots timeline Untold History* (Channel Four Television)

Chapter forty-nine

Man's inhumanity to his fellow man and women in the 21st. Century

Human trafficking is the process of trapping people using violence, deception or coercion and exploiting them for financial or personal gain.

What trafficking really means is girls groomed and forced into sexual exploitation; men tricked into accepting risky job offers and trapped in forced labour in building sites, farms, or factories; and women recruited to work in private homes only to be trapped, exploited, and abused behind closed doors with no way out.

People don't have to be transported across borders for trafficking to take place. In fact, transporting or moving the victim doesn't define trafficking, it can take place within a single country, or even within a single community.

People can be trafficked and exploited in many forms, including being forced into sexual exploitation, labour, begging, crime (such as growing cannabis or dealing drugs), domestic servitude, marriage, or organ removal.

Human Trafficking estimated figures, according to the United Nations Office for Drugs and Crime (UNODC)

- *51% of identified victims of trafficking are women,*
- *28% children and*
- *21% men*
- *72% people exploited in the sex industry are women*
- *63% of identified traffickers were men and 37% women*
- *43% of victims are trafficked domestically within national borders*

How do people get entangled in trafficking?

People trapped by traffickers are mostly trying to escape poverty or discrimination, improve their lives and support their families.

Vulnerable people are often forced to take unimaginable risks to try and escape poverty or persecution, accepting precarious job offers and making hazardous migration decisions, often borrowing money from their traffickers in advance.

When they arrive, they find that the work does not exist, or conditions are completely different. They become trapped, reliant on their traffickers and extremely vulnerable. Their documents are often taken away and they are forced to work until their debt is paid off.

MYTH: TRAFFICKING AFFECTS FOREIGNERS

Wrong. In fact, more than a quarter of all victims of trafficking found in the UK last year were British (26%), making this the most common victim nationality, followed by Albanian (16%) and Vietnamese (8%).

British people are trafficked in many ways. These could include:

- Homeless people offered jobs that turn out to come with threats and without pay
- Teenagers groomed by gangs into criminal acts such as shoplifting
- Young people and adults coerced or manipulated to act as drug couriers or dealers
- Girls and women forced into prostitution by abusive partners or by organised criminals.

County lines is when gangs and drug dealers use children to transport and sell drugs across the country, using "county line" mobile phone numbers for different regions.

All the above and more would involve trafficking.

MYTH: HUMAN TRAFFICKING INVOLVES HAVING TO CROSS AN INTERNATIONAL BORDER

Human trafficking means moving someone by means such as force, fraud, coercion, or deception, with the aim of exploiting them. It is a form of modern slavery.

You don't have to cross an international border, and much trafficking takes place within countries. It could refer to county lines. It could even mean taking someone just next door.

MYTH: MOST VICTIMS OF TRAFFICKING ARE SMUGGLED INTO THE UK

Not true. For a start many are British. But even among those that did travel to the UK, more than half of those reported to the Modern Slavery Helpline in 2018 arrived by plane (where means of transport was known).

The most common methods of travel to the UK by potential victims (PVs) in 2018 were by plane (732 PVs); bus or coach (232 PVs); car (124 PVs); boat (63 PVs); and lorry (53 PVs).

DECENT BASED SLAVERY – IN MAURITANIA

Mauritania is one of the last countries in the world where people are still born into slavery and literally owned by other people, facing a lifetime of abuse and forced labour.

Although no definitive survey was ever carried out, thousands of people are estimated to be in descent-based slavery. Born into slavery, they are literally owned by their masters.

They face a lifetime of exploitation and abuse.

Women are commonly raped and forced to bear their masters' children, who in turn also become their slaves.

People in slavery come from the Haratine ethnic group, historically enslaved by White Moors.

Whilst people in slavery in Mauritania are not chained or publicly beaten, they remain totally dependent on their masters.

Under a misguided interpretation of Islam, those in slavery are told that their paradise is bound to their master. Many believe that it is Allah's wish for them to be enslaved. Islam dictates that a Muslim cannot enslave a fellow Muslim.

It is extremely difficult to run away from slavery. Mauritania's caste – based society means that even those who escaped slavery are still considered to be part of the 'slave-caste' and are ostracised.

Slavery has been criminalised since 2007 but the law has not been implemented. A new law, passed in 2015, offered some new promise, but the government is reluctant to admit that slavery even exists in the country, let alone to seriously tackle it. Instead, it has been very hostile to anti – slavery activists, cracking down on any attempts to mobilise the Haratines.

DECENT BASED SLAVERY – IN NIGER

Communities of slave descent are among the most marginalised and impoverished communities in Niger. Historically, people were raided, enslaved, and assimilated by slave owning Tuaregs and their descendants remained trapped in hereditary slavery.

In the last two decades, many of these communities have cut ties with their masters and attempted to establish independent villages.

However, the challenges faced by these groups, who still bear the status of "slaves", are immense. In areas prone to drought and famine, these populations are usually destitute, illiterate and with very limited access to basic services. They are typically overlooked by State services and development programmes due to their social, economic, and political marginalisation.

In addition, women and girls in these communities face extra disadvantage due to discriminatory gender roles.

SLAVERY IN SENEGAL: FORCED CHILD BEGGING

One of the most prevalent forms of slavery in Senegal takes the form of forced child begging in Koranic schools.

Across Senegal, boys known as 'talibés' (boys who are sent out to beg), are sent out to beg on the streets by their teachers at Koranic schools called 'Daaras'. (This is the title used in Senegal to designate traditional Islamic schools)

Most Daaras do not charge the students for their studies, food or accommodation. Instead, the teachers force the children to beg for their keep. They must work for long hours and hand over their income.

Children who are forced to beg are commonly beaten if they fail to meet their begging quotas or suffer abuse from individuals they encounter as they beg.

Daaras are not properly regulated, so often the children are poorly educated and socially ill-equipped for future life. Most of the children attending Daaras are from remote rural areas and sometimes from neighbouring countries.

Working alongside two local partner organisations Tostan (Tostan is a US-registered 501 international non-governmental organization headquartered in Dakar, Senegal) and RADDHO (the African Meeting for the Defence of Human Rights) our three-pronged approach aims to tackle child begging through the modernisation of Daaras, child protection and access to a regular school curriculum.

Communities come together to protect children in their own towns and villages and influence local governments to allocate funds to support that process.

Our project has engaged over 300 Koranic teachers, the majority of whom now supports the modernisation of the Daaras. The teachers are supported by the communities to make improvements and look after the children better, without sending them out to beg.

We have also introduced a system where talibés are being 'sponsored' by local families in all the project areas. Over 3,000 children were 'adopted', providing them items such as soap, sleeping mats and mosquito nets.

As a result, begging has significantly decreased in these communities.

Advocating to end forced child begging.

At national level, (RADDHO) lobbies senior politicians, ministries, and Senegal's influential religious leaders to develop a law regulating the Daaras, introduce a state curriculum to all schools and criminalise forced begging.

The draft Bill is waiting to be presented before Parliament. However, it is contested by parts of the religious lobby, and further consultations have led to lengthy delays.

The Senegal President's recent announcement of a new ad-hoc initiative to remove begging children from the streets proved to be ineffective, and children returned to the street shortly after having been removed.

CHILD DOMESTIC WORK – IN TANZANIA

There are an estimated 1 million children doing domestic work in Tanzania, most of them girls.

Poverty and hardship in rural areas force children to migrate to cities to find jobs in private households. Many girls also run away from home to avoid domestic abuse or forced marriage.

Far from their families and vulnerable to exploitation, children are often denied the salaries they are initially promised. They are often forced to work long hours and have little chance of attending school and getting an education. Many are subjected to physical and sexual abuse.

Child domestic work is a traditional practice in Tanzania and a common response to poverty.

Although no reliable statistics are available, some estimates suggest that around 3% of the population in urban areas are live-in children working in private homes. Up to a third of children in domestic work are below fourteen and can be as young as ten. Over 80% of them are girls.

Child domestic workers suffer from extreme isolation and low self – esteem. Child domestic workers are extremely vulnerable. Sexual harassment and other abuses are common and hidden from sight in employers' homes. Many children must work gruelling working hours, are extremely isolated and lack care and protection.

Child domestic workers primarily come from poor, rural families. Often, families marry off their young daughters to reduce the financial burden and receive 'the bride price'. Many girls run away to the city to avoid marriage and frequently end up as child domestic workers or in other forms of child labour.

Some parents choose to send their child away to work as an alternative to early marriage, unaware of the abuse and exploitation that frequently awaits the child.

Many child – domestic workers have no or little access to education, limiting their chances to find good jobs in future.

A survey carried out in 2012 found that less than 0.5% of the children in domestic work had formal contracts; over 40% suffered physical abuse and other cruel and degrading treatment from their employers; 17% suffered sexual abuse; and over 60% did not attend school and were illiterate and innumerate.

Other common problems included little or no pay, despite working up to 60+ hours per week and working in complete isolation which limits children's movements, any social life and contact with families.

Since the early 1990s Anti – Slavery International and its partners in Africa, Asia, Latin America, and the Caribbean have been at the forefront of work to raise the visibility of child domestic workers, to promote their cause and reduce their suffering.

The isolation and dependency of these children, their frequent loss of liberty, methods of recruitment which can amount to trafficking, and low pay or no pay at all, put them in a category of human rights violation that can often be close to slavery.

FORCED LABOUR IN THE COTTON INDUSTRY

Uzbekistan and Turkmenistan are two of the biggest producers and exporters of cotton in the world. To produce this cotton both repressive governments use systems of forced labour on a massive scale.

Both countries export a vast majority of their cotton, which ends up in global supply chains and on the shelves of many high street shops worldwide.

Anti-slavery.org has worked to end forced labour in Uzbekistan's cotton industry for nearly a decade under the banner of our Cotton Crimes campaign. Recently we extended our work to Turkmenistan, which uses similar practices.

Cotton Crimes campaign:

Anti-slavery.org work in partnership with the Cotton Campaign, a wide coalition of organisations, lobbying governments, international organisations, and business to put pressure on the governments of Uzbekistan and Turkmenistan to end these abuses.

They are working to mobilise the cotton industry to ensure that no tainted cotton is in the goods we buy and lobby national government and international organisations such as the European Union and the United Nations to put pressure on the Government of Uzbekistan to end this practice.

They have gone a long way in mobilising the business to stop knowingly using Uzbek cotton in their products. Over 250 businesses have already signed the Cotton Pledge to not use Uzbek cotton.

But supply chains are so complex that it's often not easy to determine the source of the cotton in final products, so we urge businesses to proactively do more to ensure that Uzbek and Turkmen cotton does not enter their supply chains.

Anti-slavery.org have successfully convinced H&M and Nike to take more proactive steps to that end and continue to encourage others to do the same.

Our work with governments and international organisations has recently been made harder by their increasingly lenient approach towards Uzbekistan after it stopped forcing children to pick cotton on a systematic scale but replaced them with adults.

They have campaigned to stop the World Bank financing Uzbek agricultural projects, and recently campaigned against a trade deal between the European Union and Uzbekistan that that was unfortunately passed by the European Parliament in December 2016. They still have a long way to go to encourage such organisations to put more pressure on Uzbekistan to stop slavery practices.

In more positive news, the US State Department downgraded both countries in its annual Trafficking in Persons report, pointing out the lack of effort to end forced labour.

An important part of our work is documenting these abuses to counter the Uzbek government's propaganda. Anti-slavery.org have produced two short documentaries containing rare first-hand evidence from the ground, as well as other awareness raising videos.

Forced labour in cotton industries in Uzbekistan and Turkmenistan:

In a practice rooted in Soviet times, the governments of Uzbekistan and Turkmenistan force their own citizens to pick cotton under harsh conditions each harvest season.

Farmers are ordered to grow cotton or else risk financial penalties or removal from the land they farm.

During the harvest each autumn citizens such as teachers and doctors are forced out of their regular jobs to spend weeks in the fields picking cotton, often in hazardous conditions and without basic equipment.

Although younger children are no longer mobilised, local administrations routinely send older students to the fields in some districts.

Each citizen is given a daily quota. Those who fail to meet their targets or pick a low-quality crop, risk losing their jobs or face harassment from employers or the government.

The work is dangerous. People can be left exhausted and suffering from ill-health and malnutrition after weeks of arduous labour. Those working on remote cotton farms are forced to stay in makeshift dormitories in poor conditions with insufficient food and drinking water.

The government of Uzbekistan routinely harasses, intimidates, and represses citizens who attempt to monitor the cotton harvest.

Businesses are forced to contribute financially if they want to stay open during harvest time. The provision of public services such as healthcare and education are also severely affected during the harvest.

Despite widespread knowledge of these abuses, some textile traders and companies have been complicit in buying and selling Uzbek cotton. And although many companies have pledged to not knowingly use Uzbek cotton, it still ends up in global supply chains and in a lot of finished products.

Many governments and international bodies continue to promote trade with Uzbekistan and Turkmenistan without regard to ongoing human rights abuses.

Chapter fifty

China's Crackdown on Xinjiang

Xinjiang, also historically renowned as the most well-known route of the Silk Road, has a history of succession for 2,500 years and as a domino effect, several leaders and empires have competed for control over scraps of the region, let alone the entirety of it. Falling in the Northwest of China, it has become the country's largest natural gas producing region, found to have an abundance of oil and mineral reserves. The region is made up of several ethnicities, however, around 50% of its population is made up of the Uyghur, a Turkic ethnic group who happen to be predominantly Muslim.

"The first thing you notice is the quiet. Then the white strips of paper stretched diagonally across the front doors of stores that look like they were vacated in a hurry. Once you get close enough, you can read the painted serial numbers on the house walls – WB-BUK 1 to 15 on one street – that tell you no one is coming back to these homes, and that many of those who lived there have been detained." – Emily Feng, a reporter at the Financial Times.

Part of China's mission to ethnically cleanse Xinjiang, against human rights activism, autonomy and more importantly Uyghur independence includes home visits from government officials. This is an attempt to test these homes for "extremism" and to see how "loyal" these groups of people are to the government's authority. If those tested do not pass, they are put on a list, noted down as a potential threat to the Chinese state, and at risk of being sent to "re-education centres", where they are subjected to abuse, torture and whatever it may take to re-shape them into the ideal Chinese citizen. China sugar coat the inhumanity they enforce, these are concentration camps and should not be known as anything other than.

Data released the advocacy group Chinese Human Rights Defenders read that an

estimated 227,000 people were arrested in 2017, a 731% increase from the year before, and that does not include the potential 1 million innocent people who've been thrown into concentration camps in a bid to "re – educate", this past year, never to be heard from again.

"This strong rise in 2017 in arrests is consistent with all the other securitization measures, including massive police recruitment, deployment of sophisticated technologies, installation of checkpoints everywhere, etc. Re-education detainment figures are certainly on top of these numbers," explained Adrian Zenz, a social researcher at the European School of Culture and Theology who had conducted his research by using job ad postings and construction bids. "It shows the scale of the security state in Xinjiang at these different levels."

- It was only due to the heavy pressure of global media that the Chinese government recently acknowledged the existence of these centres. During a United Nations committee, when questioned on the aims of its "re-education centres" and the scope of tactics used, China reassured the UN that these were all justified methods for a righteous cause. However, evidence heavily suggests otherwise – testimonies by those freed from the centres demonstrate psychological trauma inflicted on detainees.

Life for the Uyghurs as well as other Turkic and culturally Muslim groups is pierced with trauma. Children are being sent away to state orphanages as their parents are being detained. With the detaining of thousands of wealthy Uyghur business owners, most people are stricken by poverty. Humanitarian work and potential aid is being blocked off by the Chinese government. Families beyond Xinjiang live in fear for their relatives, unable to contact them in case it bares dire consequences for their detained relatives.

China's objective is simple, to those who don't want to read between the lines, they'll believe that this is a war against terror, not dissimilar to the West post 9/11, but the fact is this, racism and more specifically Islamophobia are tools, used by colonisers to exert power and control. This is a region that oozes natural gas, oil, gold, and salt. Xinjiang supplies the country's largest supply of fruit and raw cotton – independence for the Uyghur means a loss of control over these forms of trade.

The dire silence of everyone on this matter has been shocking, articles–on "Muslims being forced to eat pork in China" barely covers the severity of this issue but unfortunately, that's all we've had to offer the Uyghurs of Xinjiang. Uyghurs are being subjected to cultural cleansing, and potential mass extermination, the millions of people detained are unaccounted – the world needs to ask why that is, not just stand by and watch.

Chapter fifty-one

George Perry Floyd

I suppose that this book came about in part because of what happened to George Floyd. I have already written about Floyd in my book **"If MY people…."** ISBN: 979-8-64509-28188,

The impact that his death had on this planet sent everyone into such a hissy fit, that it is almost impossible to see things clearly. Black Lives Matter is all we have been hearing since 25th. May 2020.

So many people turned out in Houston for his funeral, that the police in Dallas were afraid to enforce the Covid restrictions for fear of provoking riots. It would not have taken much to set the protesters off again. The police did arrest someone though, for selling hotdogs near the Funeral.

To many, Floyd was a hero, to others he was just another criminal, who despite his rap sheet did not deserve to die in the wat that he did.

It was reported that 5,000 turned out in Dallas for his funeral. But that was not as many as turned out in Dallas, on May 26th. 1934 for Bonnie Parker's funeral, 20,000 attended that funeral, and 15,000 attended Clyde Barrow's funeral at sundown the night of 25th. May 1934.

I just don't get it with American's, turning felons into heroes and giving them superstar status.

What follows can be found in my book mentioned above.

George Perry Floyd Jr. was an African American man murdered by a police officer during an arrest after a store clerk suspected he may have used a counterfeit $20 bill in Minneapolis. Derek Chauvin, one of four police officers who arrived on the scene, knelt on Floyd's neck and back for 9 minutes and 29 seconds.[2250]

After his death, protests against police brutality, especially towards black people, quickly spread across the United States and globally. As he was dying, he said, "I can't breathe," which was used as a rallying cry during subsequent protests.

[2250] Bailey, Holly (April 8, 2021). "George Floyd died of low level of oxygen, medical expert testifies; Derek Chauvin kept knee on his neck 'majority of the time'". *Washington Post.*

The City of Minneapolis settled a wrongful death lawsuit with Floyd's family for $27 million. Chauvin was convicted on two counts of murder and one count of manslaughter on April 20, 2021[2251] and on June 25, 2021 was sentenced to 22.5 years in prison.[2252] The trial of the other three officers at the scene of his death is scheduled to begin on March 7, 2022.[2253]

The first of his siblings to go to college, Floyd attended South Florida Community College for two years on a football scholarship, and also played on the basketball team.[2254] [2255] [2256] He transferred to Texas A&M University – Kingsville in 1995, where he also played basketball before dropping out.[2257] At his tallest he was 6 feet 6 inches (198 cm)[2258] and by the time of his autopsy he was 6 feet 4 inches (193 cm) tall and weighed 223 pounds (101 kg).[2259]

Floyd returned to Houston from college in Kingsville, Texas, in 1995 and became an automotive customizer and played club basketball.[2260] [2261] Beginning in 1994, he performed as a rapper using the stage name Big Floyd in the hip-hop group Screwed Up Click.[2262] [2263] *The New York Times* described his deep – voiced rhymes as "purposeful", delivered in a slow – motion clip about " 'choppin' blades' – driving cars with oversize rims – and his Third Ward pride."[2264] The second rap group he

---

[2251] Mike Hayes, Melissa Macaya, Meg Wagner and Veronica Rocha (April 20, 2021). "Derek Chauvin guilty in death of George Floyd: Live updates". *CNN*. Retrieved April 20,2021.

[2252] *"Derek Chauvin sentenced to 22.5 years in prison for the murder of George Floyd"*. CNN. *Retrieved June 25, 2021.*

[2253] Xiong, Chao (May 13, 2021). "State trial postponed to March 2022 for ex-officers charged with aiding and abetting murder in George Floyd death". *Star Tribune*. Retrieved May 13, 2021.

[2254] Fernandez, Manny; Burch, Audra D. S. (April 20, 2021). "George Floyd, from 'I Want to Touch the World' to 'I Can't Breathe'". *The New York Times*. ISSN 0362-4331.

[2255] Ebrahimji, Alisha (May 29, 2020). "This is how loved ones want us to remember George Floyd". *CNN*. Retrieved June 1, 2020.

[2256] Holton, Jennifer (May 29, 2020). "'A good guy:' College classmate, coach remember George Floyd". *WTVT*. Retrieved June 1, 2020.

[2257] Mee, Emily (June 7, 2020). "Who was George Floyd? The 'gentle giant' who was trying to turn his life around". *Sky News*. Retrieved June 4, 2020.

[2258] *"George Floyd: 'Gentle giant' killed in U.S. police custody"*. Japan Times. May 30, 2020. *Floyd, standing at an imposing 6 feet, 6 inches (two meters), became a star athlete*

[2259] "Hennepin County Medical Examiner's Office Autopsy Report". *Hennepin County*. June 1, 2020. The body is that of a normally developed, muscular and adequately nourished appearing, 6 feet 4 inch long, 223-pound male

[2260] Hall, Michael (May 31, 2020). "The Houston Years of George Floyd". *Texas Monthly*. Retrieved June 5, 2020.

[2261] *Lance Scott Walker (2019). Houston Rap Tapes: An Oral History of Bayou City Hip-Hop. University of Texas Press. p. 83. ISBN 9781477317938. Retrieved June 4, 2020.*

[2262] Julian, Gill (May 27, 2020). "Before dying in Minneapolis police custody, George Floyd grew up in Houston's Third Ward". *Houston Chronicle*. Retrieved May 30, 2020.

[2263] Burney, Lawrence (May 29, 2020). "The Rap Report: To George Floyd a.k.a. Big Floyd of the legendary Screwed Up Click". *The Fader*. Retrieved June 1, 2020.

[2264] Fernandez, Manny; Burch, Audra D. S. (April 20, 2021). "George Floyd, from 'I Want to Touch the

was involved in was "Presidential Playas" and he worked on their album *Block Party* released in 2000.[2265] An influential member of his community, Floyd was respected for his ability to relate with others in his environment based on a shared experience of hardships and setbacks, having served time in prison and living in a poverty – stricken project in Houston.[2266] In a video addressing the youth in his neighbourhood, Floyd reminds his audience that he has his own "shortcomings" and "flaws" and that he is not better than anyone else, but also expresses his disdain for the violence that was taking place in the community, and advises his neighbours to put down their weapons and remember that they are loved by him and God.[2267]

Between 1997 and 2005, Floyd served eight jail terms on various charges, including drug possession, theft, and trespass. [2268] In one of these cases the arresting officer was later investigated for a pattern of falsifying evidence, related to the Pecan Park raid, leading the District Attorney of Harris County, Texas to request a posthumous pardon for Floyd in 2021.[2269] In 2007, Floyd faced charges for aggravated robbery with a deadly weapon; according to investigators, he had entered an apartment by impersonating a water department worker and barging in with five other men, then held a pistol to a woman's stomach and searched for items to steal. [2270] Floyd was arrested three months later during a traffic stop and a 7 – year – old victim of the robbery identified him from a photo array.[2271] In 2009, he was sentenced to five years in prison as part of a plea deal [2272] and was paroled in January 2013.[2273] After Floyd's release, he became more involved with Resurrection Houston, a Christian church and ministry, where he mentored young men and posted anti – violence

World' to 'I Can't Breathe'". *The New York Times*. ISSN 0362-4331.

[2265] Altatis, Conan (June 1, 2020). "George Floyd, Kimberly Brinks' video surfaces as U.S. riots continue". *conandaily.com*. Retrieved November 16, 2020. As a member of the rap group Presidential Playas, Floyd released the album "Block Party" in 2000.

[2266] Schkloven, Emma (June 2, 2020). "Remembering Big Floyd". Big Floyd, who also appeared on a track in 2000 as part of another group, the Presidential Playas, freestyled on at least half a dozen of Screw's famous mixtapes, if not more.

[2267] Henao, Luis Andres; Merchant, Nomaan; Lozano, Juan; Geller, Adam (June 11, 2020). "A long look at the complicated life of George Floyd". *chicagotribune.com*. Associated Press. Retrieved March 29, 2021.

[2268] Jervis, Rick (June 9, 2020). "'George Floyd changed the world': Public viewing in Houston honors the man behind the social justice movement". *USA Today*. Retrieved June 11, 2020.

[2269] Barker, Aaron (April 29, 2021). "Harris County DA requests posthumous pardon for George Floyd in 2004 drug conviction". KPRC-TV. Retrieved April 29, 2021.

[2270] Rao, Maya (December 27, 2020). "George Floyd hoped moving to Minnesota would save him. What he faced here killed him". *Star Tribune*. 2020. Retrieved December 29, 2020.

[2271] Rao, Maya (December 27, 2020). "George Floyd hoped moving to Minnesota would save him. What he faced here killed him". *Star Tribune*. 2020. Retrieved December 29, 2020.

[2272] *Walters, Joanna (May 29, 2020). "An athlete, a father, a 'beautiful spirit': George Floyd in his friends' words". The Guardian. Retrieved June 4, 2020.*

[2273] *Hall, Michael (May 31, 2020). "The Houston Years of George Floyd". Texas Monthly. Retrieved June 5, 2020.*

videos to social media.[2274] He delivered meals to senior citizens and volunteered with other projects, such as the Angel By Nature Foundation, a charity founded by rapper "Trae tha Truth."[2275] Later he became involved with a ministry that brought men from the Third Ward to Minnesota in a church-work program with drug rehabilitation and job placement services.[2276] A friend of Floyd acknowledged that Floyd "had made some mistakes that cost him some years of his life," but that he had been turning his life around through religion.[2277]

In 2014, Floyd moved to Minneapolis to help rebuild his life and find work.[2278] Soon after his arrival, he completed a 90 – day rehabilitation program at the Turning Point program in north Minneapolis. Floyd expressed the need for a job and took up security work at Harbour Light Centre, a Salvation Army homeless shelter.[2279] He lost the job at Harbour Light and took up several other jobs. Floyd hoped to earn a commercial driver's license to operate trucks. He passed the required drug test and administrators of the program felt his criminal past did not pose a problem, but he dropped out as his job at a nightclub made it difficult to attend morning classes, and he felt pressure to'earn money. Floyd later moved to St. Louis Park and lived with former colleagues.[2280] Floyd continued to battle drug addiction and went through periods of use and sobriety.[2281]

In May 2019, Floyd was detained by Minneapolis police when an unlicensed car he was a passenger in was pulled over in a traffic stop. Floyd was found with a bottle of pain pills. Officers handcuffed Floyd and took him to the city's third police precinct station. Floyd told police he did not sell the pills and that they were related to his own addiction. When Floyd appeared agitated, officers encouraged him to relax and helped calm him down, and they later called an ambulance as they grew worried about his condition. No charges were filed in connection with the incident.[2282]

[2274] Shellnutt, Kate (June 5, 2020). "George Floyd Left a Gospel Legacy in Houston". *Christianity Today*. Retrieved June 1, 2020.

[2275] Kantor, Wendy Grossman (June 10, 2020). "Years Before George Floyd Cried Out for Late Mom in Final Moments, He Nursed Her After Stroke". *PEOPLE.com*. Retrieved June 11, 2020.

[2276] *Fernandez, Manny; Burch, Audra D. S. (April 20, 2021). "George Floyd, from 'I Want to Touch the World' to 'I Can't Breathe'". The New York Times. ISSN 0362-4331.*

[2277] Henao, Luis Andres; Merchant, Nomaan; Lozano, Juan; Geller, Adam (June 11, 2020). "A long look at the complicated life of George Floyd". *chicagotribune.com*. Associated Press. Retrieved March 29, 2021.

[2278] Evelyn, Kenya (June 3, 2020). "'I miss him': George Floyd's daughter speaks out for first time". *The Guardian*. Retrieved June 5, 2020. She added Floyd was a good father who wanted his daughter 'to have the best'.

[2279] Rao, Maya (December 27, 2020). "George Floyd hoped moving to Minnesota would save him. What he faced here killed him". *Star Tribune*. Retrieved December 29, 2020.

[2280] Rao, Maya (December 27, 2020). "George Floyd hoped moving to Minnesota would save him. What he faced here killed him". *Star Tribune*. Retrieved December 29, 2020.

[2281] Rao, Maya (December 27, 2020). "George Floyd hoped moving to Minnesota would save him. What he faced here killed him". *Star Tribune*. Retrieved December 29, 2020.

In 2019, George Floyd worked security at the El Nuevo Rodeo club, where police officer Derek Chauvin also worked off – duty as a security guard.[2283] In 2020, Floyd was working part time as a security guard at the Conga Latin Bistro club, and began another job as a delivery driver. Floyd lost the delivery driver job in January after being cited for driving without a valid commercial license and for being involved in a minor crash. He was looking for another job when the COVID – 19 pandemic hit Minnesota, and his personal financial situation worsened when the club closed in March due to pandemic rules.[2284] In April, Floyd contracted COVID – 19, but recovered a few weeks later.[2285]

On May 25, 2020, Floyd was murdered by Derek Chauvin, a white Minneapolis police officer, who pressed his knee to Floyd's neck for 9 minutes and 29 seconds[2286] while Floyd was handcuffed face down in the street.[2287] As seen in a witness's cell phone video,[2288] two other officers further restrained Floyd and a fourth prevented onlookers from intervening[2289] as Floyd repeatedly pleaded that he could not breathe. During the final two minutes[2290] Floyd was motionless and had no pulse, [2291] but Chauvin kept his knee on Floyd's neck and back even as emergency medical technicians arrived to treat Floyd.[2292]

Police had been called by a grocery store employee who suspected that Floyd had used a counterfeit $20 bill.[2293]

[2282] Rao, Maya (December 27, 2020). "George Floyd hoped moving to Minnesota would save him. What he faced here killed him". *Star Tribune*. Retrieved December 29, 2020.

[2283] Kates, Graham (June 3, 2020). "George Floyd and Derek Chauvin worked at same club and may have crossed paths, owner says". *CBS News*. Retrieved June 19, 2020.

[2284] Rao, Maya (December 27, 2020). "George Floyd hoped moving to Minnesota would save him. What he faced here killed him". *Star Tribune*. Retrieved December 29, 2020.

[2285] Vagianos, Alanna (June 9, 2020). "'He's Gonna Change The World': George Floyd's Family Remembers The Man They Lost". *HuffPost*. Retrieved June 11, 2020.

[2286] Forliti, Amy; Karnowski, Steve; Webber, Tammy (April 5, 2021). "Police chief: Kneeling on Floyd's neck violated policy". *Star Tribune*. Associated Press. Retrieved April 8,2021.

[2287] "Complaint – *State of Minnesota v. Derek Michael Chauvin*" (PDF). *Minnesota District Court, Fourth Judicial District, File No. 27-CR-20-12646*. May 29, 2020. The defendant pulled Mr. Floyd out of the passenger side of the squad car at 8:19:38 p.m. and Mr. Floyd went to the ground face down and still handcuffed.

[2288] "Derek Chauvin trial: George Floyd 'slowly fading away' during police arrest". *BBC.com*. March 29, 2021.

[2289] *Forliti, Amy; Sullivan, Tim (May 29, 2020). "Officer Charged With George Floyd's Death as Protests Flare". Associated Press. Retrieved April 22, 2021.*

[2290] "Prosecutors: Officer had knee on Floyd for 7:46, 1-minute error not expected to impact criminal case". *KSTP*. Associated Press. June 18, 2020. Retrieved July 24, 2020.

[2291] Thorbecke, Catherine (May 29, 2020). "Derek Chauvin had his knee on George Floyd's neck for nearly 9 minutes, complaint says". *ABC News*. Retrieved June 5, 2020.

[2292] *Hill, Evan; Tiefenthäler, Ainara; Triebert, Christiaan; Jordan, Drew; Willis, Haley; Stein, Robin (May 31, 2020). "How George Floyd Was Killed in Police Custody". The New York Times. Retrieved June 1, 2020.* (Subscription required - video @ YouTube).

[2293] Furber, Matt; Burch, Audra D. S.; Robles, Frances (May 29, 2020). "George Floyd Worked With

The medical examiner found[2294] that Floyd's heart stopped while he was being restrained and that his death was a homicide, [2295] caused by "cardiopulmonary arrest complicating law enforcement subdual, restraint, and neck compression",[2296] t hough fentanyl intoxication and recent methamphetamine use may have increased the likelihood of death.[2297] A second autopsy, commissioned by Floyd's family,[2298] a lso found his death to be a homicide, specifically citing asphyxia due to neck and back compression;[2299] it ruled out that any underlying medical problems had contributed to Floyd's death,[2300] and said that Floyd being able to speak while under Chauvin's knee does not mean he could breathe.[2301]

On March 12, 2021, the Minneapolis city council approved a settlement of $27 million to the Floyd family following a wrongful death lawsuit.[2302]

Officer Derek Chauvin was fired and charged with second – degree murder, third degree murder and second degree manslaughter.[2303] Chauvin was found guilty on all three murder and manslaughter charges on April 20, 2021.[2304] On May 12, 2021, Hennepin County District Judge Peter Cahill allowed for the prosecution to seek a greater prison sentence for Chauvin after finding that he treated Floyd "with particular cruelty."[2305] On June 25, Chauvin was sentenced to twenty two and a half years in prison.[2306]

Officer Charged in His Death". *The New York Times*. ISSN 0362-4331. Retrieved May 30, 2020.

[2294] Autopsy Report, George Floyd, Deceased, ME No.: 20–3700. Hennepin County Medical Examiner. June 1, 2020. (20 pages.)

[2295] Press Release Report: Floyd George Perry Case No: 2020–3700. Hennepin County Medical Examiner. June 1, 2020.

[2296] George Floyd death homicide, official post-mortem declares". *BBC News*. June 2, 2020. Retrieved June 2, 2020.

[2297] Brooks, Brad (June 2, 2020). "State, independent autopsies agree on homicide in George Floyd case, but clash on underlying cause". *Reuters*. Retrieved June 2, 2020.

[2298] Gors, Michele (June 1, 2020). "Family autopsy: Floyd asphyxiated by sustained pressure". KTTC. Retrieved June 2, 2020.

[2299] *Robles, Frances (June 2, 2020). "How Did George Floyd Die? Here's What We Know". The New York Times. Retrieved June 3, 2020.*

[2300] Ensor, Josie (June 1, 2020). "Independent autopsy reveals George Floyd died from 'asphyxiation' as lawyers call for first-degree murder charges". *The Daily Telegraph*. Retrieved June 2, 2020.

[2301] Ensor, Josie (June 1, 2020). "Independent autopsy reveals George Floyd died from 'asphyxiation' as lawyers call for first-degree murder charges". *The Daily Telegraph*. Retrieved June 2, 2020.

[2302] Bogel-Burroughs, Nicholas (March 12, 2021). "George Floyd's Family Settles Suit Against Minneapolis for $27 Million". *The New York Times*. 2021.

[2303] Forliti, Amy; Press, Associated (March 7, 2021). "Key points in Derek Chauvin's trial: George Floyd's cause of death, ex-cop's use of force". *ABC13 Houston*. Retrieved March 28, 2021.

[2304] *"Derek Chauvin trial: George Floyd 'slowly fading away' during police arrest". BBC.com. March 29, 2021.*

[2305] Walsh, Paul (May 12, 2021). "Judge's ruling echoes prosecution's points, setting stage for Chauvin getting longer sentence". Retrieved May 12, 2021.

[2306] *"Derek Chauvin sentenced to 22.5 years in prison for murder of George Floyd". BBC News. June 25, 2021.*

After Floyd's death, protests were held globally against the use of excessive force by police officers against black suspects and lack of police accountability. Calls to both defund and abolish the police have been widespread.[2307] Protests began in Minneapolis the day after his death and developed in cities throughout all 50 U.S. states and internationally.[2308] The day after his death, all four officers involved in Floyd's death were fired and, on May 29, third-degree murder and second-degree manslaughter charges were brought against Chauvin.[2309]

Several memorial services were held. On June 4, 2020, a memorial service for Floyd took place in Minneapolis with Al Sharpton delivering the eulogy.[2310] Services were planned in North Carolina with a public viewing and private service on June 6 and in Houston on June 8 and 9.[2311] Floyd was buried next to his mother in Pearland, Texas.

Colleges and universities which have created scholarships in Floyd's name included North Central University (which hosted a memorial service for Floyd),[2312] Alabama State, Oakwood University,[2313] Missouri State University, Southeast Missouri State, Ohio University,[2314] Buffalo State College, Copper Mountain College,[2315] and others.[2316] Amid nationwide protests over Floyd's killing, Netflix CEO Reed Hastings and his wife Patty Quillin made a $120 million donation to be split equally among Morehouse College, Spelman College and the United Negro College Fund.[2317] The donation was the largest ever made to historically black colleges and universities.[2318]

[2307] "What Defunding the Police Really Means". *Black Lives Matter*. July 6, 2020. Retrieved April 26, 2021.

[2308] Murphy, Esme (May 26, 2020). "'I Can't Breathe!': Video Of Fatal Arrest Shows Minneapolis Officer Kneeling On George Floyd's Neck For Several Minutes". KSTP-TV. Retrieved May 26, 2020. While lying face down on the road, Floyd repeatedly groans and says he can't breathe.

[2309] *Hill, Evan; Tiefenthäler, Ainara; Triebert, Christiaan; Jordan, Drew; Willis, Haley; Stein, Robin (May 31, 2020). "How George Floyd Was Killed in Police Custody". The New York Times. Retrieved June 1, 2020.* (Subscription required - video @ YouTube)

[2310] *Ling, Thomas (June 2020). "How to watch the George Floyd memorial online and on TV". Radio Times. Retrieved June 6, 2020.*

[2311] Burke, Minyvonne (June 6, 2020). "George Floyd memorial in North Carolina as sheriff's officers escort his body". *NBC News*. Retrieved June 6, 2020.

[2312] "George Floyd's Body Returns To Houston For Memorial Service, Funeral". *CBS News*. June 7, 2020. Retrieved June 9, 2020.

[2313] Russell, Lois G. (June 4, 2020). "ASU Establishes George Floyd/Greg Gunn Memorial Scholarship | Alabama State University". *www.alasu.edu*. Retrieved June 5, 2020.

[2314] "George Floyd Memorial Scholarship Established at Southeast". *news.semo.edu*. Retrieved June 6, 2020.

[2315] "Copper Mountain College announces George Floyd Scholarship Fund". *z1077fm.com*. June 6, 2020. Retrieved June 6, 2020.

[2316] "12 other universities join North Central in creating a George Floyd Memorial Scholarship". *FOX 9*. June 11, 2020. Retrieved June 11, 2020.

[2317] *Togoh, Isabel (June 17, 2020). "Netflix CEO Reed Hastings Donates $120 Million To HBCUs: 'We Hope This Will Help More Black Students Follow Their Dreams'". Forbes. Retrieved June 17, 2020.*

On May 21, 2021, Bridgett Floyd gave a $25,000 check from the George Floyd Memorial Foundation to Fayetteville State University in Fayetteville, North Carolina to be used for scholarships. On the same day, the city declared May 25 George Floyd Jr. Day.[2319]

The officers were charged with showing "deliberate indifference to [Mr Floyd's] serious medical needs" during the attempted arrest in May 2020.

Tou Thao, 36, J Alexander Kueng, 28, and Thomas Lane, 38, all testified in their own defence in the trial. They said they did not realise Mr Floyd needed medical care at the time.

Violating a person's civil rights carries various punishments but prosecutors have recommended 25 years in federal prison for each man.

Derek Chauvin, the former police officer who was filmed kneeling on Mr Floyd's neck for more than nine minutes, is currently serving a 22-and-a-half-year sentence.

Chauvin was found guilty of Mr Floyd's murder last April. He also pleaded guilty in December to his own federal civil rights charges as part of a plea agreement. Video footage of the arrest shows Keung and Lane assisting Chauvin by helping to hold Mr Floyd down. Thao, meanwhile, kept concerned bystanders away.

Over four weeks of testimony, prosecutors argued that "human decency and common sense" should have compelled the men to take action to prevent Mr Floyd's death.

"It wasn't a split-second use of force like a gunshot. Not 30 seconds, not a minute, several minutes – 569 seconds," said Assistant US Attorney Manda Sertich.

But lawyers for the defence claimed they were listening to a commander with seniority. Chauvin was a field training officer to both Lane and Kueng.

[2318] St. Amour, Madeline (June 18, 2020). "Netflix CEO Donates Millions to HBCUs". *Inside Higher Ed.* Retrieved June 23, 2020.
[2319] Jasper, Simone (May 22, 2021). "George Floyd's memory honored with scholarship at historically Black college in NC". *News and Observer.*

When asked why he did not tell Chauvin to get his knee off Mr Floyd's neck, Officer Thao testified: "I think I would trust a 19-year veteran to figure it out."

A 12-person jury deliberated for about 13 hours before returning their verdict on Thursday.

In June, the trio of defendants will be back, this time in state court, to face criminal charges for aiding and abetting Chauvin's actions.[2320]

[2320] BBC News Website – Thursday 24 February 2022

Chapter fifty-two

How can we stop man's inhumanity?

The only answer to that question is not going to be a popular one, but I must stress that the only way of stopping this in its tracks is for everyone to turn to Jesus.

Seriously is that all you've got, Jesus?

I said way back at the start of this book, that Man's inhumanity to man, was first recorded in the Bible, in Chapter four of the Book of Genesis. Even earlier in the Book of Genesis we learn of the "Fall of Man", when Adam and Eve ignored what God had told them about not eating the fruit from the tree in the midst of the Garden.

Genesis 3. King James Version

Now the serpent was more subtle than any beast of the field which the Lord God had made. And he said unto the woman, Yea, hath God said, Ye shall not eat of every tree of the garden?
2 And the woman said unto the serpent, We may eat of the fruit of the trees of the garden:
3 But of the fruit of the tree which is in the midst of the garden, God hath said, Ye shall not eat of it, neither shall ye touch it, lest ye die.
4 And the serpent said unto the woman, Ye shall not surely die:
5 For God doth know that in the day ye eat thereof, then your eyes shall be opened, and ye shall be as gods, knowing good and evil.
6 And when the woman saw that the tree was good for food, and that it was pleasant to the eyes, and a tree to be desired to make one wise, she took of the fruit thereof, and did eat, and gave also unto her husband with her; and he did eat.
7 And the eyes of them both were opened, and they knew that they were naked; and they sewed fig leaves together and made themselves aprons.
8 And they heard the voice of the Lord God walking in the garden in the cool of the day: and Adam and his wife hid themselves from the presence of the Lord God amongst the trees of the garden.

⁹ And the Lord God called unto Adam, and said unto him, Where art thou?

¹⁰ And he said, I heard thy voice in the garden, and I was afraid, because I was naked; and I hid myself.

¹¹ And he said, Who told thee that thou wast naked? Hast thou eaten of the tree, whereof I commanded thee that thou shouldest not eat?

¹² And the man said, The woman whom thou gavest to be with me, she gave me of the tree, and I did eat.

¹³ And the Lord God said unto the woman, What is this that thou hast done? And the woman said, The serpent beguiled me, and I did eat.

¹⁴ And the Lord God said unto the serpent, Because thou hast done this, thou art cursed above all cattle, and above every beast of the field; upon thy belly shalt thou go, and dust shalt thou eat all the days of thy life:

¹⁵ And I will put enmity between thee and the woman, and between thy seed and her seed; it shall bruise thy head, and thou shalt bruise his heel.

¹⁶ Unto the woman he said, I will greatly multiply thy sorrow and thy conception; in sorrow thou shalt bring forth children; and thy desire shall be to thy husband, and he shall rule over thee.

¹⁷ And unto Adam he said, Because thou hast hearkened unto the voice of thy wife, and hast eaten of the tree, of which I commanded thee, saying, Thou shalt not eat of it: cursed is the ground for thy sake; in sorrow shalt thou eat of it all the days of thy life;

¹⁸ Thorns also and thistles shall it bring forth to thee; and thou shalt eat the herb of the field;

¹⁹ In the sweat of thy face shalt thou eat bread, till thou return unto the ground; for out of it wast thou taken: for dust thou art, and unto dust shalt thou return.

²⁰ And Adam called his wife's name Eve; because she was the mother of all living.

²¹ Unto Adam also and to his wife did the Lord God make coats of skins, and clothed them.

²² And the Lord God said, Behold, the man is become as one of us, to know good and evil: and now, lest he put forth his hand, and take also of the tree of life, and eat, and live for ever:

²³ Therefore the Lord God sent him forth from the garden of Eden, to till the ground from whence he was taken.

²⁴ So he drove out the man; and he placed at the east of the garden of Eden Cherubims, and a flaming sword which turned every way, to keep the way of the tree of life.

In some denominations this is known as the Fall of Mankind. This was the original sin. Some denominations would disagree and say that sex was the original sin, but they would be wrong.

The whole point of the Bible all the wat from Genesis to Revelations is to project forward the Birth of Christ (Genesis through to Malachi) and then it takes us through HIS, Birth, Ministry, Crucifixion and Resurrection (The Gospels) then onto how we can prepare ourselves for HIS Second Coming and the end of this Age (Acts to Revelations).

When Adam eats the fruit from the forbidden tree, sin entered into this world by way of this man, hence the Fall of Mankind. Through out the Old Testament we read about how God made provision for the Hebrew peoples, HIS chosen people, could give sacrifices to God to make amends for their sins. But God had a plan that would remove the need for everyone to keep making sacrifices as an atonement for their sins. His great plan was, as Sin came into this world via a man (Adam) then God would send His son Jesus as a man to be the last sacrifice that we would ever need. Thus, because Sin came into this world via a man, Sin would be removed via a man Jesus, God's own son.

We read in 2 Chronicles 7:13-14. King James Version

13 If I shut up heaven that there be no rain, or if I command the locusts to devour the land, or if I send pestilence among my people.
14 If my people, which are called by my name, shall humble themselves, and pray, and seek my face, and turn from their wicked ways; then will I hear from heaven, and will forgive their sin, and will heal their land.

God here, is speaking to Solomon, God is not happy with the way people are behaving, with the way they behave etc. So, in verse 14 above, God tells Solomon what needs to be done. It needed to be done by the people in Solomon's day, but my friend this verse also needs to be adhered to by all of us now. God knows your heart, so there is no use in you saying that you are all good, you do not need to pay any attention to this verse.

Last year, (2020), my wife and I were in Beaumont, Texas on vacation when the Covid-19 Epidemic shut down all the airports. We were "Divinely Detained" in Texas for a total of eighteen weeks. During that time this scripture quoted above became very prevalent to the Ministry that I started whilst in Texas. But not only did the Lord lay this scripture on my heart, but within days most of the new ministry friends that I had met whilst in Texas in 2020, had all received that very same scripture.

That one scripture has shaped or influenced all that I have done since. Either in my broadcasts, or in the books that I have written since then.

You may think that because I am an Ordained Minister, that of course I would be pushing the Bible and Jesus, and you would be right.

I make no apology for that fact, but that is my main task on this Earth, to bring as many Souls to Christ as I can, and before it is too late.

Too late? Too late for what?

Well quite simply, too late for the Rapture of the Church.

The Rapture is one of last prophesies mentioned in the Bible that has not yet happened, but it will and if you are not right with God before it takes place, then News Flash – **THERE IS NO PLAN B.**

The Rapture of the Church is NOT the Second Coming of Christ.

<u>The Rapture of the Church – what does the Bible tell us?</u>

1 Thessalonians 4:16 -17 King James Version

16 For the Lord himself shall descend from heaven with a shout, with the voice of the archangel, and with the trump of God: and the dead in Christ shall rise first:
17 Then we which are alive and remain shall be caught up together with them in the clouds, to meet the Lord in the air: and so shall we ever be with the Lord.

Romans 8:23 King James Version

23 And not only they, but ourselves also, which have the first fruits of the Spirit, even we ourselves groan within ourselves, waiting for the adoption, to wit, the redemption of our body.

1 Corinthians 15:51 – 52

51 Behold, I shew you a mystery; We shall not all sleep, but we shall all be changed,
52 In a moment, in the twinkling of an eye, at the last trump: for the trumpet shall sound, and the dead shall be raised incorruptible, and we shall be changed.

Titus 2:13 King James Version

13 Looking for that blessed hope, and the glorious appearing of the great God and our Saviour Jesus Christ.

Jesus taught that HE would return to earth. He was careful to warn His disciples to be constantly prepared for this.

Matthew 24:42-51 King James Version

42 Watch therefore: for ye know not what hour your Lord doth come.
43 But know this, that if the goodman of the house had known in what watch the thief would come, he would have watched, and would not have suffered his house to be broken up.
44 Therefore be ye also ready: for in such an hour as ye think not the Son of man cometh.
45 Who then is a faithful and wise servant, whom his lord hath made ruler over his household, to give them meat in due season?
46 Blessed is that servant, whom his lord when he cometh shall find so doing.
47 Verily I say unto you, That he shall make him ruler over all his goods.
48 But and if that evil servant shall say in his heart, My lord delayeth his coming;
49 And shall begin to smite his fellow servants, and to eat and drink with the drunken;
50 The lord of that servant shall come in a day when he looketh not for him, and in an hour that he is not aware of,
51 And shall cut him asunder and appoint him his portion with the hypocrites: there shall be weeping and gnashing of teeth.

Matthew 25:1 – 13 King James Version

Then shall the kingdom of heaven be likened unto ten virgins, which took their lamps, and went forth to meet the bridegroom.
2 And five of them were wise, and five were foolish.
3 They that were foolish took their lamps, and took no oil with them:
4 But the wise took oil in their vessels with their lamps.
5 While the bridegroom tarried, they all slumbered and slept.
6 And at midnight there was a cry made, Behold, the bridegroom cometh; go ye out to meet him.
7 Then all those virgins arose, and trimmed their lamps.
8 And the foolish said unto the wise, Give us of your oil; for our lamps are gone out.

⁹ But the wise answered, saying, Not so; lest there be not enough for us and you: but go ye rather to them that sell, and buy for yourselves.
¹⁰ And while they went to buy, the bridegroom came; and they that were ready went in with him to the marriage: and the door was shut.
¹¹ Afterward came also the other virgins, saying, Lord, Lord, open to us.
¹² But he answered and said, Verily I say unto you, I know you not.
¹³ Watch therefore, for ye know neither the day nor the hour wherein the Son of man cometh.

Mark 13:37 King James Version

³⁷ And what I say unto you I say unto all, Watch.

Luke 12:37 King James Version

³⁷ Blessed are those servants, whom the lord when he cometh shall find watching: verily I say unto you, that he shall gird himself, and make them to sit down to meat, and will come forth and serve them.

They understood that the present age will end with His coming (Matthew 24:3). The assurance of His return was one of the truths with which He comforted His followers before His death (John 14:2, 3).

At the time of Christ's ascension two angels came to the group of watching disciples to repeat the promise that He will return. They declared it would be in the same manner as He went away (Acts 1:11). This clearly means His second coming will be literal, physical, and visible.

The New Testament Epistles refer often to the Second Coming, and the theme of imminence runs through all the passages of Scripture dealing with this subject. Though there would be a period of time between the first and second comings (Luke 19:11), the whole body of teaching concerning the return of the Lord emphasizes that it will happen suddenly without warning; that believer should be in a state of continual readiness (Philippians 4:5; Hebrews 10:37; James 5:8, 9; Revelation 22:10).

Believers in the early days of the Church lived in this state of expectancy (1 Corinthians 1:7; 1 Thessalonians 1:9, 10). Paul's "we" in 1 Corinthians 15:51 and 1

Thessalonians 4:17 shows that he maintained the hope he would be alive when Jesus comes back.

A comparison of passages of Scripture relating to the Second Coming shows that some speak of a visible event seen by all mankind and involving the judgment of sinners. Others describe a coming known only to believers and resulting in their deliverance from earth.

The latter is referred to among evangelicals as the Rapture. This word is not in the English Bible but in the Oxford English Dictionary it refers to the word "Rapture" as follows: ecstasy, bliss, euphoria, elation, exaltation, joy, joyfulness, joyousness, cloud nine, seventh heaven, transport, rhapsody, enchantment, delight, exhilaration, happiness, pleasure, ravishment. In the Rapture we, the Remnant of HIS Church will be transported up from the Earth to meet with Jesus in the clouds.

See here now one of the of "rapture" in Webster's Third New International Dictionary Unabridged is: "Christ's raising up of His true church and its members to a realm above the earth where the whole company will enjoy celestial bliss with its Lord." The word raptured could well be used to translate the expression "caught up" of 1 Thessalonians 4:17. Jesus said His coming will result in one individual being taken from a location while another is left. This indicates a sudden removal of believers from the earth with unbelievers left to face tribulation (Matthew 24:36-42).

Jesus spoke of His return as a time when the nations of the earth shall mourn as they see Him (Matthew 24:30). The apostle Paul spoke of the Lord's return as a time of judgment and wrath upon the wicked (2 Thessalonians 1:7-10).

In 1 Thessalonians 4:13-18, he considered a different aspect of the Second Coming. This brief passage is the most direct and clear teaching on the Rapture in the New Testament. It speaks only of believers, living and dead. Nothing is said about the wicked seeing Christ at this time. Paul described Jesus as coming in the air, but nothing is said about His feet touching the earth, as we are told elsewhere, they will at His return (Zechariah 14:4). It is the moment when 1 John 3:2 will be fulfilled, and we shall be like Him.

The same Greek word used in 1 Thessalonians 4:17 for "caught up" is used in Acts 8:39 to describe Philip's being "caught away" after baptizing the Ethiopian. The latter verse states that the Spirit of the Lord caught Philip away identifying the source of the power that will remove believers from earth at the Rapture.

In 2 Thessalonians 2:1 Paul called the Rapture "our gathering together unto him." The Greek word for "gathering" is the same as the one used for "assembling" in Hebrews 10:25, referring to the assembling of Christians for worship. It is a picture of the saints congregating around Christ at His coming for them.

The supernatural removal of godly individuals from earth is not unknown in Scripture. The outstanding event in the life of Enoch was his miraculous disappearance from earth after years of walking with God (Genesis 5:21-24). The author of Hebrews called this experience a translation, bypassing death (Hebrews 11:5).

Although some aspects of Elijah's translation differed from Enoch's, it also involved the sudden removal of a believer from the world without experiencing death (2 Kings 2:1-13).

First Corinthians 15:51-54 deals with the same event as 1 Thessalonians 4:13-18. Here also Paul spoke of the changes that will take place in both living and dead believers at the Rapture. He called this a mystery (1 Corinthians 15:51), a truth previously unrevealed but made known to him by the Holy Spirit.

In Philippians 3:21 Paul connected the Lord's coming to the time when "our vile body" will be changed – another reference to the Rapture.

Passages which pertain to the Rapture describe the coming of the Lord for His people. Passages which refer to the revelation of Christ describe the coming of the Lord with His saints. Colossians 3:4 speaks of believers appearing with Christ at His coming. Jude 14 also foresees the Lord's return with His people to execute the judgment referred to in many other passages relating to His public appearing.

Since Scripture does not contradict itself, it seems reasonable to conclude that the passages describing Christ's coming for the saints and with the saints indicate two phases of His coming. We believe it is scripturally correct to assume that the intervening period between the two is the time when the world will experience the Great Tribulation, involving the reign of Antichrist and the outpouring of God's wrath on the wicked (Daniel 12:1, 2, 10-13; Matthew 24:15-31; 2 Thessalonians 2:1-12).

Although God's people may endure severe trials before the Lord comes, the Church will be raptured before the period called the Great Tribulation.

In 2 Thessalonians 2 Paul indicated certain things must take place before the Day of the Lord (of which the Great Tribulation is a part) can begin. An individual called the man of sin (Antichrist) will appear. The mystery of iniquity has been at work since Paul's time but is being restrained by the power of the Spirit working through the true Church. Only when the Church is removed from earth by the Rapture can this man come forward publicly.

In 1 Thessalonians 5, following the passage on the Rapture in chapter 4, Paul taught about the Day of the Lord. He warned of the destruction it will bring to the wicked (vv. 2, 3). He was quick to assure Christians that those who abide in Christ will not be overtaken by it (v. 4).

Still speaking of the Day of the Lord Paul wrote: "For God hath not appointed us to wrath, but to obtain salvation by our Lord Jesus Christ" (v. 9). It seems clear that he meant the deliverance of believers from the judgments of the Day of the Lord, including the Great Tribulation.

Christians are told repeatedly in the New Testament to be watchful for the Lord's appearing. Never are they taught to watch for the Great Tribulation or the appearance of Antichrist. To expect that such things must happen before the Rapture destroys the teaching of imminence with which the New Testament is replete.

Believers are told to wait "for his Son from heaven," not the Great Tribulation (1 Thessalonians 1:10). When the signs of the end of the age are evident, they are to look up and lift up their heads in expectation of their redemption, not the Great Tribulation (Luke 21:28). The signs of the Lord's coming will be fulfilled before His public appearing, but they do not have to be fulfilled before the Rapture. Any teaching that certain events must transpire before the Rapture is out of harmony with the doctrine of imminence.

It is consistent with God's dealings with His people in the Old Testament to believe that the Church will be removed from the world before the Great Tribulation. God did not send the Flood until Noah and his family were safe in the ark. He did not destroy Sodom until Lot was taken out.

The weight of Scripture supports a pre-Tribulation Rapture. Wherever teaching about the Second Coming occurs in the New Testament, imminence is underscored. To interpose other events before the Rapture does violence to such teaching.

While Christians are looking forward to the coming of the Lord, it is well to remind themselves of Paul's words to Titus: "For the grace of God that bringeth salvation hath appeared to all men, teaching us that, denying ungodliness and worldly lusts, we should live soberly, righteously, and godly, in this present world; looking for that blessed hope, and the glorious appearing of the great God and our Saviour Jesus Christ; who gave himself for us, that he might redeem us from all iniquity, and purify unto himself a peculiar people, zealous of good works" (Titus 2:11-14).

Going to Heaven is not a given, there are conditions attached. If you meet God's conditions, then you may get caught up in the Rapture. But if you choose not to meet HIS conditions, then as I said before, there is no Plan B.

We may never totally irradicate Racial Inequality, or Human Trafficking, or Child Exploitation, but if we adhere to 2 Chronicles 7:14, then we have made a smart choice, and with the Lord's help, ad ONLY with the Lord's help we can start to make a difference, and help to take a stand against "Man's Inhumanity to Man."

If you want to more about the Rapture, I have written a book **"Does this mean that I am too late?"** It is available from Amazon Books, and larger bookstores. ISBN: 978-1-51874-818-9

Chapter fifty-three

Man's inhumanity to man

A poem By

Robert Burns

Many and sharp the numerous ills
Inwoven with our frame;
More pointed still, we make ourselves
Regret, remorse and shame;
And man, whose heaven-erected face
The smiles of love adorn,
Man's inhumanity to man,
Makes countless thousands mourn.

See how this poem by Robert Burns has been referenced to events over the years.

"More inhumanity (to man) has been done by man himself than any other of nature's causes." Samuel von Pufendorf, 1673.

"Man's inhumanity (towards man) comes from within, due to the lack of cardinal virtues." An unknown Catholic priest, date unknown.

"There is only one way in which one can endure man's inhumanity to man and that is to try, in one's own life, to exemplify man's humanity to man." Alan Paton.

"The inhumanity of man toward man is our greatest sin." Ellen G. White, 1895.

"Man's inhumanity to man is equalled only by man's inhumanity to himself." Edmund Bergler, 1949.

"Man's inhumanity to man crosses continents and decades." Anthony Venutolo, 2009.

"Why do we hunt and persecute each other? Why is our world so full of man's infamous inhumanity to man – and to woman?" Riane Eisler, 1987

"Woman's Inhumanity to Man," a lecture topic by Emma Goldman, April 1912.

"Man's inhumanity to man"—the phrase is all too familiar ... a profound silence prevailed about woman's inhumanity to woman. Women's aggression may not take the same form as men's, but girls and women are indeed aggressive, often indirectly and mainly toward one another." Phyllis Chesler, May 2009.

"Man's inhumanity to woman – War has shattered many ... women's lives." Marty Logan, 2006

"Man's inhumanity to man begins with man's inhumanity to woman." Marilyn Stasio, 2008

"More of man's inhumanity to man has been done in the name of religion than any other cause." Author unknown, circa 1929.

"This is the most tragic picture of man's inhumanity to man. I've been to Mississippi and Alabama, and I can tell you that the hatred and hostility in Chicago are really deeper than in Alabama and Mississippi." Dr. Martin Luther King, Jr., 1966

"For most of this country's history, we in the African American community have been at the receiving end of man's inhumanity to man. And all of us understand intimately the insidious role that race still sometimes plays – on the job, in the schools, in our health care system, and in our criminal justice system." Barack Obama, 2008

"Behind *Nineteen Eighty-Four*, there is a sense of injustice, a tormented sense of the way political systems suppresses individual thought. Man's inhumanity to man." Jean Eloi, 2002

"It was in the great cities of Europe and among the hovels of the peasantry that my eyes were first fully opened to the extent and consequences of man's inhumanity to man." Edward Bellamy in support of socialism.

"When man's inhumanity to man shall cease from the earth, and justice and equity reign supreme, we may well be rid of both the trust and the labour union, each, in its way, a positive detriment to society." George Frazier Miller, 1910

"The State, therefore, is the most flagrant, the most cynical, and the most complete negation of humanity. It shatters the universal solidarity of all men on the earth and brings some of them into association only for the purpose of destroying, conquering, and enslaving all the rest. It protects its own citizens only; it recognizes human rights, humanity, civilization within its own confines alone. Since it recognizes no rights outside itself, it logically arrogates to itself the right to exercise the most ferocious inhumanity toward all foreign populations, which it can plunder, exterminate, or enslave at will." Mikhail Bakunin, September 1867

"The real US healthcare issue: moral deficiency…man's inhumanity to man" Title of MSNBC article on healthcare, 27 December 2009

"All over the world we read of economic crises, social crises, ethnic conflicts and crises, national conflicts and crises, crises in family life, crises of poverty, crises of exploitation, crises of homelessness, crises of governmental oppression, crises of man's inhumanity to man and so on. The fundamental crisis is the turning away of men and women from spiritual and moral values." L. J. Mark Cooray, 1993

"Throughout all of human history, from the first murder to the present crises, the rise of socialism in America, and catastrophes, we have faced famine, depression, wars and rumours of wars, and countless examples of man's inhumanity to man." Gail B. Leatherwood, May 2009

"It has been the worst of all centuries, with more of war, more of man's inhumanity to man, more of conflict and trouble than any other century in the history of the world." Gordon B. Hinckley, 1999.

"The inhumanity of socialism as described by Edward Adams in 1913 has proven, that more inhumanity to man, since 1918, has been done in the name of socialism than any other cause. Dick Carpenter"

Chapter fifty-four
Who shook the jar?

"If you collect 100 black ants, and 100 fire ants and put them into a jar nothing will happen.

But if you take the jar, shake it violently and leave it on the table, the ants will start killing each other.

Red believes that black is the enemy, while black believes that red is the enemy, when the real enemy is the person that shook the jar.

The same is true in society.

Men versus Women

Black versus White

Faith versus Science

Young versus Old

Etc....

So, before we fight each other, we must first ask ourselves: Who shook the jar?

Sir David Attenborough OM; GCMG; CH; CVO; CBE; FRS; FRSB; FRSAFLS: FZS; FSA; FRSGS.

As Sir David Attenborough has said above, before we roll up our sleeves and start fighting, one with another, we need to sit down and first ask ourselves the question; "Who shook the jar?"

When I started out compiling this book, I had to ask myself a few questions. Such as "What do I include in this book, and what can I afford to leave out of this book?"

As I said at the outset of this book, there is a fair amount of the details contained in this one volume, that can be found online. But only if you can be bothered to do so. Not everybody will want to do so because by doing so, they could discover that their cause is not as genuine as they may think. They may discover that their reason for protesting or looting and destroying other peoples' properties, isn't something that is, and I quote, "a victimless crime." There is no such thing.

Black Lives Matter would have you think that they have always been the downtrodden. The "Woke" brigade want us all to lay down and roll over so that they can do what they want when they want.

Liberals and Socialists would have you think that theirs is the only answer to solving all of the world's problems.

The "snowflakes" would have us all believe the fake news that is growing day by day.

The ONLY answer to all of our problems is for a Global Revival and for everyone to turn to Jesus.

As the late Texas based Evangelist R. W. Schambach used to say.

"You don't have problems; you just need Jesus!"

About the author

William K Mackie is a native of Aberdeen, Scotland. A Veteran of both the Royal Navy and British Army. William tried his hand at Politics and stand - up comedy, as well as a Radio presenter. He has also appeared on TV as an extra in a drama series, as well as TV debates shows, and Quiz shows, before finally graduating in July 1997 from the University of Aberdeen with a Bachelor of Theology Degree and becoming preacher.

William worked as a self-employed Security Training Consultant until a stroke forced him to retire. He is also a former Member of the British Society of Criminology, as well as being a former Member of the Centre for Crime and Justice Studies both based at Kings College, London. He went on from there and became an Author, a Broadcaster, a Covenanter, a Missionary and more recently, a Humanitarian

Now registered as Partially Sighted, in part due to Military service, he is a Member of the Sight Scotland Veterans, formerly known as Scottish War Blinded, where he receives assistance that helps him cope with his sight loss.

William had been offered the chance of a Commission into the Royal Army Chaplains' Department as a Captain ("B" Class Commission - working with Cadets only) but had to decline due to health issues.

In 2020, William became a Baron because of his work with and for the Royal and Imperial House of Rurikovich. It was also granted because of his Services to Humanity.

In February of 2021, William became a Member of the Special Monitoring Mission of the International Human Rights Commission. Working with the Danish International Division, under HRIH Hans Maximus Cabrera Lochaber Rurikovich. In November 2021, he was elevated to the noble rank of Count of the Royal and Imperial House of Rurikovich.

The author is now also a Global Goodwill Ambassador, and he is also an advocate for the "My Body is My Body" programme, as well as being an advocate for the United Nations Sustainable Development Goals (2030), and an advocate for the "End of Female Genital Mutilation."

Most recently, he became an ambassador for the "White Ribbon – End Domestic Abuse Against Women." Campaign.

The Books by the same author
Currently available from Amazon
(Listed in the order they were published)

"Denis Law - an icon of the 20th Century" was supposed to be the only book that I would write, and it was sold to raise funds for the Regimental Museum of the Gordon Highlanders in Aberdeen.

"Do you know who I am" - [not the original title] was not meant for publication, but then it became part of a trilogy.

"You can't hear Gods voice at 4 o'clock in the morning." The title of this book came about when I had a disagreement with my then Pastor who told me that I could not hear God speaking at 4 am, in my own house unless there was a Pastor or Elder present. When I handed him my Bible and asked him to show where in the Bible it says what he had just told me. He replied, "There you go again being all charismatic."

"The devil doesn't close down churches GOD does" is the final part of the trilogy

"Yesterday's Man" is a collection of works by the late Rev Duncan Campbell, best remembered for the Lewis Revival 1949-52.

"Serving GOD not man" is the trilogy mentioned above in one volume with added chapters. So it is now a "Trilogy in four parts."

"Conflict in the Temple GOD versus Soros" This is an in depth look at Hungarian born Jew, Gyorgy Schwartz. He changed his name to George Soros, and he now owns the American Democratic Party.

"Lead me not into Temptation, I'll find it for myself" This is an in depth look at how the Christian Church globally has watered down the message of Christ and HIS Gospel, and how the morals of our society have gone so far downhill because of this, that only a Global Miracle can rectify this problem.

"Where Satan's seat is...." This is part Bible Study, part History Lesson, and part WAKE UP CALL. Revelation 2:13 Authorized King James Version, "I know thy works, and where thou dwellest, even where Satan's seat is: and thou holdest fast my name, and hast not denied my faith, even in those days wherein Antipas was my faithful martyr, who was slain among you, where Satan dwelleth."

This book above, links, Revelation 2:13 with Hitler, the European Parliament, Yasser Arafat and Obama.

"Does this mean that I'm too late?" - Looks at the Rapture and at who is most likely be left behind when the Rapture actually happens. "Hell is hot, time is short, Jesus is returning ready or not."

"The Wooden Horse of ISLAM" and in-depth look at the "Silent invasion of Islam" across Europe and America.

"Billy Sunday" This is the second in the series "Yesterday's Man" with a collection of his most notable sermons.

"Vernon Johns" Another in the "Yesterday's Man" series. This time focusing on the "Father of Americas Civil Rights Movement". This book is a joint project with Patrick Louis Cooney PhD, he granted me access to the work that he had collated on Dr Johns, but back in the 1990's Dr Cooney (an African American) was unable to publish his book, because at the time it was deemed to be racist.

"There were two wolves" I got the idea for this book from an old Cherokee tale. There are two wolves inside each of us. One is pure evil, and the other is everything nice. They are constantly fighting. Which wolf wins depends on which one you feed. In other words, you choose where you want to spend eternity.

"LORD! Your church has lost its way" In view of how many churches of all denominations have been bowing to the pressures of "Political awareness", by watering down their sermons so that their congregations do not get upset or offended. Church leaders are praying to God to ask for a blessing to their nation. If you want your nation to be blest, go back to basics with your bible in hand and STOP Legalising SIN.

"Echoes through time" This book covers Battlefield tours arranged for the Members of what was then known as the Scottish War Blinded, now known as Sight Scotland Veterans. In 2015 we went on a WW1 Battlefields Tour and visited several cemeteries., there are pictures to help visualise what we saw. In 2016, we went on a Tour of Normandy battle sites and cemeteries.

"Halloween and Christianity – A warning" Today far too many Christians thinks that it is ok to celebrate Halloween, but they are so wrong.

"If MY people…." The answer to all of the word's issues, Covid-19, corruption within Governments etc is for us ALL to return to GOD as per HIS instruction in 2 Chronicle's 7:14.

"Beyond the Beaches of Normandy" This a sequel to **"Echoes through time…."** It follows the Allies from the pre-landing preparations for the D-Day invasion to what happened once they pushed beyond the Beaches of Normandy.

Books compiled by the same author

"Agano Jipya" The New Testament in Swahili

"Biblia Takatifu" The Complete Bible in Swahili

Books by other family members

"Granny Mackie's Austerity Handbook"

By

Heather E. M. Mackie

Printed in Great Britain
by Amazon